BANKING AND CAPITAL MARKETS

BANKING AND CAPITAL MARKETS

David Adams LLB, Solicitor

Published by

College of Law Publishing,
Braboeuf Manor, Portsmouth Road, St Catherines, Guildford GU3 1HA

© The University of Law 2020

British Library Cataloguing-in-Publication Data

A catalogue record for this book is available from the British Library.

ISBN 978 1 913226 24 4

Typeset by Style Photosetting Ltd, Mayfield, East Sussex

Tables and index by Moira Greenhalgh, Arnside, Cumbria

Preface

The hardest part in writing this book was deciding what should be left out; a work entitled 'Banking and Capital Markets' could justifiably run to a dozen volumes. However, from a solicitor's perspective, banking practice is essentially 'document driven', and so Part I of this book is devoted to the fundamentals behind drafting loan facility documentation. Probably the most legally complex area of a banking solicitor's practice is that of security: Part II therefore explains the fundamental issues of secured lending. Lastly, Part III of the book introduces capital markets financing and, in particular, the process of issuing a eurobond. The reader should be aware that this book is primarily designed as an integral part of the Legal Practice Course elective, 'Banking and Debt Finance'.

In true preface tradition, I must record my thanks to the people who saved me from making countless mistakes. In particular, I must thank ex-client Ian Brown, colleagues Patrick O'Connor, David Dunnigan and Julia Machin, and ex-colleague Frances George. Following preface tradition still further, I take all responsibility for the mistakes that remain. This book is dedicated to Jayne, who supported me through the pregnancy pains of its creation whilst suffering her own, and to little Tabitha and Francesca for giving me the best incentive to finish writing.

The law is stated as at 1 October 2019 (unless indicated otherwise).

Lastly, the *Financial Times* articles reproduced throughout the book are from various years and are intended to provide contextual illustrations of topics rather than current market positions.

DAVID ADAMS
London

Contents

Table of Cases

Table of Statutes

Table of Secondary Legislation, Accounting Standards and Rules

Table of Abbreviations

ACT	Association of Corporate Treasurers
CA 1989	Companies Act 1989
CA 2006	Companies Act 2006
CD	certificate of deposit
CDDA 1986	Company Directors Disqualification Act 1986
COMI	Centre of Main Interest
CP	conditions precedent
EA 2002	Enterprise Act 2002
EEA	European Economic Area
FCA	Financial Conduct Authority
FPC	Financial Policy Committee
FRN	floating rate note
FRSs	Financial Reporting Standards
FSA 2012	Financial Services Act 2012
FSMA 2000	Financial Services and Markets Act 2000
GAAP	Generally Accepted Accounting Practice
IA 1986	Insolvency Act 1986
IAS	International Accounting Standard
IBOR	Interbank Offered Rate
ICE	Intercontinental Exchange Inc
ICMA	International Capital Markets Association
ICTA 1988	Income and Corporation Taxes Act 1988
IFRS	International Financial Reporting Standards
IPMA	International Primary Markets Association (now part of ICMA)
IRB	internal ratings-based
ISIN	International Securities Identification Number
ISMA	International Security Markets Association (now part of ICMA)
LIBOR	London Interbank Offered Rate
LMA	Loan Market Association
LPA 1925	Law of Property Act 1925
LRA 2002	Land Registration Act 2002
LSE	London Stock Exchange
MAC	material adverse change
MTN	medium term note
PRA	Prudential Regulation Authority
PSM	Professional Securities Market
RCF	revolving credit facility
RIS	Regulatory Information Service (Listing Rules, Rule 12.5)
SA 1891	Stamp Act 1891
SDRT	stamp duty reserve tax
SPV	special purpose vehicle
TLC	transferable loan certificate
UKLA	UK Listing Authority

CHAPTER 1

RAISING FINANCE: AN OVERVIEW OF PLAYERS AND PRODUCTS

> 'We're in the risk business. We take positions. We lend money. We get most of it back.'
>
> Martin Taylor, Chief Executive, Barclays Bank, reporting losses of £325m
>
> (Source: *Financial Times*, September 1998)

1.1 INTRODUCTION

Most people will never be party to litigation. Many of us, including a good few lawyers, will die without making a will. Some people will never own property, and so avoid the nuances of conveyancing, and very few people will run their own business. Almost all of us, however, will borrow money.

Whether it is to buy a car, a house, to fund education, or to bridge from one payday to the next, borrowing is almost a 'requirement' of our society. Banking services available to individuals have grown in number and sophistication over recent years, with internet banking making borrowing increasingly more accessible.

However, borrowing is not the sole preserve of the individual. Businesses must also borrow money, and they usually require more versatile, more complex, and far larger loans than individuals. Banks and business borrowers will therefore frequently rely on the skills of specialised solicitors to help establish their required financing.

This book is not about banking for individuals. It is about financing a business; and in particular it is about the solicitor's role in the two dominant forms of corporate financing: commercial loan facilities and capital markets finance. Beyond this chapter the book is divided into three parts: the first part concentrates on raising money by way of a commercial loan facility, the second deals with taking security for a commercial loan, and the third part considers raising money on international capital markets.

1.2 BORROWERS

1.2.1 Types of borrower

The most common borrowers of capital on a commercial basis can conveniently be placed into the following three broad categories.

1.2.1.1 Governments

All governments borrow; this is usually referred to as 'sovereign debt'. The borrowing may be short term, to bridge a shortfall between their income (primarily from taxation) and the money they require to fulfil their policies and meet their general obligations, or it may be long term (eg, to fund specific projects).

Local authorities and municipalities

Part of a government's borrowing may be used to fund local authorities; however, those authorities will also have the capacity to borrow for some purposes, typically to invest in infrastructure. The article at the end of this chapter illustrates local authority funding through a semi-autonomous regional entity (a 100-year loan to fund drainage construction).

1.2.1.2 Companies

By far the most prevalent borrowers are companies. These range from public companies with diverse interests and a vast network of subsidiaries to small local businesses. Furthermore, banks and other financial institutions are voracious corporate borrowers. Companies, particularly public companies, enjoy a broader range of techniques for raising money (and providing security for borrowing) than any other type of borrower. Since they are so numerous, corporates usually account for the majority of a solicitor's borrower clients. The following chapters will therefore concentrate on borrowing by a limited company, and references to 'borrower' should be read accordingly.

1.2.1.3 Others

Whilst most commercial borrowers will fall within the above-mentioned categories, there are others; partnerships, sole traders and supranational organisations (eg, the World Bank and European Investment Bank) will all raise substantial borrowing. Many educational institutions also borrow: in 2015, for example, the University of Liverpool, University College Oxford and King's College London all took advantage of low interest rates to raise capital. Bristol University followed suit in 2017, borrowing £200 million in a 40-year loan in part to develop a new campus focused on 'high-tech and digital innovation'.

1.2.2 The need for finance

It is not difficult to think of reasons why a *new* business might require considerable 'start up' capital. Assets such as premises, office equipment, and plant and machinery must be purchased or leased. Manufacturing businesses will need to buy raw materials, and almost all businesses must pay employees' wages. They will need to pay electricity bills, advertise to attract customers, and initially they may even have to run at a loss to win business from competitors.

However, most existing businesses will also need to borrow capital in order to trade successfully. Consider Rio Tinto group, a UK-headquartered global mining group. According to its latest (2018) audited accounts, the group had a net worth of almost $50 billion, with operating profit in 2018 of around $17.7 billion. It might be thought that a well-established company generating such immense profit would have little need for borrowing. However, the group had outstanding commercial borrowing of nearly $13 billion. The Rio Tinto group almost certainly has continuing working capital requirements not dissimilar to those listed above for a newly-formed business (albeit on a larger scale!), as well as requiring capital to expand its businesses through the acquisition of other operations.

1.2.3 Financing a company

There are, broadly, four methods by which a large company might raise the money it requires to run its business:

(a)   share capital;

(b)   retained profits;

(c)   loan facilities; and

(d)   capital markets instruments.

1.2.3.1 Share capital

All companies have 'ordinary' shareholders who invest money in the company in return for a 'share' in the business. This money is effectively 'non-returnable' so far as the company is concerned (other than on a winding-up), and so it can be used to invest in the company's assets on a long-term basis. Furthermore, while most shareholders expect to share in some of the profits their company makes (by way of a dividend), there is no absolute obligation on the company to provide a return on its shares.

Most companies will issue shares both on incorporation (to provide initial capital) and at a future date (to raise additional capital). However, each time a company issues more shares it will generally entail any profit which is distributed to the shareholders being spread more thinly. The existing shareholders may therefore prefer their company to borrow capital on which it pays a 'fixed' return, rather than a return linked to profits. In other words, the company can borrow money at a (relatively) fixed cost, and use it to make greater profits for its shareholders. This is known as 'gearing', or 'leverage'. (A fuller explanation of share finance is given in **Business Law and Practice**.)

1.2.3.2 Retained profit

Once a company starts trading successfully, it will make a profit. The directors will decide how to use any profit, and a substantial amount will usually be distributed to the shareholders as a return on their investment in shares. However, part (and occasionally all) of a company's profits will be retained in the company to provide working capital and to finance other funding requirements. These retained profits are shown in a company's balance sheet as 'retained profits' or 'retained earnings' (see **6.3.5**).

1.2.3.3 Loan facilities

Whilst share capital and retained profits can provide substantial levels of funding, they are unlikely to be entirely sufficient for all a company's needs. For example, share capital cannot generally be raised in small amounts on a regular basis, and only public limited companies may offer their shares to the general public. Meanwhile, the timing and amount of a company's profits are often unpredictable.

Borrowing by way of a loan (usually known as a 'loan facility') can provide a company with a flexible and 'reliable' source of funds, and allow very diverse methods of borrowing capital. An overdraft facility, for example, provides an instant source of variable borrowing, helping a company with its cash flow. Alternatively (or additionally), a company might borrow a lump sum for a period of time (known as a 'term loan') to fund a specific project. Loan facilities can cater for borrowing in a choice of currencies. Interest may be payable at a fixed or variable rate, whilst the capital may be repayable in stages through the life of the loan, or in one repayment when the loan 'matures'. The most common forms of loan facility are dealt with more fully in **Chapter 3**.

1.2.3.4 Capital markets instruments

Large companies may obtain financing from another source of funds known as the 'capital markets'. In simplistic terms, this will involve a company issuing a series of instruments (ie, a form of certificate) to investors in acknowledgement of an amount of capital it has borrowed from them (these instruments are known generically as 'debt securities'). The most common forms of capital markets debt security involve the issuer agreeing to repay the borrowed capital on a specified date (on 'maturity') and to pay interest on the borrowed capital in the meantime. The debt security may be sold by the original investor to subsequent investors at any time, allowing it to recover some or all of its capital investment before the maturity date. The subsequent investor will then be entitled to claim any remaining interest payments, and to receive the borrowed capital on maturity. The debt security can be re-sold any number of times; the issuer simply pays interest to the current owner, and repays capital to the owner at maturity.

Debt securities issued on the capital markets include bonds, notes, commercial paper, certificates of deposit, and loan stock. Raising finance through issuing debt securities is dealt with in **Part III**.

1.3 LENDERS

For most people the word 'lender' is probably synonymous with 'bank'. There are, however, two main types of commercial lender: banks and so-called 'institutional' lenders (also known as 'non-bank lenders' or, rather loosely, 'funds'). Both are intermediaries, that is they generally lend money raised from others rather than their own capital. Banks raise money primarily from depositors (eg, you and I opening savings accounts), from issuing debt securities and by borrowing from each other (see **4.9.1.2**). Individuals also 'lend' indirectly through their contributions to pension funds and insurance policies, because the institutions which receive the contributions invest them in order to raise the money they need to meet their obligations under the funds and policies. Institutional lenders usually raise money from investors by creating a series of 'funds' which then reinvest the money in various ways. These 'non-bank lenders' have become prominent participants in term loans in recent years, commonly making up at least half the syndicate (by value) once a loan is in secondary syndication (see **3.3.2**).

In basic terms, therefore, individuals and companies fund all the forms of lending outlined above by putting 'spare' cash with banks or into investment funds, and by buying debt securities. However, it is usually a bank, of one type or another, with which a borrower must initially deal in order to arrange most types of borrowing. For the sake of brevity, the generic term 'bank' is used throughout this book to refer to the financial institution which acts as lender. The main types of bank are examined below.

1.4 A BANK IS A BANK IS A BANK

To some extent, the banks which provide us with current accounts, credit cards, savings products and loans are also the bankers to businesses. However, it is helpful to distinguish commercial banks and investment banks.

1.4.1 Commercial banks

Commercial banks essentially raise money by attracting deposits and then lend that money to individuals ('retail' banking), companies ('corporate' or 'wholesale' banking), governments and others who need it. We are all familiar with the retail divisions of commercial banks such as Barclays, Lloyds, HSBC and Nat West because they have branches on most high streets (they are known as 'high street banks'). They clear cheques, provide current accounts, savings accounts, overdrafts and mortgages for individuals and many businesses. We take these services for granted, but they are so woven into our lives that even a short interruption can be traumatic, as demonstrated by the computer failure suffered by the RBS Group in June 2012 (see article below). If we lose trust in a high street bank, the consequence can be catastrophic, as demonstrated by the collapse of Northern Rock and its subsequent nationalisation in 2008. In essence then, commercial banks do what you might expect of a bank: they are intermediaries, 'moving money' to where it is required and providing basic banking services. So long as they lend prudently, it is a relatively low risk and lucrative business.

1.4.2 Investment banks

You and I are unlikely to have direct dealings with investment banks. They do not take deposits or lend in the traditional sense. The term 'investment bank' was originally used for US institutions such as Goldman Sachs, JP Morgan and Merrill Lynch; the equivalent banks in the UK, such as Barings, NM Rothschilds, Samuel Montagu and Hambros, were known as 'merchant banks'. Their origins were in financing trade in the 18th and 19th centuries (they were sometimes known as 'accepting houses' from their traditional role of accepting bills of exchange – see **17.6.4**). Over time, the role of these banks expanded and the term merchant bank was largely dropped. Modern day investment banks sell advice (for example, advising on bond or share issues, or corporate acquisitions) and underwrite securities issues. They also trade and speculate on bonds, shares and complex financial instruments, and it is these activities that can bring huge reward but also the risk of large losses. It has attracted the tabloidesque label of 'casino banking'.

1.4.3 Glass-Steagall, universal banks and 'ring-fencing'

In 1929 the US suffered the Wall Street Crash, the most devastating stock market collapse in its history. It was followed by years of economic depression. Many US banks collapsed over this period, due in part to their exposure to the stock market through their own trading and their loans to others to buy shares. This led to the Banking Act 1933 (commonly known as the 'Glass-Steagall Act' after its sponsor) which regulated the investments of many commercial banks and effectively prohibited commercial banks and investment banks from combining their businesses. The aim of the regulation was to protect depositors' money held by commercial banks from the investment risks taken by investment banks.

The European banking market had no equivalent to Glass-Steagall and, stimulated by the deregulation in the UK financial markets in the 1980s (the 'Big Bang'), European banks grew in size and complexity. Banks such as Barclays, Royal Bank of Scotland and HSBC combined retail, wholesale and investment bank services in one institution. These 'universal banks' were intended to benefit from economies of scale and reap synergies, with the capital and customer base of the commercial business feeding the investment and advisory activities of the investment banking arm. The investment business also benefited from being married to a retail business that markets knew governments would not allow to fail. In 1999, following heavy lobbying from the banks, Glass-Steagall was repealed and US banks largely followed suit through institutions such as Citigroup and JP Morgan Chase.

It would not be fair to lay the blame for the financial crisis of 2007–08 entirely at the feet of universal banks: proponents would argue that the largest institutions provide a 'full service' to customers and are better able to weather financial storms. However, many governments and regulators now see stricter bank regulation as critical and the separation of investment and commercial bank business is high on the agenda. The UK Independent Commission on Banking (the 'Vickers Report'), set up to consider reforms of the UK banking sector to promote financial stability, recommended forcing bank groups to separate their retail and investment bank businesses. This 'ring-fencing' of the retail banking business was adopted by the subsequent HM Treasury White Paper. Meanwhile, the US authorities similarly restrict banks from making certain speculative investments under the 'Volcker Rule'. Universal banks will almost certainly have to make changes to their structure as a result.

1.4.4 Central banks

All countries with developed economies have a central bank, although the functions performed by that institution will vary between jurisdictions. The central bank of the United Kingdom is the Bank of England, which was founded in 1694 as a private bank and nationalised under the Bank of England Act 1946. The main functions of the Bank of England are to act as the Government's banker (holding its main account and borrowing on its behalf) and adviser on monetary policy, to issue bank notes, to regulate the money markets by lending or borrowing and to set interest rates. The Bank of England will also help other banks with short-term liquidity problems as a lender of last resort (in September 2007 the Bank provided a short-term 'emergency' loan facility to the Northern Rock bank which feared it could not borrow sufficient short-term funds in the markets). Longer-term problems are more likely to be met with advice than money (when Northern Rock's depositors decided an 'emergency loan' signalled time to withdraw their savings, the UK Government had to nationalise the bank).

The Bank of England is also indelibly linked with UK bank supervision. In June 1988 the majority of that supervisory function was passed to the Financial Services Authority (FSA); however, from 1 April 2013 the FSA became two separate regulatory authorities: the Prudential Regulation Authority (PRA) and the Financial Conduct Authority (FCA). The PRA, an operationally independent subsidiary of the Bank of England, is the prudential regulator and supervisor of banks, building societies, credit unions, insurers and designated investment firms. The FCA is the conduct and prudential regulator for most other financial service firms.

RBS: systems down

Houston, we have a problem. Banks often plan for disasters, such as a rival bank failure, currency collapse or terrorist attacks. But Royal Bank of Scotland has been caught out by an internal IT problem after a routine software upgrade last week. This laid low the retail banking operation's payment processing system. RBS has fixed the problem, but still has to clear a backlog of client payments. Many banks have service interruptions when installing patches or upgrades. But big upsets are rare for a UK banking system that handled more than 6.5bn interbank payments (£70tn worth) in 2010, according to British Bankers' Association data.

The mess will further dent RBS's reputation, but the final cost should be manageable.

Clients will surely claim back late payment charges and other indirect costs. RBS and its Nat-West and Ulster Bank units, with almost 17m customers in total, have said clients will not be left out of pocket. The administrative cost of proving and settling claims could be burdensome for a business that generated £6bn of operating profit last year. But it is likely to be a small fraction of the £1.2bn it has provided against payment protection insurance mis-selling claims.

The Financial Services Authority does not stress test bank IT systems. But it expects banks "to take reasonable care to establish and maintain such systems and controls as are appropriate to its business", and to ensure business continuity.

The key, however, as Research In Motion, Perrier and Toyota learnt, is to communicate clearly and often with stakeholders. RBS has struggled to get ahead of the problem. It may be that a line of programming code was wrong, or the bank lost vital IT staff in its cost-cutting zeal. Either way, RBS must once again take the financial and reputational rap for its actions. "The computer says no" is no longer a satisfactory response.

Source: *Financial Times*, 25 June 2012

1.5   THE FINANCE SOLICITOR'S ROLE

This chapter has provided a very brief overview as to why a business might need to borrow money, how that money might be raised, and the role of various banks in the financing process. What part does a finance solicitor play? Newly-formed companies will usually require relatively straightforward financing: typically a simple term loan to supplement their initial shareholders' capital, together with an overdraft facility to aid cash flow and provide flexibility. Many banks provide their own specialist small business advisers, and will usually insist that basic loans are transacted on their standard form documents, with minimal negotiation. There is little requirement at this stage for a specialist finance solicitor.

Larger companies, however, will tend to have more complex financial requirements, and so both the company and the bank will frequently instruct their own specialist finance solicitors. The depth of a solicitor's involvement depends upon the stage at which they are instructed by their client. In very complicated facilities, or for specialised transactions such as an acquisition finance, project finance or securitisation, the finance solicitors will be involved at a very early stage assisting with the structure of the deal. For more straightforward facilities, the structure and basic terms of the facility will usually be agreed between the director with executive responsibility for supervising the company's finances (the 'finance director') and the company's bankers. The finance solicitors will then be instructed to draft and negotiate the loan documentation. Together with good drafting and negotiation skills, a finance solicitor must also be aware of current market practice, since this will dictate the terms that most banks are likely to accept.

Most City firms will split a large finance department into a number of areas with specific responsibilities. The common divisions are:

(a)   general banking (ie, loan facilities – acting for bank or borrower);

(b)   capital markets and securitisation (see **10.10** for a brief explanation);

(c)   project finance (ie, the financing of specific projects in which the return on investment is linked to the project itself);

(d)   asset finance (ie, the financing of the purchase or lease of specific assets such as aircraft or ships); and maybe

(e)   separate derivatives and regulatory practices.

1.6   PERSPECTIVES

Banking practice is usually a particularly constructive form of legal work; both parties will be anxious for the loan transaction to go ahead, and this invariably results in a fair degree of co-operation between them. It is important to remember, however, that each party will see certain matters from a slightly different perspective, with various matters up for negotiation. As a finance solicitor, your perspective on certain matters will therefore depend on your client. Where appropriate, this book will try to give a brief summary of both the borrower's and the bank's perspectives.

Century-long green bond bets on Washington waste   By Tracy Alloway and Vivianne Rodrigues in New York

Investors can now make a century-long return on effluent emanating from Washington following the sale of $350m worth of ultra-long "green bonds" from the District of Columbia Water and Sewer Authority.

Proceeds from the debt, which will mature in October of 2114, will be used to help finance a new drainage programme aimed at preventing excess sewage and rainwater from seeping from the US political capital into surrounding rivers.

It is the first time that debt used to fund an environmental project has been marketed with a century-long duration, and comes as sales of both green and ultra-long bonds have jumped in recent months.

The bonds fetched a yield of 4.81 per cent when they priced on Thursday, compared with the 3.37 per cent on offer from investing in 30-year US Treasuries.

While the bonds are being issued by the DC Water and Sewer Authority, meaning they resemble the municipal debt sold by government bodies, it is also the first deal in the US to come with a "green" certification from an outside agency.

The debt's environmental credentials, combined with its long duration and backing from DC Water, helped attract a $1bn order book from a wide variety of investors, people familiar with the deal said.

"These are investors that may not otherwise have been interested in DC Water previously," said Mark Kim, chief financial officer. "We had traditional municipal investors show interest, we clearly had folk looking at the century bond as a long-duration play and then we also had the green bond investors."

Sales of green bonds have totalled $18.3bn so far this year, according to figures from Dealogic, compared with just $1.66bn in the equivalent period in 2013. At the same time, issuance of long-dated bonds, or those with durations of 30 years or more, has risen 16 per cent to $109bn in the year to date.

"The environment is just very friendly for funding through capital debt markets," said Adrian Miller, director of fixed income research at GMP Securities. "Unless we see a rapid back-up in Treasury yields and a sharp widening on spreads, the primary calendar will remain very strong and will include all sorts of credits and types of bonds."

DC Water hired Vigeo, a Paris-based ethical rating agency, to opine on the environmental credentials of its drainage project. Vigeo has provided similar services for green bonds issued by EDF and GDF Suez, two of France's biggest power companies.

The bonds received an investment-grade rating of "AA" from Fitch Ratings, and will account for about 12 per cent of DC Water's debt portfolio, according to the credit rating agency.

"This is not a tool that will immediately be adopted by authorities across the country," said George Hawkins, general manager at DC Water. "But this opens up a new avenue."

Source: *Financial Times*, 10 July 2014

PART I

FACILITY AGREEMENTS

Due Diligence, Commitment Letters and the Term Sheet

'Every journey begins with a single step.'

Mao Tse-Tung

2.1 INTRODUCTION: UNDERSTANDING THE CONTEXT

Before considering loan documentation, it is important to understand that the context in which a loan facility is to be used will influence its final terms and the process of its creation. There are, very broadly, three contexts for mainstream commercial bank lending:

(a) *investment grade loans (or 'corporate credit')* – where the borrower is typically a large established company requiring cash to run and expand its business, and possibly make small acquisitions;

(b) *leveraged loans* – where the amount of debt is substantial compared to the borrower's earnings and/or its share capital (equity). Because this involves greater risk for a bank, the controls in the facility agreement are usually tighter. Leveraged loans are usually used for 'acquisition finance' in which companies, or private equity funds, buy other companies or groups.

(c) *cross-over credit* – where a borrower is borderline investment grade and so subject to controls in the facility agreement stricter than usual investment grade loans but not usually as strict as leveraged loans.

Furthermore, if the loan is for construction or purchase of a specific asset (eg an aircraft, ship, office block or power station) that will influence certain terms of the document. Almost as important as the context is the liquidity of the market: the more potential lenders there are available, the more borrowers can dictate the terms of the loan facility, whatever the context.

This book generally explains the process and terms relevant to an investment grade loan made to a company, but with an indication of certain leveraged terms, and relaxations that a strong corporate borrower might request.

If a borrower is refinancing an existing loan it will probably approach its current syndicate. Not only will there be an existing relationship, but the current facility agreement will usually form the basis of the new loan document. If it has no existing facilities, is dissatisfied with its current bank, or even requires a loan facility of a type that the current bank cannot or will not provide, then the borrower will have to approach a new institution. It should not be assumed, however, that the borrower is always the 'suitor'. When the lending market is flush with money, banks are generally more pro-active and may approach businesses with the offer of a loan.

Once initial contact has been made, a bank cannot proceed further without obtaining approval for the transaction in accordance with its internal credit procedures. Approval must always be obtained before a loan is offered. If the loan is approved, the next stage involves the drafting of an initial summary of terms (the 'term sheet') from which the loan facility will grow. This chapter explains the first steps in the lending process with a review of a typical credit procedure and term sheet.

2.2 DUE DILIGENCE

Before lending several hundred million pounds, it is necessary to know a little bit about the borrower! When a bank considers lending to a would-be borrower, its initial job is to assess the credit risk: put simply, what is the risk that the borrower will be unable to pay interest ('service' the loan), or be unable to repay the capital? If the credit risk is small, many banks will be prepared to lend to that borrower, and so the fees and margin (ie, profit) that can be charged will be driven down. Conversely, the higher the chance of default, the larger the fees and margin a bank will demand to compensate for the greater risk, and at some point the risk will become too great for the bank to offer a loan. The more information about a borrower that a bank can get, the better it can assess the risk. A bank will therefore conduct a fact-finding exercise known as 'due diligence'.

The breadth and depth of any due diligence process will depend on a number of factors (see **2.2.1**), but in broad terms it will be in two parts.

2.2.1 Initial investigation

The format and scope of the investigation will vary with the identity of the bank and the borrower as well as a number of factors, including:

(a)   the size of the loan;

(b)   the type of loan and its purpose;

(c)   whether the loan is to be secured;

(d)   whether the borrower is already known to the bank;

(e)   market liquidity (ie, whether there are numerous or few lenders willing to lend); and

(f)   whether the loan is an integral part of a larger transaction, such as a flotation or an acquisition (where the due diligence process will have to take account of the larger transaction).

There is no 'standard' due diligence procedure applied by all banks. However, a typical initial investigation for an existing borrower requiring a loan for general corporate purposes might be as follows.

2.2.1.1 Account officer

Each borrower is assigned a particular individual (usually known as an 'account officer') within the bank who provides a consistent point of contact and someone with whom the borrower's officers (in particular its Finance Director) can build a relationship. The account officer will put together a very basic package of terms for the proposed loan. This will usually cover matters such as the amount and term of the loan, repayment dates and principal financial covenants, and will be based largely on the account officer's knowledge of the borrower.

2.2.1.2 Credit analysis

The account officer's proposal will then undergo a credit analysis. Some banks will have a separate committee which meets regularly to analyse lending proposals. Many banks will rely on the account officer to create their own assessment, often with the help of a credit assessment manual which provides checklists of the points to be covered. This will also include any policy guidelines peculiar to the bank, for example, the mandatory inclusion of a material adverse change, or cross-default clause (see **Chapter 8**). The source of information for the credit analysis depends on the borrower and the proposed deal. The borrower's most recently published accounts will always be reviewed. Since a private company has nine months after its year end in which to publish accounts (a public company has six months and a (London) listed company has four months), a bank might require more current information. Smaller borrowers may be asked to produce interim accounts or management accounts. Larger borrowers (eg, those in the FTSE 250) would treat such a request with derision if the loan was for general purposes. If a borrower provides sensitive unpublished information, it will ask the bank to give an undertaking not to disclose it to third parties (a 'confidentiality letter').

As mentioned above, the scope of the analysis will also depend on the size of the loan. It is also important for any analysis to take into account the 'global' exposure the bank will have with respect to the borrower, its affiliated entities and that business sector, since these factors may affect the risk assessment.

2.2.1.3 Credit clearance

Once the credit analysis has been completed it will be sent to a credit department for sanctioning by a more senior officer of the bank. The credit department (or a 'credit committee') will see all credit requests and therefore have an overview of overall lending. They will also check that internal limits and policies, as well as any external restraints (eg, for exposure), will not be breached. Occasionally, they may defer the analysis to an industry department (which has expertise in a particular industry) or Area Credit Officer (with geographical expertise) to obtain a more specialised view of the borrower in the context of contemporary businesses.

The credit department might reject the proposal. Alternatively, they may either approve a loan on the basis of the analysis, or make approval subject to revised terms being agreed (eg, a smaller loan, stricter undertakings, or a shorter term). Once clearance has been given, the account officer can finalise a draft term sheet. If the deal is particularly complex, the account officer might involve a solicitor at this stage, to help construct the term sheet.

2.2.2 Subsequent investigation

The borrower may immediately accept the bank's draft of the term sheet, or there may be a small amount of negotiation (any major changes would require reapproval by the credit department). Once the bank and borrower have agreed the term sheet, a second phase of the due diligence process will begin. It is at this point that the bank is most likely to involve advisers (although smaller loans and 'repeats' may be dealt with largely 'in house'). The bank will instruct solicitors to put together an initial draft facility agreement on the basis of the term sheet. The bank may also instruct accountants to compile a report on the borrower.

During this stage, a solicitor might obtain copies of the memorandum and articles, the charges register and company records relating to the borrower. Obtaining a copy of a corporate borrower's registered documents (typically from the Companies Registry online service) is a quick and cost-effective way of getting information. However, the register does have its limitations. For example, the borrower may not have filed its returns properly. Whilst this may result in a fine for a company and its officers, there is no provision for compensating a third party who suffers any loss. Primarily, therefore, the bank and its advisers will turn to the borrower to supply information as 'conditions precedent' to the loan facility becoming available.

2.2.3 Ongoing information

It is important to realise that a bank's information gathering does not end with the signing of the loan document. A bank must monitor the borrower to ensure it has a reasonable chance of getting its loan repaid. This is the practical reason behind the repeated representations and undertakings in a facility agreement (see **Chapters 5** to **7**).

2.2.4 Acquisition finance

The position is different here. Traditionally, acquisition financings involve greater due diligence since they are leveraged financings with increased risk. However, in very liquid markets, with multiple bidders for each target company, due diligence may be very limited. In particular, if the target is already owned by a private equity house, due diligence may consist of just a few documents and reports about the target company made available to view for a limited time in a 'data room' (either a 'virtual' data room – ie, online – or a designated room at the vendor's solicitor). In a hostile acquisition of a public company, information will also be limited.

2.3 THE TERM SHEET AND COMMITMENT LETTER

2.3.1 What are they?

A term sheet is a document which records, in writing, the principal terms of a transaction. It is signed by the parties to the transaction, but it is not usually intended to be contractually binding (see **2.5**). Term sheets are often attached as an Appendix to a short letter (the 'commitment letter' or 'mandate letter'), which contains any legally binding terms required at the outset of the lending process (see **2.4**).

After initial meetings with the borrower to discuss the fundamentals of the proposed loan, the bank will produce a commitment letter and term sheet reflecting the terms on which it is prepared to lend. The borrower will then be given a date by which it must accept those terms by signing and returning the commitment letter (known as granting the bank a 'mandate'). Occasionally, the bank will instruct solicitors to assist in drafting the commitment letter and term sheet, but more frequently it will be produced by the bank's in-house legal department. Typically, the term sheet aims to provide an overview and will not include substantial detail (but see **2.7**).

2.3.2 Why have a term sheet?

The key reason for producing a term sheet is to focus the minds of bank and borrower on the fundamental issues of the deal. If the pricing and structure of the loan cannot be agreed in outline then there is little point instructing solicitors or performing substantial due diligence. When markets are flush with cash (as was the case for acquisition finance before the economic downturn started in late 2007) borrowers tend to have the whip hand in negotiating terms. This may result in borrowers drafting their own term sheets in an attempt to dictate terms to prospective lenders (see **2.7**).

If the proposed facility is to be syndicated (ie involve more than one lender), it will be helpful for the bank which is arranging the loan to have an accurate summary of the main terms when trying to sell the deal to early syndicate members before an information memorandum has been produced (see **Chapter 3** for further explanation).

Finally, the term sheet acts as an outline from which the bank's solicitor can extract the key information necessary to prepare the first draft of the facility agreement. Whilst not usually intended to be legally binding, neither party will expect any derogation from the broad outline of the term sheet, and so the solicitor has some certainty on which to begin their drafting.

2.4 WHAT SHOULD THE COMMITMENT LETTER COVER?

The commitment letter (also known as a 'mandate letter') is sent from the bank which is arranging the facility to the borrower. It is legally binding (unlike the term sheet which is usually appended to it) and so it contains any terms which need to be legally binding before the loan itself is executed. The key points covered in the letter are:

(a) whether the bank's obligation to arrange the facility (see **3.3.2.1**) is 'best efforts' or 'underwritten';

(b) any general conditionality to the offer to arrange, eg time limit for executing the facility document, obtaining credit committee approvals, completion of satisfactory due diligence, etc;

(c) a material adverse change provision allowing the bank to withdraw from the offer if there is a material adverse change to the market generally (known as the 'market mac') or to the borrower's situation specifically (known as the 'business mac');

(d) a 'clear market' clause in which the borrower agrees not to raise other finance whilst this facility is being arranged;

(e) a 'market flex' clause which allows the bank to change aspects of the negotiated facility agreement if it is necessary to attract other banks to participate; and

(f) provisions for the bank to recover fees, costs and expenses if the deal does not go ahead, as well as an indemnity for any losses the bank might suffer.

The intention is that the commitment letter is signed and returned by the borrower within a few days, although it must be said this is not always enforced in practice.

2.5 WHAT SHOULD A BASIC TERM SHEET COVER?

A 'sample' of a straightforward bilateral, investment grade type term sheet appears at **2.10**, although many are more complex (see **2.7**). As explained earlier, a signed term sheet is usually the first thing a solicitor will know about the transaction. If called upon to help draft the term sheet, however, there are a number of general points a solicitor should keep in mind.

2.5.1 What the term sheet should not cover

A term sheet is not a facility agreement, neither is it a first attempt at drafting. Too much detail will neutralise its purpose. For example, the term sheet may specify the *type* of undertakings (see **Chapter 7**) that are to appear in the final agreement, but it will not include a draft clause.

The aim is towards brevity; the details will need careful negotiation at a later stage. For example, the term sheet might state:

> Guarantees will be given by all material subsidiaries of the borrower.

It is not usually necessary to define what is meant by 'material subsidiary' at this stage: the term sheet simply makes it clear that guarantees will be required between companies within the borrower's group; which companies actually give the guarantees will be a focus of subsequent negotiation.

2.5.2 'Inclusive' lists

There is a danger, when listing specific points to be included in the agreement, that one party might claim during later negotiation that they believed the list to be exhaustive. Where appropriate, therefore, language such as '... including, but not limited to ...' should be used to preface a list of requirements.

2.5.3 Only specify 'unusual' provisions

It is quite common to see the following in a term sheet:

> Conditions Precedent:
>
> The facility agreement will contain the usual conditions precedent applicable to this type of facility.

This wide language can also be used with other generic terms such as undertakings, events of default or representations and warranties. Any provisions peculiar to the deal, for example a condition precedent that a borrower must win a particular contract before the loan facility can be utilised, should be referred to specifically in the term sheet.

2.6 LEGAL EFFECT OF THE TERM SHEET

The term sheet is not usually intended to be legally binding. This is because it is drafted in broad terms, and based on limited information. More detailed investigation by the bank and its advisers will follow the signing of the term sheet (see **5.2**). These investigations will guide the bank as to the terms required in the facility agreement, and occasionally may cause it to withdraw from the deal altogether although this would be unusual: term sheets have considerable 'moral' authority.

Term sheets are usually not binding as a matter of English common law. An 'agreement to agree' will not be legally enforceable if there is a material term of the future contract which has not been expressly or impliedly agreed (this is not the same as an ambiguous or meaningless term, which might be disregarded whilst the remaining terms stand). A binding contract would also require consideration. To avoid any doubt, however, it is usual practice to head a term sheet with language making clear that the parties do not intend it to be legally binding, for example:

> Please note that the terms set out in this term sheet are indicative only and do not constitute an offer to arrange or finance the Facility. The provision of the Facility is subject to due diligence, credit committee approval, the terms and conditions of the Mandate Letter and satisfactory documentation.

If any sections of a term sheet are required to be legally binding, they should be moved to the commitment letter (see **2.4**) or a separate side letter which can be made legally binding.

2.7 PRIVATE EQUITY TERM SHEETS

In acquisition finance deals, the private equity house raising debt to finance the acquisition commonly produces its own term sheet from which to negotiate the loan. In contrast to the traditional term sheet described above, these private equity (or 'sponsor') term sheets are long (90–100 pages), detailed (containing complete definitions and clauses) and favour the borrower. This strong borrower position was the result of high market liquidity in recent years, which brought stiff competition to lend but also easy syndication, allowing banks to sell almost any loans.

2.8 FROM COMMITMENT DOCUMENTS TO LOAN: DUTY TO NEGOTIATE IN GOOD FAITH?

The commitment letter and term sheet are usually intended to set parameters for negotiating the facility agreement. There is no implied duty to negotiate in good faith under English law (although many other European jurisdictions do imply some sort of duty): in other words, either party may withdraw at any time without reason. There is also long-established authority that even an express contractual obligation to negotiate in good faith would be unenforceable for lack of certainty (see *Walford and Others v Miles and Another* [1992] 2 AC 128). A surprising departure from that doctrine was delivered in *Petromec Inc v Petroleo Brasileiro SA Petrobras and Others* [2006] 1 Lloyd's Rep 121, where the Court of Appeal stated that an express obligation to negotiate in good faith may be enforceable in some cases. However, the comment was obiter (the point was not a point of appeal before the Court) and so the statement is not binding precedent. Furthermore, the Court of Appeal later chose not to follow the *Petromec* statement and reiterated the established view (see *Barbudev v Eurocom Cable Management Bulgaria* [2012] EWCA Civ 548). A similar line was taken by the High Court in *Shaker v Vistajet Group Holding SA* [2012] EWHC 1329 (Comm).

2.9 SAMPLE TERM SHEET

The format of a term sheet will depend on the type of loan facility being proposed. Set out below is an imaginary term sheet for a simple bilateral term loan to illustrate typical content and structure.

DATE 1 March 2020   SUBJECT TO CONTRACT

Borrower:	Bashum Car Rental Co Ltd (the 'Company').
Lender:	Loadido Bank plc.
Facility:	£10,000,000 term facility to be drawn in advances of sterling.
Fees:	Commitment fee at 2 per cent per annum on daily unused and uncancelled amount (payable monthly in arrear).
Purpose:	To finance part of cost of acquisition by the Company of entire issued share capital of Wrecker Rent Ltd ('Target'), together with costs and expenses in connection therewith.
Availability:	The facility will be available for utilisation for 2 months after execution of documentation.
Interest:	Floating rate interest at Loadido Bank plc's (prime bank) LIBOR + 4 per cent per annum.
Maturity:	5 years from execution of loan documentation.
Repayment:	The facility will amortise as follows:

Repayment date:	Amount:
years 1–3	zero
42 months	2,000,000
48 months	2,000,000
54 months	2,000,000
60 months	4,000,000

Prepayment:	Prepayment permitted with 5 business days' notice to coincide with any interest payment. Prepayment amounts to be no less than £50,000 or a multiple thereof, and may not be redrawn.
Security:	The facility will be secured by:

  a.   First ranking security over all shares in Target being acquired by the Company.

  b.   First ranking fixed and floating security over all current and future assets (including revenues) of the Company.

  c.   Guarantee from Target supported by first ranking fixed and floating security.

Conditions Precedent: All conditions precedent which are customary for such financings including, without limitation:

  a.   Payment of Arrangement fee.

  b.   Satisfaction with the terms of the acquisition documentation in connection with Target.

  c.   Satisfaction with the terms of financing for the balance of Target's acquisition cost, in particular as regards the equity contribution.

Representations: The usual reps and warranties in connection with this type of facility shall be included in the loan documentation, including but not limited to:

  a.   No withholding taxes on payments.

  b.   Pari passu ranking.

  c.   No material adverse change.

Undertakings: The loan documentation will include standard undertakings for this type of facility, including, without limitation, restrictions on:

  a.   Liens and encumbrances.

	b. Guarantees.
	c. Sale of assets.
	d. Loans and advances.
Financial Covenants:	The loan documentation will contain financial covenants to be negotiated, including, without limitation:
	a. Minimum net worth to be £10 million at all times.
	b. Borrowings not more than 0.5 times net worth.
Events of Default:	Customary events of default for a facility of this type, including, but not limited to:
	a. Default in payment or other obligation.
	b. Cross-default.
	c. Material adverse change.
Taxes:	All payments to be free of withholding and other taxes.
Costs:	Notwithstanding that this term sheet is 'subject to contract', the following provision shall be binding on the Company from the date hereof. All expenses in the preparation, negotiation, execution and delivery of the facility, including, but not limited to, legal fees, to be paid by the Company whether or not the facility is put in place. All expenses associated with administering the facility to be paid by the Company.
Assignment:	Loadido may transfer or assign all or part of the facility at any time.
Other:	All other standard terms for documents of this nature shall be included.
Available:	These terms will be available until 11 March 2020. In the event that documentation is not executed within 30 days of acceptance of this offer, Loadido reserves the right to renegotiate the term sheet, or withdraw the offer.
Law:	English law and jurisdiction shall apply.

Accepted by:

....

on behalf of Bashum Car Rental Co Ltd   Date ....

2.10 CONFIDENTIALITY LETTER

A bank may, at some stage in the loan negotiation, be given information about the borrower which is highly confidential. This may be information about the purpose for which the borrower requires the loan, such as a project finance, management buy out, or funding for a flotation. Alternatively, it may be information specifically concerning the borrower which the bank requires to enable it to make a decision on whether it can lend, or to enable it to form a syndicate to provide the loan (see **3.3**).

Whilst a bank is subject to common law confidentiality obligations (based on agency principles) due to the banker/customer relationship (see **8.3.4**), most borrowers will require the bank to sign a confidentiality letter. The short letter contains an undertaking by the bank not to disclose confidential information other than in limited circumstances to aid syndication. Any bank which is considering participating in the facility will have to sign the confidentiality letter before receiving any information.

PLAIN VANILLA OR BELLS AND WHISTLES?

'The Golden Rule is that there are no golden rules.'

George Bernard Shaw

3.1 INTRODUCTION

A facility agreement is a contract. In common with most commercial contracts, the detailed provisions of a facility agreement will be tailored to the specific requirements of the parties. From a wider perspective, however, there is a handful of categories within which most loan facilities can be placed. This chapter explains the most common types of facility, before providing a broad anatomy of a facility agreement as a preliminary to more detailed review in the ensuing chapters.

3.2 COMMON TYPES OF FACILITY

The three most common types of general purpose loan facility are:

(a) overdraft;

(b) term loan;

(c) revolving credit facility.

The feature which distinguishes one type of loan from another is the way in which it allows the borrower to utilise credit. Facilities with relatively straightforward mechanics were traditionally referred to as 'plain vanilla' loans, whilst any additional features were known as 'bells and whistles'. Which particular loan is appropriate for a borrower will depend largely on the purpose for which the money is required.

Before looking more closely at the features of different loan facilities, it is important to understand a further categorisation: a loan facility may be either 'committed' or 'uncommitted'. A facility is committed if the facility agreement, once executed, obliges the bank to advance monies at the borrower's request (subject to the borrower complying with certain pre-agreed conditions – see **4.7**). If the facility agreement allows the bank some discretion before advancing any loan monies, the facility will be an 'uncommitted' facility.

Committed

uncommitted

3.2.1   Overdraft facility

This is the one type of facility of which most of us have first-hand experience! The corporate overdraft is little different from the personal one, apart from its size (see also **3.2.5** below).

3.2.1.1   Purpose

In the long term, a business will survive only if its income is greater than its expenditure. From day to day, however, it is very difficult for a business to ensure that it has sufficient receipts to cover all outgoings: the week in which the employees are paid will not necessarily coincide with the business selling products, or customers paying their bills. An overdraft is, essentially, a tool to aid cash flow by providing a reserve of easily accessible money to meet any shortfall in working capital (it is sometimes known as a 'working capital facility').

3.2.1.2   Basic features

An overdraft is an 'uncommitted' facility (see **3.2**). Furthermore, it will be 'on demand', which means that it must be repaid (reduced to zero) whenever the bank demands, even if the borrower has not defaulted (ie, failed to comply with a term of the loan). This position is not quite as precarious for the borrower as it first seems; there is generally an understanding that the bank will not 'pull the plug' and demand repayment without good reason. Even so, since it is technically on demand, an overdraft must appear as a current liability on a borrower's balance sheet (see **6.3.2**).

As a result of being on demand and uncommitted, an overdraft facility does not usually require substantial documentation. It is often provided on the bank's 'standard terms', with little room for negotiation by the borrower.

An overdraft will always be subject to a maximum aggregate amount which may be borrowed at any one time and may be subject to a 'clean-down' provision (see **3.2.3.3**). If a business is being run efficiently, each utilisation of its overdraft should be temporary, and once cash flow recovers, it should be used to reduce borrowing under the overdraft.

An overdraft is a relatively expensive way of borrowing capital. Interest is calculated on the amount outstanding each day, and usually charged at a fixed percentage above the bank's base rate (see **4.9** for interest rate calculations). The bank will also charge a relatively high fee for providing an overdraft, since it requires more administration than other loan facilities.

3.2.2   Term loan

A term loan (or 'term facility': both labels are used for this type of credit) essentially provides a specified capital sum over a set period (the 'term'), with an agreed schedule for repayment (see **Table 3.1** below).

3.2.2.1   Purpose

Term loans provide a borrower with a lump sum of capital usually for a specified purpose, for example setting up a business, renewing assets ('capital expenditure'), or acquiring another business.

TABLE 3.1   £10m one-year term loan: repayment examples

Date	Total Drawn	Amortised	Type of repayment	
			Balloon	Bullet
1/1	10m	[Repayment	—	—
28/2		Holiday]	—	—
31/3		1m	—	—
30/4		1m	—	—
31/5		1m	—	—
30/6		1m	—	—
31/7		1m	—	—
31/8		1m	½m	—
30/9		1m	1m	—
31/10		1m	1½m	—
30/11		1m	3m	—
31/12	Nil	1m	4m	10m

3.2.2.2   Basic features

Term loans are usually committed facilities (see **3.2**). Typically, a borrower is allowed a short period (the 'availability period' or 'commitment period') after executing the facility agreement during which (provided it has complied with certain pre-conditions – see **4.7**) it can draw down or 'utilise' a lump sum up to a specified amount. Sometimes, a term loan will provide for an extended availability period during which the money can be drawn in a number of portions (known as 'tranches', 'advances' or 'loans') as and when required by the borrower. This allows a borrower to borrow only what it needs, minimising interest payments, and also to spread the incidence of interest payments into manageable amounts at different times.

Term loans will be repayable in accordance with an agreed timetable. The schedule of repayment may be structured in a number of different ways (see also **9.2**), most commonly:

(a)   'amortisation' – repayment in equal amounts at regular intervals over the term of the loan. There will usually be a repayment 'holiday' at the beginning of the loan;

(b)   'balloon repayment' – repayment over several instalments where the instalment amount increases in size towards maturity;

(c)   'bullet repayment' – repayment in a single instalment at the end of the term of the loan (at 'maturity').

Once the capital has been repaid it cannot then be re-borrowed (compare revolving facilities at **3.2.3**). If the loan has a bullet repayment, the borrower might negotiate a renewal of the loan at maturity, or arrange a 'refinancing' to repay the loan by taking out other borrowings. It is unusual to see a general purpose term loan with a life of more than five years, whilst acquisition finance term loans may be of a little longer tenor (though usually refinanced long before maturity) and project finance loans may be for 20 years or more.

Term loans are not usually 'on demand': the bank cannot withdraw the facility unless the borrower defaults (see **Chapter 8**). This allows the borrower to plan with certainty when it needs to fund capital repayments, and to commit borrowed money in a way that would not be possible with a loan which was on demand, such as an overdraft.

A multicurrency term loan allows the borrower to draw different tranches in different (pre-agreed) currencies. In addition, drawn amounts may be 'redenominated' (ie, converted into a different currency) at the end of an interest period. For example, a sterling tranche could be redenominated into dollars: the borrower does not receive more capital, but its interest payments and repayment would now be due in dollars, maybe matching a new income stream.

Interest on a term loan may be at a fixed rate, but more usually floats at a fixed percentage (the bank's 'margin') above the bank's base rate or LIBOR (see **4.9**).

3.2.3   Revolving credit facility

Like a term loan, a revolving credit facility (RCF) provides a maximum aggregate amount of capital, available over a specified period. Unlike a term loan, the RCF allows a borrower to draw down and repay tranches of the available capital, almost as and when it chooses throughout the term of the loan (see **Table 3.2** below).

TABLE 3.2   £10m one-year RCF: utilisation and repayment example

Date	Total Drawn	Repayment	Available
1/1	4m	—	6m
7/2	7m	—	3m
1/4	3m	4m	7m
21/6	8½m	—	1½m
7/8	5½m	3m	4½m
31/12	Nil	5½m	Nil

3.2.3.1   Purpose

The RCF combines some of the flexibility of an overdraft, allowing the borrower to draw money when it is required, with the certainty of a term loan (the RCF is usually a committed facility: see **3.2**). Not only can the borrower save money by not drawing the whole loan at once, it can also elect to repay outstanding tranches that it no longer requires. Interest payments can therefore be kept to a minimum. Like an overdraft, the RCF is a 'working capital' facility intended to meet the short-term, fluctuating capital needs of the borrower.

3.2.3.2   Basic features

Each tranche is usually borrowed for a relatively short period (eg, one, three, or six months) after which it is technically repayable. However, if the borrower has not defaulted under the loan, the tranche to be repaid can be immediately re-drawn. This is known as a 'rollover'. The RCF might appear very similar to an overdraft facility, but there are fundamental differences. The first of these is size: an overdraft will rarely exceed a few hundred thousand pounds, whereas many large companies have revolving credit facilities of several hundred million pounds. A second difference is flexibility: utilisation and repayment will usually be subject to more restrictions than an overdraft. For example:

(a)   minimum notice periods before each utilisation;

(b)   maximum and minimum amounts which may be drawn down in one tranche;

(c)   a minimum period for which an amount must be borrowed before it is repaid;

(d)   a maximum number of tranches which may be drawn at any time;

(e)   control over frequency and timing of repayment (final repayment is usually required in a bullet repayment, although an RCF can also be structured with a reducing availability through its life, mimicking term loan amortisation).

Whilst a borrower can avoid unnecessary interest costs by borrowing only as much as it requires, the bank will charge a 'commitment fee' calculated as a percentage of the undrawn facility from time to time. The commitment fee is levied to cover capital adequacy costs suffered by a bank in making a committed facility available. (Capital adequacy requirements are dealt with in more detail at **9.3.3**.)

3.2.3.3　Clean down

A clean down provision may be included to ensure the money borrowed under an RCF (and any overdraft) is used for working capital rather than for 'long term' capital expenditure. The clean down provision typically requires the borrower to reduce the amount drawn under the RCF (overdraft) to a specified sum, during a specified period and for a specified number of (consecutive) days. For example, the borrower might have to reduce these facilities to zero, for at least five consecutive business days, once a year. At first sight this provision appears rather odd. It is, however, designed to ensure that the borrower is utilising its RCF and overdraft as intended for cash flow management, and not for long-term capital purchases (contrast term loans at **3.2.2**).

3.2.4　Ancillary facilities

Syndicated facility agreements (see **3.3**) may include both a term loan and an RCF in one document. Furthermore, the borrower is typically permitted to take part of the RCF commitment as a bilateral loan with one of the syndicate banks, for example an overdraft or letter of credit facility. These are known as 'ancillary facilities'.

3.3　SYNDICATED FACILITIES

3.3.1　Bilateral or syndicated facility

Most small loans and overdraft facilities are provided by a single bank. Because they are between two parties, they are known as 'bilateral' facilities. However, banks try to avoid the risk of making large commitments to single borrowers, and so large or sophisticated facilities (eg, for a project or acquisition funding) are commonly provided by a group of banks known as a 'syndicate'. It is not unusual to find syndicates of more than 30 banks, and sometimes even larger (large facilities with multiple institutional investors, for example, may have several hundred lending entities).

3.3.2　Structuring a syndicate

The majority of syndications involve one or more banks, the 'arranger(s)', organising a group of banks to participate directly in the facility agreement. This is known as 'primary syndication'. The syndicate members will participate in the syndicate on common terms, and so agree common documentation, although they may contribute different amounts. Most importantly, each syndicate member will assume liability only for its own lending obligations: it will not undertake any responsibility for other syndicate members' commitments.

As with most banking terminology, the nomenclature is not set in stone, but the main roles of various syndicate members are explained below.

3.3.2.1　Arranger

The arranger (sometimes known as the 'mandated lead arranger' or 'MLA') is the bank responsible for advising the borrower as to the type of facility it requires, finding other banks to form the initial syndicate (known as 'primary syndication'), and negotiating the broad terms of the loan. It will either be a bank with which the borrower already has a relationship or one which has won the mandate to arrange the loan after pitching for the role. In large facilities there may be several arrangers.

Once the facility is made available, the participating banks might sell part or all of their commitment to other banks or institutional lenders (known as 'secondary syndication'). However, a borrower will usually require the arranger to retain a substantial part of the facility (known as a 'minimum hold'), since negotiation with the arranger can become more difficult if it does not have any direct interest. The facility agreement should specifically state that the arranger does not owe the other syndicate members any common law fiduciary duties, in order to prevent any argument to the contrary.

3.3.2.2   Administrative agent

Once a syndicated facility is operational, it is not difficult to imagine how the mechanics could become very unwieldy; some of the largest facilities have several hundred named lenders. To avoid a logistical headache, it is common for one bank to act as agent for the others in the day-to-day running of the loan. This bank is known as the 'administrative agent' (or simply the 'agent') and, broadly, it must act as interpreter (maintaining regular contact with the borrower and representing the views of the syndicate), counsellor (dealing with any practical problems concerning the provisions of the agreement), policeman (monitoring the borrower's compliance with its obligations), postman, record keeper and conduit for payments (it is the agent to which the borrower must usually give notices, pay interest and make repayments, and through which it will receive loan monies).

The agent is simply empowered to administer the mechanics of the facility. Any material decisions, such as a waiver of facility agreement provisions, must usually be taken by the whole syndicate, or at least by a majority (see **3.3.2.4**). The agent will carry the duties and responsibilities imposed on any agent under English law, but the facility agreement will contain provisions to limit the relationship (known as 'exculpatory provisions'), in particular:

(a)   the agent will not want any obligation to act unless instructed by the syndicate;

(b)   the agent will want the ability to delegate its functions and to take professional advice if necessary;

(c)   the agent will want syndicate members to take responsibility for their own credit assessment of the borrower. It will not want responsibility for any information it passes to the syndicate members with respect to the borrower, for the efficacy of the facility agreement, or for any security or other ancillary documents (see **3.3.4** below);

(d)   syndicate members will also be required to complete their own 'Know Your Customer' (or 'KYC') checks to comply with money laundering regulations;

(e)   the agent must be permitted to take an agency fee, as well as an indemnity for costs, losses and liabilities, from the borrower;

(f)   to the extent that costs, losses and liabilities are not recovered from the borrower under (e) above, the agent will want an indemnity from the syndicate;

(g)   the agent will always want a right to resign and the syndicate will want the right to replace it. This will entail provisions dealing with notice periods and the procedure for appointing a successor (either by the agent or by the majority lenders depending on the circumstances). Whilst the agent is agent to the syndicate, the borrower is usually given consultation rights on any replacement because the relationship between them is so important.

3.3.2.3   Security trustee

If a syndicated loan is secured, one entity (usually one of the syndicate banks) will usually hold the security on trust for the whole syndicate. This entity is known as the 'security trustee'. In civil law jurisdictions, which may not recognise the trust, a 'security agent' and 'parallel debt' structure may be used instead (see **14.14.4**). The fiduciary duties imposed upon a security agent/trustee will be more extensive than those of a simple agent.

3.3.2.4   Advantages of taking a role

There are several advantages for a bank in taking lead roles within a syndicated facility. The first is prestige: the most prestigious role is lead arranger. The second advantage to taking a leading role in the syndicate is the ability to charge fees (see **9.5**). Lastly, the 'relationship' banks within the syndicate will hope that the borrower comes to them for other financial products.

3.3.3 Tombstones

Historically, once a large deal closed, it would be announced by way of an 'advert' in the financial press with details of the borrower, deal size and main parties. This was known as a 'tombstone' (or sometimes the 'football team'), and some examples are shown at pp 30–31. The tombstone would often be cast in a perspex block and given to parties and advisers as a 'memento' of the deal. Nowadays, both the adverts and mementos are uncommon, due to their cost and the availability of alternative online advertising.

3.3.4 Liability of arrangers

In order to persuade banks to join the syndicate, an arranger will have to provide a considerable amount of information about the borrower and its group companies. This information is usually written as an 'information memorandum', referred to colloquially as the 'info memo'. The info memo is written by the arranger (or sometimes its lawyers) and, importantly, based on documents and other information provided by the borrower. It usually contains:

(a)   financial information relating to the borrower and its group companies (financial statements for previous years, financial projections over the life of the loan including capital expenditure, revenue, details of anticipated expansion, etc);

(b)   general information about the borrower's group companies; and

(c)   information about the group's business and the markets in which it operates.

Since the arranger compiles the info memo, it is potentially liable for any wrong information the info memo contains which is relied on by lenders deciding to join the syndicate. Claims might be brought for misrepresentation (see **5.5**) or negligence. In addition, the courts have confirmed that the relationship between an arranger and syndicate banks is a 'classic example' of a situation where a tortious duty of care will arise (see *Sumitomo Bank Ltd v Banque Bruxelles Lambert SA*, QBD (Commercial Court), 1 October 1996). It is therefore market practice for the arranger to disclaim responsibility for any information given to the syndicate, by including a clause in the info memo which states:

– the borrower has supplied the information and confirms it is true, complete and accurate; has been prepared with reasonable care; is not misleading; and does not omit anything material;

– the borrower confirms that any assumptions or projections it makes are reasonable and in good faith;

– the arranger has not independently verified the information; does not make any representations or undertakings with respect to it; does not take responsibility for it; and accepts no liability for loss caused by reliance on it; and

– participants in the facility acknowledge the info memo is not a valuation of the borrower's credit; that it is not a recommendation to participate; and that they should make their own independent assessment of the documentation and the borrower.

A broad disclaimer of responsibility will also appear in the loan agreement.

The effectiveness of such disclaimers has been questioned. First, as a general proposition, courts tend to apply a strict interpretation to limitation clauses, particularly if they claim to exclude all liability. More specifically, the Unfair Contract Terms Act 1977 will allow a disclaimer of liability for negligence or misrepresentation only if it satisfies a reasonableness test under the Act. Secondly, the disclaimer and warranty clauses are often drafted too narrowly. They should cover:

(a)   excluded, as well as included, information;

(b)   oral, as well as written, information.

Thirdly, the arranger is almost certainly under a duty not to withhold relevant information, and also under a duty to answer fully any specific questions.

However, in *IFE Fund SA v Goldman Sachs International* [2007] EWCA Civ 811, the Court of Appeal ruled that the disclaimer language commonly used in information memoranda is effective to deny an arranger's liability for the accuracy of information and to deny responsibility for updating it. More recently, the judge in *Raiffeisen Zentralbank Osterreich AG v The Royal Bank of Scotland plc* [2010] EWHC 1392 (Comm) considered (*obiter*) that the standard disclaimer language in RBS's info memo (and other transaction documents) was effective to avoid RBS making representations and taking responsibility for information. The judge decided that if commercial parties wished to conduct business on that basis, they were entitled to do so.

Finally, in the 'Golden Belt' case in 2017, the judge found the arranger bank of a sukuk bond issue liable to certificate holders for improper execution of a key transaction document (see **20.9**).

3.4 LEVERAGED ACQUISITION FACILITIES

Leveraged acquisition financing usually involves more than one source of lending in order to raise the maximum amount of debt. Until recently this would typically consist of a 'senior' facility providing a term loan and a revolving credit facility ('revolver'), and a 'mezzanine' facility providing a second term loan. If the borrower defaults, the senior lenders enjoy first right to repayment and control of enforcement processes. The mezzanine lenders (so called because they sit between the senior lenders and the shareholders in terms of priority) only get repaid if the senior lenders are fully reimbursed. The shareholders (the 'equity') only recover money if the seniors *and* the mezzanine get fully repaid. The greater risk taken by the mezzanine lenders (often known as the 'mezz') is compensated by a higher interest rate. Mezzanine facilities have become rare in recent years, and leveraged deals have instead seen a combination of a senior facility (term and revolver, or just a revolver) and a 'high yield bond' issued by the borrower. The rights of enforcement and priority between the senior lenders and the high yield bondholders vary widely depending on the deal structure.

3.5 OTHER FORMS OF SHORT-TERM LENDING

3.5.1 Standby facility

A standby facility is a generic name for a facility which a borrower does not intend using under normal circumstances but may need to utilise if other uncommitted funding is unexpectedly unavailable (see also swing-line facility at **3.5.3**). It may include a 'utilisation fee', payable (in addition to interest) if the facility is actually drawn.

3.5.2 Bankers' acceptance

A bankers' acceptance is a bill of exchange (essentially a written acknowledgement by one party that it owes a second party money at a future date) which a bank has agreed to be responsible for paying when it falls due. The borrower which asked the bank to accept its bill must eventually reimburse the bank, but in the meantime it is effectively borrowing short term from the bank.

3.5.3 Swing-line facility

A swing-line facility is a facility which is usually made available to a company which has a commercial paper programme ('commercial paper' is a short-term – between one day and one year – uncommitted debt security ('IOU') issued by a company to investors). The swing-line facility can be utilised on very short notice (eg, by a telephone request) to allow the borrower to pay back any maturing commercial paper which it is unable to re-issue ('rollover').

Chapter 17 provides a short explanation of MTNs, bills of exchange and commercial paper.

3.6 WHICH FACILITY IS APPROPRIATE?

This chapter has outlined the common forms of loan facility. It should be appreciated that, rather like primary colours, these can be mixed and matched to suit an individual client's requirements. Furthermore, within a particular type of facility, the mechanics of utilisation, interest payment and the repayment schedule can fundamentally alter its complexion. A banking solicitor must therefore understand their client's needs and business in order to establish the most appropriate facility and properly negotiate its terms.

3.7 ANATOMY OF A FACILITY AGREEMENT

Banks must lend to make money; businesses must borrow to thrive. The ultimate aim of borrower and bank is therefore the same: both want the loan in place as soon as possible. The loan contract could of course be made orally. It is generally accepted, however, that the certainty of a written facility agreement is preferable, especially from an evidential point of view. But how can a facility agreement which might be summarised in a 10-page term sheet grow to a 150-page document? To answer that question, it is important to realise that the provisions in a loan document are almost all designed to protect the bank's position, since it is the bank which is most likely to suffer in the event of any uncertainty or ambiguity.

3.7.1 A bank's concerns

In broad terms, a bank will want to ensure three things:

(a) its fees are paid;
(b) it receives interest on the loan;
(c) it eventually gets its loan capital back.

These aims may be best served by ensuring that:

(a) the loan monies are used only for a specific purpose(s);
(b) the borrower does not do anything which might put its ability to service and/or repay the loan at risk;
(c) the borrower is monitored to give early warning of any possibility that it might be unable to service or repay the loan; and, in some cases,
(d) all monies due to the bank are secured over the borrower's assets.

These areas of concern provide the pattern for most facility agreements (the first draft of which is usually produced by the bank's solicitor). First, the agreement will need clauses to cover the use and flow of the borrowed money, for example:

(a) amount and purpose;
(b) fees;
(c) interest payment;
(d) repayment;
(e) maturity;
(f) early termination by the bank.

Secondly, there will be a number of clauses designed to protect the bank's profit margin in the event that certain costs or other circumstances change, for example:

(a) withholding tax is imposed (the 'gross-up clause');
(b) regulatory capital costs increase (the 'increased costs clause');
(c) the bank's borrowing cost is not covered (the 'market disruption clause');
(d) it becomes illegal for the bank to lend to the borrower (the 'illegality clause');
(e) other unexpected costs are incurred (indemnities).

Thirdly, the facility agreement will usually contain provisions allowing the bank to keep a check on the borrower's 'financial health', and to deal with the possibility of things going wrong, for example:

(a)   conditions to be met before utilisation ('conditions precedent');

(b)   information from the borrower about its status and business ('representations');

(c)   promises by the borrower about things it will do, or will not do ('undertakings');

(d)   events allowing the bank to cancel the loan ('events of default'); and, in some cases,

(e)   security over the borrower's assets.

Lastly, there will be a number of provisions which the bank's solicitor insists are necessary for smooth operation of the agreement, for example:

(a)   a governing law clause;

(b)   provisions for transferring the loan to another lender; and

(c)   provisions for serving notices.

The clauses in a facility agreement can therefore be classified into four main groups.

(a)   'Mechanics' clauses (ie, clauses dealing with the mechanics of making the money flow).

(b)   Margin protection clauses (ie, clauses protecting the bank's profit).

(c)   General protection clauses (ie, clauses connected with the bank's willingness initially to make the loan, and then to allow it to continue).

(d)   Boiler plate clauses (ie, provisions governing the relationship between the parties, and enforcement of the agreement).

3.7.2   A borrower's concerns

The borrower's primary concern is flexibility. It wants the money to achieve its aims, and the fewer strings that are attached the better. In particular, the borrower wants the bank (and so the facility agreement) to recognise that there are bound to be highs and lows on the road to corporate success, and so if the bank sticks with it, everything will be fine in the end … probably.

The main areas to be negotiated, therefore, will relate to the monitoring of, and restrictions on, the borrower. The solicitors must try to negotiate a document which both bank and borrower feel is an acceptable and workable compromise. The mechanics will, to a large extent, be a function of the terms agreed initially between bank and borrower, and recorded in the term sheet (see **Chapter 2**). The boiler plate will contain provisions affording protection for the bank, or (occasionally) the borrower, and provisions 'oiling' the mechanics. These will usually be included as a matter of accepted market practice. **Chapters 4** to **9** will focus on the detail of loan documentation.

3.8   MATCHED FUNDING

Before exploring loan facilities further, it is important to understand a concept that permeates many of the mechanics clauses. Most facility agreements assume that when the borrower requests a utilisation, say for £10 million, the facility banks will fund their commitment by borrowing £10 million from other banks in the London interbank market. This is known as 'matched funding'.

Loans in the interbank market are typically short term (eg one, three or six months) and never longer than a year. Thus, if a borrower requests £10 million under a three-year term loan, the banks might take an interbank loan of £10 million for, say, six months. After six months, the interbank loan must be repaid and so the bank will take a second interbank loan for £10 million to repay the first. The interest payable on the first interbank loan ('LIBOR') is recovered from the borrower and the process is repeated through a succession of these 'interest periods' (see **4.9.2**) until the borrower repays the £10 million at the end of three years.

The matched funding assumption drives numerous provisions in the facility including interest periods (**4.9.2**), repetition of representations (**5.2.4**), repayment, prepayment and break costs (all at **9.2**). It should be noted, however, that loan facilities will not actually *require* the banks to fund this way, and in fact interbank market lending has reduced dramatically since 2007.

3.9 FURTHER READING

Stephen Valdez and Philip Molyneux, *An Introduction to Global Financial Markets* (8th edn, Macmillan, 2016).

Geoffrey Fuller, *Corporate Borrowing: Law and Practice* (5th edn, Jordans, 2016).

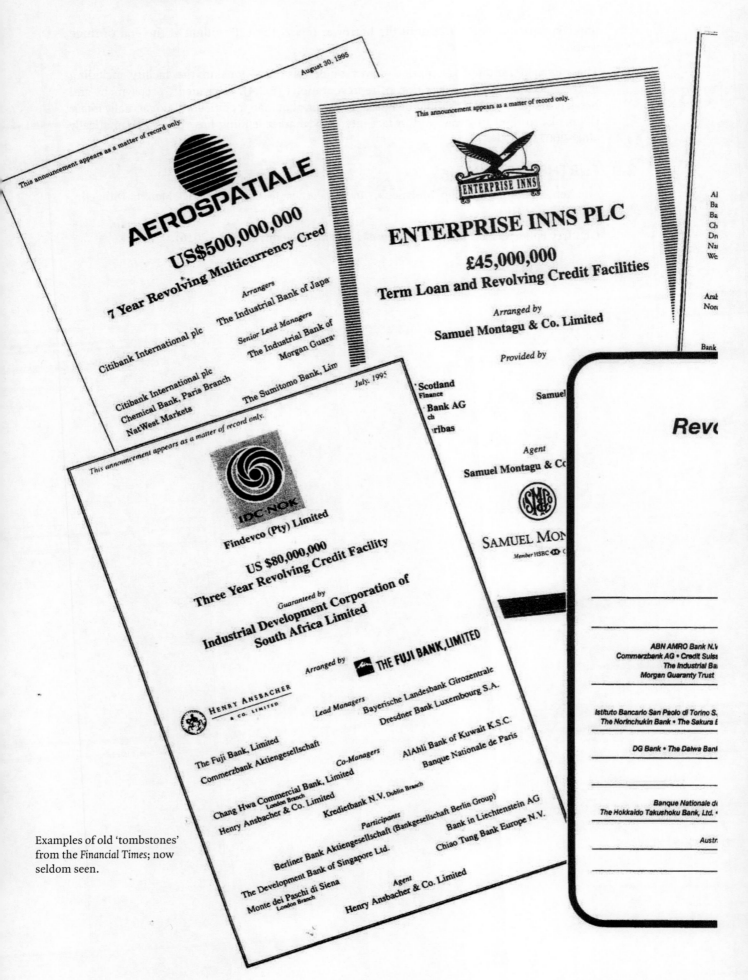

Examples of old 'tombstones'
from the *Financial Times*; now
seldom seen.

definitions are almost mini-clauses and they should be drafted with great care, particularly since any mistake is likely to occur more than once. Finally, you should not negotiate a definition before checking where it is used and thus the full effect of any changes.

4.5 THE FACILITY

The facility clause outlines the type of facility (or facilities) the bank will provide under the agreement, as well as the amount to be made available. From a borrower's perspective it is important to include this clause to create an obligation on the bank to lend (albeit conditional – see **4.7**).

Many facility agreements contain both a term loan and an RCF. The leveraged acquisition market has at times seen several term facilities in one document, traditionally labelled 'Facility A' (an amortising term loan), 'Facility B' and 'Facility C' (bullet term loans with different duration, margin and maybe prepayment rights and other terms), as well as an RCF. Each bank in a syndicated loan will agree to provide a proportion of the total facility, and this is known as the bank's 'commitment'. The clause will specify that their obligations are 'several' (and not 'joint and several') to ensure that each bank is liable to provide only its own commitment.

4.5.1 Why 'facility'?

In common usage, the terms 'loan facility' and 'loan agreement' tend to be interchangeable. There are, however, two technical reasons why the use of 'loan facility' might be more appropriate in the document:

(a) The term 'agreement' suggests that the borrower has agreed to borrow money, and is obliged to draw down. The term 'facility' reflects the fact that the loan is available if the borrower wants to use it, but without an obligation to borrow.

(b) If a document acknowledges or creates debt, it may be classified as a 'debenture' (*Levy v Abercorris Slate and Slab Co* (1887) 37 Ch D 260). If facility agreements are debentures, they may then be 'specified investments' under the Financial Services and Markets Act 2000 (Regulated Activities) Order 2001 (SI 2001/544). This in turn would trigger licensing requirements for banks (or other entities) which carry on certain 'regulated activities' with respect to 'specified investments'. Most loan facilities are deliberately drafted to create a commitment to lend, and the mechanics to do so, but not to create or acknowledge a debt. Labelling them as 'facilities' is intended to reinforce that position, and UK regulators have to date accepted that they fall outside the Financial Services and Markets Act 2000 (FSMA 2000) regime. Unhelpfully, in 2014, the Court of Appeal decided that a loan agreement is an instrument which creates and acknowledges debt and is therefore a debenture (see *Fons Hf v Corporal Ltd and Another* [2014] EWCA Civ 304). Fortunately, however, the Financial Conduct Authority has indicated that it does not consider the *Fons* decision to have altered its interpretation of FSMA 2000 with respect to loan facilities.

How, then, can a bank prove that a borrower owes it any money? The account records kept by a bank showing the total amount outstanding (the bank's 'book') and certified by an appropriate officer of the bank are, under English law at least, prima facie evidence of the borrower's obligations (the facility agreement will usually require the borrower to accept the account records as conclusive evidence). In some jurisdictions (eg, the United States) the bank's account records would be insufficient evidence of debt. In that case, a certificate is issued acknowledging each utilisation (known as a 'promissory note').

4.5.2 Facility office

The facility office (or 'lending office') is the particular branch of a bank through which a loan is made ('booked'). The facility office will be specified in the facility agreement, and is the place where the borrower must make interest payments and capital repayments. The location of the facility office is of particular concern to a borrower for tax reasons (see **9.3.4**).

4.6   PURPOSE CLAUSE

4.6.1   Control

The bank will want the facility agreement to state explicitly how the loan monies can be used. It is the first point of control which a bank can use to protect its money and maximise the probability of being repaid. The wording may be relatively wide, for example:

> The Facility is to be used for general corporate purposes.

or

> The proceeds of the Facility will be used to support the general corporate requirements of the Borrower.

This would at least make it clear that the borrower must not place the first utilisation on the '2.30' race at Epsom.

Sometimes, however, a purpose clause will be more specific. For example, restricting the use to 'working capital' purposes will probably exclude making a substantial acquisition. If the bank has assessed its credit risk (see **2.2**) on a particular project which the borrower is to finance with the loan monies (known as 'project finance'), or it has taken security over particular assets on which it will want the loan monies spent, the purpose clause should be drafted accordingly.

Some purpose clauses state that money should not be used for certain purposes (eg, an investment in particular industries). The purpose clause might also contain restrictions which are driven by the bank's constitution or policy.

Two matters closely connected with the purpose clause are those of capacity and authority. The questions of whether a borrower has the capacity to enter into a transaction, and who is authorised to bind the borrower, are invariably determined in accordance with the law of the borrower's domicile (for companies, this is the country of incorporation). The position for companies incorporated under English law is considered briefly below.

4.6.2   Capacity

Banks will want to ensure that the borrower has unrestricted capacity ('power') to borrow under the facility and, where required, to give a guarantee and/or security. In the case of English registered companies, the Companies Act (CA) 2006, s 39 provides a helpful starting point (adopting a provision introduced in the CA 1989) by stating:

> The validity of an act done by a company shall not be called into question on the ground of lack of capacity by reason of anything done in the company's constitution.

This gives helpful protection for third parties but, since the stakes are high in lending transactions, the bank's solicitors will typically check that there are no specific restrictions on the requisite powers in the borrower's constitution. If there is any doubt about the borrower's capacity, the transaction may need to be approved by an appropriate shareholders' resolution.

4.6.3   Authority

As well as ensuring the borrower has capacity, the bank must be sure that whoever executes the facility agreement and any other documents on behalf of the borrower has authority to do so. Typically the borrower's directors will approve the transaction in a board meeting and will execute the relevant documents. Once again there is, ostensibly at least, a pertinent provision in the CA 2006, where s 40 says:

In favour of a person dealing with a company in good faith, the power of the directors to bind the company, or authorise others to do so, is deemed to be free of any limitation under the company's constitution.

Again, whilst this is helpful, it does have limitations: for example, what exactly is meant by the requirement to 'act in good faith', the need for non-directors to be given authority, and the possibility that an inquorate board meeting might fall outside the provision. In practice therefore, the bank's solicitors will check the borrower's constitutive documents for any restrictions on directors' powers and remove them or obtain overriding shareholder approval. There will also be a requirement for a board meeting which identifies and approves the transaction and execution of all associated documents.

Finally, it should be remembered that there are a number of institutions other than limited companies which may seek to borrow, such as partnerships, building societies or local authorities, all with different common law or statutory powers. Companies that are charities are also subject to certain exceptions to ss 39 and 40 of the CA 2006. A solicitor must therefore consider the legal status and nature of a borrower, and then assess its legal capacity and what action is required to provide proper authority (local authorities have been particularly problematic, eg, *Credit Suisse v Allerdale Borough Council* [1997] QB 306, where the local authority's guarantee was held void for being ultra vires).

4.6.4   Resulting trust

Another reason for including a purpose clause is an attempt to create a resulting trust if the purpose fails. For example, imagine a loan made specifically to fund a new factory for borrower B. After two months, B's orders suddenly dry up and it stops work on the factory. If the purpose of the loan was specified then, since that purpose has failed, any money which has been drawn down but remains unspent (and identifiable) will be held by B on resulting trust for the bank (*Barclays Bank Ltd v Quistclose Investments Ltd* [1970] AC 567). While B is solvent, the question of whether unspent monies are held on trust or in contract is largely irrelevant. On its insolvency, however, any money held on trust by B must be paid to the bank, irrespective of any claims by other creditors. If held under contract, the money would become an asset of B to be shared between its creditors in accordance with the liquidation process.

4.7   CONDITIONS PRECEDENT

4.7.1   Purpose

Conditions precedent (CPs) are, as their name suggests, specific conditions which a bank requires a borrower to fulfil before part or all of a facility agreement takes effect. The CPs provide tangible evidence that the representations and warranties (see **Chapter 5**) are met. The clause is usually found near the beginning of the loan facility, but if there are numerous CPs to satisfy, they may be listed in a schedule at the back of the agreement.

4.7.2   Condition precedent to ... ?

Usually, the substantial parts of a loan document will come into effect as soon as it is executed by all the parties, but the borrower will not be able to utilise unless and until the CPs are satisfied. This has a number of advantages for the bank. First, the borrower is locked in to the main provisions of the agreement. This means the bank's fees are payable and remedies for default apply.

Secondly, the representations, warranties, undertakings, events of default and boiler plate (see **Chapters 5** to **9**) will all become operative as soon as the document is executed. This means the bank can begin monitoring the borrower, even whilst the borrower is trying to satisfy the CPs.

4.7.3 Watch out for …

4.7.3.1 Waivers

If a borrower believes it cannot satisfy one or more CPs before 'closing' (ie the date when the facility is intended to be available), it will have to ask the banks for a temporary or permanent waiver. Most of the CPs, aside from the legal opinions, are within the borrower's control and so it, through its solicitors, must collect the necessary paperwork and deliver it to the bank's solicitor before execution. In practice, however, the bank's solicitor also takes responsibility for ensuring that the CPs are either satisfied (or waived) and they may have to write a 'CP confirmation letter' to the agent confirming the position. If the loan is for a specific purpose, for example an acquisition, then timing of the CPs and first utilisation will almost certainly be tied in to the acquisition timetable.

4.7.3.2 Uncertainty

It is possible that a CP could be so vague as to make the agreement void for uncertainty. For example, a condition in a contract which stipulated that the sale was 'subject to the purchaser obtaining a satisfactory mortgage' was held to make the entire contract void in *Lee-Parker v Izett (No 2)* [1972] 2 All ER 800. It is, however, common to see wording requiring a CP document to be 'in form and substance satisfactory to the banks'. This is probably certain enough in legal terms, although it may trouble the borrower (see **4.7.6**).

4.7.4 Typical conditions precedent

Obviously the form of the CPs will depend entirely on the particular transaction, but a general purpose term loan is likely to require fewer CPs than a multi-currency term and RCF funding an acquisition. Many CPs to a facility agreement are fairly standard, however, and those most commonly seen are mentioned at **4.7.4.1**.

4.7.4.1 Documentary

Common CPs might include:

(a) current constitutional documents (eg articles of association) of the borrower and any companies giving guarantees or security;

(b) a board resolution approving the terms and conditions of the facility agreement and authorising signatories (usually the directors);

(c) a list of names of authorised signatories, together with a specimen of their signatures;

(d) a shareholders' resolution from any guarantor, approving the guarantee (if there are any possible corporate benefit issues associated with it);

(e) legal opinions from the bank's lawyers confirming the validity of the agreement and effectiveness of any security (see **Chapter 16**);

(f) a comfort letter from the borrower's parent (see **13.2.2**);

(g) insurance policies (including any 'Keyman' insurance (see **7.6**));

(h) certificates of title for any properties;

(i) executed security documents, together with any documents of title (eg, share certificates) which those documents require;

(j) copies of any other related documents (eg, fee letters, hedging agreements, intercreditor, and of course the loan facility executed by all parties);

(k) in an acquisition finance, 'Reliance Letters' allowing the bank to rely on expert due diligence reports on the target, commissioned by the purchaser;

(l) management accounts;

(m) payment instructions notifying the bank where loan monies should be paid;

(n) any consents or licences which are necessary in connection with the purpose of the loan;

(o) an agreement for an agent for service of process to be appointed by a borrower which is domiciled abroad (see also **9.8**).

If a borrower does not want to provide an original document then a 'certified copy' might be sufficient. This is a copy which has been signed, usually by a director or secretary of the borrower, as a true copy of the original as at a given date. Clearly, certified copies of board minutes are acceptable; certified copies of share certificates are usually not. If the borrower is based overseas and original documents are likely to be in a language other than English, the facility agreement should require the borrower to provide translations.

4.7.4.2 Other

Most CPs entail providing documentary evidence. However, it will also be a condition of utilisation that no event of default is continuing (see **Chapter 8**) and CPs might include less tangible things such as obtaining a listing, being granted a licence, or obtaining competition clearance.

4.7.5 Conditions subsequent

In some transactions, notably acquisition finance bids which are required to happen quickly, some of the usual CPs are made 'conditions subsequent'. For example, the borrower may be required to give share security over its subsidiaries as a condition precedent, but the remaining security as a condition subsequent within, say, 90 days of utilisation.

4.7.6 CPs – the bank's perspective

A bank looks to the CPs, alongside the representations (see **Chapter 5**), to satisfy it of the borrower's position before any money is utilised. The bank simply lists what it requires.

4.7.7 CPs – the borrower's perspective

The borrower must approach a list of CPs with some caution: can they be achieved within the required time? The potentially problematic CPs for the borrower are those where a third party is involved. The form and availability of accountants' reports, licences and opinions should all be agreed early in the countdown to signing. There are solutions to most problems, provided they are addressed in good time: a bank may be less flexible if a problem is sprung on it at the last minute in what looks like tactical timing.

Another potential minefield for a borrower is wording, such as 'in form and substance satisfactory to the bank' (see **4.7.3.2**). This gives a bank plenty of discretion to decide that something is not satisfactory and utilisation cannot be made. Wherever possible, an agreed form should be settled in advance, for example with respect to board minutes and legal opinions. These are sometimes appended in draft form in a schedule to the agreement, so that all parties know what is required. If a form cannot be agreed in advance, qualifying the bank's discretion with the word 'reasonable' gives a borrower some comfort.

Lastly, this is one area where the borrower in a syndicated loan might press for acceptance of documents to be in the discretion of the agent or, if not, a simple majority of the syndicate. The agent is likely to be the entity with which the borrower has the best relationship, and so may be more flexible. Majority decisions entail persuading a number of banks, but at least avoid dissenting minorities causing trouble.

4.8 AVAILABILITY

4.8.1 Single utilisation facility

The availability or 'utilisation' clause deals with the mechanics of when and how the borrower can actually borrow money under the facility. A simple term loan facility might allow the money to be utilised in one amount on a specified day. The utilisation clause will essentially say: satisfy the CPs, repeat the representations, and so long as you are not in default we will comply with your utilisation request.

4.8.2   Multiple utilisation loan

More sophisticated facilities might allow the borrower to utilise in a number of tranches (or 'loans') as and when required, up to the available amount. Tranches must be utilised within a specified 'commitment period' (see **3.2.2**). Revolving credit facilities offer even more flexibility, allowing repeated utilisation and repayment throughout the term of the facility. A bank will invariably charge a 'commitment fee' during any commitment period (see **9.5**). In either case, the availability clause must cater for multiple utilisation.

4.8.2.1   Notice of utilisation

A fundamental premise of syndicated facility mechanics is that banks will use the interbank market to fund large advances (sometimes known as 'matched funding') (see **3.8**). They will therefore require the borrower to give notice of utilisation. The notice period will depend on the currency: in the London market, currencies other than sterling will technically require a minimum of two clear business days for the bank to fund, whereas sterling could be funded on the day of request. In a syndicated loan, however, the banks will usually require notice no later than the third business day before the day of utilisation for eurocurrencies, or the first business day before for sterling (the extra time allows syndicate members to sub-participate the loan if required – see **Chapter 10**). Often the facility document will specify the latest time in a day when a request can be received (eg, 11 am). If the facility is a revolving one, where fees are usually higher to buy flexibility, the bank is more likely to accept a shorter notice period.

Some utilisation provisions require the borrower's request to be not more than a specified period (eg, two weeks) before the money is required. This is a purely practical point to avoid the situation, not unknown among sovereign borrowers, where a borrower puts in a request several years in advance!

Once a utilisation notice is given, a borrower is usually committed to taking the money requested. Once again, this is based on the assumption that banks will have matched funded a facility, and that 'funding loan' cannot be cancelled without penalty.

4.8.2.2   Representations and defaults

In its utilisation request, a borrower must confirm there is no current default (and that utilisation will not result in a default) (see **Chapter 8**). In a facility allowing multiple utilisations, those requirements must be complied with each time a utilisation is requested.

4.9   FLOATING RATE INTEREST

Banks are intermediaries and so the interest they charge on their loans must cover their cost of raising money as well as an element of profit to keep their shareholders happy. The majority of commercial loans will bear interest at a floating rate: the interest rate will vary through the life of the loan to reflect the fluctuating cost to the bank of raising money in the market. Floating rate loans are usually based on 'base rate' or more commonly an Interbank Offered Rate (IBOR), and these concepts are explored below.

4.9.1   Base rates

Commercial banks raise loan capital in a variety of ways, but primarily through attracting depositors and through issuing debt securities (see **Chapter 17**). Along the way they will also incur regulatory costs (see below and **9.3.2**). A bank's base rate amalgamates all those costs to provide a general cost of raising funds. Base rate is then typically used to charge interest (often with a margin) on bilateral loans to individuals and small to medium businesses. Each commercial bank will have its own base rate, though they may be very similar or identical.

The Bank of England also publishes a base rate (the 'official rate') which is decided by its Monetary Policy Committee each month and is designed to influence economic activity and control inflation. The official rate influences the economy because it is the rate at which the Bank lends to financial institutions (primarily through the short term sale and repurchase of gilts) and so it will eventually affect a bank's cost of funding. Thus, while commercial banks' base rates will not usually be as low as the official rate, they will broadly speaking follow its movements.

4.9.2 LIBOR

Large commercial facilities, which are typically syndicated, will not usually use base rates to calculate interest. Instead, a floating rate is usually the sum of two or maybe three elements:

(a)   LIBOR (or equivalent): representing the main cost of funding (see **3.8** and below);

(b)   margin: generating the bank's profit and covering regulatory capital costs (see **9.3.3**); and very rarely

(c)   mandatory cost: the cost to the bank of its regulatory fees and deposits (although this element is now typically not included in the London market, see **9.3.2**).

LIBOR stands for 'London Interbank Offered Rate' and is the interest rate charged for loans between banks in the London interbank market. The interbank market is intended to provide banks with liquidity: quickly accessible, short-term loans allowing banks to meet their lending commitments or put excess funds to work. As mentioned at **3.8**, large commercial loan facilities typically *assume* that banks will fund their commitments by borrowing on the interbank market (although it is never an *obligation*, and the recent financial crisis and its repercussions have resulted in a much reduced volume of interbank lending). LIBOR rates will vary depending primarily on:

(a)   the currency of the interbank loan;

(b)   the duration of the interbank loan;

(c)   the credit standing of the borrowing bank; and

(d)   the liquidity of the interbank market.

A LIBOR-based interest rate definition must therefore specify the first three variables. In addition, since LIBOR rates fluctuate throughout each day (in contrast, base rates might only change every few months), the definition should specify the date (eg the first day of each interest period) and time (typically 11am when the market is most active) at which the rate is to be set. Lastly, each bank effectively has its own LIBOR rate. To simplify calculating the interest rate for syndicated loans, most facilities use an average rate calculated and published on market screens (see below).

4.9.3 Screen rate (LIBOR and Euribor)

In 1986, the British Bankers Association (BBA) started publishing an averaged LIBOR rate known as 'bbalibor' or the 'screen rate' (or simply 'LIBOR'). It was intended to provide an easily accessible, impartial benchmark rate for the borrowing costs of a variety of currencies, over different maturities, in the London interbank market. This screen rate has become widely used across financial products and markets internationally, and it appears in almost all syndicated facility agreements. The rate is calculated by asking a panel of banks to submit estimated rates at which they could borrow unsecured funds if they were to do so by 'asking for and then accepting interbank offers in a reasonable market size just prior to 11am'. The highest and lowest quartile (ie 25%) of submitted rates are discarded and the remaining quotes are averaged.

However, in the wake of the 2007/08 financial crisis, several banks on the rate setting panel were found to have manipulated the screen rate by making false submissions. The motivation was in part to create a healthier picture of the bank's credit quality during the financial crisis, and in part down to individuals collaborating to influence financial trades. In 2014, following recommendations of a Government-commissioned review (the Wheatley Review), administration of the LIBOR screen rate was taken from the BBA and awarded to Intercontinental Exchange Inc (known as 'ICE'). In addition, five currencies (Australian, Canadian and New Zealand dollars as well as Danish Krone and Swedish Krona) were dropped from LIBOR quotation on the basis that they were 'both difficult to support using trade data, and not heavily used by market participants'. For similar reasons, the number of maturities calculated for the five currencies that are still quoted (Sterling, US Dollars, Euros, Swiss Francs and Japanese Yen) were reduced from 15 to 7.

On taking over, ICE deliberately used the same methodology to calculate LIBOR as had been used by the BBA so that contracts referring to the 'bbalibor' screen rate could adopt ICE LIBOR without the need for renegotiation. The rates can be accessed directly from ICE or through third party 'redistributors' (eg Bloomberg or Thompson Reuters).

Other interbank rates

Financial markets outside of London have their own interbank rates, for example Mibor in Mumbai, Tibor in Tokyo, and Hibor in Hong Kong. In the eurozone, there is a euro equivalent of the ICE LIBOR mechanism, known as Euribor, which is calculated and published by Thomson Reuters. It is calculated by asking a panel of around 18 banks throughout the European Union each to submit the rate at which they are concluding, or can conclude, euro loans in the interbank money market. The highest and lowest 15% of rates are discarded and the remainder averaged to give the Euribor rate.

LIBOR replacements

Despite being used across more than $350 trillion of financial contracts, LIBOR's days are numbered as regulators worldwide demand markets move away from estimated forward looking rates and the perceived vulnerability of a ubiquitous benchmark. For example:

- the EU Benchmarks Regulation (Regulation (EU) 2016/1011) requires administrators of interest rate benchmarks to prioritise data from *actual* market transactions over observations of third party transactions, indicative quotes or expert judgment;
- the Financial Stability Board (an international body that monitors and makes recommendations about the global financial system) has recommended that benchmark rates be anchored in transactions and objective market data as far as practicable; and
- the Financial Conduct Authority has specifically told London market participants that they should not rely on LIBOR being available after 2021.

The as yet unanswered question is what will replace the 30-year-old LIBOR benchmark. Replacements are likely to be based on overnight interest rates such as the Sterling Overnight Index Average (SONIA) and equivalents for other currencies (eg SOFR for US dollars, ESTER for the euro and SARON for Swiss francs). These rates reflect the average interest that banks pay to borrow overnight from other financial institutions. Their big advantage is that they are based on actual transactions and therefore reliable, accurate, freely available and difficult to manipulate. However, they have some key disadvantages against LIBOR, including:

(a) they are sometimes known as 'risk free rates' because they do not include any premium for term (ie length of borrowing) or credit risk (ie risk of the counterparty's ability to repay); however, loan markets usually want to take account of those risks; and

(b) since they are not published as forward looking 'term rates', eg setting a rate for the next one, three or six months, parties cannot know in advance how much interest will be due at the end of those periods.

Loan, bond and derivatives markets are all currently working on LIBOR replacements.

4.9.4   Alternatives to the screen rate

If loan facilities use a screen rate to calculate interest, they need to legislate for the rate either not being available or being insufficient to cover the banks' actual funding costs. Options might include:

(a)   *interpolation* which involves using rates quoted for a shorter and longer tenor than that required to calculate ('interpolate') the required tenor (eg using rates for 1 month and 3 month tenors to calculate a 2 month rate);

(b)   *shortening the interest period* to a tenor that is available;

(c)   *using historic interest rates* if they are available, for example a rate quoted the previous day, although this is controversial and so uncommon;

(d)   *using reference banks* which involves asking a small group of 'reference banks' (typically three) to quote their own LIBOR rates for the currency and tenor required and taking an average of those rates. However, reference banks may be unable to give accurate LIBOR rates for the same reason as the screen rate is unavailable, namely a reduced or non-existent interbank market in some currencies and tenors; and

(e)   *cost of funds* which requires each bank in the syndicate to provide the agent with its *actual* cost of funding the loan, which will be added to the margin (and mandatory cost if charged) to create individual interest rates for each bank. This clause is usually used as a last resort (it is administratively burdensome) and only if none of the above solutions are available. Cost of funds can also be invoked if syndicate banks with more than a given percentage of commitment (eg 50%) notify the agent that the rate of LIBOR (either the screen rate or one of the above alternatives) does not cover their cost of funds.

4.10   FIXED RATE INTEREST

Fixed rate interest is unusual in commercial loan facilities. The fixed rate must cover the banks' costs of funding, and provide a profit, through the life of the loan, and since their fund raising may be at a floating rate, they will not want to be caught out by unexpected upward interest rate movements. Fixed rates therefore tend to be unattractively high. However, borrowers looking for fixed rate liability under their loans may be able to use hedging (see **4.14**) or possibly look to the capital markets (see **Part III**).

4.11   INTEREST PERIODS

A simple loan might require a borrower to pay interest at regular intervals throughout the term of the loan. More sophisticated agreements will divide the life of each tranche into successive 'interest periods' of varying duration. Interest periods are primarily used to support matched funding (see **3.8**) so that:

(a)   the chosen interest period will (theoretically at least) be mirrored by the bank's interbank loan (the borrower's choice is often limited to one, three or six months, since these are the most common interbank funding periods);

(b)   the LIBOR rate is recalculated at the start of each interest period and applies for the duration of that interest period (hence the 'floating rate' loan is really a succession of different fixed rates);

(c)   interest is payable at the end of each interest period;

(d)   the borrower can usually select the duration of each interest period, giving it some control over the rate it pays and timing of payment to match income;

(e)   repayments (and prepayments) are required to coincide with the end of an interest period, when the bank will (theoretically) be repaying its interbank loan. If the borrower prepays mid interest period, it will be charged 'break costs'. These are typically the difference between total interest the bank would have received to the end of the broken interest period, less the interest it can raise by lending the prepaid amount in the interbank market. Strong borrowers will argue they should not pay margin or mandatory cost for the remaining period but just the difference between the LIBOR on the loan and the current LIBOR (if less); and

(f)   some of the representations will be repeated on the first day of each interest period.

4.12   APPORTIONMENT: THE 'DAY COUNT FRACTION'

Interest rates are almost invariably quoted at an annual rate. However, interest payments are usually due several times a year (ie, at the end of each interest period). The bank and borrower must therefore agree the basis on which the annual interest will be apportioned between each interest period (known as the 'day count fraction'). For domestic sterling facility agreements in the London market, the traditional basis for calculating interest is known as '365/365': the annual interest rate is applied to the principal outstanding, and the result is multiplied by the actual number of days in the interest period and then divided by 365.

> **EXAMPLE**
>
> If the annual rate of interest is 6%, and the principal outstanding is £200, then:
>
> Total interest due each year = £12
>
> In February (non-leap year) the interest due will be:
>
> $$\frac{(12 \times 28)}{365} = \text{approx. } 92$$

Interest paid under this method will therefore reflect the exact number of days in the interest period (other currencies and other markets may use methods which 'approximate' periods, for example treating each month as exactly one-twelfth of a year – see **19.4.3**).

4.13   RATCHETS

Some facility agreements provide for their margin to vary in accordance with the health of a borrower, which is measured through monitoring its financial ratios (for cross-over or leveraged facilities) or credit rating (for investment grade facilities) (see **17.11**). These 'margin ratchets' are intended to reflect the variation in risk borne by the bank, and provide an incentive for the borrower to perform well. If the ratios (or rating) worsen, the margin increases; if they improve, the margin falls and the loan is 'cheaper'.

4.14   HEDGING

While most commercial loans will carry floating rate interest, this does leave borrowers vulnerable to upward swings in the floating rate on which they are based (eg LIBOR). This is particularly acute for leveraged borrowers, which typically have large loans with relatively high margins. Many leveraged borrowers therefore manage ('hedge') their exposure to interest rate fluctuation by entering into an interest rate swap (a type of derivative). Essentially, the borrower contracts to periodically pay a fixed amount to another party (the 'counterparty') in return for an amount which varies in line with the floating rate of interest under the loan facility. The borrower therefore knows (and can budget for) its fixed obligations under the swap whilst also knowing it will receive income from the counterparty to meet its floating rate obligations under the loan.

Not all borrowers will hedge their interest obligations (the swaps can be expensive), and if they do, they may only hedge a proportion of their exposure. Typically, the syndicate banks will want to provide the hedging as it is lucrative 'ancillary' business.

4.15 DEFAULT INTEREST

If a borrower fails to pay any sum due under a facility agreement, there will invariably be a provision for default interest. This will charge a rate of interest on any overdue amount (eg, interest, capital or fees) which is a fixed rate above the usual interest rate payable, ie:

(a) LIBOR (at the rate applicable to each day the amount is overdue); plus

(b) the margin; plus

(c) Mandatory Cost Rate (though this is now rarely charged; see **9.3.3**); plus

(d) default interest of around 1%.

If the default interest rate is so high that it appears to punish the borrower, it may be deemed a penalty for breach of contract and hence unenforceable. The test for penalty clauses was recently recast by the Supreme Court in *Cavendish Square Holding BV v El Makdessi; ParkingEye Ltd v Beavis* [2015] UKSC 67 as follows:

> The true test is whether the impugned provision is a secondary obligation which imposes a detriment on the contract-breaker out of all proportion to any legitimate interest of the innocent party in the enforcement of the primary obligation. The innocent party can have no proper interest in simply punishing the defaulter. His interest is in performance or in some appropriate alternative to performance. In the case of a straightforward damages clause, that interest will rarely extend beyond compensation for the breach ... But compensation is not necessarily the only legitimate interest that the innocent party may have in the performance of the defaulter's primary obligations.

In other words, any amount that is beyond compensatory is in danger of being unenforceable. In practice most facility agreements settle for a rate between 1% and 2%.

A bank will usually justify the additional rate as compensation for increased risk of lending to a defaulting borrower.

4.16 BASIS POINTS

Traditionally, banks were able to charge a relatively large margin, which would usually be measured in minimum amounts of 0.5%. In the 1980s, however, borrowing became a 'buyer's market', as the number of products increased and world markets shrunk. Banks were forced to trim their margins and, as a result, a smaller measure was required. Margins are now measured in 'basis points'. One basis point (or 'bp') is 0.01%. Thus, 1% is 100 basis points. If LIBOR is running at 2%, then loan interest of 85 basis points above LIBOR is a rate of 2.85%. Sometimes (particularly in capital markets), 1% is referred to as one 'point', and a basis point is referred to as a 'tick'. Most loan documents will simply refer to percentages.

SUMMARY

This chapter has dealt with the following aspects of a facility agreement:

(1) Who? ... the parties to the agreement.

(2) When? ... the date, and the conditions precedent to be satisfied.

(3) What? ... the type of facility and the definitions clause.

(4) Why? ... the purpose of the facility, and the interest payable.

(5) Where? ... the availability of the facility.

Most of these provisions deal with the mechanics of lending. The conditions precedent and purpose clause give only a crude control over the borrower. The following four chapters, however, deal with the most important control aspects of a facility agreement (and thus often the most heavily negotiated), namely the representations, undertakings and events of default.

REPRESENTATIONS

> 'Put all your eggs in one basket, and watch that basket!'
>
> Mark Twain

5.1 INTRODUCTION

A bank will want to lend only if it is happy with the 'status quo' of a borrower. A facility agreement will therefore contain statements which the bank requires the borrower to make about various matters. These representations (also referred to as 'representations (or just 'reps') and warranties') are made on signing the facility agreement and usually repeated periodically thereafter. The first part of this chapter deals with these representations in the facility agreement. Representations and warranties under general contract law are discussed at **5.5**.

5.2 REPRESENTATIONS IN A FACILITY AGREEMENT

5.2.1 Contractual remedies

Throughout the due diligence process (see **2.2**), the borrower will provide facts, records, forecasts, business plan, documents of title and other unpublished material (eg, management accounts). The most important pieces of information are effectively recorded in the facility agreement as representations: statements of fact made by the borrower and, sometimes, by the guarantor(s) confirming their position.

The three primary reasons for including borrower representations in the facility agreement are:

(a) to elicit information (part of the due diligence process);

(b) to provide a 'drawstop' (money may not be borrowed) if they are untrue; and

(c) to allow the bank to call a default (see **Chapter 8**) if they are untrue.

The borrower should therefore consider the representations carefully before agreeing to them. A bank will also be entitled to various legal remedies in the event of a misrepresentation, and these are examined at **5.5** below.

5.2.2 Examples of common representations

The representations should provide disclosure of any circumstances which might affect the bank's decision to lend, and as such they will be tailored specifically to a particular borrower and particular loan; however, some of the areas commonly covered are outlined below.

5.2.2.1 'Legal' representations

The first group of representations (known as the 'legal' representations) relate to the validity of the borrower, any guarantor and the loan documentation.

Status

A borrower will be required to state that it is duly incorporated under the laws of its 'original jurisdiction' (ie its jurisdiction at the date the facility is signed) and the representation will be repeated (see **5.2.4**) to ensure the jurisdiction is not changed. The borrower will also represent that it has power to own its assets and carry on its business. In some jurisdictions (eg, the United States) the relevant authorities will produce 'certificates of good standing' to confirm that a borrower is up to date in filing information and paying taxes: reference should be made to these, if appropriate.

Binding obligations

The borrower must confirm that the obligations it undertakes in the facility agreement and associated documents are legal, valid, binding and enforceable. It has become commonplace to qualify this representation by any general principles of law which limit the borrower's obligations and which are referred to in the legal opinion addressed to the bank (see **Chapter 16**), for example insolvency procedures, equitable principles or public policy issues. Banks should resist this qualification applying to other representations since it puts risk back on to the banks.

Non-conflict

Borrowers must usually state that entering into the facility agreement will not conflict with any laws or regulations, their constitutional documents, or any other agreement or instrument to which they are a party. Clearly this is important from a practical point of view: the bank does not want a borrower immediately to be in default under another contract, or in breach of a law, as a result of signing the loan. However, there is also an important legal issue which the third element of this representation is designed to tackle. If entering the loan causes the borrower to breach an existing contract, the other party to that contract might sue the bank in tort for 'procuring a breach of contractual relations' (or 'interference with contractual relations'). The representation that there is no conflict with other agreements should protect the bank, since the tort requires the bank to act with knowledge or indifference to any conflict. Banks should therefore beware of borrowers limiting the representation to 'material' breaches of other contracts, since that would not protect them from the tortious claim (though the claim itself may not be material).

Power and authority

It might be thought that the question of whether a borrower has the power to enter into the loan facility is one for a solicitor to answer rather than the borrower. Indeed, it will usually be addressed in the legal opinion given to the bank (see **Chapter 16**). If, however, the borrower had no authority to take the loan, suing its solicitor is of only limited comfort to the bank. A borrower must therefore represent that it has the power and authority to enter into the loan, and to perform its obligations. Breach of the representation (as with other representations) will lead to a default and allow the bank to refuse advances or demand repayment ('acceleration'). This is particularly important for this type of representation which cannot usually be remedied.

Validity and admissibility in evidence

The borrower must represent that it has done everything required to ensure that the facility agreement is admissible in evidence in its jurisdiction of incorporation. This will be particularly important if the borrower is incorporated in a different jurisdiction from the governing law. It might include the need for government or regulatory authorisations: if these are extensive, they may be included in a schedule to the facility. Sometimes the facility itself must be signed before obtaining the authorisation, in which case it should be made a condition to utilising the loan ('a condition precedent', see **4.7**) or an undertaking to obtain authorisation within a specific time-frame.

Governing law and enforcement

The last of the common 'legal' representations is that the law governing the facility agreement, and any judgment obtained in relation to it, will be recognised and enforced in the borrower's jurisdiction of incorporation. For obvious reasons this is not a negotiated clause.

All six of these 'legal' representations are usually repeated (see **5.2.4**).

5.2.2.2 'Commercial' representations

The second group of representations (known as the 'commercial' representations) relate to the commercial position of the borrower.

Deduction of tax

The borrower will be required to represent that it is not required to deduct tax from payments made to banks which are defined as 'Qualifying Lenders' (those banks usually exempt from withholding tax or which benefit from a double tax treaty). This is primarily aimed at ensuring there is no withholding tax imposed on interest payments which would mean the banks getting less interest than expected, or the borrower having to increase its interest payment under the gross-up provisions. This representation is not repeated because ongoing tax issues are dealt with in a separate section of the facility agreement (see **9.3.4**).

No filing or stamp duties

Stamp duties are a form of document tax imposed on the execution of certain instruments (ie written documents). In the United Kingdom, stamp duty is imposed on the transfer of 'stock', 'marketable securities' and 'interests in partnership', with rates ranging from 0.5% to 1.5% of the consideration or market value of the property being transferred (known as *ad valorem* stamp duty). Failure to pay stamp duty within 30 days of execution will usually mean that the document is not admissible in evidence or accepted for registration purposes. It may also entail penalties and interest on late payment. Whilst ad valorem UK stamp duty will not usually apply to a loan facility or related documents, a representation that none is payable is required to protect against possible foreign duties of which the bank is unaware. This representation is not usually repeated unless new borrowers accede to the facility agreement.

There is a separate UK regime imposing stamp duty on the transfer of land.

No event of default

The borrower must represent that there is no event of default (see **Chapter 8**) continuing, or which might reasonably be expected to occur as a result of utilising the facility. In addition it must represent there is no event of default under any other of its agreements which would have a material adverse effect (this is usually a defined term) on the facility agreement. It is hard for a borrower to argue against giving this representation: any negotiation will focus on narrowing the definition of 'material adverse effect'. The bank will insist that this representation is repeated. It is therefore important that the representation refers to 'event of default' and not the LMA definition of 'default' or 'potential event of default' (see **8.6**).

No misleading information

This representation – that the borrower has not supplied information to the bank which is misleading – will usually have three points of focus. First, it will state that the information provided for the information memorandum (see **3.3.4**) was true and accurate. Secondly, it will state that the financial projections prepared by the company's directors (and which usually appear in the information memorandum) are based on recent information and contain reasonable assumptions. Thirdly, it will state that all other information provided to the banks was true, complete and accurate at the time it was given.

The borrower will want to negotiate this clause in at least two ways. It will want the representation to apply only to written information it has provided; oral discussions will be considered too numerous to remember in detail and represent as accurate. This is usually acceptable to banks, unless key oral representations were made; after all, proving what was said would be problematic unless it was recorded. The borrower will also want the representation qualified to say the information was 'true and accurate in all material respects'. Again, this is usually acceptable to the banks. It is not usually necessary to repeat this representation.

Accounting principles

The bank will have closely reviewed the borrower's accounts as part of its due diligence procedures, and it will base lending decisions on the information they provide. Under UK GAAP (Generally Accepted Accounting Practice) a company may use a variety of policies in compiling its accounts as long as they give a 'true and fair view'. A similar principle applies under International Financial Reporting Standards (see **6.9.1.2**).

The borrower will therefore be required to represent that the original financial statements it provided to the bank were prepared in accordance with the relevant GAAP, consistently applied, and give a 'true and fair view' (or equivalent). The borrower will also give an undertaking to deliver future accounts on the same basis, but with a proviso to deal with any change in policies or practice (see **7.4.4.3**).

A third limb of this representation usually states that there has been no material adverse change in the business or financial condition of the borrower since a particular set of financial statements. This is because the financial statements may date from some time earlier, for example audited accounts are produced only annually. The representation effectively brings them up to date, in a material sense at least.

If it is to be repeated (it usually won't be if the facility has a material adverse change event of default – see **8.3.14**), there is a point for negotiation on the third limb: should it refer to material adverse change from the original financial statements produced when the facility agreement was executed, or should it refer to the latest financial statements? If the borrower performs well financially in the first few years, referring to the original financial statements is a less severe test, since the good performance will build a cushion for later bad performance. If it refers to the most recent financial statements, the 'no material adverse change' test ratchets up with each improved set of financial statements. Conversely, if a borrower performs poorly from the start, measuring against the latest financial statements allows it to keep failing incrementally so long as no one year is 'material'. If the failure was measured against the original financial statements, the cumulative failings would eventually become a material adverse change and the borrower could not make the representation.

Ranking

The borrower is invariably asked to represent that any claims the bank may have under the loan documentation will rank at least *pari passu* (equally) with any other unsecured creditors, other than as a result of any preference through insolvency regulations (eg, for unpaid employees' wages). In fact this simply states the position under current English law, but if the representation is repeated it protects the bank (by becoming an event of default) if the law should change. In addition, some jurisdictions (eg, Spain) allow a borrower to favour some unsecured creditors over others (eg, by notarisation), and so it may be a provision that overseas syndicate members want to see in the facility (see also **7.6**).

Litigation

A bank needs to know about any litigation (or similar proceedings), existing or threatened, in order to assess the risk and effect of an unfavourable judgment. The consequences may not just be a heavy fine; they might include loss of licences, bad publicity affecting trade, or cross defaults into other agreements.

The borrower might have a problem with an unqualified statement that it faces no current or threatened litigation, particularly if the statement is to be periodically repeated (see **5.2.4**). Most large companies have a number of law suits in which they are involved at any one time. They may involve minimal amounts, they may be a 'try on' by a rival or creditor, or they may be started by the company itself to protect its intellectual property. The solution might be to use a disclosure letter (though these are now uncommon: see **5.2.3**) to include an element of de minimis or materiality (see **11.5.3** and **11.5.5**); to draft the representations to exclude frivolous and vexatious claims; to refer to the 'reasonably likely outcome'; or perhaps to use a combination of all the above.

The CA 2006 made 'derivative actions' (ie, shareholders bringing claims against directors in the company's name) easier to bring, and so litigation representations are likely to include claims against the borrower group's directors.

Winding-up proceedings

A bank will want to know that no insolvency proceedings in any form have been started or are threatened against the borrower. At first sight this might seem eminently reasonable. However, non-payment may be due to a genuine mistake or disagreement, and it is not uncommon for creditors to threaten a company over relatively small unpaid amounts. The borrower should press for a de minimis provision and wording to exclude debts which it disputes in good faith. This representation is usually repeated (unless covered by an undertaking or event of default).

Encumbrances

If a loan is to be secured over the borrower's assets, the priority and effectiveness of the bank's security might be compromised by any existing security (see **Chapter 12**). In practice, the bank's solicitor will have obtained a company search on the borrower and examined its register of mortgages and charges. In addition, the bank will usually require a representation by the borrower that there are no encumbrances other than those disclosed before execution (see **5.2.3**). A bank might also require a representation from the borrower that it has valid title, in its own name, to all property over which security is to be given. This representation does not usually require repetition.

Environmental

If a borrower breaches environmental laws, it might result in any one or more of a fine, clean-up costs, business disruption, reputational issues or asset degradation. In some instances, its lender may also incur direct liability ('lender liability') if it is found to have 'knowingly permitted' contamination or if it takes possession of contaminated land. Environmental liability may arise in various contexts, but there are two main areas which are most commonly relevant in England and Wales (alongside the common law of nuisance): contaminated land, primarily under the Environmental Protection Act 1990, and water pollution, governed by a patchwork of legislation.

A bank's main defence against these risks is due diligence before lending, the detail and extent of which will depend on the nature of the borrower's business operations. An expert report on environmental issues may be commissioned by potential purchasers in a leveraged acquisition, and banks may be able to view and even rely on that report. Another simple piece of due diligence is to include a representation in the facility agreement that the borrower is in compliance with all environmental laws and has obtained, and complies with, all environmental licences necessary for its business. This representation is usually subject to materiality and is typically not repeated because it will be coupled with an environmental undertaking looking forward.

Catch all

From time to time, banks have asked for a representation that there is 'nothing the borrower has omitted to tell the banks that if it had told them they would not want to lend'! Most borrowers resist this on the basis that it is almost impossible for them to know if they have complied.

5.2.3 Disclosure letter

When a bank's solicitor is preparing the first draft of the representations, they will try to make them as wide as possible. For example, the borrower may be required to state that it has no litigation against it. However, most businesses will be sued, from time to time, albeit that it may be of no real significance to the bank. A would-be borrower is therefore forced to say that it cannot give the representation, the bank will ask why, and any litigation is revealed. The first objective of the representation has been achieved.

Assuming the bank is not unduly worried by the disclosed litigation, it could simply include it in the representation as a specific exception. An alternative solution, however, is to keep the representation 'clean' and use a separate document to deal with anything which would otherwise amount to a breach. This document is known as a 'disclosure letter'. The disclosure letter is essentially an agreed list of specific items which would ordinarily prevent a borrower from making a representation but which the bank has agreed to waive. The representations in the loan document are then made subject to anything in the disclosure letter.

If a disclosure letter is used (they are now uncommon), the borrower should be wary of pegging a disclosure to one particular representation, because it may breach more than one. The disclosure should therefore be worded to modify all the representations. At the same time, the bank should be sure that the disclosure is a full and accurate one so that it can properly judge whether it may be waived. Using a disclosure letter to soften the representations is very effective when they are first given, but can lead to problems for the borrower if they are to be repeated (see **5.4**).

5.2.4 Repetition of representations

Representations are used in many commercial agreements: the purchaser of a house or business, for example, will want numerous representations from the vendor. Unlike many agreements, however, a loan document provides for a continuing relationship, and a bank may therefore want the representations repeated from time to time. Since a representation can be made only as at a given date, the question arises as to when it should be repeated. Some agreements require the representations to be deemed repeated every day throughout the life of the loan (known as 'evergreening'). However, most facility agreements require them to be given on execution and then repeated immediately prior to each utilisation, and on the first day of each interest period (see **4.9**).

If the representations are deemed repeated, the loan document will often specifically state that they are to 'survive' the execution and first utilisation. Some agreements will require a certificate to be provided periodically, by an officer of the borrower, confirming that the representations are still correct (or that there has been no default). Both measures prevent a borrower from arguing that the representations were merely initial pre-conditions of lending. Furthermore, any claim for misrepresentation will depend on the innocent party showing reliance on the representation (see **5.5.1**). Reliance may be harder to prove on a deemed repetition, and so the additional emphasis provided by requiring a certificate or specifying repetition may be helpful.

Some practitioners believe that it is better not to deem someone to have made an incorrect statement and will instead use undertakings (**Chapter 6**) and events of default (**Chapter 8**) to allow the bank to respond to changes during the term of the loan.

5.3 REPRESENTATIONS – THE BANK'S PERSPECTIVE

There is an element of *caveat emptor* which applies when a bank makes a loan: essentially, there is no common law obligation on a borrower to disclose information which might be pertinent to the bank's decision to lend. The representations will need careful drafting to achieve the required disclosure. Some representations are best cast in very wide terms, for example that a borrower has 'no litigation, arbitration, or similar proceedings pending or threatened'. However, a representation that a borrower 'has insurance' could benefit from being more specific.

Sometimes a borrower will ask to qualify its 'legal' representations by any qualifications used in the bank's legal opinions. This may be accepted for the 'binding obligation' and possibly 'governing law' representations, but a 'blanket' application is not appropriate or necessary. Remember, from the bank's perspective, the representations are about 'risk allocation', allowing them to take action if a situation is not what they had been led to believe.

5.4 REPRESENTATIONS – THE BORROWER'S PERSPECTIVE

If a representation is untrue when made or repeated it will trigger an event of default, and therefore borrowers will want to negotiate wide margins for error. A repeated representation should avoid the need for an undertaking or an event of default on the same issue, but, at the very least, any concessions negotiated in drafting any equivalent or related events of default or undertakings (such as de minimis provisions) should be reflected in any representations which are to be repeated (see **5.2.4**). A borrower should never repeat a representation that there is no 'potential event of default' or equivalent, since breach would turn a 'potential' into a 'full' default.

There is a particular danger for the borrower if the representations are to be deemed repeated. The bank will argue that when representations are first made, they should be tightly worded in order to flush out any problems (by way of a disclosure letter: see **5.2.3**). However, on repetition, the disclosure letter is ineffective against new breaches.

EXAMPLE

A borrower is asked to give a representation that it is not involved in litigation or a dispute of any kind. However, the borrower has a small dispute currently running with a distributor in the United States. The bank suggests the representation remains, but that the borrower lists exact details of the dispute in a disclosure letter. The bank considers the letter and decides that the dispute is in fact trivial, and the loan may go ahead. The representation has therefore served its purpose by exposing the dispute, and allowing the bank to dismiss it as inconsequential to lending. If, however, the agreement provides that the representations are deemed repeated then any new dispute, even although it may be as inconsequential as the first, will cause a default. The disclosure letter is effective only in the first instance.

A borrower will sometimes ask for the representations to be qualified with, 'to the best of our knowledge and belief'. Whilst this might at first sight seem quite reasonable, it confounds the true purpose of the representations, which is to lay the risk of unknown problems on the borrower rather than the bank. The qualification is therefore acceptable to banks only in very limited circumstances (eg, with respect to knowledge of threatened legal proceedings or market information) and may carry the caveat 'after due and careful enquiry'.

Borrowers may want to negotiate a materiality qualification to many of the representations. This is largely a question of risk allocation between the banks and the borrower. The borrower should ensure any materiality qualification will not make a representation too uncertain to be given (using a minimum monetary amount, where appropriate, can help). A borrower should also check whether representations are given in relation to just itself, or whether they also include a defined 'group' or even all its subsidiaries. Is it able to give what is required, or should the representation be limited, for example, to 'Material Subsidiaries'?

Lastly, a borrower should be careful about any information it provides during negotiations. If the information is false, it may be liable for misrepresentation under general law in addition to any sanctions in the facility agreement (see **5.5**).

5.5   REPRESENTATIONS IN CONTRACT LAW

5.5.1   Representations

A representation is a statement of fact, made to induce the party to whom it is addressed to enter into a contract. The statement may be oral or written, and if it is drafted into the contract it also becomes a term of that contract. If the statement is untrue, it constitutes misrepresentation. The due diligence process (see **2.2**) will inevitably involve the borrower in making numerous representations. If a borrower makes a false statement during negotiations, when might it be actionable by the bank under the general law?

5.5.1.1   Misrepresentation Act 1967

The right to claim for contractual misrepresentation is governed by the Misrepresentation Act 1967 (as amended). A claim will be recognised only if the misrepresentation was of a material fact, was intended to induce a party to contract, and did induce the party to contract. The Act effectively places misrepresentations into two categories, one of which is sub-divided.

Fraudulent misrepresentation

A misrepresentation is fraudulent where it is made knowingly, or without any belief in its truth, or recklessly. The test is subjective, ie what did the maker truly believe?

Non-fraudulent misrepresentation

If the maker honestly believed the statement they made was true, the misrepresentation is not fraudulent. Non-fraudulent misrepresentation may be one of two types:

(a)   *Negligent misrepresentation.* Negligent misrepresentation presumes that a representation was made negligently. The test here is objective, ie the 'reasonable person' type test.

(b)   *Innocent misrepresentation.* If the maker can show that they had reasonable grounds to believe their statement was true, then s 2(1) says the misrepresentation will be innocent.

If the borrower makes a true statement but then learns before the loan document is executed that it has ceased to be true, it must notify the bank or it may be liable for misrepresentation.

5.5.1.2   Remedies for misrepresentation

The reason for categorising misrepresentation is that each category allows a slightly different remedy.

Rescission

Whatever form the misrepresentation takes, the innocent party has a prima facie right to rescind the contract they were induced to enter. Rescission aims to put the parties back into their pre-contractual position. The right to rescind may be lost in two particular circumstances.

First, s 2(2) of the Misrepresentation Act 1967 (as amended) gives a court the discretion to award damages instead of rescission in non-fraudulent cases. The court may exercise this discretion if it feels that the remedy of rescission is too drastic in the circumstances, particularly since the misrepresentation was not fraudulent. The court will lose this discretion if the right to rescind has been lost (see below).

Secondly, rescission is an equitable remedy and will not be available if, for example:

(a)   it is impossible to restore the pre-contractual position;

(b)   bona fide third party rights have been acquired;

(c)   the innocent party, knowing of the misrepresentation, takes action affirming the agreement; or

(d)   there is undue delay in seeking relief.

Damages

If the misrepresentation is innocent but not negligent, there is no right to damages. Damages may, however, be awarded in lieu of rescission as long as the right to rescind is not lost to an equitable bar (see above).

Negligent misrepresentation and fraudulent misrepresentation both entitle the innocent party to damages, under the Misrepresentation Act 1967, s 2(1) and the tort of deceit respectively. In both cases, however, any damages will be on a tortious basis and, therefore, a bank would get no compensation for loss of bargain or profit (see *Smith New Court Securities Ltd v Scrimgeour Vickers (Asset Management) Ltd* [1997] AC 254, HL, for a comprehensive guide to determining damages for fraudulent representation inducing a plaintiff to buy property).

5.5.1.3   *Hedley Byrne & Co Ltd v Heller & Partners Ltd* [1964] AC 465

There is a claim for negligent misstatement in the law of tort, based on the judgment in *Hedley Byrne v Heller*. This depends on there being a relationship between two parties that gives rise to a duty of care. This might occur, for example, if the borrower's in-house accountant provided information to a bank. The rule in *Hedley Byrne v Heller* is, however, eclipsed by the Misrepresentation Act 1967 in a situation of inducement to contract, because the onus of proof in the latter is more favourable to a claimant.

5.5.2   Application to a facility agreement

The most important remedies for misleading and inaccurate information are built into the facility agreement, typically as events of default. The general law on misrepresentations is therefore only relevant in the unlikely event that a material representation was not caught by the facility agreement, or the facility agreement was unenforceable.

It should be clear by now that a borrower would be hard pressed not to make oral and written representations in the negotiations leading to executing a facility agreement. If any of those statements is untrue, the bank may have a claim for misrepresentation, which has the advantage over an event of default in that it might give a remedy even if the facility agreement is invalid.

5.6   CONCLUSION

The purpose of the representations is threefold. First, while the loan is being negotiated, they will force the borrower to disclose information and discuss problems. Secondly, after execution of the loan, the bank will not be obliged to lend unless the representations are (materially) correct. Lastly, once money has been lent, a breach of representation will allow the bank to pursue the remedies provided by the facility agreement, which ultimately includes demanding repayment (see **Chapter 8**).

A REVIEW OF COMPANY ACCOUNTS

'Fear is that little darkroom where negatives are developed.'

Michael Pritchard

6.1 INTRODUCTION

Chapter 4 considered some of the more important operative provisions at the beginning of a loan document. **Chapter 5** concentrated on how a bank gleans information concerning a borrower. This chapter 'steps back' from the loan document to provide a basic review of company accounts.

Most readers will now protest earnestly that they want to be lawyers, not accountants, which is why they are reading these pages in the first place. However, if they are required in a facility agreement, financial covenants will be keenly negotiated and no banking solicitor can feel entirely comfortable producing a document where a whole section is beyond their comprehension. Furthermore, to fully understand a business you must understand its accounts. A basic grasp of company accounts is therefore essential. The following summary is not intended to be highly technical, specialised, or comprehensive, but a broad introduction.

The observations in this chapter are based on UK GAAP, a compilation of legislation, accounting standards and accepted practice. However, comparison is made with International Financial Reporting Standards (IFRS) on key issues and terminology; and in any event, the UK regime is increasingly converging with IFRS principles. European listed companies must publish *consolidated* accounts under the IFRS (sometimes referred to as International Accounting Standards or 'IAS') pursuant to EU Regulation No 1606/2002.

6.2 FINANCIAL STATEMENTS

Why is a company required to produce accounts? The requirement was originally driven by the principle that members should know how the directors are running their company. Under ss 394–396 of the CA 2006, a company's directors must provide the following financial statements for its shareholders:

(a) a balance sheet (as at the last day of the company's accounting period); and

(b)   an income statement (sometimes known as a profit and loss account),

and, under UK GAAP, a cash flow statement (see **6.6**).

These statements must be delivered to members (and registered at the Companies Registry) once a year, and so are often known as 'annual accounts'. Under s 442 of the CA 2006, they must be produced no later than nine months (or six months for public companies – four months if listed on the London Stock Exchange – see the Disclosure and Transparency Rules, DTR 4.1.3) after the end of the company's financial year, accompanied by a directors' report and an auditor's report (see **6.5**). Parent companies must produce group accounts: a consolidated balance sheet and consolidated profit and loss account (see **6.6**).

In order to understand financial covenants, it is necessary to understand the basic content and structure of financial statements.

6.3   THE BALANCE SHEET

6.3.1   What does it show?

A balance sheet (sometimes known as a 'statement of financial condition') lists all of a company's assets and all of its liabilities at a given date. The total value of the assets less the liabilities gives a figure known as the 'net assets' (aka 'net worth', 'shareholders' funds' or 'equity'). In theory, the net assets figure shows the value left to the shareholders if the company were to repay all its debts on the balance sheet date, but this assumes the 'book value' of all the assets and liabilities is accurate and realisable (which is unlikely, see **6.3.7**). In practice, however, the net assets figure is helpful because:

(a)   if it is a reasonable size, it gives a 'cushion' to allow for the assets being overvalued (or liabilities undervalued) which provides some comfort to creditors;

(b)   it is dissected in the bottom part of the balance sheet into a number of 'reserves' showing where asset value derived from and how much can be distributed to shareholders (see **6.3.5**); and

(c)   some facility agreements impose a net worth covenant which requires the borrower to maintain a minimum value of assets (see **7.3.3.2**).

If a small company were to list its assets and liabilities, it might look something like this:

EXAMPLE 1

Balance sheet as at 31 December 2019

	£	£	£
ASSETS			
Word processors	1,000		
Money at bank	600		
Delivery van	3,500		
Warehouse	8,000		
Money owed by customers	350		
Unsold stock	3,000		
Petty cash	175		
Licence	1,500		
TOTAL		18,125	

	£	£	£
LIABILITIES			
Long-term loan	6,000		
Overdraft	460		
Money owed to creditors	1,150		
TOTAL		7,610	
TOTAL OF ASSETS LESS LIABILITIES			10,515

CAPITAL AND RESERVES	
Called-up capital	5,500
Share premium account	1,500
Profit and loss account (reserves)	3,515
TOTAL	10,515

6.3.2 Grouping of assets and liabilities

The example at **6.3.1** is essentially correct, but in practice the published accounts will show assets and liabilities in groups, and list a total value for that group, rather than list them individually. The groups will usually be as follows.

6.3.2.1 Fixed assets

Fixed assets (known as 'non-current assets' under IFRS) are assets a company intends to retain on a (relatively) permanent basis. In the example at **6.3.1** this will include the word processors, the van, and the warehouse. Essentially, these are assets which the company needs to run its business. They may not be easily or quickly realisable. Fixed assets are sub-divided into 'tangible' (such as those listed above), 'intangible' (such as licences, patents, copyrights or acquired goodwill) and 'investments' (such as long-term shareholdings in other companies).

6.3.2.2 Current assets

Current assets are cash and other assets which a company expects to turn into cash in the ordinary course of its business (usually within 12 months). It is these liquid assets that the company intends to use to pay its short-term liabilities. The current assets therefore form part of the company's 'working capital', essential for maintaining its liquidity (see **3.2.1**). Current assets will include any stock which the company holds, money owed by customers (debtors) and any cash. Current assets are usually listed in order of permanence.

6.3.2.3   Current liabilities

Current liabilities are liabilities which the company must pay within 12 months of the balance sheet date. They are usually labelled in a balance sheet as 'Creditors: amounts falling due within one year'. They will include most trade creditors and any short-term loans, including any overdraft facility and any repayments of long-term loans falling due (see **3.2.1**). Current liabilities would also include any dividend declared but unpaid (eg, because it is awaiting shareholder approval).

6.3.2.4   Long-term liabilities

Long-term liabilities are liabilities which the company need not settle until more than 12 months after the balance sheet date, for example long-term loans. They are usually labelled as 'Creditors: amounts falling due after more than one year'.

6.3.3   Ordering of assets and liabilities

Rather than simply listing the groups of assets and then subtracting all the liabilities (as in Example 1 at **6.3.1**), a balance sheet re-orders these items slightly. First, it will list the groups of fixed assets. It will then show the current assets and the current liabilities, then deduct the latter from the former to show 'net current assets' (or 'liabilities'). This provides an indication of whether the company can cover short-term liabilities with its current assets.

Finally, the long-term liabilities are listed and then subtracted from the above figure to give a total value for the company once all its liabilities have been paid. This is the amount which belongs to the shareholders, and would be returned to them if the company was wound up at that point. Thus the re-written balance sheet from Example 1 would look like this:

EXAMPLE 2

Balance sheet as at 31 December 2019

	£	£	£
FIXED ASSETS			
Tangible assets	12,500		
Intangible assets	1,500		
CURRENT ASSETS			14,000
Stock	3,000		
Debtors	350		
Cash at bank and in hand	775		
		4,125	
LESS CREDITORS: amounts falling due within one year			
Trade creditors	1,150		
Bank overdraft	460		
		1,610	
NET CURRENT ASSETS			2,515
TOTAL ASSETS LESS CURRENT LIABILITIES			16,515
LESS CREDITORS: amounts falling due after more than one year			
Borrowings			6,000
NET ASSETS			10,515
CAPITAL AND RESERVES			
Called-up capital			5,500
Share premium			1,500
Retained profit			3,515
			10,515

Some balance sheets will present the equation in a different order:

Assets = Shareholders' funds (ie capital and reserves) plus liabilities

6.3.4 The 'balancing bit': capital and reserves

As explained at **6.3.3**, the top part of the balance sheet calculates a figure representing all the company's assets less all the debts it owes (in Example 2, that figure is £10,515). These are the 'shareholders' funds' referred to at **6.3.1** – the amount which would be paid back to shareholders if the company were wound up. The bottom part of the balance sheet, headed 'Capital and reserves' (or 'Equity'), takes the figure representing shareholders' funds and shows its origins and whether it is freely distributable to shareholders.

It is important to understand that amounts shown in reserves do not represent money held in an account or specific assets; they are simply retained value in the company.

6.3.4.1 Share capital

This is the total amount of money which shareholders have invested in the company through buying shares. It is divided into:

(a)   called-up share capital, ie the nominal value of the shares which has either been paid by the shareholders, or called to be paid ('nominal' or 'par' value is the value attributed to shares when they are first issued, usually £1); and

(b)   share premium, ie any amount paid for the issued shares over and above their nominal value.

6.3.4.2   Retained profit

This is profit which directors have, over time, retained in the company instead of distributing it to shareholders. The retained profit entry (known as 'retained earnings' under IFRS) is part of a company's 'reserves' (see also revaluation reserve at **6.3.6.1**).

6.3.5   Restrictions on disposal of assets

One of the reasons for splitting the shareholders' funds into categories showing their origins is that there is statutory control over the value of assets which must remain in a company to meet creditors' claims. Essentially, ss 641–653 of the CA 2006 prohibit a company from returning the money paid for its shares to the shareholders (other than under very restricted circumstances), theoretically maintaining a minimum value of assets in the company to meet the demands of creditors. The amounts of paid-up share capital and premium are shown separately because the restrictions on disposing of assets representing the value of the latter are slightly less than for the former.

EXAMPLE 3

The rules outlined above can be illustrated using the figures from Example 2 (see **6.3.4**). On the current figures, the company may pay up to £3,515 to its shareholders because this figure simply represents profits that the directors decided not to distribute at an earlier date. However, the company must keep sufficient assets so that (once all its liabilities are paid off) there is £7,000 worth of assets remaining. Of that £7,000, however, £1,500 is share premium. In limited circumstances (see CA 2006, s 610), for example funding scrip issues (effectively turning premium into share capital), or writing off expenses of issuing shares (instead of reducing the retained profit reserve), assets representing that premium may be disposed of and, in the second example, the value of the company's assets may be reduced to £5,500.

Thus the different categories into which the capital and reserves are divided show the value of assets which cannot be returned to shareholders ('non-distributable' reserves) and the value which may be disposed of freely, or under restricted circumstances.

6.3.6   Miscellaneous

Having reviewed the fundamental aspects of the balance sheet, there are a number of other matters which commonly occur, and which may be conveniently dealt with at this point.

6.3.6.1   Revaluation

Tangible assets are initially recorded on the company's balance sheet at cost. In time, that value is likely to become inaccurate because the assets have depreciated (see **6.3.6.2**) or more rarely appreciated. If an asset is 'revalued' upwards in the balance sheet, this will increase the net assets figure. This in turn means the shareholders' funds will increase, which must be shown under the capital and reserves. The increase cannot be included in the retained profit reserve in the balance sheet, however, because it is only an estimation of the assets' extra worth. It is shown as a separate line in the accounts labelled 'revaluation reserve', which indicates that it is not yet an amount of shareholders' funds which may be distributed. (The exception is if the gain reverses revaluation losses on the same asset which were previously deducted from the retained profit amount.)

The main advantage of upward revaluation to a company is that a higher net asset value usually increases borrowing power and improves the debt to equity ratio (see **7.4.3**). The disadvantage is that the shareholders might expect a higher return.

6.3.6.2   Depreciation and impairment

Most fixed assets will have a period over which their value is used up (their 'useful life'). Initially, these assets are shown on the balance sheet at cost, and at each subsequent balance sheet date the value is reduced: this is known as 'depreciation'. The amount by which the asset is depreciated is then charged as an expense against profit for that year in the income statement. So if a laptop is bought for £300 and judged to have a useful life of three years (ie before needing replacing), its balance sheet value after one year will be shown as £200, after two years £100 and after three years £0. Each year, £100 of depreciation expense will be deducted from profit in the income statement.

In addition to depreciation, fixed assets may be subject to impairment. Essentially, a company must ensure that the (depreciated) value of an asset (or group of assets) shown on the balance sheet is not materially different from what it is actually worth (its 'fair value') at that date. If an asset value has to be reduced to show its fair value, this is known as an 'impairment' and, like depreciation, it is charged against the income statement as a cost for that year, reducing profit. The method used to determine fair value and regularity of its application varies between asset classes.

6.3.6.3   Provisions

Provisions are amounts which are set aside out of a company's profits to cover 'a present obligation as a result of a past event for which it is probable that a transfer of economic benefits will be required'. They ensure a cost is charged against the accounting period in which it occurs, even if it has not yet been paid. Provisions will commonly be made for deferred tax, pension costs and structural changes. They will appear in the balance sheet as a form of liability, usually as 'provisions for liabilities and charges'. Provisions will reduce the profits in the profit and loss account (see **6.4**), which in turn reduces the retained profit figure in the balance sheet.

6.3.7   'Snapshot'

The balance sheet is always given 'as at' a certain day. This is because a list of everything owned, and everything owed, can be accurate only at one given moment in time: the list will change each time an asset is disposed of, or a new liability incurred. The balance sheet is therefore often said to provide a 'snapshot' of the company's assets.

6.3.8   Bank's balance sheet

The majority of assets on the balance sheet of a commercial bank will be loans it has made to customers and other banks. Conversely, its key liabilities will be deposits by customers and other banks. A typical commercial bank balance sheet is set out below by way of illustration.

Balance sheet
As at 28 February 2017

	Notes	2017 £m	2016 £m
Assets			
Loans and advances to customers	11	**3,962**	3,353
Cash and balances with central banks		**377**	423
Loans and advances to banks	13	**26**	25
Derivative financial instruments	14	**1**	–
Financial investments – available for sale			
Investment securities	15	**398**	317
Intangible assets	16	**146**	118
Property, plant and equipment	17	**44**	39
Other assets	19	**840**	224
Total assets		**5,794**	4,499
Liabilities			
Customer accounts	20	**4,101**	3,209
Other deposits	21	**509**	247
Other borrowed funds	22	**311**	299
Derivative financial instruments	14	**21**	18
Other liabilities	23	**106**	107
Provisions for liabilities and charges	24	**15**	16
Total liabilities		**5,063**	3,896
Equity			
Called up share capital	25	**566**	436
Retained earnings	26	**164**	166
Other reserves	27	**1**	1
Total equity		**731**	603
Total equity and liabilities		**5,794**	4,499

6.4 INCOME STATEMENT

6.4.1 Introduction

The retained profit figure on a balance sheet has already been explained at **6.3.5**. Essentially, it shows profit that a company has made but which the directors have not distributed to the shareholders. This figure is a cumulative total of retained profit (less any losses) from year to year since the company started trading. A shareholder will also want a breakdown to show exactly how the company made a profit, or loss, in a particular year. This gives rise to the second financial statement required by the CA 2006, the income statement (also known as the 'profit and loss account').

6.4.2 Period of income statement

Whilst the balance sheet is an inventory of assets and liabilities, and so has to be made at a specific date, the profit or loss that a company makes must be calculated over a specific period. The income statement required by the CA 2006 calculates the profit, or loss, made over a period (generally 12 months) ending with the date of the balance sheet. There is, however, nothing to prevent a company's directors from drawing up an income statement for a different period (see **6.5**).

6.4.3 Structure of income statement

The income statement shows whether a company has made a profit or a loss over a period. The calculation is very straightforward: income less expenses. The income shown in an income statement is income generated by the company's business activities, and does not include money raised by issuing shares or borrowing. The expenses shown are expenses of a 'revenue' nature (ie, day-to-day costs of running the business), and do not immediately include 'capital' expenses (such as plant and machinery) which are instead deducted by way of depreciation or amortisation.

In order to analyse a company's profit or loss, it is convenient to consider its trading in two stages:

(a)   The profit made on buying-in or manufacturing, and then selling the products of the business. This is essentially the money a company raises by selling its products over a period (its 'turnover'), less the price it paid for them. If the company manufactures its products, then the direct costs of producing the products as well as the cost of the raw materials must be deducted from turnover. This figure is known as the 'gross profit'. If a company is making a loss at this stage it is in serious trouble.

(b)   From gross profit, a company must then deduct all the general overheads of running the business, for example advertising costs, administration expenses, etc. This will produce a figure known as the 'net profit'.

The structure of an income statement reflects those two stages outlined above.

EXAMPLE 4

Income statement for the year ended 31 December 2019

	£	£	£
Turnover	110,000		
Cost of sales	58,000		
Gross profit		52,000	
ADMINISTRATION			
Salaries	31,000		
Stationery	240		
Telephone	930		
Electricity	576		
Auditors	325		
General Expenses	925		
	33,996		
SALES			
Advertising	4,300		
Carriage	1,105		
	5,405		
FINANCIAL			
Interest	1,670		
Professional fees	215		
Bad debts	350		
Depreciation	645		
	2,880		
TOTAL EXPENSES		42,281	
NET PROFIT on ordinary activities before TAXATION		9,719	
TAXATION		2,517	
PROFIT on ordinary activities after TAXATION		7,202	
Extraordinary items		2,405	
		4,797	
Dividends			3,000
Retained profit for the year			1,797
Retained profit brought forward			1,718
Retained profit carried forward			3,515

6.4.4   Points to note on the income statement

6.4.4.1   Turnover

Turnover is the total amount of money the business has generated from sales over the previous 12 months.

6.4.4.2   Cost of sales

Cost of sales is the basic cost to the company of buying the products which were sold during the year. To calculate the cost of the stock which was sold, the account will add the cost of stock held at the start of the year (opening stock) to the cost of stock acquired during the year, and then subtract any stock unsold at the end of the year (closing stock). For example, a company starts the year with stock costing £1,000, spends another £4,500 buying stock during the year, but has stock costing £2,300 left at the end of the year. The total cost of stock held *during* the year is:

$$£1,000 + £4,500 = £5,500.$$

However, the cost of stock *remaining* is £2,300. That means stock costing £5,500 − £2,300 = £3,200 was sold during the year.

If the business makes the products which it sells, the 'cost of sales' becomes 'cost of manufacture'. If the company is in the service industry, a similar calculation will be required to ascertain the cost of providing the service.

6.4.4.3   Net profit

In an income statement, 'net profit' is gross profit less all expenses of the business. In one sense, this is a true measure of the profit the directors have managed to make for the year. The more efficiently the business is run, the lower expenses will be and the higher the net profit figure. Whilst tax deductions are still to be shown, those are effectively beyond the directors' control.

6.4.4.4   'Exceptional' items

Exceptional items are material items of income or expense that, due to their size or irregular occurrence, are required by UK accounting standards to be disclosed separately. This might be by way of a separate line on the face of the income statement or by way of a specific note in the accounts. Examples include the profit or loss on sale of an operation, fundamental restructuring costs and the profit or loss on disposal of certain fixed assets. The term 'extraordinary items' is sometime also used in this context, but these are actually highly abnormal and would not be expected to occur in practice.

International Financial Reporting Standards have a similar requirement but use the term 'material items'.

6.4.4.5   Dividends and retained profit

Once any tax, extraordinary or exceptional items have been deducted from the net profit, there will be a final figure representing a profit or a loss made from the company's trading throughout the year. If the figure shows a profit, the directors must decide whether it should be used to pay a dividend to the shareholders, or retained in the company as investment.

6.5   DIRECTORS' REPORT, AUDITOR'S REPORT, AND NOTES TO THE ACCOUNTS

The CA 2006 (s 415) requires the directors of a company to include a report with the annual accounts. This normally appears before the balance sheet and income statement. There are prescribed items to be summarised in the directors' report, although they are usually dealt with in minimal detail. These items include the principal activities of the company, any changes in the business through the year, any anticipated changes in the business, recommended dividends, charitable and political donations, the directors' names and any interests they have in the company's shares or debentures.

Annual accounts will require certification by the company's auditors. This appears as a report to the members immediately after the directors' report. If the auditors are satisfied with the accounts, their core opinion for the consolidated accounts of a UK listed company (which would have to follow IFRS) might typically be worded:

> In our opinion:
>
> - the financial statements, defined below, give a true and fair view of the state of the Group's and of the Company's affairs as at (... year end date ...) and of the Group's profit and of the Group's and Company's cash flows for the year then ended;
> - the Group financial statements have been properly prepared in accordance with International Financial Reporting Standards ('IFRSs') as adopted by the European Union;
> - the Company financial statements have been properly prepared in accordance with United Kingdom Generally Accepted Accounting Practice; and
> - the financial statements have been prepared in accordance with the requirements of the Companies Act 2006 and, as regards the Group financial statements, Article 4 of the IAS Regulation.
>
> This opinion is to be read in the context of what we say in the remainder of this report.

If the auditors are not happy with some aspect of the accounts, they must 'qualify' their report by clearly stating any problems they have discovered. Any such qualification is potentially damaging to a company because it will suggest the financial statements are not reliable. A bank may insist that a material qualification to the accounts will trigger an event of default (see **8.3**).

Lastly, the accounts will invariably include notes, cross-referring to a numbering system against certain entries in the income statement and balance sheet. These notes to the accounts break down the figures on the face of the accounts, providing detailed information on performance and accounting policies adopted by the company.

6.6 CASH FLOW STATEMENTS

As well as Companies Act requirements to produce a balance sheet and income statement, FRS 102, sections 3.10 and 3.17 require companies to produce a cash flow statement. A cash flow statement will show the source of cash coming into a business (from operating activities, from investments and from raising share capital and borrowings), and the destination of cash going out, over a period (typically the accounting year). The cash flow statement is created by taking the net profit figure from the income statement and adjusting it by adding back any non-cash deductions and then taking account of any other cash movements not reflected in that net profit figure. For example, the income statement will have deducted depreciation on fixed assets to calculate the net profit figure. However, depreciation does not represent real cash spent, and so that amount will be added back to the net profit figure. Once all other items of cash inflow or outflow are included (that were not included in calculating the net profit figure), the end result shows whether the company generated more cash than it spent over the period, or vice versa.

An IFRS-based cash flow statement should be near identical to the UK GAAP version.

6.7 CONSOLIDATED ACCOUNTS

When a company has one or more 'subsidiary undertakings', it must produce combined accounts for itself and its subsidiaries, known as 'consolidated accounts' (or 'group accounts'). Essentially, under s 1162 of the CA 2006, a 'subsidiary undertaking' is a company (or partnership, or unincorporated association) in which the parent:

(a)   has a majority of the voting rights; or

(b)   is a member and has the right to appoint or remove a majority of its board of directors; or

(c)   has the right to exercise a dominant influence:

    (i)   by virtue of provisions in the undertaking's memorandum or articles, or

    (ii)   by virtue of a control contract; or

(d)   is a member, and controls a majority of the voting rights through an agreement with other members; and

(e)   an undertaking is a parent undertaking in relation to another undertaking, a subsidiary undertaking, if:

    (i)   it has power to exercise or actually exercises a dominant influence or control over it, or

    (ii)   it is managed on a unified basis with the subsidiary undertaking.

The requirement for consolidated accounts is based on the premise that a parent company's business is likely to be closely linked with that of any subsidiary undertaking. The shareholders of the parent should therefore be provided with financial information on the whole group.

A subsidiary undertaking must continue to produce its own balance sheet and income statement. A parent producing consolidated accounts must produce its own balance sheet, but is not obliged to publish its own income statement. The exemption from producing accounts which applies to small and medium-sized companies (see **6.9.1**) also applies to the obligation to produce consolidated accounts.

Note that European listed companies must produce their consolidated accounts in accordance with IFRS.

6.8   MANAGEMENT ACCOUNTS

Management accounts are financial summaries produced from time to time by a company's directors. They may be a breakdown of figures within the balance sheet and income statement (eg, a manufacturing account), they may be financial projections, or they may be an interim balance sheet or income statement drawn up over a period of one month or more. The board will use the management accounts to monitor the business through its financial year, and help it to make changes and predictions. They may, for example, use them to decide whether to declare an interim dividend.

Unlike final accounts, management accounts do not have to be shown to the shareholders, or lodged at the Companies Registry. Whether a bank has sight of management accounts will depend on the size of the borrower and its relationship with the bank. A borrower will usually be reluctant to provide management accounts: the detail they provide makes them very sensitive, since they may expose information which is hidden behind the broad approach of the published accounts. Any disclosure will often be subject to a confidentiality undertaking.

6.9   ACCOUNTING REGULATIONS

Having reviewed the basic form of company accounts, this chapter concludes with a summary of the regulations which govern them.

There are three main sources of UK regulation affecting company accounts:

(a)   the CA 2006;

(b)   FRSs; and

(c)   the UKLA's 'Listing Rules'.

Together with accepted accounting practices, these form 'UK GAAP' (Generally Accepted Accounting Practice).

6.9.1 Companies Act 2006

The CA 2006 requires the directors of every company to produce a balance sheet and income statement (though this is referred to as a 'profit and loss account' in the Act) for each financial year (ss 394–396). It also requires a directors' report (s 415) and auditors' report (s 495) to accompany the accounts (see also **6.5**). The Act then provides a range of rules relating to the content of those accounts, and the format in which they must be presented.

The CA 2006 also requires copies of the accounts and reports to be:

(a)   sent to every member, debenture holder, and anyone entitled to receive notice of general meetings (s 423). This must be done at least 21 days before (b) below;

(b)   laid before the company at a general meeting (unless, in the case of a private company, this requirement is dispensed with by elective resolution); and

(c)   delivered to the Registrar of Companies, for publication.

The requirements at (b) and (c) must both be satisfied within nine months of the financial year end in the case of a private company, and within six months if a public company (four months if a UK listed company).

The CA 2006 also requires quoted companies to publish their annual accounts and reports on a website (s 430).

6.9.1.1 'Small' and 'medium-sized' companies

Delivering accounts

In the case of 'small' and 'medium-sized' companies, the requirement to deliver accounts to the Registrar is modified. 'Medium-sized' companies may provide the Registrar with an abbreviated income statement. 'Small' companies need not provide the Registrar with an income statement, and may send an abbreviated balance sheet. They may also have a reduced directors' report. The parameters for qualifying as a 'small or medium-sized' company (which is estimated to account for more than 99% of British companies) are currently (CA 2006, s 382 and s 466):

		'Small'	'Medium'
1.	'Turnover' not more than	£10.2m	£36m*
2.	'Balance sheet total' not more than	£5.1m	£18m*
3.	Average employees not more than	50	250

*net of group transactions

Any two criteria must be satisfied.

Auditing requirements

'Small' companies can also qualify for full or partial exemptions from auditing their accounts under the CA 2006 (see s 477).

In addition, under s 482, a company which is a 'non-profit-making' company may enjoy exemption provided it is subject to a form of 'public' audit.

(Note that certain companies are specifically excluded from these exemptions, for example public companies, banking or insurance companies, and members of an 'ineligible group' (see CA 2006, s 384).)

6.9.1.2 True and fair view

There is a fundamental requirement under the CA 2006 (s 393) that the accounts should provide a 'true and fair view'. This principle overrides all others. It is primarily the directors' responsibility to ensure that the accounts give a true and fair view, although it must also be addressed in the auditor's report (see **6.5**). Under the IFRS, the equivalent concept is 'fair presentation'.

6.9.2 Financial Reporting Standards (FRSs)

Whilst the CA 2006 provides some regulation as to the content and format of company accounts, it does not provide detailed guidance but instead requires that they provide a 'true and fair view' (s 393). In order to satisfy the true and fair view requirement, the directors will typically either follow UK Financial Reporting Standards (FRSs) or the international equivalent (International Financial Reporting Standards (IFRSs) and International Accounting Standards (IASs)).

FRSs are created by the Financial Reporting Council, an accounting industry body, and from 1 January 2015 comprise just five standards: FRS 101 to 105. The standard applicable to most UK companies is FRS 102 and the accounts will follow its guidance (or those of the international standards) or else justify any derogation from them.

6.9.3 The Listing, Disclosure and Transparency Rules

The UKLA's Listing, Disclosure and Transparency Rules impose some additional accounting requirements on London-listed companies. First, the Listing Rules require listed companies to prepare their annual report and accounts in accordance with the company's national law and in all material respects with national accounting standards or IFRS (LR 9.8.2R).

The information to be included in the listed company's annual report and accounts is outlined by LR 9.8.4. DTR 4.1 requires the annual report to be published within four months of the financial year end. DTR 4.2 requires a half-yearly (unaudited) financial report to be published no later than two months after the period to which it relates.

6.9.4 Summary accounts

Lastly, s 426 of the CA 2006 allows a listed company to substitute a summary of its full annual accounts for sending to consenting members. This is to avoid the expense of sending a full account, but the proviso is that the members retain the right to receive the full accounts on request.

SUMMARY

(1)   The balance sheet lists all a company's assets, and deducts all its liabilities. The value then remaining belongs to the shareholders. The assets and liabilities fluctuate, and so the calculation can be made only for a particular day (a 'snapshot'), usually the company's year end.

(2)   The income statement (sometimes known as the 'profit and loss account') shows a company's income over the 12 months immediately before the balance sheet date. It then subtracts related expenses of the business over that period to show the profit or loss the company has made. That figure is then combined with any previous retained profit and the total is the retained profit figure at the bottom of the balance sheet.

(3)   The cash flow statement shows all the cash brought into the company less all the cash spent by the company over the same period as the income statement.

(4)   The balance sheet, income statement and cash flow statement must be prepared annually by the directors in order to show the shareholders how their company has been run. They are also deposited at the Companies Registry and are an invaluable source of information for lenders and creditors. The most useful analysis of company accounts comes from comparison with previous years and with results for similar businesses (see also **7.4.4**).

UNDERTAKINGS

'Why didst thou promise such a beauteous day,
And make me travel forth without my cloak
To let base clouds o'ertake me in my way,
Hiding thy bravery in their rotten smoke?'

William Shakespeare

7.1 INTRODUCTION

Representations are about information: undertakings are about control. The greater the control a bank has over a borrower, the better it can safeguard the money it has lent. Undertakings are one of the main provisions in a facility agreement which help a bank to monitor and control a borrower once the agreement is executed. As with representations and events of default, they may apply not just to the borrower, but also to guarantors and other members of the borrower's group.

7.2 WHAT IS AN UNDERTAKING?

7.2.1 Form and purpose

In a facility agreement, an undertaking (also known as a 'covenant') is simply a promise given by the borrower to the bank. It may involve a promise to do (or not to do) something, or to procure that something is (or is not) done by a third party within the borrower's control.

The purpose of the undertakings in a facility agreement is to protect the loan monies, as far as possible, by controlling the assets and activities of the borrower and, sometimes, group companies. Control is achieved using up to three different categories of undertaking:

(a) *Financial covenants* – traditionally known as financial *covenants* (not *undertakings*), these are financial targets which the borrower is required to meet during the life of the loan relating to profit, generation of cash or net worth. They are designed to check adherence to (and so are set with reference to) the borrower's projected performance under its business plan (see **Chapter 8**).

(b) *Information undertakings* – these are promises to provide the banks with information with which they can check the borrower's compliance with the provisions of the facility agreement.

(c) *General undertakings* – these are designed to control the business in general terms by, for example, prohibiting disposals, maintaining insurance and not diversifying from the key business.

These groups are examined more closely at **7.3–7.5** below.

An undertaking will require a borrower to meet certain standards (primarily financial) and to supply the bank with specific information in order to test those standards. Thus the undertakings allow the bank to monitor a borrower's status.

The undertakings are given 'teeth' by making a breach of them an event of default (see **Chapter 8**). The bank will then have an opportunity, amongst other things, to cancel its commitment and demand repayment.

7.2.2 Undertaking or representation?

There is an overlap between undertakings and the representations dealt with in **Chapter 5**. Certain points may be covered using either type of clause.

> **EXAMPLE 1**
>
> A (repeated) representation such as:
>
> 'There are no encumbrances over the borrower's property'
>
> may be recast as an undertaking:
>
> 'The borrower will ensure at all times that there are no encumbrances over its property'.

> **EXAMPLE 2**
>
> An undertaking such as:
>
> 'The borrower will ensure it retains a majority shareholding in X Co'
>
> may be recast as a (repeated) representation:
>
> 'The borrower has a majority shareholding in X Co'.

The choice of whether to use a repeated representation or an undertaking will often depend on the drafting preference of the solicitor. In either case, the likely result of a breach is an event of default. However, some practitioners feel uncomfortable with deeming a borrower to repeat representations, and then relying on a deemed misrepresentation to call a default. They prefer a borrower to represent the position at signing and at the same time promise (undertake) that it will maintain the position throughout the term of the loan. Once that promise has been given, it will apply at all times (until the facility ends) and create a default immediately it is broken: in contrast, a repeating representation is tested only at the time of repetition (typically at the start of each interest period).

Note also that using a representation followed by an undertaking allows a strict initial test (the representation) followed by a more relaxed test (the undertaking) going forward. This ensures the banks elicit maximum information initially, but avoid a 'hair trigger' once the money has been lent.

In addition, a breach of a representation may give remedies under the Misrepresentation Act 1967 (see **5.5.1**), whereas a breach of an undertaking may give remedies of specific performance or an injunction (although note that specific performance is a discretionary remedy, and the courts will not order specific performance where damages are an adequate remedy (almost always the case for a facility agreement), and are particularly averse to granting specific performance of loan contracts).

7.3 FINANCIAL COVENANTS

7.3.1 What are financial covenants?

Financial covenants are undertakings which impose financial targets or limitations on a borrower. They are invariably seen in leveraged financings, may be used for cross-over credits, but are unusual for investment grade borrowers. The sections below concentrate on (maintenance) financial covenants seen in leveraged acquisition facilities, but project financing, real estate financing and some bond documents also use their own tailored forms of financial covenants. There are two broad types of financial covenant used in the London loan markets: maintenance covenants, and incurrence covenants.

Maintenance covenants

These are the most common form of financial covenant in the London market and are explained in a little more detail at **7.3.3**. They require the borrower to *maintain* a specified level of financial performance and are tested regularly over the life of the loan facility. The targets set in the financial covenants are based on the predictions for the borrower's performance shown in the directors' business plan (but usually allowing for a degree of underperformance against those predictions, known as 'headroom').

Maintenance covenants allow the banks to monitor the borrower's performance, to impose some control on what the borrower does with its money, and sometimes to incentivise the borrower. It is important to note, however that maintenance covenants measure *past* performance: the figures they use are for a period that has already taken place. They may indicate a positive or negative trend and so warn the bank of potential breach, but they will not tell the bank whether the borrower will meet its next interest payment.

The result of breaching the maintenance financial covenants is an event of default.

Incurrence covenants

Incurrence covenants also set financial targets, but the borrower has to show compliance only if it wants to do specified things, for example disposing of large assets, acquiring new companies or paying dividends. If the borrower does not do the specified things, it will not *incur* the covenants (ie they will not be tested). Incurrence covenants originated in high yield bonds, a US product which has found a foothold in the London market as bank liquidity has been reduced. Some leveraged loan facilities have also adopted incurrence-style financial covenants and are colloquially known as 'covenant lite'.

7.3.2 Form of financial covenants: limits and ratios

Some financial covenants simply set a financial limit which a borrower must attain, eg, net worth of at least £50 million, or a maximum amount of capital expenditure allowed each year. However, most financial covenants compare two figures derived from the borrower's accounts: the most common of these are explained below.

7.3.3 Examples of financial covenants

7.3.3.1 Ratios

There are no 'rules' for computing ratios; however, there is little point in comparing figures which have no logical connection. For example, comparing a company's fixed assets to its share premium would produce a ratio, but a fairly meaningless one. The more common ratios used by banks in leveraged financing are set out below.

Leverage ratio

A leverage ratio compares the amount of debt a company has at a moment in time to the profit (or 'earnings') it has earned over a period (usually a year) leading up to that time. The ratio is typically written as:

Net Debt : EBITDA

'Debt' is usually defined as commercial borrowing (eg loan facilities, bonds, finance leases and equivalents) and will not include short-term trade creditors (eg suppliers who give the borrower, say, 90 days to pay for goods). The amount of debt is typically reduced by the amount of freely available cash held in the borrower at that date (hence the term 'net' debt) on the basis that the cash is 'unused' borrowings and could in theory be used to pay back the debt. If the covenants are tested against the figures for a group of companies then the debt figure will come from consolidated accounts and be 'consolidated net debt'.

'EBITDA' stands for 'earnings before (taking into account) interest, tax, depreciation and amortisation' and is a measure of profit. Profit is a key indicator of the success of a business, and EBITDA is an ingredient in most financial covenants, though it is not an accurate measure of how much cash a business is generating (see 'Fixed charge cover ratio' below). Exceptional items (see **6.4.4.4**) will typically be excluded from EBITDA to give a figure representing the underlying trading performance of the borrower.

Banks will set the leverage ratio at a level which is acceptable to the market for a particular borrower and its sector, but a 'typical' acquisition financing might see a ratio of between 4 and 5 to 1.

A leverage ratio is sometimes known as a 'debt cover' ratio, but note that 'gearing' is strictly the ratio of net debt to net worth.

Interest cover ratio

The interest cover ratio measure a borrower's ability to cover the interest payment and fee obligations under its borrowing. The ratio is typically written as:

EBITDA : Net Finance Charges

The term 'EBITDA' has been explained above.

Finance charges are fees and interest payments (but not capital repayments) due under the borrower's main debt obligations (commercial borrowing and equivalents). Any interest earned by the borrower from its investments is usually deducted from interest payable (hence the term 'net' finance charges). Again, the interest cover ratio will depend upon the borrower and sector, but a ratio of 2 to 1 is not uncommon.

Cashflow cover ratio (aka 'fixed charge cover' or 'debt service cover')

A cashflow cover ratio looks at the ability of a borrower to generate enough cash (rather than profit) to pay *all* amounts due under its borrowing. The ratio is typically written as:

Cashflow : Net Debt Service

Cashflow is, broadly, the amount of cash the borrower has generated from its business, less the amount it has spent, over a given period (typically a year). The definition usually starts with EBITDA but then adjusts the items included and excluded to represent cash movements more closely (EBITDA includes non-cash items and makes non-cash deductions). This is a similar concept to the cash flow statements discussed at **6.6**, though not quite as 'pure' (a strong borrower will negotiate out some cash expenditure from the cashflow definition, and it will not include cash from borrowing under loan facilities, bonds, etc).

Net debt service will include fees and interest payments due under the borrower's commercial borrowing and equivalents (like the interest cover ratio), but will also include any capital repayments due. The cashflow cover ratio is typically set at 1:1.

In addition, the cashflow definition is used as a starting point for calculating whether the borrower has produced more cash than the bank believes the borrower needs to run its business. This 'excess cash' is usually taken by the bank and used to prepay the loan, thereby reducing the leverage, under a provision known as a 'cash sweep'.

7.3.3.2   Limits

The following financial covenants may be set as minimum or maximum financial limits with which the borrower must comply.

Minimum net worth

A minimum net worth financial covenant aims to ensure the company maintains a minimum value of assets in the business. The definition of 'net worth' will vary slightly between agreements, but is intended to represent the difference between the borrower's assets (at their value in the latest accounts) and the borrower's liabilities. The starting point is therefore the paid-up share capital of the borrower together with any reserves (essentially the 'shareholders' funds' in the balance sheet (see **6.3.1**)).

If a bank has to look to a borrower's fixed assets to repay the loan, the borrower is almost certainly in severe financial difficulty and will probably be wound up. Most calculations of 'net worth' will therefore exclude any assets which may have little or no value if the borrower is in liquidation (these will generally be the so-called 'intangible assets'). The definition of 'net worth' is therefore likely to be headed 'tangible net worth' and (if otherwise included) exclude the following:

(a) *Goodwill.* Goodwill is the difference between the price paid for a business by a purchaser and the aggregate fair value of that business's assets and liabilities. Under UK GAAP (and IFRS), the amount paid for goodwill when buying another company may be shown on the acquiring company's balance sheet. Since a business that is not trading successfully will probably be worth little more than the value of its tangible assets (unless there are particular items such as a brand name which can be identified and sold off separately), goodwill is usually excluded from the calculation.

(b) *Capitalised research and development costs.* Research and development costs are usually entered as an expense in the P&L account for the year in which the expense was incurred. However, in some circumstances, these costs may be lumped together (capitalised) and treated as an asset in the balance sheet, if, amongst other things, it is reasonably certain that they will be recovered once the product to which they relate is developed. This capitalised amount is then 'amortised' (gradually deducted as an expense against profit over time) to spread the cost over a period as a form of accrual (see **6.3.8**). Most definitions of 'net worth' will require any costs capitalised in this way to be excluded because they do not represent a tangible asset.

(c) *Patents, copyrights, concessions, licences, etc.* Patents, copyrights and similar assets are likely to be excluded from a definition of 'net worth' because they are often not transferable (ie cannot be sold) or would be worth little or nothing on insolvency.

(d) *Payments on account.* Payments on account, where a borrower has received money in advance of providing any product or service, are also usually excluded from the net worth calculation since they would have to be repaid if the borrower did not perform.

(e) *Unaudited revaluation.* If the borrower has written up the value of fixed assets (eg, freehold or leasehold property) after the date of the last audited balance sheet, the increase may not be permitted to count towards 'net worth' until it is confirmed by the auditors. This is to avoid the borrower over-inflating the value in order to meet its financial covenants.

(f) *Tax provisions.* Any provisions for the payment of anticipated tax liability (see **6.3.7**) would usually be added back (ie, increasing net worth for the purpose of measuring compliance with the covenant).

Capital expenditure

This financial covenant puts a limit on the amount the borrower can spend on 'long-term' assets of the business (ie 'capital expenditure') over a given period. The aim of this covenant is to limit expansion of the business and help retain cash to service the debt. This covenant is known colloquially as the 'capex' covenant.

Borrowing

A bank will want to limit a borrower's exposure to other creditors, and this may be achieved through a financial covenant capping total borrowings. A borrower may ask for the cap to be linked to its tangible net worth, so that it remains relevant in the context of the borrower's size (and it then becomes a gearing ratio). Since there are many different ways for a corporate borrower to raise money, the definition of 'borrowings' (or 'financial indebtedness') must be fairly sophisticated. The following transactions are likely to be included in the definition because their commercial effect is similar to borrowing:

(a)   *Finance leases and instalment credit agreements.* Some leasing arrangements are structured to finance the use of the leased asset by one lessee (known as 'finance leases'). The lessee will usually be required, over the life of the lease, to pay instalments to the lessor equivalent to the full value of the leased asset together with a return on the capital value. The lessee is usually responsible for maintaining the asset, and early termination of the lease will incur a heavy penalty. The effect of these leases is very similar to borrowing a capital sum and paying it back in instalments, and the asset and capitalised obligation must be recorded in the lessee's balance sheet. Finance leases are used to fund assets such as computer hardware or heavy machinery, and frequently feature in aircraft financing.

   Other types of agreements under which the borrower is effectively given credit and repays capital by instalments will also be defined as 'borrowing'. The most common example is a hire purchase agreement.

(b)   *Deferred purchase agreements.* Deferred purchase agreements allow for the purchase price of an asset or services to remain outstanding for a period of time, and will usually be defined as 'borrowings'.

(c)   *Capital instruments.* Capital instruments, for example bonds, notes and commercial paper, are borrowing methods explained in **Part III** of this book.

(d)   *Guarantees and indemnities.* Where the borrower has given a financial guarantee, indemnity or any other form of financial assurance in respect of any transaction, that will usually be included as 'borrowing'.

7.3.4   Using financial ratios

7.3.4.1   Defining terms

Accounting is certainly more akin to an art than a science. The CA 2006 and accounting standards allow a company some discretion in the format and content of financial statements and the way certain events are presented (see **6.9**). To avoid ambiguity, the financial covenants should therefore be carefully drafted, and terminology should be specifically defined, rather than relying on standard accounting terms.

7.3.4.2   Information for testing

Under the CA 2006, all companies must produce some form of year end accounts, while (London) listed companies must also produce 'interims' – an unaudited report on their activities and profit and loss for the first six months of their financial year. These will provide figures with which a bank can test the financial covenants it has set for the borrower. If a bank wants to test a borrower's compliance more frequently than twice a year, what figures can it use? (Note that whilst banks will usually have a right to request financial information at any time (see **7.5**), they will not usually do so without suspicion that the borrower is in trouble.)

The solution is to require the borrower to supply a 'compliance certificate', signed by two directors, confirming that the financial covenants have been met on the requisite date: typically every 'quarter' (3 months). The compliance certificates must usually be accompanied by a set of financial statements covering the certified period, and may also contain confirmation that there has been no default.

7.3.4.3 Changes to GAAP and accounting policies

A bank will want to ensure that each new set of financial statements delivered by the borrower adopts the same accounting policies and practice used for the accounts the borrower originally supplied and on which the financial covenants were set. However, GAAP evolves from time to time and borrowers may legitimately wish to modify the policies they apply. The usual solution to this problem is to allow the borrower to modify policies and follow changes to GAAP as long as its auditors provide a description of changes necessary to reflect the new financial statements as if written under the original policies and practice. This allows the bank still to check compliance with the financial covenants, and is known as a 'frozen GAAP' provision. To avoid the frozen GAAP provision becoming a long-term burden, there will also be provision for the bank and borrower to negotiate re-setting of the financial covenants to neutralise the accounting policy change (and, if they cannot agree, to use a third party 'expert' to advise on necessary changes).

7.3.4.4 Equity cure

Traditionally, borrowers could not cure a breach of a financial covenant: it was seen as a 'mathematical' test to be met at a given time, and failure to do so would require a waiver to avoid default. However, strong equity sponsors in acquisition financings have negotiated the right to inject cash into a borrower to help it meet its financial covenants. This right is known as 'equity cure' and usually works by reducing debt, either by actual prepayment or by leaving the money in an account which reduces 'net debt'.

Equity sponsors would prefer to treat the new cash as if it is profit made by the borrower (ie, increasing the borrower's EBITDA). Under this method, the ratio works for them (ie, they need inject less cash to get the same result) but it is less commonly given. Equity cure monies will, however, be treated as positive cashflow when testing the fixed charge cover ratio.

7.4 INFORMATION UNDERTAKINGS

The effectiveness of most provisions in the facility agreement will depend on the bank receiving a regular supply of information from the borrower. The nature and extent of the information undertakings will depend on the type and size of loan, but might include those discussed below.

Syndicated facilities will require sufficient copies of any information to be delivered to the agent to supply the syndicate banks.

7.4.1 Financial information

The bank will require financial information to monitor the borrower's financial wellbeing and to check for any breach of the financial covenants. The main sources (not all of which are always required) are as follows:

(a) Year end accounts (and interims, or possibly even pro forma quarterlies, if appropriate), including consolidated accounts if the borrower has subsidiary undertakings (see **6.6**). An investment grade borrower is typically given between 120 and 180 days (after its financial year end) to deliver its annual accounts, and up to 90 days to deliver interims.

(b) Management accounts (ie unpublished pro forma accounts produced by companies for internal use), which might include cash flow statements, income statements and a cash flow forecast. These might form the basis of the financial statements used to accompany quarterly or monthly compliance certificates.

(c) A forecast of the borrower's performance, usually in the form of projected balance sheet, income statement and cash flow statements for the financial year ahead. Sometimes a commentary of the borrower's actual performance as against its forecast performance is also required.

(d)   A certificate, provided on each covenant testing date, which shows compliance with all the financial covenants (a 'compliance certificate').

(e)   A 'sweep-up' provision requiring the borrower to provide any other information within its control, which relates to the financial condition or operation of the borrower, and which the bank requests. A well-advised borrower would negotiate this requirement subject to no material cost (at least prior to any default). A bank would not usually use this provision unless it suspected the borrower might be in breach.

7.4.2 Shareholder documents

A bank may ask for copies of all information sent to the borrower's shareholders, although a borrower might feel that this smacks of a 'trawling' process. A compromise might be to send the bank any information which the borrower is required, by statute, to send to its shareholders. This 'filter' should ensure the bank receives only the relatively important information.

7.4.3 'Know Your Customer'

In an effort to combat money laundering, regulators require tight monitoring of banks' clients, a process referred to as 'Know Your Customer' or 'KYC'. Banks will make initial KYC checks before the facility is executed. In addition, an undertaking by the borrower to supply information reasonably requested by any lender in order to fulfil ongoing KYC obligations is now standard. Lenders will give a similar undertaking to each other.

Borrowers may, not unreasonably, ask to limit this undertaking to information within their possession or control, or which they can obtain with reasonable endeavours. This would avoid a breach of undertaking beyond their control (and leave the banks to rely on the illegality clause if necessary – see **9.9.3**).

7.4.4 Insurance

Most banks will require a borrower to maintain adequate insurance for its major assets, even if the loan is unsecured (see **7.5.1.1**). As a check to ensure the policies are renewed, a bank may include an undertaking requiring the borrower to produce copies of insurance policies or certificates if requested and to notify the bank of any material changes to insurance cover.

7.4.5 Notification of default

There will invariably be an undertaking requiring the borrower to notify the bank if it defaults under the loan. The undertaking may also require the borrower to notify the bank of any 'potential' events of default that might occur (note that failure to notify would therefore cause a default, even if the potential event of default itself has been, or might be, cured (see **8.6**)). The definition of 'potential event of default' is therefore critical, because it determines the sensitivity of the undertaking.

The undertaking will require written confirmation, to be given by the directors at the bank's request, confirming that there has been no default or potential event of default. This may be useful, to put pressure on the borrower if the bank fears it is in difficulty but has no evidence of default.

7.5 GENERAL UNDERTAKINGS

The final set of undertakings comprises those under which the borrower promises to do, or not to do, something. The aim of these positive (or 'affirmative') and negative undertakings is usually to preserve the borrower's assets, and to ensure there is not a fundamental change in the business on which the bank assessed its lending risk.

Once again, the exact form of these 'general' undertakings depends on the circumstances of each particular loan. However, it is possible to identify a number that are commonly used.

7.5.1 Positive undertakings

Positive undertakings require some sort of positive action by the borrower, or by an entity within the borrower's control.

7.5.1.1 Insurance

The bank will usually require the borrower to keep all its major assets insured. This may be because the bank holds some form of security over the assets, but it also avoids the borrower losing assets which it cannot replace, with a subsequent loss of income. In the case of very small borrowers, or in an acquisition finance, the borrower will sometimes employ one or more managers who the bank sees as crucial to the ongoing success of the business. In such a situation, the bank may make it a condition of lending that the borrower obtains, and maintains, 'Keyman' insurance over the life of these individuals. If the insured should die, a lump sum will be paid to the borrower, which will bolster the borrower through a potentially difficult time and help to fund a replacement for the 'key' manager.

7.5.1.2 Consents, licences and laws

An undertaking will also usually be included requiring the borrower to ensure that it maintains all necessary consents, authorisations and licences to perform its obligations under the loan document. Similarly, a borrower must invariably undertake to comply with all laws if failure to do so might have a 'material adverse effect' (usually a defined term). Compliance with environmental laws is often covered in some detail in a separate undertaking.

7.5.1.3 Access to information and assistance

Very occasionally, an undertaking is included which requires a borrower to give the bank access to its books and records. The bank may also require the right to inspect the borrower's assets. In either case the borrower will want reasonable notice, and availability restricted to within office hours.

7.5.2 Negative undertakings

Negative undertakings prohibit the borrower from doing something, or require the borrower to ensure something is not done by an entity within the borrower's control.

7.5.2.1 Negative pledge

One of the most important negative undertakings is the so-called 'negative pledge'. This is an undertaking by the borrower not to create any security (other than to the bank) over its assets. Where the bank is unsecured, the purpose of this clause is self-evident. However, even if the bank has taken security, it may insist on a negative pledge to help protect its floating charge security (see **13.3**). Furthermore, a secured creditor is more able to pursue a debtor's assets than an unsecured creditor, and so the former may be more willing, or more able, to precipitate any action.

A borrower may want certain exceptions 'carved out' of the negative pledge to ensure that it can carry on business as usual, for example:

(a) security that might be necessary under equipment leasing, or hire purchase arrangements. Control on this type of transaction should be achieved through specific undertakings if necessary;

(b) liens arising under the common law, statute, and in the ordinary course of business. A trading company has little control over these occurring (eg, an asset which is retained by a third party until payment for services). The bank may want to restrict any carve-out to allow liens only on amounts overdue for a maximum of, say, 30 days;

(c)   cash collateralisation (ie depositing money by way of security) that may be necessary as part of the borrower's business arrangements;

(d)   security which pre-dates the facility;

(e)   security which the borrower acquires through purchasing an asset or business over which the security already exists (this may carry a proviso that the borrower obtains release of the security within a few months of acquiring the asset);

(f)   netting or 'set-off' arrangements between group companies, and any cash management arrangements with clearing banks;

(g)   retention of title clauses, allowing a creditor to recover assets from the borrower. If this carve-out is permitted, it should usually only be on the basis that the clause is not registered as a charge;

(h)   project finance, in which a borrower is lent money to finance a specific project, for example a factory. Banks to a project finance will want security over the asset being funded, but since that will not impinge on the existing assets of the borrower, there is an argument that it should be outside the negative pledge; and

(i)   a 'de minimis' amount (also known as a 'basket') allowing an aggregate amount of debt for which the borrower may create any security.

In addition, a borrower might ask for 'carve-outs', allowing security between companies in its group; new security which replaces existing security (eg, on a refinancing of existing debt); and security given in relation to 'factoring' (selling its debts).

Sometimes the negative pledge contains wording which attempts to create security for the bank automatically in the event that the undertaking is breached. This provides that, if the borrower gives security to a third party (so breaching the negative pledge), it is deemed to create equal security for the bank, at the same time and over the same assets. There are some doubts as to whether this type of provision is effective under English law, the fundamental problem being that the new security would probably fail for lack of registration.

7.5.2.2   Pari passu ranking

The negative pledge clause will often be accompanied by an undertaking under which the borrower is to ensure that:

> The claims of the bank rank at least pari passu with the claims of all other present or future unsecured and subordinated creditors, except for those preferred by bankruptcy, insolvency, liquidation or other similar laws.

Whilst the negative pledge ensures that the bank's right to repayment is not subordinated to secured creditors, a 'pari passu' undertaking tries to ensure that the bank is not subordinated to unsecured creditors. In fact, drafting this as an undertaking (ie, a promise to do it) arguably looks a little awkward, and some practitioners prefer to use a repeated representation or event of default instead (see **5.2.2**).

7.5.2.3   Disposals and acquisitions

Any substantial disposal of assets (other than trading stock) may affect the borrower's ability to service the loan and might also indicate cash flow problems. A bank will usually, therefore, restrict, if not prohibit, the disposal of assets (including shares) other than disposals in the ordinary course of trading or in exchange for comparable or superior assets.

The undertaking may allow the disposal of obsolete assets, though any disposals of shares, businesses or land may require the bank's consent (on the basis that even if the borrower does not 'need' them, they are likely to be of value). Alternatively, or in addition, the clause might allow disposals at arm's length up to a maximum aggregate annual value (a 'basket'), or be tied in to mandatory prepayment (see **9.2.3**).

A bank will also typically want to restrict a borrower from making substantial acquisitions of shares or a business: there may be restrictions on mergers, and almost always an undertaking that there will not be any substantial change to the general nature of the business (see **8.3.6**).

7.5.2.4 Lending

Allowing a borrower to lend carries risk of non-repayment, and so a depletion of assets. The borrower will probably have to give an undertaking not to lend, other than in the ordinary course of its business (eg, trade credit) or within the group of companies 'controlled' by the facility agreement and any security.

7.5.2.5 Shares and dividends

With some borrowers (in particular under leveraged facilities), a bank may require an undertaking from the borrower not to make any distributions to its shareholders without the bank's consent or meeting a financial test. This is to avoid money leaving the company before the bank is satisfied that the loan can be serviced. The bank may agree that the undertaking will not apply to the borrower's subsidiaries, since that would prevent profits being hived-up to the borrower to help it meet its obligations (sometimes known as 'dividend stripping').

Care must be taken if the borrower has issued any preference shares. Under the borrower's articles of association, these shares might provide the holder with a fixed rate of dividend which must be paid if the company's profits reach a pre-ordained amount. The undertaking should take account of any such obligations on the borrower to avoid inducing a breach of contract. Lastly, if the borrower has subsidiaries, then the bank may require that the borrower undertakes not to allow those subsidiaries to issue shares to third parties. This will prevent dilution of the borrower's holding, with the subsequent reduction in value.

7.5.2.6 Auditors

In older documents, banks sometimes sought an undertaking from borrowers that they would only appoint auditors whose size and status were satisfactory to the bank. More recently, such provisions have been seen as potentially anti-competitive and, from 17 June 2016, the statutory Auditors and Third Country Auditors Regulations 2016 (SI 2016/649) mean that any contractual clause that restricts an audited person's choice of auditor has no legal effect.

7.5.2.7 People with significant control

Since 6 April 2016 (following an amendment to the CA 2006 made by the Small Business, Enterprise and Employment Act 2015) most UK incorporated companies have been required to keep a register of individuals and certain entities that have 'significant control' over them. If a company fails to comply with this 'people with significant control' regime, the sanctions may prevent security being taken or enforced over the company's shares. Secured facilities will therefore usually include an undertaking that the group companies will comply with the relevant requirements.

7.6 UNDERTAKINGS – THE BANK'S PERSPECTIVE

It is important to understand that the undertakings control the borrower's business and so the decision on which to include, and how restrictive they are, is very dependent on the context of the loan. For example, a loan to a large investment grade company for general corporate purposes is perceived as very low risk and so will contain very few undertakings. Leveraged acquisition finance is more risky and so may warrant more controls over assets, borrower activities and 'cash leakage' from the group (eg by shareholder distributions). The level of undertakings is also driven by current market conditions, for example if a borrower has several sources to raise debt, banks may relax demands in order to win business (see the article on p 85).

When drafting undertakings for a bank (and advising on their enforcement), a solicitor should be aware of the provisions relating to 'shadow directorship' in the CA 2006, IA 1986, Company Directors Disqualification Act 1986 (CDDA 1986) and FSMA 2000. A 'shadow director' is, in broad terms, a person in accordance with whose directions or instructions the directors of the company are accustomed to act (the definition is almost identical in all four statutes – see ss 251, 251, 22 and 417 respectively), with an exception for professional advisers. If a bank uses the undertakings in its facility agreement to force a borrower to take certain action, it seems possible that the bank might be a 'shadow director'. The time of greatest risk is usually when a borrower is in financial difficulties: in an attempt to preserve its assets, a bank may be tempted to persuade the borrower's directors to take certain action under threat of enforcement of security, or even liquidation.

In *Re A Company (No 005009 of 1987)* [1989] BCLC 324, a company was allegedly managed in accordance with the bank's suggestions under threat of the bank otherwise appointing an administrative receiver. The judge held that this was arguably a case of shadow directorship, although the allegation was in fact dropped later in the case. In a more recent case *Re PFTZM Ltd* [1995] BCC 280, a company which could not meet its obligations under a secured loan was subject to weekly management meetings with the lending bank's staff in order to monitor the business. It was held that the bank was not acting as a shadow director, but simply trying 'to rescue what they could out of the company using their undoubted rights as secured creditors'.

The implications of being a shadow director include taking on the duties and responsibilities of an executive director (in so far as common law rules or equitable principles apply – see CA 2006, ss 170–177). Perhaps more seriously from a bank's perspective, a shadow director may be held liable for wrongful trading under the IA 1986, s 214(7), and may have to contribute to a company's assets on its liquidation. This is of particular concern to a bank involved in a workout or refinancing. Lastly, the provisions of the FSMA 2000 will apply equally to shadow directors as to executive directors (s 417).

7.7 UNDERTAKINGS – THE BORROWER'S PERSPECTIVE

A borrower is unlikely to be able to negotiate a loan that is 'undertaking free'. However, it is important to all parties that the facility agreement (in particular, a long-term loan) is workable in practice. In particular, the provision of financial projections and management accounts can be very time-consuming if they are not already part of the directors' remit. Furthermore, any failure to provide information on time may result in default, even if the information itself was satisfactory. The borrower's solicitor will therefore need to ensure that the undertakings are not too tight and, where possible, are subject to materiality or a de minimis. Any time limits for producing information, or for achieving a target, must be attainable. Requests for information should be 'reasonable' requests wherever possible. The borrower should also try to negotiate cure periods for as many breaches as possible (see **8.3** and **8.7**). Lastly, as with representations, the borrower will try to limit the number of companies subject to the undertaking, by, for example, referring only to 'Material Subsidiaries'.

Covenants in spotlight as banks reduce 'headroom' on company debt

By Anousha Sakoui

Mark Pain describes it as one of the most difficult periods of his 25-year career - involving round-the-clock work at an incredible intensity.

The finance director of Barratt Developments is referring to four months spent renegotiating the housebuilder's finances, at a time when the UK property market had nosedived.

It is an experience being lived by a growing number of companies having to face the fact that they can no longer refinance themselves out of trouble, unlike previous years, when debt financing was abundant and on easy terms.

"This is a turbulent river and we have crossed it, but there are still some on the other side," says Mr Pain.

Many companies are already in talks with lenders to ease debt terms, in particular waiving or resetting so-called covenants as earnings deteriorate.

The bad news is that banks have cut the margin for error they allow companies on meeting financial targets linked to earnings or other measures of ability to pay debt.

This so-called "headroom" has shrunk in bank lending terms this year by a third to about 20 per cent, according to research from analysts at Deloitte.

Covenants are financial ratios or limits that provide lenders with red flags warning of any sign that a company may start to struggle to meet debt repayments.

Advisers say more companies are struggling to meet these financing terms. Mike Duncan, chairman of the global banking practice at Allen & Overy, the law firm, believes this will worsen by the end of the year.

Barratt agreed with lenders to reset covenants, including swapping its interest cover-based covenant with a cash-flow covenant, highlighting banks' growing focus on the ability of companies to generate cash as they try to ride through the next few years, rather than profitability.

Barratt also had its leverage covenant and minimum tangible net worth covenants relaxed, which would allow it to make writedowns on its land bank.

Other covenants in the spotlight are based on the size of the loan relative to the value of the assets. Property companies are at risk of breaching these triggers as real estate prices plunge.

Mr Duncan says banks seem relatively relaxed about breaches for good quality commercial assets that still pay interest, but he expects them to be worried if rental income falls.

Banks balance the need to set these covenants tight enough to keep a grip on performance but loose enough to avoid breaches. Mr Duncan says initial breaches are more likely to be waived and covenants reset for a fee. A second breach is more of an issue

This year banks have, unsurprisingly, increased the covenants they place on loan financings, reversing the pre-credit crunch trend of ever-loosening terms.

Once a company realises it is close to breaching, or has breached, tests it is thrown into talks with banks in an attempt to get waivers.

In the Barratt example, the board was taken aback by a big drop in orders in the first week of April. Concerned about a £400m debt refinancing due in 12 months, Mr Pain started talking to banks. As the sector remained under pressure into May, stress tests of finances started to indicate it could struggle to meet covenants.

The process can be fraught. After a series of meetings with banks and private placement noteholders, which had the same covenants as its bank debt, Mr Pain finalised the creditor sign-off on a restructuring of its finances mere hours before a trading update to the market early last month.

For banks, though, the growing concern is that many existing financings carry so few, or such loose, covenants that by the time a company is forced into talks it will be too late.

Because covenants and the negotiations around them are carried out behind closed doors, the scale of the problem is hidden. Some believe the number of companies struggling with covenants could be double what has been reported in the press.

Covenant measures

* **Leverage** - a measure of borrowings relative to earnings. For an investment grade company, debt divided by earnings before interest, tax, depreciation and amortisation (Ebitda) typically has to be kept below 3.5-3.75. For a leveraged buy-out for example, with more speculative grade debt, it can be much higher

* **Interest cover** - the ratio of interest cost to earnings before interest and tax. Generally set at about 3:1-3.5:1 for an investment grade company. Ensures that profitability is enough to ensure a company can meet interest payments

* **Capex** - places a restriction on the amount a company can spend on capital expenditure over a period of time. More common in buy-out financing

* **Debt service or cash flow** - monitors that a company has enough cash to cover both principal and interest repayments on debt. More common in buy-out financing

* **Tangible net worth** - measures the value of a company's tangible assets

An example of renegotiating breached covenants.
Source: *Financial Times*

EVENTS OF DEFAULT

> 'It is impossible to live without failing at something, unless you live so cautiously that you might as well not have lived at all – in which case you will fail by default.'
>
> JK Rowling

8.1 INTRODUCTION

The events of default dictate the circumstances in which a bank can terminate its loan early or take other action to reduce risk. Because of this, they will be among the most heavily negotiated clauses in the whole agreement. The events of default also dovetail with many other operative parts of a facility agreement.

8.2 WHY HAVE EVENTS OF DEFAULT?

If one party breaches the provisions of an agreement, an 'injured' party may seek a remedy for breach of contract. The type of remedy available for breach of contract (under English law) will depend on the type of term that has been breached:

(a) *Conditions.* Conditions are terms which are fundamental to a contract. Breach of a condition may allow the injured party to terminate the contract and claim damages, or to affirm the contract and claim damages.

(b) *Warranties.* Warranties are terms which are not considered fundamental to the contract (see also **5.5.2**). Breach of a warranty will not allow the injured party to terminate the contract, but merely to claim damages for any loss arising from the breach.

(c) *Intermediate (or innominate) terms.* Intermediate terms are a creature of judicial invention created to bridge the gap between conditions and warranties. They will usually be terms which are capable of being breached either in a trivial, or in a fundamental way. The remedy available on the breach of an intermediate term will be either damages, or damages and termination, depending on the effect of the breach on the contract.

In addition, if a party to the agreement makes a false representation to induce the other party to contract, the remedies for misrepresentation may be available (see **Chapter 5**).

However, if a borrower breaches a term of the facility agreement or is guilty of misrepresentation, a bank will not want to rely on common law or statutory remedies. If the breach is serious, a bank must be able to take immediate action. Events of default are events, specified in the facility agreement, which provide the bank with a contractual right to suspend or cancel any commitment, put the loan on demand, or immediately demand repayment of all outstanding principal and interest (known as 'acceleration').

8.3 COMMON EVENTS OF DEFAULT

In common with most of the other operative provisions, the events of default will be tailored to meet the requirements of each particular loan, bank and borrower. There are, however, certain events of default which will appear in most facility agreements, and these are explained below.

8.3.1 Late payment

Banks are highly sensitive about punctual payment by the borrower, not least because they themselves may have borrowed specifically to fund the loan (the bank will therefore have its own loan to service, matched with the income stream from its loan to the borrower – see **3.8**). Even if the bank has funded a loan from its own resources, it may conduct other business on the basis that the loan will be repaid on time and that it can re-invest the repayment. In either case, therefore, a bank will require default interest to be paid on the overdue amount (see **4.15**). There is usually also a general requirement to indemnify the bank against any costs associated with a default.

A further concern for the bank is that since a borrower's payment commitments are established in the facility agreement, those commitments should be accounted for in the borrower's projected cash flow requirements. A missed payment probably means a missed budget and may signal serious cash flow problems.

The inclusion of a default for late payment will be non-negotiable, and will usually cover late payment of any amount due under the agreement, including fees and expenses, as well as interest and repayments of principal. However, a borrower may argue, not unconvincingly, that accidental errors do occur. Furthermore, technical problems may also unavoidably delay payments, especially where financing is cross-border, or in a foreign currency. If, therefore, late payment is due to an administrative error or for technical reasons, a bank will sometimes allow a borrower three to five further business days in which to make payment (known as a 'cure period' or 'grace period'). The bank may, however, limit the errors to those of third parties and not the borrower. A bank's solicitor should ensure that any default interest and indemnity provisions are drafted so that they will run from the date when the payment is overdue, and not from the end of any grace period. A borrower may ask that any grace period should run only from when the bank notifies the borrower in writing that it has not received payment, though this is very rarely conceded.

Default for late payment is the most important event of default. The other events of default effectively play a 'supporting role': they are trying to predict situations which may lead to late payment.

8.3.2 Breach of representation

A bank will always want the option to call a default if one of the written representations proves to have been incorrect or misleading when made. The problem with this default is that it is often drafted very widely. A typical clause might provide for default if:

> Any representation or statement made or deemed to be made in, or in connection with, this agreement, or any document connected with this agreement, is or proves to have been incorrect or misleading when made or deemed to be made.

Thus, the default will cover statements made in connection with the document, as well as within the reps and warranties clauses. This might include anything from the inflated valuation of an important asset, to a mistake in the accounting reference date of a minor subsidiary.

A bank will therefore often concede some softening of this event of default. Usually this takes the form of a requirement for either the misstatement, or its consequences, to be 'material' or have a 'material adverse effect' (see also **11.5.3**).

8.3.3 Breach of undertaking

A breach of undertaking will be expressed as an explicit event of default in much the same way, and for the same reasons, as a breach of a representation. It is not uncommon to see a grace period in this event of default, and sometimes a materiality qualification too.

8.3.4 Breach of financial covenant

As mentioned at **7.3.4.4**, some equity sponsors in acquisition financings have negotiated 'equity cure' rights to avoid a default on breach of a financial covenant. A further concession sometimes requested by strong borrowers is a so-called 'Mulligan' provision. This works either:

(a) to prevent the bank calling an event of default unless the borrower breaches a financial covenant on two consecutive testing dates (this is a 'true' Mulligan and is rarely, if ever, seen); or

(b) to allow the bank to call a default on the first breach of a financial covenant, but to lose that right if it fails to call a default before the borrower meets the financial covenant on the subsequent test date (arguably not a true Mulligan and probably reflecting the commercial position in any event).

The term 'Mulligan' originates from a golfing expression, meaning a player is allowed a second tee shot without penalty.

8.3.5 Cross-default

Cross-default is a key event of default, and one which will be heavily negotiated. Imagine that a borrower defaults under another loan or financial contract (ie, other than the facility agreement). The other party to that contract may be in a very strong position to force terms on the borrower. These might include extra payment, additional security, or some other form of preferential treatment. The borrower may have done nothing to trigger a default of the facility agreement, and so the bank would have to sit and watch its position being eroded. A cross-default clause operates by automatically defaulting the borrower under the loan in the event that it defaults under certain other types of agreement (see also **5.2.2**). This ensures that the bank is also in a position to 'influence' the borrower and, if necessary, to protect its position by accelerating the loan. A cross-default clause also effectively gives a bank the benefit of the default provisions in other agreements to which the borrower is a party.

Because of the 'domino' effect which a cross-default might have, it is usually limited by:

(a) being confined to defaults which occur under other documents providing 'financial indebtedness' (eg, loans, bonds, notes, acceptance credits, finance leases, guarantees, etc – see also **7.3.3**); and

(b) including a threshold amount below which the default will not apply (a 'de minimis').

Other aspects that might be negotiated include the following:

(a) A borrower will often argue that the cross-default should operate only if the other default will have a material effect on its ability to perform its obligations under the facility agreement.

(b) A cross-default might be set to trigger at different points in the initial default, for example if:

(i) the borrower simply fails to pay an amount due under another agreement; or

(ii) the creditor under another agreement obtains a right to demand early repayment; or

(iii)   the creditor under another agreement actually exercises a right to demand early repayment (known as a 'cross-acceleration' clause).

A borrower would prefer option (iii) but banks will resist relying on just a cross-acceleration. Their concern is that the borrower will 'favour' the party with the benefit of a default (eg by paying fees, increased margin or giving them security) to persuade them not to accelerate.

(c)   Sometimes a borrower will ask for a carve-out (ie, an exception) for any defaults with respect to unpaid debts which the borrower is disputing in good faith. This is, however, strongly resisted by most banks. Pure debt disputes are seldom bona fides. Furthermore, a bank will not want to be arguing whether or not a dispute is in 'good faith' at a time when it might want to take action.

(d)   If the borrower is part of a group, a bank will often want the cross-default provision to extend to a default by any other companies in the group. A bank will argue that financial difficulties in a subsidiary will usually have an effect on the parent because of intra-group guarantees and letters of support. Furthermore, a bank will argue that a parent should not let a subsidiary default without good reason: if there is good reason then the event of default can be waived. However, a borrower will usually persuade a bank to limit any cross-default into its 'material' or 'principal' subsidiaries from time to time.

One issue for a bank is the evidential problem of finding out when a borrower has defaulted under another agreement. If a borrower knows that a default in another agreement will cross default into its loan then it has little incentive to reveal the first default. The fact that this in itself may cause the borrower to breach its representations when they are repeated is of little consequence; the bank will still be no wiser, and the borrower has simply defaulted twice instead of once. Furthermore, a bank is subject to an implied duty of confidentiality with regard to a customer's affairs (see *Tournier v National Provincial and Union Bank of England* [1924] 1 KB 461). This limits the availability of any information about defaulting borrowers 'in the marketplace'. A bank will therefore have to resort to its knowledge of the borrower's obligations under other agreements (through initial due diligence and subsequent information covenants), and its monitoring of the borrower's financial position.

8.3.6   Change of business

The type of business in which a borrower is involved plays a large part in the bank's initial risk assessment when agreeing to lend. A change in that business would entail a change in risk, and so be unacceptable to the bank without its consent. It will therefore usually be an event of default if the borrower makes any material change to its business, ceases to carry on any material part of its business, or disposes of a material part of its business ('material' may be defined, eg, with reference to net worth). The point at which outsourcing would trigger a 'change of business' is open to some debate.

8.3.7   Change of control

There are several reasons why a bank will be concerned about any change in control of the borrower. However, it almost invariably triggers mandatory prepayments, rather than an event of default (see **9.2.3**).

8.3.8   Insolvency and related proceedings

The insolvency of a borrower will, without question, be an event of default. Any negotiation of this clause will simply relate to the timing of default. From a bank's perspective, an event of default should give it the ability to take action at the first sign of any problem. If a bank holds security, it will at least want the option to enforce it as early as possible to optimise its position with regard to other creditors and to preserve the borrower's assets. Typical triggers for this event of default are: 'inability to pay debts as they fall due' (see below), 'assets worth less than liabilities', 'ceasing to make payments on debts', 'negotiating with creditors to reschedule debts' (though borrowers might want to carve out negotiations with banks under the facility) and 'declaration of a debt moratorium'.

Some clauses may make reference to the two insolvency tests in s 123 of the IA 1986. Section 123(1) deems a company unable to pay its debts if it has not paid a debt three weeks after service of a statutory demand or court order (if the debt is over £750). Section 123(2) deems a company unable to pay its debts if the value of its assets is less than its liabilities. In *BNY Corporate Trustee Services Ltd v Eurosail-UK-2007-3BL Plc & Others* [2011] EWCA Civ 227, the Court of Appeal analysed the meaning of s 123(2) for the first time. The Court rejected the simple test that a company was insolvent merely because its 'liabilities (however assessed) exceed its assets (however assessed)'. It said that s 123(2) 'applies to a company whose assets and liabilities (including contingent and future liabilities) are such that it had reached a point of no return'. The case confirms that simply showing, at face value from a company's balance sheet, that its liabilities exceed its assets is not enough to satisfy the s 123(2) test.

In addition to insolvency itself, there will also be triggers related to insolvency *proceedings*. Typically this will include any corporate action, legal proceedings or other procedure or step (these last two being particularly important since the Enterprise Act 2002 introduced out of court appointment of an administrator) taken in relation to, for example:

(a)   a moratorium, winding-up, dissolution, administration, reorganisation or arrangement with a creditor;

(b)   the appointment of a liquidator, receiver, administrator, administrative receiver (or the equivalent in another jurisdiction); or

(c)   the enforcement of any security over the borrower's assets.

From a borrower's perspective, once the bank 'pulls the plug' its problems are likely to get worse, especially if it is subject to cross default clauses in other documents. Ideally, therefore, a borrower wants any event of default to trigger as late as possible. A borrower might argue, therefore, that a creditor might 'take steps' to appoint an administrator as a method of forcing payment which the borrower disputes. It will typically ask for a remedy period, a carve-out for debts that are genuinely disputed (so long as proceedings are dismissed within, say, 30 days), or even a default limited to the actual appointment of an administrator, a receiver or similar officer.

8.3.9   Proceedings

If a borrower becomes involved in any material litigation, arbitration or similar proceedings, the bank will usually want the ability to call a default. A borrower will argue that this default should not be absolute but should be subject to a de minimis figure (see **11.5.5**). An alternative for the borrower is to draft the event of default so that it is only triggered by proceedings which will (the bank will want 'might') have a material adverse effect on the borrower's ability to perform its obligations under the loan.

8.3.10   Unlawful performance

A bank will invariably want to call a default if it becomes unlawful for a borrower to continue to perform its obligations under a facility agreement. Similarly, a bank may also want an event of default if the borrower should lose any consents or authorisations necessary for it to perform its obligations under the loan. The borrower will want to introduce some element of materiality into both these clauses. A borrower may also argue that this should not be included as a default, since it has no control over the law, and ask instead for a provision for mandatory prepayment for illegality.

8.3.11   General default

A provision will often be included in a facility agreement which makes it an event of default if the borrower fails to comply with any 'other obligations' (ie, other than representations and undertakings) under the facility agreement. This clause will invariably be drafted with a relatively long 'cure period' of perhaps 30 days. Specific events of default, which aim to pick up all the fundamental situations in which the bank may want to terminate the loan, will still stand, but the general default clause will 'sweep up' any minor defaults and make them actionable by the bank if the borrower cannot cure them.

8.3.12 Qualified accounts

In leveraged transactions it is not uncommon for a bank to include an event of default which is triggered if the borrower's accounts are qualified by the auditors (see **6.5).** A borrower will want to limit any default to a qualification which has a material adverse effect on its ability to perform its obligations under the loan facility.

8.3.13 Repudiation

Most facility agreements will make any actual, or attempted, repudiation by the borrower (ie words or conduct indicating it does not regard itself as being bound by the facility) an event of default. This provision is rarely negotiated.

8.3.14 Material adverse change

The material adverse change event of default, known colloquially as the 'MAC' clause, also acts as a 'sweep up' provision. It allows a bank to call a default if there is a material adverse change in the borrower's position or circumstances which might prevent it from complying with any provisions of the facility agreement. The potential breadth of this event of default means that many borrowers will try to exclude it, arguing that a detailed facility agreement which contains a raft of undertakings, financial covenants and events of default should not require such a 'catch all' provision. If a MAC clause is included (most banks' lending policies require it), it is always heavily negotiated.

A strong MAC clause might read as follows:

> Any event or circumstance occurs which the Majority Lenders believe might have a material adverse effect on the ability of the Borrower to perform or comply with its obligations under this Agreement

The first negotiation point for a borrower is to ensure the threshold for 'Majority Lenders' is as high as possible (commonly 66⅔%): the more banks that need to agree there is a MAC, the better. Borrowers might also ask for 'reasonably' (commonly accepted) and for 'might' to be replaced by 'will' (less common).

Negotiation will then turn to the phrase 'material adverse effect'. If this is left undefined, the uncertainty as to what it means might actually benefit the borrower in some circumstances. Equally, its breadth could be problematic, and so it is usual to have a definition of 'material adverse effect' along the following lines:

> Material Adverse Effect means a material adverse effect on:
>
> (a)   the business, operations, property, condition (financial or otherwise) or prospects of the borrower;
>
> (b)   the ability of the borrower to perform its obligations under the finance documents; or
>
> (c)   the validity or enforceability of the finance documents or the rights or remedies of any lender under the finance documents.

A strong borrower might argue for the removal of paragraph (a), on the basis that if it can perform its obligations under the document, and that document is valid and enforceable (ie paras (b) and (c)), then it should not be defaulted. It might also argue that (b) should refer to 'financial obligations'. If paragraph (a) is not negotiated out then a borrower might argue that it should be linked to (b) by 'and' being inserted between them. Focusing on (a) itself, the borrower might try to negotiate out the wider language, such as 'prospects', 'or otherwise' and maybe 'property'.

Lastly, there is a view that, as long as the borrower demonstrates that it can comply with all its obligations under the agreement (particularly any financial covenants – see **7.3**), it would be difficult for a bank to argue that any material change had been 'adverse'.

Such MAC clauses are not commonly used to default a borrower; a bank must be very sure of its case to use the MAC clause to demand repayment, but may be more willing to use it as a 'draw-stop' (ie to prevent new borrowing). The most common use for the MAC, therefore, is to threaten possible default and thereby persuade a borrower to start a dialogue with the bank (see **8.5** below). However, in *BNP Paribas v Yukos Oil Company* [2005] EWHC 1321 (Ch), the court upheld the validity of accelerating a loan based on a MAC event of default (it must be said the facts allowed a very clear argument for a MAC).

8.4 EVENTS OF DEFAULT AND OTHER CLAUSES

Ideally, the events of default should not overlap with any of the representations or undertakings. For example, if the borrower gives a repeating representation that there is no litigation, there should be no need for a litigation event of default (just a default on breach of representation). If for some reason there is both a repeating representation or undertaking and a specific event of default for the same circumstances, care should at least be taken that they are not contradictory: any carve-outs to the repeating representation or undertaking must be reflected in the event of default. Remember that a disclosure letter will circumvent a representation only with respect to breaches existing when the letter is accepted (see **5.2.3**).

8.5 ACTION ON DEFAULT

If an event of default occurs, a bank will want a number of different options, which might include:

(a) cancelling any undrawn commitments if part of the loan has not been utilised; and/or

(b) putting all or part of the facility 'on demand', and taking over the selection of interest periods (see **4.9**); and/or

(c) demanding immediate repayment of part or all outstanding capital and interest, as well as any cash collateral for contingent liabilities (eg, bills of exchange or letters of credit); and/or

(d) enforcing any security it holds.

The bank may choose not to exercise any of these options. It may feel that the event of default is not serious enough to terminate the loan, but that it justifies demanding additional fees from the borrower. Alternatively, the bank may use the default as an opportunity to insist that the borrower gets 'around the table' with the bank to discuss its business plans.

A bank will want these remedies available 'on or at any time after an Event of Default has occurred and until it is waived ...'; a borrower will want to add '... or remedied'. It is not unusual for banks to allow this request, but they should be aware that it has at least two implications. First, if the borrower can unilaterally remedy an event of default, it will have little incentive to disclose it when it occurs; if it must be waived, the borrower is more likely to disclose. Secondly, what constitutes a remedy of certain types of default is not always clear, and ambiguity usually favours the borrower. Some facilities will try to specify what 'remedy' means for different events of default (but this is cumbersome) or else will say 'remedied to the satisfaction of the bank' (but this is less helpful to the borrower).

In the case of a syndicated loan, the agent will often be given discretion as to what action to take on an event of default, but with an overriding obligation to act in accordance with any instructions of the majority banks (either in number or value). Giving the agent this autonomy allows a faster response in time-critical situations, but at the price for the agent of taking on potential liability for wrong decisions (through action or inaction). Clearly, a borrower would want the most considered response possible, and so it may prefer that any default decision (and decisions in relation to a particular event of default) is taken by the entire syndicate, or a large majority of them.

If the loan is terminated and all outstanding amounts are immediately repayable, 'default interest' will apply until the amounts are settled in full (see **4.15**).

8.6   GRACE PERIODS, DEFAULTS AND POTENTIAL EVENTS OF DEFAULT

Some events of default will include a specified time period during which the borrower is permitted to remedy the event or apply for a waiver from the banks. During this 'grace period', the borrower is typically prevented from borrowing new money (known as a 'draw stop'). However none of the other options available to banks on an event of default (see **8.5**) will apply unless the grace period expires before the borrower can remedy or obtain a waiver.

An event of default with an in-built grace period is sometimes referred to as a 'potential event of default'. It is worth noting, however, that the Loan Market Association (LMA) facilities, a widely used suite of market standard documents, do not use the term 'potential event of default'. Instead, they define a 'Default' to mean:

> an Event of Default **or** any event or circumstance specified in Clause [   ] (Events of Default) which would (with the expiry of a grace period, the giving of notice, the making of any determination under the Finance Documents or any combination of any of the foregoing) be an Event of Default.

The equivalent of a 'potential event of default' is then described as 'a Default other than an Event of Default'.

Borrowers must undertake to tell the banks as soon as they are aware of a 'potential event of default', but there are a couple of points they will want to argue:

(a)   borrowers under a revolving credit facility (RCF) will argue that the draw stop within a grace period should not prevent them rolling over a maturing RCF loan on the basis that this is not new borrowing; and

(b)   borrowers should not agree to give a *repeating* representation that there are no 'potential events of default' (or equivalent) since if one occurs they will be unable to repeat the representation, which will then trigger a full event of default!

8.7   EVENTS OF DEFAULT – THE BANK'S PERSPECTIVE

A bank will generally consider demanding early repayment of a loan as a 'last resort': recovering capital will usually involve selling assets, and this might mean winding up part or all of the borrower's business. However, the threat of recalling a loan can be used as a very potent negotiating tool. If a default occurs, the borrower is effectively at the bank's mercy, and the 'price' of not recalling the loan might be increased fees, a greater margin, tighter financial covenants or renegotiation of other terms. Any changes will be justified as consideration for the bank agreeing to continue despite the 'risk' of ignoring the default.

A borrower will sometimes argue that it should not be defaulted on the basis of events which are beyond its control, for example, a change in the law. Any such argument will be strongly resisted by the bank, because events of default are not based on 'fault' but on risk: they are situations in which a bank feels that the borrower's ability to perform the facility agreement may be compromised, and therefore it should have the right to terminate the facility agreement or take other appropriate action (see **8.5**).

Events of default do present some risk to the bank. The bank must ensure that it is justified in calling an event of default. Withdrawing a loan facility is likely to destroy a borrower's business, not least because of cross-default into other agreements. If a bank wrongly calls an event of default it may be sued by the borrower for breach of contract or in tort. In *Concord Trust v The Law Debenture Trust Corporation plc* [2005] UKHL 27, the House of Lords ruled that the wrongful calling of an event of default was not a breach of contract, but simply an ineffective action. However, the *Concord* decision was given in the context of default under a bond; it would not apply to a loan facility which was not fully utilised and where calling the default prevents further borrowing (see also **19.2.4.4**). Because of the consequences of calling a default, a bank will want the events of default drafted as clearly as possible (see also **Chapter 11**).

8.8 EVENTS OF DEFAULT – THE BORROWER'S PERSPECTIVE

The borrower must obviously be very cautious when agreeing to the events of default because, if triggered, they give the banks the option to terminate the loan. Any breadth in the wording of the events of default will work for the borrower not just because it provides leeway, but also because a bank will be cautious about 'grey areas'. It is also true that a bank will not usually withdraw a loan without considerable provocation.

CHAPTER 9

BOILER PLATE, MECHANICS AND MISCELLANEOUS CLAUSES

'The fox knows a little about many things. The hedgehog knows only one thing, but it is a very big thing.'

Isaiah Berlin, Philosopher

9.1 INTRODUCTION

The preceding chapters have reviewed the main provisions of a loan facility in the order in which they will most usually be found in the agreement. Initial operative clauses will usually be followed by representations, undertakings and events of default (the only logic to this order is a vague chronology). The last three areas will be the most heavily negotiated, and unique to each facility agreement. In contrast, the remaining provisions are often seen as rather 'unglamorous', using standard clauses, and of minor consequence. The colloquial title for these clauses, the 'boiler plate', is far from inspiring, and many of them are in the back end of the document. Yet these provisions control some important areas: they seem unimportant only until something goes wrong. This chapter looks at the main 'boiler plate' clauses and funding mechanics, as well as at one or two miscellaneous items.

9.2 REPAYMENT, PREPAYMENT AND CANCELLATION

The following clauses are part of the mechanics of funding and settlement ('funding mechanics').

9.2.1 Repayment

The repayment clause is arguably the most important provision in the agreement. As part of the funding mechanics, it will appear before the representations, undertakings and events of default. The form of repayment will depend on the type of facility: a non-amortising loan will simply refer to a fixed date; if the loan is amortising, tables listing the amount to be repaid on specific dates are usually attached as schedules to the agreement. An overdraft is usually on demand and so does not strictly require a repayment date.

9.2.2 Prepayment

Most loans will allow (and in certain circumstances require) a borrower to repay capital before the dates envisaged by the facility agreement. This is known as 'prepayment'. Without some form of contractual provision, a borrower probably has no right to prepay a loan. (See *Hooper v Western Counties and South Wales Telephone Co Ltd* (1892) 68 LT 78: while this related to debt securities, at least one Commonwealth case has drawn the same conclusion for a loan facility.) From a borrower's perspective, the ability to pay down the loan as soon as spare capital is available will save interest payments. Furthermore, rates of both interest and margins will fluctuate: if there is a sustained downward movement, borrowers may refinance existing loans (either with their existing bank or a new one) part way through their term. Prepayment rights are usually also given against individual banks that have triggered payments under a gross-up clause (see **9.3.3.3**) or increased cost clause (see **9.3.1.6**).

A bank is usually happy for the borrower to prepay, but there are a number of points which the bank's solicitor will want to ensure are covered, and these are mentioned below.

9.2.2.1 Broken funding

As explained at **3.8**, large commercial loans may be funded by interbank lending ('matched funding'). If a borrower prepays part of the loan, the bank may be left to service an interbank loan without an equivalent interest stream from the borrower. Alternatively, the bank would have to terminate the interbank loan early and incur breakage fees (there is usually no provision for prepayment in interbank borrowing).

Facility agreements will therefore usually include a 'break costs' clause (see **4.11**) under which the borrower must reimburse the bank for matched funding losses it incurs as a result of prepayment. Break costs will be avoided if the borrower can ensure that any prepayment is always made at the end of an interest period.

9.2.2.2 Prepayment fee

Some banks will ask for a prepayment fee (or 'prepayment premium') to cover the administration costs of early repayment. Loans for leveraged acquisitions (see **3.4**) may feature 'call protection', which is an extra amount payable by the borrower if it prepays within a given period (eg 12 months) of utilisation. Call protection is intended to compensate lenders for their 'investment' being ended prematurely. It will not usually apply to banks in senior facilities, but may be required by funds lending to a mezzanine facility to reflect the way in which they raise capital and that they are less able to quickly re-invest any prepaid amounts.

9.2.2.3 Order of application

In amortised loans, banks traditionally resist treating a partial prepayment as an early settlement of the next repayment amount due. This is primarily because the bank will want a borrower to continue to demonstrate the financial control necessary to maintain the steady repayment regime envisaged by the facility agreement. A bank may insist that any prepayment is treated as satisfying the final repayment obligations first (ie, prepayment will be applied against repayment obligations in inverse order of maturity), or else that the prepayment is spread across all the scheduled repayment amounts, reducing each one rateably. Taking the prepayment off the 'back end' of the loan reduces the life of the loan, which in turn reduces the bank's risk; using the rateable approach reduces exposure but maintains the relationship. Strong borrowers will be allowed to apply any prepayment as they choose.

In a simple syndicated facility, prepayments will usually be distributed to the banks in proportion to their advances ('pro rata'). In structured leverage deals, with more than one level of debt, prepayment provisions are more complex.

9.2.2.4 Preference

If the borrower was to become insolvent within six months of a prepayment (extended to two years for connected parties), there is a risk that a liquidator or administrator could apply to set aside the prepayment as a preference under the IA 1986, s 239. The risk of a successful preference claim is typically remote because the borrower would have to be influenced by a desire to produce the preferential effect, and it is also a defence to show that the borrower was solvent at the relevant time (taking into account the repayment). Nevertheless, if the loan is secured, a preference claim could be particularly problematic, and security documents may purport to keep the debt and related security 'alive' in such circumstances (see **15.2.9**).

9.2.3 Mandatory prepayment

In some circumstances a borrower will be *required* to prepay the facility, known as 'mandatory repayment'. In an investment grade facility there are usually only two circumstances requiring mandatory prepayment:

(a)   if it becomes unlawful for a bank to lend to the borrower. This is typically due to sanctions being imposed, for example the EU and US both impose wide-ranging sanctions against various countries from time to time, which may prevent banks lending to borrowers associated with the regimes. In a syndicated facility, the borrower is usually required to repay just the affected bank and not the whole syndicate; and

(b)   if there is a change in control of the borrower. Control is typically defined as the ability to remove half or more of the directors, the ability to dictate how the company is run, the holding of a majority of the shares in the borrower, or the ability to cast more than half the shareholder votes. The bank's concern is that the borrower may be run differently or supported less by the new entity in control, and it will require prepayment of the whole amount outstanding.

In a leveraged facility there are likely to be additional mandatory prepayment events. In general terms, these are events which the banks see as an opportunity to take cash from the borrower to reduce the outstanding debt (reduce the 'leverage'), rather than repay completely, and typically include:

(a)   if the borrower disposes of certain fundamental assets other than in the ordinary course of business (and assuming the proceeds are not required to purchase a replacement asset);

(b)   if the borrower receives insurance monies for an asset it is not replacing;

(c)   if the borrower generates more cash than it is deemed to require to run its business (this is known as an 'excess cash sweep');

(d)   if the facility is required to fund an acquisition and the purchase price is subsequently adjusted downwards due to a revaluation event; and

(e)   if the borrower subsequently raises funds through an issue of shares or debt securities.

These events usually result in repayment of part of the facility pro rata across the banks. In some acquisition financings, however, the mezzanine lenders (see **3.4**) are allowed to forgo their share of any prepayment (because they may be funds which do not have the flexibility of bank lenders to accept early repayment). Mandatory prepayment is a useful alternative to default since it will not usually trigger a cross-default.

9.2.4 Cancellation

If a loan provides a commitment period over which the borrower is allowed to utilise the facility (see **4.8.2** and **3.2.2**), the bank will almost certainly charge a fee for making the facility available during that period (known as a 'commitment fee' (see **9.5**)). However, a borrower may realise part way through the commitment period that it will not require the full amount of the available facility. Many loans allow the borrower to cancel any available amounts during the commitment period and so save on commitment fees (although sometimes a bank will charge cancellation fees!). A syndicate of banks will therefore want any cancellation to reduce their commitments rateably. A borrower must be sure that any cancellation fee is not prohibitive and that cancellation is available in the smallest multiples possible in order to give maximum flexibility.

Commitments may be mandatorily cancelled if there is an event of default during the commitment period, and will be automatically cancelled to the extent they are undrawn at the end of the commitment period.

The following clauses are usually considered part of the 'boiler plate'.

9.3   MARGIN PROTECTION

The interest rate charged by a bank on a syndicated loan is typically calculated by adding a margin to the estimated cost of lending (see **4.9**). If the cost of lending rises, the bank must be able to pass any increase to the borrower to protect its margin (thereby protecting its profit). This section looks at the main threats to the margin and how the bank might protect against them.

9.3.1   Regulatory capital

As explained in **Chapter 1**, banks are intermediaries: the money they lend is largely raised from taking deposits and borrowing from various sources, including other banks. If a bank cannot recover the money it has lent, there is a danger that it may be unable to repay depositors and other lenders. In an attempt to reduce this risk, banks are required to maintain 'regulatory capital'. This is essentially a minimum level of assets each bank must maintain to create a 'buffer' which can absorb any losses from its lending activities. The concept is explained in more detail below, but the key point is that banks build the cost of regulatory capital into the margin: if the costs increase, they need the ability to recover the increase or else their margin will be eroded.

From 2013, the regulatory capital requirements began a 10-year period of change, and so the following paragraphs briefly explain the origins and evolution of the rules.

9.3.1.1   Origins of regulatory capital – the Basel Committee

In the mid-1980s, a group of 12 nations set up a committee to discuss creating a joint policy on regulatory capital (those involved were Luxembourg plus the 'G10' – the self-styled 'group of 10 most advanced economic nations', which actually number 11!). After several years the so-called 'Basel Committee' (they met in Basel, home to the Bank for International Settlements) came up with some 'Proposals for the International Convergence of Capital Measurement and Capital Standards'. Those proposals (known as the 'Basel Capital Accord') were adopted by all major banking jurisdictions, and implemented by 'local' legislation. More recently, a second, more sophisticated version of the Basel regime was adopted by most jurisdictions (the US being a notable exception). This new regime, commonly known as 'Basel II', was fully implemented in the UK from January 2008. However, the global banking crisis which began in late 2007 prompted regulators to revisit the regulatory capital regime, and 'Basel III' is being implemented in stages from 2013 through to 2023 (see **9.3.1.5**).

9.3.1.2   Basic proposition of Basel regimes: assets backed by capital

As mentioned earlier, the key proposition underpinning the Basel regimes is that a bank needs to recover its assets (primarily loans) to repay its depositors: if there is a risk that an asset cannot be recovered in full, it must be backed by 'capital' to create a 'buffer'. This capital buffer is known as 'regulatory capital'. The starting point for the amount of regulatory capital a bank must hold is 8% of the value of each asset: so making a £100 loan would require a bank to have £8 of capital. However, this is just a minimum requirement. First, a regulator can increase the percentage for individual institutions or across the market if it feels it is necessary. Secondly, the risk of a particular loan (or other asset) not being recovered will vary and so assets are 'risk weighted' to calculate whether more or less than 8% capital should be held.

9.3.1.3 Risk weightings

Under Basel I, the calculation of counterparty credit risk (ie, for loans, the risk of a borrower being unable to repay) was relatively crude, grouping diverse borrower types into single risk categories. Basel II introduced a more sophisticated regime for risk weighting assets, allowing banks to use either a 'standardised' approach or an 'internal ratings based' ('IRB') approach.

Under the standardised approach, banks apply counterparty risk weightings as pre-determined in the regulations. For example, a corporate borrower with a high credit rating might be risk weighted at 20%, meaning only £1.60 of regulatory capital (20% of £8) must be allocated to each £100 lent to that borrower. A borrower with a lower rating might get 100% weighting (£8 regulatory capital per £100 lent), whilst a high risk borrower might attract 150% weighting, requiring £12 regulatory capital allocated to every £100 lent. See **17.11** for an explanation of credit ratings.

The IRB approach allows a bank to use its own internal model to calculate the risk of recovery from different counterparties (albeit that the model must be pre-approved by its regulator). There are two IRB versions: 'foundation' and 'advanced'. The former relies in part on the regulator's risk assessment figures to populate the model; the latter allows a bank to use its own data. Most large banks will use the IRB advanced approach.

9.3.1.4 Types of capital

So, a bank will use either the standardised or an IRB approach to calculate the amount of regulatory capital it requires. This then begs the question, 'what is capital'? The first notion to disabuse is that it is cash in an account: in fact, regulatory capital is simply a numerical target which can be made up of many different assets. Basel II split capital into three types: 'Tier 1, 2 and 3 capital'.

Tier 1 capital included ordinary share capital, verified net profits and certain reserves (these represent assets in the bank which are permanent, able to absorb losses, rank behind depositors, and do not carry an unavoidable maintenance cost such as interest or compulsory dividends).

Tier 2 capital had less 'permanence' than Tier 1 and/or might incur fixed costs, and included cumulative perpetual shares, subordinated debt and revaluation reserves.

Tier 3 capital was the least 'stable' of all, for example short-term subordinated loans or non-verified profits.

Under Basel II, at least half a bank's regulatory capital had to be core Tier 1 capital, and Tier 3 capital could only be used to cover limited regulatory capital requirements.

9.3.1.5 Basel III and Basel IV

The collapse of Lehman Brothers bank in late 2008, and the banking crisis which followed, spurred regulators to look again at bank supervision and to tighten regulatory requirements, including regulatory capital, even further. Basel III is being phased in from 2013 to 2023 and is a much more stringent regime than Basel II. Furthermore, part way through that implementation (2017), the Basel Committee has proposed further 'tightening' of the Basel III requirements, in what the industry have dubbed 'Basel IV'. The details are beyond the scope of this book, but the key changes include the following:

(a)   Banks must have a greater percentage of Tier 1 capital and the regulatory capital must contain a greater degree of 'common equity' (ie ordinary shares and retained profits).

So-called 'hybrid capital' (financial products designed to be treated as equity but behave more like debt) is being phased out.

(b) Tier 2 capital is simplified, whilst Tier 3 capital is abolished.

(c) Deductions from capital (certain assets that actually reduce a bank's capital, eg loans to other banks) are increased.

(d) The overall minimum capital ratio remains at 8% (though see **9.3.1.2**), but the effect of the other changes mentioned here mean that it will be the equivalent of around 14% under the Basel II rules.

(e) The IRB risk models (see **9.3.1.3**) are tightened (and, under Basel IV, more standardised).

(f) Two new buffers of capital are introduced. The capital conservation buffer is imposed if a bank is facing financial difficulties, in an attempt to prevent it from paying large dividends. The countercyclical buffer requires banks to build up extra reserves during periods of high economic growth, providing a 'grain store' for more straitened times.

(g) There is an increase in the capital requirement for global and domestic 'systematically important banks'. There is also an increase in capital required to back loans to other financial institutions and certain derivatives.

(h) There is a liquidity requirement encouraging banks to hold enough liquid assets to deal with periods of high depositor withdrawal. (Northern Rock Bank required emergency loans from the Bank of England in 2007 because it suffered a liquidity crisis (a 'run on the bank'): it had one of the highest regulatory capital ratios of any bank at the time.)

(i) There is a new leverage ratio which compares the bank's assets *before* they are risk weighted to its Tier 1 capital.

9.3.1.6 Increased costs clause

Maintaining regulatory capital in accordance with the Basel rules carries a cost, and this is passed to the borrower as part of the margin on a loan. If regulations change and the cost of capital increases, this would eat into the margin and reduce the bank's profit. The increased costs clause in a facility agreement purports to allow a bank to pass on any increase in regulatory costs to the borrower. It is a difficult provision for banks to use because calculating the cost of capital is not straightforward, and going 'cap in hand' to the borrower raises relationship and market perception issues. Borrowers will, however, try to limit its application solely to changes which affect the banking market, or a borrower type, in general. One point to watch out for during the implementation of Basel III is that many increased costs clauses specifically exclude costs due to implementing Basel II, on the basis that banks should have already factored those costs into their margin. However, Basel III is technically an 'amendment' to Basel II and so arguably would fall within the exclusion: if a bank wishes to claim for Basel III increased costs, that should be mentioned specifically in the drafting.

9.3.2 Mandatory cost

As explained at **1.4**, the main regulator for UK banks is the Prudential Regulation Authority (PRA). The PRA funds itself by leveraging fees against regulated entities and, until recently, most facility agreements gave banks the opportunity to recover these costs from the borrower. A formula attached as a schedule to the facility agreement converted the costs into a percentage, and this 'mandatory cost' could be added to the interest rate. That meant any fluctuation in the costs could be passed to the borrower when interest was charged, protecting the banks' margin. However, since the level and applicability of mandatory cost varies between lenders, calculating and distributing costs for a large syndicate was complicated. As a result, from late April 2013, the Loan Market Association (LMA) withdrew the schedule calculating mandatory cost from its market documentation, and most banks stopped overtly calculating and charging it.

9.3.3   Withholding tax

Withholding tax is not a threat to the margin per se, but it is a potential threat to a bank recovering the full amount of interest it is expecting.

9.3.3.1   What is withholding tax?

Under the Income Tax Act 2007 (ITA 2007), there are certain circumstances in which a person paying interest must deduct tax from the payment before it is made. This is known as 'withholding tax' or 'deduction at source', and (like the more familiar PAYE) it is a tax imposed on the recipient of the payment but collected from the payer, providing a very efficient mechanism for tax collection. The withheld tax is either sent to HM Revenue and Customs (HMRC), or it may sometimes be netted off against any tax credit of the withholding party. Withholding tax does not apply to repayments of principal, nor on repayment of the discount element of a loan issued at a discount.

9.3.3.2   Withholding tax and banks

The section of the ITA 2007 which is of primary concern to a bank receiving interest payments is s 874. Under s 874, interest payments may be subject to UK withholding tax at a rate of 20% if they have a 'UK source'. Various factors will determine whether interest has a 'UK source', including the borrower being a UK resident, a loan being secured on assets in the UK, and payments being made from or through the UK.

There are, however, several exceptions to s 874 of particular relevance to commercial loans.

'Short' interest

Essentially, s 874 applies only to 'yearly' interest, which case law suggests is interest payable under a debt which is capable of having, and is intended to have, a term of at least 12 months. Interest on a debt for less than 12 months, known as 'short' interest, will not therefore be subject to withholding tax. This may be relevant for '364 day' facilities (see **3.2.4**) and bridging loans.

Some types of loan will be difficult to classify under this definition, for example, a loan which matures after six months but which may be rolled over by the borrower. HM Revenue and Customs therefore has some discretion, and may apply a 'hindsight test' which allows it to re-classify the type of interest once a loan has been running for a time. There is clear authority for the importance of intention (see Lord Denning MR in *Corinthian Securities v Cato* [1970] 1 QB 377). Paradoxically, the classification of 'annual' or 'short' interest depends only on the term (or intended term) of the loan, and has nothing to do with when the interest is actually paid.

Interest subject to corporation tax

Withholding tax will not apply to interest paid 'on an advance from a bank (as defined in ITA 2007, s 991) if, at the time when the payment is made, the person beneficially entitled to the interest is within the charge to corporation tax as respects the interest' (ITA 2007, s 879).

The requirement therefore has two elements to be satisfied before interest can be paid gross:

(a)   interest must be paid on an advance from a *bank* (essentially, an institution authorised as a deposit-taking institution under the Financial Services and Markets Act 2000); and

(b)   the person entitled to the interest is within the scope of *corporation tax* (at the time the interest is paid, and with respect to the interest).

Similarly, s 930 of the ITA 2007 exempts interest paid by a company if the payer reasonably believes that the beneficial owner of the interest is subject to UK corporation tax.

Interest paid by a bank

Section 878 of the ITA 2007 exempts interest paid by a bank in the ordinary course of its banking business.

The implications of withholding tax are discussed at **10.6**. If s 879 of the ITA 2007 applies, it imposes an obligation to withhold tax on anyone 'by or through whom' the payment is made. A syndicated loan will usually require the borrower to make interest payments to one of the banks as agent for the others (see **3.3.2**). When an agent bank pays the other syndicate members their share of the interest, it is someone 'through whom' the interest is paid. Will the agent be forced to deduct withholding tax a second time as it passes through its hands? Remarkably, the ITA 2007 is silent on this point. In practice, however, the view is that the 'double hit' will not occur, and this is supported by judicial authority (on the ICTA 1988, predecessor to the ITA 2007) in *Grosvenor Place Estates v Roberts* (1960) 39 TC 433.

Double tax treaties

A bank can also avoid UK withholding tax if the interest is paid to a person resident overseas in a jurisdiction which enjoys a double tax treaty with the UK. The provisions and application of these treaties are complex, but in brief they may provide for most or all of the tax on interest payments to be levied in the country of the recipient. The country of the payer does not therefore tax the payment. UK treaties with the USA and many European countries provide for no tax to be collected in the payer's country. Treaties with some jurisdictions, eg Australia, reduce the amount of tax which must be withheld rather than extinguish completely.

These tax treaties do not apply automatically; treaty qualifying banks must complete an application form, and have it certified by their home tax authority and then filed with HMRC. It can take HMRC several months to process an application. However, banks may apply to HMRC for a 'passport'; if a UK entity borrows from a 'passported' bank, the treaty application will be expedited, with the time taken to process it reduced to a few weeks.

The residence of a bank that is not lending out of a UK facility office is therefore of great importance to a borrower. If it is resident outside the UK and not in a jurisdiction which has a double tax treaty with the UK, the borrower may have to withhold tax and so suffer the gross-up provisions (see **9.3.4.3**).

9.3.3.3 Provision for change in withholding tax – 'grossing-up'

Many banks will benefit from the exceptions under the ITA 2007, and will not suffer deduction of tax from interest payments. Furthermore, a borrower will usually be required to give a representation that all payments to be made under the loan will be free of any deductions. However, a bank will want to provide for any change in the situation, or for any unforeseen withholding tax, particularly if a loan has a non-UK element when interest might be paid from non-UK sources and be subject to withholding tax imposed by other jurisdictions. One solution is to provide for an indemnity from the borrower, under which it agrees to pay any withholding tax itself whilst paying the full amount due under the loan to the bank. However, in many jurisdictions the indemnity will not work, because the withholding tax will be levied on the amount indemnified.

A facility agreement will therefore usually include a 'gross-up clause', requiring all payments to be made 'free and clear' of withholding tax. If a deduction is required by law, the borrower will be obliged to gross up the payment so that the bank receives the full amount due after deduction of any tax. This is particularly important if a bank has match-funded its obligations (see **3.9**) because interest on interbank market loans is not subject to withholding tax (ITA 2007, s 878), and so any withholding by the borrower would leave a bank short of money to meet its interbank interest obligation.

Typical drafting for a gross-up clause would be:

If a deduction is required by law to be made by an Obligor, the amount of the payment due from that Obligor shall be increased to an amount which (after making any deduction) leaves an amount equal to the payment which would have been due if no deduction had been required.

EXAMPLE

A UK borrower has to make an interest payment of £1,000. The bank receiving payment does not fall within the ITA 2007 exceptions, neither is it subject to a relevant double tax treaty, and the payment will be subject to withholding tax, currently at 20%. This would mean the bank receives only 80% of £1,000, or £800. If the loan contains a 'gross-up' provision, then the borrower must pay the bank an amount (X) sufficient to ensure that £1,000 remains after deducting 20% tax.

Thus 80% (or $^4/_5$) of X = 1,000

$X = 1,000 \times {}^5/_4$

X = £1,250

The borrower must make a payment of £1,250, of which £250 (20%) goes to HMRC, and £1,000 to the bank.

It should be understood that the gross-up clause is usually a 'last resort' provision: neither bank nor borrower wants to apply it because it will be costly for the borrower and strain its ability to meet regular loan payments.

Borrowers should ensure that the gross-up provisions only apply to banks that were exempt from withholding tax when they joined the syndicate. The borrower then only takes the risk of a change in tax law.

9.3.3.4   Tax credits

Withholding tax is simply a method of collecting tax on interest payments. If UK tax is withheld by a UK borrower, a UK bank can offset the tax against its corporation tax liability, and so the net result for a bank is simply a cash flow disadvantage. A borrower might then reasonably ask that once a bank gets tax credit for any withholding tax that has been paid, it reimburses the borrower. However, banks will strongly resist any borrower claim for an absolute right to reimbursement on the basis that it is in practice very difficult to allocate a tax credit to a particular facility and borrower. Any credit due back to the borrower is therefore usually left to the determination of the bank.

9.3.3.5   Other taxes

The borrower will usually be required to indemnify the bank against liability for any other taxes (apart from corporation tax in its jurisdiction of residence or the jurisdiction in which its relevant 'facility office' is located) which might be imposed on the bank after payment has been made.

9.3.4   Right to prepay

If the cost of the loan does increase, and a bank chooses to claim under one of the clauses outlined above, it is usual to give the borrower a right to prepay the loan. Whilst this might not always be practical for the borrower, it can be valuable in the case of a syndicated loan where one bank is subject to increased costs imposed in its own jurisdiction. In this case, the borrower usually has the option of just prepaying that one bank's commitment.

9.4   COSTS AND EXPENSES

A bank will usually require a borrower to indemnify it against the 'incidental' costs it incurs in setting-up and running the loan. These might include any costs in connection with the following:

(a)   The negotiation, preparation and execution of the loan document, any security documentation, and any supplemental documents.

(b)   The registration of the loan and ancillary documents, including any stamp duty or similar tax. In the UK, a straightforward facility agreement is not currently subject to stamp duty, although a nominal fixed duty is levied on instruments transferring property by way of security (eg, shares). The Stamp Act 1891 (SA 1891), on which the present system is based, does not actually state who is accountable for the duty, and the main sanction for non-payment is that the unstamped document will not be admissible in evidence in civil proceedings (SA 1891, s 14(1)). Many jurisdictions have much higher duties, particularly with regard to security documentation.

(c)   The preservation and enforcement of the bank's rights under the loan and ancillary documents. This may also include the costs of investigating any potential, or actual, event of default it believes may have occurred.

The costs identified at (a) above are usually covered by an indemnity from the borrower in the mandate letter (see **2.4.5**) as well as in the loan document. Indemnities for the costs in (b) and (c) are usually contained in the loan document. The borrower will only want to cover 'direct' costs which are 'reasonably incurred', although it is harder to argue the later qualification in circumstances where the borrower is at fault. In a syndicated loan, the agent bank will also want an indemnity for costs from the syndicate banks since most will be incurred on their behalf.

9.5 FEES

9.5.1 Types of fee

In addition to paying interest and reimbursing certain of a bank's expenses, a borrower will also have to pay fees to the bank as compensation for additional work or responsibility. Common examples include the following.

9.5.1.1 Front end fees

Front end fees are usually paid shortly after signing or are recovered by withholding part of the initial utilisation. The bank in a bilateral loan may charge a 'front end fee' (also known as a 'facility' fee) in return for the initial work it must do to put the loan together (eg, due diligence and negotiation). It may be a lump sum, or be calculated as a percentage of the loan.

In a syndicated loan the arranging bank is responsible for the initial work in organising the facility, taking a leading role in due diligence and negotiation, and also for putting together the syndicate. The arranger's front end fee is usually larger than in a bilateral loan, and is known as the 'arrangement fee'. The arranger may have to use part of this fee in offering a 'participation fee' to attract other banks to the syndicate. The amount of fees remaining once the arranger has paid any participation fees is traditionally known as the 'praecipium'.

9.5.1.2 Underwriting fee

A syndicated loan may involve a small initial group of banks who intend other banks to join the syndicate and take some or all of their commitment, but who agree to provide the entire loan between them if necessary. These initial banks underwrite the syndication, taking the risk that they may have to provide a larger part of the facility than they would want. Risk has its price, and the borrower will pay for this use of the underwriting bank's balance sheet by way of an underwriting fee (calculated as a percentage of the underwritten sum).

9.5.1.3 Commitment fee

The various costs that a bank must factor into pricing a loan were considered at **9.3.** They included a provision for regulatory capital which, essentially, requires a bank to back its lending with capital. The cost of meeting these requirements is covered by the margin a bank charges. However, regulatory capital provisions also apply, albeit on a reduced scale, to money which a bank is committed to lend but is as yet unutilised. A fee is therefore charged on any committed but undrawn money to cover the related regulatory capital costs. This 'commitment fee' is usually between 25% and 50% of the margin, and is charged in both bilateral and syndicated facilities on any unutilised (and uncancelled) commitment. The commitment fee is often drafted to run from signature of the facility agreement, even if the borrower has not yet satisfied the conditions precedent.

Some documents use a 'facility fee'. This is payable on both unutilised amounts (replacing a commitment fee) and utilised amounts, but with margin on utilised amounts reduced to compensate.

9.5.1.4 Agent's fee

A bank which takes on an agency role (eg, administrative or security agent – see **3.3.2**) will demand a fee to compensate for the extra responsibilities involved.

9.5.1.5 Cancellation fee

Some facilities are put in place but are never used. A common example is acquisition financing, where a company needs funding to bid for a target company. If the bid fails, the loan will never be utilised. If this is likely, the banks may try to incorporate a cancellation fee in the facility agreement (also known as a 'drop dead fee').

9.5.1.6 Utilisation fee

Facilities that are intended to be used only rarely, or not at all (eg, standby or swing-line facilities) may carry a utilisation fee. The utilisation fee will apply if the facility is used regularly, or borrowing under it exceeds a minimum amount.

9.5.2 Fee letter

A bank will usually want the details of its fees to be put in a letter separate from the loan facility (other than, usually, the commitment fee). The 'fee letter' provides confidentiality from syndicate members, other borrowers and the market generally: breach of its terms will carry the remedies of default under the facility.

The facility agreement will specifically refer to the agent's fees (though not usually the amount) to avoid any argument that its fee letter arrangement with the borrower is a secret profit in breach of its fiduciary duties. Likewise, any individual fee to an agent should be expressed as payable to the bank individually, to demonstrate it is not a fee to be distributed among the banks in an agency role. Conversely, the facility agreement should specify when a fee is to be paid to the agent or lead manager to be split amongst the syndicate.

9.6 REMEDIES, WAIVERS, PARTIAL INVALIDITY AND AMENDMENTS

9.6.1 Remedies and waivers

Most facility agreements will contain a boiler plate clause along the following lines:

> The rights and remedies of the Bank under this agreement:
> (i)   shall not be waived by any failure, or delay, in their exercise;
> (ii) are cumulative, and shall not exclude or restrict its rights and remedies under any other agreement or the general law; and
> (iii) may be exercised in whole, in part, and as often as necessary.

Sub-clause (i) tries to avoid the borrower using the equitable doctrine of 'laches' (a form of estoppel) to preclude the bank exercising a right or remedy after unreasonable delay. Note, however, that case law suggests that continued performance of a contract will be inconsistent with a termination of a contract and result in the loss of a right to terminate (see *Tele2 International Card Company SA v Post Office Limited* [2009] EWCA Civ 9).

Sub-clause (ii) provides, first, that if the bank has more than one right or remedy under the agreement, it is not confined to using only one of them. This sub-clause also tries to avoid any merger of rights between, say, the facility agreement and a security document (there is authority that a superior security right will merge with an inferior one and the latter is effectively lost). Lastly, the sub-clause avoids any suggestion that the rights under the agreement should replace any rights under general law.

Sub-clause (iii) tries to avoid an argument that, in exercising any rights or remedies, the bank has only 'one bite at the cherry'.

The effectiveness of any of these clauses cannot be guaranteed, and the best advice to a bank is usually to act quickly and decisively, and to keep the borrower informed of any action it takes.

9.6.2 Partial invalidity

There is a danger, albeit remote, that an illegal or invalid clause might make an entire agreement unenforceable. The following type of clause is therefore commonly included in a facility agreement:

> If any provision of this agreement is prohibited, unenforceable, void or invalid, that shall not invalidate, or otherwise affect the enforceability of, the remaining provisions hereof.

This type of clause tries to enhance the possibility of a court severing an invalid section, allowing the other provisions to stand. Under English law there are two underlying principles in relation to severance:

(a)   a court will not construct a new contract: any severance must leave the original contract standing and not alter its basic scope or intention; and

(b)   a court will not sever if to do so is against public policy.

In *Goldsoll v Goldman* [1915] 1 Ch 292, the court formulated the 'blue pencil test': a provision may be severed only if it is possible to do so simply by 'running a blue pencil' through the invalid provisions. Whether or not the type of damage-limitation clause outlined above has any influence on a court's willingness to sever is open to debate.

9.6.3 Amendments and waivers

Under English contract law, no alterations to the provisions of an executed document will be effective without the agreement of all the parties. It is not difficult to imagine the logistical problems this might cause for a syndicated loan with numerous banks. In addition, a requirement for unanimity can result in the 'tail wagging the dog', since even banks with the smallest commitment will have a right of veto over a waiver or an amendment. Most syndicated facilities will therefore allow amendments and waivers to most of their clauses to be agreed by a majority of the syndicate. 'Majority' is typically defined as votes representing either 66⅔% or a simple majority of commitments.

There are two provisions related to amendments and waivers that have become common in leveraged deals during the recent 'borrowers' market':

(a)   'Yank the bank' – this colloquial term refers to a clause allowing the borrower to take a bank out of the syndicate if the bank votes against an amendment or waiver which a requisite majority of banks voted to allow. Usually, the dissenting bank can be removed only if the borrower can find another lender to take the commitment, but sometimes the borrower is allowed to prepay the dissenting bank's commitment.

(b)   'Use or lose' – another colloquial term, a 'use or lose' (also known as 'snooze and lose') provision says that if a bank does not vote on an amendment or waiver decision within a given time (eg, 10 days) then that bank's commitment is disregarded in calculating whether the borrower gets the required majority. An even more aggressive (and therefore rarely, if ever, seen) version, known as 'delay and it's OK', deems a bank to have voted 'yes' to an amendment or waiver if it fails to vote within a specified number of days.

Whilst these clauses are borrower friendly, they are also popular with agents since they help with 'syndicate management'.

9.7 FORCE MAJEURE

There will be circumstances in which the parties to a contract consider that performance of their obligations is, through no fault of any party, no longer possible. A 'force majeure' clause attempts to define those circumstances, typically natural disasters or war, but it might be any circumstance which the parties could neither foresee nor prevent. The clause might provide that the obligations under the contract are suspended until the circumstances have passed, or that the contract is immediately terminated. In either case, however, there will not usually be sanctions on either party since, by definition, there is no blame.

Most facility agreements do not include a specific force majeure clause but rely instead on provisions for increased costs (see **9.3**), illegality (see **9.2.3**), and material adverse change provisions (see **5.2.2** and **8.3**).

9.8 GOVERNING LAW AND JURISDICTION

Clearly, it is crucial to the parties to know and, if possible, control the law and jurisdiction which will apply on enforcement of a facility agreement. It is important to recognise two separate issues: the governing law of a document is different from the jurisdiction where a disputed document will be judged. If English courts have jurisdiction, they will rule on an agreement governed by Icelandic law: they must simply apply Icelandic law principles rather than English law principles.

9.8.1 Governing law

9.8.1.1 Common law rules

In English common law, the governing law of a contract (also known as its 'proper law') will determine issues which include the validity of the original document and any amendments (eg, sufficiency of consideration), interpretation of clauses and remoteness of any damages. The parties are free to choose the governing law provided their choice is bona fide and legal, and not contrary to public policy (see *Vita Food Products Inc v Unus Shipping Co Ltd (in Liquidation)* [1939] AC 277). However, for most contracts, including facility agreements, the common law rules have been largely superseded by statute.

9.8.1.2 Rome I Regulation

The Rome I Regulation on the law applicable to contractual obligations (593/2008/EC) must be applied by EU Member States (except Denmark) to all contracts concluded on or after 17 December 2009 and determines which law is applicable to them. It replaced, with minor amendments, the Rome Convention with the same objective. The Regulation, like the Convention before it, allows complete freedom to choose the governing law of a contract (either expressly or impliedly), although the public policy, and certain 'mandatory rules' (eg, competition law, consumer protection) of the jurisdiction in which a dispute is heard, may supersede the governing law if necessary. If the choice of governing law is not express or reasonably certain, a court will attempt to identify the country with which the contract is 'most closely connected'.

9.8.1.3 Rome II Regulation

From 11 January 2009 the Rome II Regulation allows parties to choose the governing law of non-contractual obligations (eg, claims in tort). The choice will be upheld if: the claim falls within Rome II (some claims are excluded, eg those arising from voluntary trusts); the context is a commercial activity; and the choice of law was freely negotiated. In addition, if all the elements of a claim are outside the UK, non-English law provisions may still apply in limited circumstances. The usual election is for the governing law for non-contractual obligations to be the same as for contractual obligations.

9.8.1.4   Factors affecting choice

The party most likely to sue under a facility agreement is the bank, and so it is the bank which decides the governing law. It may choose the law of its own country, because it is familiar and accessible. Alternatively, it might consider using the law of the borrower's country, because that is where the contract will need to be enforced, and is probably the location of most of the borrower's assets. However, many overseas banks choose English law to govern loan documents because it is relatively sophisticated and stable, the legislation processes are (relatively) predictable, and it is considered 'creditor friendly'.

The jurisdiction in which the assets are situated will normally provide the governing law for any security documentation over those assets.

If the parties do not choose a governing law, the English courts will first look for any implied choice: the choice of jurisdiction will often be a strong influence. If no implied choice is evident, the courts will take a pragmatic view and look to factors such as nationality or residence of the parties, the currency of the loan contract and the place of execution or performance of the agreement. The issues of contractual capacity and authorisation of a party (see **4.6.2**) are determined by the law where it is domiciled.

9.8.2   Jurisdiction

A jurisdiction clause specifies the jurisdiction(s) in which the facility agreement may be enforced in court. The two main reasons for stipulating this are (i) to avoid litigation in unfavourable jurisdictions, and (ii) to enable the contract to be enforced as expected.

The three regimes that will usually apply to a contract giving jurisdiction to English courts are:

(a)   the Brussels I Regulation on jurisdiction and enforcement (Regulation No 44/2001), which binds all EU members (including Denmark);

(b)   the 2007 Lugano Convention, which binds EU members, Denmark, Norway, Iceland and Switzerland; and

(c)   English domestic law.

(Note that the Brussels I Regulation and the Lugano Convention are, for all practical purposes, the same.)

Which of these regimes applies (if any) can be a complex question. Broadly, however, if a party is domiciled in the EU, the Brussels I Regulation applies; if domiciled in Iceland, Norway or Switzerland, the Lugano Convention applies. If a party is domiciled outside the EU or EFTA then English domestic law will apply unless the parties have chosen exclusive jurisdiction of a Member State.

Simplistically, and with exceptions for certain types of contract (eg insurance, consumer and employment contracts), all three regimes allow parties to agree that particular courts can have exclusive or non-exclusive jurisdiction.

Some facility agreements contain one-sided (also known as 'unilateral' or 'asymetric') jurisdiction clauses. These purport to allow the bank to sue either in the named jurisdiction or any other competent jurisdiction, whilst requiring the borrower only to sue in the named jurisdiction. The validity of this kind of clause was called into question by a decision of the French *Cour de cassation* (Decision No 11-26.022, 26 September 2012). The French court decided that a clause of this sort did not meet the requirements of Article 23 of the Brussels I

Regulation (now Article 25 of the recast Brussels Regulation) and, as a result, was ineffective to confer jurisdiction on the named court. However, there are decisions in other EU Member States to the contrary, and most loan documents include one-sided jurisdiction clauses whilst recognising the risk that they may be challenged.

Similar considerations will apply to choosing jurisdiction as when choosing governing law. A bank might want to take advice from a solicitor as to which forum is likely to be quickest, or may be most sympathetic to its case (frequently, a clause will specify several jurisdictions in which any proceedings might be brought). The court which is given jurisdiction will enforce the agreement under the chosen governing law on the basis of evidence from local experts. It should be borne in mind that this is likely substantially to inflate any enforcement costs.

The governing law and jurisdiction clauses are typically found at the end of the document, but you should read them first to make sure you are qualified to review it!

9.8.3 Agent for service of process

If any of the obligors in the facility is not an English registered company and does not have a branch or other place of business in Great Britain, the service of any English court documents on that obligor would require service 'out of jurisdiction' – a time-consuming process when time is of the essence. Fortunately, r 6.11 of the Civil Procedure Rules 1998 allows parties to use any contractually agreed method of service instead of serving out of jurisdiction:

(1) Where—

(a) a contract contains a term providing that, in the event of a claim being started in relation to the contract, the claim form may be served by a method or at a place specified in the contract; and

(b) a claim solely in respect of that contract is started,

the claim form may, subject to paragraph (2), be served on the defendant by the method or at the place specified in the contract.

The usual 'contractually agreed method' is to appoint a conveniently located third party to receive documents on the obligors' behalf, known as an 'agent for service of process'. Using an agent for service of process gives a certain address for service and will avoid a bank having to apply to court for leave to serve a foreign corporation. Several companies offer these services (for a fee), for example The Law Debenture Trust Corporation plc in the UK, and CT Corporation System in New York. Subsidiaries of the borrower are sometimes used, but this runs the risk that the subsidiary might be dissolved or sold. Using Consuls or Ambassadors is not a good idea either, in case they claim immunity to proceedings! Note that, strictly, an 'agent for service of process' is different from a 'process agent' who is someone appointed to *serve* court documents.

9.9 MISCELLANEOUS

9.9.1 Inter-bank provisions

A syndicated facility agreement will contain a section dealing with the relationship between the various syndicate banks, appointing the agent bank(s) and specifying their powers to act on behalf of the other banks. It will usually contain provisions on matters such as monitoring defaults, liability for actions and information, resignation of agent banks, and indemnities. It will also deal with sharing of money in the event that some banks receive payment, or recover money, from a borrower and others do not. All of these matters need careful consideration by banks, borrowers and their solicitors.

9.9.2 Set-off

A facility agreement will usually contain a specific authority from the borrower giving the bank a right (but not an obligation) to set off credit balances in favour of the borrower against any amounts due but unpaid (see **13.5**). The borrower will be prohibited from exercising set-off. This is, in part, to prevent a defaulting borrower from making a counterclaim against the bank (eg for breach of duty) and then setting off the two claims as an excuse to delay repayment of the loan (note the counterclaim can still be made, but not set-off; see eg, *Credit Suisse International v Ramot Plana OOD* [2010] EWHC 2759 (Comm)). (See **9.9.4** for borrower set-off against a defaulting lender.)

9.9.3   Notices

The boiler plate will contain the provisions under which a borrower and bank give notice to each other. Mundane as this might appear, it can be very important, since many of the rights under the document cannot be exercised without notice. Communications must be written, and sent either:

(a)   by post. Banks will sometimes want a notice sent to the borrower to be deemed to arrive a certain number of days after posting, but will never accept a reciprocal arrangement. Always beware of deemed receipt: it has led to litigation in times of postal strikes (see *Bradman v Trinity Estates plc* [1989] BCLC 757); or

(b)   by fax. Fax is almost instantaneous, but the problem is knowing whether it has been received: there is little that can be done if a borrower, suspicious of bad news, simply turns off its fax machine.

Perhaps surprisingly, e-mail can typically only be used for communication between bank and borrower, where they have both pre-agreed. Similarly, posting information on a web page (eg, accounts) may be allowed but only if pre-agreed.

9.9.4   Defaulting lender provisions

As a result of the chaos that ensued when Lehman Brothers bank collapsed in 2008, many borrowers and lenders now consider including provisions in the mechanics and boiler plate of the facility agreement which deal with a lender becoming insolvent (or otherwise defaulting on its obligation to lend), known as a 'defaulting lender'. The defaulting lender provisions typically cover some or all of the following:

(a)   Allowing the borrower to cancel any undrawn commitment of a defaulting lender. This is to avoid complications in dealing with an insolvent lender or its acting insolvency practitioner (eg administrator or liquidator). The borrower will hope that another bank will take up the commitment, but this will not be mandatory.

(b)   If the defaulting lender retains a commitment, no commitment fee is payable on the basis that it will almost certainly be unable to lend if required to do so.

(c)   If the defaulting lender retains a commitment it will not be allowed to vote on any decisions under the facility (it is 'disenfranchised'). This is because it may be very difficult to get a response from a defaulting lender (or its insolvency practitioner), and in any event its perspective on issues such as waiver requests is likely to be very different from that of the 'non-defaulting' banks.

(d)   The defaulting lender may be forced to transfer its participation (ie, money already advanced) in the facility to another lender at par (ie, face value rather than market value).

(e)   Any amount lent by a defaulting lender under a revolving credit facility is automatically turned into a term loan. This is to avoid the borrower having to repay that part of the revolver and then finding it is unable to re-draw from the defaulting lender.

(f)   The identity of a defaulting lender may be disclosed by the agent to the borrower.

(g)   If the defaulting lender is also the facility agent, payments and notices may be made directly between banks and borrower rather than through the agent. In addition, the defaulting agent can be removed by a majority vote of the remaining banks. This avoids the obvious problem of having an insolvent entity as the conduit for all payments and allows the loan mechanics to continue as smoothly as possible.

Some borrowers have suggested that they should be allowed to exercise set-off against defaulting lenders (usually a borrower is prohibited from doing so – see **9.9.2**). However, banks should strongly resist this since it causes issues with the pro-rata sharing provisions in the facility (see **9.9.1**), it can prevent Credit Default Swap (see **Glossary**) protection and makes the facility ineligible for certain central bank liquidity schemes (which, in essence, allow banks to temporarily swap illiquid assets (eg certain loans) for liquid ones (eg government securities) to aid bank liquidity).

9.10 SCHEDULES

The schedules appear at the very end of a document, after all the operative provisions but before the execution clause. They attach lists of information which could be included in the operative provisions but which would make them rather clumsy, for example, banks' commitments, condition precedent documents, repayment dates and amounts, as well as the mandatory costs formula. The schedules may also contain any agreed drafts of the documents required under the loan, such as utilisation requests, transfer certificates (see **Chapter 10**), compliance certificates, accession deeds, confidentiality undertaking and the form of any guarantee (if not built into the facility itself) and/or security to be provided, or sometimes the terms on which security will be given ('security principles').

9.11 EXECUTION

Where a syndicated loan requires a party to perform several defined roles, it is conventional for a bank to execute separately for each of those roles. For example, a bank would sign three times if it were a participating bank, the administrative agent and the security agent. If it signs only once, it must be made clear that this is in respect of all the bank's roles. Note that s 44(6) of the Companies Act 2006 requires that if a director is signing a document as director for more than one company (quite common for large groups), they must sign separately for each company.

If the loan involves a large syndicate, it may not be possible to find a date on which all the members are available to attend a signing meeting. There are three possible solutions:

(a)   the documents may be sent to each signatory in turn. This can be a rather cumbersome process, however, and may stretch the execution over several days;

(b)   the absent party may appoint someone to sign on its behalf under a power of attorney, which should be created by a deed. Section 7(1) of the Powers of Attorney Act 1971 (as amended) allows an attorney to sign in their own name, or that of the principal. The borrower's solicitor should check the power of attorney document for expiry, powers, and any conditions or limitations, before accepting an attorney's signature; or

(c)   the document may be executed in counterparts. This allows identical copies of the document to be signed simultaneously in as many different locations as necessary. This may be done in a number of ways, but care must be taken due to the judgment in R (*on the application of Mercury Tax Group and Another*) *v HM Revenue and Customs Commissioners and Others* [2008] EWHC 2721, which criticised poor practice in execution of deeds, and also because of the Law of Property (Miscellaneous Provisions) Act 1989. One of the following methods is therefore usually used for execution in counterparts:

(i)   The printed documents are sent to each party by post or courier. Each party signs its own document and confirms that it has done so (without any amendments) to the solicitor coordinating the documents. Once all parties have signed and confirmed, the facility is treated as executed and the parties then return their respective (whole) documents to the solicitor. The 'original agreement' is technically the composite of all the counterparts.

(ii)   The documents are circulated by e-mail or made accessible via an online platform, with instructions to print off the full document and then proceed as for (i) above.

Signatories may be asked to scan the signed document as a PDF and e-mail it back (or upload to a platform) as proof of execution, though this PDF is evidential only and not an 'original'. As a practical matter, it is important to check that signatories have the facilities to print and scan large documents. Also, be aware that print sizes vary between some countries (eg the US and UK), and so the document will run to a different number of pages and the execution clauses will appear on different numbered pages (which can look odd when collating the originals). Solutions include sending documents by pdf (which has the added advantage that parties cannot alter the document), or removing the page numbers from the execution pages.

(iii)   The documents are circulated by e-mail with instructions to print off and sign the signature pages only, then to scan the signed pages into a PDF and return them together with an electronic copy of the (unsigned) document in a single e-mail. The true 'original' document is the electronic version and any hard copy created is merely evidential. This method therefore cannot be used where hard copy originals are required, for example for registration at the Land Registry.

(iv)   The documents are circulated by e-mail with instructions to print, sign and return just the signature pages to the solicitor coordinating the documents, as evidence of the document being signed. Strictly, this will mean that there is no 'original document'. This method cannot be used for executing deeds (due to the *Mercury Tax Group* ruling) or agreements with provisions for the sale or disposition of interests in land (because of s 2(1) and (3) of the Law of Property (Miscellaneous Provisions) Act 1989).

(v)   Just the signature pages are circulated (sometimes with a latest draft of the agreement) for signature in advance of the final documents being agreed. The pages are signed and returned to the solicitor coordinating the documents. When the documents are in agreed final form, the solicitor is authorised to affix the signature pages and the document treated as executed. As with method (iv), this method cannot be used for executing deeds or agreements with provisions for the sale or disposition of interests in land. The key issue, if using this method, is to ensure that there is clear authority from a party to attach its pre-signed signature pages to the relevant version of the document.

If executing in counterparts the document should ideally have a clause specifically allowing execution by counterparts to avoid any argument by a party that it did not realise that its signature alone could make the document 'live'.

The solicitor may produce 'conformed copies' (see **Glossary**) for each party or a CD containing copies of the original documents as appropriate.

Lastly, the location of execution may be important for tax purposes, with documents often needing to be executed 'offshore' (ie outside certain jurisdictions).

9.12   US AND ENGLISH LAW LOAN FACILITIES

The examination of loan facility provisions in the previous chapters is based on a document governed by English law to be used in the European syndicated loan market. Other jurisdictions and legal systems will have their own nuances which must be reflected in the loan document. By way of example, this section outlines some key differences between an English law facility agreement and one governed by US law and aimed at US lenders.

What drives the differences?

A number of factors will create differences between US and English law loan facilities and associated documents such as security agreements:

(1)   The insolvency regimes are different, although English law administration is quite similar to the US law equivalent ('Chapter 11') and both are far more 'creditor friendly' (they favour lenders) than most European regimes.

(2)   It is generally easier to take security over all of a borrower's assets under US law, and the registration and enforcement regimes are more standardised (under the Uniform Commercial Code). English security law is very flexible but relatively complex, having evolved over centuries of case law (although the recently simplified registration regime is helpful).

(3)   The US is a more litigious environment, which allows unconnected third parties to purchase and pursue legal claims and provides a more favourable costs regime for litigants.

(4)   The US market has more 'institutional investors' lending in the loan market, leading to greater liquidity and a convergence between loan and bond market terms. This last factor drives most of the points listed below.

Key differences in facility agreements

The following features are common in, and originated from, US law facilities, although they may also appear in some English law facilities.

Call protection

Call protection is a US phrase for an early prepayment fee. It entitles the lenders to an extra fee if the loan is refinanced within a specified time of signing (usually 12 months). If incurred, call protection is typically payable as a fee of around 1% of the facility amount.

Limited amortisation

Another commercial term driven by institutional investors is that it is common to have an annual amortisation of around 1% per annum on the term loan 'B' (ie the term loan taken by institutional investors). This is simply to provide a current return on the facility.

'Covenant lite'

English leveraged loan facilities generally use 'maintenance' financial covenants: the borrower is obliged to show at regular intervals (usually every three months ('quarterly')) that it is maintaining the financial performance it predicted in its business plan. Within a given period of each testing date, the borrower must submit a compliance certificate to the agent bank confirming that it has met the financial covenants. This is quite onerous. US leveraged facilities generally contain just a single financial covenant or 'incurrence'-style covenants, which are only tested ('incurred') if the borrower wants to take certain specified actions (eg make further acquisitions or disposals). Cashflow covenants, which are common in London market leveraged facilities, are not typical in the US market. The US-style financial covenant packages are colloquially known as 'covenant lite' and are similar to those found in high yield bonds.

MAC event of default

US law facilities would typically not include a material adverse change (MAC) event of default. They would usually include a MAC representation, but breach would only usually prevent further utilisation of the revolving credit facility and could not be used to accelerate the loan.

Majority lender votes

Votes requiring consent of 'majority lenders' in US law facilities usually just require a simple majority. English law documents typically require two thirds.

Loan transfer

US facilities will typically allow the term loan to be freely transferred without borrower consent, although revolving credit facilities are more likely to require consent. English law facilities for the London market are more likely to require borrower consent, not to be unreasonably withheld or delayed, sometimes coupled with a 'white list' of institutions that lenders can transfer to freely.

Novation, Assignment and Sub-participation

'The only permanent thing is change.'

Heraclitus

10.1 INTRODUCTION

Glance at a bank's balance sheet and it will contain the usual list of assets you might expect to find in a company: buildings, office equipment, and perhaps a few safes. The big difference is a large entry in the current assets under 'loans and advances' (see the sample balance sheet at **6.3.3**). As with other assets, a bank spends money to acquire loans, and they in turn produce money for the bank. However, once a bank has made a loan it might not keep it until it matures.

In one sense, a bank may use its loans like fixed assets: 'purchase' them, keep them for a time to earn an income, and then dispose of them. This chapter examines how banks dispose of their loans: an exercise known as 'asset sales'.

10.2 WHY SELL A LOAN?

Since the main purpose of a bank is to lend money, it might seem strange that it would want to dispose of its loans, but there are a number of common reasons for doing so.

10.2.1 Realising capital

A bank may want to realise some of the capital it has tied up in long-term loans in order to improve its liquidity. This would allow it to take advantage of any new lending opportunities which give a better return. Alternatively, a bank might decide to concentrate on a particular market and to sell any loans that do not 'fit the bill'.

10.2.2   Risk management

A bank may decide that its loan portfolio has become distorted. Too much emphasis on one type of loan or one type of borrower carries risk, and a bank may sell some existing loans to allow it to make others.

10.2.3   Balance sheet

A bank's ability to lend is subject to internal and external requirements to retain a percentage of its capital as cover for its loans ('regulatory capital' – see **9.3.3**). If a bank's capital is entirely allocated, it cannot participate in new loans (unless they carry a zero risk weighting), no matter how attractive or lucrative they might seem. Therefore, unless the bank can raise more capital, it must sell some existing loans to release capital for backing new ones.

10.2.4   Profit

A bank may see an opportunity to make some short-term profit by selling a loan. For example, if interest rates start to fall, an existing fixed interest loan might become very marketable. Conversely, if a borrower has defaulted or is performing badly, a lender may choose to sell its participation at a discount to crystallise any loss (see also **10.6**).

10.2.5   Prestige

A bank will sometimes want an initial involvement in a facility because it is particularly high-profile or important, for example the London 2012 Olympics financing. It may, however, choose to sell some or all of its share of the loan once it has derived any benefit to its market profile. Some forms of asset sale will allow a bank to keep its name to a loan but to lay off the lending risk.

10.2.6   Syndication

A bank may, either alone or with a small group of banks (Lead Arrangers), sometimes provide the full amount of a loan but bring in other banks to form a syndicate 'post-closing'. This 'postponement' of syndication allows large loans to be made quickly.

10.3   MOVING RIGHTS AND OBLIGATIONS

Before looking at how a bank might sell its assets, it is necessary briefly to consider the legal analysis of transferring a contractual role to another party. Most contracts operate by giving rights and obligations (liabilities) to each party. One party's rights will usually constitute another party's obligations. Under most facility agreements, a bank's fundamental obligation is to lend money (the borrower has a right to borrow), whilst its fundamental rights are usually to receive interest and eventual return of capital (the borrower is obliged to service and repay the loan). There are many other rights and obligations in a facility agreement, and since facility agreements are primarily designed to protect the bank, most rights are in favour of the bank and most obligations rest on the borrower.

In order to fully dispose of a loan, a bank must dispose of both its rights and its obligations, and this is where problems might arise. Under English law, rights under a contract (other than very personal rights) can be transferred at the instigation of the party entitled to them; contractual obligations can be moved only with the consent of the party to whom the obligation is owed. In other words, a borrower must agree to any change in a bank's obligations.

The rule is intended to prevent a party being prejudiced by the change in identity of an obligor. This can be illustrated by a simple example. Imagine that you lend your neighbour £500 on the understanding that she will pay you back in two weeks' time. You have known her for three years, she has a very well-paid job, and you obviously know where she lives. The chances of your neighbour fulfilling her obligation to pay back the money are good. Two weeks later your neighbour politely informs you that she had decided to lend the £500 to her brother who is a student in Spain, and so the obligation to repay you now rests with him. Not only have your chances of repayment probably fallen, but enforcing the obligation to repay has become much more difficult. It should now be clear why obligations cannot be transferred without the consent of the party to whom they are owed: you remain entitled to demand repayment of the £500 from your neighbour.

10.4 SELLING ASSETS

10.4.1 Summary

A bank can dispose of an asset in several different ways with different consequences. The most common methods are:

(a)   novation;

(b)   legal ('statutory' or 'disclosed') assignment;

(these two methods both result in the selling bank disposing of the asset completely)

(c)   equitable (or 'undisclosed') assignment;

(d)   sub-participation;

(e)   risk participation.

(Using any of these last three methods will entail the selling bank retaining some involvement in the asset.)

On examining all of these methods in more detail, it is important to keep in mind that the basic aim of a bank in selling an asset is to remove the risk associated with it.

10.4.2 Novation

10.4.2.1 What is novation?

The only way in which a party can effectively 'transfer' all its rights and obligations under a contract is with the consent of all the parties involved. This type of transaction is known as a 'novation', a term with its origins in Roman law. Novation involves one party's rights and obligations under a contract being cancelled and discharged, whilst a third party assumes identical new rights and obligations in their place. Novating a facility agreement simply means that a new bank is put in place of the old one. It is the most straightforward, and therefore most commonly used, transfer method under English law.

The new bank assumes identical rights and obligations with respect to the borrower as applied to the existing bank. This method is often contemplated in the original loan documentation, allowing the new bank to step into the facility agreement in place of the existing bank.

In strict legal terms, a novation does not transfer rights and liabilities: it cancels an existing contract and replaces it with another. The borrower's promise to perform its obligations in favour of a new bank is consideration for the existing bank releasing the old debt.

10.4.2.2 Advantages of novation

The main advantages in disposing of a loan by way of novation are as follows.

Moving obligations

Novation is the only proven method of moving contractual obligations as well as rights. In particular, this allows the existing bank to dispose of a loan which has an unutilised commitment (eg, under an RCF). Conversely, the new bank achieves a relationship with the borrower as if it were a party to the facility agreement.

Risk transfer

Novation can fully remove a loan (including any undrawn commitments) from the existing bank's balance sheet and so exclude it from any regulatory capital requirements.

Easy syndication

If the original facility agreement includes transfer certificates (see **10.4.2.3**), the existing (and any subsequent) bank can take on a large commitment without the delay of putting an underwriting syndicate together, knowing that it will easily be able to sell all or part of its commitment.

10.4.2.3   Disadvantages of novation

The main disadvantages of novating rights and obligations under a facility agreement are as follows.

Consent

The consent of all the parties involved in the original loan document is required, including any parties which have guaranteed the borrower's performance under the original facility agreement. This puts a great deal of power in the borrower's hands. Even if all parties are agreeable to a novation, a syndicated loan will present the logistical problems involved in organising the borrower, any obligors, and all the syndicate members to sign the document necessary to effect a novation.

One neat solution to the problem of consent, found predominantly in syndicated loans, is the use of 'transfer certificates'. The facility agreement will contain a clause under which the parties agree in advance that a bank may dispose of (by novation) any or all of its commitment. This is effectively an open offer to take a loan. To accept the offer, a new bank (together with the existing bank) must simply execute a transfer certificate, though the facility agreement may specify circumstances in which borrower consent is required (see **10.13**). A pro-forma certificate will usually be included as one of the schedules to the facility agreement. Transfer certificates can be used to dispose of all or part of both a bank's participation and/or its commitment.

A recent Australian case (*Goodridge v Macquarie Bank Limited* [2010] FCA 67) held that a prior agreement to novation in a loan agreement was invalid and simply an 'agreement to agree'. However, in *Habibsons Bank Ltd v Standard Chartered Bank (Hong Kong) Limited* [2010] EWCA Civ 1335, the Court of Appeal criticised the *Goodridge* decision. While this rebuttal was *obiter*, it is a very useful affirmation of the viability of standard transfer provisions in loan facilities, and so properly drafted transfer certificates should still be effective.

Note also that even if transfer certificates are used, the facility agreement may still require the borrower's consent to transfer in specified circumstances.

A system similar to the transfer certificate is the transferable loan certificate (TLC). The only significant difference is that the TLC operates through the agent bank issuing certificates and keeping a register of transfers. The TLC was originally devised to avoid stamp duties which are no longer in force, and so it is now relatively uncommon.

Secured loans

Since novation replaces existing obligations with new ones, it probably restarts the time periods ('hardening periods') during which the security might be set aside as a transaction at an undervalue, or preferred transaction, under the IA 1986, ss 238–241. The time limits for any floating charge being avoided under the IA 1986, s 245 might also be restarted (see **14.9** – although the likelihood of a liquidator using any of these provisions against a novation must be small). The other danger of security being re-dated to the time of each novation is that it might lose its priority over other security (see **14.3**). The favoured way to resolve these potential problems (in common law jurisdictions at least) is to appoint a security trustee to hold any security granted under the loan on trust for the banks. The banks participating in (or committed to) the facility will be beneficiaries of the security under the trust and may vary from time to time whilst the security remains. If the relevant jurisdiction does not recognise trusts, a 'parallel debt' structure might be used.

Disclosure

For obvious reasons, it is difficult to hide the identity of a transferee bank using novation.

10.4.3 Legal assignment

10.4.3.1 What is legal assignment?

Assignment is simply the transfer of rights. The Law of Property Act 1925 (LPA 1925), s 136 provides that an assignment of debts and other choses in action (ie, rights enforceable by legal action rather than possession) will only be recognised 'at law' (a 'legal assignment') if it is:

(a)   in writing and signed by the assignor;

(b)   absolute (ie, unconditional); and

(c)   notified in writing to any person(s) against whom the assignor could enforce the assigned rights.

In order to be 'absolute' in the context of loan transfers, an assignment must transfer the whole of the debt owed to the existing bank (see *Walter and Sullivan Ltd v Murphy (J) and Sons Ltd* [1955] 2 QB 584) (and cannot be 'by way of charge') (see **12.6**). If any one of the conditions for legal assignment is not fulfilled, the assignment will be an equitable one (see **10.4.4**). Legal assignments are also known as 'statutory assignments'.

An assignment can transfer only rights and not obligations – see **10.4.3.3**.

The assignment of some contracts is governed by legislation other than the LPA 1925. Of particular relevance in a banking context are bills of exchange and promissory notes (assignment of which is regulated under the Bills of Exchange Act 1882), and shares in registered companies, the rights under which are transferred in accordance with the CA 2006.

10.4.3.2 Advantages of legal assignment

Rights transferred

Subject to any restrictions in the loan facility and the 'disadvantages' discussed at **10.4.3.3**, legal assignment is an effective method of transferring rights under a facility agreement without requiring the borrower's consent.

Borrower's payments

On receiving notice of an assignment, the borrower is obliged to pay any monies due under the assigned loan to the new bank.

Secured loan

Any security, or a bank's rights as beneficiary of any security sharing agreement, may be assigned along with the debt, but is usually held by a Security Trustee or under a parallel debt structure (see **10.4.2.1**).

10.4.3.3 Disadvantages of legal assignment

Obligations not transferred

An assignment cannot transfer the assignor's obligations. Therefore, the existing bank cannot assign any undrawn commitments, which makes assigning a revolving credit facility problematic. In addition, any obligations the existing bank owes to its fellow syndicate members will not be transferred. Some facility documents therefore include assignment mechanics which purport to assign the existing bank's rights, release the existing bank from any obligations relating to that part of its commitment, and require the new bank to assume equivalent obligations.

Rights not transferred

The rights under a contract can be assigned without consent only in 'cases where it can make no difference to the person on whom the obligation lies to which of two persons he is to discharge it' (*Tolhurst v Associated Portland Cement Manufacturers (1900) Ltd* [1902] 2 KB 660). The test is an objective one and so, for example, the character of an assignee will be ignored. In a banking context, there is a danger that any indemnity provisions for increased costs (see **9.3**) might be unassignable without consent because they are 'personal' (eg, they may vary substantially with the jurisdiction of a bank). The standard transfer provision will usually deal with this issue (see **10.13**).

10.4.4   Equitable assignment

An assignment which does not meet any one (or more) of the provisions required for legal assignment under the LPA 1925, s 136 will (as long as there is an intention to assign) be an equitable assignment.

10.4.4.1   Differences between legal and equitable assignments

As a purely procedural matter, an equitable assignee (ie, the new bank) must join the assignor (the existing bank) in any action on the debt (*Three Rivers DC v Bank of England* [1995] 4 All ER 312). However, significant differences between legal and equitable assignments arise only if the obligor (ie, in the case of loan transfers, the borrower) is not given notice of an assignment (see **10.4.4.3**).

10.4.4.2   Advantages of equitable assignments

Partial assignment and non-disclosure

If a bank wants to assign part of an outstanding loan, it must use an equitable assignment. Likewise, if a bank wants to assign an outstanding loan without disclosing the identity of the new bank to the borrower, it must use an equitable assignment.

In all other material respects, equitable assignments share the advantages of legal assignments (see **10.4.3.2**).

10.4.4.3   Disadvantages of equitable assignments

Payments

If the equitable assignment is not notified to the borrower, it will not know the identity of the bank to which its debt has been assigned, and it is entitled to continue making payments through the existing bank. In some circumstances, this may be an advantage to the existing bank: some assignments allow the assignor to retain a percentage of the interest paid on the assigned loan. In that situation, the existing bank will be happy to receive payments from which it can skim its entitlement.

However, the new bank buying a non-disclosed assignment must rely on the borrower to pay its money, and on the existing bank to pass it on. It is therefore taking a double credit risk. Furthermore, if the borrower should become insolvent the new bank might have the near impossible task of tracing any monies which the existing bank received from the borrower but did not pass on.

Subject to equities

If the equitable assignment is unnotified, a new bank will be subject to all 'equities' (eg, mutual rights of set-off) which arise between the existing bank and the borrower, even *after* the loan is assigned (until notification of assignment).

10.4.4.4 Form of notice of assignment

The rights of a bank taking an assignment depend almost entirely on whether notice is given to the borrower. In light of the issues outlined above, a notice of assignment (legal or equitable) should require a borrower to confirm:

(a) the amount of the existing bank's debt;

(b) that it has no rights of set-off or counter-claim against the existing bank;

(c) that it has no notice of other assignments of the same debt;

(d) the facility agreement has not been varied; and

(e) that it will pay amounts due and payable under the underlying contract to the new bank's order.

10.4.5 Sub-participation

10.4.5.1 What is sub-participation?

The main reason why a bank is interested in novation and assignment is that they both enable it to remove loans from its balance sheet. There is, however, a way to achieve the same objective whilst leaving the original loan in place, known as 'sub-participation' (or sometimes 'funded participation' (to differentiate from 'risk participation' – see **10.4.6**) or simply 'participation', although this is confusing because it is also the label for a bank's share of a loan).

Sub-participation (which has no technical legal meaning) is an arrangement under which an existing bank matches part or all of its loan to a borrower with a deposit it takes from a new bank (the 'sub-participant'). So far, this sounds like the inter-bank funding described at **4.9**. However, in a sub-participation the new bank agrees that its deposit will be serviced and repaid only when the borrower services and repays the loan from the existing bank. The sub-participant has effectively taken on the risk of the first loan: if the borrower fails to make a payment due under its loan from the existing bank, the existing bank will not have to pay the new bank.

The existing bank's obligations to the new (sub-participant) bank match, and are conditional upon, the borrower's obligations to the existing bank.

There are two aspects to sub-participation which it is important to appreciate at this stage. First, the transaction does not involve any transfer of rights or obligations: the existing bank's contractual relationship with the borrower is unaffected. Secondly, since the sub-participation agreement is an entirely separate contract to the initial facility agreement, the new (sub-participant) bank will not have any rights directly against the borrower. This is known as a 'non-recourse' transaction. Any security provided by the borrower will remain with the existing bank.

10.4.5.2 Advantages of sub-participation

Risk transfer

Sub-participation will effectively remove a loan from inclusion in the existing bank's regulatory capital requirements, other than in respect of undrawn commitments (see **10.4.5.3**).

Consent

Unless there is a prohibition in the original facility agreement (which is unlikely), an existing bank may sub-participate without the consent of the borrower. The only problem the existing bank might face is in providing information about the borrower to a new bank, since all banks owe a duty of confidentiality to their clients (set out in *Tournier v National Provincial and Union Bank of England* [1924] 1 KB 461). An existing bank intending to sub-participate will therefore want to include a clause in the original facility agreement allowing it to release information about both the borrower and the loan, without a breach of duty.

Non-disclosure

An existing bank does not have to disclose a sub-participation to the borrower (unless it has a confidentiality issue – see above), and most sub-participations will be 'silent'. The advantage to both existing bank and borrower is that the relationship between them is maintained despite the risk being laid off.

10.4.5.3 Disadvantages of sub-participation

Sub-participant's credit risk

A new (sub-participant) bank must take a credit risk on both the existing bank and the borrower. If the borrower goes into liquidation, the new bank receives only what the existing bank can reclaim (because of the non-recourse nature); and if the existing bank goes into liquidation, the new bank will usually have to claim as an unsecured creditor. This double risk will be reflected in the new bank's fees for sub-participation.

Risk transfer

Funded sub-participation may not be fully effective to off-load the (entire) risk of undrawn commitments if it simply results in the existing bank taking a risk on the new bank instead of the borrower. The sub-participation agreement must ensure that the existing bank is put in funds in time to meet the borrower's demands for utilisation in order effectively to remove the risk.

10.4.6 Risk participation

Risk participation is a form of participation which acts like a guarantee. The risk participant bank will not immediately place any money with the existing bank, but will agree (for a fee) to put the existing bank in funds in certain circumstances (typically on any payment default by the borrower). Risk participation might be provided by a new bank as an interim measure before it takes full transfer of a loan.

A more common use for risk participation is to cover so-called 'unfunded' assets (ie, assets under which an existing bank has a potential outlay such as guarantees, letters of credit or swaps). If the existing bank's customer fails to meet its reimbursement obligations under these products, the new bank will put the existing bank in funds.

10.5 GLOBAL TRANSFER AGREEMENT

Sometimes a deal requires a large amount of simultaneous transfers, for example if a small number of banks initially underwrite the loan but then transfer to several dozen new banks after the closing. To avoid preparing a large number of transfer certificates, a Global Transfer Agreement may be used. This is simply a new contract which amends (and restates) the facility agreement to add a new schedule of commitments. The logistical advantages are obvious, though it is very transparent: all banks will see who else is lending and the 'level' of their commitment, and this will not suit all deals.

10.6 DISTRESSED AND PAR LOANS

Originally, the main market for asset sales was for so-called 'distressed debt' (also known as 'impaired debt'). Distressed debt is corporate debt which a bank is prepared to sell at a price below the amount outstanding, usually because it believes the debt may be repaid late, or repaid only in part.

At the end of 1996, however, a number of banks formed the 'Loan Market Association' (LMA), intending to enhance trading in (primarily) performing loans known as the 'par market'. The LMA, which now has a very substantial membership, has produced standardised documentation, settlement procedures, and agreed a code of practice for market activity, all of which has helped create a more active and efficient secondary market.

10.7 TAX IMPLICATIONS

Detailed analysis of the tax implications of asset sales is beyond the scope of this book. Briefly, there are usually two main types of tax which might affect asset sales: stamp duty (or stamp duty reserve tax (SDRT) payable on some undocumented transactions) and withholding tax.

Sub-participation does not involve any transfer of rights, and so will not attract stamp duty. Novation will not usually involve a transfer of property for stamp duty purposes and so will not normally attract the tax. If, however, the asset has rights other than those normally associated with a debt (eg, rights to acquire property) stamp duty or SDRT may apply. Assignment may prima facie attract stamp duty or SDRT; however, exemptions for transfer of loan capital (Finance Act 1986, ss 79(4) and 99(5)(a)) can often be used to avoid any duty.

In all asset sales between banks, and involving a UK resident/domiciled borrower, the relevance of withholding tax on interest payments will depend largely on whether the exemption under s 879 of the ITA 2007 applies (see **9.3.4**). The s 879 exemption will apply to loans which have been assigned as long as the advance was initially made by a 'bank' and the assignee is beneficially entitled to the interest and within the charge to UK incorporation tax at the time interest is paid. If the loan is novated (see **10.4.2**), however, this probably creates a new advance and so must be made to a 'bank' to ensure s 879 still applies.

10.8 FINANCIAL SERVICES AND MARKETS ACT IMPLICATIONS

Section 19 of the FSMA 2000 provides that:

> No person may carry on a regulated activity in the United Kingdom or purport to do so unless he is an authorised person or an exempt person.

This 'general prohibition' may impinge on some asset sales.

The only certain way for a bank to avoid the implications of the FSMA 2000 when selling participations, is probably to ensure that it is authorised to do so under the Act.

10.9 BORROWER TRANSFERS

Facility agreements will invariably prohibit a borrower from transferring any of its rights or obligations under the agreement without consent from the bank(s).

10.10 OTHER JURISDICTIONS

If a borrower (or any other obligor, such as a guarantor) is registered or domiciled in a jurisdiction other than England and Wales, there may be issues of local law which impinge on asset sales. Generally, sub-participations are unlikely to face problems because they use a contractual agreement completely outside the loan document and which will not affect the borrower. Novations and assignments may require consents of, or notices to, local regulatory bodies (or to the borrower) before being recognised. The golden rule is to get advice from a 'local' lawyer.

10.11 SECURITISATION

Sometimes a bank will want to sell not just one or two loans at a time but a whole group of loans together. Securitisation is a technique which allows banks to 'sell' a large portfolio of loans (or other income-producing assets), thereby freeing up capital to re-invest. In very basic terms, securitisation involves the owner of a pool of assets (the 'originator') transferring them to a specially formed company (a 'special purpose vehicle' or 'SPV'). The SPV funds its purchase of the assets by issuing debt securities (it is therefore known as the 'issuer'). Coupon and redemption of the debt securities are met with, and secured over, the asset pool.

10.12 ASSET SALES – THE BANK'S PERSPECTIVE

Most banks will require the flexibility to sell a loan if they decide it is necessary or desirable. They will, however, usually be receptive to a borrower's feelings towards maintaining some form of lending relationship during the term of the loan and allow some restrictions (see **10.12** below). In current markets, many entities other than traditional banks are involved in buying loans on the secondary market. A bank's solicitor should therefore ensure the facility transfer language allows transfer not just to other banks but also to trusts, funds, or other entities engaged in buying loans. (Some facilities restrict transferees to other 'financial institutions': in *Argo Fund Ltd v Essar Steel Ltd* [2005] EWHC 600 (Comm) the court gave a helpfully wide interpretation to the phrase 'financial institution'.)

10.13 ASSET SALES – THE BORROWER'S PERSPECTIVE

At first sight, the identity of the bank might appear to be of little importance to a borrower. After all, on novation, assignment and sub-participation the provisions of the facility agreement will apply to the existing bank(s) or any of their successors. However, a borrower's relationship with its lenders will be crucial if it requires waivers to actual or potential defaults, if it wants to make changes to the loan documents going forward, or needs tolerance in interpreting provisions.

Investment grade borrowers might look for a 'club loan' in which a small number of 'relationship' banks provide the facility and no transfers are made in normal circumstances. Most facilities, however, will allow transfer but subject to obtaining the borrower's consent (other than for transfers between existing lenders or their affiliates), such consent not to be 'unreasonably withheld or delayed'. There are then substantial negotiations to modify the consent requirement, for example:

(a) borrower consent may be deemed given if they do not reply within a given timeframe (eg five business days);

(b) transfers to a borrower's competitors may be prohibited on the basis that the competitor might then obtain sensitive information about the borrower;

(c) transfers to certain types of fund may be prohibited on the basis that they acquire debt for motives other than pure lending (eg to take control of the borrower or agitate in other ways): the difficulty is in agreeing a generic definition for such funds;

(d) a list of named institutions to which banks can transfer without consent may be pre-agreed (known as a 'white list'). Less commonly there may be a list of named institutions to whom no transfers can be made (a 'black list'); and

(e) banks will usually want complete freedom to transfer without borrower consent if an event of default is continuing. Ironically this is the time when borrowers most need a stable, sympathetic syndicate and so they will usually resist this if possible.

Finally, the difficult credit conditions during 2008 and 2009 saw many loans trading at substantially less than their face value (below par). This prompted borrowers to consider buying back portions of their own loan debt: buying the debt at a discount is a cheap way to prepay. Most facility agreements did not specifically address whether a borrower could buy back the loan, but there may be issues with prepayment restrictions, pro-rata sharing between lenders, restrictions on cash usage, and issues with novation (see the *Financial Times* article below). Most loan facilities now include specific mechanics to deal with borrower debt buy-back. These mechanics either prohibit buy-back completely, or restrict which borrower-related entities might buy. Even if buy-back is allowed, the buying entity is usually required to allow all the syndicate banks a chance to sell (rather than approach specific banks). Furthermore, any debt they purchase will lose the associated voting rights to stop borrower entities interfering with votes.

10.14 FURTHER READING

Geoffrey Fuller, *Corporate Borrowing: Law and Practice* (5th edn, Jordans, 2016).

Debt buy-back sparks loans policy revision

Martin Arnold and Anousha Sakoui

Phones 4U has bought back some of its debt and with it joined a growing legion of companies capitalising on record-low debt prices.

The UK mobile phone retailer, owned by Providence Equity Partners, has bought £25m ($45m) of its debt at about 75 per cent of face value, according to a person familiar with the company.

Providence has already invested $2.5bn (£1.4bn) buying debt in its own and other buy-out deals, and recently hired Thomas Gahan from Deutsche Bank in the US to head its new capital markets group.

The news follows an ever-increasing number of mainly private equity-backed companies and their shareholders buying up their own debt either as an investment or in an attempt to reduce leverage as they navigate the global financial crisis.

However, lenders are not always supportive. One concern is that these debt buy-backs could allow shareholders or the company to build a blocking stake in the debt and influence future debt renegotiations or even block lenders from enforcing a default.

In response, the Loan Market Association, a trade body representing lenders, has published revised loan documentation that includes the ability to prohibit borrowers from buying back debt and stop shareholders or their affiliates voting debt they have bought back in negotiations with lenders - in a bid to avoid conflicts of interest. Borrowers can be allowed to buy back debt under certain conditions.

These buy-backs can happen in different ways.

The first is for a private equity company to buy its portfolio company's debt through a special purpose vehicle it owns, then consolidate it with the rest of the group - either selling the vehicle to the business or contributing it as equity ñ reducing leverage.

Another way is for the private equity group to use its own fund or a separate debt fund to buy the debt for investment purposes.

However, private equity groups with separate debt funds, such as KKR and Permira, say they have solid Chinese walls between their credit and buy-out teams.

Amadeus, the BC Partners and Cinven-owned travel IT company, has asked lenders' consent before doing a buy-back and has been negotiating the terms of it - a process investors generally prefer.

After discussion with lenders, the company has limited the size of the debt buy-back to €320m (£254m) and agreed not to vote in lender negotiations, according to a person familiar with the company.

Blackstone's German plastic film producer Klöckner Pentaplast has also been buying back debt, helping it reduce leverage. Earlier this year, it bought back about €25m of mezzanine, or subordinated, debt at about 20 to 30 per cent of face value, but has bought more since.

However, in spite of concerns, some banks may ultimately see these moves as a way to reduce the risk of a debt restructuring.

"Banks don't really want to end up owning the equity in these companies, so there is an alignment of interest between the debt and equity," said Peter Combe, chief executive of Permira Debt Managers, the €800m debt fund set up by the UK private equity group last year.

Source: *Financial Times*, 30 September 2008

DRAFTING TIPS

'I am a bear of very little brain, and long words bother me.'

Pooh Bear, in *Winnie-the-Pooh* by AA Milne

11.1 INTRODUCTION

Probably the hardest task of a banking solicitor is drafting the documentation. Having identified the issues which affect their client and having negotiated those issues (usually at some length), the solicitor must return to their office and create a document to reflect what the parties have agreed.

Most solicitors' firms have a house style of drafting documents to which they encourage adherence. Furthermore, like most skills, drafting legal documents is best learnt and perfected through practice. The aim of this chapter, therefore, is not to produce a set of drafting rules, but rather to highlight some of the issues and techniques which commonly arise in the context of drafting loan documentation. If there is a 'golden rule', however, it is this: work out what you want to achieve before putting pen to paper (or finger to key).

11.2 CREATING THE DOCUMENT

In order to put the techniques explained below into context, it is important to appreciate the way in which a facility agreement is created. Since a written facility agreement is primarily used to benefit the bank (see **3.7**), the drafting of the document traditionally starts and remains in the control of the bank's solicitor (although in some acquisition financings, where the sponsor's solicitor has drafted the term sheet, they may also draft the loan). The bank's solicitor will produce a first draft from the term sheet (see **2.3.2**), which will then be sent to all parties for comment. The borrower and its solicitor are likely to have a number of clauses which they want deleted or varied, and will annotate the first draft accordingly (this is usually the only time when the borrower's solicitor does any substantial drafting). Once the marked-up draft has been seen by all parties, a conference call or (more rarely) meeting is arranged to discuss the points that it raises. There then ensues a series of e-mail exchanges, telephone calls or meetings which will attempt to resolve all the issues, with the bank's solicitor periodically producing amended drafts of the agreement to reflect substantial changes.

The burden of drafting which the bank's solicitor must shoulder is partly offset by the fact that in creating the document they know what they have, and have not, included. The borrower's solicitor must not only review the provisions that are in the draft agreement, but also identify any points which should be included for their client's protection but which are not. It is worth noting that the LMA (see **10.5**) has produced a series of widely-used term and revolving facilities (as well as intercreditor agreements and security agreements) for investment grade and leveraged deals, the former having been 'blessed' by both the LMA members and the Association of Corporate Treasurers (ACT – akin to a representative body for borrowers). These are widely used to provide conformity to the loan market and a first draft which eliminates some basic negotiation.

11.3 THE AIMS OF DRAFTING

There are a number of aims to bear in mind when creating or amending a facility agreement.

11.3.1 Certainty

The primary reason for having a written facility agreement is to create certainty between the parties. The document must be drafted to reflect what has been agreed.

Certainty may help to avoid litigation: in a case before the House of Lords (reviewing the interpretation of a guarantee), Lord Jauncey said:

> I find great difficulty in understanding the desire of commercial men to embody so simple an obligation in a document which is quite unnecessarily lengthy, which obfuscates its true purpose and which is likely to give rise to unnecessary arguments and litigation as to its meaning. (*Trafalgar House Construction (Regions) Ltd v General Surety & Guarantee Co Ltd* [1995] 3 WLR 204)

11.3.2 Ambiguity

Despite the general requirement for certainty, there are circumstances in which a party will want some ambiguity drafted into the facility agreement, for example, a requirement for 'reasonableness' when the bank exercises a right (see **11.5.6**). Any uncertainty will usually work in favour of the borrower and against the bank.

11.3.3 A workable document

There are two elements to a document being 'workable'. First, it must be reasonably user-friendly from the parties' point of view. A borrower in particular will not be happy with drafting which can only be understood by its solicitor. The borrower must be able to refer to the document from time to time in order to check what it can and cannot do. Whilst many facility agreements are long and complicated, the language need not be: the best documents are those which have simple language and are easily understood.

Attention to detail can also improve a document from the client's point of view. For example, putting a meaningful heading to each main clause and including a list of clauses at the front of the document is very helpful. When referring to a clause number, it is good practice to add the heading of the clause as well as the number. For example, 'subject to clause 16 (permitted disposals) the borrower may … '.

Secondly, the drafting must work in practice as well as in theory. For example, it is of little use drafting a clause which provides for interest payment dates to fall on a certain date each month if it does not also provide for what happens when that day is not a 'business day' when bank and borrower are open.

11.4 TEMPLATES AND PRECEDENTS

At some stage, most legal drafting will rely on the use of templates and/or precedents. Most firms have a set of template documents on their word-processing system which have been compiled over some years and which represent their most commonly used documents (eg, term loans, RCFs, guarantees and debentures). These templates can be used as a starting point for the bank's solicitor to create the first draft of the facility agreement. If the document to be drafted does not have a template, it is common practice to cannibalise precedent documents, ie those drafted for previous transactions, making alterations as required. The use of templates and precedents not only avoids 're-inventing the wheel', it also helps to maintain the house style of a particular firm.

There are two potential pitfalls in using precedents: first, failing to ensure conformity of terminology (for example, a precedent clause might define the borrower as 'the Borrower', whereas the document which is being created might use 'the Company'); secondly, precedents are negotiated documents, meaning standard clauses may have been changed or removed.

11.5 DRAFTING TECHNIQUES

Templates and precedents are particularly useful for boiler plate clauses, since these often require minimal alteration between documents. However, those clauses which are likely to require heavy negotiation (eg, representations, undertakings and events of default) are also likely to need substantial re-drafting. This section outlines some of the more common drafting techniques which can be used to achieve a compromise in these clauses.

11.5.1 Clause construction

When drafting a clause from scratch which must incorporate a right or obligation (eg, undertakings), it is worth remembering a principle of clause construction devised by George Coode, and outlined in *Skills for Lawyers*. In 1843, Coode suggested the following order for clause construction:

(1)   Refer to any exceptions first: eg 'Subject to ... '.

(2)   Next, set out the circumstances or conditions upon which the legal right or obligation depends, using the present tense: eg 'If X does [...] and Y does [...]'.

(3)   Next, set out the right or obligation using the active and avoiding the passive: eg 'X must do 1, 2, 3, 4 and 5'.

(4)   Finally, put the provision into paragraphs and give it a heading.

For example, a provision that the borrower can draw money only if the conditions precedent have been satisfied, notice has been given in the required form, and no event of default has occurred, might be drafted as:

> **4.1   Availability of loan**
>
> Subject to no event of default having occurred under clause 7, if the Borrower:
>
> (a)   satisfies all the conditions precedent listed in clause 3; and
>
> (b)   delivers to the Agent a notice of utilisation in accordance with clause 9;
>
> the Banks will make available to the Borrower a term loan facility up to a maximum amount of £10,000,000 (ten million pounds).

The advantage of using this technique is that any provisos to the right (or obligation) created by the clause are clearly stated in the first part of the clause. However, many banking documents will not conform to this style. It is quite common to see the phrases 'subject to' or 'provided that' in the middle of a clause. For example:

> The Banks will make available to the Borrower a term loan facility up to a maximum amount of £10,000,000 (ten million pounds) provided that no event of default has occurred under clause 7, the Borrower has satisfied all conditions precedent ...

11.5.2 Qualifying an obligation

Many obligations will be drafted as absolute. For example, an undertaking might provide: 'the borrower will not change the date of its financial year end without the bank's consent'. It would not be appropriate to draft this as 'the borrower will use its best endeavours not to change its financial year end without the bank's consent'.

However, a borrower may argue, particularly where an obligation involves a third party, that it is inappropriate to make an obligation absolute. The usual qualifiers are 'reasonable', 'all reasonable' or 'best' endeavours. For example:

> The borrower will use *all reasonable endeavours* to prevent any circumstances occurring which would result in any person taking any action or making a claim against them under any environmental laws ...

What, then, is the difference between 'reasonable', 'all reasonable' and 'best' endeavours? Whilst there is plenty of pertinent case law, the meaning of each phrase will depend on its context. However, in general terms the case law can be summarised as follows:

'*Reasonable endeavours*' is the least onerous. It requires a party to adopt and pursue *one* reasonable course of action in order to achieve the result, bearing in mind its own commercial interests and the likelihood of success. It does not require the party to exhaust every course available to it.

'*All reasonable endeavours*' requires a party to explore *all* avenues reasonably open to it, and explore them all to the extent reasonable. However, the party is neither obliged to disregard its own commercial interests, nor required to continue trying to comply if it is clear that all further efforts would be futile.

'*Best endeavours*' is the most onerous and requires a party to take steps which a prudent, determined and reasonable obligee, acting in its own interests and desiring to achieve that result, would take. It is not an absolute obligation, though, and would not include actions which would lead to financial ruin, undermine commercial standing or goodwill, or have no likelihood of being successful.

It is worth noting that 'all reasonable' and 'best' endeavours are very similar, and some judges have held there is no practical difference (eg *Rhodia International Holdings v Huntsman International LLC* [2007] All ER (D) 264 and *Jet2.com Ltd v Blackpool Airport Ltd* [2011] EWHC 1529 (Comm)). What is common ground, however, is that the onus is on the obligor to show it has met the required level of 'endeavour'. Finally, 'endeavour' is sometimes replaced by 'efforts', but since most case law is based on 'endeavour', that is the more certain term to use.

Since the meaning of these phrases is inherently uncertain, it might be worth specifying parameters in some circumstances. For example, indicating acceptable expense, time limits, whether legal action is required or even any steps the party is not expected to take might be helpful. The downside is that these are yet more points to negotiate and so more often than not the generic wording is used.

11.5.3 Materiality

It is often the case that a borrower will not object to a clause (eg, an event of default) in principle, but finds that it is too tightly drafted. A common compromise for this sort of provision is to qualify the clause with 'materiality'. For example, an absolute provision under which the borrower will be defaulted in the event that it 'is in breach of any licence necessary for operation of its business' has no regard to the varying scale and consequences of any breach. A provision which defaults the borrower only in the event of a breach which 'may have a material adverse effect on its ability to perform its obligations under the facility agreement' is far more palatable for the borrower. A material adverse change event of default clause is an obvious example of the use of 'materiality' (see **5.2.2** and **8.3**).

Unfortunately, any clause which calls for a judgment may hold some danger for a bank. What does 'material' mean in the context of 'a material adverse effect'? A bank will be wary of calling a default only later to be proven to have acted negligently (see **8.8**). This is another case of uncertainty acting in the borrower's favour. The best solution from the bank's point of view is to define 'material'. However, quantifying 'material' might be very complicated, or even impossible. The next best solution for a bank is to be specifically entitled to make the decision as to what is 'material'. Thus wording such as 'material in the opinion of the bank' will avoid any argument. In a syndicated loan, the agent bank might prefer any discretion with respect to important decisions (eg, events of default) to be exercised by a 'majority' of the banks rather than the agent (see **9.6.3**). This may delay the process, but it relieves the agent of a difficult responsibility.

11.5.4 'Would' or 'might'

Some clauses (eg, certain events of default) will be drafted so that they are triggered by events which 'might' have particular consequences. For example, a borrower could be asked to give a representation that it:

> ... is not subject to any litigation, arbitration, or similar proceedings which might affect its ability to perform its obligations under the facility agreement.

From the borrower's point of view, this is clearly preferable to providing an absolute warranty that it is not subject to any such proceedings whatsoever. However, it is arguable that almost anything 'might' occur: the Earth might be overrun by aliens. A borrower will sometimes argue, therefore, that the word 'might' should be replaced by the word 'will' or 'would'. This can give a bank problems. To be certain that something will cause something else can be very difficult. The parties will usually agree to some form of compromise, such as 'is reasonably likely to ... ', or 'will in the bank's opinion'.

11.5.5 De minimis

De minimis non curat lex is the general legal principle that some breaches of duty or mistakes are too trivial to attract a legal remedy. In common parlance a 'de minimis provision' is one which excludes minor breaches of a term. It is another technique for softening the effect of a provision but, unlike some of the methods (eg, materiality) outlined above, without the risk for the bank of creating uncertainty. For example, a cross default clause (see **8.3.5**) might provide for a default '... if the Borrower fails to pay any indebtedness when it falls due'. This would mean the borrower could be defaulted for failing to pay the milk bill on time. A de minimis provision might add '... if the Borrower fails to pay any indebtedness in a principal amount exceeding £50,000'.

The level at which a de minimis is set is crucial; it must allow the borrower sufficient 'leeway' to run its day-to-day business, whilst not being so high as to prevent the provision which it modifies from operating effectively. The level of the de minimis provision will therefore largely depend on the nature of a borrower's business. One problem with de minimis provisions is that they can allow a multitude of minor breaches, which might together be as 'harmful' as a large breach. To overcome this problem, some de minimis provisions will set an aggregate outstanding maximum.

11.5.6 Reasonableness

The effect of most provisions can be altered substantially simply by inserting the word 'reasonable'. For example:

(a)   in the bank's reasonable opinion;

(b)   take all reasonable steps;

(c)   reasonably likely to have an effect;

(d)   use reasonable endeavours;

(e)   consent not to be unreasonably withheld.

This is a powerful tool for the borrower to reduce the severity of a provision. The real value for a borrower is the difficulty for the bank in making an objective decision about what is 'reasonable' in a given situation. Once again, the word introduces uncertainty into a provision, which will make a bank hesitate before calling a default.

11.6 KEY WORDS

Some of the words and phrases which occur in many loan documents, and which can cause some confusion, are explained below.

11.6.1 'Subsidiary'

It is quite common for a bank to require a parent company to guarantee any loans it has made to the parent's subsidiaries (and occasionally vice versa) (see **13.2**). Such 'cross guarantees' effectively breach the companies' status as separate legal entities vis-à-vis each other. Furthermore, a parent company may simply be a 'holding company', with most of the group's business being run through its subsidiaries and with no substantial assets of its own other than shareholdings. For these reasons many of the undertakings and events of default in a facility agreement may be drafted to take account of, or apply to, other companies in the borrower's group. The definition of 'subsidiary' in the facility agreement is therefore very important. Most agreements will usually refer to one of the two definitions in the CA 2006.

The CA 2006 uses two different concepts of 'subsidiary'.

11.6.1.1 Section 1159 (as supplemented by Sch 6)

For a company to be its subsidiary, the 'parent' company must:

(a)   hold a majority of the voting rights which can be exercised at a general meeting of the 'subsidiary'; or

(b)   be a member of the 'subsidiary' and have the right to appoint or remove its directors who together control more than half the voting rights at board meetings; or

(c)   be a member of the 'subsidiary' and control, pursuant to an agreement with other shareholders, a majority of the voting rights which can be exercised at a general meeting of the 'subsidiary'; or

(d)   be a holding company of another subsidiary which is itself the holding company of the 'subsidiary'.

In determining the voting rights, etc, of the 'holding company', the voting rights of its subsidiaries and certain nominees and trustees are taken into account.

11.6.1.2 Section 1162 and Sch 7

Section 1162 and Sch 7 provide a definition used in the CA 2006 in relation to financial statements (see full explanation at **6.6**). The important difference from s 1159 is the concept of 'subsidiary undertaking', whereby the ability to exercise a 'dominant influence' over a company (or partnership, or other unincorporated association) makes it a 'subsidiary undertaking' for accounting purposes. This might include joint-venture arrangements which a company would not usually consider to be a subsidiary.

A bank will always want as much control over the borrower as possible and so it will favour a wide definition of subsidiary in the facility agreement, usually the definition under s 1162 of the CA 2006. It is probably best to set out the definition in the loan document, rather than simply refer to the section number, in order to avoid any problems if the statutory definition is amended after the agreement is executed.

If a borrower is part of a large group of companies, it might ask that the provisions in the facility agreement apply only to its 'material subsidiaries' (ie, those worth over a certain amount). Subsidiaries may grow in size and importance, and so the bank will want the definition to embrace 'material subsidiaries from time to time', to catch any non-material subsidiary which becomes 'material' at a future date.

In *Enviroco Ltd v Farstad Supply A/S* [2009] EWCA Civ 1399, the Court of Appeal decided that a company ceased to be a subsidiary of its holding company when the subsidiary's shares were secured to a bank by way of legal mortgage. To prevent subsidiaries subject to a legal mortgage falling outside the controls of a facility agreement, it is worth considering amending the definition of 'subsidiary' to include companies which would qualify under s 1159 of the CA 2006 *but for* any legal mortgage of their shares (see also **15.2.2.6**).

The concept of 'subsidiary' varies widely internationally. It is therefore very important when dealing with foreign borrowers or foreign banks to be quite clear as to the scope of the 'subsidiary' definition.

11.6.2 Notwithstanding

'Notwithstanding' is most remarkable for the fact that it is one word and not three! It means 'in spite of', and so pushes aside the clause(s) to which it refers. For example: 'Notwithstanding the prohibition in clause 29 (giving security), the Borrower may provide a guarantee', means the borrower can give a guarantee whatever clause 29 might say.

The opposite effect can be achieved with the phrase 'Subject to...'. For example, 'Subject to the prohibition in clause 29 (giving security), the Borrower may provide a guarantee', means the borrower can give a guarantee only if clause 29 does not prevent it from doing so.

11.6.3 Definitions

Since, by its very nature, a definition will be repeated frequently throughout a document, it is particularly important to ensure that it is correct. Some of the points to watch out for include the following.

11.6.3.1 'Means' or 'includes'

Using the word 'means' will give a precise definition and avoid uncertainty. For example, '"Security" means a fixed charge or a floating charge'.

However, using the word 'includes' makes the definition much broader and less certain. For example, '"Security" includes a fixed charge or a floating charge'.

Imagine a facility agreement incorporating a negative pledge which prohibits the borrower from giving any 'security'. Under the first definition, the borrower could be safely advised that giving a mortgage, pledge or lien would not breach the agreement, but not under the second definition. This is an example of drafting which is deliberately imprecise in order to benefit the bank: a precise definition of 'security' carries a risk that the bank might not think of everything to be included, and it may not cover new products.

11.6.3.2 Law of Property Act 1925, s 61 and the Interpretation Act 1978

Section 61 of the LPA 1925 applies, amongst other things, to all deeds and contracts made after 1925 and, unless the context otherwise requires, will deem:

(a) 'month' to mean a calendar month;
(b) 'person' to include a corporation;
(c) the singular to include the plural (and vice versa);
(d) the masculine to include the feminine (and vice versa).

Under the Interpretation Act 1978, any reference to statutory provisions in a document will be deemed (subject to contrary intention) to be a reference to those provisions as amended or re-enacted from time to time. Curiously, but perhaps because most solicitors are cautious by training, many commercial documents explicitly state the provisions deemed by these two statutes. However, sometimes the 1978 Act provision is excluded to avoid amended legislation from bringing new meaning to a document (eg, if the definition of 'subsidiary' in the CA 2006 was changed under new legislation).

11.6.3.3   Eiusdem generis rule

The eiusdem generis rule of interpretation means that where general words follow a list of specific words, they are taken to be limited to categories of the same kind as the specific words. If a definition or other clause includes a list which is intended to be non-exclusive, the eiusdem generis rule can be avoided by the use of words such as 'whatsoever' to emphasise generality.

11.7   TIME COMPUTATIONS

Time limits are a crucial element in facility agreements. Most notice provisions and certain events of default will revolve around timing. Provisions dealing with timing will require careful drafting, and may be subject to certain statutory implied terms.

Unless specified otherwise, reference to a 'month' will mean a calendar month (LPA 1925, s 61). Furthermore, unless there is a contrary intention, the courts are likely to hold that:

(a)   the day on which an event occurs is not included when calculating a period which runs from the occurrence of that event (*Lester v Garland* (1808) 15 Ves 248). For example, the calculation of a period '21 days after giving notice', will not include the day on which notice is given (unless wording such as 'including' or 'commencing on' is used);

(b)   the period of a 'month' (or 'months') will end on the day which has the same date in the subsequent month (see *Dodds v Walker* [1981] 2 All ER 609). For example, two months from 20 March will be 20 May. If this rule would not yield a date (eg, one month from 31 August), the period is taken to end on the last day of the month in which it expires (eg, 30 September). The period will end at midnight on the appropriate day;

(c)   if a period is stated as 'not less than 3 months nor more than 6 months', the rule outlined in (b) above will apply. For example, if a notice is to be given 'not more than 3 months nor less than 2 months before cancellation', then cancellation on 30 November may be notified from 31 August to 30 September (inclusive);

(d)   notice of 'at least' or 'no fewer than' 21 days will usually exclude the day on which notice is given and the day on which it expires. The same effect is obtained by the expression '21 clear days';

(e)   'day' is a calendar day (ie, including all holidays, and not just a 'business day').

These implied rules will probably reflect the parties' intentions in most cases. However, since they are particularly critical in loan documents, timing provisions should be very specific. For example, a period of time should specify whether it is to include the day on which it begins or ends. A period should be stated as '21 clear days' if that is what is intended. Most documents will also specify that time limits or payment dates will always end by close of business on a 'business day' (usually defined as a day on which banks are generally open for business in London). If the end of a particular period will not fall on a 'business day', provision should be made for it to be deemed as falling on the 'business day' which immediately precedes it, or next follows it, as required. Loans which involve funding in currencies other than sterling will have to source those currencies in their country of origin (eg, a bank in London providing a US$ loan will have to borrow the dollars in, say, New York). This means that the 'business day' definition in the loan should specify that funds can be drawn only on a day on which both London and New York are open for business.

Repayment dates are usually contained in a schedule to the document, which specifies the exact date and time by which the money is to be received.

SECURED LENDING

COMMON FORMS OF SECURITY

'Protection is not a principle, but an expedient.'

Benjamin Disraeli

12.1 INTRODUCTION

What would you do if someone failed to repay money you had lent them? Your options might range from forgiving the debt to threatening bankruptcy, but ultimately your only effective sanction is probably to sue them for the unpaid amount. Litigation has its drawbacks: it is usually expensive, protracted, and obtaining enforcement of a judgment may take too long to be effective. Furthermore, if you have to litigate to recover a straightforward debt claim, it probably means the debtor cannot pay because it is insolvent. Its assets must almost certainly be shared with other creditors, and the bottom line is that you will probably recover only part of the money due to you.

Taking security as a bank is all about increasing the likelihood of getting repaid. There are many ways to achieve this, but most rely on giving a bank direct recourse to a borrower's property in the event of the borrower's default. This will usually avoid the need for litigation, may ensure priority over other creditors, and will almost certainly hasten recovery of the debt. This chapter provides an introduction to some of the more common types of security, **Chapter 13** looks at 'quasi-security', **Chapter 14** develops some of the issues which can arise on taking security and **Chapter 15** briefly examines a typical security document.

Whilst security might be used to support almost any type of obligation, the following four chapters concentrate on security for loan transactions. For the sake of continuity, therefore, the text will generally refer to the giver of the security as the 'borrower', and the holder of the benefit of the security as the 'bank'.

12.2 CATEGORISING SECURITY

Security arrangements are sometimes categorised into 'consensual' (ie, agreed between the parties) and 'non-consensual' (ie, arising at law). It is probably more helpful, however, to categorise the main types of loan security according to their effect, that is:

(a)   security which merely gives the bank rights over an asset (eg, fixed or floating charge – see **12.3**);

(b)   security under which 'ownership' (ie, legal or equitable title: see below) in the secured asset is transferred to the bank (eg, a mortgage and assignment – see **12.4**); and

(c)   security under which the bank has actual (or 'constructive') possession of the secured asset (eg, pledge or lien – see **12.5**).

Each of these categories is examined below. At this stage, however, it is worth clarifying some terminology. In everyday language, the words 'ownership' and 'possession' are virtually interchangeable. However, in the context of security interests, the two terms have distinct meanings: 'ownership' means having title to an asset (legal or equitable); and 'possession' means having physical possession of an asset. These are the meanings attributed to 'ownership' and 'possession' in this book.

12.3   GIVING RIGHTS OVER ASSETS

The cornerstone of most loan security will be the charge. Charges may be 'fixed' or 'floating' and are always 'equitable' (other than the 'charge by deed expressed to be by way of legal mortgage' (LPA 1925, s 87) which is arguably not a true 'charge' anyway – see **12.4** – and other statutory charges, which are rarely seen).

12.3.1   Fixed charges conferring rights not possession

Probably the most certain way to ensure that a secured asset is available to meet unpaid monies is to take possession of it (known as a 'pledge' – see **12.5.1**). This will prevent the borrower disposing of the asset, or diminishing its value in any way. Consider, however, some typical assets of a trading company: machinery, vans, office equipment and premises. Giving a bank physical possession of those assets would simply prevent the borrower from running its business. If it is impractical, or impossible, for a bank to take possession of an asset, an alternative is to give it rights over the asset which:

(a)   prohibit the borrower from disposing of the asset without permission;

(b)   attempt to maintain the asset's value whilst it is in the borrower's hands; and

(c)   allow the bank recourse to the asset in the event of the borrower's default under the loan.

This is the aim of a fixed charge.

A fixed charge does not immediately transfer ownership or possession, but allows a borrower to use the charged assets (subject to conditions designed to maintain their value, and a prohibition on disposal) unless and until any 'enforcement event' occurs as specified in the charge document. On an 'enforcement event', under its contractual rights in the charge document, the bank may require the borrower to sell the asset, or the bank may take possession of, and sell, the asset, or appoint a receiver to do the same (this carries less risk for the bank since the receiver acts as the borrower's agent). The fixed charge simply gives the bank a claim over the charged assets in priority to other creditors. If the borrower sells an asset subject to a fixed charge, the rights created by the charge usually remain with the asset.

Some security documents will refer to fixed charges as 'specific equitable charges'.

12.3.2   Floating charges

12.3.2.1   What is a floating charge?

There will be certain of a borrower's assets for which a fixed charge is not an appropriate form of security. For example, any stock in trade subject to a fixed charge could not be sold without the bank's consent. This might not be a problem if the borrower is a boat-builder selling two or three boats a year. Consider, however, the problems that would be caused by taking a fixed charge over the stock in a sweet shop: clearly, it would be unworkable. The unsuitability of a fixed charge to secure assets which a borrower might want to deal with quickly and at some unspecified future date (ie, the borrower's current assets – see **6.3.2**), led to the development, from the late 19th century, of the floating charge.

A floating charge secures a group of assets which may fluctuate from time to time. The assets secured by a floating charge are identified generically, for example a borrower's 'trading stock' or its 'undertaking and assets' (fixed charges may also use generic descriptions, or alternatively refer to individual assets). Unlike a fixed charge, a floating charge specifically allows the borrower to deal with the charged assets in the ordinary course of business (which is very widely construed). This allows a borrower to sell its stock and dispose of its other current assets so that it may continue trading and make money which (in theory at least) it will eventually use to repay the secured loan. Conversely, any assets which are acquired after the floating charge is formed but which fall within the identified group will be subject to the charge.

The freedom to deal with assets, which is the very advantage of the floating charge, does give rise to a very important question: what is to stop a borrower from disposing of all its current assets, leaving the floating charge 'empty'? This is, in fact, a very real problem, and is one reason why a bank prefers to take a fixed charge over an asset whenever possible. The problem is minimised, however, through the concept of 'crystallisation'.

12.3.2.2 Crystallisation

Each floating charge document will incorporate a mechanism through which the borrower's freedom to deal with the assets over which it floats can be frozen. This is known as 'crystallisation'. On the occurrence of certain events (see below), the floating charge will effectively become a fixed charge with respect to any of the assets over which it previously 'floated', and which remain in the borrower's ownership. The borrower will then be unable to dispose of those remaining assets without the bank's consent. Most charges provide for crystallisation to be simultaneously effective over all the assets secured by the charge. There is, however, no reason why a floating charge should not be partially crystallised (ie, preventing only a selection of the secured assets being dealt with) as long as the charge document specifically provides the power to do so.

The effectiveness of this mechanism is entirely dependent on the sensitivity of the trigger for crystallisation. There are two ways in which crystallisation might occur: under common law, or under the terms of the document creating the charge.

Crystallisation under common law

Case law has established a number of events which will cause a floating charge to crystallise, all of which are triggered by a cessation of the business as a going concern, or by a prohibition on the borrower using its charged assets:

(a) *The borrower's liquidation.* Crystallisation will occur when a winding-up order is made (including a voluntary winding-up, even if merely for reorganisation), but not simply when a petition to wind up is presented.

(b) *An administrative receiver, or receiver, is appointed by the bank.* If the bank appoints a receiver or an administrative receiver, this implies that the borrower's authority to deal with the asset has been withdrawn and thus it will crystallise a floating charge. There is authority that a floating charge will not be crystallised (under common law) merely by the crystallisation of another floating charge (since it does not necessarily signify the end of trading). The making of an administration order which is not intended to prevent the borrower continuing to run as a going concern will probably not crystallise a floating charge at common law.

(c) *The borrower ceases to carry on business.* A floating charge will crystallise if the borrower ceases trading for any reason (including where the borrower has disposed of its assets to such an extent that it can no longer carry on its business).

(d) *Intervention by the bank.* Most forms of intervention by a bank which prevent a borrower dealing with its charged assets will cause crystallisation at common law.

Under the charge document

Crystallisation will also occur in any of the circumstances agreed contractually between the borrower and bank in the charge document. These are important to alleviate any uncertainty about crystallisation at common law. These will usually consist of an immediate right to crystallise the floating charge at any time by giving notice to the borrower (a borrower may request the proviso 'if the bank reasonably believes the secured assets are in jeopardy … ', etc), and a number of specified events which will crystallise the charge without any action by the bank, for example the appointment of an administrator. This second group of events is often referred to as 'automatic crystallisation' (somewhat confusing, since the term might be thought more applicable to the common law situations which cause crystallisation, outlined above). A lender may sometimes be asked to provide a certificate of non-crystallisation (eg, to a purchaser of the borrower's assets).

12.3.2.3 Post-crystallisation

The most widely accepted legal analysis of a floating charge is that it creates an immediate security interest, but does not attach to any individual asset until crystallisation (in contrast to a fixed charge, which attaches immediately – ie, it encumbers the charged assets with the rights it creates). On crystallisation, a floating charge effectively will become a fixed charge. However, this 'fixed charge' will rank behind any fixed security created before it crystallised and will be subject to any third party rights of set-off (see **13.5**), including legal or equitable rights, which accrued prior to the crystallisation. However, crystallisation does not, in itself, create a new charge to be registered under the CA 2006 (*Re Manurewa Transport Ltd* [1971] NZLR 909).

The charge document will contain the powers which can be exercised by the bank (see **Chapter 15**) and will invariably include the power to appoint a receiver to run the business and realise the charged assets. Crystallising a floating charge will create an effective stranglehold on a borrower: without the use of its current assets it cannot usually make any money. A bank will therefore not take crystallisation lightly, and frequently it is a precursor to the appointment of a receiver.

12.3.2.4 Weaknesses of a floating charge

The floating charge suffers from a number of weaknesses to which the fixed charge is immune.

Fixed charges and administrator's costs

A floating charge is vulnerable to later fixed charges, although this may be alleviated by a prohibition on creating further security (see **14.2.2** and **14.3**). Floating charges also rank behind the costs and expenses of an administrator appointed to the borrower; the administrator can use any of the floating charge assets to fund the administration costs.

In addition, all liquidation expenses (other than litigation expenses) have automatic priority over floating charge holders, and are recoverable from the assets of the company (see the Insolvency (Amendment) Rules 2008 (SI 2008/737)).

Preferential creditors

Any proceeds realised from assets secured by a floating charge must be used to pay any 'preferential debts' of the company before meeting claims under the floating charge (IA 1986, s 40). 'Preferential debts' are defined at s 386, and specified fully in Sch 6 to the IA 1986, as modified from 15 September 2003 by the Enterprise Act 2002 (EA 2002) (s 251). The main preferential debts are now limited amounts of outstanding employees' wages and pension scheme contributions. The preferential status previously accorded to 'Crown creditors' (eg, PAYE contributions, VAT, social security contributions, etc) was abolished by the EA 2002.

These now rank as unsecured creditors. However, the Act also provides for an amount of the company's property which would otherwise go to floating charge-holders (the 'prescribed part'), to be set aside to pay unsecured creditors. The amount of this 'fund' is determined by statutory instrument from time to time. It is currently 50% of the first £10,000 of the prescribed part and 20% thereafter, subject to a maximum amount of £600,000 (see IA 1986, s 176A).

Avoidance of floating charge

As well as the provisions concerning transactions at an undervalue and preferences (see **14.9**) which can apply to all forms of security, the IA 1986 provides for specific circumstances in which a floating charge can be set aside by the court on the application of a liquidator or administrator (s 245). The degree of vulnerability of a floating charge will depend on whether or not it is granted to a 'connected person'.

12.3.2.5 Charge to connected person

If a company grants a floating charge to a 'connected person' (this includes a director, their close relatives, their business partners and their close relatives – see s 249 of the IA 1986) then it might be set aside if it was granted within two years of the onset of a company's insolvency.

12.3.2.6 Charge to unconnected person

A floating charge granted to a person not 'connected' with the company might be set aside if it was given within 12 months of the onset of the company's insolvency, provided that the company was either insolvent when it gave the charge, or became insolvent as a result.

However, a floating charge will not be invalid in either case to the extent that it is in return for valuable consideration (ie, money, goods, services or the reduction of any debt) given on or after the creation of the charge. The underlying debt will remain unsecured if the floating charge is set aside.

The concept of a 'floating charge' is very much a product of the English legal system (and derivative systems) and so may not be recognised or have an equivalent in other jurisdictions.

12.4 TRANSFER OF OWNERSHIP

12.4.1 Mortgages

A fixed charge creates a new equitable proprietory interest in the secured assets, giving the holder rights to the asset ahead of unsecured creditors. An alternative way to provide security over assets is by transferring ownership (ie, legal or equitable title) to the bank, along with a right to sell on default and an obligation to re-transfer title on satisfaction of the debt. This form of security interest is known as a 'mortgage'. The transfer of title may enhance a bank's ability to realise the security if necessary, and in the meantime prevents a borrower from selling the secured assets. A mortgage can therefore be thought of as an 'enhanced' charge, since it gives rights over an asset which are backed with a transfer of legal or equitable title. As Professor Goode explained in *Legal Problems of Credit and Security*, '... a mortgage is a right of appropriation (= charge) plus a transfer of ownership ...'. Subject to contrary intention (and statutory restrictions in the case of land), a (legal) mortgage entitles the bank to take immediate possession of the mortgaged asset. However, possession is not required to perfect the security (it is 'non-possessory' security) and, for reasons of practicality, most banks will not take possession of mortgaged assets before default.

12.4.2 Mortgages over land

Many types of asset can be secured by way of a mortgage, although many of us associate it with land because we give security over our homes. Under the LPA 1925 (as amended by the Land Registration Act 2002), the only way to create legal security over freehold or leasehold land is by way of 'a charge by deed expressed to be by way of legal mortgage' (LPA 1925, s 87). The terminology is not particularly helpful (it is not a 'true' charge, neither does it actually transfer legal title like most legal mortgages), but the net result is to provide the bank with rights equivalent to granting it a 3,000-year lease (or, for leasehold, a lease for one day less than the borrower's lease).

12.4.3   Legal and equitable mortgages

If a mortgage does not transfer *legal* title, it will be an equitable mortgage. Equitable mortgages can be created with less formality than their legal equivalent, and may result from any of the following, depending on the circumstances:

(a)   a written agreement by a borrower that the property is to be secured by way of equitable mortgage;

(b)   an agreement to provide a legal mortgage if the borrower intended the agreement to have immediate effect (the most common example being a purported legal mortgage over property not yet owned by the borrower);

(c)   a mortgage over an equitable interest; or

(d)   a purported legal mortgage that does not comply with all the necessary formalities. For example, in the case of land, a failure to register the mortgage at the Land Registry (which may be accidental or intentional).

In reality, there is little practical difference between an equitable mortgage and an equitable fixed charge.

As between equitable and legal security interests, the former can be ignored by a bona fide purchaser (or 'security taker') for value of the legal title to an asset without notice (actual or constructive) of the equitable security. However, the 'disadvantage' is largely overcome if the equitable security is registered under CA 2006, ss 860–894 (see **14.2**), because this provides notice of the security to anyone searching, or who is deemed to search, the register. An equitable mortgage may not benefit from the 'automatic' powers vested in legal mortgagees under LPA 1925, s 101, which include the power of sale (although these powers should be specifically given in the security document).

12.5   GIVING PHYSICAL POSSESSION

For the reasons of practicality explained at **12.3.1**, the most common forms of debt security are 'non-possessory': that is, the bank does not take immediate physical possession, but simply takes certain rights over the charged assets. However, there are circumstances in which a security interest involves possession of an asset from the outset.

12.5.1   Pledge

A pledge is a way of creating security by the actual (or constructive) delivery of a tangible movable asset to a creditor, to be held until the performance of an obligation (eg, repaying a debt). The bank will take possession while the borrower retains ownership. The best known example of a pledge is placing an article with a pawnbroker.

12.5.1.1   Rights of the pledgee

The security created by a pledge is essentially the possession of an asset. A pledged asset must therefore be 'delivered' by the borrower. This can be achieved by physical delivery, or by vesting control (sometimes known as 'constructive delivery' – eg, having the keys to a safe deposit box) with, in either case, an intention to create security. Some assets may be pledged by delivery of documents; however, the pledge will fail if the document does not effectively provide control. For example, simply holding the share certificate of a registered share does not give sufficient control (even if accompanied by a 'blank' stock transfer form) because the share certificate is not a document of title and it does not give the right to vote or receive dividends.

Since it does not transfer rights of ownership, a pledge will end as soon as the pledged asset is returned to the borrower. A pledge will confer certain implied rights, the most important of which is the right to sell the pledged assets to meet a defaulted debt.

12.5.1.2 Problems with taking a pledge

There are a number of practical difficulties with taking pledges. A bank will probably want to take a pledge only over valuable assets. This will lead to problems of keeping the pledged assets secure (imagine a pawnbroker taking a pledge over a Stradivarius violin) both on delivery to the bank and on return. Furthermore, the bank will probably be liable as bailee while it holds the pledged assets, and this may entail insurance costs.

There is no legal requirement to document a pledge. However, to avoid any argument that an asset has merely been deposited for safe-keeping, a 'letter of pledge' or 'memorandum of deposit' is usually provided by the borrower to evidence the terms of the pledge. One advantage of pledge security is that it does not require any form of registration: giving up possession is notice to third parties ('perfection').

12.5.1.3 What assets may be pledged?

A pledge involves the delivery of an asset into the possession of a creditor, therefore the asset must be capable of actual (or constructive) delivery. The most common types of asset to be pledged are therefore bearer instruments, such as bills of exchange, promissory notes and bearer bonds (see **18.2.2**). More substantial assets may be 'constructively pledged' by placing them in a location (eg, a warehouse) only accessible to the bank.

12.5.2 Lien

A lien is the right to retain possession of another person's property until they settle an obligation. The term 'lien' derives from the word 'ligamen', meaning 'binding'. Liens arise automatically under English law in certain types of commercial relationship. There are three main types of lien.

12.5.2.1 Common law (or particular) liens

A common law lien allows retention of the goods under which the debt arises. If, for example, a customer refuses to pay for their dry-cleaning, the cleaner has a right to retain the clothes in lieu of payment.

12.5.2.2 Statutory (or general) liens

Statutory liens allow certain persons to retain any goods in their possession against any obligation owed to them by the owner of those goods. Stockbrokers, bankers, solicitors and innkeepers all benefit from statutory liens, which arise by operation of law and without the need for any agreement.

Common law and statutory liens are both types of legal lien. Legal liens will usually require actual possession of the property which has been rightfully acquired. Unlike a mortgage or pledge, legal liens will not generally confer any right to sell the property. A banker's lien is an exception, however, allowing the retention and sale of any securities and cheques deposited by a customer.

12.5.2.3 Equitable liens

An equitable lien does not require possession of the property to which it attaches (usually land) and will give a right of sale through application to the court.

It is also possible for a lien to be created by contract. However, if the contract provided for any right of sale the 'lien' would be little different to a pledge.

12.6 ASSIGNMENT

Chapter 10 explained how a bank wanting to sell a loan could transfer its rights under the facility agreement by way of assignment. An assignment may also be used to create a mortgage over certain forms of asset.

The most common assets secured by assignment are a borrower's rights against a third party ('choses in action'), for example debts, and rights under various contracts. As with an assignment by way of sale, an assignment by way of security can be legal or equitable: it will in effect create a legal mortgage if it complies with s 136 of the LPA 1925 (a 'statutory assignment' – see **10.4.3**); otherwise it will create an equitable one (see **10.4.4**) (notice that assignment 'by way of charge' is expressly excluded from s 136 and so assigning rights by way of security will constitute a legal assignment only if it is an absolute assignment with a proviso for re-assignment on satisfaction of the secured obligation). Assignments by way of security will always include a provision (either explicit or implied) for reassignment on satisfaction of the debt. Priority between assignments depends on notice being given to the third party (see **14.3.3**).

12.7 SOME TERMINOLOGY

Unfortunately, the area of loan security suffers more than its fair share of overlapping and interchangeable terminology. Documents and statutes use identical terms to describe entirely different things, and the legal meaning of terms is often subtly different to their colloquial meaning. Some of the terms which have multiple meanings are explained below.

12.7.1 Debenture

At common law, a 'debenture' is any document which a company issues to acknowledge, or create, a debt.

But beware! In common banking parlance a 'debenture' is the name given to the document under which a borrower creates the security for a secured loan, usually incorporating fixed and floating charges along with other security interests (see **Chapter 15**).

12.7.2 Charge

A 'charge' is the appropriation of assets to the satisfaction of a debt. Strictly speaking, a charge does not transfer any ownership in property, but simply creates certain rights over it: in other words, it creates an equitable security interest. Used in this sense, there are only two forms of charge, fixed and floating (see **12.3).**

But beware! The term is used colloquially (even in statutes and case law) as a generic label for almost any type of security, including mortgages, liens and assignments.

12.7.3 Security/securities

The term 'security' refers to the provision of rights against a person's assets which are intended to enhance the probability of recovering a debt claim against them.

But beware! In common banking parlance the terms 'security', or 'securities' refer to the instrument (ie, the 'piece of paper') in which a borrower acknowledges debt, or to investments such as shares, debentures, stock, bonds, bills of exchange and other forms of tradeable debt (see **Part III**).

12.7.4 Statutory definitions

The confusion which can arise in terminology is illustrated by statutory definitions. In the LPA 1925, 'mortgage' is defined to include 'any charge or lien on any property for securing money or money's worth'. Under the IA 1986, 'security' means 'any mortgage, charge, lien or other security' (s 248(b)). In the CA 2006, the term 'charge' includes a 'mortgage'.

The statutory definitions are also often inclusive rather than specific. The 'moral' of this maze of terminology is that the label given to an instrument is not always a reliable indication of the type of security it provides; it is important to examine its substance.

12.8 FURTHER READING

Richard Calnan, *Taking Security: Law and Practice* (4th edn, Jordans, 2018).

Roy Goode, *Commercial Law* (5th edn, Penguin, 2017).

Roy Goode, *Legal Problems of Credit and Security* (6th edn, Sweet & Maxwell, 2017).

Geoffrey Fuller, *Corporate Borrowing: Law and Practice* (5th edn, Jordans, 2016).

QUASI-SECURITY

13.1 INTRODUCTION

Chapter 12 examined the most common methods by which a bank might take security in order to increase the likelihood of recovering a borrower's debt. However, there are various other ways a bank might choose to enhance its prospects of repayment, which are not strictly security interests because they do not create any rights 'in rem' (ie, rights over the asset). This chapter explains some of the more common types of 'quasi-security' before considering the main reasons for taking loan security.

13.2 THIRD PARTY SUPPORT – GUARANTEES AND COMFORT LETTERS

A bank will frequently look for a third party willing to support the borrower's repayment obligations. The generic name usually given to such third parties (together with the borrower) is 'obligor', and the two most common forms of third party support are the guarantee (which may be secured on the guarantor's assets) and the comfort letter. Guarantors are sometimes known as 'sureties'.

13.2.1 Guarantees

13.2.1.1 What is a guarantee?

A guarantee is a form of undertaking by one party to answer for another party's liabilities, usually on its default. In the context of a loan, the guarantor will frequently be a company in the same group as the borrower. For example, a bank might make a loan conditional on receiving a guarantee of the borrower's obligations from its parent company. Furthermore, the company which has given the guarantee may be required to give security over its own assets to support its potential liability under the guarantee. As well as providing a second source of repayment, a parent company will also guarantee punctual performance of the borrower's obligations under the facility, to encourage supervision of the borrower by the parent.

13.2.1.2 Guarantees and indemnities

Before considering guarantees further, the strict legal differences between the terms 'guarantee' and 'indemnity' should be appreciated (although the guarantee document will usually purport to contract out of these limitations – see **13.2.1.3**).

A guarantee creates a 'secondary' obligation which relies on there being a valid primary obligation between two parties other than the guarantor (the main implications of which are explained at **13.2.1.3**).

An indemnity creates an obligation to indemnify a party for a specified loss which it may incur. Unlike a guarantee, an indemnity creates a 'stand alone' (or primary) obligation which is independent of the liability or default of another party. In general terms, an indemnity is more 'robust' than a guarantee: most loan facilities therefore contain a guarantee plus an indemnity, in case the guarantee fails.

13.2.1.3   Legal implications of a guarantee

Once a contract is classified as a guarantee there are a number of consequences at common law (most of which the bank will want to vary), including the following.

Consequences of being a secondary obligation

(a)   Since the guarantee creates a 'secondary' obligation, the guarantor will not be liable unless the borrower's debt becomes due. Most banks will therefore require that the 'guarantee' is 'on demand' and payable as if a 'principal debt': once the borrower defaults, the bank can immediately demand performance from the guarantor (see eg, *McGuinness v Norwich and Peterborough Building Society* [2010] EWHC 2989 (Ch)).

(b)   If the contract between bank and borrower (the primary contract) is void (or if the borrower's obligation is discharged), the guarantor's obligation will fall away. A bank will therefore usually include a provision that the guarantee survives failure of the underlying obligation, as well as an indemnity within the guarantee document in order to create a primary obligation on the 'guarantor' if the guarantee fails.

(c)   If the contract between bank and borrower is varied in any material way without the guarantor's consent, the guarantor is released from the guarantee (even if the variation was not prejudicial to the guarantor). Similarly, certain acts which might be prejudicial to the guarantor (eg, if the bank fails to register security for the debt) will void the guarantee. This issue commonly arises where the facility which the guarantee supports is to be increased. In *Triodos Bank v Ashley Charles Dobbs* [2005] EWCA Civ 630, the Court of Appeal considered a guarantee which purported to allow 'any amendments, variation, waiver or release of an obligation' by the borrower, without reference to the guarantor. The Court held that any amendment or variation must be 'within the general purview of the original guarantee' (a test adopted in *Trade Indemnity Co Ltd v Workington Harbour and Dock Board* [1937] AC 1). In *Triodos* the guarantee was held not to survive an increase of the underlying facility, in part because the facility was to be used for a different purpose. The fact that the guarantor *knew* of the amendments made no difference – he had to *consent* with a clear understanding of the facts.

More recently in *Maxted, Lorimer v Investec Bank PLC* [2017] EWHC 1997 (Ch), the High Court held that amendments to a loan (including an increase in amount and extension of the term) *were* within the purview of guarantees given by the borrowing company's directors. Nevertheless, when faced with material changes to a facility, most lawyers will be reluctant to rely on 'saving language' in a guarantee, however wide, and will ask guarantors to confirm that their existing guarantees cover the changes. Helpfully, the judge in *Maxted* confirmed that if facility amendments were beyond the purview of the guarantees, this could be cured by the guarantors consenting to them.

Other key rights (usually waived or postponed)

(a)   A guarantor may use most rights of set-off or counter-claim which the borrower has against the bank (and which arose before the borrower defaulted) to reduce its liability under the guarantee.

(b)   Once it has paid out under the guarantee, a guarantor will be entitled to reimbursement from the borrower. This right will arise through an implied or actual indemnity between the borrower and guarantor.

(c)   The guarantor will also be entitled to any security the bank holds for the borrower's debt, under the doctrine of subrogation. Subrogation arises only once a guarantor has paid the full amount to which it is liable under the guarantee (and does not arise automatically for an indemnity).

(d)   If there is more than one guarantor of the debt, any guarantor that pays out will have a right to claim back a share of the payment from the co-guarantors (a right of 'contribution').

The problem with all these rights from a bank's perspective is that it may not want the guarantor to enforce them immediately (eg, if the subrogated security secures borrowings in addition to the guaranteed loan). The guarantee document should therefore postpone the rights until such time as the bank has been repaid in full and no longer requires the security. It will also want any obligation of contribution to be waived in respect of any subsidiary it wants to sell (eg, on enforcement of security).

13.2.1.4   General considerations for a bank's solicitor

In addition to the points mentioned above, a bank's solicitor should take account of the following:

(a)   The governing law of a guarantee should, if possible, mirror that of the other loan documents as this will make enforcement easier.

(b)   If the contract is legally a guarantee it must be evidenced in writing before it can be enforced (Statute of Frauds 1677, s 4). As with any other contract, a guarantee is enforceable only if it is given for consideration. In particular, there is a danger that a guarantee will be void for past consideration if it is pre-dated by the obligation it supports. The problem can be resolved by creating the guarantee document as a deed.

(c)   A guarantee should be expressed as 'continuing' to avoid the rule in 'Clayton's case' (see **14.6**) and to help it to survive variations to the primary obligation (but see **13.2.1.3(c)**)

(d)   The guarantee should provide that the bank's evidence of the borrower's liability is conclusive (at least in the first instance) to avoid any argument on enforcement.

(e)   As with any other contract, a company must have the requisite power to enter into a guarantee, and its officers must be properly authorised. The CA 2006, s 172 requires a director to 'act in the way he considers, in good faith, would be most likely to promote the success of the company for the benefit of its members as a whole'. The section provides a (non-exhaustive) list of the factors to which directors must have regard in fulfilling this duty. In approving a guarantee, the directors must consider this duty together with the factors, and the board minutes should reflect that they have done so. Directors usually get comfortable with the s 172 duties (see **14.10** for more detail), but other jurisdictions will have different rules, and guarantees are often prohibited or limited to amounts actually received by the guarantor.

(f)   A guarantee is capable of being 'financial assistance' under the provisions of CA 2006, ss 678–680 (see **14.11**).

13.2.1.5   Insolvency Act 1986

A guarantee is arguably capable of being a transaction at an undervalue (because, unlike a borrower granting security, it usually increases the guarantor's liabilities) and, in limited circumstances (eg, where the guarantor had previously only given third party security, with no guarantee), a preference, and so being set aside under IA 1986, ss 238 and 239 respectively (see **14.9**).

13.2.1.6   Counter-indemnity

A guarantor will usually want an express counter-indemnity from the borrower (ie, a contractual right to claim back any money it pays to the bank – see 'Guarantor's rights' at **13.2.1.3**).

13.2.2   Comfort letters

Sometimes a parent company or other potential obligor will refuse to provide a guarantee. It may be contractually prevented from doing so (eg, by a negative pledge style undertaking; see **13.3**), or a company might not wish to create a contingency on its balance sheet. In such cases, the bank might demand a comfort letter from the company. Comfort letters (also known as 'support letters', or 'letters of intent') are usually given by a parent company in respect of a subsidiary. They range from a simple written acknowledgment of the fact that the subsidiary is undertaking the obligations created by the loan, to a statement of intention to maintain an interest in, and support for, a subsidiary, and to ensure it is capable of fulfilling those obligations (sometimes known as a 'keep-well' agreement).

Comfort letters are not normally intended to be legally binding but are used to reassure a bank that the parent company is aware of, and supports, its subsidiary's borrowing and other general or specific activities. They will require careful drafting. Statements of the comforter's 'intention' or 'policy' will not usually amount to an actionable undertaking. However, words such as 'guarantee' and 'undertake' may be binding. The general phrasing of comfort letters is usually deliberately vague so that the terms are not certain enough to be enforced under English contract law.

The test for determining whether a comfort letter has legal effect is to analyse it as though it were a contract. Was there offer and acceptance, intention to create legal relations and consideration? Did the issuer of the letter promise to do something? Has it failed to do that thing? Has the recipient of the letter suffered loss as a consequence of the failure? What is the measure of damages for the breach? In the seminal case of *Kleinwort Benson Ltd v Malaysia Mining Corpn* [1989] 1 All ER 785, a parent company's comfort letter stated: 'It is our policy to ensure that the business of [subsidiary] is at all times in a position to meet its liabilities to you under the above arrangements.' The Court of Appeal held this to be a statement of fact (ie, that this was the parent's policy) at the time rather than an undertaking actually to support the subsidiary going forward. However, the conclusion depended entirely on the facts – in this case, the parent had previously refused to give a guarantee or accept joint liability, which suggested that it did not intend the comfort letter to be binding. In contrast, the recent Australian case of *Gate Gourmet Australia (in liquidation) v Gate Gourmet Holding AG* [2004] NSWSC 149 found a 'comfort letter' to be legally binding. The key points were that the letter included technical language, was provided to reassure directors that their otherwise insolvent company could continue to trade, and made statements which were clearly promises, not just statements of fact.

In the case of *Re Atlantic Computers plc (in administration); National Australia Bank Ltd v Soden* [1995] BCC 696, it was held that the common intention of the parties to a comfort letter must be ascertained by reading it as a whole. The final paragraph of the letters in question, which asserted that they 'were not intended to be a guarantee' and that they were 'an expression of present intention by way of comfort only', was sufficient to show that they did not amount to a contractual promise.

A solicitor should be aware that even if the tests outlined above are not fulfilled, comfort letters may still be treated as binding in jurisdictions other than England and Wales.

13.3   NEGATIVE PLEDGE

There is a sense in which a negative pledge provision (one which prohibits a borrower granting security to third parties – see **7.5.2.1**) provides a form of security, because it is arguably a restriction on how the borrower may use its assets. There is, however, little doubt that a negative pledge clause is not technically a security interest (although it might provide a claim in tort for damages against a third party which induces a borrower to breach the prohibition, and there is an argument that the third party holds any such security on trust for the negative pledge holder). The Companies Act 2006 security registration form MR01 includes a tick box notification if the 'terms' of the security include a negative pledge.

13.4 RETENTION OF TITLE

Retention of title arrangements are dealt with in **Business Law and Practice**. In essence, a retention of title clause allows a seller to retain legal title to goods which have been supplied to a buyer until the buyer settles its account. If payment is not forthcoming, the seller can recover the goods from the buyer. A retention of title clause therefore acts as a type of security interest for the seller. This is clearly not of any use to 'secure' a loan. However, the existence of such a clause may undermine a bank's security: if a borrower does not have beneficial ownership of an asset, it cannot usually grant security over it. Where the borrower's business makes it appropriate, a bank should consider requiring representations and/or warranties to the effect that the borrower is not party to any agreements which contain a retention of title clause.

A bank should also check if any assets which are in a borrower's possession are actually subject to a finance lease (see **Glossary**), in which case ownership of the leased asset technically remains with the finance company (although usually subject to contractual rights of the borrower).

13.5 SET-OFF

13.5.1 What is 'set-off'?

Imagine that you take a loan from your bank for £1,500. You also have a current account with that bank into which your salary of £1,100 per month is paid. The money in that current account is owed to you by the bank. If you default on the loan repayment the bank will not want to let you draw your salary from the current account and then have to make a demand against you for the £1,500. It would prefer to keep the £1,100 towards payment of the loan, and then demand the balance of £400. This is known as 'set-off'. It is not a security interest (and so not registrable) but a right to set a debt owed by a creditor to a debtor against the debtor's debt, and so reduce or extinguish that debt. Remember that facility agreements typically prohibit the borrower from exercising set-off against the bank (see **9.9.2** and **9.9.5**).

13.5.2 When is set-off available to the bank?

The right of set-off is a complex area of law. In general terms, however, there are three ways in which a bank is *likely* to have a right of set-off against a borrower.

13.5.2.1 Equitable right of set-off

Broadly, a bank may set off a liquidated debt owed to it by a borrower against a liquidated debt owed by it to that borrower.

13.5.2.2 Contractual set-off

Most security documents supporting a loan will enhance the equitable right of set-off by allowing the bank to set off unliquidated (ie, contingent) claims.

13.5.2.3 Set-off on liquidation

Both equitable and contractual rights of set-off may be affected by the liquidation of a borrower when, in certain circumstances, r 4.90 of the Insolvency Rules 1986 (SI 1986/1925) provides for mandatory set-off. Basically, any 'mutual' credits, debts or dealings can be set off so long as the bank did not know of the petition for insolvency against the borrower when it gave credit. From 1 April 2005 the Insolvency (Amendment) Rules 2005 have rewritten r 4.90 and allowed set-off of contingent claims against a company.

There is a statutory right of set-off under the Statutes of Set-Off dating from the 1700s, but this is now of little real significance.

The right of set-off is particularly important if a debtor is in danger of becoming insolvent (but no petition has been lodged), since it allows access to the debtor's unsecured assets (ie, cash) without risk of being a transaction at an undervalue or a preference under IA 1986, ss 238 and 239.

13.5.3 Banker's right of combination

There is an implied right under common law which is peculiar to banks and which allows them, subject to contrary agreement, to combine two or more accounts of a borrower. If one account is in debit (ie, overdrawn), an account in credit can be used to 'repay' the overdraft. This is sometimes known as 'bankers' set-off', but is more correctly the right of 'combination'.

13.6 WHY TAKE SECURITY?

The introduction to **Chapter 12** stated that 'Taking security as a bank is all about increasing the likelihood of getting repaid'. There are a number of peripheral reasons for taking security.

13.6.1 Appointing an administrator or administrative receiver

If a bank wants to enforce security it will invariably do so through a third party, and usually when the borrower is, or is about to become, insolvent. Until late 2003, a bank with security (including a floating charge) over all (or substantially all) of the borrower's assets would usually appoint an administrative receiver with wide-ranging powers to manage the company and sell off assets to repay the bank. However, the EA 2002 changed the insolvency landscape. To understand the current position, it is necessary briefly to consider two procedures both before and after the 2002 Act took effect.

13.6.1.1 Administration pre-Enterprise Act 2002

The administration procedure was introduced by the IA 1986. A court had to consider that one (or more) of four specific purposes would be achieved before making an administration order and appointing an administrator. The first, and key, purpose was to ensure 'the survival of the company, and the whole or any part of its undertaking, as a going concern'. To help achieve the purposes, an administrator was given wide powers to run the company and, crucially, a moratorium (or 'freeze') applied to the rights of all secured and unsecured creditors. This took effect immediately on presentation of the petition for administration.

The idea of a moratorium was unpopular with banks which, as the major creditors of a company, wanted the ability to enforce their security whenever they chose. They therefore lobbied for, and won, the right to block an administration order if they held security (which included a floating charge) over all, or substantially all, of a company's assets. This was achieved by appointing an administrative receiver under IA 1986 (s 9).

13.6.1.2 Administrative receivership pre-Enterprise Act 2002

An administrative receiver is defined in IA 1986, s 29(2), as:

(a) a receiver or manager of the whole (or substantially the whole) of a company's property appointed by or on behalf of the holders of any debentures of the company secured by a charge which, as created, was a floating charge, or by such a charge and one or more other securities; or

(b) a person who would be such a receiver or manager but for the appointment of some other person as the receiver of part of the company's property.

The term 'debenture' 'includes … bonds and any other securities of a company …' ('securities' is not defined).

Therefore, as long as a bank held security (which included a floating charge) over 'all or substantially all' of a borrower's assets, it could appoint an administrative receiver, with wide-ranging powers to manage the business and sell assets to repay the bank debt and, crucially, the power to block an administration order and moratorium. This was a critical part of a bank's security package, because it allowed the bank to take control if it wanted to realise its security.

13.6.1.3 Enterprise Act 2002

The EA 2002 was enacted to assist small businesses and made reforms to competition law, consumer protection law, personal bankruptcy law and corporate insolvency law. From 15 September 2003, it significantly amended the law relating to administration and administrative receivers; the key changes are explained below.

13.6.1.4 Administration post-Enterprise Act 2002

The four original purposes of administration were replaced by three new ones with more emphasis on corporate rescue. They essentially require the administrator to:

(a) *attempt to rescue the company as a going concern* – if this is not reasonably practical, or would not produce the best result for the creditors as a whole;

(b) *attempt to achieve a better result for creditors than if the company were wound up;* and (only if the administrator thinks the first two purposes are not reasonably practical)

(c) *realise the company's property to distribute to secured or preferential creditors, so long as the administrator does not unnecessarily harm the interests of the creditors as a whole.*

These purposes apply regardless of who appoints the administrator.

The appointment of an administrator was streamlined: as long as the company is or is likely to become insolvent, an administrator may be appointed:

(a) by court order (as previously);

(b) out of court by the holder of a 'qualifying floating charge'. This is essentially the same definition as under IA 1986, s 29(2) (see **13.6.1.2**), as long as the floating charge document also states that the EA 2002 applies to it, or it purports to allow the holder to appoint an administrator or administrative receiver; or

(c) out of court by the company or its directors.

13.6.1.5 Administrative receivership post-Enterprise Act 2002

Perhaps the most significant change for banks is that the ability to appoint an administrative receiver, and so block an administration order, was abolished other than in limited circumstances. In addition to any floating charges created before 15 September 2003, there are eight 'exceptions' under which an administrative receiver *may* still be appointed: the 'capital market' exception, 'public–private partnership' exception, 'utility projects' exception, 'urban regeneration projects' exception, 'project finance' exception, 'financial markets' exception, 'protected railways and other companies' exception and 'registered social landlord' exception. Suffice it to say these are intended to apply to 'specialised financing' and not to general commercial bank lending (see IA 1986, ss 72B–72G, inserted by EA 2002, s 250, for further details).

The EA 2002 does allow 'grand fathering'; in other words, if a bank was able to appoint an administrative receiver before the 2002 Act took effect (15 September 2003), it will retain the right (see IA 1986, s 72A, inserted by EA 2002, s 250).

In summary, where the bank holds a 'qualifying floating charge' created after 15 September 2003, but does not fall within one of the eight statutory exceptions, it will be permitted to appoint an administrator only to realise security on insolvency. The bank's administrator must consider the two prior purposes of administration before realising assets on the bank's behalf.

Further details on these procedures can be found in **Business Law and Practice**.

13.6.2 Peripheral benefits to security

Banks will not typically take security with the intention of enforcing it; they will want a borrower to service the loan from cash flow generated by the business and repay in accordance with its business plan. However, taking security may have peripheral benefits which enhance typical borrower undertakings. For example, taking fixed security will help to prevent a borrower disposing of assets and ensure they remain in the business to create value, enhancing disposal undertakings. It may deter other banks from lending to the borrower, enhancing the negative pledge. It may also dissuade unsecured creditors from taking action to wind up the borrower. Finally, directors of small businesses may be required to give personal guarantees and security, not just to provide another source of repayment but also to act as an incentive to ensure the business prospers.

13.6.3 Costs

Chapter 9 explained the requirement of regulatory capital imposed by central banks. Secured loans will carry less risk for a bank than unsecured loans, and compliance with regulatory capital requirements will make some types of secured loan 'cheaper' than unsecured loans.

13.7 SECURITY – THE BANK'S PERSPECTIVE

It is important to understand that not all loans are secured: taking security is expensive and time-consuming, and not usually necessary unless the bank thinks there is a real risk of insolvency or a specific need to preserve assets. Investment grade loans are unsecured; highly leveraged loans almost always secured. Whilst enforcement of most types of security will be a last resort, until that time a secured bank has greater control over the borrower and greater leverage to get the borrower 'around the table' to talk if a problem should arise.

A bank's solicitor should check that the borrower and any other party providing security has capacity to do so (see also **4.6.2**). For example, the articles of some companies will allow them to provide a guarantee only if it is matched by an indemnity from the guaranteed party. A check should also be made that there is no existing negative pledge.

13.8 SECURITY – THE BORROWER'S PERSPECTIVE

The borrower is invariably liable for all (reasonable) costs of providing security, which will include solicitors' fees, registration costs and, in some jurisdictions, notarial fees and stamp duty. As mentioned at **13.7** above, not all loans are secured, although more specialised lending for large assets (eg, for a ship or aircraft) or financing a project ('project finance') will always be secured over the asset or project in question. Leveraged loans are also secured, although borrowers have negotiated two 'concessions' in recent years. First, in most acquisition financings only share security is provided at 'closing' (ie, when the loan is available). The borrower is then given anything up to 120 days to provide the remaining asset security.

Secondly, it is now common to agree 'security principles' early in the negotiation. These are pre-agreed parameters for the type and extent of security to be given (particularly where multiple jurisdictions are involved), the costs that can be incurred, and any obligations on the borrower (eg, giving notice of an assignment).

13.9 FURTHER READING

Richard Calnan, *Taking Security: Law and Practice* (4th edn, Jordans, 2018).

Roy Goode, *Commercial Law* (5th edn, Penguin, 2017).

Roy Goode, *Legal Problems of Credit and Security* (6th edn, Sweet & Maxwell, 2017).

FURTHER ISSUES ON TAKING SECURITY

'Borrow £1 million, and you are in trouble; borrow £1 billion, and the bank is in trouble.'

Old banking adage

14.1 INTRODUCTION

There are three key steps to creating a valid security interest:

(a) creation: that is, agreement to create a particular security interest between debtor and creditor (usually by executing a security document);

(b) attachment: that is, ensuring that the security interest binds on specific assets; and

(c) perfection: that is, ensuring the security interest is valid against third parties, giving priority (often achieved by registration).

The two previous chapters examined aspects of creation and attachment. This chapter looks at some of the issues associated with perfection and priority.

14.2 PERFECTION THROUGH REGISTRATION

14.2.1 The purpose of registration

The point has already been made that the safest way to secure an asset is to take possession of it (take a 'pledge'), but practical considerations dictate that the overwhelming majority of loan security is non-possessory. This gives rise to a problem: if a borrower retains the secured asset, what is to stop it, albeit fraudulently, selling or re-securing the asset to an unsuspecting third party? The problem is alleviated by a statutory requirement (under CA 2006) for the registration of (non-possessory) security interests: placing the security contract on a public register creates a system of actual and deemed notice to third parties. In addition, the nature of the secured asset may entail registration under a different statutory regime (see **14.2.3**).

14.2.2   Companies Act provisions

14.2.2.1   The regime

The requirement for companies to register certain security interests at Companies House is longstanding. The primary aim is a mechanism to give third parties notice of the security and thereby make it valid against their claims (where relevant).

On 6 April 2013, after some years of consultation, an updated and simplified Companies Act security registration regime came into force. The new regime is found in ss 859A to 859Q of the CA 2006 and applies to companies and limited liability partnerships (LLPs) registered in the United Kingdom (ie England and Wales, Scotland and Northern Ireland). The key requirements are outlined below.

14.2.2.2   What must be registered?

Like the old regime, the new one applies to 'charges' created by companies and LLPs. The term 'charge' is defined to include mortgages (s 859A(7)), and 'charge' in this section (**14.2.2**) should be read to include 'mortgage'. By implication the regime does not apply to pledges or liens for which actual or constructive possession of the secured asset by the security holder operates as notice to third parties.

The old regime identified fixed charges which had to be registered by reference to the assets they secured (*all* floating charges were registrable), but its interpretation and application was ambiguous in places. As a result many practitioners registered every charge taken over any asset. The new regime starts from the premise that *all* charges (remember this includes mortgages) *may* be registered, with the following three (minor) exceptions (s 859A(6)):

(a)   a charge in favour of a landlord on a cash deposit given as security in connection with the lease of land;

(b)   a charge created by a member of Lloyd's to secure its obligations in connection with its underwriting business;

(c)   a charge excluded by any other Act.

The old language (s 860) *required* registration of certain charges. Whilst registration has technically now been made 'voluntary', the consequences of failure to register are such that chargeholders will almost always wish to do so (see **14.2.2.7**).

14.2.2.3   Who may effect registration?

Section 859A(2) allows either the company that created the charge or 'any person interested in the charge' to deliver the documents required for registration. A 'person interested' would include the chargeholder as well as the legal advisors to the company or chargeholder. In practice, it is almost invariably the chargeholder (or more specifically its solicitor) who applies for registration since it has most to lose from failure to do so (see **14.2.2.7**).

14.2.2.4   What is required for registration?

Registration is effected by delivering a 'section 859D statement of particulars' (s 859D), a certified copy of the instrument creating or evidencing the charge (if there is one) and the requisite fee. The 'statement of particulars' will usually be a form MR01 for a company (or MR08 where there is no charge instrument) or the equivalent forms LLMR01 and LLMR08 for a limited liability partnership. The form MR01 is much simpler than its predecessors (MG01 and Form 395), providing limited information about the company and security being registered. This is because, unlike previously, a copy of the entire security instrument is made available on the Companies House register. Conveniently, form MR01 can also now be registered online.

In recognition of the fact that the charge instrument may contain sensitive information and will appear as a public document, s 859G allows certain details to be obscured in the certified copy (known as 'redaction'). Information which can be redacted is essentially:

(a) personal information relating to an individual (other than the name of the individual): for example, the date of birth, a residential address, mobile or personal telephone number, and in some circumstances the occupation or email address of the individual;

(b) the number or other identifier of a bank or securities account of a company or an individual;

(c) a signature.

Redaction usually involves obscuring the information in the certified copy using a black marker pen. The paragraph certifying it as a true copy of the original should state 'save for material redacted pursuant to s 859G'.

14.2.2.5 What is the time limit for registration?

The registration documents must be delivered before the end of 21 days beginning with the day after the date of creation of the charge (s 859A(4)). Weekends and public holidays will count towards the 21 days. The Companies House London Counter closes at 5pm, but packages delivered after that time are posted through a mailbox and stamped with the delivery time; postings up to midnight are treated as being received on that date.

If there is a defect with the submission, it must be corrected within the 21-day time limit for submission. The Registrar has power under the Companies Act to rectify incomplete or internally inconsistent submissions, and many firms pre-authorise Companies House to email them asking for instructions to make any necessary changes. For more serious errors, the forms will be returned to be resubmitted. In either case, the 21-day time limit keeps running, and so the best advice is to submit registration early and without errors! There is a useful checklist on the back page of the form MR01 highlighting the most common mistakes in submissions, which include (depressingly) entering the wrong company number, and forgetting to sign the form or include the fee.

Whilst there is provision at s 859F for the company (or a person interested) to apply to court for an extension to the 21-day period, there is no guarantee it will be granted and in practice this is never relied upon. If the registration deadline is missed, it is usually resolved by re-taking new security: an expensive and highly embarrassing situation to explain to the client.

14.2.2.6 What is the effect of valid registration?

A validly registered charge is valid against a liquidator, administrator and any creditor of the company that created the charge, although it will not prevent the terms of a charge being challenged (eg as floating not fixed) or challenge as a preference, transaction at undervalue or similar process.

The form MR01 also has a 'tick box' for noting whether the terms of the charge include a negative pledge. The intention is to put anyone who searches the register on notice of the negative pledge. The theory is that if a subsequent fixed charge is created over assets subject to a prior floating charge, the fixed chargeholder would have knowingly breached the negative pledge and would be forced to hand over any proceeds of the fixed charge. This has not been tested in court.

14.2.2.7 What is the effect of invalid registration?

Failure to register a charge within the 21-day period has the following consequences (s 859H):

(a) the security is void against a liquidator, administrator and any creditor of the company; and

(b) the amount secured by the void security becomes immediately payable.

In accordance with
Sections 859A and
859J of the Companies
Act 2006.

MR01

Particulars of a charge

Companies House

Go online to file this information www.gov.uk/companieshouse	**A fee is be payable with this form** Please see 'How to pay' on the last page.

✓ **What this form is for** You may use this form to register a charge created or evidenced by an instrument.	✗ **What this form is NOT for** You may not use this form to register a charge where there is no instrument. Use form MR08.	For further information, please refer to our guidance at: www.gov.uk/companieshouse

This form **must be delivered to the Registrar for registration within 21 days** beginning with the day after the date of creation of the charge. If delivered outside of the 21 days it will be rejected unless it is accompanied by a court order extending the time for delivery.

You **must** enclose a certified copy of the instrument with this form. This will be scanned and placed on the public record. **Do not send the original.**

1   Company details

For official use

Company number

Company name in full

→ **Filling in this form**
Please complete in typescript or in bold black capitals.

All fields are mandatory unless specified or indicated by *

2   Charge creation date

Charge creation date   d d   m m   y y y y

3   Names of persons, security agents or trustees entitled to the charge

Please show the names of each of the persons, security agents or trustees entitled to the charge.

Name

Name

Name

Name

If there are more than four names, please supply any four of these names then tick the statement below.

☐   I confirm that there are more than four persons, security agents or trustees entitled to the charge.

06/16 Version 2.1

MR01
Particulars of a charge

4   Brief description

Please give a short description of any land, ship, aircraft or intellectual property registered or required to be registered in the UK subject to a charge (which is not a floating charge) or fixed security included in the instrument.

Brief description

Please submit only a short description If there are a number of plots of land, aircraft and/or ships, you should simply describe some of them in the text field and add a statement along the lines of, "for more details please refer to the instrument".

Please limit the description to the available space.

5   Other charge or fixed security

Does the instrument include a charge (which is not a floating charge) or fixed security over any tangible or intangible or (in Scotland) corporeal or incorporeal property not described above? Please tick the appropriate box.

☐   Yes

☐   No

6   Floating charge

Is the instrument expressed to contain a floating charge? Please tick the appropriate box.

☐   Yes   Continue

☐   No   Go to **Section 7**

Is the floating charge expressed to cover all the property and undertaking of the company?

☐   Yes

7   Negative Pledge

Do any of the terms of the charge prohibit or restrict the company from creating further security that will rank equally with or ahead of the charge?
Please tick the appropriate box.

☐   Yes

☐   No

8   Trustee statement ❶

You may tick the box if the company named in Section 1 is acting as trustee of the property or undertaking which is the subject of the charge.

☐

❶ This statement may be filed after the registration of the charge (use form MR06).

9   Signature

Please sign the form here.

Signature

X   X

This form must be signed by a person with an interest in the charge.

06/16 Version 2.1

MR01
Particulars of a charge

👤 Presenter information

You do not have to give any contact information, but if you do, it will help Companies House if there is a query on the form. The contact information you give will be visible to searchers of the public record.

Contact name

Company name

Address

Post town

County/Region

Postcode ☐☐☐☐☐☐☐

Country

DX

Telephone

✔ Certificate

We will send your certificate to the presenter's address if given above or to the company's Registered Office if you have left the presenter's information blank.

✔ Checklist

We may return forms completed incorrectly or with information missing.

Please make sure you have remembered the following:
- ☐ The company name and number match the information held on the public Register.
- ☐ You have included a certified copy of the instrument with this form.
- ☐ You have entered the date on which the charge was created.
- ☐ You have shown the names of persons entitled to the charge.
- ☐ You have ticked any appropriate boxes in Sections 3, 5, 6, 7 & 8.
- ☐ You have given a description in Section 4, if appropriate.
- ☐ You have signed the form.
- ☐ You have enclosed the correct fee.
- ☐ Please do not send the original instrument; it must be a certified copy.

❗ Important information

Please note that all information on this form will appear on the public record.

£ How to pay

A fee of £23 is payable to Companies House in respect of each mortgage or charge filed on paper.

Make cheques or postal orders payable to 'Companies House.'

✉ Where to send

You may return this form to any Companies House address. However, for expediency, we advise you to return it to the appropriate address below:

For companies registered in England and Wales:
The Registrar of Companies, Companies House, Crown Way, Cardiff, Wales, CF14 3UZ.
DX 33050 Cardiff.

For companies registered in Scotland:
The Registrar of Companies, Companies House, Fourth floor, Edinburgh Quay 2, 139 Fountainbridge, Edinburgh, Scotland, EH3 9FF.
DX ED235 Edinburgh 1
or LP - 4 Edinburgh 2 (Legal Post).

For companies registered in Northern Ireland:
The Registrar of Companies, Companies House, Second Floor, The Linenhall, 32-38 Linenhall Street, Belfast, Northern Ireland, BT2 8BG.
DX 481 N.R. Belfast 1.

ℹ Further information

For further information, please see the guidance notes on the website at www.gov.uk/companieshouse or email enquiries@companieshouse.gov.uk

This form is available in an alternative format. Please visit the forms page on the website at www.gov.uk/companieshouse

The charge remains valid against the company creating it unless and until that company goes into liquidation or administration. The old regime made failure to register a criminal offence (the company and every officer who was in default was liable to a fine), but the new regime has repealed that provision.

14.2.2.8 Documents to be kept by the company

The old regime required the company to keep its own register of charges, but that will not apply for charges created after 6 April 2013. There is still an obligation on the company to keep the following documents available for inspection at its registered office (s 859P) or acceptable alternative location (s 859Q(2)):

(a)   a copy of every instrument creating a charge capable of registration under the CA 2006;

(b)   a copy of every instrument that amends or varies a charge capable of registration under the CA 2006;

(c)   a copy of any documents containing particulars required for registration if those particulars are not in the charge instrument;

(d)   a copy of any translation required as part of the registration (see CA 2006, s 1105).

The documents may be certified copies (other than the translation) and be available without charge to a creditor or shareholder, and to any other person on payment of a prescribed fee.

14.2.2.9 Security release and memorandum of satisfaction

At some point, all or part of the secured debt will be repaid and the security will be wholly or partially released. Some security documents may purport to allow a bank to retain the security for a period even after repayment as 'insurance' against the repayment being clawed back under the IA 1986 (see **15.2.9**). Alternatively, they may deem the debt and security to 'continue', even after the repayment, if the security agent considers clawback a possibility. In practice, the efficacy of such provision is questionable.

Security might also be released to allow for disposal of a particular asset. Release is usually achieved by a deed of release drawn up by the borrower's solicitor. Whilst there is no statutory requirement to notify Companies House of security release, the borrower will want to keep the register up to date for third parties and creditors. Form MR04 can be used to update the register for partial or full satisfaction of a charge.

14.2.2.10 Property acquired already subject to a charge

Under the old regime, if a company acquired property subject to a charge, registration was required within 21 days of acquiring the property. Failure to comply was an offence, although it would not make the charge void. The new regime simply allows a company (or person interested) to register a charge which already exists on property it acquires (assuming the charge would have been capable of registration if the company had created it) – see s 859C. There is no time limit, and non-registration does not constitute an offence or make the acquired charge void.

14.2.2.11 Overseas companies

The Companies Act registration requirements apply to companies and limited liability partnerships registered in the United Kingdom. Previous iterations of the regime left ambiguity as to whether they also applied to overseas companies in some circumstances. The uncertainty was aided and abetted by an unhelpful judgment in *Slavenburg's Bank NV v Intercontinental National Resources Ltd* [1980] 1 All ER 955, leading to attempted registration of security apparently unconnected to the UK (known as 'Slavenburg registrations'). However, the Overseas Companies (Execution of Documents and Registration of Charges) (Amendment) Regulations 2011 (SI 2011/2194) helpfully determine that any charge created by an overseas company on or after 1 October 2011 will not require registration at Companies

House. This applies even if the secured asset is within the UK or the security document is governed by English law. Note, however, that there remains an obligation on overseas companies to register charges at 'specialist' asset registries such as Land Registry, the UK Intellectual Property Office, the Aircraft Mortgage Register and the relevant port of registry for any UK registered ship.

14.2.3   Registration requirements for specific assets

Brief mention must be made of certain registration requirements for specific assets sited in England or Wales, or registered under English law. The most notable statutory regimes for registration of non-possessory security are:

(a)   land – registered land (under the Land Registration Act 2002 (LRA 2002) and Land Registration Rules 2003, SI 2003/1417 (from 13 October 2003)) at District Land Registry;

(b)   ships – (under the Merchant Shipping Act 1894) registered at the ship's port of registration;

(c)   aircraft – (under the Mortgaging of Aircraft Order 1972, SI 1972/1268) in the UK Aircraft Mortgage Register maintained by the Civil Aviation Authority; and

(d)   intellectual property, for example patents and copyrights – under various statutory provisions.

14.2.4   Security created by individuals: Bills of Sale Acts 1878 and 1882

The Bills of Sale Acts 1878 and 1882 impose registration requirements on security created by individuals. The Acts require most written, non-possessory charges given by an individual or a partnership over tangible property to be registered in prescribed form at the Supreme Court as a bill of sale (the Bills of Sale Acts require each charged asset to be identified in the register, which is the main reason why it is impracticable for individuals or partnerships to give floating charges). Furthermore, IA 1986, s 344 requires most forms of assignment of a trader's book debts to be registered as a bill of sale if they are to be valid against a trustee in bankruptcy.

14.3   PRIORITY OF SECURITY

This is a complex area, and what follows is therefore a summary of the main rules.

14.3.1   Priority between charges and mortgages

Fixed charges and mortgages

Generally, fixed charges and mortgages rank in order of creation (provided they are properly registered). At common law, a legal mortgage will take priority over an existing equitable security interest, only if the legal mortgage was taken bona fide, for value and without notice of the prior equitable security. Registration in accordance with s 860 of the CA 2006 gives notice to anyone who has, or ought to have, searched the register, which will usually protect a prior registered equitable security.

Fixed and floating charges

A fixed charge (and a mortgage) will rank in priority to a floating charge. This is because a floating charge, ostensibly, allows the chargor to deal with the charged asset, and this will include granting security over it. However, this vulnerability can be minimised if the floating charge contains a restriction on creating further security (a negative pledge) and the later fixed charge-holder has actual or constructive notice of the prohibition, eg through registration – see **14.2.2.6**. Notice of the negative pledge probably would not void the fixed security but rather require the fixed security holder to surrender any proceeds.

Priority between floating charges over the same assets is governed by their time of creation (if properly registered): an earlier charge will take priority even if the later one has crystallised.

Remember that, under the Companies Act registration, the date of the charge from which priority can be calculated is not the date it is registered but the date it is created. This means that a search made on the day of registering a charge might not show a charge created within the last 21 days, which would have priority over a charge created more recently.

14.3.2 Priority for security over land

The priority between interests in security over land is a complicated area. Of primary importance, however, is the priority between registered mortgages. Under the registered land system, the bank proposing to take a legal mortgage must first complete a 'priority search' at the Land Registry. The priority search will show any existing encumbrances over the registered land as well as any recent actual or proposed dealings with the land. Assuming the priority search does not reveal other encumbrances, dealings or existing priority searches, the bank will have a period of 30 working days within which to register the new legal mortgage and take priority. Registration within that period will ensure priority even over an earlier dated unregistered legal mortgage if it does not have the benefit of a priority search.

14.3.3 The rule in *Dearle v Hall*

The case of *Dearle v Hall* (1828) 3 Russ 1 established a rule of priorities which now applies to all assignments or charges of equitable interests and any interest (legal or equitable) in debts. In order to ensure priority, notice of the charge or assignment must be given to the third party which owes the obligation. For example, if C is owed £1,000 by D, and C assigns the debt to its bank B as security for a loan, B can perfect the assignment by notifying D that its debt is assigned. However, if B fails to notify D, and C later assigns D's debt to E, then E's assignment will gain priority over B's if E notifies D first.

As mentioned above, the same rule applies to charges. The rule will not apply, however, where a subsequent assignee (or chargee) (ie, E) knows of the earlier assignment (ie, to B) when taking its assignment. Thus, registration of the security at the Companies Registry will usually defeat the rule.

14.4 CONTRACTUAL SUBORDINATION

14.4.1 Contractual priority arrangements

The previous section discussed the order of priority between various security interests and nothing can be done directly to vary that order. It is possible, however, for creditors to decide between themselves on the order in which they will benefit from claims against a defaulting debtor. Such priority arrangements are frequently used in large financings which involve several 'layers' of debt: if the borrower defaults, the order in which the banks will have their loans repaid is contractually prearranged. The document creating these rights is usually known as an 'intercreditor agreement', 'subordination agreement' or 'deed of priorities'. These are complex documents and the legal issues surrounding the effect and effectiveness of contractual subordination are unsettled. However, the key provisions are outlined below.

14.4.2 A typical arrangement

How do these subordination arrangements work? A typical intercreditor agreement will restrict its participants so that:

(a) the participating lenders are divided into an agreed order of priority for repayment of their credit. 'Senior creditors' enjoy top priority, whilst 'subordinated creditors' rank below them. Subordinated creditors are further subdivided, for example 'mezzanine', 'loan notes' and sometimes 'high yield', all of which enjoy different levels of priority among the subordinated group;

(b)   no participating bank may enforce any security or otherwise proceed against the borrower without the agreement of the senior banks (or occasionally only with majority consent);

(c)   when any security is enforced, or any money received after a specified event (eg, a potential default by the borrower), either:

   (i)   subordinated creditors agree contractually not to claim against the borrower until the senior creditors are repaid, thereby maximising the assets available to satisfy senior debt (usually known as 'contingent debt subordination'), or

   (ii)   subordinated creditors agree to hold any money they receive on trust for senior creditors (known as a 'turnover trust'). This is more robust than contingent debt subordination and maximises return in all circumstances. Some practitioners take the view that this type of subordination creates a proprietory interest over the debt which requires registration as a charge under the CA 2006. However, the court in *SSSL Realisations Limited* [2004] EWHC (Ch) 1760 held that the turnover trust in that case did not create a charge: it did create a proprietory right, but since it was limited to the debt owed there was no charge over the 'junior' creditor's property.

(d)   the pooled money will then be distributed in accordance with the agreement. Thus the 'senior' banks will be paid back first. Once they have been repaid in full, any remaining money will be used to repay the 'mezzanine' and other subordinated creditors, as appropriate.

Subordination occurs in other ways. For example, ordinary shareholders (equity) will be automatically subordinated to all other creditors (debt), because they cannot usually distribute the company's assets and realise their capital until all creditors of the company are repaid (known as 'structural subordination'). Subordination between shareholders can be achieved by issuing preferential shares which carry rights to participate in the distribution of assets before other shareholders.

14.4.3   When is contractual subordination used?

Why would a bank agree to postpone its claim to, and even share its security with, other banks? The main incentive is that, generally, the greater the risk, the greater the margin. Provided the borrower does not default, the subordinated banks will ultimately get a better return on their loans. All banks will want to diversify their lending to create a mixture of risk and, when a syndicate is formed, some banks will be looking to make less risky loans and will participate only as senior banks: other banks will accept subordinated positions because they can take more risk (see also **9.3.3**).

Contractual subordination might also be used where an unsecured bank requires any debts to a borrower's directors or parent company to be subordinated to its own. Alternatively, an existing bank might benefit by allowing new finance into the borrower to enhance the business. The only way to attract new finance might be to release some existing security, or to agree subordination to the new bank.

Subordination agreements are usually executed as deeds. The borrower is usually a party.

14.5   TACKING

Tacking is the ability to secure new advances under existing security. It will depend on whether the secured asset is unregistered land, registered land or personalty.

14.5.1   Unregistered land

New advances relating to unregistered land can be 'tacked' onto an existing mortgage (or charge) under s 94 of the LPA 1925 if:

(a)   an arrangement has been made to that effect with the subsequent mortgagees; or

(b)   the mortgagee had no notice of subsequent mortgages when it made the new advance; or

(c)   where the mortgage imposes an obligation on the first mortgagee to make further advances.

14.5.2 Registered land

In the case of registered land, there are specific provisions brought in by the LRA 2002, s 49. In outline, these allow a mortgage (or charge) holder to tack if:

(a)   it has not received notice of the subsequent security; or

(b)   the new advance is under an obligation already on the register when the subsequent charge was created; or

(c)   the maximum amount of the first charge was agreed and on the register when the subsequent charge was created.

14.5.3 Personalty

Mortgaged/charged personalty is subject to the provisions of LPA 1925, s 94. Thus any actual or constructive notice of a subsequent mortgage/charge will end a prior mortgagee's/chargee's right to tack unless the conditions in (a) or (c) at **14.5.1** are fulfilled.

14.6   RULING OFF ACCOUNTS

When a borrower makes a payment to a bank, the borrower may (subject to any contrary agreement) instruct the bank as to which account it should be appropriated (although see the banker's right of combination at **13.5.3**), or which loan should be repaid (but see **9.2.2**). However, in the absence of instructions or specific agreement, the rule laid down in *Devaynes v Noble* (1816) 1 Mer 572 (known as '*Clayton's case*') will apply. In a banking context the rule says that money paid to the bank will discharge the borrower's debt in the chronological order in which the debt was incurred. If this rule applied, there might be circumstances in which a bank would be disadvantaged, particularly if it was providing a secured revolving account (eg, an overdraft or RCF). This is best explained by way of example:

EXAMPLE

Bank provides a secured RCF for Borrower. Borrower draws two tranches as follows:

1 January – £2,000

1 March – £4,000

On 1 February, Bank also provides Borrower with an unsecured overdraft of up to £5,000. On 1 April, Borrower makes a payment of £2,000 to Bank, with no instructions as to whether it should reduce the overdraft, the RCF, or be put into a new account. If there is no other agreement between them, the rule in *Clayton's case* means that the £2,000 will be treated as repaying the debt which was incurred earliest – it will reduce the secured RCF.

There are several reasons why this might disadvantage Bank:

(a)   If Borrower is in financial difficulty, Bank might prefer the £2,000 to reduce the unsecured overdraft rather than the RCF which has the benefit of security.

(b)   Even if the overdraft was secured, new security may be more vulnerable to being set aside than older 'hardened' security (see **14.9**): Bank may prefer newer secured loans to be repaid first.

(c)   Finally, if Bank learns that Borrower has organised a loan from another lender secured by second ranking security, in certain circumstances new advances would rank behind the second loan. Therefore, as the RCF was repaid and re-drawn, it would lose priority to the new loan.

To avoid problems (a) and (b), banks may insist that they can choose where payments are appropriated in some circumstances (eg, where payments are not received in full). The third problem is usually dealt with by allowing a bank to 'rule off' an account if it learns that a borrower has taken a second secured loan. This means that the original secured loan (which has priority to the new secured loan) is preserved ('ruled-off') and not treated as repaid by any amounts received from the borrower until the first bank can ensure that any new advances it makes will rank ahead. In addition, security should be specified as securing all amounts due from time to time from the borrower to the bank, and banks should include a negative pledge in their loan facility and debenture.

The rule in *Clayton's case* may also affect guarantees. Subject to contrary agreement, once a guaranteed liability has been fixed in value, any payment by the borrower to the bank will be deemed to reduce the guaranteed debt, placing any other debts which are outstanding beyond the guarantee. This can be avoided by specifying the guarantee to be 'continuing', or alternatively an 'all monies guarantee'.

14.7   FIXED OR FLOATING CHARGE?

14.7.1   Which is preferable?

Chapter 12 outlined the main differences between fixed and floating charges, but which is preferable if the bank has a choice? The principal advantages of the floating charge are:

(a)   it allows the borrower to deal freely with the charged assets in the ordinary course of business (though this is a disadvantage to the bank if there are no assets left on enforcement);

(b)   in restricted circumstances, it allows the bank to appoint an administrative receiver (see **13.6.1**), who may manage the borrower's business, and also block an administration order (a floating charge taken primarily for this reason is known as a 'lightweight' or a 'phantom' floating charge). After changes made by the EA 2002, this is relevant only to 'specialised' financial structures (eg, project finance, housing finance and capital markets – see **13.6.1.5**);

(c)   the holder of a 'qualifying floating charge' (as defined by IA 1986, Sch B1, para 14) can appoint an administrator using an out of court procedure. It can also choose the identity of an administrator by intervening in a third party's court application.

The main disadvantages (for the bank) are:

(a)   on insolvency a floating charge will rank behind any fixed security and preferential creditors (see **12.3.2**);

(b)   a floating charge might be vulnerable to later fixed charges, even if it contains a negative pledge which is registered (see **14.3**);

(c)   a floating charge can be set aside under wider circumstances than a fixed charge (see **12.3.2**);

(d)   some of the proceeds realised from a floating charge may be allocated to unsecured creditors (see **12.3.2**);

(e)   the proceeds of a floating charge may be taken by a liquidator to cover their expenses;

(f)   the borrower is free to deal with the assets until crystallisation.

Because of the disadvantages listed above, banks are inclined to take a floating charge where 'necessary' (eg, for stock), giving them the right to appoint an administrative receiver in some circumstances (see above), and to declare all other charges as fixed. However, as explained below, the nature of a charge is not determined by its label, but by its effect.

14.7.2 Recognising a floating charge

If the name of a charge is not conclusive proof of its nature, how is it determined as fixed or floating? The most commonly quoted description of a floating charge is that of Romer LJ in *Re Yorkshire Woolcombers Association Ltd* [1903] 2 Ch 284:

> I certainly do not intend to attempt to give an exact definition of the term 'floating charge', nor am I prepared to say that there will not be a floating charge within the meaning of the Companies Act 1900, which does not contain all the three characteristics that I am about to mention, but I certainly think that if a charge has the three characteristics that I am about to mention it is a floating charge. (1) If it is a charge on a class of assets of a company present and future; (2) If that class is one which, in the ordinary course of the business of the company, would be changing from time to time; and (3) If you find that by the charge it is contemplated that, until some future step is taken by or on behalf of those interested in the charge, the company may carry on its business in the ordinary way as far as concerns the particular class of assets I am dealing with.

Subsequent cases have emphasised the third characteristic identified by Romer LJ. Thus, if a charge allows a borrower to deal with the charged assets without the bank's consent, it almost certainly will not be a fixed charge, even if it is called a 'fixed charge': a fixed charge requires the bank to exhibit control over the charged asset. Similarly, if a borrower is not free to deal with secured assets without the bank's consent, the security will be fixed even if it is described as 'floating' in the security document (*Russell Cooke Trust Company Ltd v Elliott* [2007] EWHC 1443 (Ch)).

14.8 HARDENING PERIODS

When new security is granted, there is often a reference made to its 'hardening period'. This refers to a period during which the security is vulnerable to provisions in the IA 1986 for setting aside certain transactions. The primary concerns are as follows.

14.8.1 Transactions at an undervalue (IA 1986, s 238)

An administrator or a liquidator can apply to court to set aside a transaction in which a company received either no consideration, or significantly less consideration than it provided (a 'transaction at an undervalue'), and which was entered into within two years of winding-up. The transaction must either have been made when the company was insolvent, or have resulted in the company's insolvency (this is presumed if with a connected person). Furthermore, if the directors can show the transaction was entered into in good faith, and with reasonable grounds to believe it would benefit the company, it cannot be set aside.

14.8.2 Preferences (IA 1986, s 239)

A 'preference' is a transaction in which a company intentionally benefits a creditor (or a surety or guarantor) by enhancing its position in the event that the company becomes insolvent. Providing new or enhanced security can be a preference. As under s 238, a transaction will be set aside only if it was made when the company was insolvent, or results in insolvency. A liquidator or an administrator can apply for a transaction to be set aside if it was made within six months of winding-up, although if the transaction was with a 'connected' person (this includes a director, their close relatives, their business partners and their close relatives – see s 249) the time limit is extended to two years. A transaction will not be a preference unless the company was influenced by a desire to put the preferred person in a better position on winding-up (this is a rebuttable presumption in the case of a connected person). Granting security in an attempt to ensure 'survival' is therefore probably not a preference.

A director might also be warned that any involvement in an insolvent company giving a transaction at an undervalue or a preference may lead to their disqualification under the CDDA 1986.

14.8.3   Floating charges (IA 1986, s 245)

Floating charges can be set aside if not granted for valuable consideration, and if granted within a given period before the company's insolvency (see **12.3.2**).

14.9   CAPACITY

One of the first things that should be checked by the bank's (and strictly, the borrower's) solicitor is the capacity of a borrower to provide security (if lack of capacity is discovered early enough it can usually be rectified). The issues as to a company's capacity to give security are largely the same as those which apply to its capacity to borrow, discussed at **4.6.2**.

Trustees are something of a 'special case'. Most of their powers and limitations will be found in the deed creating the trust, which will need careful review. Under the Trustee Act 1925, s 16, trustees (including personal representatives) are given the power to grant security, provided that the borrowing is for the purposes of the trust and is authorised by the trust deed, or under general law. This power applies whatever the trust deed might provide, but does not apply to trustees of charitable property.

14.10   CORPORATE BENEFIT

It is not uncommon for a bank to require additional security from a borrower's parent, subsidiary or sister company. This might be necessary to make up for a deficiency in the borrower's assets and reduce an otherwise unacceptable risk of lending. Alternatively, it might reduce the cost of the loan. However, it is necessary for a company providing a guarantee, indemnity or real security to prove it derives sufficient 'corporate benefit' from granting the security: s 172 of the CA 2006 requires a director to 'act in the way he considers, in good faith, would be most likely to promote the success of the company for the benefit of its members as a whole'. The section provides a (non-exhaustive) list of the factors to which directors must have regard in fulfilling this duty. In approving a guarantee or security, the directors must consider this duty together with the factors, and the board minutes should reflect that they have done so.

At first sight, it might seem difficult to justify a company giving a guarantee or security for another company's loan as being in its best interests. When can a director justify their company securing another's obligations? This is really a commercial question of substance: what are the benefits and risks of providing the security? In crude terms, the greater the risk, the more benefit the company must derive as a consequence thereof. A parent company might justify supporting a subsidiary because directly or indirectly it will normally receive dividends from its shareholding. A subsidiary securing its parent (eg, an 'up-stream' guarantee) could argue that the support from its parent (eg, financial, marketing, product development) provides sufficient corporate benefit. This argument is more tenuous if the company is a small fish in a large group pond, but can be strengthened by a down-stream support letter (see **13.2.2**).

If a company believes there is insufficient corporate benefit to provide security, there is authority to suggest that it may still be given, provided that:

(a)   the company's shareholders unanimously direct the security to be given; and

(b)   the company is not insolvent either at the time of giving the security, or immediately following the giving of the security.

Remember that other jurisdictions will have different rules which might limit or prohibit guarantees and security given to group companies, particularly upstream.

14.11   FINANCIAL ASSISTANCE

Under the CA 2006, s 678, a public company and any of its subsidiaries are generally prohibited from directly or indirectly providing financial assistance (which includes giving guarantees and security) to any person in order to purchase the public company's shares.

14.12 APPLICABLE LAW

14.12.1 Security interests

The legal system which governs a security interest will dictate how the security will be perfected (eg, notice, registration, etc) and how it may be enforced. Under the provisions of English law (and most other jurisdictions) the legal system applicable to a security interest will depend on whether the secured assets are movable or immovable. Security over immovable assets will, for purely practical reasons, be governed by the legal system of the place where the assets are physically situated (known as the 'lex situs'). The most common types of immovable assets include land, buildings, and heavy plant and machinery.

Ascertaining the legal system applicable to tangible movable assets is slightly more complicated. Generally, the *lex situs* of the asset when the security is created will determine the validity of its creation and perfection. However, if the asset is moved into another jurisdiction then the rules of that legal system may supersede the original lex situs with regard to perfection and enforcement. Local lawyers must therefore be instructed to ensure that any necessary steps are taken to maintain the validity of the security. These issues are of particular importance for valuable assets which regularly move between jurisdictions, such as ships and aircraft.

Security over intangible assets (eg, debts) is usually subject to the governing law of the contract creating the asset, but the law of the place of performance of the asset (eg, where the debt is to be paid) is also relevant.

14.12.2 Insolvency proceedings

From 31 May 2002, the EU Insolvency Regulation (EUIR) came into force in all EU Member States except Denmark. The EUIR provides rules that dictate which system of insolvency law applies in a 'cross-border' insolvency situation: in other words, it resolves conflicts of law situations but does not change the substantive insolvency laws currently in existence.

Under the EUIR, the main insolvency proceedings will be opened in the jurisdiction of the entity's Centre of Main Interest (COMI). The rather vague definition of COMI is where an entity 'conducts the administration of his interests on a regular basis' (Preamble 13). More helpfully, there is a rebuttable presumption that the COMI is in the jurisdiction of an entity's registered office (Article 3(1)), although factors such as location of employees, head office, board meetings and where the company does most of its business can influence the COMI. There can only be one COMI, but it can change over time.

There are two main circumstances in which assets may be subject to insolvency proceedings in jurisdictions other than the COMI. First, assets outside the COMI which are subject to 'rights in rem' (broadly, security interests) are basically unaffected by the COMI proceedings. Secondly, supplemental proceedings may be brought in a jurisdiction where a company has an 'establishment'. An 'establishment' is defined, in best euro-speak, as 'any place of operations where the debtor carries out non-transitory economic activity with human means and goods' – in essence a branch. Any supplemental proceedings will only apply to assets within the jurisdiction of the establishment.

The EUIR applies to companies, partnerships and individuals with their COMI in an EU Member State (other than Denmark), but not to most regulated entities (eg, banks, insurance companies) which have separate regimes. As of 26 June 2017, the original EUIR was 'recast' by Regulation (EU) 2015/848 to improve the efficiency of the process. Key changes include clarification of jurisdiction and COMI concepts, new rules on secondary proceedings and improved registration of, and information about, proceedings.

14.13   UNCITRAL MODEL LAW

In April 2006, the Cross-Border Insolvency Regulations 2006 (SI 2006/1030) came into force in England and Wales. These Regulations implemented the main provisions of the 'Model Law' on Cross-Border Insolvency devised by UNCITRAL (the United Nations Commission on International Trade Law). The Model Law aims to facilitate cross border insolvencies by providing a framework for dealing with problematic issues, for example where creditors, debtors and assets are located in different jurisdictions. Where the Model Law covers the same ground as the EUIR then the EUIR takes precedence.

14.14   OTHER CONSIDERATIONS ON TAKING SECURITY

When a solicitor is advising on security issues, there are a number of peripheral points to be covered, including the following.

14.14.1   Prior security

Copies of any existing charges (and other security interests) should be checked to ascertain the extent of their influence, and also to check for negative pledges. A subordination agreement may be necessary (see **14.4**).

14.14.2   Notification requirements

It may be necessary to notify third parties such as licensing authorities and landlords.

14.14.3   Overseas registration

Security interests over property situated overseas may need to be registered in the jurisdiction in which it is situated: some property may be incapable of being the subject of security, and rules about enforcement and insolvency may be very different from those of English law. Local lawyers should be instructed.

14.14.4   Parallel debt structures

In common law jurisdictions, security for a syndicated loan will be held by a security trustee (usually one of the lenders): legal title to the security is held on trust and the syndicate banks are the beneficiaries. This allows the syndicate members to change (as the loan participation is traded) without danger of the security being treated as renewed (and so losing priority or hardening periods).

Civil law jurisdictions do not recognise trust structures, and so a 'parallel debt' structure may be used instead. In a parallel debt structure, a security *agent* will hold the security on behalf of the syndicate. However, most jurisdictions will only allow a party to hold security to the extent it is owed a debt. A parallel debt structure therefore creates a debt owed to the security agent in the same amount as the debt owed to the bank syndicate. At first sight it looks as though the borrower has to repay its loan twice, but the two debts run in parallel. Thus, in normal circumstances, the borrower repays the syndicate, and any amount it repays is deemed to reduce the debt to the security agent at the same time. If the syndicate is repaid in full, the security agent debt is treated as repaid in full. On a default, however, the security agent becomes entitled to demand repayment of the debt owed to it and enforce the security if necessary. For every amount the security agent recovers, the syndicated debt will be deemed to reduce by the same. Therefore the borrower only ever has to repay the amount it borrowed, because the debts reduce 'in parallel'.

Most civil law jurisdictions recognise some form of parallel debt structure. They are still not quite as effective as a trust structure, however: the syndicate takes a risk on the security agent becoming insolvent (think Lehmans!), whereas if a security trustee became insolvent the trust assets would not be part of its estate.

14.15 FURTHER READING

Richard Calnan, *Taking Security: Law and Practice* (4th edn, Jordans, 2018).

Roy Goode, *Commercial Law* (5th edn, Penguin, 2017).

Roy Goode, *Legal Problems of Credit and Security* (6th edn, Sweet & Maxwell, 2017).

SECURITY DOCUMENTATION – DEBENTURES

> 'Men lend their money to traders on mortgages or consignments of goods because they suspect their circumstances and they will not run the risk of their general credit.'
>
> Lord Mansfield (*Foxcroft v Devonshire* (1760))

15.1 INTRODUCTION

The document creating multiple security interests (eg charges, mortgages, assignments) for a secured loan is commonly known as a 'debenture', for a reason explained at **15.2.1**. This chapter briefly examines the typical structure of a debenture.

15.2 STRUCTURE OF A TYPICAL DEBENTURE

Most banks have their own short standard form security agreement, consisting of two or three pages of closely typed terms which are not usually open to negotiation. They will use these for creating security over small, straightforward loans. However, more complex secured loan facilities will require a longer and more sophisticated 'debenture', which is usually drafted by the bank's solicitor. The broad structure of most debentures is similar to other commercial documents, ie: date, title and parties; preamble; definitions; operative provisions; schedules; and execution. The main operative provisions are explained below.

15.2.1 Covenant to pay

The first clause in the operative part of a debenture is usually the 'covenant to pay'. This clause acknowledges the debt obligation of the borrower to the bank and may refer to a specific debt obligation, or to all debts between the bank and borrower (known as an 'all monies' clause). A typical all monies covenant to pay might read:

> The Borrower covenants with the Lender that it shall, on demand of the Lender, pay, discharge and satisfy the Secured Obligations in accordance with their respective terms.

Acknowledgment of the borrower's debt obligations has two key purposes. First, it brings the document within the common law definition of 'debenture' (ie 'a document which either creates a debt or acknowledges it' (see *Levy v Abercorris Slate and Slab Co* (1887) 37 Ch D 260)). This in turn satisfies one of the conditions to appointing an administrative receiver under s 29(2) of the IA 1986 (see **13.6.1.2**), though note that the transaction must still fall within one of the eight exceptions listed in ss 72B–72G (see **13.6.1.5**).

Secondly, in a syndicated loan, the covenant to pay is addressed to the security trustee (often labelled the 'Security Agent') who holds security on behalf of the syndicate. This allows the security trustee to demand repayment, and thereby enforce the security, on behalf of the syndicate members.

The phrase 'on demand' is intended to prevent the Limitation Act 1939 operating against the bank until it makes a demand. It does not, and should not, alter the payment obligations in any facility agreement which it secures (see *Cryne v Barclays Bank plc* [1987] BCLC 548 in which it was held that the words 'due, owing or incurred' meant that demand under the debenture could be made only when the loan was due under the facility agreement which it secured).

Some debentures refer to monies owing or incurred 'on any account whatsoever', but this wording may be inadvisable because there is a danger that it would not include certain types of obligation (eg, loan stock – see *Re Quest Cae Limited* [1985] BCLC 266).

15.2.2 Charging clause

The second clause in a debenture is usually the charging clause. This clause specifies which of the borrower's assets are charged to repay the debts acknowledged in the covenant to pay, as well as how each type of asset is secured. The following paragraphs examine some of the issues which arise with respect to charging particular assets.

15.2.2.1 Land

A debenture will usually secure leasehold and freehold land by way of a 'charge by way of legal mortgage' (see **12.4**). Details of any registered land which is to be secured will be included in a schedule to the debenture, so that the security can be registered at Land Registry under the LRA 2002 (the schedule will also usually list details of unregistered land for ease of reference). The terms of any leases to be secured should be checked to ensure they do not prohibit particular forms of security interest being granted over them (eg, a prohibition on assignment or sub-letting). Future acquired land cannot be secured by legal mortgage, and is therefore secured by a separate equitable mortgage or charge over the property as soon as it is acquired. (The borrower may then be required subsequently to 'upgrade' this to a legal mortgage – see **15.2.3**.)

15.2.2.2 Fixed plant and machinery

A mortgage of land will automatically secure any assets which are, or become, permanently fixed to the secured property (known as 'fixtures'), and it is not strictly necessary to list these individually. There may, however, be other assets which will not be 'fixtures' but are nevertheless fixed assets (eg, certain plant and machinery), and so the charging clause should specifically mention 'buildings, trade and other fixtures, and fixed plant and machinery' if these are to be secured.

15.2.2.3 Cash deposits (bank accounts)

There are circumstances in which a bank may want to take security over a cash deposit made with it. For example, the bank might have provided a performance guarantee in return for which it demands a cash deposit from the guaranteed party. 'Cash deposit' does not entail a suitcase full of used banknotes; rather it involves the borrower opening an account with the bank into which it credits the required amount. The obvious way to secure the account is for the depositor to create a mortgage or charge over it in favour of the bank. However, in 1987, a controversial first instance decision by Millett J in *Re Charge Card Services* [1987] Ch 150 included the following statements (emphasis added):

> [a debt] ... cannot be made the subject of a *legal* or *equitable mortgage* in favour of the debtor, since this requires a conveyance or assignment by way of security, and this operates as a conditional release;

and

> a *charge* in favour of a debtor of his own indebtedness to the chargor is conceptually impossible.

In other words, a depositor could not *charge* or *mortgage* (ie, assign by way of security) its account with a bank *to that bank*. The argument for this proposition was based on the fact that an account is a debt owed by a bank to a depositor, and a debt is simply a right to sue the debtor for the amount owed. If that right were charged, or mortgaged, in favour of the debtor it would be giving the debtor the right to sue itself: this would simply cancel (or reduce) the debt. Millett J's judgment (at least with respect to the invalidity of a charge in these circumstances) was criticised by practitioners and legal commentators.

In October 1997, in *Morris v Agrichemicals Ltd* [1997] 3 WLR 909 (also known as 'BCCI No 8'), the House of Lords, led by Lord Hoffmann, declared that a *charge* in favour of a person over the benefit of a deposit made with that person, by another, is not a conceptual impossibility. It must be assumed, since Lord Hoffmann did not opine otherwise, that an assignment (mortgage) of the account to the bank remains ineffective.

How should a depositor provide a bank with security ('cash collateral') over a deposit (ie, an account) with that bank? It is important that the means of enforcing a cash collateral arrangement is by set-off – contractual set-off prior to winding-up, and mandatory set-off after winding-up (see **13.5**): any security granted over the account is intended to ensure that the money is in the account when the bank needs to set off. Therefore, the bank should usually require (assuming the depositor will not have unhindered access to the account – otherwise (b) will probably be a floating charge and (d) will not usually be appropriate):

(a)   an express (contractual) right of set-off;

(b)   a fixed charge over the account (assuming the depositor will not be allowed to withdraw any money without the bank's prior consent);

(c)   a prohibition on the depositor assigning the account (to deal with the fact that a bona fide purchaser, for value, without notice could defeat the fixed charge); and

(d)   if the depositor's obligation is contingent, a 'flawed asset' arrangement (that is, the deposit only becomes repayable at the same time that the depositor's debt becomes due and unpaid). This protects the account from a liquidator until the bank can exercise its rights of set-off.

Note that an assignment (mortgage) will usually be possible if security over an account is given to a security trustee or an agent bank on behalf of a syndicate, and that none of these issues will apply if a borrower gives security over an account held with a third party bank.

15.2.2.4   Goodwill

Any goodwill held by a borrower is probably automatically secured as an inseparable part of the borrower's secured 'undertaking'. However, to avoid any uncertainty, a debenture will usually specifically secure the borrower's goodwill (as well as intellectual property rights) by way of a fixed charge.

15.2.2.5   Book debts

Book debts (also known as 'receivables') are the monies owed to a borrower by its debtors, and a bank will want to secure them with a fixed charge or, for single large debts, possibly an assignment (see **12.6**). The fact that book debts are usually a valuable asset means there has been considerable litigation over what constitutes fixed security (remember, if security is deemed floating not fixed, it will increase the amount available to preferential creditors). Most cases suggest that book debts have two elements, the debt and the proceeds of the debt, and that a bank must show control over both elements to achieve fixed security over either (eg, *Re Brightlife* [1987] Ch 200; *Re Keenan Bros* [1986] BCLC 242). Taking control over the debt element is usually uncontroversial: the bank must prevent the borrower doing anything other than collecting in the debt (eg, not allowing any discounting, factoring or assigning of the debt). Controlling the proceeds, however, is more difficult, because the borrower usually needs access to them to run its business.

In the early 1990s there was a run of judgments which moved against the previous cases and was much more in favour of the banks. The leading case was *Re New Bullas Trading* [1994] 1

BCLC 485, where the Court of Appeal blessed a debenture allowing fixed security over the unrealised debt and floating security over the proceeds (the New Bullas debenture required the realised debts to be paid into a specified account and then released under the directions of the creditor (ie, fixed security), but with the proviso that an absence of creditor's directions would automatically release the account monies from the fixed charge into a floating charge).

Many debentures subsequently used the *New Bullas* approach; however, the decision was subject to judicial criticism (see *Re Westmaze Ltd* (1998) *The Times*, 15 July, *Chalk v Kahn and Another* [2000] 2 BCLC 361 and *Agnew and Another v Commissioner of Inland Revenue* [2001] UKPC 28, [2001] 3 WLR 454 ('Brumark')). Most recently, the House of Lords in *National Westminster Bank plc v Spectrum Plus Limited* [2005] UKHL 41 held that to create a fixed charge over book debts, the chargee must control both the debt and its proceeds; the exact degree of control required to avoid recharacterisation remains unclear.

In summary, while total control over both debt and proceeds will definitely give fixed security, such tight restrictions may be commercially unworkable. The vexed question for practitioners, still unanswered by the courts, is how much control (if any) may be given to the borrower without fixed security being lost.

Take note that bank accounts may not be considered 'book debts' and so the charge should refer to them expressly if they are to be secured.

15.2.2.6 Shares

Shares may be in registered form (in which a register of legal owners is maintained by the company), in bearer form (where legal ownership is generally determined by possession of the share certificate) or 'dematerialised' (where they are held and traded electronically – see below). Registered shares are the most common form, and they are usually secured in one of two ways (for companies incorporated in England and Wales):

(a) Creating a legal mortgage by transferring the shares into the bank's name and issuing a new share certificate to that effect. This method is not common because it creates greater administration issues and potential liabilities for the bank as owner of the company (eg, under the Pensions Act 2004). In *Enviroco Ltd v Farstad Supply A/S* [2009] EWCA Civ 1399, the Court of Appeal decided that a company ceased to be a subsidiary of its holding company if the holding company gave a legal mortgage over the subsidiary's shares. However, there was no suggestion that the company then became a subsidiary of the mortgagee (the bank). The debenture will allow the bank to sell the shares on default of the borrower and provide for re-transfer when the loan is repaid.

(b) Creating an equitable mortgage (or charge) by taking custody of the share certificate together with a stock transfer form executed by the borrower, but with the transferee's name and other details left blank. The security document should also contain a power of attorney allowing the bank to complete the stock transfer form and submit it, with the share certificates, to register a new owner (see **15.2.8**). The bank can then enforce the security by completing the transfer form with its own name, or that of any purchaser. The advantage of this method is that the bank does not have the 'inconvenience' of ownership pre-enforcement (eg, voting, passing dividend and shareholder information back to the borrower, etc) and does not run the risk of the company whose shares are secured becoming a subsidiary of the bank (before enforcement).

In either case, enforcement of the security will not require further involvement of the borrower. The bank's solicitor should ensure that the shares are fully paid up, that (in the case of (a) above) any stamp duty payable on the transfer form has been paid, and that there are no restrictions on transfer in the articles (eg, pre-emption rights). In the case of bearer shares, security is usually achieved simply by taking delivery of the share certificate and a memorandum of deposit (ie, a pledge). The matter is more complex if the shares are held in a depository or clearing system (see also **19.2.7**), or are traded on an electronic transfer system, and details are beyond the scope of this book.

15.2.2.7 Stock in trade and sundry assets

A borrower's stock, sometimes known as 'inventory', is by definition an asset the borrower needs to sell and so will typically be secured by a floating charge.

15.2.2.8 Contracts

Companies are typically party to a wide range of contracts, some of which will include valuable rights. Contractual rights are choses in action and so may be secured by way of assignment (legal or equitable) or a charge. Which of these security devices is used will depend on a number of factors, including for example whether:

- the contract is specified as 'non-transferable';
- the borrower needs to alter the contract from time to time;
- it is preferable for the borrower to enforce the contact rights;
- all or only part of the contract is to be secured;
- the counterparty can be notified; and
- the contract has specific features (eg an insurance contract).

15.2.3 Further assurance clause

A debenture will usually include an undertaking by the borrower to do anything necessary in order to perfect the security (this is sometimes known as a 'further assurance' clause). This might include execution of any documents required by the bank, the conversion of an equitable mortgage to a legal mortgage, the deposit of any documents of title, or even the provision of additional security to ensure that the bank obtains the full security anticipated in the debenture.

15.2.4 Undertakings

Most debentures will contain a number of undertakings, the most common being:

(a) a negative pledge. This may be included even if the facility agreement contains a negative pledge to help ensure registration at the Companies Registry (and therefore notification) of its terms;

(b) an undertaking to execute, at the bank's request, a legal mortgage in place of an equitable one;

(c) an undertaking to provide the bank with any documents of title it might request;

(d) an undertaking to repair and maintain land, and insure all assets, together with a power of attorney allowing the bank to do these things (and recover any expenses it incurs) if the borrower does not.

Care should be taken not to duplicate (except in the case of (a) above), or conflict with, similar clauses in any loan documentation.

15.2.5 Crystallisation clause

If it creates a floating charge, the debenture will specify when the floating charge crystallises (see **12.3.2**). This will usually be:

(a) at any time the bank notifies the borrower in writing (although a borrower may resist the bank being able to crystallise the floating charge at will, and insist that it is linked to a default under the facility agreement, or at least a perception that the assets secured by the charge are in jeopardy); and

(b)   automatically on specified events, for example on any demand by the bank for repayment, on a petition for the winding-up of, or an administration order in relation to, the borrower, or if the borrower ceases to carry on a substantial part of its business.

15.2.6   Enforcement

The bank will have a right (subject to contrary agreement) to immediate possession of any assets over which it has a legal mortgage. However, this right of possession does not extend to assets over which the bank has merely an equitable mortgage or charge. The debenture should therefore give the bank an express contractual right to take possession of the charged assets on specified 'enforcement events' (ie, events of default). Debentures will also give banks enhanced powers to sell, lease and appropriate secured assets on enforcement.

The bank should also be given the right, on an enforcement event, to appoint a receiver of the secured property, an administrator and, if permitted, an administrative receiver – see **13.6.1**. These individuals are licensed insolvency practitioners and are usually appointed as agents of the borrower, selling assets to meet the borrower's obligations to the lender, to avoid the bank being liable for any of their acts or omissions. They will also be extended any enhanced rights given to the bank (see above).

15.2.7   Collection of debts

A debenture will usually require the borrower to collect in any debts and claims of the business 'promptly', and to pay them into specified accounts (see **15.2.2.5**).

15.2.8   Power of attorney

A debenture will invariably provide the bank and any receiver it appoints with a power of attorney. This will allow the bank to carry out any of the borrower's obligations under the debenture which the borrower fails to honour (for example perfecting security) and assist in the event of an enforcement of security. The instrument creating a power of attorney must be executed as a deed and, provided it is given to secure a proprietary interest of the donee and also expressed to be 'irrevocable', it will survive the borrower's liquidation (Powers of Attorney Act 1971, s 4). Powers of attorney are strictly construed and therefore will need to be widely drafted to cover the bank's needs.

15.2.9   Redemption of the security

The debenture must provide for the release of the security once the secured obligations are satisfied. However, in the unlikely event that a repayment is deemed a preference under the IA 1986, s 239 (see **9.2.2.4**), there is a danger that the bank would have to surrender the amount repaid having already released its security. Some debentures therefore purport to allow the bank to retain security for a period even after repayment: this is usually struck out as unworkable. Alternatively, the debenture may allow the bank, if it believes a preference (or similar) claim is possible, to deem the debt and related security to 'continue' even after repayment. Once again this is unproven and probably not workable.

There are no strict formalities for the discharge of security, other than for registered land for which the requisite form should be filed with the Registrar. The borrower will usually be made liable for any costs involved in discharging the security.

15.2.10   Administrative provisions

As with any other commercial agreement, a debenture will contain a number of boiler plate clauses concerning administrative matters, such as notice periods, interpretation, service of documents, and costs and expenses.

15.3 EXECUTION

Debentures should be made by way of deed. Under the Law of Property (Miscellaneous Provisions) Act 1989, a document will not be a deed unless:

> it makes clear on its face that it is intended to be a deed ... whether by describing itself as a deed or expressing itself to be executed or signed as a deed or otherwise.

The introduction or execution (or preferably both) of a debenture should be drafted accordingly. A debenture should be created as a deed because:

(a) it avoids any doubt as to sufficiency of consideration;

(b) it is necessary because debentures invariably create a power of attorney (see the Power of Attorney Act 1971, s 1);

(c) it is necessary if a debenture conveys or creates a legal estate in land (LPA 1925, s 52); and

(d) it is necessary if the bank is to take powers under LPA 1925, s 101.

A debenture should also be expressed as being made by the borrower 'in favour of the bank' (rather than 'between' borrower and bank) to ensure that it can be enforced by a party other than the bank (eg, a receiver or attorney).

Note that, from 6 April 2008, a company can execute a deed by the signature of one director whose signature is witnessed (CA 2006, s 44).

LEGAL OPINIONS

'There is nothing in the world so easy as giving an opinion; consequently, in general, there are few things so utterly valueless.'

Charles William Day, *The Maxims, Experiences, and Observations of Agogos*

16.1 INTRODUCTION

Legal opinions were first introduced in the USA, where they were required by banks' auditors in order to confirm the enforceability of loan documentation inter-state. It is now usual for banks in the UK, making either substantial loans or capital market investments (see **Chapter 17**), to require a legal opinion. This chapter briefly explains the typical structure and content of a legal opinion relating to loan documentation.

16.2 WHAT ARE LEGAL OPINIONS?

16.2.1 Purpose

Legal opinions relate only to matters of law and not to matters of fact. In a banking context, legal opinions will usually confirm that all the documents associated with the loan are legally valid and enforceable. The opinion will also highlight areas which may be problematic (eg, on enforcement), helping the bank to assess any associated risk. The opinion does not, however, provide a guarantee that the borrower will service or repay the loan, a confirmation of commercial efficacy for a transaction, or a complete risk assessment. In one sense, a legal opinion is simply a written statement by a solicitor that they have done their job properly.

16.2.2 Who provides the opinion?

The opinion is usually provided by the bank's solicitor (who will have created and negotiated the loan documentation) and is addressed to the bank. Generally, only an addressee may sue the solicitor if the opinion proves wrong, although the solicitor will owe a general responsibility to anyone they know has relied on their advice. If the transaction involves a syndicate (or underwriters), the opinion may be addressed to the agent bank on their behalf, or be addressed to each of them individually (so that they can each sue on it individually).

A lawyer can only opine on the law of the jurisdiction in which they are qualified. Therefore, if an opinion is required on an overseas matter, it will be necessary to instruct local lawyers.

16.2.3 When are opinions used?

There are three situations in which legal opinions will almost always be required:

(a) *Large loans.* If a bank makes a large loan with complex documentation, and external lawyers are involved, the bank will want an opinion, (usually) given by the bank's lawyers, that the documents are legal, valid and binding. Banks will not usually require legal opinions for small, unsecured loan transactions: the fact that a bank's in-house legal department has 'signed off' on the loan may be sufficient for the bank's internal procedures.

(b) *Secured lending.* Where a bank takes security for a loan, it will usually want an opinion to confirm the priority and enforceability of the security, and to outline any risks associated with those issues.

(c) *Overseas jurisdictions.* If a bank is providing money to a borrower incorporated outside England and Wales, or is taking security falling under an overseas jurisdiction (see **14.12**), it will invariably require a legal opinion from a local lawyer with respect to the enforceability, legality, priority, etc, of the relevant documents.

Even if the loan is a repeat of an earlier one (a re-financing), the bank may still require a new opinion (even if the opinion is identical to the previous one) in order to update its effect (see below).

A bank will usually make the delivery of a satisfactory legal opinion a condition precedent to the loan being drawn down (see **4.7.4**). If this is the case, a borrower ideally should insist that the bank and the opining solicitors agree the form of the opinion in advance of executing the facility agreement (it will then appear as a schedule to the facility agreement). Unfortunately, this does not always happen, and many 'eleventh hour' problems are due to disagreement over the content of legal opinions.

16.2.4 Form of the opinion

Legal opinions are invariably written in the form of a letter on the solicitor's headed notepaper, addressed to the bank and signed in the firm's name (it is common policy that only partners may sign legal opinions). The date of the letter is very important, since a legal opinion can be given only at a particular date, taking account of the law as it stands at that time.

Most legal opinions will follow a similar format:

(a) preamble;

(b) assumptions;

(c) opinion; and

(d) qualifications.

Some firms will put the assumptions and qualifications into a schedule in order to emphasise the actual 'opinion'.

More detail on each section is given below.

16.3 PREAMBLE

The first section of the opinion will specify the addressees and then briefly outline the form of the loan transaction (eg, the parties, the type of loan, the maturity date, etc). The opinion will then usually provide two lists: the first will be a list of all the documents in respect of which the opinion is given (in addition to the facility agreement, this will normally include any security documents and guarantees); the second list will specify the documents which the solicitor has reviewed in order to give the opinion (which, in addition to the documents opined upon, will probably include board and shareholders' resolutions, memorandum and articles, security registration forms, etc).

Usually, the legal opinion will be delivered after the documents to which it refers have been executed. However, the timing of some transactions may make this impossible, and the opinion will need to refer to unexecuted documents. In this case, the opinion should be clear that it refers to a specific draft and assumes the executed document is unchanged from that draft.

Lastly, the preamble to the opinion will also contain a record of any searches (eg, at the Companies Registry and Companies Court) on which the opinion relies, together with the dates on which they are made.

16.4 ASSUMPTIONS

All opinions will be based on certain assumptions of fact (remember, the opinion only addresses the law) which the opining solicitor must make. The most common assumptions include:

(a)   that all signatures appearing on the reviewed documents are genuine;

(b)   that the documents submitted to the solicitor as originals are authentic and complete;

(c)   that the documents submitted to the solicitor as copies are complete and conform to the original document (which was itself authentic);

(d)   that any resolutions were properly passed at quorate meetings which were duly convened and held;

(e)   that the documents on which the opinion relies (as listed) remain accurate;

(f)   if the opinion predates the execution of the documents on which it opines, that those documents are executed unchanged;

(g)   that any searches (see above) remain unchanged;

(h)   that (since the date of the relevant search) the companies to which the opinion relates have not become subject to any type of insolvency procedure;

(i)   that no foreign law would affect the conclusions reached in the opinion;

and, if the opinion covers security documents:

(j)   that the bank had no notice of any prohibition or restriction on creating the security, or notice of any other security in the same assets;

(k)   that immediately after providing any guarantee (or other security), each obligor was fully solvent, and that the provision of the guarantee (or security) was in good faith, for the benefit of the obligor and did not constitute financial assistance.

The assumptions will also often be followed by a list of limitations, for example that the opinion is based solely upon the law of England and Wales, that no opinion is expressed as to the title of any obligor with respect to the secured assets, and that no opinion is expressed as to matters of fact.

16.5 OPINION

At this point the actual opinion appears, usually in the form of a series of numbered statements. The actual opinion will be quite short by comparison with the overall length of the letter: the vast majority of the paragraphs are assumptions and qualifications. The exact form of a legal opinion will be a matter for negotiation between the bank and its solicitor. It might relate only to the borrower and the facility agreement, or it might include some or all of the obligors and other transaction documents. However, for a straightforward domestic loan facility, the matters which are most commonly opined upon (either by the bank's, or sometimes the borrower's, solicitors) are as follows:

(a)   That the borrower was properly incorporated and is not in liquidation. If the loan is secured, the bank might want this opinion to cover any main obligors. In the USA, it is common to opine that a company is of 'good standing', meaning it has paid all due taxes and other substantial levies necessary for it to continue in business; however, this phrase has no technical meaning in English law.

(b)   The borrower has the requisite power to enter into and perform the facility agreement, and has taken any action necessary to authorise execution of the facility agreement. The first part is essentially a statement that borrowing under the facility agreement is intra vires for the borrower. Once again, this will occasionally be worded to include main obligors, with respect to their security. The second part covers any procedural matters which were necessary, such as board meetings. The opinion will usually assume that the necessary procedures were validly performed.

(c)   The execution, delivery and performance of the facility agreement will not contravene English law, any regulation applicable to companies (incorporated in England and Wales), and will not violate any provision of the borrower's memorandum and articles. This is essentially a declaration that the facility agreement is not illegal, is properly constituted so as to bind the borrower, and would be upheld in the courts if sued upon (although the remedy cannot be predicted with any certainty). Under English contract law, an agreement which is illegal at the time it is formed will not be enforced by the court. One of the functions of the legal opinion, therefore, is to ensure the loan documents are not illegal ab initio. The consequences of a contract which becomes illegal after execution can be dealt with in the contract itself (see **9.9.3**).

(d)   Payments made by the borrower will not be subject to UK taxes (ie, withholding tax), and no taxes are payable on execution or registration of the facility agreement. The implications of withholding tax and grossing-up provisions are dealt with at **9.3.4**. The second part refers primarily to stamp duty (the result of non-payment being non-enforceability of the document on which the stamp duty is due).

(e)   All necessary registration, filings, licences and consents have been obtained in order to validate the loan document. Some jurisdictions may impose exchange controls or other requirements. Almost all jurisdictions will have a registration system for non-possessory security.

16.6   QUALIFICATIONS

The statements made in a legal opinion will never be unequivocal. They will always be subject to a number of qualifications or provisos. In a similar way to the disclosures against warranties (see **5.2.4**), the qualifications to an opinion allow the opining solicitor to modify general declarations. The most common qualifications are as follows:

(a)   The validity, performance and enforcement of the facility agreement may be affected by insolvency proceedings (and similar processes). The opinion may give particular examples, such as the powers of administrators and administrative receivers under IA 1986 (as modified by the EA 2002), and the provisions for setting aside transactions at an undervalue and preferences under IA 1986, s 423 and ss 238–239 respectively.

(b)   Any declaration in the opinion that the facility agreement is enforceable must be read on the basis that equitable remedies are at the discretion of the court (eg, specific performance and injunctions are not usually available if damages would be an adequate alternative).

(c)   A provision purporting to create a fixed charge may be construed as creating a floating charge (see **14.7**).

(d)   The enforcement of some security rights is controlled by law. For example, a mortgagee has duties to both the borrower and any prior mortgagees.

(e)   Any claims under the loan may be affected by lapse of time (ie, under the Limitation Acts), by any rights of set-off or counter-claim. Provisions in the facility agreement absolving the bank of liability for default may not be effective in court.

(f)   The opinion can only take account of the law of England and Wales.

(g)   A court may refuse to entertain proceedings if a claim has been, or is being, brought elsewhere.

(h)   Certain specific provisions may not be upheld by a court, most notably default interest (which may be declared penal – see **4.9**), provisions for severability (see **9.6**), and provisions requiring a borrower to pay the costs of litigation on enforcement. Evidence which might be held as conclusive under the facility agreement will not necessarily be acceptable to a court.

16.7   FOREIGN COUNSEL LEGAL OPINIONS

If the facility agreement is governed by English law but a borrower (or guarantor) is incorporated outside of England and Wales, the banks will usually require a legal opinion from counsel in that jurisdiction. Ideally, any foreign counsel opinion should be similar to the English law opinion: following the layout and using similar assumptions and reservations helps the client to review and understand the opinions.

16.7.1   What should the opinion cover?

Focusing on the opinion, the following issues should usually be covered:

(a)   *Borrower's status*: confirmation that the borrower is duly incorporated, duly organised and validly exists in its jurisdiction. Specific terms may be appropriate in certain jurisdictions, such as 'good standing' (see **16.5** at (a)).

(b)   *Authorisation*: that the borrower has the power and authority to execute the transaction documents and perform the obligations they contain.

(c)   *No legal conflict*: that there is no breach of law, regulation, treaty, etc, nor any conflict with the constitutional documents of the borrower. Sometimes the opinion will be provided by the borrower's own internal counsel, in which case the opinion should cover conflict with existing contracts to which the borrower is party.

(d)   *Legal, valid, binding and enforceable*: that the transaction documents bind the borrower and are not contrary to public policy.

(e)   *Filings, registrations and consent*: confirmation that it is not necessary or desirable to file, register, notarise (which usually involves reading and executing the documents in front of a notary – quite common in civil law jurisdictions), stamp (a type of document tax) or take any other action to make the documents legal, valid, enforceable and admissible in evidence.

(f)   *Withholding tax*: lenders are very sensitive to withholding tax being imposed (see **9.3.4**) and so will want confirmation that it is not applied in the local jurisdiction.

(g)   *Domicile*: confirmation that the lenders will not become domiciled in the local jurisdiction by virtue of the transaction documentation, and conversely that it is not necessary for the lenders to take domicile or establish a place of business in the jurisdiction to enforce the documents.

(h)   *Choice of law*: that the choice of governing law for the documents (eg English law) would be recognised and enforced if the lenders needed to enforce the documents or take proceedings in the local jurisdiction. Also, that any *judgment* obtained under the governing law of the document would be enforced.

(i)   *Lender's claims rank pari passu*: it is unusual for opinions to be given on ranking among secured parties, but usually a statement that the debt will rank at least *pari passu* (equally) with unsecured and unsubordinated creditors will be given.

(j)   *Jurisdiction and agent for service of process*: confirmation that the borrower's submission to jurisdiction (that is, agreeing that claims under the documents will be heard in a specific jurisdiction) is valid and cannot be revoked. Also, confirmation that the appointment of an agent in the jurisdiction of the governing law (an 'agent for service of process') is valid and cannot be revoked.

And if it is a secured loan:

(k) *Valid security:* that the borrower has created a valid and effective security interest over the relevant assets, and that it covers future as well as current advances.

16.7.2 Additional issues

Other issues that may be covered in the foreign counsel's opinion include:

(a) no limitation on paying interest (prohibited in some Middle-Eastern countries);

(b) no exchange control (preventing recovery of security or debt from the jurisdiction);

(c) that the borrower is solvent; and

(d) that the borrower cannot claim immunity to proceedings.

And if guarantees or security are being taken:

(e) whether there are any restrictions on providing guarantees and security (for example, the amount of guarantees is often limited by law); and

(f) whether there are issues with financial assistance (most jurisdictions prohibit or limit a company assisting the purchase of its parent's shares).

It is probably also worth asking whether any documents need translating into the local language (eg to be enforceable or notarised).

Foreign counsel will need as much information as possible, both at the start of the transaction and as it progresses, and details inevitably change. It is important, therefore, to keep a dialogue open throughout the transaction, notifying the counsel of new information and, in particular, of any delay to closing.

16.8 CONCLUSION

The examples of matters opined upon, and the assumptions and qualifications given above, are designed to provide an idea of the areas commonly covered. All of these will vary between transactions, depending on the nature of the loan, the documents involved in the transaction, any international aspects of the deal and the requirements of the bank. The format of most legal opinions will, however, closely follow that outlined above.

Lastly, on the basis that it is a necessary expense in providing the loan, it is invariably the borrower who must pay the solicitor's fees for producing any opinions.

PART III

CAPITAL MARKETS

INTRODUCTION TO INTERNATIONAL CAPITAL MARKETS

'When investing money, the amount of interest you want should depend on whether you want to eat well or sleep well.'

Wall Street dictum

17.1 INTRODUCTION

The preceding two parts of this book have dealt with aspects of raising finance by way of a commercial loan. In certain circumstances, however, entities with substantial borrowing requirements may turn to a different source of funds known as the 'capital markets'. This part of the book introduces the capital markets, the most common instruments that are used to raise finance on those markets, and the process of issuing one such instrument, the eurobond (also known as 'International Bonds' or just 'bonds').

17.2 WHAT IS A CAPITAL MARKET?

17.2.1 Investment capital

A capital market is not a marketplace in the sense of a physical place, such as a trading floor with people waving their arms and trading in securities. It refers instead to the vast amount of capital available from financial institutions, pension funds and investment funds (and a few high-net-worth individuals) which want to buy securities, either to hold as an investment or to trade. References to the 'market' are more accurately references to the borrowing requirements of potential issuers, and the funds available from investors. The 'size' of a market refers to the amount of funds available from the participants and the tradeability of the securities issued. An 'illiquid' market means that the participants are unwilling to buy new or trade in issued securities.

The international capital markets are subject to an even more confusing array of terminology than commercial bank lending. The terms used in this section of the book are given their most common meaning, but different participants in the capital markets may have different terminology for the same thing or process, and no terminology should be thought of as definitive (eg, strictly speaking, commercial bank lending is a 'capital market', but colloquially the phrase refers to debt and equity securities only).

17.2.2 Comparing debt securities to loan facilities

There are some fundamental differences between raising money through the capital markets and borrowing by way of a loan facility. The main differences include:

(a) In a capital markets issue a borrower traditionally issues a document (or documents) evidencing the debt obligation (known as 'debt securities', 'instruments' or more colloquially 'bonds') in return for the money it receives from lenders. The borrower is therefore known as the 'issuer'.

(b) Whilst the vast majority of loan facilities are (at least initially) provided by banks, a wide variety of institutions, and some individuals, 'lend' by purchasing securities on the capital markets. The lenders in the capital markets are known as 'investors' (although they are not just investors in the traditional sense of holding on to the investment until it matures, but also speculators who buy securities hoping to sell them at a profit prior to their maturity).

(c) Since the potential number of investors is far greater than lenders offering commercial loans, the amount of funds available to an issuer is potentially much larger and interest rates lower. This wide investor base allows a borrower's debt (and therefore any risk) to be spread among numerous 'investors'. Furthermore, the regulatory capital costs associated with most commercial loan facilities (see **9.3.2** and **9.3.3**) will not apply to capital markets investors. These factors help reduce the cost of raising money on capital markets.

(d) **Chapter 10** explained how loan facilities can be sold, but despite the advent of the LMA most 'asset sales' have a limited market. In contrast, the capital markets are well established and geared towards the relatively quick and simple trading of debt. The ability to sell securities easily and quickly provides liquidity to the market: more investors are prepared to buy knowing that they can sell prior to maturity and realise their capital if necessary. The liquidity of the market means investors are prepared to accept lower yields, which reduces the cost of borrowing for the issuer.

(e) The more extensive market means that the size and maturities of the debt can be more varied than for most commercial loans. An investor can usually invest in smaller 'participations' in a capital markets issue than in a loan facility. Certain debt securities can be significantly longer term than commercial loans, for example 30-year Gilt-edged securities (government bonds).

(f) A listed bond issue inevitably involves 'publicity', whereas a syndicated loan can remain confidential.

(g) Generally speaking, the undertakings and events of default in the terms and conditions of capital markets securities are less onerous and restrictive than in a facility agreement. There is no specific relationship bank monitoring compliance with wide-ranging financial covenants as there would be in a loan facility, although a trustee will have a basic role of overseeing standard undertakings (see **19.2.4**).

17.3 DOMESTIC AND EUROMARKETS

Capital markets may be either 'domestic' markets, or 'euro' markets (also known as international markets).

17.3.1 Domestic markets

A 'domestic' market is the market in a currency in its country of origin. Raising sterling in the UK, euros in France or US dollars in the United States are all examples of using domestic markets. When currencies are raised in their domestic markets, they are usually subject to control by that country's central bank or relevant central monetary authority (eg, the FCA and the Bank of England in the UK, or the Securities Exchange Commission and Federal Reserve Bank in the USA). The largest domestic capital market is the USA.

17.3.2 Euromarkets

17.3.2.1 The meaning of 'euro'

'Euro' is a prefix used very frequently in capital markets terminology: there are 'eurobonds', 'euronotes' and 'eurocurrencies'. 'Euro' does not imply the involvement of European currencies, money deposited in Europe or, indeed, necessarily indicate any 'European' connection. The term 'euro' simply refers to a currency held outside the currency's country of origin.

17.3.2.2 Eurocurrencies

Imagine a large UK exporter, such as Jaguar cars, which receives several millions of US dollars every year in payment for the cars it sells in the USA. If Jaguar invests those dollars outside their country of origin (eg, in an issue of securities in the UK) they are 'eurodollars'. There is a large number of exporters in this country earning currencies from all over the world, as well as many financial institutions which find themselves holding foreign currencies as a result of various transactions (these are sometimes known colloquially as currencies 'on holiday'). In London, therefore, as in any financial centre of a country which has a modicum of international trade, there is ownership of a large pool of the most common foreign currencies. The organisations owning these currencies will invest them by lending them to other institutions which require dollars, yen, sterling, etc. This creates the eurocurrency market.

17.3.2.3 Eurosecurities

Securities issued to attract the pool of eurocurrencies are known as 'euro' securities or, sometimes, 'international securities'. For example, if Tesco plc issues dollar denominated bonds in London, they are 'eurobonds'. A bond issued in London to raise sterling from *overseas* investors (rather than *domestic* investors) may also be regarded as a eurobond. The euromarkets 'globalised' the world's capital markets, providing an issuer with access to a much greater source of funds than in its domestic market alone. Any currency which is held outside its 'natural' country in sufficient quantity is likely to be targeted by the euromarkets.

(Note that the 'euro' prefix is sometimes still used colloquially, but will not appear on the face of the instrument. Furthermore, most practitioners will simply refer to 'bonds' or 'notes' (rather than 'eurobonds' or 'euronotes') and for simplicity the term 'bond' will generally be used below.)

17.3.2.4 Why use eurocurrencies?

Why should an issuer be particularly interested in the eurocurrency markets? What is wrong with borrowing dollars from US investors, or yen from the Japanese? Why do institutions keep foreign currency to invest instead of exchanging it for the currency of their own country? The answer to these questions lies within the origins of the euromarkets. In the late 1960s and early 1970s, the US Government put strict controls on interest rates and levied taxes on non-nationals issuing bonds in the USA (a form of exchange control). Investors avoided the interest rate restrictions by lending dollars outside the USA, and companies issued dollar denominated bonds outside the USA to avoid the US Government tax. The dollar and other euromarkets evolved, therefore, because they were immune to any domestic restrictions. Today, there are fewer domestic controls, and eurocurrencies are no longer 'refugees' from monetary restraints. However, having established an abundant (and therefore relatively cheap) source of funds, the euromarkets continue to flourish.

17.3.2.5 'Foreign' securities

A eurocurrency instrument taps into money which is held outside of its country of origin. This is not the same as tapping into money held outside the *issuer's* country. For example, if a German company issues sterling securities in Germany (or France, Switzerland, Japan, etc – ie anywhere outside the UK) it is a 'euro' issue, since it is aimed at sterling owned outside the UK. However, if a *non-British* company issues a sterling instrument (to 'domestic' investors) in the UK, this will raise currency in its country of origin, and so it is not a 'euro' issue but rather a 'foreign' issue. Foreign issues are known in the markets by highly colloquial names: an instrument issued by a non-British company in the UK to raise sterling from the UK domestic market is known as a 'bulldog'. Likewise, if a foreign company issues a dollar instrument in the US domestic market it is known as a 'yankee', and a yen instrument in Japan raising local yen is a 'samurai', etc.

17.4 DEBT AND EQUITY SECURITIES

'Securities' were defined at **12.7** as instruments in which a borrower (or more accurately an 'issuer') acknowledges a debt or an investment. The best-known securities are probably shares in listed companies which are traded on the stock market. Raising finance through share issues (known as 'equity' securities, since they provide equity in the issuer) is the subject of **Public Companies and Equity Finance**. This book is primarily concerned with debt securities which, in legal terms, are more similar to a straightforward debt obligation under a loan than to a share (although certain equity linked securities (see **17.5.5**) initially have the characteristics of a debt obligation but may be exchanged or converted into equity securities). There are a number of important differences between typical debt and equity securities.

17.4.1 Equity securities (ordinary shares)

In general terms:

(a)   they are essentially a non-returnable investment. An investor can realise its investment capital only by selling the shares or winding up the company;

(b)   an investor has no absolute right to receive a return on its investment (a 'dividend');

(c)   an investor will rank behind all other creditors of the company (ie, those owed 'debts') in the event of a winding-up;

(d)   an investor will take equity (a share) in the issuer, and is usually (although not always) given the power to vote on major issues at shareholders' meetings.

17.4.2 Debt securities (bonds)

In general terms:

(a)   the investment will have a maturity date on which the issuer must redeem the security by repaying the investor. Most debt securities are tradeable on established markets, allowing an investor easily and quickly to realise the capital value of the instrument prior to its maturity;

(b)   under the terms and conditions of the security it holds, an investor will have the right to receive a regular return on its investment (an interest payment or 'coupon'), or the investment may be issued at a 'discount' to its face value on redemption at maturity (see below);

(c)   the investment may occasionally be secured, although it will more commonly be unsecured and rank behind all secured and preferred creditors and pari passu with all other unsecured creditors (but ahead of the equity investors) in the event of the winding-up of the issuer;

(d)   with the exception of equity linked securities where the original debt obligation may be exchanged for equity (see **17.5.5**), an investor does not take any equity in the issuer, or have any rights over the issuer other than basic rights to call an event of default if coupon or principal are not paid or undertakings (which are very basic) are breached.

The following section explains the characteristics of the most common debt security structures found in the capital markets.

17.5 BONDS AND NOTES

A bond is a certificate of debt under which the issuer obligates itself to pay the principal to the bondholder on a specified date, usually (there is no hard and fast rule) three years or more after the date of issue.

The main characteristics of a bond are:

(a)   it is a debt obligation (although some bonds may have conversion rights into equity) made by way of a transferable instrument (see **18.3.1**) with a medium- or long-term maturity;

(b)   initially, it is sold by way of marketing to a wide number of investors through a syndicate of financial institutions, or it is sold to a small group of specifically targeted investors (known as a 'private placement');

(c)   it is a marketable instrument (ie, it has an established secondary market);

(d)   it may or may not be listed on a recognised stock exchange (see **21.8**);

(e)   it will bear interest (usually payable semi-annually), or be issued at a discount to its face value on redemption.

Until relatively recently, the term 'note' was reserved for securities with a short maturity (eg less than three years) or with a floating rate coupon: everything else was a 'bond'. However, the terms are now almost interchangeable and 'note' is probably used more commonly than 'bond'. Confusingly, there are no written rules; the cognoscenti just know which terms are used in the market. As a rule of thumb you should refer to:

(a)   'floating rate notes', not 'floating rate bonds' (see **17.5.2**);

(b)   a 'global note', rather than a 'global bond' (see **18.2.1**);

(c)   securities issued under a programme as 'notes', not 'bonds' (see **17.6**);

(d)   securities issued under a securitisation as 'notes', not 'bonds'.

If in doubt, use the term 'note' rather than 'bond'.

Bonds are probably the most widely used debt security on the capital markets. They can take a number of different forms, the most common of which are explained below.

17.5.1 Fixed rate bonds

Many bonds are issued on a 'fixed rate' basis. This means that the rate of interest (known as the 'coupon': see **17.5.4**) they yield for the investor is fixed at the time of issue and will not change during the life of the bond. The interest is usually payable annually (or semi-annually in the case of some 'emerging markets' issuers) in arrear, an infrequent return on investment compared with most loan facilities. The rate of interest will depend primarily on the market conditions prevailing at the time of issue, the credit rating of the issuer (see **17.11**), and the length of maturity of the bond. The starting point of the interest calculation will be based on the rate offered at that time on a government security (eg, a treasury bill) of similar maturity. A margin will be added to reflect the issuer's creditworthiness and the maturity of the bond (the longer the maturity, the higher the interest rate, since investors must wait longer for the return of their capital), and the composite rate is then shown on the bond as a single figure. Fixed interest bonds without any special features are known as 'straight bonds' or 'plain vanilla bonds'.

17.5.2   Floating rate notes

Floating rate notes ('FRNs') pay interest which fluctuates in accordance with a variable benchmark rate, which (if it is issued in London) is usually the LIBOR (see **4.9**) for the currency in which the bond is issued. The interest rate payable on the FRN is the benchmark rate plus a margin (in a similar way to floating rate loan facilities – see **4.9**), for example US$ LIBOR plus 50 basis points (0.5%). The rate is recalculated each time the interest is paid in order to reflect the then current benchmark rate. Floating rate notes will usually pay interest more frequently than fixed rate bonds (eg, quarterly) in order to reflect the changing market rate.

Floating rate notes appeal to issuers such as financial institutions which lend at a floating rate and so want to borrow at a floating rate to achieve 'matched funding' (ie, when the interest rate falls, they will receive less money from their lending, but will also be paying less for their borrowing).

17.5.2.1   Reverse FRNs

Under a reverse FRN, the interest rate payable on the bond rises or falls in the opposite direction to a benchmark level of market interest rates. This type of bond might appeal to investors who believe that general interest rates are likely to fall from the current level and want to speculate. Alternatively, they may be used to hedge an exposure that an investor has in a particular currency.

17.5.3   Variable rate bonds

Some bonds have a rate of interest which varies throughout their term, although, unlike FRNs, the rate does not vary freely in accordance with an underlying benchmark. Under a variable rate bond, the variation of interest rates is restricted, or is designed to alter in accordance with a pre-determined schedule. This type of bond can be structured in a variety of ways.

17.5.3.1   'Step-up' or 'step-down' bonds

In a 'step-up' bond, the initial fixed interest rate moves up to another (pre-determined) fixed rate after a given time. For example, a 10-year bond with a fixed rate of 3% for the first five years and 5% for the remaining five years (there may be more than one step). In a 'step-down' bond, the interest rate reduces rather than increases.

17.5.3.2   Collars

A bond which is subject to a 'collar' is similar to an FRN in that its rate of interest will vary in accordance with a benchmark rate (eg, LIBOR); however, the rate of interest payable is subject to an upper and a lower limit. These limits are known as the 'cap' and 'floor' respectively, and turn the underlying FRN into a variable rate bond. The advantages of a collar are that it guarantees a minimum return for the investor, and a maximum outlay for the issuer.

17.5.4   Zero coupon bonds

Zero coupon bonds do not pay any interest. The term 'coupon' refers to the interest on a bond and is derived from the fact that interest on definitive bearer bonds is claimed by tearing off perforated coupons at the side of the bond instrument and presenting them for payment. It might be thought strange that any investor would purchase an instrument which bears no interest. However, the amount which the investor pays for a zero coupon bond on its issue is less than its face value (ie, the value printed on the bond) on redemption. The bond is said to be issued at a 'discount' (a bond issued at substantially less than its face value is known as a 'deep discount bond'). The investor's return is achieved on maturity, when the issuer will redeem the bond at its face value.

> **EXAMPLE**
>
> Imagine that an instrument with a face value of $100, and a maturity of 12 months, is sold on issue at a discount of 10%, ie at $90. On maturity, one year later, the investor can claim $100 from the issuer. The investor will have made a return of $10 on a one-year investment of $90 – equivalent to an interest rate of a little over 11%.

The investor's return is represented by the difference between the cost of the bond at issue and its value when redeemed, spread over the term of the bond. There is therefore a gradual appreciation in the amount for which the bond might be sold as the date of maturity becomes closer. The investor can therefore make a partial return on its investment even if it sells the bond before it matures. The size of discount given on the issue of a zero coupon bond will reflect the return available to an investor purchasing interest-bearing bonds at the same time as the issue of the zero coupon bond (otherwise the bonds would not be attractive to investors). Furthermore, as interest rates fall, the price of a zero coupon bond already in issue will rise since the yield it offers to maturity can be lower yet still compete with equivalent interest-bearing bonds. Zero coupon bonds are usually favoured by investors who prefer to be taxed on a capital gain than on income.

17.5.5   Equity linked bonds

Although this section of the book is focusing on debt instruments, it is important to recognise that some bonds are linked to the equity (ie, the share capital) of the issuer. These are known as 'equity linked bonds' and they provide an investor with the opportunity to obtain some form of equity interest in the issuer (in which case the issuer must clearly be a company), or a related company. There are three main types of equity linked bond:

(a) convertible bonds;

(b) bonds with warrants; and

(c) exchangeable bonds.

The typical characteristics of these instruments are explained below.

17.5.5.1   Convertible bonds

Convertible bonds provide the bondholder with an option to convert (or sometimes the issuer with an option to force conversion of) the bond into shares in the issuer, at some stage after issue. The bondholder's option to convert usually exists throughout the life of the bond. However, the bond may include a condition that the option is available only during a specific period, or expires after a given date.

Once a bondholder converts, the issuer will create new shares to be given in exchange for the bond, which is then redeemed in consideration for the issue of shares (thereby extinguishing the debt obligation of the issuer). The directors should ensure that there are no restrictions on allotment in the company's articles (see CA 2006, s 550); and, since the new shares are effectively issued for cash consideration, the existing shareholders may have pre-emption rights to be disapplied (under CA 2006, ss 561–573).

A convertible bond will also specify the 'conversion price'. This is the price at which the shares a bondholder receives in exchange for its bond will be valued upon conversion. For example, if the bondholder converts its convertible bonds with a total face value of $10,000 at a conversion price of $25 per share, it will receive 400 shares. The conversion price of the shares is invariably higher than their market value at the time the convertible bond is issued. The difference between the two is known as the 'conversion premium'.

The main attraction of convertible bonds from an investor's point of view is that they provide a potential high return with a limited risk. The bondholder may be happy simply to retain the steady fixed income from the unconverted bond (although this will usually be less than a similar non-convertible bond issued at the same time), particularly if the issuer appears to have a policy of not paying dividends. However, if the issuer performs well, the bondholder can take advantage of any resultant rise in its share price by exercising its conversion rights and selling some or all of the shares it has received on conversion.

From an issuer's perspective, the interest rate it must offer on a convertible bond will be less than an equivalent non-convertible bond, due to the added attraction of convertibility. The convertible bond also allows an issuer effectively to defer equity financing if it feels that its share price is currently undervalued and is therefore reluctant to raise equity finance at that time.

Convertible capital bonds (also known as 'CoCo bonds') are a type of convertible bond that converts into equity at the happening of a defined event as opposed to the issuer's or investor's option. The trigger point is typically related to a bank's regulatory position, for example a decrease in regulatory capital.

17.5.5.2   Bonds with warrants

Bonds with warrants are bonds which are issued as two securities: an interest-bearing security (the 'bond'), and an option to purchase shares in the issuer which can be exercised by the bondholder (the 'warrants'). The bond element will pay a fixed rate of interest and have a specified maturity, and will always remain as a debt obligation whether or not the warrants are exercised. The warrants provide the bondholder with a right to buy shares at a pre-determined price, either within a specified time period (a 'narrow exercise period', found in most European-style warrants), or at any time (a 'wide exercise period', found in US-style warrants).

The warrants are intended to provide an incentive for investors to purchase the bond and also allow the issuer to have a lower coupon (as for convertibles – see **17.5.5.1**). The warrants are detachable instruments, allowing a bondholder to trade them (as a right to buy shares in the issuer) separately from the bonds. Like convertible bonds, bonds with warrants are, to some degree, a speculative investment since the value of the right to take equity depends on the future market value of the issuer's shares.

17.5.5.3   Exchangeable bonds

Exchangeable bonds are similar in nature to convertible bonds, sharing the characteristics of an option to convert the debt into an equity interest. The difference is that the shares for which the bond can be exchanged are not shares in the issuer of the bonds but shares in a related company, such as a parent or subsidiary. Exchangeable bonds are less common than convertible bonds.

17.5.5.4   Conclusion

Equity linked bonds are debt instruments when they are issued and do not confer any 'shareholder' type rights on the investor until such time as the debt instrument converts or changes, in accordance with its terms and conditions, into some form of equity instrument.

17.6   OTHER DEBT SECURITIES

17.6.1   Medium term notes

Medium term notes (usually referred to as 'MTNs') are very similar in form to bonds or FRNs, other than the way in which they are issued. Bonds and FRNs are usually issued as a 'one off' issue for that issuer (a 'stand-alone' issue), for example 5,000 bonds at US$10,000 each, with a five-year maturity to raise US$50,000,000 for ABC Plc: MTNs, however, are issued in several series (ie, separate sets of issues) through a 'programme'. Essentially, an MTN programme involves the issuer and an arranger agreeing a set of legal documentation under which the issuer can issue notes of varying currencies and maturities (usually between one and 30 years), and bearing fixed, floating or variable rates of interest. The MTN programme may provide that the notes are issued in either bearer or registered form; and if in bearer form, they may be held as global notes or in definitive form (see **18.2**). The agreed documentation will specify the terms and conditions of any series of notes which are issued, as well as provide an information memorandum to be used for selling the notes to investors (this will need updating periodically). The programme will state an initial aggregate amount which it intends to raise through the series of issues.

The programme will also appoint a number of 'dealers', one of whom (although not always the same one) acts as a lead manager to each separate issue of notes. The advantage of an MTN programme is that it allows an issuer to issue a wide variety of notes at very short notice (since the majority of the necessary documentation is already in place).

17.6.2   Commercial paper

Commercial paper is a type of security providing issuers (which include large companies, banks and building societies) with short-term borrowing in the capital markets. It is issued through a programme, in a similar way to MTNs. An entity wishing to issue commercial paper must first find a bank willing to set up a programme for an agreed maximum amount of borrowing. The bank will then usually appoint a number of dealers, who will be responsible for finding buyers for the commercial paper in return for a commission. Commercial paper issues are not usually underwritten (ie, there is no guarantee that an issue will be sold), but conversely the issuer is not under any obligation to issue.

Commercial paper is usually unsecured, sold at a discount rather than being interest bearing (for withholding tax reasons) and is almost always in global form (see **18.2.2**). Commercial paper is usually available in various maturities of up to 365 days, although in practice, maturities will often be just one or two months. When the issuer wants to raise money, the dealers will sell the requisite amount of commercial paper under the programme (the dealers will sometimes suggest to the issuer that it is a good time to issue paper of a certain maturity under the programme). Whilst the programme specifies a maximum amount of paper which may be issued, it is a 'rolling' maximum limiting the amount which can be outstanding at any one time.

17.6.3   Certificates of deposit

Certificates of deposit (known as 'CDs') are quite literally certificates (ie, receipts) issued by a bank or building society in return for a deposit of money made with them in the form of a loan. They are negotiable instruments issued in bearer form. CDs issued and payable in the UK (known as 'London CDs') usually have a maturity of no more than five years and may bear interest (which is more common), or be issued at a discount. The advantage to a lender of investing spare cash in a CD is that it receives a very good rate of interest (because the loan is not repayable until the CD matures), but it can recover capital at any time by selling the CD in the market. The issuer, meanwhile, has the advantage of a deposit which it knows is not repayable until maturity. CDs are unsecured obligations and, like commercial paper, any issue, if it is intended to trade in the London market, is bound to follow British Bankers' Association guidelines.

Ten-year gilt yields touch record low

By Robin Wigglesworth and Mary Watkins in London

The UK's 10-year borrowing costs touched a record low of just 1.407 per cent as fears over Spain's economic and financial malaise caused investors to head for highly rated assets outside the eurozone.

While the UK's bond yields fell across the curve, the 10-year benchmark bond yield of Germany, another haven asset in the eurozone crisis, edged up slightly to 1.17 per cent. The move indicated that investors are concerned that its creditworthiness may be impaired by possible rescues of the single currency area's stricken members.

Yields on US Treasuries were also lower, with five-, 10 - and 30-year bond yields hitting record lows in US intraday trade. By early afternoon in the US, five-year Treasuries were trading at 0.56 per cent, 10-year bonds at 1.43 per cent and 30-year Treasuries at 2.51 per cent.

While gilts later moved back to 1.47 per cent, analysts said the fact that Treasuries, gilts and Bunds continued to flirt with record lows

reflected investors' rush into the few remaining bond markets seen as relatively safe.

Government bonds of Europe's "soft core" countries have also rallied since the European Central Bank stopped paying interest on deposits held by banks at the ECB, but investors have continued to flee the eurozone's struggling periphery.

Analysts say that many investors have lost faith with eurozone policy makers and their ability to get to grips with problems in Spain and Italy.

Divyang Shah, global strategist at IFR Markets, said the latest bout of market volatility reflected the view that "eurozone negative tail-risk scenarios are now back on the radar screens".

Investors are weighing up a range of possible scenarios, from an early exit of the eurozone by Greece to a full sovereign bailout for Spain.

Mr Shah said the lack of stimulus for the eurozone economy

would do little to keep investors from putting "their funds anywhere else but the safety of the safest of sovereign bonds of Bunds, core eurozone, gilts and Treasuries".

Other so-called semi-core members of the eurozone have also benefited from the flight away from southern European economies.

But the 10-year bond yields of Finland, the Netherlands, Austria and France – eurozone countries that have enjoyed a strong rally in their government debt markets in recent weeks – all climbed higher on Monday. The 10-year bond yields of Norway and Sweden, two highly rated non-euro countries, eased slightly.

The euro fell against the US dollar and Japanese yen, underlining the "flight to safety", but edged up against most other currencies, particularly those of emerging markets, which are smaller and less liquid than the major global currencies.

Source: *Financial Times*, 23 July 2012

17.6.4   Bills of exchange

A bill of exchange was, originally, simply an instrument recognising a trade debt. Rather than demanding immediate payment for goods, a seller draws up a document under which the buyer of the goods promises to pay for them after a specified period, such as three months. This form of credit is a 'trade bill of exchange'. Trade bills of exchange may be sold, at a discount, in the capital markets. Whilst the seller gets slightly less money than if it had waited for the buyer to pay under the trade bill, it gets the money earlier. Some bills of exchange will have payment of the amount due under them guaranteed (or 'accepted') by a bank. These are known as 'bank bills' or 'accepted bills'. Because they carry less risk of non-repayment, accepted bills will be sold at a higher price (ie, less discount) than identical non-accepted trade bills.

Accepted bills also provide large companies with a form of very short-term finance. A company can establish an agreement with a bank allowing it to issue bills of exchange (up to an aggregate amount) which the bank will 'accept' (ie, undertake the payment obligations) in return for a fee. This is known as an 'acceptance credit facility': there is no underlying trade debt. The company can then sell the accepted bills to raise short-term money.

17.6.5   Treasury bills

Treasury bills are capital markets instruments which work in a similar way to bills of exchange and are used by governments for short-term borrowing in order to balance their cash flow. In London, the Government auctions treasury bills to banks and other financial institutions every Friday. The treasury bills do not bear interest, but are sold at a discount.

17.7   PRIMARY AND SECONDARY MARKETS

When a security is issued, it is offered on what is known as the 'primary market'. The primary market involves the sale of securities by an issuer to investors in order for the issuer to raise the money it requires. If the investor holds the security until it matures, the transaction will have been confined to the primary market. However, most investors will want the ability to sell a security before it matures, allowing them to realise its capital value early. This is known as the 'secondary market', in which investors and traders can buy and sell securities already in issue.

Certain investors will buy securities to hold as a 'long-term' investment, ie until the security matures. Other investors buy securities in order to 'play' the market, ie to sell them when their value rises. These investors may hold a selection (or 'book') of securities (in the same way as an equity investor holds a portfolio of shares in various companies), which they trade on the market (some financial institutions act as brokers, buying and selling securities on behalf of their client investors). These investors are generally known as 'traders'. An instrument with an established secondary market is usually known as a 'marketable instrument'.

Whilst an issuer usually has no direct part to play in it, the secondary market will have an effect on its ability to issue in the primary market. This is because one of the most important features of any security instrument, both at and after issue, is its marketability. Some of the factors affecting marketability include:

(a)   the identity of the issuer and its credit rating;

(b)   the type of security being issued;

(c)   the number of potential investors that can be offered the issue (ie, are there any regulatory or practical restrictions?).

Marketability may also be enhanced if the securities are listed on a regulated market. For example, many domestic and eurosecurities are listed on the London Stock Exchange which provides regulated information about the issuer (in the form of listing particulars). This encourages investors to take the securities on issue, and provides an indication of market interest and value of particular securities which is helpful in launching and pricing a new issue. Although the securities may be listed on a stock exchange, they may (particularly in the case of bonds) still be traded in the secondary market 'off exchange' (see **21.8.1**).

17.8   CLEARING SYSTEMS

17.8.1   What is a clearing system?

Originally all eurobonds took the form (known as 'definitive form') of paper certificates which represented a debt to be paid by the issuer to whoever possessed the bond (the 'bearer') at maturity. However, these definitive 'bearer bonds' are difficult to trade rapidly in large numbers and are vulnerable to theft or loss in the same way as cash. To speed trading and improve security, 'clearing systems' were developed which allowed the bonds to be left safely in a vault and for trading to take place through accounts. There are a number of clearing systems worldwide which deal with trading bearer (and other) securities. However, in the international eurosecurities markets, there are two systems of paramount importance: the Euroclear system and the Clearstream Service (which is part of the Deutsche Börse Group), commonly referred to as 'Euroclear' and 'Clearstream'.

Euroclear was created by Morgan Guaranty Trust Company of New York in 1968. It is now owned largely by 'user shareholders' with a core operation in Brussels and subsidiary operations in Paris, Amsterdam and London. Clearstream was created (originally as 'Cedel') in 1970, and operates primarily from Luxembourg and Frankfurt.

17.8.2   Operation of the clearing systems

Euroclear and Clearstream are not confined to dealing with bonds. Both clearing systems will accept most common forms of securities which are actively traded in the international capital markets, for example bonds, notes, debenture stock, commercial paper, certain certificates of deposit (depending on their place of issue) and some types of shares. However, in order to explain the clearing systems' processes, this section concentrates on bond issues.

Euroclear and Clearstream operate in similar ways. The primary purpose of a clearing system is to avoid the physical handling of bearer instruments on issue and on subsequent trading. Therefore, the actual bond certificates (which may be in definitive bearer form or global form – see **18.2**) are invariably passed on to a bank known as a 'depositary' (see **19.2.7**) for safekeeping, and the clearing system works through a series of 'book entries' (akin to depositing cash with your bank and debiting your account to pay debts rather than withdrawing cash). In order to participate in a clearing system, an investor will have two accounts with the system (although some investors will use accounts held by their bank or broker who act as nominee for them):

(a)   a securities clearance account to and from which the securities are credited (the account does not usually allocate the holder specific bonds, ie the bonds in a particular issue are fungible); and

(b)   a cash account (like a current account) through which all payments from the sale or purchase of securities must pass.

Each issue of securities is allocated a unique code number, known as its ISIN (International Securities Identification Number), from which is derived the 'Common Code'. The Common Code is used as a label to identify the particular *issue* each time the clearing system is instructed to deal in securities, and it should not be mistaken for a security device, nor a way of identifying individual bonds within an issue (other issue identification numbers are sometimes seen, eg 'sedol' – used by the London Stock Exchange). If a bondholder wants to sell some bonds on the secondary market, it instructs the clearer, which reduces the seller's securities clearance account by the requisite number of securities and credits them to the securities clearance account of the purchaser. At the same time, the cash account of the purchaser is debited, and the cash account of the seller credited, to represent payment for the securities. Euroclear and Clearstream also allow trading between their two systems since each has securities and cash accounts with the other (this is known as the 'bridge').

Clearing systems have a function in both the primary and secondary markets. In the primary market, they will accept a new issue of bonds onto their systems, so long as it has complied with any regulations applicable to it (eg, selling restrictions – see **18.2.1**). On the closing date of a new issue, the requisite number of bonds will be credited to the securities clearance accounts of the syndicate members and can then be transferred to the accounts of the investors (see **21.10**).

The clearing systems also keep a record of interest payment dates and redemption dates for each issue, and will 'present' the securities for payment when appropriate. The bondholders therefore avoid the need to present the coupons or certificates themselves. The clearing systems will also act on investors' instructions with respect to any options or conversion rights which might be attached to the securities. The legal position of securities held in a clearing system is discussed in **Chapter 18**.

17.9   INTERNATIONAL CAPITAL MARKETS ASSOCIATION

The International Capital Markets Association (ICMA) was formed in July 2005 by the merger of the International Primary Markets Association (IPMA) and the International Securities Markets Association (ISMA). ICMA is the association for financial institutions which play an active role, usually as managers, underwriters and traders, in the primary and secondary bond markets. ICMA is a trade association, as opposed to a statutory body, created by participants in the international capital markets with a view to establishing recognised standards of market practice. Membership of ICMA brings a financial institution the status and recognition, from other institutions and issuers, necessary to take a major part in large euromarket deals. Members of ICMA include banks, members of recognised stock exchanges, licensed dealers in securities and affiliated organisations.

ICMA is a self-regulating body, and the ultimate sanction for non-compliance with its recommendations is expulsion from the Association. In order to appreciate the gravity of expulsion, it is important to understand that the euromarket works with something of the aura of a 'members' club'. An institution which breaches ICMA rules will soon become known to other euromarket institutions, and they may become reluctant to deal with the offender. Persistent or serious breaches will eventually result in an offender being unable to raise a syndicate, and being left out of invitations to join other syndicates.

ICMA publishes, and periodically updates, recommendations to its members in relation to both debt and equity issues in the form of a handbook (non-members must comply with the recommendations if they hope to join the institution). The areas typically covered include the following:

(a) The timing of a bond issue. In particular, ICMA regulates the time which must elapse between the various stages of the issuing process (eg, the minimum time which managers should be allowed to review documentation prepared by the lead manager – see **21.5**).

(b) The minimum content of certain documents (eg, the invitation telex).

(c) The timescale to be allowed for payment of fees and commissions to the managers.

These, and other ICMA regulations, are dealt with in more detail in **Chapter 19**, which explains the process of issuing a bond.

17.10 THE ISSUERS

The following types of entity use capital markets for raising money:

(a) companies, including banks and financial institutions (recent examples include General Electric (€2.25bn, due 2029, and €2bn, due 2037), Volkswagen (€956m, average life 4.1 years));

(b) governments/sovereign (ie, government-owned) entities (eg, Iraq ($1bn, due 2023), Greece (€3bn, due 2022), Argentina ($2.7bn, due 2117));

(c) public authorities (eg, City of Berne (SFr 180m, due 2025);

(d) supranationals (eg, the European Investment Bank (€75m, due 2030)).

Each entity will need the authority to issue bonds. English companies should be authorised in their constitutive documents to issue debt securities; whilst governments and public bodies are likely to be authorised by statute or statutory instrument.

17.11 CREDIT RATING

When an investor is deciding whether to purchase or make a particular investment, the most important factor affecting its decision is the risk of non-payment. The higher the risk that an issue may not be serviced or repaid, the greater the return an investor will demand. Some institutions, such as pension funds and investment funds, are limited by their constitution as to the risk they can take when investing their funds.

Investors in the international capital markets are particularly sensitive to risk, and most issuers and/or their individual debt security issues will therefore be given a credit rating. Official ratings for the euromarkets are provided by specialist independent rating organisations, the best known of which are the US firms, Moody's Investors Service, Standard and Poor's, and Fitch Ratings, Duff & Phelps. A credit rating is an opinion on the risk of default on payment, and will be based on a number of different factors, including an issuer's current financial statements, past and projected performance, management, market position and operating environment.

The ratings are split into two broad categories: 'investment grade' and 'speculative grade'. The range of Standard and Poor's long-term debt ratings (which are very similar to those used by Fitch), together with their brief explanation of each grade, are shown below.

Standard and Poor's ratings

AAA Highest rating, ability to repay interest and principal extremely strong.

AA   Very strong capacity to repay interest and principal.

A   Strong ability to pay, but somewhat susceptible to adverse economic conditions.

BBB Adequate capacity to repay debt, but more subject to bad economic conditions. Lowest investment-grade rating.

BB   Any debt rated this grade or below has significant speculative characteristics.

B   Has vulnerability to default but presently has the capacity to meet interest payments and principal repayments.

CCC Vulnerable to non-payment.

CC   Currently highly vulnerable to non-payment.

C   Typically in arrears on payment or liquidation petition filed, but payments still continuing.

D   Debt is in default.

Moody's ratings

Aaa Bonds of the best quality.

Aa

A

Baa Lowest form of investment grade.

Ba   Speculative elements.

B

Caa

Ca

C   Lowest rated class of bonds.

If a bond issue is to be individually rated, a rating will be assigned at launch of the issue (there is an appeals procedure for issuers who are unhappy with the proposed rating). The rating given to an issue is then periodically reviewed: if the risk has increased, the rating will fall (and vice versa). Ratings of issuers themselves are also periodically reviewed. A rating above the dotted line (ie, BBB or Baa) is known as 'investment grade', but anything below the line carries an increasing degree of speculation as to whether the issuer will be able to meet its obligations. To provide greater flexibility within their main gradings, Standard and Poor's may modify grades between AA to CCC by adding a + or – symbol to show relative standing within the main grade (eg, AA– or BBB+). Moody's achieve a similar effect by applying 'numerical modifiers', 1, 2, and 3 ('1' being better than '2', etc) to classifications between Aa and Caa inclusive (eg, A2 or Baa1).

Issues with a lower rating must try harder to attract investors, and so generally pay a higher coupon; hence, they are known as 'high yield'. Credit ratings are not only available on fixed income securities; they are also provided for short-term investments, and even some syndicated loans.

The recent financial crisis has led to a new focus on rating agencies and the way ratings are produced. The agencies attracted criticism from some quarters when bonds given high quality ratings became worthless. This was less prevalent with plain vanilla bonds raising corporate debt, but more so among notes issued as part of complex, securitisation-based structures. Critics claimed that investors made decisions to buy paper based on the credit rating of a product, rather than fully understanding the structure and risks explained in the prospectus. In addition, the rating agencies are paid by the issuer (or originator) to give a rating, and the issuer wants the best rating possible to keep the coupon low. Some felt this gave rise to a conflict of interest. Lastly, rating agencies have also been criticised for exacerbating recent government financial crises, for example by suddenly downgrading bonds for countries such as Greece, Spain and Portugal.

As a result, the rating agencies have been subject to some litigation, and regulators across Europe and in the US have looked to regulate the rating agencies more closely. This has ranged from requiring agencies to hold licences, to requiring more transparency as to their rating methods and documentation.

17.12 FURTHER READING

Stephen Valdez and Philip Molyneux, *An Introduction to Global Financial Markets* (8th edn, Macmillan, 2016).

THE FORMS AND LEGAL CHARACTERISTICS OF A BOND

'Within three months – that's a month before this bond expires – I do expect return of thrice three times the value of this bond.'

William Shakespeare, *The Merchant of Venice*

18.1 INTRODUCTION

Chapter 17 explained the concept of raising finance on the capital markets and examined the characteristics and structures of various debt securities. The remainder of this part of the book concentrates on bonds, since they are probably the most common form of debt security issued on the capital markets.

18.2 THE FORM OF A BOND

The first eurobond issue is generally accredited to Autostrade, the Italian motorway operator, and was launched in 1963. As was mentioned in **Chapter 17**, early investors in the eurobond market held printed bearer certificates with tear-off coupons attached which were used to claim interest. These certificates are known as 'definitive bearer bonds'. As the eurobond market grew, holding and trading these physical certificates became impractical. In 1968 Euroclear was created to store the definitive bonds safely and to record transfers between investors through an account system. As this 'clearing system' grew in size and sophistication (Clearstream, then known as 'Cedel' started in 1971), printing definitive bonds was seen as largely unnecessary other than in specific circumstances. Thus definitive certificates are rare today and bonds take on other forms, most typically:

(a) temporary global form, followed by either:
  (i) permanent global form, or
  (ii) definitive form (which may be bearer or registered); or
(b) permanent global form from the outset.

This chapter explains what these terms mean and when the different forms of a bond are used.

18.2.1   Temporary global form

18.2.1.1   What is a temporary global note?

When a bond is first issued, it will almost certainly not be in the form of certificates. The total debt obligation of the issuer will, instead, usually start life as a single document known as a 'temporary global note'.

The temporary global note document is a wordprocessed document, prepared by the lead manager's solicitor, and which represents all the bonds to be offered under that particular issue. It will be executed by an authorised officer of the issuer and 'authenticated' by the fiscal agent (or principal paying agent) (see **19.2**). All the terms and conditions which apply to the bonds (see **19.4**) will be attached to, or incorporated in, the temporary global note. The document will also have a schedule attached to it on which the fiscal agent (or principal paying agent) can record all exchanges of the temporary global note for definitive bonds, as well as interest payments (if any) which are made during the life of the temporary global note.

18.2.1.2   Why use a temporary global note?

As the name suggests, the temporary global note exists only for a short time. There are two reasons why bonds are initially issued as a single document in temporary global form.

Time constraints

Once an entity has decided to raise money through a bond issue, the process of issue will usually proceed relatively quickly. Many bond issues (in particular, eurobond issues) have a time scale of three to five weeks between launch (ie, when the offer is announced) and closing (ie, issue of the bonds). This timetable is primarily driven by market practice: issuing a bond is intended to be a relatively quick way for a borrower to raise finance, and the markets therefore have an expectation to fulfil (a short period between launch and issue also minimises the risk that the market moves and the price of the bonds becomes unattractive to potential investors). However, such a short timetable makes it difficult to complete the security printing and necessary 'authentication' of the certificates which represents the final definitive form of a bearer bond. Producing a temporary global note allows the issue to close, and be placed in a clearing system, before the final certificates are ready.

Selling restrictions

In order to understand the second reason for producing a bond in a temporary global form, it is necessary to appreciate the concept of 'selling restrictions'. Most jurisdictions impose restrictions on securities being offered or sold within that jurisdiction. Many of these restrictions are imposed on issues made to the public in order to protect unsophisticated investors. However, they may also be driven by policies of investment control or taxation (a detailed analysis of these restrictions is beyond the scope of this book).

In order to avoid contravening any restrictions which might apply to it, a bond will include contractual restrictions on the institutions selling the issue (the 'syndicate'). These are known as 'selling restrictions'. For example, the syndicate might be contractually prohibited from selling bonds to 'US persons' if this would require registration of the issue with the Securities Exchange Commission (an elaborate and costly procedure) (there are exceptions to these rules and procedures to follow in order to benefit from those exceptions, commonly known as 'safe harbours').

The most commonly applicable selling restrictions are those imposed under US tax and securities laws. Some of these require that definitive bonds cannot be delivered for a period (usually 40 days) after issue (known as a 'lock-up' period). More commonly, there will be a restricted period during which definitive bonds may be offered only to certain investors. In either case, the use of a temporary global note helps to ensure compliance with the restrictions.

18.2.2 Permanent global and definitive forms

Once any lock-up period expires, the temporary global note must be exchanged for either a permanent global note (as the name suggests, this is a permanent version of the temporary global note), or bonds in definitive form (in other words, separate certificates representing each bond).

18.2.2.1 Permanent global note

As with the temporary global note, this is a wordprocessed document (as opposed to being security printed) prepared by the lead manager's solicitor, and which represents all the bonds in issue. The permanent global note is issued on the closing date of the issue (see **21.10**), and is usually held by a bank known as the 'common depository' for safe-keeping on behalf of the clearing systems (but see 'New Global Notes' at **19.2.7**).

The main advantage of using a permanent global note rather than definitive bonds is cost, since the permanent global note is not security printed. However, it does prima facie leave bondholders without a bearer instrument with which to prove ownership. In circumstances where it is important that the investor has legal ownership of the debt obligation represented by the bond, the terms and conditions require the issuer to print definitive bearer bonds and distribute them to the investors. The permanent global notes state the circumstances in which definitives should be printed, most commonly:

(a)   if any bondholder requires a definitive bond, in order to prove their legal entitlement to the bond in which they have invested, in connection with legal proceedings, eg in a tax dispute;

(b)   if the bondholder requires definitive forms in order to trade the bonds (ie, physically to deliver the bond certificates) because the clearing systems have for some reason ceased to operate, preventing trading through the clearing systems with reference to the global note; and

(c)   on or following a default by the issuer (where the bondholder might need to sue the issuer).

However, even if the global note states that the issuer must print definitive bonds (providing the investor with legal ownership), the issuer may refuse to comply with that condition. There are various methods which practitioners use to avoid this problem. The first solution is to provide investors with direct rights of enforcement in the text of the global note itself, which is executed by the issuer. The second is for the issuer to execute a unilateral deed of covenant (a 'deed poll') in favour of the bondholders from time to time. This contains a declaration by the issuer to pay those persons shown as investors on the relevant accounts at the clearing systems, and provides a contractual link between the issuer and the investors on which an investor can sue the issuer for breach of the terms of the bonds. A third solution is to appoint a trustee to the issue which holds the issuer covenant to pay on trust for the bondholders: the trustee can then enforce on the bondholders' behalf. Whichever solution is used, the documents make it clear that they are 'alternatives': the debt is paid only once.

18.2.2.2 Definitive form

A bond issued in 'definitive form' can be either a 'bearer' or 'registered' instrument.

Bearer bonds

The most familiar bearer instrument to most people is currency (eg, a £5 note), and bearer bonds share similar characteristics. They are security printed documents in order to make forgery very difficult, the issuer's debt obligation is printed on the bond itself and ownership can be transferred by physical delivery. A bearer bond has the following basic features:

(a)   *A promise to pay.* The face of the bond will include a simple statement to pay principal (and, if relevant, interest). For example:

I promise to pay the bearer $US10,000 on the 12th November 2020, in accordance with the terms and conditions contained herein.

The bearer bond will be signed by at least one officer of the issuer, although the signature is part of the security printing rather than being an original on each definitive bond instrument. However, each instrument is individually 'authenticated' (ie, signed) by the fiscal agent (or paying agent), and will not be valid until this is done.

(b)   *Terms and conditions.* The terms and conditions of the bearer bond will be printed on the reverse of the bond itself, together with the addresses of the relevant paying agents. The main terms and conditions are reviewed in **Chapter 19**.

(c)   *Coupons.* If the bond bears interest, coupons will be printed on the right-hand side of a bearer bond which must be torn off and surrendered to the paying agents in order to claim each interest payment as it falls due (the coupon is probably a bearer document itself). The name and address of the paying agents will be printed on the reverse side of each coupon.

(e)   *Talons.* The maximum number of coupons which can be attached to a eurobond is 27 (under ICMA rules). If a bond carries more than 27 interest payment dates (eg, a bond paying semi-annual interest with a maturity of 14 years), the final coupon (at the top left of the coupon sheet next to the bond) will be known as a 'talon'. The talon can be exchanged for a further sheet of coupons in relation to the remaining interest payments once all the coupons on the first sheet have been claimed.

Registered bonds

Registered bonds create a promise to pay the person whose name appears on a register of bondholders held by the issuer (or its agent for this purpose) rather than the holder of the actual bond certificate. Registered bonds can be transferred only by an entry on the register; title will not pass by physical delivery of the bond instrument. The terms and conditions of the bond will be printed on the reverse of the instrument.

Most bonds are issued in bearer form and registered bonds are rare. However, bond issues which are intended to be placed in the US but not registered with the Securities Exchange Commission are usually in registered form to take advantage of registration exemptions.

18.3   LEGAL NATURE OF A BOND

18.3.1   Transferability

In order to attract investors, the debt obligation of a bond must be easily transferable. Bonds will achieve transferability in one of two ways:

(a)   creating the bond as a bearer instrument, allowing transfer by simple physical delivery. This is the most straightforward way to achieve transfer, although the vulnerability this creates means that bearer bonds will usually be traded through a clearing system; and

(b)   making the bond a registrable instrument so that transfer is effected by a document of transfer and an entry on the register confirming that transfer has taken place (in a similar way to registered shares).

There is, however, an important legal difference between bearer bonds and registered bonds. Only bearer bonds can be 'negotiable'.

18.3.2 Negotiability

Negotiability of a bond is of paramount importance in order to ensure that it is freely marketable (and should be distinguished from transferability or assignability (see **10.4.3**)).

18.3.2.1 Achieving negotiability

In deciding on negotiability it is first necessary to decide which jurisdiction is applicable. Usually, the jurisdiction in which the 'negotiation' takes place is relevant: in the case of a bearer bond this will be the place where the bond is delivered. In a conflict of laws situation, negotiable instruments are usually treated as chattels because the debt claim is represented by a tangible document rather than a simple 'book entry'.

Under English law, there are two ways in which negotiability can be achieved.

By statute

The Bills of Exchange Act 1882 confers negotiability on bills of exchange, promissory notes and cheques. However, the Act requires conditions as to amount and unconditionality of an instrument before they can be negotiable, and bonds invariably fall foul of those conditions (eg, a floating rate of interest or grossing-up provisions will make bonds 'uncertain' and therefore outside the provisions of the Act).

By mercantile custom

It is an established principle of English common law that an instrument can achieve negotiability simply because it is customarily treated as negotiable in the 'markets' in which it is usually traded. The financial community treats definitive bearer bonds (but not registered bonds) as negotiable, and therefore definitive bearer bonds have achieved negotiability by mercantile custom.

18.3.2.2 Consequences of negotiability

The consequences of negotiability work in favour of a transferee who purchases the bond bona fide, for value and without any actual notice of a defect in title (known as a 'holder in due course'). A negotiable bond purchased by a 'holder in due course' will have the following benefits:

(a) the purchaser can obtain better title than the seller (eg, if the seller obtained the bond dishonestly);

(b) the purchaser will take a clean legal title to the bond and is entitled to payment in full, notwithstanding any claims of set-off or other defence which the issuer may have had against any previous holder;

(c) the purchaser can sue the issuer directly in the case of a dispute over the bond, and does not need to join the transferor in a claim (although a bond issued under a trust deed will usually give the trustee the power to act on behalf of the bondholders);

(d) if a 'holder in due course' presents a stolen bond, the issuer must pay out on that bond as well as on any replacement bond it has issued to the original bondholder. Because of this risk, an issuer will not usually provide a replacement bond without first obtaining an indemnity from the original bondholder to the effect that they will recompense the issuer if it has to pay out on the original bond.

18.4 COMPARING REGISTERED AND BEARER BONDS

Having examined the legal consequences of negotiability, the differences between registered and bearer bonds can be examined.

18.4.1 Title

A bona fide purchaser for value without notice (of defects in title) of a bearer bond can obtain better title than the seller; but the purchaser of a registered bond, which is not a negotiable instrument, will not obtain good title if the seller stole the bond certificate and was able to obtain a transfer in the register.

18.4.2 Claims and defences of an issuer

Negotiable bearer bonds will always be sold free from any claim the issuer might have against a previous holder. The purchaser of a registered bond is, in principle at least (although this may be varied under contract), subject to the rights the issuer might have against the transferor, such as set-off.

18.4.3 Priorities

A purchaser of a bearer bond will usually take the bond free of any equities (ie, third party claims), for example a person for whom the bond was held on trust. A purchaser of a registered bond will only take the bond free of competing interests of which they had no actual or constructive notice.

18.4.4 Anonymity

Bearer bonds can be held anonymously since the issuer will not know at any time who owns the bond. An issuer will know the identity of the registered holder of a registered bond, although the true beneficial ownership may lie behind a nominee holder.

18.4.5 Transfer

Bearer bonds are transferred by delivery. The similarity to cash of bearer bonds makes them vulnerable to theft if they are transferred by physical delivery, and most bearer bonds are therefore traded through clearing systems (see **17.8**). The transfer of a registered bond requires the execution of an instrument of transfer, and the filing of the instrument and the original bond certificate with the issuer or its agent for that purpose (whoever maintains the register of bondholders), and finally an amendment to the register. This whole process can take some time and is a lengthier process than the physical delivery of a bearer bond, or its transfer within a clearing system which is effected by book entries.

Rate shift poses a risk for Yankee trade

By Robin Wigglesworth in London and Nicole Bullock in New York

A shift in a key financial rate risks damping the 'Yankee trade' of European companies selling US dollar-denominated bonds and swapping the proceeds into euros, a popular funding strategy.

The five year euro-dollar basis swap, effectively the annual cost for European companies when they borrow dollars and exchange them for euros, has moved from a negative 67 basis points at the start of the year to a negative 37bp on Thursday.

That means that the effective annual cost for a European company selling a five-year bond yielding 3 per cent and swapping the proceeds from the sale into euros has increased from 2.33 per cent late last year to 2.63 per cent.

The fall in the basis swap rate reflects the improvement in market sentiment surrounding the eurozone debt crisis, which has eased funding conditions for European companies.

Although the rate is still favourable for dollar issuance, if the cost of entering into a swap with banks is factored in, euro-denominated bond issuance has become more enticing, bankers said.

"Swapping euros into dollars is now much more attractive than it has been for a long time," said Chris Marrow, head of European corporate debt markets at Credit Suisse. "Over the next few weeks and months this could encourage more European borrowers to stick to euros."

Longer-dated swap rates have also moved sharply this year. The 10-year euro-dollar swap rate is now a negative 25bp, versus a negative 47bp at the start of the year.

"European issuers are still getting a discount to issue in the US," said Ryan Preclaw, a US-based credit strategist at Barclays. "It is just not quite as much of a discount."

Euro-denominated debt issuance has soared this year, but the 'Yankee trade' has remained popular, particularly with multinational companies that have operations in the US or those whose borrowing needs are so big that the US remains the most viable market.

European companies have sold $42.3bn of bonds in the US in the first three months of the year, the most active quarter for the funding strategy since the first quarter of 2011, according to Dealogic data. Overall, European companies sold $106bn of Yankee bonds last year, according to the data provider.

A top debt syndicate banker based in London doubted that the recent move in the swap rate would slow the 'Yankee trade'. Once companies have done the initial paperwork required, it is relatively easy to be a repeat bond issuer in the US

"It's getting more competitive, but it's still cheaper to borrow in dollars," he said. "Even after two doses of [European Central Bank loans to banks] it's still quite a difference."

The banker estimated that euro issuance would become more attractive if the five-year swap rate hit a negative 20 bp. Given the cost, and complexity, of entering into currency swaps with banks, more companies would at that level eschew dollars for euros, he said.

Source: *Financial Times*, 22 March 2012

18.5 THE LEGAL EFFECT ON BEARER BONDS HELD IN CLEARING SYSTEMS

As explained at **18.2** above, it is now unusual for definitive bearer bonds to be printed and held in a depositary. However, if they are, it is important to understand the legal rights of the various parties with respect to the bonds. Some investors may not actually be 'participants' in a clearing system (ie, they will not have their own accounts in a system) but will rely on a financial institution which is a participant to act as their nominee. In that case, a definitive bearer bond transaction will involve a chain of parties:

Investor ⟶ Participant ⟶ Clearing System ⟶ Depository

In basic terms the investors (ie, bondholders) give the bond to a participant (ie, an entity holding accounts with the clearing system – assuming the investor is not a participant itself), which must give the bond to the clearing system (eg, Euroclear or Clearstream), which in turn gives the instrument to a depositary bank for safekeeping. The danger for an investor is that if any of these parties goes into liquidation in possession of the investor's bearer securities, the investor will be left to claim as an unsecured creditor. The way to avoid this risk is to ensure that the proprietary rights over the securities remain with the investor and are not vested in any of the other parties in the chain. In the event of another party's liquidation, the investor can therefore simply reclaim the bonds. The following sections examine each relationship in turn.

18.5.1   Investor – Participant

The law governing the relationship between the investor and the participant will usually be the governing law they have chosen in the documentation acknowledging their transaction (see also **9.8**). Under English law, the deposit of bearer securities with a participant will result in the investor passing legal title to the participant, but the investor retaining beneficial ownership. The participant therefore takes all the rights against the issuer such as payment of coupon and principal, and any conversion rights. However, the participant must account for any payments it receives, must comply with the investor's instructions as to any rights under the security, and must transfer the securities back to the investor at their request. The investor can also demand the return of the bonds in the event of the participant's liquidation and they will not become part of the participant's general pool of assets.

18.5.2   Participant – Clearing system

The two main clearing systems for bonds, Euroclear and Clearstream (see **17.8.1**), are (respectively) Belgian and Luxembourg entities, and the terms and conditions of the clearing systems will be construed in accordance with the local law. For the sake of simplicity, we will assume that the clearing system being used is Euroclear in Belgium.

Under general Belgian law, participants depositing bearer securities in Euroclear would have contractual rights against Euroclear for the return of their securities. However, general Belgian law is modified under a specific decree, so that the participants retain a proprietary right of ownership in the securities credited to their securities clearance account. Therefore, if Euroclear should become insolvent, the participants will not be unsecured creditors but will have the right to the return of the securities which are credited to their securities account.

18.5.3   Clearing systems – Depository

The final link in the chain is that between the clearing system and the depositary bank where the bearer instruments are held for safekeeping. This relationship is subject not only to the local law of the relevant clearing system, but also to the law of the jurisdiction in which the depository is situated. It is therefore important for the participant to ensure that the proprietory rights in the bearer securities are not in any way transferred to the depositary bank. The clearing systems will usually ensure that this is the case before using a depository; however, some participants may want a legal opinion from local lawyers to confirm that this is the case.

With careful planning and legal advice, therefore, an investor with bearer securities can avoid taking a credit risk on any of the other parties involved in the clearing system process.

18.6   FURTHER READING

This chapter has provided a brief overview of the legal 'chain' of rights over a bond: for a more thorough examination, see the excellent *Interests in Securities* (Oxford University Press, forthcoming 2020) by Dr Joanna Benjamin.

CHAPTER 19

ISSUING A BOND – THE PARTIES AND DOCUMENTATION

19.1 INTRODUCTION

The next three chapters concentrate on the parties, documents and process involved in the issue of a eurobond. The reason for examining a eurobond is that they are among the most common form of debt security and something of a paradigm for debt securities issued in the London markets. Many of the matters which are dealt with will, however, also apply to issues of other types of bond and other debt securities.

The characteristics of a bond were explained at **17.5**, and the concept of eurocurrencies was explained at **17.3.2**: a eurobond is a bond which is issued to attract eurocurrencies. In other words, it is a bond denominated in a globally recognised currency which is not the currency of the country in which the bond is issued. It is generally agreed that the very first eurobond was issued in 1963 by Autostrade (the Italian motorway authority) in London, arranged by SG Warburg (now part of UBS) for US$15,000,000. However, the real increase in these bond issues came in the early 1980s, reflecting a reduction in the size of the syndicated loan market caused by the imposition of more severe regulatory capital requirements (see **9.3.3**). Banks facing restrictions on lending turned instead to the lucrative fees available from underwriting bond issues.

19.2 PARTIES TO A BOND ISSUE

19.2.1 The issuer

The various entities which might issue debt securities on the capital markets were listed at **17.10**. The key question for a lawyer is whether the issuer is a 'debut issuer', in which case the prospectus will need drafting from scratch, or has issued before, when the existing prospectus can probably just be updated. By definition, eurobonds will raise a currency that is not 'indigenous' to the country in which they are issued. If the issuer does not have a specific requirement for that currency, it will enter into a derivative or foreign exchange transaction to exchange the money for a currency it can use.

19.2.2 Lead manager

The lead manager to an issue will be a financial institution such as an investment bank, and it will have a role similar to the arranger in a syndicated loan (see **3.3.2**). It will be responsible for arranging the bond issue and managing the issue process, from receiving its mandate through to the issuer receiving funds. The lead manager will advise the issuer on the structure, timing and pricing of the issue, and so takes the credit for success and responsibility for the failure of the issue to sell. If the issue is to be listed, the lead manager will usually be the 'sponsor' required by the UKLA to provide confirmations (eg, of compliance with the Listing Rules) for listing.

19.2.3 Syndicate

The lead manager will recruit a number of 'co-managers' to join them in a 'syndicate'. The syndicate are effectively a distribution network for the issue, using their contacts and knowledge of the market to find investors ('book building'). In most bond issues on the London market, the syndicate agree with the issuer to take all the bonds, even if they cannot find investors. This gives the issuer the reassurance of knowing the exact amount of the funds it will receive. The syndicate (in return for a fee) take the risk that the issue is not fully subscribed by investors, in which case they will buy the unsold bonds (they may sell any such bonds in the secondary market at a lower price in order to clear their books, or they may retain the bonds in the hope that demand for them increases and they make a profit on a sale). The names of the syndicate will appear on the prospectus in order of contribution to the amount of the issue that they have sold, and if equal in alphabetical order. In some US issues and some high-yield UK issues, the syndicate will only have to use 'reasonable endeavours' to sell the securities, and a separate group of banks will 'underwrite' (ie, purchase) any unsold bonds to give the issuer certainty of funds.

19.2.4 Fiscal agent and trustee

A bond issue will use either a fiscal agent (under a fiscal agency agreement), or a trustee (under a trust deed). The legal effect of each arrangement is quite different.

19.2.4.1 Fiscal agent

The fiscal agent is appointed by, and is the representative and agent of, the issuer and not the bondholders. It is primarily responsible for paying principal and interest to the bondholders. The fiscal agent will also have certain administrative functions, including the publication of notices to the bondholders and acting as a depository for the issuer's accounts and other financial information which is open to inspection by the bondholders (although it has no duty to review or investigate such information). The fiscal agency agreement will appoint the fiscal agent and explicitly state that it does not owe the bondholders any duty of care.

19.2.4.2 Trustee

A trustee is initially chosen and appointed by the issuer (through its advisers) but represents the interests of the bondholders. The property held on trust is the issuer's covenant to pay the bondholders. The trustee's powers and duties are recorded in a trust deed, but it will also owe the bondholders a duty of care under common law trust principles. The trustee can act on behalf of bondholders in certain situations (see below for more details). Trust arrangements are a concept peculiar to common law jurisdictions and will not usually be recognised by civil law jurisdictions. In a bond transaction, the trustee is likely to be either a professional trust association (eg, The Law Debenture Trust Corporation), or a subsidiary of a bank or other financial institution, whose sole function is to act as a trust corporation.

19.2.4.3 Choosing between a trustee and a fiscal agency

The majority of bond issues will use a fiscal agency rather than a trustee, primarily because of cost considerations. However, there are specific circumstances in which a fiscal agent is insufficient and a trustee must be appointed. These include the following.

Secured issues

If the bonds are secured, a trustee is required to hold the security. This is primarily due to the impracticality of providing individual bondholders with a right to part of the security, which would have to be transferred every time the bond changed hands. Any such transfer may restart 'hardening periods' (see **14.9).** Therefore, the trustee holds the security on trust for all the bondholders from time to time. A fiscal agent cannot perform this function since it is the agent of the issuer and so acts in the issuer's interests.

Subordinated issues

If bonds are to be issued which are subordinated to (ie, ranking behind) the repayment of another bond issue, the same trustee may be appointed to both senior and junior issues to ensure effective subordination (although it is now quite common to achieve subordination contractually through the terms of the issue, creating 'contingent debt').

19.2.4.4 Advantages of using a trust arrangement

Under a trust arrangement, the trustee has legal ownership of any claims that the bondholders (ie, the beneficiaries) have against the issuer. There are advantages of using a trust arrangement for both the issuer and the bondholders.

Advantages for the issuer

The advantages of using a trust arrangement from the issuer's perspective are based on the possibility of dealing with one sophisticated party representing the bondholders, rather than dealing with a group of individuals. For example:

(a) Only the trustee can act in the event of a default by the issuer (albeit that it can act only within the terms of the trust deed under which it is appointed, or on the direction of a specific majority of bondholders). This will usually lead to a more considered approach towards a default than might be the case if the bondholders could precipitate action individually. The issuer can deal with a professional trustee rather than a disparate group of potentially less sophisticated bondholders with varying views and requirements. Furthermore, many trust deeds will provide the trustee with authority to waive technical events of default where it sees fit. The trustee therefore protects the issuer from 'rogue' bondholders.

Interestingly, in *Concord Trust v The Law Debenture Trust Corporation plc* [2005] UKHL 27, the House of Lords held that if a trustee mistakenly called an event of default (ie when no event of default had actually occurred), this was not a breach of contract, but simply an 'ineffective action'. This is some comfort to trustees who had feared they might be sued for wrongfully calling a default; however, an action in tort (for negligence or interference by unlawful means) may lie in some circumstances (though not on the facts in *Concord*).

(b) A trustee can be given power to agree certain amendments to the terms of a bond without calling a meeting of bondholders (eg, to approve a restructuring of the issuer's group), providing the issuer with greater flexibility.

Advantages for the bondholders

There are a number of important advantages for a bondholder in creating an issue with a trust arrangement:

(a) If an event of default occurs, the bondholders can rely on a professional entity (the trustee) to pursue the situation on their behalf. Individual action by each bondholder, which can be expensive and difficult to pursue, is not necessary since the trustee will act on their behalf. Class actions are fraught with difficulties because of the variety and disparity of bondholders.

(b) Most bond issues are unsecured, and so if an issuer is facing financial difficulties, the bondholders are very vulnerable. A trustee acting on behalf of all the bondholders is more likely to achieve a moratorium, or a negotiated resolution with other creditors, than bondholders would if they acted as individuals.

(c)   If the bondholders need to make a collective decision, the trustee can chair any meetings and make recommendations.

(d)   After a default, an issuer must make any payment through the trustee rather than to individual bondholders. This avoids a powerful bondholder negotiating themselves a good deal at the expense of minority bondholders.

(e)   A trustee will have investigative and monitoring powers which a fiscal agent will not. It is not, however, usual practice in bond issues for the trust deed to create any specific duties of investigation for the trustee: it will usually act simply as a medium for receiving certain information, such as the issuer's annual accounts, notices and certificates of compliance which must be available for inspection by the bondholders. The common law duty to act with due diligence in the best interests of the beneficiaries (ie, the bondholders) is still applicable irrespective of the contractual requirements of the trust deed, for example, if the trustee is given the power in the trust deed to request financial information from the issuer then it has a positive duty to do so if it would be in the best interests of the bondholders.

19.2.4.5   Advantages of using a fiscal agent

The primary advantage to the issuer of appointing a fiscal agent rather than a trustee is cost. A trustee will require its own solicitor (whose fees must be met by the issuer) to advise on the trust documentation, and a trustee's fees during the life of the bond will reflect the substantial responsibilities it must undertake. By way of contrast, there is considerable competition to take the high profile and prestigious role of fiscal agent. This drives down the fiscal agent's fees, and it is not unknown for institutions to take on the fiscal agency role for no remuneration provided that they are also awarded another role in the issue (eg, as the common depositary bank).

19.2.5   Listing agent

When listing on certain exchanges a listing agent must be appointed by an issuer to communicate with the listing authority on its behalf, to lodge the necessary documents with the listing authority, and to advise the issuer on the listing rules and process (see also **21.8**). The concept of Listing Agent for the UKLA was removed with the introduction of the FSMA 2000 on 1 December 2001.

19.2.6   Principal paying agent and paying agents

A paying agent is an agent of the issuer responsible for co-ordinating payments of principal and interest under the bond. It will receive payment monies from the issuer and distribute them to the appropriate paying agents, who pay the bondholders resident in their jurisdictions. If an issuer uses a fiscal agent, it will usually take the role of principal paying agent. However, if the issuer uses a trustee structure (or if the fiscal agent does not have a 'presence' in a jurisdiction in which interest payments must be made) a principal paying agent (or further paying agents) will be appointed.

19.2.7   Depository and common depository

A depository is a bank appointed on behalf of a clearing system dealing with a particular issue to act as 'safe keeper' of the temporary global note, the permanent global note, and any definitive bearer bonds traded through a clearing system. If an issue uses more than one clearing system, each system must use the same depository and it will be known as the 'common depository'. There are only a limited number of international commercial banks which have been approved by the clearing systems to perform the role of depository. The common depository will hold part of an issue for Euroclear and part for Clearstream, and transfers can be made between the two systems (see **17.8**).

As well as providing a 'hole in the ground', using a depository also allows the bonds to be kept in jurisdictions other than those of the clearing systems, giving rise to tax and other advantages. The use of a depository to hold the bonds is sometimes known as 'immobilisation' (not to be confused with 'dematerialisation', whereby paper securities are dispensed with altogether, and the rights are recorded and traded electronically).

There is one circumstance in which a global note cannot be placed with a common depository. Some issuers will want their securities to be recognised by the European Central Bank as 'eligible collateral' for the euro central banking system (known as 'Eurosystem'). These securities can be used to support exposure in Eurosystem and so are popular with certain investors. From July 2006, securities are only eligible as Eurosystem collateral if their global form is held by the clearing system themselves and not at a common depository. This is known as a 'New Global Note' structure (or 'NGN') for bearer notes and 'new safekeeping structure' ('NSS') for registered notes.

19.2.8 Legal advisers

Separate legal advisers will be appointed by the issuer and the lead manager. If the issue involves a trust arrangement, the trustee will also instruct solicitors, although they will sometimes use the same firm as the lead manager with an 'information barrier' between the individuals acting for each party. Most bond issues are governed by English law. However, if the issue involves an overseas jurisdiction, irrespective of whether the bonds themselves are governed by English law, lawyers from that jurisdiction must be instructed to ensure compliance with local laws and regulations.

The role of legal advisers in an issue primarily involves the preparation of documentation (the principal documents will be produced initially by the solicitors to the lead manager – see **Chapter 21**). The solicitors will also be involved in the due diligence process, and will have to produce a legal opinion for the transaction.

19.2.9 Auditors

Auditors will be involved in the issue process whenever the issuer is an entity which produces accounts (primarily companies and certain quasi-governmental entities). The lead manager and its legal advisers will want to review the issuer's accounts for at least the previous three years. If the issue is to be listed, the audited accounts may have to be published, or incorporated by reference, in the prospectus (or listing particulars). The issuer's auditors will be asked to provide a comfort letter addressed to the lead manager and the syndicate, confirming that there has been no material change in the issuer's financial condition since the last published accounts, and a 'consent letter' consenting to the publication of their report in the offering document (see **19.3**).

19.3 DOCUMENTATION OF A BOND ISSUE

19.3.1 List of required documents

A typical bond issue involves a substantial number of documents. The principal documents required are listed below in two sections:

(a) documents relating to the underwriting, subscription and distribution of the bonds; and

(b) documents which relate to and constitute the bonds themselves.

19.3.1.1 Underwriting, subscription and distribution

(a) mandate letter;

(b) initial syndicate communication (formerly known as 'invitation telex');

(c) allotment confirmation (formerly known as 'allotment telex');

(d) prospectus or other offering document;

(e) subscription agreement (or underwriting agreement);

(f)   agreement among managers;

(g)   auditor's report and consent letter;

(h)   auditor's comfort letters;

(i)   legal opinions.

19.3.1.2   Bonds and related documents

(a)   fiscal agency agreement (including paying agency agreement) (or trust deed);

(b)   paying agency agreement (if no fiscal agent);

(c)   temporary global note;

(d)   permanent global note (or definitive form bond);

(e)   deed of guarantee (if the issue is guaranteed and there is no trust deed);

(f)   deed of covenant (if no trustee, and bonds are in permanent global form).

19.3.2   Mandate letter

Once the issuer has awarded an institution the mandate to act as lead manager for the proposed bond issue, there will be a series of meetings and/or an exchange of correspondence which results in a letter (or sometimes telex or fax) which confirms the fundamental terms of the issue. This is known as the 'mandate letter'. It will also authorise the lead manager to announce the issue and allow them to invite other institutions (co-managers) to form a syndicate which will distribute the issue. The mandate letter is usually prepared by the lead manager.

19.3.3   Initial syndicate communication

The initial syndicate communication (formerly known as the 'invitation telex') is the document sent by the lead manager to prospective co-managers (lead managers and co-managers together form the 'syndicate') inviting them to participate in the issue by subscribing for the bonds on their issue. If the issue is being underwritten (see **19.3.6**) the communication will also request the co-managers to give an underwriting commitment. The initial syndicate communication is prepared and sent, by e-mail, by the lead manager (having usually been checked by its solicitors) on the day the issue is launched (see **21.7**).

The requirement to send an initial syndicate communication, and its minimum content, are governed by ICMA rules. The communication must provide summary information about the issue and its basic terms and conditions. It may also provide a brief description of the issuer and its business, as well as any guarantor, and will also outline the timetable of the issue.

19.3.4   Allotment confirmation

Once they have received a response from the co-managers indicating the level of investor interest they have each garnered, the lead manager decides how to allocate the issue: allocation is at the sole discretion of the lead manager. In a traditional 'retention' structure, the lead manager then notifies the co-managers of their allocation (which the co-managers will then on-sell to their investor clients). Where a 'pot' system is used, the co-managers reveal the identity of the investors they have identified to the lead manager, who then notifies them directly of their allocated amount. The investors will then pay the purchase price to the lead manager, who in turn pays the co-managers a commission for finding the investors. The pot system is just a way of dealing with allotments and does not affect underwriting obligations of the co-managers. Payment and transfer instructions will also be provided, which the lead manager will give to the clearing system at closing (see **21.10**).

ICMA rules require that allotments are made within 24 hours after the launch of the issue.

19.3.5 Prospectus or listing particulars

The prospectus is the document which provides detailed information about an issue for potential investors. If the issue is to be listed on the London Stock Exchange Professional Securities Market ('PSM') then this document is known as the 'listing particulars'. Since these 'selling documents' are at the heart of any bond issue, they are examined separately in **Chapter 20**.

19.3.6 Subscription agreement/underwriting agreement

The subscription agreement is a contract between the issuer, the lead manager and the co-managers which records the basis on which the issuer will sell, and the managers will buy, the bonds on issue. The syndicate members will be subscribing for the bonds on the basis that they will keep very few, or none, of those bonds for themselves ('for their own book'). Before they agree to subscribe (ie, before they sign the subscription agreement) the syndicate members will have lined up investors who want to take the bonds.

As explained at **19.2.3**, most London market bonds work on the basis that the syndicate will subscribe for all of the bonds between them, even if they cannot place them with investors. Under the terms of the subscription agreement, the liability of the syndicate members to the issuer of an issue is joint and several (compare this with a syndicated loan in which each bank's liability is restricted to its commitment). Therefore, whilst the managers will agree between themselves how many bonds they will each subscribe for (in the 'agreement among managers'), the subscription agreement allows an issuer to require any one manager to subscribe for the entire bond issue if necessary. If the issue uses underwriting banks instead, the subscription agreement will contain the terms of the underwriting (and may be called an 'underwriting agreement').

The subscription agreement will also cover the following matters:

(a) Conditions precedent to the issue. These might include legal opinions to the managers, auditors' consent and comfort letters, and a closing certificate confirming there has been no material adverse change to the issuer's representations and warranties.

(b) The pricing of the issue (ie, the interest rate payable on the bonds and, if appropriate, the price at which convertible bonds can be converted into shares).

(c) Fees and commissions payable to the managers. These will usually include a 'selling commission' (also known as a 'selling concession') and a 'management/underwriting commission', both calculated as a percentage of the principal amount of the bonds.

(d) Costs and expenses to be paid by the issuer. These are likely to include costs in connection with preparing and printing the bonds and documentation of the issue, any costs of listing, advertising costs, and the fees and expenses of the trustee (if one is used). There is also likely to be a provision under which the issuer pays for all or part of the syndicate's legal costs.

(e) Representations and warranties given by the issuer to each of the managers. These will include representations of fact, for example that any (material) information supplied by the issuer in connection with the issue (particularly with respect to the offering circular) is true and accurate in all material respects, as well as representations of law, for example that the issuer is validly existing and incorporated (the subscription agreement will also contain indemnities given by the issuer to the managers in respect of any misrepresentation).

(f) A representation from the managers that they will comply with all applicable selling restrictions (see **18.2.1**).

(g) A force majeure clause (see **9.7**), allowing the lead manager to terminate the syndicate's obligations under the subscription agreement (other than pre-existing liabilities). Force majeure is typically triggered when financial, political or economic conditions change such that the lead manager believes they are likely materially to prejudice the success of the issue. There is a standard ICMA force majeure clause which is usually used.

19.3.7   Agreement among managers

The agreement among managers is a contract between the lead manager and the co-managers. Its main purpose is to record the number of bonds which each member of the syndicate has agreed to take. However, the agreement also covers payment and allocation of the managers' commission (these are governed by ICMA rules). The agreement among managers also delegates power to the lead manager to act on behalf of the syndicate in certain circumstances. ICMA has produced a standard form of agreement among managers which is incorporated by reference in most bond issues.

19.3.8   Auditor's report, consent letter and comfort letters

The prospectus or other offering document may include extracts from the latest set of accounts for the issuer, but not necessarily the entire set of statutory accounts filed at Companies House. The issuer's auditors will therefore be required to 'sign off' on the extract to confirm it is consistent with the annual accounts (the 'auditor's report').

The auditors will be asked to provide a consent letter containing the report and consenting to the printing of their report in the prospectus (or listing particulars), and comfort letters, addressed to the managers, which essentially confirm:

(a)   that there has been no material adverse change in the issuer's financial position since the latest audited accounts; and

(b)   that any unaudited financial information contained in the offering document is correct.

There will usually be two comfort letters, the first given at the execution of the subscription agreement (the 'signing'), and the second, updating the first, at the time of the closing. The comfort letters are as important to the managers as the legal opinions, and will be legally binding on the auditors (although auditors will often attempt to limit their liability).

19.3.9   Legal opinions

Legal opinions are required by the lead manager and (usually) the co-managers and the trustee. One legal opinion will be required from the lead manager's solicitors with respect to the binding nature of the documentation, and a second will be required from the issuer's solicitors confirming the due incorporation of the issuer, that all necessary consents have been obtained, the position regarding taxation, and enforceability of the contractual documents against the issuer. Opinions from local lawyers will be required if the issue involves other jurisdictions.

19.3.10   Fiscal agency agreement

The fiscal agency agreement is a contract between the issuer, the fiscal agent (as fiscal agent and principal paying agent), and any other paying agents which have been appointed. The fiscal agency agreement records the structure through which the bondholders will receive payment of coupon and principal. Payments to bondholders are made through paying agents, because the issuer will not have the administrative capability to make the payments itself. If the issue uses a trust arrangement then it will require a 'principal paying agent' (usually a bank); if a fiscal agent is used, it will perform the function of a principal paying agent. Further paying agents will need to be appointed if an issue requires payments to be made in jurisdictions outside that of the principal paying agent (although they will often be branch offices of the principal paying agent).

Bonds will usually be held in a clearing system, and so payment will involve funds flowing through that system.

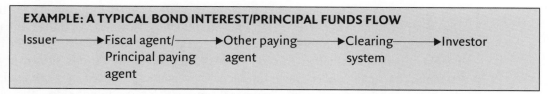

EXAMPLE: A TYPICAL BOND INTEREST/PRINCIPAL FUNDS FLOW

Issuer ──▶ Fiscal agent/ ──▶ Other paying ──▶ Clearing ──▶ Investor
Principal paying   agent   system
agent

The fiscal agency agreement will also document the following matters:

(a)   the procedure for authentication of the temporary global note and definitive bonds;

(b)   the process necessary to exchange the temporary global note for definitive bonds;

(c)   the issue of replacement bonds (eg, on loss or theft of the original);

(d)   the procedures for convening the bondholders' meetings;

(e)   fees and expenses of the paying agents.

The fiscal agency agreement will also contain the full terms and conditions of the bonds, as well as the forms (if any) of temporary global notes, permanent global notes and definitive bonds, which will appear in a schedule to the agreement.

19.3.11   Paying agency agreement

If a bond issue uses a trust arrangement, the trustee is not responsible for making any payments of coupon or principal. A 'principal paying agent' (together with any other paying agents if necessary) must be appointed under a separate agreement with the issuer. This is known as the 'paying agency agreement', and it will cover similar payment matters to the fiscal agency agreement (see **19.3.10**).

19.3.12   Trust deed

If a trustee is employed as opposed to a fiscal agent (see **19.2.4**), a trust deed will be required to cover the following matters:

(a)   creation of the trust relationship;

(b)   the trust property (the issuer's covenant to pay);

(c)   the trustee's powers and duties;

(d)   appointment and removal of the trustee;

(e)   the requirements for, and organisation of, bondholders' meetings;

(f)   some monitoring of the issuer's financial position.

19.3.13   Deed of guarantee

Some corporate issuers (usually for tax reasons) may use a subsidiary company to issue securities and thereby raise finance for the parent or group. These subsidiaries may be formed solely for the purpose of the issue (often known as 'special purpose vehicles' or 'SPVs'), or they may be general finance vehicles through which the group does most, or all, of its financing. In either case they are often little more than shell companies with few assets. Such a company is unlikely to attain 'investment grade' status (see **17.11**), and therefore the parent company will need to guarantee the SPV's (or the finance vehicle's) obligations under the bond in order to lift the credit rating of the issue. The guarantee may be endorsed on the bond itself, or it may be made as a unilateral declaration of guarantee, by the parent company, in a deed of guarantee.

19.3.14   Deed of covenant

If a note is in permanent global form (ie, there are no definitive bonds) then the legal owner of the note is the common depositary bank since it is the bearer (holding the note on behalf of the clearing system). However, in the event of non-payment, the common depositary will not bring a claim against the issuer on the bondholders' behalf. Furthermore, whilst the global note is exchangeable for definitives, the issuer may be unwilling to comply with this condition if it is in a non-payment situation. The bondholders are left unable to enforce their claim.

One solution to this problem is to use a trust structure (see **19.2.4**), whereby the trustee holds the issuer's covenant to pay on trust for the bondholders. However, for those bond issues which do not use a trust structure, it is necessary to create a document which gives the bondholders a right to sue the issuer in accordance with their bond allocations shown in the clearing systems. That document is known as a deed of covenant: a promise to pay executed by the issuer in a deed poll (ie, a unilateral document), and which gives bondholders the right to claim against the issuer in accordance with their bond allocation shown on clearing system accounts.

19.4 TERMS AND CONDITIONS OF A BOND

19.4.1 Comparison with a facility agreement

The terms in a bond are generally both fewer and shorter than the terms in most commercial facility agreements. There are also standard terms for bonds which are used in international capital markets, and substantial variation from, or heavy negotiation of, the standard terms is unusual. The reason for this standardisation is to provide instruments which are familiar to investors, without complex terms, making them easily tradeable.

A bondholder will usually have five main concerns:

(a)   the issuer's and the issue's credit rating;
(b)   the amount of its investment;
(c)   the return it will receive on its investment;
(d)   when it is able to redeem its investment;
(e)   its rights on the issuer's default ranking pari passu with any other holders of the same or similar debt instruments of the issuer.

A bondholder will not be concerned with the detailed business of the issuer, or with intricate financial covenants unless it is a 'high yield' bond. Unlike the borrower in a loan transaction, the issuer of a bond will not make detailed representations and warranties to the investor. The issuer will provide information about itself and its finances in the prospectus (or listing particulars), and investors will normally rely on this in making their decision to invest. Liability for the content of these documents is discussed in **Chapter 20**.

19.4.2 Where are the terms and conditions found?

The terms and conditions of a bond govern how the instrument operates once it has been issued. Unlike most commercial loan transactions, a bond issue involves numerous documents relating to the funding. Several of those documents will contain a complete set of terms and conditions of the bond, for example:

(a)   in the temporary global note;
(b)   on the back of the definitive bearer (or registered) bond, or in the permanent global note;
(c)   as a schedule to the fiscal agency agreement (or trust deed);
(d)   sometimes in the paying agency agreement (if there is a trustee);
(e)   in the prospectus (or listing particulars).

The debt obligation is evident in the bond itself (whether in temporary global, definitive, or permanent global form) and is the property held on trust if a trustee is appointed (see the covenant to pay in the trust deed).

19.4.3 Specific terms and conditions of a bond

19.4.3.1 Preamble

The preamble is a short initial paragraph which may confirm the authorisation of the issue by the board (or other authorising body) of the issuer, and which lists the parties to, and dates of, all relevant contractual documents entered into in respect of the issue. This list will include the trust deed, fiscal agency agreement and paying agency agreement.

19.4.3.2 Form, denomination and title

This short clause will state the form (eg, bearer, registered or global) the bonds will take, the amounts in which they are issued (eg, US\$10,000 and US\$100,000 and also known as 'par value' or 'denomination'), and a statement as to how title to the bonds will pass (eg, for bearer bonds, title will pass by delivery).

19.4.3.3 Status

The status clause will specify the characteristic of the debt obligation and its ranking amongst other debt obligations of the issuer, indicating to the bondholder how it stands vis-à-vis other creditors of the issuer. Bonds are usually unsecured and rank pari passu with all other unsecured creditors. However, bonds may be secured or subordinated. (Banks may issue subordinated bonds so that the proceeds of the issue will supplement their 'Tier 2 Capital' for regulatory capital purposes: see **9.3.3**.)

19.4.3.4 Negative pledge

The negative pledge in a standard bond transaction will almost always be less onerous than the negative pledge required by the lenders in a commercial banking transaction (see **7.5.2.1**).

> **EXAMPLE**
>
> So long as any of the Bonds or Coupons remains outstanding, the issuer will not create or permit to subsist any mortgage, charge, lien or other form of security interest or encumbrance upon the whole or any part of its undertaking, assets or revenues present or future to secure any present or future indebtedness in the form of bonds, notes, debentures, loan stock or other securities, or any guarantee of or indemnity in respect of such indebtedness, unless the Issuer's obligations under the Bonds and the Coupons are secured equally and rateably therewith or have the benefit of such other security, guarantee, indemnity or other arrangement as shall be approved by an Extraordinary Resolution of the Bondholders.

This form of negative pledge simply ensures that the issuer will not issue debt securities ranking higher than the current issue, unless the bondholders of this current issue receive identical rights. Any stronger form of negative pledge would be unworkable, since (unlike restrictive terms in a facility agreement) it would require a bondholders' meeting to obtain a waiver of this term.

19.4.3.5 Coupon

If a bond carries a fixed coupon, the rate will be determined on or before the launch date, and the coupon will be payable annually in arrear. If the coupon is at a floating rate, the method of calculation is explained in the interest clause, and the coupon payment dates are specified. The coupon payment dates will usually be the same dates in the appropriate months depending on the commencement date of the issue itself (eg, if quarterly – 15 August, 15 November, 15 February and 15 May). Since those days may not be days on which banks are open, a 'business day' definition must be introduced into this condition (see **11.7**).

The 365/365 basis for calculating domestic loan interest was explained at **4.9**. For fixed rate bonds issued *before* 1 January 1999, the convention was to use the '360/360' basis in which each calendar month is treated as having 30 days, so that one-twelfth of the annual interest rate will accrue for each month irrespective of the actual number of days in that month. However, fixed rate bonds issued *after* 1 January 1999 usually use the 'Actual/Actual' convention. Unfortunately, there are at least three different interpretations of this convention, but the most commonly adopted will probably be the ICMA method (r 251), ie actual days elapsed over the product of the number of days in a coupon period and the number of coupon periods. For floating rate notes (and syndicated loans, for most currencies other than sterling), the 'Actual/360' or '365/360' basis is usually used. This applies the 'annual' rate (x%) to the principal sum as if it were x% per 360 days. Over a calendar year, therefore, the interest charged is actually slightly more than the 'annual' rate and is different for months of different lengths.

> **EXAMPLE**
>
> If the annual coupon is 6%, and the principal sum is £200, then the '365/360' basis requires interest of £12 to be paid every 360 days: ie 3.33p per day or approximately £12.17 per calendar year.

19.4.3.6 Payments

The mechanics for payment under a definitive bearer bond are relatively simple, requiring surrender of the bond for payment of principal, and surrender of the relevant coupon for interest. Surrender and payment are effected through the paying agents, who are agents of the issuer (in contrast with facility agreements where payments are made through the agent which is an agent of the lenders). Most bonds, however, will be held in clearing systems, and so payments will be made from the paying agents directly to the clearing systems which credit the money to the relevant cash account of each bondholder.

19.4.3.7 Redemption and purchase

The bond will usually specify three occasions on which it may be redeemed:

(a)   On maturity (usually 'at par', ie at face value).

(b)   For tax reasons. As with a facility agreement, an issuer will not want to maintain a bond issue if a change in tax law or practice renders its borrowing more expensive. A bond will therefore include a 'tax redemption clause' permitting redemption of the entire issue if, as a result of a change in tax laws, the issuer is required to gross up payments of interest or principal. The issuer must redeem the whole issue, and not just part.

(c)   Re-purchase. There is no legal reason why an issuer should not purchase its own bonds in the secondary market, and the terms will specifically permit this. However, if the bonds are listed on the London Stock Exchange, the Listing Rules generally require the issuer to notify all the bondholders of its intentions, through a Regulatory Information Service (RIS) – see Rule 12.5. Any purchases which are made by tender offer to the bondholders generally must be made to all the bondholders.

19.4.3.8 Taxation

An issuer will be required to gross up payments to investors in very limited circumstances, since the issuer has little control over the bondholder's identity and tax domicile. Any grossing-up obligation is usually restricted to taxes imposed by the issuer's own jurisdiction and would benefit only 'non-domestic' investors (see also **9.3.4**).

19.4.3.9 Events of default

The events of default in a bond issue are almost invariably less onerous and less detailed than in a facility agreement. Any default for non-payment of interest will have a grace period (often as much as 14 days) as a matter of course. Cross-default clauses are often subject to a high minimum threshold (ie, de minimis).

19.4.3.10   Prescription

The prescription period is the time in which a bondholder must claim principal and coupon, usually 10 years and five years respectively, from the due date for payment. The prescription periods avoid the issuer looking to statutes of limitation to limit its liability. At the end of the prescription period, the debt is actually extinguished not just action barred. (This is important to avoid the situation where an investor may search for an applicable jurisdiction with a limitation period which only views action barring as procedural, and with a longer limitation period than the prescription period.)

19.4.3.11   Replacement of bonds and coupons

This provision deals with lost, stolen, defaced or destroyed bonds. The risk to an issuer of simply replacing a 'lost' bearer instrument has already been mentioned: if the original bond is presented for payment, the issuer will have to honour the payment obligations on both original and replacement (this also applies to replacement coupons). The condition for replacement of bonds and coupons therefore provides that the bondholder claiming a replacement must indemnify the issuer in respect of any payments the issuer has to make on the original bond or coupon and pay all expenses of the issuer in making such a replacement (including any tax). Any mutilated or defaced bonds will have to be surrendered before a replacement is issued.

19.4.3.12   Meetings of bondholders and modification

The procedure for convening bondholders' meetings and the conducting of business thereat is provided for in the fiscal agency agreement (or trust deed). The trustee (or, if no trustee, the issuer) convenes meetings, either on its own initiative or at the request of bondholders holding at least 10% in aggregate of the principal amount of the bonds. Bondholder meetings are usually convened only when there is a problem with the issue or the issuer, or if any modifications of the terms and conditions are required. The conditions governing meetings are usually in standard form. Notice must generally be given to all bondholders through publication in an appropriate newspaper (eg, the *Financial Times*), and strict quorum requirements must be met for meetings to modify the terms and conditions. Matters on which bondholders might be asked to vote include the following:

(a)   a postponement, reduction or cancellation of principal or interest;

(b)   the release of any security or guarantee;

(c)   a change in the currency of the bonds;

(d)   waiver of any event of default;

(e)   appointment of a new trustee;

(f)   reorganisation of the issuer (eg, on a merger);

(g)   if there is no trustee, the appointment of a bondholders' committee to represent bondholders in a liquidation or reorganisation.

Under English law, there are no specific statutory requirements as to when a majority can bind a minority of bondholders. However, in order to protect the minority, English euromarket practice dictates that the majority of bondholders required to pass an extraordinary resolution is 75% (the matters listed above will usually require an extraordinary resolution). Certain civil law jurisdictions have precise statutory requirements as to which matters require a majority vote. A trustee is usually given power to approve minor modifications, or waive a minor breach of the terms and conditions, provided that such action is not materially prejudicial to the bondholders.

19.4.3.13   Notices

In a commercial loan transaction, the lenders' names and addresses appear in the parties clause, a schedule and on the signing pages of the loan document. However, the identity of bond investors will not be known, and therefore notice can be given only by one or more of an RIS, the FCA or a national newspaper (usually the *Financial Times* and, for issues listed on the Luxembourg Stock Exchange, the *Luxemburger Wort*) (see Rule 9.6). If bonds are listed on the London Stock Exchange, copies of any notices to bondholders must also be given to the Exchange. Notices of meetings for holders of London listed debt securities in bearer form must usually be placed in a leading national newspaper circulating in the UK, and a copy of the notice must be sent to the Company Announcements Office of the London Stock Exchange. When bonds are held in clearing systems, notices must also be sent to the systems, which have a duty to notify the relevant securities account holders.

19.4.3.14 Further issues

An issuer is usually permitted to issue further bonds with the same terms and conditions as the bonds in the issue: in other words, it may increase the size of the issue. Any such further issue will be allowed without the consent of the bondholders (which would be a time-consuming and difficult process). Any further issue will have the same ISIN number in the clearing systems and will be treated as part of the original issue once it has gone through the same 'lock up' provisions. In order for a further issue to be treated by the clearing systems as 'fully fungible' (ie, the new instruments are indistinct from those of the original issue), it must have exactly the same terms and conditions in all respects as the original issue.

19.4.3.15 Governing law and jurisdiction

These are standard boiler plate clauses (see **9.8**). The governing law will usually be English, with a submission to the non-exclusive jurisdiction of the English courts. For certainty and ease of enforcement, all documents in the issue process should have the same governing law.

CHAPTER 20

BOND PROSPECTUS AND LISTING PARTICULARS

20.1 INTRODUCTION

International bonds are usually listed, primarily for tax efficiency and because of investor demand (see **21.8.1**). The jurisdictions most commonly used for listing a London-based bond issue are Ireland, Luxembourg and of course London itself. All three of these bourses are subject to the EU penchant for market harmonisation in the guise of the Financial Services Action Plan and, more recently, Capital Markets Union. These projects focused on creating uniform disclosure requirements for securities prospectuses across the EU. This chapter looks primarily at a London listing for a stand-alone bond, and the requirements for producing a disclosure document to inform potential investors about the issue and issuer.

20.2 OBTAINING A LONDON LISTING

Listing a bond in London actually involves two (closely connected) separate events:

(a) admission to the 'Official List'; and

(b) admission to trading on one of two markets, one 'regulated' and one 'unregulated'.

These stages are described below.

20.2.1 Admission to the Official List

The phrase 'admission to the "Official List"' means satisfying the legal requirements for a London listing.

There is a veritable 'regulatory waterfall' which eventually ends in the 'pool' of listing rules. The bulk of the requirements derive from the EU regime which governs prospectuses. This regime was revised in July 2019 by a new Regulation (Regulation (EU) 2017/1129) and underlying legislation (including Delegated Regulations 2019/980 and 2019/979). The new regime is commonly referred to as the Prospectus Regulation or 'PD3' and replaced the previous EU prospectus regime in full. The relevant EU legislation has direct effect and does not need to be implemented in Member States, but Part VI of the UK Financial Services and Markets Act 2000 (and certain derivative regulations) is also relevant for a UK listing, empowering the Financial Conduct Authority (as the 'competent authority') to implement the

UK Listing Rules. The FCA delegates this task to a division known as the United Kingdom Listing Authority (the UKLA). Finally, the UKLA's implementation of the Listing Rules takes the form of the Listing Rules (LR), Prospectus Regulation Rules (PRR) sourcebook and the Disclosure Guidance and Transparency Rules (DTR) sourcebook in the FCA Handbook.

If a bond issue complies with the Listing Rules, it will be eligible for admission to trading.

20.2.2 Admission to trading

The phrase 'admission to trading' means placing the bond on one of the markets for listed securities run by the London Stock Exchange (LSE). Two markets involve listing:

(a)   The London Stock Exchange's 'Main Market' is an EEA 'regulated market', for the purposes of many EU Directives and Regulations. It has stricter rules than the Professional Securities Market (see below) and requires publication of a UKLA-approved disclosure document known as a 'prospectus' which complies with the Prospectus Regulation – see further below.

(b)   The Professional Securities Market (PSM) is an 'unregulated market' (that is, with 'locally created' rules) commonly used for bonds. It has a slightly more relaxed regime than the Main Market, although disclosure requirements are substantially based on the Prospectus Regulation, and results in publication of a UKLA-approved disclosure document known as 'listing particulars' rather than a prospectus.

For completeness, note that bonds may also be admitted to trading on a further exchange-regulated market, launched in mid-2017, known as the International Securities Market (ISM). In the case of the ISM, the disclosure rules were created by the London Stock Exchange (rather than the UKLA), and the London Stock Exchange (rather than the UKLA) reviews the admission particulars. Bonds admitted to the ISM may still benefit from a tax advantage (see **21.8.1**) but, unlike the PSM, there is no listing.

20.3   WHEN IS AN APPROVED PROSPECTUS REQUIRED?

A prospectus approved by the UKLA is essentially required (as a prerequisite) if a bond issue is to be offered to the public or admitted to trading on the Main Market. If the issuer's 'home state' (usually the jurisdiction of the issuer's incorporation in the case of equity, but subject to a case-by-case choice for many types of debt issue – see FSMA 2000, s 102C) is not the UK but the prospectus has been approved by another EEA 'competent' authority as satisfying disclosure requirements, the prospectus will be accepted by the 'host state' listing authority (eg the UKLA in the UK). This 'mutual recognition' or 'passporting' of a prospectus is usually subject to a few additional requirements such as a translation of the transaction summary (see **20.4.1.3**).

There are two groups of exceptions to producing an approved prospectus, one relating to the type of bonds and the other relating to the type of offer.

20.3.1 Bonds which are exempt from producing an approved prospectus

Certain exempt securities are listed in the Prospectus Regulation, the Prospectus Regulation Rules (PRR) sourcebook and also in Sch 11A to the FSMA 2000. These exemptions relate to very specific types of issue (for example, one guaranteed by an EEA government or local authority) and most are not usually relevant for a corporate bond issue.

20.3.2 Offer types which are exempt from producing an approved prospectus

Even if the bond is offered to the public, in the UK there are exemptions from producing an approved prospectus provided that the bond is not admitted to trading on a regulated market (eg if it is admitted to trading on the PSM rather than the Main Market in the UK). These exemptions are found in the Prospectus Regulation at Article 1.4 and are referenced in s 86 of the FSMA 2000 and in PRR 1.2.3. The exemptions focus on offers which are not targeting the 'general public'. For a corporate issuer, the main exemptions are:

(a) an offer which is made to or directed at 'qualified investors' (for example, governments, central banks and entities authorised or regulated to operate in financial markets);

(b) an offer which is made to or directed at fewer than 150 persons (other than 'qualified investors') per EEA State;

(c) the minimum consideration which may be paid by any person pursuant to the securities offer is €100,000 (or equivalent);

(d) where the securities have a minimum denomination of €100,000 (or equivalent), often referred to as a 'wholesale' offer;

(e) where the total consideration for the securities is less than €8 million. This exemption derives from Article 3.2 of the Prospectus Regulation.

20.4 CONTENTS OF A PROSPECTUS

20.4.1 Authority, format and general content

20.4.1.1 Authority

The UKLA derives its authority to insist upon the issue and publication of a prospectus or listing particulars from s 79 of the FSMA 2000, which provides that the Listing Rules can require that securities may not be admitted to the official list unless:

(a) listing particulars have been submitted to, and approved by, the competent authority and published, or

(b) in such cases as may be specified by listing rules, such document ... as may be so specified has been published.

20.4.1.2 General content

Assuming the bond issue requires a prospectus (see **20.3.1** and **20.3.2** for exceptions), Prospectus Regulation Rule (PRR) 2.1.1 replicates the general content requirements contained in Article 6 of the Prospectus Regulation on the 'necessary information' to be contained in the prospectus:

1. ... a prospectus shall contain the necessary information which is material to an investor for making an informed assessment of:

   (a) the assets and liabilities, profits and losses, financial position and prospects of the issuer and of any guarantor;

   (b) the rights attaching to the securities; and

   (c) the reasons for the issuance and its impact on the issuer.

The level of detail required in a prospectus will depend on whether it is a 'retail' (ie 'non-exempt') or 'wholesale' (ie 'exempt') offer. The 'wholesale' regime requires less detailed disclosure, but applies only if the securities are denominated at or above €100,000. A new feature from July 2019 permits lighter disclosure for smaller denomination securities which are admitted to trading on a professionals only segment of a regulated market.

20.4.1.3 Prospectus format

The format of a prospectus is outlined at PRR 2.2 which references Articles 6, 10 and 8 of the Prospectus Regulation. There are two options for stand-alone bond issues: either a single document or as three separate documents. The three separate documents are:

(a) a 'registration document', which contains information relating to the issuer;

(b) a 'securities note', which contains the information relating to the bonds; and

(c) for retail deals only, a 'summary', which must be written in a concise manner and with a maximum of seven sides of A4. The strict table format required under the old regime was replaced in July 2019 with a more flexible approach, albeit with fairly detailed specified content.

The advantage in using the three documents is that the registration document is valid for 12 months and so can be re-used for any number of issues during that period. However, most stand-alone issues use a single document format.

Lastly, Article 8 of the Prospectus Regulation (PRR 2.2.3) allows the issuer of a debt programme (eg an MTN programme) to use a 'base prospectus' (containing the main information on issuer and programme) and a 'final terms' document (which contains information on each particular securities issue under the programme).

20.4.1.4   Listing particulars

If a bond issue is to be admitted to trading on the PSM (this tends to be a minority), or is being admitted to trading on the LSE but does not require a prospectus under the Prospectus Directive, then listing particulars must be prepared. FCA Handbook, Listing Rule 4 details the content and format of listing particulars, and does so largely by incorporating selected parts of the Prospectus Regulation regime. Listing particulars will therefore usually look like a 'low fat' version of a PD3 prospectus.

20.4.2   Responsibility for information

The Prospectus Regulation permits Member States to determine prospectus responsibility. In the UK, s 84(1)(d) of the FSMA 2000 allows the PRR to specify who is responsible for a prospectus, and for a bond PRR 5.3.5 specifies that this includes:

(a)   the issuer;

(b)   anyone who accepts (and the prospectus states as accepting) responsibility;

(c)   the offeror (if this is not the issuer);

(d)   the person requesting admission to trading (if this is not the issuer);

(e)   any guarantor (in relation to information on them or the guarantee); and

(f)   anyone else who has authorised the contents of the prospectus.

In the case of a bond (and most other non-equity related securities) the issuer's directors are *not* required to take responsibility for the prospectus. In terms of disclosure about prospectus responsibility, Annex 7 of Commission Delegated Regulation 2019/980 (PR 2.3) requires each of those responsible to make a declaration in the prospectus along these lines:

> [ ] accepts responsibility for the information contained in this document. To the best of their knowledge and belief the information contained in this document is in accordance with the facts and does not omit anything likely to affect the import of such information.

Liability for errors and omissions is considered in more detail at **20.7**.

20.4.3   Key information relating to the issuer

For general prospectus disclosure, the Prospectus Regulation (and therefore the PRR in the FCA Handbook) makes a distinction based on the type of securities, the type of issuer and the denomination of securities. For bonds, different disclosure Annexes apply for 'wholesale' or 'retail' debt. For wholesale (or 'exempt') debt securities – that is, with a minimum denomination of €100,000 – the relevant disclosure annexes are Annexes 7 and 15. For retail (or 'non-exempt') securities – that is, with a denomination of less than €100,000 – the relevant disclosure annexes are 6 and 14. Additional or alternative disclosure annexes may apply depending on whether bonds are convertible, asset-backed or derivatives, or, for example, if the issuer is a bank or sovereign entity.

For the purposes of this chapter, the retail regime is used to illustrate the sort of information to be disclosed. The content requirements for wholesale debt are fairly similar, although, as might be anticipated, they are slightly less detailed (requiring fewer explanatory sections, in view of the greater experience of the investors likely to be buying larger denominations) and less stringent about the basis on which financial information must be prepared. Similarly, in most circumstances, there is no need to include a summary section at the front of the prospectus for wholesale debt.

The minimum disclosure requirements for information relating to the issuer under the more onerous 'retail' regime include the following:

20.4.3.1 Persons responsible

The responsibility statement mentioned at **20.4.2** above.

20.4.3.2 Financial information

Audited accounts covering the last two financial years (unless the issuer is under two years old) to include a balance sheet, income statement, cash flow statement and accounting policies. If the issuer prepares consolidated accounts it must use those in the registration document.

In the interests of creating a uniform disclosure, all financial information must be prepared in accordance with International Financial Reporting Standards (IFRS – see **6.9.5**) or a third country 'equivalent'. In the past, US, Japanese, Canadian, South Korean and Chinese GAAP have been determined to be 'equivalent' for EU purposes.

20.4.3.3 Risk factors

Issuers must also disclose risk factors that may affect the issuer's liability to fulfil its obligations under the securities. Risks must be specific to the issuer – for example, risks relating to an issuer's sphere of business or industry. From July 2019, risks must also be grouped into categories, with the most material risk in each category listed first.

20.4.3.4 Information about the issuer

Unsurprisingly, information about the issuer itself is considered vital. So the name, registration number, place and date of registration, registered office address and any 'recent events particular to the issuer which are to a material extent relevant to the evaluation of the issuer's solvency' must all be included.

20.4.3.5 Business overview

The prospectus must describe the issuer's activities, new products and markets. It must also include a statement that there has been no material adverse change in the prospects of the issuer since its last published audited accounts (or explanation why this statement cannot be made). Any profits forecasts or estimates are strictly regulated.

20.4.3.6 Administrative, management, supervisory bodies and shareholders

Names, business addresses and functions of directors (or equivalent) must be disclosed and, to the extent known to the issuer, the identity of any 'controlling' shareholders.

20.4.3.7 Material contracts and displaying documents

The prospectus must summarise any material contracts 'not entered into in the ordinary course of the issuer's business' which could result in any member of the group being under an obligation or entitlement that is material to the issuer's obligations under the securities. Finally, the prospectus must provide a hyperlink to certain 'display documents' (eg the memorandum and articles, reports, valuations, etc) which may be inspected.

This 'issuer information' appears in the registration document if a three-part prospectus is used.

20.4.4 Key information relating to the bonds

The minimum disclosure requirements for information relating to the bonds (where securities have denominations of less than €100,000) are outlined in Annex 14 of Commission Delegated Regulation 2019/980. They include the following:

20.4.4.1 Use of proceeds

The document must disclose why the money is being raised, the estimated total cost of the issue and some detail as to each principal intended use of the proceeds.

20.4.4.2 Information about the securities

Details as to the type (eg registered or bearer), currency, ranking, coupon, maturity and governing law of the securities must be included. The securities document must also give details of the terms and conditions of the offer, for example, the total amount, methods for paying up the securities and delivery back, pricing details, and the name and address of any paying agents.

20.4.4.3 Repeated information

Remember that the securities and registration documents may be issued as stand-alone documents, and so some of the information is common to both, for example the responsibility statement and risk factors. Under Article 19 of the Prospectus Regulation, an issuer may incorporate certain information by reference into the prospectus. However, there are limits on the scope of what may be incorporated and it must first have been approved by the competent authority of the Home Member State, or filed with or notified to the FCA and must be available via hyperlink. The summary document must not incorporate information by reference.

This 'bond information' appears in the securities document if a three-part prospectus is used.

20.5 GENERAL DUTY OF DISCLOSURE

Aside from the specific disclosure mandated in the PD3 regime Annexes, in drafting the prospectus it is important to remember the general overarching obligation in Article 6 of the Prospectus Regulation for a prospectus to contain:

> the necessary information which is material to an investor for making an informed assessment of:
>
> (a)   the assets and liabilities, profits and losses, financial position and prospects of the issuer and of any guarantor;
>
> (b)   the rights attaching to the securities; and
>
> (c)   the reasons for the issuance and its impact on the issuer.

The prospectus must therefore contain information which the market reasonably needs and expects to receive so as to make an 'informed assessment' of the issuer's general position and the rights attached to the securities.

Article 6 also states that in determining what information is required to comply with this obligation, account must be taken of 'the type of securities and their issuer'. The information must be written in an easily analysable, concise and comprehensive form.

There is a similar general disclosure obligation for listing particulars in s 80 of the FSMA 2000, which also requires consideration of:

(a)   the nature of the persons who are likely to consider acquiring the securities;

(b)   the fact that certain matters may reasonably be expected to be within the knowledge of professional advisers of any kind which those persons may reasonably be expected to consult; and

(c) any information available to investors or their professional advisers by virtue of requirements imposed by listing rules, by any other legislation or by a recognised investment exchange.

Finally, the Prospectus Regulation now requires all 'retail' prospectuses (for securities with denominations of less than EUR 100,000) to be drafted in 'plain language'. In the case of the UK FCA, this is likely to reflect the previous UK approach to retail prospectuses where some additional descriptive text and guidance for investors on how to navigate the prospectus was mandated for securities targeted at retail investors, largely as a 'consumer protection' measure. It is not yet clear how other EEA jurisdictions will address the new 'plain language' requirement for retail prospectuses.

20.6 PROSPECTUS DIRECTIVE REGIME AND 'GRANDFATHERING'

Although the Prospectus Directive regime (Directive 2003/71/EC, as amended) was replaced in full from July 2019, issuers may continue to use a prospectus approved prior to 21 July 2019 under the national laws which implemented the Directive for the remainder of the 12 month life of the prospectus – and even to supplement the prospectus under the old (pre-21 July 2019) rules.

20.7 OMISSION OF INFORMATION

In most cases, if certain information is mandated by the disclosure regime, the issuer's directors have little choice but to comply, however difficult or unpalatable that may be. The requirements for bonds are, however, generally less wide-ranging than for equity issues, reflecting the more sophisticated investor base of the former. The Rules list limited circumstances in which the UKLA can authorise the omission of information. Under Article 18 of the Prospectus Regulation (PRR 2.8), an exemption from the duty to disclose (whether that duty arises under the Rules, s 87A or s 80) may be granted if:

(a) disclosure would be contrary to the public interest, for example, information relating to important defence contracts;

(b) disclosure would be seriously detrimental to the issuer of the securities (provided that omitting the information would not be likely to mislead a potential investor as to any facts the knowledge of which is essential in order to make an informed assessment); or

(c) the information is of minor importance only and not such as to influence the assessment of the assets and liabilities, financial position, profits and losses and prospects of the issuer.

Since one of the issuer's responsibilities is to ensure compliance with the FCA Handbook, LR and PRR requirements, and to submit the listing particulars to the UKLA, both the issuer and issuer's solicitors will prepare the annotated copy of the listing particulars and the 'non-applicable' letter (see **21.8.3**). If it is within the specific requirements of the LR or PRR, or within the general duty under the FSMA 2000, the information must be included unless the UKLA allows omission. The consequences of failing to include the required information are examined at **20.7**.

20.8 LIABILITY FOR PROSPECTUS AND LISTING PARTICULARS

Misstatements in, and omissions from, the prospectus or listing particulars can give rise to both civil and criminal liability on the part of those responsible. All of the procedures outlined below apply to both a prospectus and listing particulars, but for simplicity this section refers only to 'prospectus'.

20.8.1 Civil liability

20.8.1.1 The Financial Services and Markets Act 2000

Compensation under s 90

Section 90 of the FSMA 2000 applies to both a prospectus and any supplementary prospectus (or listing particulars and supplementary listing particulars). It provides that anyone responsible for those documents is liable to compensate any person who acquires any of the securities and suffers loss in respect of them 'as a result of any untrue or misleading statement in the [prospectus] or any omission from them of any matter required to be included' under the general disclosure obligation. Certain defences are available, however.

Liability under the section is far-reaching. In this context, two points are particularly worthy of note. First, the section is concerned with a loss suffered by a person who has 'acquired' any of the securities. This may include not only the original investors on the marketing of the securities, but also subsequent purchasers on the secondary market. Secondly, the person concerned must establish that they suffered loss in respect of the securities 'as a result of' the offending statement or omission. Most commentators consider that this condition is satisfied if, for example, the price paid for the securities is higher than it would be but for the error or omission. It is not necessary for the investor to have relied on the prospectus in deciding to invest, or, indeed, even to have read them. That said, if the investor knows of the error or omission at the time of investing, their loss cannot be said to arise as a result of it.

Defences

A number of defences are available to a person facing a claim for compensation (see Sch 10 to the FSMA 2000):

(a)   That at the time the prospectus was submitted to the UKLA they reasonably believed, having made such enquiries (if any) as were reasonable, that the statement was true and not misleading, or that the matter the omission of which caused the loss was properly omitted. This is not sufficient on its own, however. The person must also establish one of four other facts, namely that:

    (i)   they continued in that belief until the time when the securities were acquired; or

    (ii)   they were acquired before it was reasonably practical to bring a correction to the attention of persons likely to acquire the securities in question; or

    (iii)   before the securities were acquired they had taken all such steps as were reasonable for them to have taken to ensure that a correction was brought to the attention of those persons; or

    (iv)   they continued in that belief until after the commencement of dealings in the securities following listing, and the securities were acquired after such a lapse of time that they ought in the circumstances to be excused.

(b)   Where the alleged loss arises as a result of an expert's statement, and that the person defending the claim reasonably believed that the expert was competent to make or authorise the statement in the prospectus and had consented to its inclusion in the form and context in which it was included. Again, this defence is available only if one of four facts, broadly similar to those referred to in paras (i)–(iv) above, is also established. This is not a defence for the expert in question. It is a defence for the issuer if confronted with a claim arising out of some error contained in an expert's report which forms part of the prospectus (eg, the accountants' report).

(c)   That before the securities were acquired they had published a correction 'in a manner calculated to bring it to the attention of persons likely to acquire the securities' (or, as the case may be, a statement that the expert was not competent or had not consented); or, at the very least, that they had taken all such steps as were reasonable for them to secure such publication, which they reasonably believed had taken place before the acquisition.

(d) That the loss arose from an official statement or one contained in a public official document, which had been accurately and fairly reproduced in the prospectus.

(e) That the investor knew that the statement was false or misleading, or knew the matter which had been omitted.

(f) Where the potential liability arose from a failure to provide a supplementary prospectus, and that they reasonably believed that the change or new matter did not warrant them.

20.8.1.2 *Hedley Byrne v Heller*: negligent misstatement

Misstatements in a prospectus may give rise to liability in tort under the rule in *Hedley Byrne & Co Ltd v Heller & Partners Ltd* [1964] AC 465. Liability arises if a person suffers loss having relied upon a misstatement and the person who made the misstatement owed a duty of care to the one suffering loss on the faith of it. For a duty of care to arise in these circumstances, a special relationship must exist between the person giving the information and the person relying on its accuracy.

Applying the principle to misstatements in a prospectus, it is thought that those assuming responsibility for the prospectus owe a duty of care to those applying for securities in the company on the marketing of those securities, but not to subsequent trading on the secondary market (see *Caparo Industries v Dickman* [1990] 1 All ER 568 and *Al Nakib Investments (Jersey) v Longcroft* [1990] 3 All ER 321). The inability of a subsequent purchaser to bring a claim for negligent misstatement contrasts with the position in relation to liability under the FSMA 2000 (see **20.8.1.1**); so too does the requirement that the claimant must have relied on the misstatement to their detriment.

20.8.1.3 The Misrepresentation Act 1967

A person may be able to rescind the contract for the acquisition of the securities and/or claim damages under the Misrepresentation Act 1967 if they acted upon an incorrect or misleading statement contained in the prospectus, or an omission from it. Under the 1967 Act, a claim for damages may be made only against the other party to the contract. So, for example, a manager, but not a purchaser in the secondary market, would have a claim against the issuer under the Act (see also **5.5.1**).

20.8.1.4 Contract

If an investor subscribes for and receives securities at the time of their issue (ie, in the primary market), they will have entered into a contract and the prospectus will form part of that contract because of the representations and warranties in the subscription agreement. If the prospectus is wrong or misleading, the investor may be entitled, under normal contractual principles, to rescind the contract and/or sue the other contracting party for damages.

As part of the subscription arrangements, the syndicate of managers generally obtain a number of warranties from the issuer (see **19.3.6**). These warranties are usually supported by appropriate indemnities. If an investor, who does not have the benefit of those warranties, brings a claim against a member of the syndicate, that syndicate member may seek recompense from the issuer under the terms of the warranties and indemnities.

20.8.2 Criminal liability

20.8.2.1 The Financial Services Act 2012 (FSA 2012), ss 89 and 90

Section 397 of the FSMA 2000 was repealed in April 2013 and replaced by new, similar offences in ss 89 and 90 of the FSA 2012. These sections make it a criminal offence for any person knowingly or recklessly to make a misleading, false or deceptive statement, promise or forecast, or dishonestly to conceal any material facts, if they do so for the purpose of inducing another person to enter, or offer to enter into a 'relevant agreement' (or refrain from doing so), or to exercise or refrain from exercising rights conferred by a relevant investment. Liability also attaches if the person is reckless as to whether such actions will produce this effect.

Section 90 of the FSA 2012 provides that a person is guilty of an offence if they 'do any act or engages in any course of conduct which creates a false or misleading impression as to the market in or the price or value of any relevant investments' if they intend to create that impression and thereby to induce another person to acquire, dispose of, subscribe for or underwrite those investments. It is also an offence recklessly or knowingly to create such an impression with a view to creating a gain for oneself or a loss for someone else.

A person charged with an offence under s 397(3) has a defence if *inter alia* they can prove that they reasonably believed that their act or conduct would not create such an impression.

Depending on the circumstances, a misstatement in the prospectus might give rise to charges on both counts. Each offence is punishable by imprisonment and/or a fine.

20.8.2.2 Other provisions

Errors in, and omissions from, the prospectus may also give rise to criminal penalties under other provisions, for example the Theft Act 1968 (misleading statements by a company's officers with intent to deceive the members or creditors) or the Fraud Act 2006 (fraud by false representation or by failure to disclose information where there is a legal duty to do so).

20.9 THE 'GOLDEN BELT' CASE

An interesting decision was delivered in *Golden Belt 1 Sukuk Company v BNP Paribas and others* [2017] EWHC 3182 (Comm) involving Sharia-compliant fixed income capital markets instruments known as 'sukuk', which are very similar to bonds. The case involved a key transaction document (a form of credit support known as a promissory note) which was not properly executed under Saudi law because the signature was laser printed rather than handwritten. The court held that an 'arranging' bank owed a duty to investors (ie holders of sukuk certificates) to exercise reasonable care to ensure the promissory note was properly executed. The claimant's losses were not decided at first instance and the defendant appealed, but the parties settled before the appeal could be heard. Despite the novelty of the decision and certain factual peculiarities of the case, it serves notice of a potential liability for arrangers, and at the very least they should ensure that they benefit from robust disclaimer language in the prospectus.

20.10 OTHER JURISDICTIONS

This chapter discusses liability for the information contained in listing particulars under English law only. Other jurisdictions may impose different liabilities, either statutory or common law, which may also apply to an issue irrespective of what law the issue is governed by as a result of the nationality of the investor. Liabilities imposed by US law can be particularly onerous.

ISSUING A BOND – THE PROCESS

Thank goodness for that . . . the last chapter!   David Adams

21.1 INTRODUCTION

Having briefly examined the parties and documents involved in a bond issue, this chapter concentrates on the actual process which an issuer must go through to issue the bonds.

One of the reasons why an issuer might choose to raise money on the euromarkets is the speed of the fund-raising process. The time between the issuer first instructing an investment bank to arrange the issue ('mandate') and when the issuer receives the money ('closing') may be as little as three weeks for a stand-alone bond (although five to six weeks is more usual). In order that an issue can be achieved this quickly, the bond market (through ICMA recommendations) has developed a guideline timetable for the issue process. Each party involved in the issue must be aware of the timetable, but it is usually the responsibility of the lead manager and its solicitors to monitor and 'police' the process.

21.2 THE STAGES OF A BOND ISSUE

The basic stages of a bond issue are as follows:

(a)   Mandate.

(b)   Due diligence.

(c)   Documentation process begins.

(d)   Marketing.

(e)   Launch and syndication.

(f)   Listing (both application to the UKLA and to the relevant exchange).

(g)   Signing.

(h)   Closing.

See Figure **21.1** below. This is the usual order in which each stage of the issue process occurs, although not every stage will be completed before the next one begins. The substance of each stage is explained below.

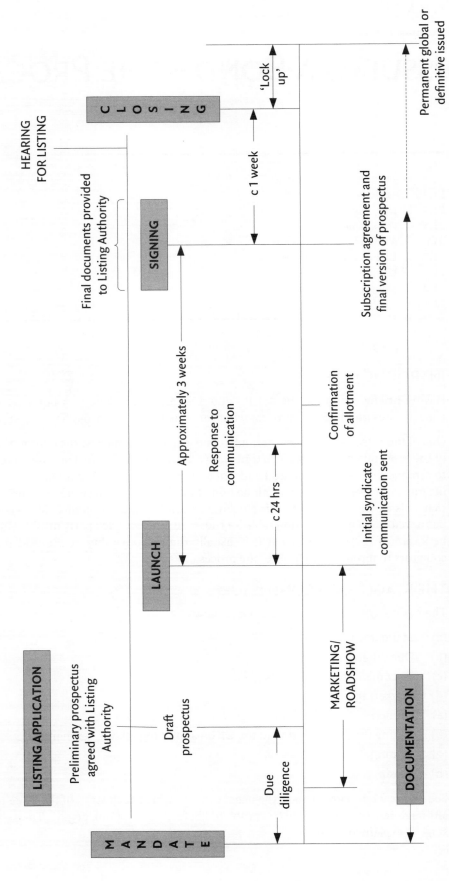

Figure 21.1 Paradigm timeline for a plain vanilla bond by a debut issuer

21.3 MANDATE

It should by now be clear that the question of the best way for a particular company to raise finance is a complex one. The company's directors will usually have lengthy meetings with investment banks and its own accountants before deciding whether an issue of debt securities is appropriate. Once the decision has been made, however, the first stage is for the company to instruct an investment bank to lead-manage the issue. This is known as the 'mandate'.

Once appointed, the lead manager will first advise as to the most appropriate structure for an issue (ie, which type of security) and the best market to target. For example, the lead manager may know that Japanese investors are particularly interested in the type of business the company runs, and suggest that the issue is targeted towards them. The lead manager will therefore approach its Japanese clients within its investor base, and will choose syndicate members which can 'bring in' Japanese investors.

The issuer and lead manager must first agree a number of important matters. These will include the marketing strategy, the decision whether to list, the identity of the fiscal agent (or trustee) and paying agents, and the fee structure. Once agreed, they will be recorded in the 'mandate letter' or 'term sheet', which is drafted by the lead manager. The basic terms and conditions of the bonds (such as price and status) will also be included in the mandate letter. The legal advisers will often have had little or no involvement up until the end of this mandate process.

21.4 DUE DILIGENCE

The due diligence process for a loan facility was explained in **Chapter 2**. Bond issues will also require a due diligence process in which the lead manager ascertains and verifies the information it needs for the issue (which is driven primarily by the information required to be included in the prospectus or listing particulars). The extent of the due diligence process will depend on a number of factors, including:

(a)   whether the lead manager already has a working relationship with the issuer;

(b)   the date of the issuer's latest audited accounts;

(c)   whether the issuer has previously issued euromarket securities and, if so, how recently;

(d)   the intended market for the issue (eg, an issue involving US investors will tend to require a more detailed due diligence process, since US investors are more litigious than most!);

(e)   the term of the bond (ie, the length of time until maturity);

(f)   whether the issue is rated: an unrated issue may require more due diligence than one which is fully rated; and

(g)   whether the issue is equity linked (eg, the debt is convertible into shares).

As a general rule, the due diligence process for an issue of equity linked securities will be more 'in depth' than for a straight debt issue, since investors in the former may become shareholders in the issuer (which represents a completely different risk to a straightforward debt investment).

The due diligence process will usually involve meetings between the lead manager and its solicitors, the relevant officers of the issuer (eg, the finance director, managing director, and other officers with particular knowledge of the business), and the issuer's auditors (both internal and external). The lead manager will usually conduct the meeting by asking detailed questions of the other parties in order to obtain sufficient information to be able to proceed with the issue and to prepare the prospectus (or listing particulars). An alternative approach to due diligence is for the lead manager to draft a list of detailed questions which is sent to the issuer. However, whilst this method is less time-consuming, it is also less flexible, and is more suited to frequent issuers, with high credit ratings, where there are likely to be few or no problems with the issuer and the information memorandum (or listing particulars) will be relatively straightforward.

The due diligence process helps with providing material for the prospectus (and listing particulars) and also in checking that appropriate matters are being disclosed. Although, ultimately, a prospectus is an issuer's document and the issuer will take full responsibility for the content, a lead manager has a vested interest in ensuring that the disclosure document for any deal with which they are associated is accurate and not misleading (see **20.6**). Obtaining the comfort letters in agreed form from the issuer's auditors (see **19.3.8**) is also part of the due diligence process following analysis of the issuer's accounts.

21.5 DOCUMENTATION

The principal documentation involved in a bond issue was discussed at **19.3.1**. The preparation and negotiation of these documents is the responsibility of the lead manager's solicitors. Preparation of the contractual documentation is expedited by the fact that most of the documents required for a bond issue comply with market accepted standards (eg, the agreement among managers will almost invariably use the ICMA standard form, and will not require any input by the solicitors). If the bond issue is to be listed, a draft of the prospectus or listing particulars must be sent to the appropriate listing authority. The UKLA usually requires a period of at least 10 working days in which to review a prospectus prior to its intended publication (or 20 working days if the issuer has not previously admitted securities to trading or made a public offer – see PRR 3.1.6). However, in any event, early application is encouraged, and most solicitors would want the draft particulars to reach the Authority at least three weeks before publication.

Preparation of some of the documents will continue through signing, and the process is only really complete on closing when the last documents of the issue are executed. The solicitors will prepare agendas for both signing and closing, which act as checklists.

21.6 MARKETING

An important role of the lead manager is to help the issuer's directors in making presentations to potential investors (these are sometimes known as 'roadshows'). The roadshows are intended to familiarise potential investors with the issuer's business and portray the issue as a good investment. The roadshow may be held in a number of different countries in order to widen the audience of potential investors, although they are not usually necessary for well-known issuers for whose securities there is usually a regular demand. Solicitors are not generally involved in the roadshow process; however, the roadshow material should be scrutinised by the solicitors and the lead manager's compliance department to ensure it complies with ss 21 and 25 of the FSMA 2000 (which put restrictions on advertising).

Sections 21–25 of the FSMA 2000 make it an offence for any person other than an 'authorised person' (ie, authorised to carry on regulated activity under the FSMA 2000) to 'in the course of business, communicate an invitation or inducement to engage in investment activity' (or to cause the same) in the UK, unless its contents have been approved by an authorised person (or an exemption applies). The prohibition is widely drafted, albeit with various exemptions.

21.7 LAUNCH AND SYNDICATION

The launch date is when the bond issue is confirmed by formal public announcement. The date will be agreed between the issuer and the lead manager. Launch must await the completion of any due diligence and marketing processes and will, so far as possible, be effected when market conditions are most favourable (eg, avoiding launches of other competing issues).

On the launch date, the issue will be announced to the market (usually through online trading screens) and the lead manager will send the initial syndicate communication to the financial institutions they have chosen to invite into the syndicate (the lead manager will already have spoken to the syndicate to gauge their interest, and so the invitation is merely a formal communication). The invitation shows the 'price' of the bonds (unless it is an equity linked deal, when pricing will not be made until the date of signing of the subscription agreement) as well as the fees and commissions the syndicate banks will receive. These are sometimes referred to as the issuer's 'all in cost' of funds, although it does not include legal fees, printing costs and agency fees.

The co-managers are usually required to respond to the invitation within 24 hours of receipt. Acceptance does not constitute a binding contract to subscribe: that is the purpose of the subscription agreement. It does, however, constitute a significant 'moral' obligation on the co-managers. Once all the co-managers have responded, the lead manager will know the level of interest in the issue, and can notify each co-manager of the number of bonds it is expected to take at issue by way of a confirmation of allotment. (Note that the sequence is slightly different if a 'pot' system is used – see **19.3.4**.)

Once the confirmation of allotment has been sent, the draft subscription agreement is sent to each co-manager. The ICMA recommendations allow the co-managers at least two working days in which to review the agreement before it is to be signed.

21.8   LISTING

A listed bond is one which is formally quoted, listed or capable of being traded on a recognised stock exchange. Bond issues are not always listed, either through choice or an inability to comply with the stock exchange requirements. Most listed bonds will be listed on the stock exchanges in London, Ireland or Luxembourg.

21.8.1   Reasons for listing

Unlike most share issues, bond issues are not generally listed in order to use the exchange as a marketplace. Most trading (even of listed bonds) will take place away from the exchange (known as 'over-the-counter' trading) between banks and other financial institutions by telephone or online. The primary reason for listing a bond issue is to demonstrate that it has satisfied the requirements of the exchange. Since those requirements are generally intended to protect investors, attaining listed status makes securities more marketable. Some entities, such as pension funds and unit trust funds, are precluded (by legislation, regulation or their constitution) from investing in securities which are not listed. An issue must therefore be listed to attract their funds.

One specific advantage of obtaining a London listing of bonds is the 'quoted bond exemption' from UK withholding tax. This exemption allows a UK issuer to pay gross interest on both bearer and registered bonds. A listing on a number of other stock exchanges, including Ireland and Luxembourg, will also enable the securities to qualify for the same exemption.

There are two main disadvantages associated with listing an issue: cost and timing. Listing authorities will charge a fee, whilst legal fees and lead managers' fees will be considerably higher for a listed issue because of the additional time involved in a listing application (particularly for a first-time issuer).

The timetable for issuing a listed bond will usually be longer than an unlisted one (particularly with respect to new issuers), because the UKLA will require time to review the documentation of an issue and the due diligence process will often be more in-depth.

21.8.2   Listing requirements

The requirements of the UKLA for admission to listing with respect to a bond issue are found in Listing Rule 2. The Stock Exchange reserves the right to impose any special condition it considers appropriate in the interests of protecting investors. Specific requirements of most types of bond issuer include the following:

21.8.2.1 Status

The issuer is duly incorporated (or validly established) and is operating in conformity with its constitution. If the issuer is a UK incorporated company, it must not be a private company.

21.8.2.2 Securities

The main conditions relating to the securities are:

(a)   the securities must conform with the law of the issuer's place of incorporation, be authorised under the issuer's constitution, and have any necessary statutory or other consents;

(b)   the securities must be freely transferable;

(c)   the securities must have an expected aggregate market value of at least £200,000 (unless securities of the same class are already listed). The Stock Exchange will allow a lower value if it is satisfied there will be an adequate market for the securities;

(d)   the entire class of a security must be listed;

(e)   convertible securities must convert into securities which are themselves listed on the London Stock Exchange or another 'regulated, regularly operating, recognised open market'.

The London Stock Exchange also has criteria for determining whether an applicant is suitable for membership.

21.8.3 Application procedure

The application procedure for listing bond securities on the UKLA Official List is found in LR 3, supplemented by LR 17, and in PRR 3. The main requirements of the procedure include the following:

21.8.3.1 '10 clear business day documents'

In general, issuers (through their sponsor) must submit two copies of specified documents to the UKLA at least 10 clear business days prior to their intended publication (see PRR 3.1.6). For a bond issue, these documents comprise the requisite application form, the prospectus (which must usually be annotated to indicate compliance with the relevant paragraphs of the Prospectus Regulation Rules), two letters (the 'non-applicable' letter and the 'omission of information' letter) explaining why certain information does not appear in the prospectus and requesting the omission of information respectively, with contact details of individuals who can answer any UKLA queries. The 10-day time limit will not strictly apply to a bond issue, although a later submission might risk a delay to the listing. The UKLA will return copies of the documents with any comments it has.

21.8.3.2 Marked-up documents

Any 10-day documents which the UKLA amends (or which are altered after submission to the UKLA) must be re-submitted with the changes marked up.

21.8.3.3 '48-hour documents'

Listing Rule 3.4.4 requires the following documents, in final form, to be submitted at least two business days prior to the consideration of the listing application:

(a)   a complete application for admission of the securities, and either:

    (i)   the approved prospectus or listing particulars; or

    (ii)   a copy of a prospectus approved by another Member State (under the 'passporting' regime).

21.8.3.4 Listing charge

On the day of consideration of the listing application, the issuer must pay the appropriate listing fee (Listing Rule 3.2.2).

21.8.4 Continuing obligations

The responsibilities imposed on an issuer do not end once its securities are listed. There is a variety of 'continuing obligations' which the Listing Rules and Disclosure and Transparency Rules require an issuer to fulfil, primarily with regard to disclosing financial statements.

21.9 SIGNING

A signing meeting is usually held within two weeks of the issue being launched, although it may be longer if the UKLA is slow to approve the prospectus. The signing is usually a simple meeting of the parties and their advisers, although it will occasionally be held as a more formal ceremony.

The lead manager and its solicitors must be sure that certain aspects of the issue process have been completed before the signing. Fundamentally, they must ensure that:

(a) the prospectus (or listing particulars) is in an agreed form (and agreed by the relevant listing authority);

(b) the other contractual documents (ie, paying agency agreement, trust deed (or fiscal agency agreement), legal opinions and auditors' comfort and consent letters) are in final form;

(c) the issuer (and any guarantor) has executed any resolutions necessary to authorise the issue, and has appointed an authorised signatory of the global note;

(d) the common depository has been appointed.

At the signing meeting, the subscription (or underwriting) agreement is executed by the issuer and the syndicate members, and takes contractual effect. If the issue is to be listed, final copies of the prospectus will be signed by the issuer to be sent to the UKLA. There is also a substantial number of peripheral documents to be produced and/or executed at the signing meeting, and the lead manager's solicitors will produce a signing agenda, which is distributed before the meeting, to ensure that nothing is overlooked.

21.10 CLOSING

The closing is the final stage of the issue process, and usually takes place approximately one week after signing. It is the time when the issuer receives its funds and the bonds come into being, creating the issuer's debt obligation.

The lead manager's solicitors will produce an agenda to ensure that all the necessary matters are completed. Essentially, there are two sets of procedures which must take place at closing: documentary procedures and payment procedures.

21.10.1 Documentary procedures

The following matters are the responsibility of the lead manager and its solicitors, and must be completed before the closing meeting:

(a) Admission to listing, if relevant, must be confirmed (subject to closing) by the relevant authorities.

(b) The conditions precedent to the subscription agreement must be satisfied.

(c) The auditors' closing comfort letter and the issuer's closing certificate must be in agreed form.

(d) The legal opinions must be in agreed form.

(e)   All other documents associated with the issue must be executed or in an agreed form (those that have been executed in advance will be held 'in escrow').

It is vitally important that as many of these matters as possible are dealt with before the closing date to minimise the risk of any problems. This is primarily because the lead manager and 'would be' bondholders will have ensured that funds are already in place, awaiting instructions for transfer to the issuer on a successful completion. Any delay or, worse still, cancellation of the completion will be very expensive. The closing meeting is traditionally attended by the issuer (or its solicitor if it has already executed the necessary documents), the lead manager and its solicitors, the depository, and the fiscal agent (or trustee). Nowadays, it is fairly common for documents to be exchanged via email and for closings to happen 'electronically'.

By the end of the completion meeting, the following documents should be executed (some may have been executed beforehand):

(a)   Trust deed (if appropriate).

(b)   Fiscal agency agreement or paying agency agreement.

(c)   Auditors' closing comfort letter.

(d)   Legal opinions.

(e)   Issuer's closing certificate.

(f)   Payment instructions from lead manager to the depository.

(g)   The temporary global note.

(h)   The permanent global note (if any).

(i)   Receipts between issuer and lead manager acknowledging payment and delivery.

The temporary global note is authenticated (ie, signed) by the fiscal agent (or paying agent) in order to give it legal effect, and is delivered to the depository for safe-keeping.

After closing, any documents still to be lodged with the UKLA (or relevant exchange) must be sent by the listing agent; the definitive bearer bonds (if relevant) must be security printed (this may take several weeks) and authenticated before the temporary global note is exchanged for the definitive bonds (alternatively, the temporary global note is exchanged for the permanent global note), in either case only after the relevant lock-up period.

21.10.2   Payment procedures

The payment procedures, also known as the 'closing mechanics', or 'payment against delivery procedures', involve the depositary and are adopted in most bond transactions. Co-ordination of the payment procedures is the responsibility of the lead manager.

21.10.2.1   Prior to closing

The lead manager will have notified the clearing system of the names and amounts of bonds to be allotted to the account of each syndicate member. Each syndicate member will also give payment instructions to the clearing system to the effect that its cash account is to be debited with the amount of money it must pay for the bonds, and the money credited to the lead manager's new issues account. The instructions are phrased so that the debit will be made only if the syndicate member is credited with the requisite number of bonds in its securities account (payment against delivery). The lead manager will also instruct the clearing system to debit its new issues account with the total amount of the issue to be paid to the account of the common depository, who will hold it until the temporary global note has been issued and delivered (ie, payment against delivery: see **21.10.3**).

21.10.2.2   At closing

The following matters occur 'simultaneously' at closing. The lead manager will authorise release of its payment instruction to the depository to transfer the money (already placed with the depository) representing the issue amount to the issuer. The depository will then transfer that money to the issuer's bank account once it receives the temporary global note.

The closing is now complete: the issuer has its funds and the depository holds the temporary global note on behalf of the clearing system. The clearing system will have credited the securities accounts of each syndicate member with an interest in the number of bonds for which they have subscribed, and each of their respective cash accounts will have been debited with the appropriate amounts.

21.10.3   Payment against delivery

Figure 21.2 below shows the flow of payments and bonds at closing for both Euroclear and Clearstream participants.

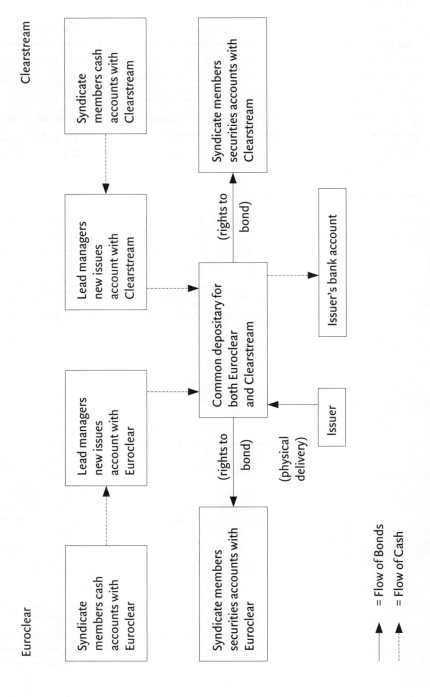

Figure 21.2 Closing procedures payment against delivery (Classic Global Note structure)

Glossary

Acceleration	Declaring a loan due and payable before the scheduled repayment date, usually as a result of an event of default
Accordion facility	Also known as a 'trombone facility', it allows the borrower to approach some or all syndicate members after signing and request an extension of available commitment. It is uncommitted, but if the borrower persuades some banks to lend more, the other syndicate members cannot object to the increased commitment being added to the loan
Accrued interest	The interest which is being earned on a loan, bond or other security on a daily basis between two interest payment dates. Secondary dealings in securities such as bonds or notes will usually take place on an accrued interest basis so that they will be bought and sold at a price which includes the accrued interest, ie market price plus interest which has been earned on that loan, bond or note but not yet paid (sometimes known as the 'dirty price')
Advance	A utilisation of money under a loan facility (now more commonly known as a 'loan')
All in cost	The entire cost of the transaction quoted to the borrower or issuer by the lenders or lead manager, which includes fees payable to the lenders or managers. All in cost will not usually include legal costs
Alphabet facilities	A facility with different tranches of debt repayable at different times, and usually labelled 'A', 'B' and 'C' facilities
Amortisation	The repayment of a debt in stages
Ancillary facility	A bilateral facility, for example an overdraft or derivatives facility, between a borrower and one of its syndicate banks which is drawn as part of a syndicated revolving credit facility
Arbitrage	Making a profit through the small differences in price between markets, for example buying shares on the Tokyo exchange and selling them in Singapore. Usually low risk, but requires high volume to make money
Arranger	Usually, the bank or financial institution responsible for arranging a loan transaction (including the syndication)
Asset backed security	A security which has its interest and capital repayments provided by a generic group of assets (eg, mortgages) which produce income (aka securitisation)
Asset stripping	Acquiring a business with a view to breaking it up and selling the most lucrative parts rather than developing it (euphemistically: 'rationalisation')
Authentication	In securities issues, the physical signing by the fiscal agent or principal paying agent of a security (eg, bond or note) in order to give it legal effect
Authorised institution	Under the provisions of the Financial Services and Markets Act 2000, in the UK only 'authorised institutions', as defined in the Act, may accept deposits in the course of a deposit-taking business

Availability period	The time during which a borrower may draw down (or 'utilise') advances under a loan (also known as 'commitment period')
Back office	The various 'non-profit centre' operational departments of a bank or financial institution which deal with the 'behind the scenes' activities of the organisation (eg, the settlement and accounts departments). 'Front office' activities include trading and lending
Balloon repayment	A final repayment of principal on a loan transaction which is substantially larger than earlier repayment instalments
Bankers' acceptance	A bill of exchange, drawn on and accepted by a bank. By accepting the bill of exchange the bank is accepting full liability to pay the bill on maturity as the primary obligor
Base rate	A fluctuating interest rate, peculiar to individual banks and used by them as a reference point for lending rates to individuals
Basis point	One hundredth of one percentage point (eg, 45 basis points is 0.45%)
Bells and whistles	Additional features of a debt transaction which are designed to attract investors
Bible	Complete set of conformed copy documents relating to a particular transaction
Bilateral facility	A loan facility between one bank and one borrower
Bill of exchange	A form of short-term IOU widely used to finance trade and provide credit
Bona fide	In good faith. A bona fide purchaser is one who believes they are entitled to buy, and the seller is entitled to sell
Book loss or gain	The difference between the original cost or book value of a security and its current market value (excluding accrued interest), ie an unrealised loss or gain
Brady bond	Paper issued in exchange for distressed commercial bank debt (particularly emerging market countries)
Bridge financing	Interim financing used before the intended long-term financing is put in place
Broker	A person or institution acting as an agent for buyers and/or sellers and charging a commission for its services, but who does not buy for its own account
Bullet repayment	Repayment of a debt obligation in a single instalment at the maturity date of the debt (ie, no amortisation)
Business day	A day on which banks are open for business in the relevant financial centre
Call option	In relation to a bond or note issue, a term which gives the issuer the right, but not the obligation, to redeem its securities before their specified maturity, normally at a specified price on a specified or determinable date. A premium may be payable on the exercise of the call option (cf 'put option')
Carve out	An exception to a representation or undertaking
Certificate of deposit	A negotiable bearer instrument evidencing a time deposit with a commercial bank, either interest-bearing or issued at a discount

Clawback clause	A clause enabling one party to retrieve money already paid out. Often found in the agency provisions of syndicated facility agreements enabling an agent to recover money already paid out by it to a party, wrongly believing that the agent had received the corresponding payment from another party. This allows an agent to distribute money (eg, repayment instalments) to the bank syndicate without confirming receipt of the payment from the borrower, knowing that if it does not receive the monies from the borrower it may 'clawback' the monies paid out to the syndicate
Clean down	A requirement for the borrower to reduce its drawing under a revolving credit facility to zero (or a specified reduced amount) for a given period (eg, five days in every year) to demonstrate it is not being used for capital expenditure
Clean-up period	The period (commonly 90 days) after an acquisition during which the new owners are allowed to remedy any events of default without the banks taking action
Clearing system	An organisation through which purchase and sale transactions of securities are handled and cleared. The main systems in the euromarkets for bonds and notes are Euroclear and Clearstream
Club loan	A facility provided by a small number of banks taking a similar level of commitment
Collateral	The assets over which security is granted
Commercial paper	Very short-term debt securities (eg, between a week and a few months' maturity) issued under a programme typically by borrowers requiring working capital funding
Commitment	The specified amount of money agreed to be lent by a bank in a 'committed facility', or agreed to be invested by a manager in a bond or note issue
Commitment fee	An annual percentage fee payable to a bank on the undrawn portion of its 'commitment' under a 'committed facility'. The commitment fee is usually paid quarterly in arrear
Commitment period	See 'Availability period'
Committed facility	A financing or credit arrangement in which a bank is obliged to lend up to a certain agreed limit of money for a defined period of time, usually subject to a predetermined set of conditions
Conformed copy	A record copy of a final executed document in which all signatures and any other handwritten words (eg, dates or alterations) are printed in typed form. Conformed copies are used to make up the transaction 'bible'
Coupon	Refers to both the stated rate of interest on a bond or note, and also to one of a series of actual coupon certificates attached to a bond or note, evidencing interest payable at a specified date
Credit default swap (CDS)	A derivative used to hedge risk against default of an entity ('reference entity') or specific lending obligation (the 'reference obligation'). Essentially, the buyer pays a premium to the seller of the CDS to buy protection against loss on default. If the entity or obligation defaults, the seller will pay the buyer the par value of the defaulted obligation (usually a loan or bond): in return the buyer usually has to transfer the obligation in question to the CDS seller to recover what it can

Cross default	An event of default triggered by a default in the payment, or the potential acceleration of repayment, of other indebtedness of the same borrower or issuer
Data room	A place in which information about a target company up for sale can be viewed by potential purchasers. It may be a room at the vendor's solicitor, or may be a 'virtual' room online
Debt push down	Usually refers to moving debt around a group of companies (typically from parent companies down to operating companies) to maximise tax advantages. For example, an operating company making profits can use interest payments to reduce its corporation tax, whereas a holding company earning only dividends cannot
Deep discount securities	Non-interest bearing securities issued at a large discount to their face value
Dematerialised	Usually referring to securities which are not represented by physical certificates but are traded through an electronic exchange
Derivatives	Financial instruments that derive their value from underlying financial products and markets such as interest rates, exchange rates, share prices, etc (examples include options, futures, swaps)
Discount	The difference between the price of a security and its face value
Distressed debt	Debt which is, or which the lender believes will be, non-performing (ie, repaid late, partially, or not at all) and which is usually sold for substantially less than the value of principal outstanding ('below par')
Double dipping	A means of structuring finance leases to utilise the tax benefits on capital investments in more than one jurisdiction
Double taxation treaty	An agreement between two countries intended to limit the double taxation of income and gains, under the terms of which an investor in one country may be able to apply for an exemption or reduction in the taxes imposed on their income or gains by another country, or from their own country on the basis that such income or gains have already had tax levied on them. This type of treaty encourages trade and financial transactions between countries
Drag along	Usually refers to certain investors being forced to accept something if a percentage of other (usually higher ranking) investors voted in favour
Drawdown	See 'Utilisation'
Drawstop	An event under a loan facility which prevents a borrower from utilising the loan
Earn out	In an acquisition finance, where the purchase price for the acquisition varies in accordance with the performance of the business post acquisition
Eligible bill	A banker's acceptance which can be re-discounted at (ie, sold to) the Bank of England
Emerging market	A jurisdiction in which the debt and capital markets are new or developing areas (often 'developing' countries) (see also 'LDC')
Equity cure	In an acquisition financing, the ability of the private equity 'owners' to put cash into the borrower which is treated as reducing debt or increasing profit (or cashflow) to 'cure' what would otherwise be a breach of financial covenants

Equity kicker	A warrant or option to buy, or exchange, debt for equity and which is attached to certain debt instruments (generally found in leveraged management buy-outs)
Equity of redemption	A chargor's right to reclaim secured assets on repayment of the secured debt with interest and costs
Escrow arrangement	Documents held 'in escrow' are executed documents given by one executing party to a third party (usually a solicitor) to hold to its order until a certain condition is satisfied, or event occurs. On the satisfaction of such condition or occurrence of event, the third party will usually be obliged to release the documents out of escrow to the other executing party
Exploding bridge	A facility in which the interest rate increases dramatically after a given period to act as an incentive to the borrower to refinance the facility
Face value	The nominal or par value of a security, rather than its market value at any particular time. It will be the amount due to the holder of the security on its maturity but exclusive of any interest or premium
Facility office	The branch or office of a bank through which the funds for a facility are provided. Also known as the 'lending office'
FCA	The Financial Conduct Authority is one of three new bodies (see also FPC and PRA) which took over regulatory functions from the Financial Services Authority in 2013. The FCA has responsibility for conduct issues across the financial services industry.
Finance lease	A means of financing whereby one lessee acquires the use of an asset for most of its useful life (eg, an aircraft). Lease payments during the life of the lease are sufficient to enable the lessor to recover the cost of the asset, plus a return. The lessee takes the risks and rewards of ownership (so, eg, is responsible for insuring the asset), and may acquire the asset at the end of the lease
Finance vehicle	A subsidiary company, usually incorporated 'offshore', for use by its parent company for issuing debt securities and then 'on lending' the proceeds to the parent or other companies in the group. The finance vehicle (aka 'special purpose vehicle') will be used only for these purposes and is unlikely to have any assets of its own. The issue of securities by a finance vehicle will therefore have to be guaranteed (usually by the parent company)
Foreclosure	A rarely used form of security enforcement which involves extinguishing the chargor's equity of redemption
FPC	The Financial Policy Committee is one of three new bodies (see also FCA and PRA) which took over regulatory functions from the Financial Services Authority in 2013. The FPC has responsibility for macro prudential regulation
Front end fee	A fee calculated as a percentage of the principal value of a loan or issue of securities, which is payable once at commencement of the loan or at issue of the securities, as opposed to an annual percentage fee payable each year (also known as 'arrangement fee')
Front running	A practice, usually prohibited in the commitment letter, in which an arranger sells part of its commitment outside of the normal process during primary syndication, thereby achieving an advantage over other arrangers in the syndicate

FSA	Financial Services Authority. Now abolished, but responsible for regulating the UK financial services industry between 2001 and 2013. The FSA's functions are now the responsibility of the PRA and FCA
FSMA 2000	The Financial Services and Markets Act 2000
Fungibility	An object is said to be 'fungible' if it can be replaced by another object and still fulfil any obligation to which it is subject. Fungible objects are therefore described by weight, quantity or value, rather than specific description (the most common example is cash)
Fungible securities	Securities of the same issue, which are kept in the clearing system where the book-keeping is such that no specific securities are assigned to customer accounts by their serial numbers
Gilts	Securities issued by the British Government
Governing law	The jurisdiction to which the terms and conditions of transaction are subject
Grace period	The period of time given to a borrower or issuer in which it is allowed to remedy an event of default
Grey market	The 'market' in a new security issue, among financial institutions, which commences on the launch of a new issue (ie, before it is available to trade to the 'public') and ends when the securities are formally available at closing of the issue
Gross-up	A borrower/issuer may be required to gross-up payments it has to make to the lenders/investors, meaning it must make additional payments to compensate for withholding taxes, or similar deductions, which would otherwise reduce the amounts actually received by the lenders/investors
Headroom	Refers to the difference between a borrower's projected performance (eg, in its business plan) and the lower targets set for it to attain under its financial covenants
Hedge fund	A fund which is allowed to take relatively high-risk and 'innovative' positions with investors' money, eg agreeing to sell securities they do not yet own ('shorting')
Hedging	An activity employed by financial institutions or corporate treasurers to protect against loss due to market fluctuation in certain investments held by that organisation. Hedging is usually performed by counterbalancing a current sale or purchase of an investment by another future sale or purchase. The aim is to ensure that any loss on the current sale is offset by the profit on the future sale
High yield bonds	A bond (or note), usually considered a more risky investment than standard corporate bonds and which therefore yields a higher rate of interest (or substantial discount) to attract investors
Hive down	Refers to the transfer of assets from a parent down to one or more of its subsidiaries ('hive up' is the opposite)
ICMA	The International Capital Markets Association, the regulatory body in the bond market, formed in July 2005 by the merger of the International Primary Markets Association (IPMA) and the International Securities Markets Association (ISMA)

Information barrier	An artificial barrier restricting communication between different areas within an organisation, allowing them to act for parties who may have conflicting interests. The concept originated in securities houses, but may also be used within large firms of solicitors
Information memorandum	A document produced by the borrower and arranger of a syndicated facility to inform potential participants about the deal
Infrastructure finance	Providing finance for the acquisition of 'infrastructure' assets or businesses such as water, gas or electricity suppliers, ports, airports, telecommunications, windfarms, and transport franchises.
Interim facility	A short-form loan agreement, usually lasting only 30 days, which allows the bidder in an acquisition finance to demonstrate that it has immediate funds with which to purchase the target. The short-form facility is really just a negotiating tool to show serious intention to bid and to move quickly, and is often not utilised; the intention is to negotiate the usual 'long-form' loan documents to replace the short-form facility before it expires
IPO	'Initial Public Offering', ie the first ever issue of (usually equity) securities by a particular entity
Issuing house	The financial institution which organises and arranges the issue of new securities, also known as the 'lead manager'
Lending office	See 'facility office'
Letter of credit	A written undertaking by a bank (the issuing bank) given at the request of, and in accordance with, the instructions of the applicant (the buyer) to the beneficiary (the seller), to effect a payment up to a stated amount of money, within a prescribed time limit, and usually against the production of stipulated documents
LIBID (London Interbank Bid Rate)	The rate of interest quoted by banks operating in the London Interbank Market at which they are willing to borrow money (ie, bid for deposits in a particular currency)
LIBOR (London Interbank Offered Rate)	The rate of interest quoted by banks in the London Interbank Market at which they are willing to lend money, ie offer deposits in a particular currency. Note that 'ICE LIBOR' is an average rate calculated by asking a panel of banks to submit rates based on the question, 'At what rate could you borrow funds, were you to do so by asking for and then accepting interbank offers in a reasonable market size just prior to 11 am?'. (See also **4.9.3.**)
London Approach	Guidelines issued by the Bank of England encouraging support for troubled debtors rather than sale of distressed debt
London Code of Conduct	Published by the Bank of England: a guide to best practice in the wholesale money markets in London
London Stock Exchange	The London Stock Exchange plc (which trades as 'the London Stock Exchange') is the international stock exchange for the UK, but not the Republic of Ireland
Management buy-in (MBI)	The purchase of a business by 'external' managers. As with MBOs, most of the funding is from outside investors
Management buy-out (MBO)	The purchase of a business by its management (and sometimes employees). The managers invest a small amount of money, but most of the finance is provided by outside investors such as venture capitalists

Mandate	The authorisation from a borrower or issuer to its chosen arranger or lead manager to conduct the relevant transaction on the agreed terms. Usually given in the form of a letter signed by both parties
Margin	(a) in relation to floating interest rates, the rate of interest charged by the bank over and above the relevant cost of funding, such as Libor;
	(b) in relation to some financial markets (eg, the futures market), a deposit required to be paid by members of the relevant exchange for each transaction they carry out;
	(c) 'margin lending' is where the loan amount is of a lesser value than the amount of collateral given for the loan
Market flex	A term written into a commitment letter allowing the arranger unilaterally to change the terms of a facility if it cannot successfully syndicate
Matched funding	The process of matching a loan (asset) with a deposit (liability) of the same maturity
Maturity	The date upon which a debt is finally repayable
Mezzanine finance	Usually high interest-bearing debt which ranks behind the 'senior debtors' so far as repayment is concerned. It is sometimes seen as halfway between debt and equity in terms of risk and reward
Monolines	Companies which provide a guarantee of debt securities issued by lower-rated issuers in return for an insurance premium. This 'monoline insurance' or 'wrap' can raise an issue rating from 'A' to 'AAA', so attracting more investors and reducing coupon for the issuer
New Global Note structure	A structure which requires global notes to be held by clearing systems (and not a common depository) to ensure they are eligible as collateral in the euro central banking system ('Eurosystem')
Non-recourse	A non-recourse loan is one with no comeback (or recourse) to a guarantor or parent company of the borrower. Non-recourse loans are usually used to finance a special project or purpose over which they are secured
Note	A widely used alternative label for 'bond' – see **17.5**
Off balance sheet liabilities	Obligations of a company which do not appear on its balance sheet. These can be of concern for lenders since they disguise the extent of the commitments entered into by a company
Opco/Propco finance	A finance technique in which an existing business puts ownership of its real property (ie, land and buildings) into one SPV (the 'Propco') and its operating assets into another (the 'Opco'). The Propco can raise finance for the business on very favourable terms because it only owns land, whilst the Opco leases the real property back from the Propco so that the business keeps trading
Option	The right, but not the obligation, to buy or sell an instrument at a specified price and up to a specified time in the future
Over-the-counter (OTC)	The purchase and sale of securities and other financial instruments which take place away from any stock exchange or other official financial exchange (eg, futures exchange).
Paper	Colloquially, securities such as bonds, notes, certificates of deposits and commercial paper

Par	The principal amount (the initial issue price) at which an issuer agrees to redeem its securities on their maturity (see also 'face value')
Parallel debt	A structure used in jurisdictions that do not recognise a security trustee. A parallel debt provision provides for a security agent to be owed an equivalent sum to that due under a loan facility (ie, two 'parallel' debts). This allows the security agent to hold security for the full amount of the loan. As the facility debt is repaid, the security agent debt is reduced 'in parallel' (and vice versa), so that the borrower only repays one debt.
Pari passu	Equally and without preference
Perpetual bonds or notes	Bonds or notes which have no scheduled maturity date and therefore are redeemable only under any call option that the issuer may have under their terms and conditions. Events of default in such issues will be very basic and will give rise to a winding-up procedure and not to redemption
PIK	Payment in kind, usually referring to a facility in which the borrower can roll-up interest and add it to principal to be paid when the loan matures (cf 'cash pay' where interest is paid as it falls due). May be found in mezzanine facilities for acquisition finance
Plain vanilla	A colloquial term used to describe securities or loan facilities with no additional features such as warrants, call options, multi-options, etc
PRA	The Prudential Regulation Authority is one three new bodies (see also FPC and FPC) which took over regulatory functions from the Financial Services Authority in 2013. The PRA is responsible for prudential regulation.
Private equity	A private equity house (also referred to as the 'sponsors', 'venture capital', 'equity' or the 'investors') is an organisation that creates funds by raising money from institutions, banks and high net worth individuals to invest in the acquisition of other companies or groups.
Private placement	An offer of securities made to a limited and prearranged number of investors
Professional Securities Market (PSM)	The PSM is a market created by the London Stock Exchange in July 2005 to enable companies to raise capital by issuing securities to professional or institutional investors. The key feature of the PSM is that it is 'unregulated' or, more precisely, 'exchange regulated' and so has a very flexible regulatory regime (eg, no requirement to report under IFRS, no restrictions on type or value of securities, etc).
Project finance	The financing of a specific project (eg, building a power station or toll road), the revenue from which will provide the lenders with repayment of their investment. The project also provides security for the lenders
Promissory note	An unconditional promise in writing, signed by the debtor, undertaking to pay a specific sum on demand, or at a fixed or determinable date in the future
Purple Book	Colloquial name for the old rules of the Financial Services Authority relating to listing on the London Stock Exchange. Now replaced by the Prospectus Rules, Listing Rules and Disclosure Rules
Put option	If contained within a bond or note issue, it will give the holder of the securities the right to call for an early redemption of the securities prior to their scheduled maturity (cf 'call option')

Redemption	The repurchase or repayment by an issuer (or borrower) of outstanding securities (or loans), in accordance with their terms, with the effect of extinguishing the outstanding debt
Repurchase agreements ('repos')	In capital markets, repos entail two simultaneous transactions: the purchase of securities (the 'collateral') by an investor from a bank or dealer; and the commitment by that bank or dealer to repurchase the securities at a specified higher price (or the same price with charges) on a specified future date (or on call). Repos are primarily used as a means of short-term funding and are governed by market standard terms and conditions
Rescheduling	In relation to debt obligations, the renegotiation and agreement of revised terms of a loan facility (usually involving the spreading of interest and capital repayments over a longer period) as a result of the borrower being unable to comply with the original terms
Reuters screen	A telecommunications system, subscribed to by banks and financial institutions, which provides regularly updated financial information relevant to banking and securities trading
Reverse flex	A clause in commitment documents for a loan that requires the arranger to push for lower pricing if the loan appears oversubscribed during syndication. The arranger is usually incentivised by taking a share of any cost saving
RIS	Regulatory Information Services: companies which provide information services to the capital markets and have been approved by the FCA Listing Rules as a vehicle for members to make announcements (see Listing Rules, Appendix 3 for a list of RISs)
Rollover	The renewal of a loan which has become repayable under a revolving credit loan facility
SEC (the Securities and Exchange Commission)	The US Federal Government agency charged with overseeing the US domestic securities market
Secondary market	The trading of securities which are already issued
Settlement	The process of clearing the paperwork involved in trading securities: ensuring the purchaser receives its securities and the seller its money. Purchases and sales must be reconciled between the different financial institutions involved in the trades. Settlement is dealt with by an institution's 'back office'
SPA	'Sale and purchase agreement' or 'share purchase agreement': the contract governing the acquisition of the target in an acquisition finance
Spread	Generally, the difference between two prices, but the term has other meanings in specific contexts
Standby letter of credit	A letter of credit issued by a bank as a form of guarantee. A beneficiary of arrangement will be able to make a drawing on the letter of credit merely by providing a certificate of non-payment of the underlying debt
Stapled financing	In an acquisition finance, where the bank advisers to the vendor offer a loan package to potential bidders for acquiring the target (the loan terms are 'stapled' to the back of the information memorandum relating to the target)

Stock lending	A transfer of securities from 'lender' to 'borrower' to meet a pre-existing contract of the borrower to sell securities. The 'loan' requires the borrower to replace the securities in due course, and cash collateral of 102–105% of the securities' value is usually taken
Structured finance	A financial structure specifically designed for a particular borrower
Subordination	A creditor is subordinated if its claim against the borrower ranks behind one or more other creditrs on insolvency. Subordination can be achieved by way of taking security, by contractual arrangements or by debt structuring (ie, lending at different levels of company within a group of companies) or a combination of all three
Swap	The exchange of one product for another, usually currencies, interest streams, or securities
T bill (Treasury bill)	A security issued by the US Government
Ticking fee	A fee to cover an arranger's commitment costs, and payable from when the arrangers underwrite a loan to when the loan documentation is signed
Toggle facility	Allows a borrower to chose whether to pay interest as it falls due, or roll it up and add it to the capital repayment ('payment in kind')
Tombstone	An announcement, usually placed in the financial press such as the *Financial Times*, made by either the borrower/issuer or the banks/lead manager, and announcing an issue of securities or provision of a loan facility. Tombstones are not intended as an advertisement to entice prospective purchasers, they simply contain a brief description of the issue or facility and a list of the participating banks or managers. The names of these banks or managers appear as a vertically presented list, hence the name 'tombstone'
Transferable loan instruments	Transferable loan instruments (TLIs) are a structured method of assigning a fully drawn commitment. They allow a bank to convert the repayment instalments due to it into debt instruments which mirror the terms of the facility agreement.
UK Listing Authority (UKLA)	The colloquial name for the division of the Financial Services Authority responsible for admission of securities to listing
Utilisation	The borrowing of money under a loan facility (sometimes known as 'drawdown')
Withholding tax	A tax deducted at source on certain payments (usually interest or dividend payments)
Workout	Common term for the long-term rescue of a defaulting borrower by its bank(s) (and other creditors)
Zero coupon bond/ note	A non-interest bearing bond or note issued at a discount to its face value

Bibliography

Commercial lending

There are few, if any, books dedicated to the documentation of facility agreements; however, the following books address many of the legal issues that loan documentation raises:

Geoffrey Fuller, *Corporate Borrowing: Law and Practice* (5th edn, Jordans, 2016)

A good technical review of certain aspects of corporate borrowing.

Philip Wood, *Law and Practice of International Finance* (Sweet & Maxwell, 2019)

This is a series of 9 volumes, of which the most relevant are Volume 3: *Comparative Law of Security Interests* and Volume 5: *International Loans, Bonds, Guarantees and Legal Opinions*.

Security

Richard Calnan, *Taking Security: Law and Practice* (4th edn, Jordans, 2018)

An exceptionally well written and thorough review of security issues: if you only read one book on security, make it this one.

Roy Goode, *Commercial Law* (5th edn, Penguin, 2017)

Professor Goode's well-known book covers a number of aspects of taking security, as well as being an invaluable reference work for general commercial practice.

Roy Goode, *Legal Problems of Credit and Security* (6th edn, Sweet & Maxwell, 2017)

A surprisingly readable collection of Professor Goode's lectures which covers a number of basic security issues in some depth.

Peter Ellinger and Eva Lomnicka, *Modern Banking Law* (5th edn, Oxford University Press, 2011)

Particularly useful review of secured lending.

Capital markets

Geoffrey Fuller, *The Law and Practice of International Capital Markets* (3rd edn, LexisNexis Butterworths, 2012)

A very useful text: *the* book for capital markets lawyers.

Dr Joanna Benjamin, *Interests in Securities: A Proprietary Law Analysis of the International Securities Markets* (Oxford University Press, forthcoming 2020)

Stephen Valdez and Philip Molyneux, *An Introduction to Global Financial Markets* (8th edn, Macmillan, 2016)

This is an excellent introduction to many different areas of banking and capital markets. Readable and informative.

General

Christopher Stoakes, *Know the City* (2018, Christopher Stoakes Ltd)

A witty and readable demystification of the markets, players and products in the City of London. A very useful jargon-buster.

Michael Brett, *How to Read the Financial Pages* (5th edn, Random House, 2003)

An unbeatable guide to jargon and concepts of the City in general and the financial world in particular. Aimed at laymen not lawyers, but contains very clear explanations and examples.

Michael Lewis, *Liar's Poker* (Hodder, 1999)

This is the story of the author's training and trading at the investment bank Salamon Brothers. The first half of this book is an hilarious account of investment banking; the second half is drier and more informative, but by this time you will be hooked. (Worth reading just to find out how to play 'liar's poker'.)

Index

THE INSIDERS CLUB

THE INSIDERS CLUB

Life on the Innside - Book 1

ECHO MILLER

Edited by
JAMES MILLINGTON

CHU & CHOTHER
PUBLICATIONS

To Innocence & Unfiltered Joy,
Please don't become extinct.

To Empathy, Grace, & Compassion,
May the world embrace you. May the future be bright.

To Imperfection,
You take such a beating, but without you, we are boring and far less beautiful.

To Bittersweet Life,
Thank you for the sweet....and, I guess, the bitter too.

A beautiful portrayal of an autistic person's inner world. Wrote a book with four autistic primary characters and got it all-the-way right.

Takes us on a journey of inclusion and what it truly means. Recommended for anyone trying to understand what it means to be on the spectrum.

I am a parent of kids with special needs and I can honestly say this book helped me understand a bit better what life might be like from their perspective. Read it!

Author's Note

Is this book for people who are autistic?*

Maybe. Although there are characters in this book who are on the spectrum, it was written to introduce a way of living that might be unfamiliar to readers who don't share that diagnosis. Being able to relate to a character can be a meaningful experience. However, a character can't represent the full experience of an autistic person in the same way that one with dark hair can't define all people who are brunette.

For sensitive readers: The story contains <u>Emotional Content.</u> Multiple views of Autism Spectrum Disorder (ASD) are presented. Some characters will hold opinions and use language that may be offensive. In this work of fiction, good and bad imaginary things happen to imaginary people. No imaginary animals were hated or harmed in the making of it.

Some <u>language</u> may upset some readers. A few hurtful words serve a purpose and do not reflect the views of the author. There's no curse word over a level 2. If you want to know what that means, you'll have to read the book. (For those truly concerned about coarse language, no "f" bombs will assault your eyes or sensitivities.)

<u>Other Notes:</u>

At the time of publication, the social skills books mentioned in the story do not exist, but the movies mentioned are real. Have fun playing along and guessing the movie lines. Quotations used from films are a unique form of speech called *Delayed Echolalia*. All works cited herein are the property of their respective owners.

The hardest part of writing this book was to imagine "my people" suffering. But without some obstacles and challenges, there can be no story. For those of you who are struggling, my heart is with you. My intention is that the world would embrace you exactly as you are in this moment. You are worthy.

This is a work of fiction. None of the characters represent anyone living or deceased.

*At the time of publication, there is much debate over identifying someone on the spectrum as an autistic person or a person with autism. Out of respect for all points of view, both phrases are used in this book.

Day 1: Inn Over Your Head

Chapter One

KEEGAN

A friendly smile and eye contact are key to establishing new relationships.

- Social Eyes

Keegan Harris stretched his eyes to the size of ping pong balls and arched his eyebrows so high they almost touched his hairline. With great effort, he tried to show every tooth. In the bathroom mirror, he thought his version of a smile appeared alert and full of energy. Yesterday his brother said that expression made him look deranged, so Keegan added "smile practice" to his morning routine.

Remembering the restroom had the best acoustics, he spoke to his reflection. "It's a different day and that's ok." He rubbed a dime-sized amount of goo through his long, wet curls and pulled his favorite tag-less, cotton jersey over his head. The yellow T-shirt with the black zigzag stripe fell softly against his skin.

He closed his eyes and brushed his cheek against the sleeve. The tip of his nose dragged against the fibers. He couldn't stomach the slightest hint of mildew. Not today. Not ever. A quick sniff confirmed that the garment was clean, but the memory of that stench made him gag. His throat constricted and his stomach caved in. When the episode had passed, he grinned. "No breakfast, no barf."

The shirt passed the softness standard and odor evaluation. Its sunny color matched his hair. His fashionable nod to Charlie Brown was a great look for the day that would shape the rest of his life.

Last night, Keegan had been too excited to sleep. He'd set multiple timers around his suite to make sure he didn't fall behind schedule. Freshly showered and mostly clothed, he had time to spare.

At this early hour, the building was extra-quiet, providing the ideal opportunity to research friendship one more time. He ventured into his private living room. A collection of rocking and spinning sculptures decorated the space. The frenetic movement disrupted the still air of solitude. Sunlight streamed through the window. The glass barrier was a source of comfort and frustration.

Keegan followed a ray of light. The beam highlighted a poster on the opposite wall, resting on the words, "Autism, it's different than you think."

He snorted. "You're telling me."

On his way to the bookcase, he passed through floating dust particles. He squinted and mumbled, "Sunshine snow" to no one in particular. A cursory touch with his fingertip left no visible trail on the shelf. Not enough of the sneezy stuff had gathered to classify the room as dirty. Determined to unravel a few social mysteries before interacting with others, he chose three books and settled into his desk chair.

He tasted the salty breeze ruffling the drapes near his workstation. The flavorful wind destroyed his concentration. Keegan closed *Social Security: Building Confidence for Social*

Encounters and added it to the small pile on his desk. He pulled the curtain, but left the window partly open.

His suite was nestled in the newest part of his family's community for people with disabilities. The Retreat on Ainsley Avenue was a protective bubble located in Oak Bay, Texas, just six blocks from the gulf coast. Whenever he left the property, he was not simply part of the world; he was smothered by it. Immersed in the chaos of sensory overload, he interpreted the sudden rush of information as a wild party where mostly good things happened. When he was alone, he tried to understand society's puzzling behaviors. He poured over hundreds of guides to help him navigate the complex system of social interaction. But out of his entire collection, not one volume explained the steps necessary to forge close, long-lasting friendships.

The first step, getting "out there," hadn't been easy. His parents had reinvented their life's purpose to create an "out there" *inside* the Retreat. His mom said they'd banked everything on bringing the mountain to Muhammad. Keegan had no idea who Muhammad was and the property didn't even include one small hill. His parents had given up dreams of retirement and invested their life savings into creating this unusual colony. If someone named Muhammad was coming to visit, he was certain they'd have a special place just for him. There'd be a mountain. It might be made of bean bags, but his parents would be sure to meet his needs.

Keegan's books about autism didn't answer many questions. Each page listed characteristics about a difference he couldn't see. One described his social experience as living behind a pane of glass, always on the outside looking in. At his height, he thought looking down through a skylight was a better description. The people who tried to interpret the spectrum but weren't actually on it confused him. He pushed the stack of books across his desk.

Inside the 500 square feet he called home, the Internet offered a path of entry to the rest of the world. He woke the computer with a tap on its keyboard. His own face stared back at him from the laptop's tiny media player. The online version of himself waited patiently. The program plastered the word PAUSE across his motionless features. Keegan leaned back in his new ergonomic desk chair. His mouth curled into a satisfied smile. In just two weeks, the interview had 100,000 views. He pushed the PLAY triangle and his voice filled the living area.

"I don't mean to be controversial, but I love breakfast. I saw this movie and—"

The reporter interrupted his revelations about films named for the most important meal of the day. Her eyelashes fluttered. "Who's Ainsley?"

Keegan spread his long, pale arms wide, imitating the game show models he'd seen on TV. With a professional flourish he said, "My dead friend."

The journalist peered into the camera. She sounded like a host for a preschool television program. "He must have been special for you to name this entire complex after him."

Aerial footage panned across Ainsley Avenue's grand lawn to the recreation center. The drone soared around the cottages and back toward the rehabilitation clinic.

A buzzing timer drew Keegan's attention. While trying to silence the horrible sound, he knocked over the family portrait on his desk. After he placed the picture back in its proper place, he smoothed the masking tape covering his sister's face. With shaking hands, he twisted the timer's dial back to zero. Today's grand opening for the Inn on Ainsley Avenue would put his hosting skills to the test.

He'd overheard his parents discuss how many residents would make the Inn a good investment. Over the course of this weekend, he needed to convince enough people to fill the rooms on one side of the hallway. If the project failed, it would be disastrous for more people than he could count. He had to succeed for his family and for his future.

He should have finished getting dressed. Mother claimed he was much more charming when fully clothed. Instead, he dragged the progress bar across the video until he saw his father standing in front of the construction site.

The interviewer held the mic below her chin. "Do you have plans to buy more property in our area to expand your vision? Another business, perhaps?" Mr. Harris wore his serious face.

Once Keegan had suggested he add a cape to his suit coat. The simple embellishment would have set his dad apart from the boring business guys who wore suits. But Bill Harris wasn't flashy. His hair was a darker shade of blond, short and straight as a board where Keegan had lighter, messy ringlets. His dad's wardrobe consisted of suits, ties, and "smart casual" golfer gear. With or without a cape, in his son's eyes, he was still a superhero.

Bill's square jaw bobbed. "We're steadily growing. The demand for appropriate housing for people with special needs is enormous."

A strange titter spilled out of the reporter.

Keegan played that bit over and over. It didn't match the types of giggling he'd heard before.

"Well, you've certainly brought a lot of attention to our area, thanks to your relationships with pro golf—"

Keegan pressed the black beanie against his skull so hard it removed any urge to smile. After years of preparation and construction, his father was going to miss the orientation weekend. The PGA tour should have changed their date. When he closed the browser, the word "unacceptable" slipped from his mouth. He tore a new piece of masking tape and stuck it on the portrait over his father's face. "Absent people get taped. Now you match Kiara."

Palming two unsharpened yellow pencils, he took his spot on the sofa, and slowly exhaled. He took a pencil in each hand

and shook them in front of his face. Sometimes he lost track of time staring at things while waving his pencils, but the activity helped him think.

The black shoes he'd selected to wear today rested on a cushion nearby. Polished to perfection, these were the third pair in a series of identical shoes. On the first shopping trip, his mother had fallen into a coughing fit when she checked the price on his choice, a pair of formal loafers covered in black crystals. The style they purchased, the one she'd called sensible, hadn't stirred up her allergies. Every time his feet grew, his parents had replaced them with duplicates.

Five years ago, a smaller version of the same shoe had taken him to the event that put this entire project in motion: his first funeral.

Keegan had been worried about what to expect at a funeral. He'd searched his social skills books, but there wasn't a chapter on sad gatherings. His mother told him it was inappropriate to entertain the crowd to lighten the mood. Looking back, those sparkly shoes would have been wasted on that occasion.

His friend Ainsley, the center of attention, waited inside a shiny black box near the front row. Keegan's new shoes were hidden under the bench in front of him. Seated on the back row, Keegan spent his time drawing pictures. He tried to focus on his artwork, but using only one hand had been a challenge. He needed his other hand to pinch his nose. The aroma from the flowers combined and twisted into a repulsive odor that threatened to choke him. Giant bouquets were a poor choice for the ceremony. This funeral was a quiet, sad party and these beautiful decorations cut off everyone's air supply. The guests' eyes glistened with tears.

Every eye watered since coughing and dry heaving were not allowed.

A silver-haired man wearing wingtips covered with polish and scuff marks sat beside him on the bench. The gravel in his voice matched his scratched shoes. "How did you know Ainsley?"

"We've been friends since I was three. We went to many of the same therapies together."

"Is that so?"

Keegan hadn't known how to answer that question. The man might have called him a liar. Since his mother had begged him to remain calm and not turn the event into what she called "The Keegan Harris Show," he returned to his drawing. Creating an illustration for his sympathy card challenged him. He struggled to get the cocoon just right.

"You don't act the way Ainsley did. He was very"—the old man scanned the ceiling—"fidgety."

"Mom says I don't behave the way anyone else does." Keegan hoped his tone wasn't too cheery for the funeral. "I try. I've got lots of books about social skills."

"You do?"

The old guy doubted every answer Keegan offered. The suspicious nature of elderly people presented him with a new mystery. Before he considered any of the social rules, the words shot out of his mouth. "You look like you've had a lot of birthdays."

The man rewarded his guess by revealing his yellow teeth through a crooked smile. "I have," he nodded.

A Primer on Conversation recommended Keegan ask another polite question. "Did you know Ainsley for a long time?"

"Since he was a baby, but I didn't see him often. What do you remember about him?"

Keegan bragged that his friend, Ainsley Mitchell, played melodies on any instrument. He even invented his own music, although not many appreciated when he produced interesting sounds. Most people acted as though they couldn't see Ainsley because he didn't talk. Keegan paid close attention to his friend. He kept his shoelaces tied and protected him when the boy held his ears and rocked. He told the gentleman Ainsley was smart, talented, and passionate about his art. When Keegan ran out of words, he presented the first greeting card he'd ever created.

The old, weathered hands trembled as he read it. His voice sounded so dusty it cracked. "You know something, kid?"

Keegan's mind raced. He knew lots of things, but many teachers had warned him about info-dumping, so he remained silent.

"You're going to change the world." The stranger wiped a tear from his eye, stood, and walked away, taking the card with him.

Within a matter of weeks, Keegan had worn those same shoes to his second funeral. This time, Ainsley's mother hid inside a black box. The original drawing had been intended for her. According to his own mother, Cheryl Mitchell had died from a broken heart. He wondered if he should have made another copy and delivered it to her. Would it have changed her world?

Since then, Keegan had worn the same style of shoes to birthday parties, weddings, and more fundraising galas than he could count. He'd also created a greeting card business with the hope he'd discovered a way to bring the change the world desperately needed.

Keegan glanced at the community newspaper on his coffee table. Headlines about a fire, several robberies, and a few disappearances shared the front page. The story about their new building was buried on the eighth page. The world needed more than a simple greeting card.

Another timer rang in the kitchen. He stopped wiggling his pencils and squeezed his feet into the elegant footwear.

From the kitchen, Luke's lazy Texas twang distracted him from his memories. "I can handle things for a while, Nic, but don't leave me hang—"

Keegan walked to the kitchenette to tend to the alarm and greet his brother. Luke stood in the doorway with his phone wedged between his shoulder and cheek. His mouth hung open, frozen mid-sentence. Shirtless, he rubbed a towel over his shaggy wet hair. Dad's lounge pants puddled around his ankles.

Keegan recognized that dropped jaw. "What?"

Luke shook his head. "Nicola, I gotta go. Yeah. You know how it is here. Get back soon." He tossed his phone onto the table, wrapped the towel around his neck, and hitched the pants at the waist. "Keeg, I don't think you want to wear those shoes."

"I always wear these on special days." They matched his black cargo shorts and the black crooked stripe on his yellow Charlie Brown T-shirt.

"True." Luke bit his thumbnail. "Today is special, but not fancy. Your regular sneakers would be fine." He swished his hand in the air. "I'm here because there's a security alert about an open window."

"Yeah. I want to let the new smell out and the old, regular air in."

"Ma will be happy you've kept your room clean and smelling fresh."

"I'm showing it off later. It needs to look and smell good."

"Speaking of, let's find something more appropriate for your feet." Luke swept his damp, brown hair into a haphazard man bun. "Did you get a copy of The Tribune this morning?"

Crouched inside the walk-in closet, Keegan spoke over his

shoulder. "Yeah. It's on my desk. There's a story about our grand opening."

Luke called from the other room, "It's mentioned on the front page."

Keegan's head swiveled around. "We're on page eight."

"I'll find the article. You find your shoes."

Keegan chose his black high-tops with the star in the logo. At the very least, today deserved a starry shoe.

The tone of Luke's voice shifted as he returned to the bedroom. "They included a picture of the Inn. The headline says, 'More Residents Expected on Ainsley Avenue.'" He cleared his throat. "'Despite tax hikes and a dwindling economy, Oak Bay's population is expected to increase with additional housing at The Retreat on Ainsley Avenue. The Harris family's private compound continues to bring more people with disabilities to our region. Bill Harris' connection to the Professional Golf Association continues to draw media attention to our formerly quiet, traditional community.'" Luke bit his lip. He continued in a soft, near whisper. "'Some residents question the city's infrastructure for supporting such a facility, expressing concerns about traffic, safety, education, and...'" His voice trailed off as Keegan finished tying the long, white laces. "Would you mind if I borrowed this? I want to finish reading it later." He folded the paper and jammed it under his armpit.

"What's wrong? Don't throw it out. It might be good for the scrapbook."

"Nothing's wrong, buddy. I just don't want us to get—"

"Off-task?" Keegan filled in.

Luke nodded. "Yep. That's just what I was thinking." He tapped the top of his brother's foot. "Nice choice."

Keegan followed the social custom and commented on his brother's appearance. "Those are Dad's pajama pants."

Luke gathered a few inches of extra waistline into his hand.

"That makes sense." He paced across the room, dragging the excessive length, and sighed. "You sure they're not yours?"

"Yes. You are un-tall. Your belly is bigger than mine but not as big as Dad's...yet."

Luke's dimples appeared. A few strands of hair fell when he looked at the floor. "Dang, dude. Good morning to you, too."

Luke touched the back of a giant frame leaning against the wall. His brother's Southern drawl stretched the word "bro" into something with more than one syllable. Luke had a way of making short words longer or combining several words into one sound. He didn't speak English; he spoke Texan: "Wuhjuhdby?"

Keegan considered the coded question. Once he completed his brother's brainteaser, he puffed out his chest and held his head high. "It will display a collage of *personal* photos."

Luke turned the frame around to see the front. "Twenty pictures! That's more than the one our sister had in high school."

Keegan's eyebrows bobbed. "It says 'Best Friends' in the center." He leaned his head back and stretched his arms out wide. "My room will be like Kiara's."

Luke flapped his arm around in a circular motion. "Are you gonna get rid of these neon lights and hang ballet stuff everywhere too? I bet we still have some of that pink paint leftover." He flashed his teeth. "We could make this look *exactly* like her old room."

Keegan responded to the error using his serious voice. "No." His eyebrows flattened. He squeezed the woven bracelet Kiara had given him years ago. "Just pictures of friends."

Luke held his hands up. There wasn't a cop in the room, but he looked like he was being arrested. "Alright. Sorry."

With a huff, Keegan let himself drop on the bed. A scowl settled on his face.

The bed sagged when Luke joined him. "I didn't mean it, Keeg, I promise. You can keep your room just the way you like it."

Keegan spun the bracelet on his long, slender wrist. "Was it easier to make friends back in the 1900s?"

"I…" Luke scrunched up his face. "What?"

"In olden times, like the 80s, the movies made it seem simple."

Luke wrestled with his hair. He spoke with a rubber band between his teeth. "Your guess is as good as mine."

"You're an adult."

"I'm not that much older than you or Kiara." He rearranged his topknot. Covered with a towel, his shoulders crept toward his ears. "I'm too young to remember the 1900s. Why don't you ask Mom and Dad?"

"They're the right age but they don't know what it's like to make friends now."

"Dude, they meet new people All. The. Time."

Keegan grimaced. "Philanderers."

Luke rolled back on the bed and howled with laughter. "Philanthropists."

Irritation filled Keegan's mouth and coated his words. "People who give donations aren't real friends, Luke."

"You better think of them that way. They helped us build this place. Keeg, their money financed your dream."

Keegan massaged his forehead. "I started my words in the wrong place. I wanted to talk about *The Breakfast*—"

Luke sat up and held his hand out. "Stop."

"It premiered in Los Angeles, California on February seventh." To add emphasis, he stared at his brother's Adam's apple and hoped it looked like eye contact. "Nineteen hundred and eighty-five, Luke. Right in the middle of the 80s. It's an important film."

"Bro, you're obsessing again. We've talked about that

movie thirty thousand times. I'm sure you've told me that already." Luke smirked and executed the family's signature move, the Harris head-tilt. "Are you nervous? Dude, you came up with some great group activities. Everything's gonna be fine. Relax."

Keegan's knees bounced to a silent rhythm. Special days always gave him extra energy. "I just want to have friends."

Luke patted him on the shoulder and stood. "You already do. And you'll have more of them." He shuffled back over to the empty frame. "Don't worry. You'll fill this in no time. Ya might want to buy another one…for symmetry." He glanced at the wall of neon lights. "Your room is becoming so trendy and stylish."

Keegan noted his brother's clothing. "I hope you'll wear something fancier than a wet towel."

Luke gripped the loose pants with one hand and raced toward the kitchen. As his face tipped toward the clock, his eyebrows shot up. He snatched his phone and sprinted to his room, calling, "Level three!"

Keegan's wide smile pushed his cheeks to the edge of his face. His brother had a knack for calming his nerves and restoring his confidence, and Luke's use of their cursing code brought peace of mind that foul language wouldn't pollute the event. He would replace the towel with appropriate apparel.

After this weekend, Keegan Harris would issue Loneliness an eviction notice. He would remain inside his cozy bubble and simply include more people in it. The future tenants would find the accommodations on Ainsley Avenue to be top notch. The Inn was superb. With flawless social skills and a schedule rooted firmly in the wisdom of 80s movies, orientation was going to be perfect.

Chapter Two

COPPER

Pennies from heaven

After almost two decades, Copper Munro knew how to move through his house undetected. Skulking was the best way to avoid disturbing his mother. Pearl Munro worked three jobs, and whenever she had the morning off, she insisted on making him a *real* breakfast. Unfortunately, her version of cooking guaranteed *real* indigestion.

Without making a sound, he turned the handle and slid into the pantry. He closed the door behind him with a soft clunk. Copper made himself as lean as possible in the tight space. He sucked his stomach in and searched the shelves for Toaster Treats. Amongst a wide array of instant food, two boxes of the delicious pastries sat unopened. He considered his options. Usually, he saved the ones filled with strawberry jam to share with his brother. That package hadn't been touched for weeks. He took a foil packet from the blueberry box and slunk into the larger part of the kitchen.

Copper listened to the quiet morning. He heard his heartbeat, the soft hum of the air conditioner, the ticking wall clock, and his mother's white noise machine blasting through her bedroom door.

He removed a container of orange juice from the refrigerator and placed it on the countertop with exaggerated care. If he'd wanted to use a real glass, he was out of luck. Two people lived in this house, both over the age of eighteen, but the kitchen was child-proofed. He grimaced. More like Copper-proofed. Only one cupboard remained free of the toddler safety locks, the one containing plastic cups. His mother may have been over-protective, but she wasn't cruel. Like a good little pet, he had access to fresh water. He could have tipped the carton into his mouth and been done with it, but he wasn't an animal. Plastic would suffice. Moving with stealth, he slipped to the cabinet, and snatched a light blue acrylic tumbler.

He double-checked the clock. The Entrée Network's *Sunrise Surprise* would begin soon. He wondered if today's episode would include chef Pascal Chevalier, whose culinary skills surpassed every other chef on television. Copper frequently imagined preparing a fabulous meal in this very space with Chef Chevalier. He hated to miss the program, but after breakfast, he needed to finish packing.

He turned his attention to the cup and carton. If he had to go along with his mother Pearl on her new scheme, she should at least allow him to pour his own juice. It sloshed onto the counter. Copper drained the cup's contents. Flavored with the acidity of independence and the sweetness of freedom, it was the most gratifying gulp of orange juice he'd ever tasted.

A crystal paperweight shaped like a giant diamond sat on a stack of cooking magazines. The recipes he'd carefully selected sat under the fake jewel, exactly where he'd left them two months ago. Out of all the suggestions he'd posted on the refrigerator door, Pearl had only prepared one. Torn from the pages of *Working Mother Magazine*, its selling point was having five ingredients, most of which were found in cans and boxes. Such a crude meal would horrify Chevalier. Copper replaced the juice with a smirk.

He inspected the small kitchen with its mysterious locked drawers and cabinets. The toaster waited in the corner, ready to warm the Toaster Treat's filling into sweet, molten lava. He imagined the next few days and realized this moment of peace was like whipped cream on top of a burned waffle of a weekend. If his mother smelled something in the toaster, she'd interrupt what had been a semi-civilized start to the day. *Extra whipped cream*, he thought. It'd be foolish to start gnawing away on annoyance and stress when he could savor the sweet topping of solitude instead. He tore open the foil packet and stuffed the cold, pale beige pastry into his mouth. Orange juice dripped from the counter's edge. The forgotten foil wrapper floated to the floor and landed on top of a small, sticky puddle. A trail of crumbs marked his path as he trudged toward the stairwell.

At the top of the stairs, bits of sheetrock dangled from a hole in the ceiling. He could almost see into the attic, but, at this hour, it was still too dark. White powder covered the staircase. With each step, puffs of powder formed ankle-high clouds. Despite Copper's previous efforts with the vacuum, his feet had ground the dust deep into the carpet fibers.

Glitter flashed in the air. He wasn't sure what made him feel light-headed. It could have been tilting his head back after climbing the stairs or the avalanche of memories that fell from the damaged ceiling. Dark, foggy circles formed around the outer edge of each eye, narrowing his field of vision. Any time the rings blocked his view completely, his knees buckled. He'd learned the hard way that when the world turned to fuzzy darkness, he needed to stay close to a wall if he didn't want to fall. He dropped to his hands and knees, braced himself against the wall, and crawled to his room.

Copper sat on the bedroom floor with his head between his knees. After some slow, deep breaths, his vision returned. He fixed his gaze on a poster from his favorite video game, *Passage*. He'd spent years staring at that robot, thinking about his past and anticipating his future. The present had been like waiting for dough to rise in a refrigerator: cold, long, and lonely. He expected becoming a man and the official transition to adulthood would bring better days.

The first time he'd played *Passage*, his older brother Sterling had been diagnosed with the flu. Their mother bought the game to entertain them while she was at work. Sterling played it for an hour, then passed the controller. Copper took to the game instantly. He was a natural. Sterling's light blue eyes widened, his teenage voice thick with flu goo. "I knew it. You're smart! I'm going to tell everyone at school what you can do." That was the first time Copper had heard anyone call him smart.

In the days that followed, Pearl had complained that her youngest son was a little obsessed with *Passage*. He played through the single player version in about three hours. Then he worked through it with the developer commentary on. Next, he memorized the dialogue from the robots that tried to shoot his character.

As Sterling watched Copper win, his health improved. Soon he rallied enough to play the cooperative levels. They worked as a team, creating special pathways, solving puzzles, and avoiding the robots' deadly lasers.

Sterling recovered from his illness and they'd continued to spend time together. Days spent playing *Passage* were magical. The activity provided a rare opportunity for them to focus on a task and share the experience. They could truly be together. Connect. As a result, Copper snatched up every officially licensed product. He amassed a large collection of posters, action figures, and T-shirts. Most of their conversations revolved around the game. Sometimes, when there was nothing more to say, one of them would quote the battle bot's deceptively friendly voice: "Knock knock. I see you!" It always made the other one laugh.

Passage had bridged the gulf between them and solidified their bond. They used the concept of the game to communicate. Eventually, their chats centered around planning for the future. Sterling had explained that he would shoot a path from high school to college. He would solve some puzzles to earn his degree. That piece of paper would provide a door to a job that paid good money. Then he could create an escape hatch. Once Copper finished high school, he could leap through and move in with his brother. Sterling promised autism would not hold Copper back. His big brother would help him reach his goals, teach him how to be a man, and make sure he'd have the best life possible. They never talked about what robots might be hiding around certain corners or what kind of deadly lasers would be fired in the real world. Copper had never thought to ask.

The robot on the poster had a catchphrase in the game. "Are you still there?" Without Sterling, Copper would be stuck looking at those same four walls until the day he died. He pulled the poster off the wall and rolled it up. Thinking of the past was a waste of time. All those plans and promises shared a coffin with Sterling.

He abandoned his quest to remain undetected. The closet door covered with *Passage* stickers ricocheted off the door stop. As Copper grabbed a T-shirt with a battle bot on the front, his stomach twisted. Grief tried to wring out the remnants of last night's dinner along with this morning's blueberry pastry.

Pearl's idea of fun, sleeping on some strange street called Ainsley Avenue, sounded like torture. Just thinking about it made his face grow hot. With an iron grip on the shirt, he stumbled across his room and sat on the bed. He touched his forehead. Surely, his mother wouldn't make him go on this so-called adventure if he was sick.

The T-shirt would be the last item he packed. When he dragged his duffle bag across the bed, a shiny penny hit the floor. He immediately thought of his brother. Sterling had collected pennies. Tears drenched Copper's face. *It's all my fault.* He placed the penny in his pocket. Whatever painful experience Pearl had planned for him, if it was a punishment, he deserved it.

Chapter Three

KEEGAN

Clues for conversation starters can be found by making observations about another person's appearance.

- Charming Chatter

Keegan dashed to the closest patch of shade, defending his milky skin from the harsh summer sun. The climate already compelled him to be an inside person. If not for the saving grace of the sea breeze, the Lone Star steam sauna would be unbearable. From the shadow of an enormous oak, Keegan Harris waited for his new life to begin.

To steady his racing heart, he thought of all that was the same this morning. The salty, roundabout breeze continued to shape the trees. The lopsided, windswept leaves nudged lost seagulls toward the coast. Pelicans plunged into the bay, their splashing symphony a prelude to the construction crew's daily concert of beating and banging. Pale blue scrubs paraded across the grand lawn sidewalks as the medical staff traded places during shift change.

Keegan leaned against the wall of the Inn. He hoped the visitors would arrive soon. He could no longer sit patiently in his suite while the minutes dragged on. Change was in the air. He had a future of excellence to pursue. Over the last few years, change had slowly crept into his life. The moment his family had decided to create the community, he transformed. Gone were the days of being a protective friend to one boy. Now he would be a champion for an entire population of people he'd never met.

After Ainsley's funeral, the Harris family was more determined than ever to serve and support people who were interesting and a little different. So Keegan helped with awareness campaigns and fundraisers while traveling the coastline on their search for utopia. People who were different needed safe places that didn't simply keep them alive but encouraged them to thrive. His family spread this message far and wide. Different, not less. Delayed, not done. Awareness, Acceptance, and Action. Unable to locate or afford perfection, they'd purchased several undeveloped acres and a few blocks of older homes in a sleepy beach town.

Their crew renovated and redesigned not only homes, but the lives of all who took part in the work. Most reported feelings of inspiration, higher self-esteem, and a renewed sense of purpose while bringing the dream to life. Keegan's personal development kept pace with the growth of the project. Each part of the process offered new adventures and increased his desire to interact with the world.

Shielding his eyes from the sun, he admired the first buildings his family had designed for the estate. As fans of the atomic ranch era of architecture, they built the Terrace rehabilitation lodge and the Courtyard extended stay facility to look both retro and brand new. They remodeled the 1950s bungalows so that they no longer appeared sad and shabby. Each came equipped with a small, manicured lawn, but that was where the similarity ended. His mother enjoyed the challenge of combining form and function with variety. Different exteriors helped full-time, independent residents navigate the property and locate their home with ease.

He was proud to be making a community for people with disabilities. With customized levels of support, the brochures advertised a higher quality of life. From the outside looking in, it seemed they'd delivered on that promise. But living in his parent's home and building the community hadn't been enough for Keegan. He couldn't change the world simply by visiting it.

Changing Minds and Behaviors stated that change could excite in a good way or be unexpected and scary. Keegan had learned that change could be so much more than good, unexpected, or scary. Change that came about as a result of innovation fell into the awesome category, even if that social skills book didn't list it as an option.

His dream was to create semi-independent housing for people like him. For those with scattered skills, the Inn blended a hotel lifestyle with a supervised college dorm experience. This stepping stone toward independent living was exactly what he needed. Finally, Keegan had a home of his very own. If everything went exactly according to plan, his parents could relax with full, happy hearts. Soon, his new best friends would step through the Inn's double doors. Once they agreed to move in, he would be safe, accepted, and able to work harder than ever to fulfill his destiny.

A dog barked a few blocks away. Keegan could tell it wasn't on the property, but his knuckles still went white. He held his pencils in an iron grip. He should have been born holding one in each hand. They were a vital extension of himself. They were his favorite thing in the entire world. His lifeline. These wooden wands, fondly referred to as "stim sticks," regulated reality. They brought reassurance he would be ok no matter what happened.

He positioned them horizontally in front of his eyes. Below each eraser, the metal bands reflected a bright sparkle from the sun. His mind replayed his father's warning: *You'll knock the nose off your face, son.* He moved the pencils five inches away from his eyes.

Waving the pencils produced the illusion of several ghost-like duplicates trailing the original. Through this blurred perspective, events unfolded in frames like an old movie reel played at a reduced speed. His therapists called the repetitive movement "*stimming.*" He didn't care what they called it. As long as he had his pencils, he determined how fast life appeared to be moving. Keegan controlled the speed of everything.

He stared at the tree-lined street. Twenty-two blurs later, a black limousine fully entered his makeshift animation, stopping in front of the Inn. A man wearing white gloves exited from the driver's seat. He touched the rear door handle on the passenger side and stumbled backward. The shiny door flew open. A teenaged boy popped out.

Struggling to control his thoughts, Keegan wiggled his pencils and repeated his comfort phrase. "It's a different day, and that's ok. The Inn on Ainsley Avenue is officially open."

He wanted to concentrate on the young man. Styled to perfection, the boy's clothing complemented his light brown skin. Wearing a prep school uniform complete with solid black sneakers, he looked like an advertisement for a back-to-school sale. But then Keegan's desire to examine the limo door shattered his focus. *What makes fancy doors fly open with a slight touch? Was it a safety hazard or a safety feature for emergency exits? Was there an emergency?* He stole another look at the young man's shoes. They were tied properly. He breathed a sigh of relief. One safety disaster averted.

A second passenger exited the vehicle. He carried the biggest stim stick Keegan had ever seen. A tiny ray of sunlight reflected off the brass-wrapped bottom. The sparkle from the cane's tip made a wonderful streak as it shot forward and smacked the back of the teen's leg. The boy jerked to a stop and gaped at the Inn with wide-eyed wonder. A single tear rolled down his cheek as he admired its beauty.

The older man gripped the cane too tightly, so Keegan could barely see the shiny ornament on the top. With the man's hand obscuring the surface, the metal would not reflect much. Boring. Keegan squinted and studied the gentleman. He wore a serious face decorated with wrinkles, angry eyebrows, and a mouth held firmly in a flat line. His boxy shoulders tilted toward the sidewalk. The man's sadness and anger washed over Keegan like the tide that sucked him into the sea and threw him back onto the beach. The experience was jarring and unwelcome. Someone needed to get that guy two canes. If he could stim properly, his mood would improve.

Keegan sauntered to the giant oak tree. He resumed wiggling his puny pencils and imagined what it might be like to wield two walking sticks. He'd need to be stronger. He squeezed his eyes shut. His mother would never allow it because he might hit someone by accident. Maybe they could rig up levers and pulleys to shake them at a certain time of day. They'd be big enough that everyone could enjoy the mesmerizing, twinkling trails. He opened his eyes and resolved to draw a massive stim stick machine and present it to her. This giant kinetic sculpture would make a relaxing addition to the outdoor area of the sensory spa.

The sound of wheels rolling over concrete drew him away from his preoccupation. A dark-skinned woman in a pale yellow dress dragged a small suitcase behind her. She stayed a few paces behind the older gentleman. The teen flinched away from the old man's grasp. Keegan decided the boy didn't want his shirt to get wrinkled. Before he could finish analyzing this social puzzle, he was distracted by the lady's beaded braids. When she turned to look his way, the braids moved away from her neck like swings on a carnival ride. She fluttered her hand. Keegan quickly shoved his pencils into his pocket and returned the gesture. He liked smiley types and hoped she would stay.

The town trolley brakes squeaked behind him, and Keegan's heart leapt in his chest. With the new trolley stop located right in front of the Inn, his home had become an official destination. He ran toward the vehicle, swinging his arms in the air. A disheveled businessman staring at an electronic tablet stepped off the small bus. He stood on the curb blocking the trolley's exit. As he raised his tablet to take a picture of the Inn, the sleeve of his wrinkled, white shirt bumped Keegan's arm. Instead of a traditional greeting, the man muttered some numbers. His clunky, brown lace-up Oxfords shuffled through old leaves as he entered the Inn.

Terrance, the trolley driver, recognized Keegan. "Your hair is still wet under that hat. Busy day?"

Keegan almost sang the words, "Yes! The Inn is finally open. Our community is growing!"

"You look mighty sharp in that shirt. Is that the same one the kid wears in the comics?"

Keegan ran his hands down his lean torso and checked his hands. His palms weren't bleeding. He'd need to research the word sharp and find out if it was a multiple-meaning word. "Yes, but don't worry. I'm not changing my name to Charlie and I refuse to get a beagle. No dogs allowed on Ainsley Avenue. That's my number one rule." He mentally scrolled through his social skills lessons. Terrance might have complimented him, so the appropriate response was to say something kind in return. "Your streetcar is super-clean and your bald head is very shiny today."

Terrance chuckled and pulled away from the curb. A man

sitting at the back of the bus held up his center finger to show Keegan the tattoo on his hand. It looked like a cross between the Avengers symbol and the Star Trek emblem.

Keegan studied the fountain in the center of the traffic circle. It resembled the letter A. Maybe the man got tattooed as a tribute to the community. Someone should teach him how to wave. *Gesturing: I'll Show You* had clear rules about which fingers stretched upward without offense. Not wanting to disappoint a fan, he flapped his hand back.

A squirrel darted near his feet searching for food, startling him. Rather than curse, he thought, *Level two!* Then he noticed his socks didn't match and his shoelaces were untied, so he bent down and made several knots to resolve the serious situation. He stacked half a dozen knots above the star logo on both shoes. Six should be enough to hold them all day.

So far, this morning was going very well. He was on task and his social skills were on point. Orientation would be outstanding.

As he drifted back to a shady spot near the front of the Inn, he scooped several acorns from the sidewalk. He set about the business of placing each one in a perfect line on the ground, as he waited for the last guest to arrive.

Chapter Four

COPPER

Earn an honest penny.

Nestled in hedges and trailing vines, a black box squawked, "Ms. Munro! So good to see you again. Come in!" A mechanical device buzzed and the gate unlocked. It clacked open and clanged shut when Copper's mom closed it behind them. Copper held his ears. "I already hate it."

Pearl Munro swept her hand across her forehead. She gathered the long auburn waves that usually hung loose around her shoulders and fanned the back of her neck. "Babydoll, we've talked about this. It's two nights. Give it a chance." She took a deep breath and dragged him onto the grounds.

The buildings on Ainsley Avenue formed a U-shape around a long, narrow lawn. A large fountain highlighted the traffic circle at the far end. The tree-lined street and old-fashioned architecture should have felt like a step back in time. For Copper, they represented the new terrain of an uncertain future. With the Inn on the left and the Welcome Center on the right, he knew he'd reached a fork in the road of his life. He examined the large structure made of glass and flat planes.

The stacked stone walls near the double doors added warmth to the Inn's facade, but it didn't look like home.

Pearl took his hand, pulling him toward the Welcome Center. "Come on, Baby. We're supposed to start over here."

Copper felt his mother tugging his arm, but his feet refused to move. Body rigid, his senses intensified. His heartbeat and the distant fountain splashing vibrated in his ears, competing for his attention. Warm, salty wind hammered his face. He sucked the hot, mid-August coastal air through his nose. By the end of this ordeal, his lungs would be brined like one of Chef Chevalier's turkeys.

He should have worn the heavy sunglasses Pearl offered him this morning, but they made his nose tired. He needed more nose muscle. His head wobbled toward the Inn again. A short woman wore a mass of color and texture that masqueraded as a dress. When she spoke, the big, loose sleeves floated hypnotically. Her hands flipped and fluttered, gesturing toward a thin giant dressed like Charlie Brown. He balanced on white crane legs, holding his hands up in front of him. He stared straight ahead, ignoring the kaleidoscopic whirlwind standing next to him.

Copper kept his eyes trained on the scene. "Mother, this is a school for the blind!"

"Copy Pie, many people will be here—"

"Shhh!" Copper interrupted.

Ms. Crazy Sleeves sang out, "My hair is getting so gray. I'm going to get it colored... Whoops! I mean, painted, a different color. You don't want the new residents to say, 'There goes Keegan's grandma!'"

There was movement near their feet. Acorns had been arranged in straight, even lines decorating the walkway, but one rolled into the grass, ruining the effect.

Copper's head snapped up at the sound of the word "No!" The blind beanpole's eyebrows slanted at a sharp angle.

His companion adjusted his black beanie. Her voice had the lilt of a songbird. "You seem a little feisty. Are you nervous? Is it already too busy?"

The angry giant was immobile except for something in his hands. While Ms. Sleeves sang every word, Charlie Brown's tone lacked all musicality. "I like people, but I won't know you with paint on your hair and neither will my father."

He thrust his arm high into the air then lowered it with a sweeping arc. He bent at the waist, executing an impressive theatrical bow. His voice boomed, "A new visitor has arrived!"

The flapping sleeves spun around. "Oh? That must be the Munro family!" She smoothed the front of her dress and glided toward them.

Copper searched the area for the missing studio audience and soundstage. Stunned by the amount of fanfare yet lack of applause, he stumbled as Pearl pulled him forward to close the gap.

"Hello! I'm Andrea Harris, director of The Retreat." Ms. Sleeves pointed over her shoulder at slim Charlie Brown. He waved a pair of pencils in front of his face. "That's my son, Keegan. He lives in the building right behind us. That's the Inn."

Pearl stuck out her hand. She selected her extra-high-pitched, speaking-to-strangers voice. "I'm Pearl Munro and this is my son, Copper."

Copper quietly thanked heaven that his mom hadn't introduced him as the dreaded "Copy Pie." The ladies grabbed each other's hands, then Pearl waved at the overgrown boy several paces away.

The world grew quiet and still. Awkward. Copper lowered his face to avoid engagement. Andrea Harris' hand stretched in his direction.

Shifting his weight from side to side, Copper's feet crushed a few acorns. He pinned his elbows to his ribs. "I don't touch people when I meet them." He reached into his pockets and squeezed this morning's one-cent windfall. Fingernails dug half-moon indentions into his palm.

Pearl's shoes scratched the pavement. "Oh, Copy. Babe, can you try to be a little…" She shook her head, wearing a pre-puke expression.

Ms. Harris smiled. "That's ok; he's right. Our customs are so weird sometimes! It's nice to meet you, Copper."

Pearl's elbow nudged him. His mother always poked, pushed, nudged, and prodded. Copper softened his belly and shoulders. He raised his head to a neutral position. "I'm Copper Munro. It's nice to meet you, Andrea Harris."

His mother's phony voice seemed tired. "It looks like Keegan's about your age. You should go say hello."

On command, he approached the pasty tower named Keegan. "I've been told that I should say hello."

There was a long, quiet pause.

"So… hello, I guess."

The Keegan kid was apparently trying to shake the yellow paint off his pencils. If he was blind, he had mythical levels of mental focus. The white string bean sucked in air and made strange sounds. When those noises transitioned into humming, Copper's head threatened to explode. He hated noisy mysteries. If his blood pressure had been a teapot, it would be whistling by now. His words came out like a growl. "What is up with the pencils?"

Keegan didn't turn in Copper's direction, but his hands became still and the humming stopped. "I'm animating. My autism gives me power." He finally turned, but only to inspect Copper. "I stim. Do you?"

Copper's mouth fell open. The guy wasn't blind.

Keegan used a louder voice. "You know, stim. Short for stimulation."

Copper had never met someone who proudly announced

their autism diagnosis. He wrung his hands. He wasn't sure what it meant to stim, even if it was short for stimulation. "I have autism, but I don't carry pencils."

The skinny boy shifted his gaze. Copper turned around to see what the sky-scraping Charlie Brown found so interesting. Their mothers were chatting a short distance from the gate. Maybe Keegan liked the gate or maybe he was planning to escape.

The irritating humming returned. It seared Copper's cheeks. Screeching birds, car horns approximately two streets south, the ladies' blathering, and Keegan's incessant noise poured over him. The commotion stole his breath. The dark, fuzzy halos reappeared around the edge of each eye. He wanted to scream, but that would only add to the noise level. If he couldn't compose himself, Copper would faint in front of these strangers. Without his brother Sterling, or a wall in the middle of the sidewalk, he had nothing to lean on.

He needed to regain control. With counterfeit confidence, he staked his claim on the moment. "My name is Copper Munro. I don't have any power. I am here to be punished."

Chapter Five

_____

KEEGAN

Speak less. Listen more.

- *How To Contain Your Crazy*

Andrea Harris led the small group to the Inn's lobby. She organized the guests, and the guardians shuffled off to another location on the property. Keegan shrugged. He enjoyed performing for larger audiences, but, as Director of the Retreat, his mother was the boss.

He tried not to worry that the latest arrival had described orientation so harshly. After all, that was how things went in the breakfast movie. Maybe Copper had seen it and was playing along. Either way, it was important to trust the wisdom of the famous writer-director John Hughes. He was the expert on the mysterious ways that young people form lasting bonds.

From now on, Keegan's life would be divided into two classifications: before friends and after friends. Yesterday, the coffee table's surface had reflected the wall art and the Edison-style lightbulbs. Last night, he'd sat in the lounge chairs and watched the light fixture make patterns in the shadows. But now, the presence of new people transformed the space. Two guys sat in the lounge chairs against the blue wall. Today, the table reflected their chests, elbows, and necks. Shadows and shoes covered the floor.

The teenager from the limousine sat in Keegan's favorite chair and brushed invisible lint from his clothes. If interior decor made a statement, the super-snuggly womb chair was the room's bright orange exclamation point. Keegan resisted the urge to reclaim his treasured seat. He looked at all three of the young men. Soon they would be a family…even the fierce redhead.

Everyone waited for the Resident Trainers to start the meeting, but his brother was nowhere in sight. The other trainer, Nicola, should have joined them, but Keegan hadn't seen her all morning, and the guests needed some entertainment. *Life at the Inn shouldn't be boring.* He touched his pocket for reassurance—the pencils were right where he left them. After a regal flourish, he began. "Welcome. I'm Keegan Harris. My parents, along with kind and generous donations from local business owners and the Professional Golfers' Association, have created the Retreat on Ainsley Avenue. The Inn is a brand new building and we will respect it." He touched his chest while making sure he practiced his best posture. "Don't worry; orientation will be perfect."

He thought about his favorite inspirational 80s movies. Usually there was a bunch of drama and arguing. Then people talked about their problems and dreams. That was the magical step when everyone became close friends. Once he figured out the pattern, he realized he could create a fast track to friendship. There wasn't time for arguing and drama; they could skip to the good part. Keegan bounced his eyebrows. *Time to get personal.* "I'm going to change the world with my greeting cards." He strode toward a small cabinet underneath the television and removed a card from the drawer. "This is my favorite in my 'Just Say Hello' collection." He read the front. "'Hi.'"

Not one guest looked at Keegan.

He continued. "The inside says, 'What's your favorite question?'" He clapped his hands and held the card in front of his body. He wanted to say "Ta-da," but Luke had warned him about showing off. Boasting hadn't made the list of recommended behaviors for social competency—patience was a trait that had been mentioned in several volumes. He gave his guests some time to applaud, but silence filled the room. This crowd needed access to his library.

A warm hand touched his shoulder. "Keeg, I love that card. Thanks for helping out. I'll take it from here."

He quickly scanned his brother's appearance. His brown, wavy hair hung loose around his shoulders. He'd paired an unbuttoned blue and white checked shirt with a plain white T-shirt underneath. Faded jeans skimmed the top of his motorcycle boots. The tear on the left knee probably helped keep him from overheating.

Luke cracked his neck from side to side, grabbed two of the hard, stackable chairs, and passed one to Keegan. He spun his own chair around backward and straddled it. Mother had taught them the proper way to sit in chairs. Backward was incorrect. The itch of irritation clawed at Keegan's neck. Today needed to be flawless.

Keegan leaned against the back of the chair with his legs stretched out before him. His butt barely touched the edge of the seat, transforming his body into a delightful inclined plane. He considered his options. His brother was a leader. Adopted at age 10, Luke didn't have Harris DNA, so he did things a little differently. To maintain the peaceful, fun ambiance, Keegan decided not to coach his brother on the proper way to sit on a chair. Even though Luke wasn't autistic, he was still a good guy.

"My name is Luke. I'm a Resident Trainer at the Inn. Welcome to Orientation. We'll get to know each other and take a tour of the property before lunch."

The businessman set his electronic tablet on the coffee table. "At precisely what time will we tour the grounds? I do not have a schedule." He stood and paced the perimeter of the lobby. "A schedule is of vital importance in order to avoid chaos. Someone neglected to email the daily agenda. I consulted my inbox four times upon arrival. Perhaps there's been some technical difficulty." He approached Luke. "May I obtain documentation outlining the scheduled activities? Also, I'd like to synchronize our watches." He resumed his parade of agitation.

Luke rubbed his stubbly cheeks. He stretched, rose from his seat, and soothed with calm, slow words. "Sure. First, I'm gonna pass out these papers real quick. Your room numbers are printed at the top. We're going to get to know each other and see how you do as a group. Learn as much as you can." He continued distributing the papers. "Take notes on this page. Later we'll use them for a game."

His signature lopsided smile was met by blank faces. He chewed his lower lip until one of his dimples appeared. "I'll go grab that schedule." He raised his radio. "Is Nicola on the property yet?" The keys on his belt loop rattled as he jogged away.

Chapter Six

COPPER

Throw a penny in the fountain. Make a wish.

As soon as the rock star cowboy left the room, Copper raced to the window. He had to figure a way out of this mess. If he could just fix things at home, Pearl would quit crying all the time and his life could go back to normal.

The construction site on the other side of the lawn gave him an idea. He flipped his paper over, grabbed a pen from the coffee table, and caught up with the pacing man. The Pacer's wrinkly Shar-Pei forehead was topped with bushy brown hair. His shirt had way too many buttons. A real leather belt was wrapped around his waist. Getting dressed in those clothes must take forever. Bundled up like a teacher, he was probably brilliant. Copper steadied the pen, ready to take notes, and asked the Pacer, "How much would it cost to get some sheetrock for a ceiling?"

The Pacing Professor looked at his watch, sighed, and moved his beady green eyes toward the ceiling. A few elaborate light fixtures and several recessed lights spruced up the most overlooked part of an interior. Thin blue plastic covered the fluorescent bulbs. The man had studied the ceiling for a long time.

Copper was desperate to speed up the process. He added, "Don't factor in the fancy lighting. Just the sheetrock."

Keegan pounced. "Aren't the lights wonderful? That blue film calms down the lightbulb."

Pinched between the tongs of tension and anxiety, Copper needed answers before he burst. He stamped his foot. "The plastic does nothing to make the sound of the light go away."

"How many square feet is the ceiling?" asked Professor Belt and Buttons.

"In here? Who cares? I want to build a different ceiling."

"A ceiling requires sheetrock, nails, texture, paint, a person to do the work…" The Professor tapped the screen on his tablet.

Several minutes passed. Keegan resumed his habit of stimming and humming, which made the man lose focus and forget the question. Copper looked toward the hyper stimmer. Since his parents had just finished building the Inn, he might have paid attention to some of the details. He decided to ask him. Paper flapping behind him, he tightened his grip on the pen and crossed the room.

Keegan's slouch all but guaranteed he'd slide off the seat and have a hard landing on his backside. Charlie Brown Beanie Boy held two pencils in one hand, with his arms folded in front of his chest.

Copper flashed his teeth and asked, "What do you think, Keegan?"

"Ceilings are important so they're very expensive. They must cost about the same as a gluten-free chocolate cake." Keegan moved the pencils in front of his face.

Copper's pulse raced. Surely someone here would be useful. He turned to the boy in the orange chair. His brown skin and pale eyes were an unusual combination. Even though he wore a standard issue school uniform, he was ready for the spotlight. Copper only watched the Entrée Network and vintage television shows, so he wasn't well versed in pop culture. But this kid was probably famous— famous people and fashion models probably didn't mind starched clothing. During televised cooking competitions, the contestants revered celebrities. Offering the universal sign for submission, Copper held his palms facing the ceiling. "Is there any chance you know something about the price of sheetrock?"

The boy displayed the whitest teeth Copper had ever seen. His smile stretched so far, his cheeks spilled over the edges of his face. He looked happy, but the veins on top of his hands bulged as he squeezed the fabric of his shorts. "My name is Joel Goodson. I deal in human fulfillment. I grossed over eight thousand dollars in one night."[1]

That level of wealth made Copper's heart soar. He'd never had that kind of money. Whatever it was, human fulfillment must be in high demand. Maybe this kid could use a partner. If his mom could learn about the industry, she wouldn't need three jobs. "This is great! How much does a ceiling cost?"

Prep School Magazine Model sprang to his feet. With one hand over his eyes and the other pointing to the sky, he declared, "You make no friends. You trust nobody. And you make damn sure you're the smartest guy in the room whenever the subject of money comes up."[2] His outburst hit Copper like a bolt of lightning.

Keegan's voice blasted from behind. "Cursing!"

Copper trembled. "I don't need trouble."

Someone touched his shoulder. He reeled to find the source of foreign pressure. Luke withdrew his hand and slid between him and the angry teen.

The boy's baby-soft cheeks became pink. With tears in his eyes, he sank to the floor and sobbed. "Show me the money!"

He looked up at Luke and whispered, "Help me. Help you. Help Meeeee, help you."[3]

Luke hugged the ranting schoolboy. "Is it Tom Cruise day, Tyler? C'mon, buddy. It's alright." He helped the crazy, handsome boy with too many names back into the orange chair.

Joel Goodson Tyler? The boy's terrible response to such a simple question forced Copper to scrutinize the people in the room. Keegan stopped waving his pencils.

The Professor stood stock-still. When his eyes met Copper's, he shrugged and said, "Five hundred dollars or more…" He looked at his scuffed leather shoes and mumbled, "For a ceiling."

The Inn on Ainsley Avenue was no ordinary place. Copper's mother hadn't simply abandoned him. She'd trapped him in an insane asylum.

Straight out of some Cool Guy Handbook, Luke threw his neck to the side, tossing brown hair away from his face. "Keeg, please move my chair closer to Tyler. I'm going to hand out the schedules." Luke distributed the printed copies. "These should also be in your email accounts, in case you prefer electronic information."

At this, the Professor's lips bent upward.

The model maniac and human fulfillment expert, Tyler, took the second piece of paper, wiped his cheeks, and flicked a small piece of lint from Luke's shirt. "Captain, my captain."[4]

With half a laugh, Luke tucked some of his long, floppy hair behind his ear. "Alright! I know this one." His hand moved to his chest. After clearing his throat, he pledged, "Seize the day boys. Make your lives extraordinary."[5]

A storm of fury burned Copper's face to a crisp. He returned to the window. Pearl was out there somewhere, probably howling with laughter. There was no way he'd be able to endure this freak show for an entire weekend. He'd had enough. He whirled to face the crowd. "Hey Rockstar Cowboy, I'm used to being confused by people, ok? Almost every moment of my life is a damned—"

Keegan cut in. "Cursing!"

"—riddle." Copper continued. "I hate it. I don't want to be here. And I can't listen to gibberish all day."

Keegan hopped out of his chair and wagged his cartoon-like limbs. "Hey! You're doing it wrong. First, let's stop using foul language. Second, you're going to live here. And third, we are *all* going to be best friends." The beanpole pouted.

Before Copper could reply, the Professor interjected. "False. That's the first lie they teach you in school. Simple proximity to people, in age or location, doesn't convert them into trustworthy companions." He shifted his attention back to his tablet.

"Guys, guys! Orientation is a chance for you to get acquainted with us and the property. Let's try to remove the pressure from the room." Luke stared at Copper. "Please, sit down."

Copper shuffled back to his seat.

Luke grinned. "I've never been called Rockstar Cowboy before. That's kind of cool, actually." He looked at his phone and said something about nickels.

The sound of the central air conditioner and the buzzing lights bombarded the air. A ticking clock added to the constant racket. He hadn't ever understood what people meant about background noise. For him, each sound registered at the same level. He became more stressed and the volume increased. When it reached a crescendo, he shut down. The world became muffled. His ears felt like they'd been stuffed with warm cotton.

"Ok. Spoiler alert: each of you is on the autism spectrum. As far as I know…"

Copper only caught small bits and pieces of Luke's speech. Like a bad phone signal, the words cut in and out.

"...only other thing you have in common..."

He could hear the dull roar of blood rushing through his veins. A pulse in his ear matched his heartbeat. Darkness crept in from the edges of his eyes. Soon he wouldn't see anything, even if his eyes were open. He picked through the garbled noise to find Luke's voice.

"...labels mean jack squat because every human being is different. Oh, crap..."

Copper put his head between his knees.

...In the distance, someone mumbled, "Cursing" and "Level two..."

He closed his eyes and slowed his breathing. The group carried on. He could not mentally adjust the noise levels, but the Resident Trainer's words sounded clearer again.

"Shoot! Anyone know what jack squat means? Never mind. All y'all are different, ok? We'll make this an easy game. Let's go around the circle. Say your name and a little something about yourself."

Keegan coughed. "Info dumping!"

"Right. Tell us three things about yourself." Luke corrected. "We'll start with Jay."

Copper raised his head. If his punishment involved two nights at the Inn, he'd be able to hurry home and forget this nightmare ever happened. But if not, he needed to pay attention. As long as he looked past the phantom glitter sparkling in the air, he could see.

The Professor held up his index finger. "My name is Jay Simmons." He peeked at his schedule and stuck a second finger into the air. "My room is 506." His third finger poked out. "In precisely 98 minutes, I will go there." He held up his tablet with both hands and snapped pictures of the lobby.

Luke's chair squeaked. "Maybe I should introduce myself as an example. I'm Luke Bachman-Harris. As a Resident Trainer, I help people get adjusted to their new home. If you choose to live here, we'll talk about your goals, monitor your progress, and help you sort through any problems. You can come to me with questions and I'll do my best to help. I'm interested in music, so if you ever hear a good song, I'd love for you to share that with me. I look forward to knowing each of you."

The flash on Professor Jay's camera lit up Luke's face. "Luke Bachman-Harris, what is the number for your residence?"

"I'm in the first room on your hall. Number 500. My name is on the door." He shook his hair again. "Keeg, it's your turn."

Keegan stood. He made a hand gesture similar to a ringleader for the circus. "Once again, I'm Keegan Harris." He bowed. "Blah, blah, blah. I hate repeating." He reached into his back pocket and unfolded a notecard. "This is from my new line of postcards. They feature friendly life tips. See the picture of the spider on the front? The caption says, 'A spider is not a snack.' That's some solid advice." He smiled and waited. Eventually he added, "My room is 502." As soon as his body slid back into his chair, Jay photographed the human ramp.

Luke looked toward Copper and flung his hand out. "Go ahead."

A small groan escaped while Copper calculated his sentences. "I'm Copper Munro. I like nicknames." He wiggled his feet. "Um… I did not plan to come here. I don't know what to say."

Luke leaned forward in his chair. "You have an interesting name. Is there a story behind it?"

Copper exhaled and relaxed his shoulders. In his day program, he'd been stuck at the mercy of other people, and sometimes appearing agreeable made life easier. So he took a deep breath and tried to reset himself from a rolling boil to a simmer. "My mom is named Pearl. She married a man named Steele for a short time. She wanted to use gemstone names for girls and metallic names for boys. Something about how all of her kids were precious." There was no response. He shifted in his seat. "She had Sterling and me. I don't have any sisters."

Luke pulled out his pen. "You bring up a good point. Raise your hand if you have any brothers or sisters." Luke held his pen in the air and Keegan stretched his clutched pencils toward the sky. They were the only ones with hands up. They looked at each other and said, "Kiara" at the same time.

Copper winced. "Is that enough?"

Jay snapped Copper's photo. "502 has been accounted for. What's your room number?"

Copper ruffled his orientation sheet. "I'm in 504." He whispered, "Weirdo" to himself.

Jay scribbled some notes. "504. Ginger. An adequate response."

Luke turned toward the mad model. "Tyler, you're next. Say hello to everyone."

Tyler's leg bounced. "Say hello to my little friend!"[6]

Keegan giggled and clapped.

Luke held his finger up to his lips until Keegan hushed. "This is Tyler Ramsey. When he gets nervous, sometimes he uses movie lines to communicate. Some of his words may sound unusual. Tyler, tell the guys where you've been living with your grandfather the last few months."

Tyler's voice took on a warm, rich tone. He sounded like an announcer from a tourism ad. "All I'm saying, mon, is if we walk Jamaican, talk Jamaican, and is Jamaican, then we sure as hell better bobsled Jamaican."[7]

The room erupted into laughter. Everyone except Tyler. But he relaxed his shoulders and smiled.

Keegan patted him on the shoulder. "I love movies...

especially from the 1980s. That's good, except for the profanity."

Tyler stretched his hand toward the hem of Keegan's T-shirt, but the Busybody stepped just out of reach saying, "Don't worry; some of the best people I know don't talk at all or they communicate in unique ways. Wait until you meet my Australian uncle."

"Tyler is a lot of fun. Y'all be kind and help him feel welcome." Luke looked at the room. "I guess that's everyone for—"

Jay spoke over his camera's shutter sound effect. "What room number?"

"Tyler, can you tell everyone your room number?"

"Nobody puts Baby in a corner."[8]

Keegan sat up straight and folded his arms, looking like someone who got to lick the spoon. "That means he's in the big corner room. 508."

Jay punched on his tablet screen. "Thanks, 502."

Luke's phone vibrated. He ran his thumb over the screen, twitched his mouth, and said, "Jay, I hope you'll learn their names. You may be living together."

Professor Jay touched his wrinkled forehead. "Numbers are easier."

"So we should call you 506?"

Jay shook his head and studied his page of notes. "I apologize for the repetition. My notations are insufficient. Please repeat your name, 502."

Keegan sprang across the room. He spoke, using his full voice, into Luke's ear. "Was only part of that in English?"

Luke shoved his phone in his pocket. "I got it. Watch this, Keeg." He stacked his chair in the corner. "I'll make it easy for ya. I'm Luke." With the tip of his finger, he poked his chest. "Apparently, a rockstar cowboy." He nudged his brother with his elbow. "This is Keegan, the stimming greeting card poet."

He waved his hand in a circular motion. "We've got our fiery, natural element Copper, movie-loving Tyler, and you"—he rubbed his stubbly chin and grinned—"just-the-facts Jay."

One of Luke's eyes blinked. He warmed his hands. His rings rubbed against each other. Rings knocking and keys tingling—Copper reconsidered his nickname. *Rockstar Cowboy, Jingles the human wind chime, or just Luke for short?*

The Resident Trainer's voice cut through his thoughts. "How are we doing on our schedule? Walk and talk, guys. It's tour time."

Chapter Seven

KEEGAN

A good host makes his guests comfortable and engages each in conversation.

- Politely Perfect

Jay followed Luke so closely, he almost stepped on his heels. Instead of admiring the property, he squinted at his watch, counting, "45, 46, 47…"

Keegan stopped the group and gave a thorough demonstration of looking both ways before crossing the street. Traffic only traveled in one direction on that part of the road, but he was a firm believer in caution. "Always practice safety. It's a rule."

In his best impersonation of a tour guide, Luke walked backward on the central lawn. "The Welcome Center is an office for Ms. Harris. It's attached to an art studio and a small gallery. If the funding comes through, we'll add a larger space for exhibits and live performances."

Jay stopped counting. "How many artists live here?"

"I'm artistic!" Keegan jumped and spiraled like a top before gravity drew his feet to the ground.

Copper picked a penny off the ground. "I thought you said autistic."

Keegan beamed. "I'm both!" He pulled off his black beanie and spun it on his finger. Whenever his hair dried underneath a hat, his curls shot out in every direction.

Jay's eyes widened.

Keegan sang, "Crazy hair; don't care."

Luke continued, "They designed the Retreat so folks can develop their interests. We want to help people find their place in the world, Jay. If that place doesn't exist, we'll build it."

Keegan slapped Luke's hand in a perfect display of friendly agreement, a well-placed high five. Retracing his steps, he found Tyler at the back of the pack. He presented his cap to Tyler. "You used to be much more...muchier. You've lost your muchness."[1]

Tyler placed the hat on his head and pulled one of Keegan's long, blond ringlets into a wavy line. When he let go, the coil snapped back like a spring. In the style of a movie trailer narrator, he announced, "There is a place, like no place on earth. A land full of wonder, mystery, and danger. Some say, to survive it, you need to be as mad as a hatter"—he pulled the cap on tighter and grinned—"which, luckily, I am."[2]

Keegan skipped away and fell into step with Copper, who seemed immune to Keegan's infectious charm and abundant energy. The grumpy redhead preferred to stare at the construction site in the distance. He was so passionate about building materials. Maybe checking on the sensory spa's progress would improve his mood. Copper's jaw clenched. "Why does it look like the Brady Bunch lives here?"

"Looks like Copper's a fan of old TV shows." Luke nodded and blinked one eye.

"They're on TV every afternoon at Pleasant Grove," Copper replied.

"Pleasant Grove? Is that the name of your…" Luke, unable to find the next word, shrugged.

Arms folded in front of his chest, Copper's voice rose. "My day program."

Luke nodded. "Gotcha. Do you like that show?"

"They always play ancient programs." Copper rested his hands on his hips. "I change it to the Entrée Network as soon as possible."

Unlike his younger brother, Luke hadn't studied game show model movements. His hands waved around nonsensically. "Some of these buildings have been here for a while. We've remodeled the interiors and built some new structures to blend in. Maybe it's nostalgic, but we thought this style would be more relaxing. Andrea said less visual clutter would help our residents."

Jay tapped his watch and strode to the front of the group. "205, 206, 207…"

Sensing a common interest, Keegan swooped in. He brought his face close to Copper's and bent down to establish eye contact. "Mom loves Brady Bunch houses. She always wanted to live in one. Old TV shows are the best! They tell you when to laugh."

Copper waved his hand in front of his face. Keegan wasn't sure if he was trying to stim or signal irritation. To make his guest more comfortable, Keegan added, "Don't worry; none of these buildings tell you when to laugh!" Four leaps later, he caught up with the others. "Laughing buildings. Copper is hilarious!"

The group stopped in a shady spot near a wall made of honeycomb-shaped concrete. Jay referenced his tablet. "The map says this is the Recreation Center. We may not have time to go inside."

Keegan pushed open the door. "We can hurry. The basketball club hasn't played in here today. Don't worry; it won't smell."

Luke snickered as they filed into the building. "You'll get used to us. Keegan has a lot of worries and a hypersensitive nose. He always notices how everyone and everything smells."

It was Keegan's turn to walk backward. "It's one of my top concerns."

Jay tapped his watch.

"Right!" Keegan ran through the rooms, labeling each one. "Gym, exercise room, mixed-use activity room, lounge, and media room. We'll hang out in here later," he sang. He turned his arms into airplane wings and "flew" out the door.

Chapter Eight

COPPER

Penny ante

When they finally arrived at the construction site, some tension left Copper's body. The sight of scaffolding and equipment strewn everywhere was inspiring.

Keegan twirled with outstretched arms. "This is going to be our Sensory Spa. It will be a special place to relax with lights, fidget toys, and soft music. We need it to get powered up, build our ideas, and become the future. Mom said I can add my whimsical touches to make it spectacular, as soon as the workers have finished."

Copper found another lost penny and shoved it in his pocket. "It sounds amazing." Drawn to the sound of men working, he slowly distanced himself from the group.

Keegan's voice echoed off the concrete floor. "It should be completed soon. We'll have a grand opening in October."

In the next room, Copper found two men wearing overalls and masks were painting the textured walls. Cords trailed from their ears into their pockets. He seized his chance. "How much does sheetrock cost?"

The workers, stopped to look at him, crinkled their eyes, nodded, and went back to work.

Luke startled him. "Come on back. I don't want you to step on a nail or something."

The rest of the group had been waiting in the doorway. Keegan was in his element. Copper couldn't decide which moved faster: Keegan's mouth or his pencils: "...there might be an indoor swing in it, but I also want an outdoor playground with lots of swings," he said.

The Professor flinched. His glowing device hung at his side. "But playgrounds are customary for small children!"

"Swinging is *fun*. Playgrounds are for fun *people*. And we've designed this one to be inclusive for *fun people* who have different abilities." Captain Stilts looked closely at Jay's face.

Copper counted to himself: *one, one thousand, two, one thousand, three, one thousand.* Keegan was holding Jay's gaze a little longer than most people. Therapists loved to teach that skill, but Copper hated it. There's too much information in a face. The constantly morphing facial expressions distracted the brain from the words being said.

The Professor seemed like an average white guy who loved buttons. He wasn't ugly, he just didn't smile very much. Jay might have been the oldest person at orientation. Copper couldn't tell what the man was feeling—Pearl said that wasn't his gift. Whenever people stared at him, his stomach turned.

Still staring, the human tower called Keegan bent down and inspected Jay like he was an unusual bug. "Are you someone who hates fun? That would be really sad. I can't tell if you grew up to be surly or if you are having a feisty day. I need to know so I can make you my friend."

Luke stepped in between them. "Keeg, remember to stand back this far." He bent Keegan's skinny arms at the elbow and held his hands out in front. Keegan moved back far enough that his fingertips didn't touch anyone.

"Jay is new here. Let's let him get used to things," whispered Luke. "Did you see how I did that? I breathed words using a tiny bit of air. That's whispering."

Copper heard the whole exchange. He wanted to laugh but stopped himself. He needed to get serious about solving his own problems. His thoughts veered back to the painters' creased eyes and his sense of frustration returned.

Luke's talk with his brother didn't seem to mean much. The blond curls bounced as he ran toward the back of the building. "These are the Cottages. Most of our full-time residents live here." As they followed Keegan's trail, Tyler snuck up behind Jay and tucked the man's tag back under his collar.

Copper dragged his feet and lingered with the Resident Trainer. "Do people ignore you, Luke?"

"Sometimes. Did you need something?"

"I asked those painters a question, but got no response. They studied me, then dismissed me like I hadn't said a word. I bet they had sad smiles under those masks. I see those all the time. They're the worst."

"What do you think sad smiles mean?"

"I don't know." He wasn't about to dredge up those memories now.

"It's possible Benny and Tony didn't understand you. What was your question?"

"I need to learn about the price of sheetrock for a ceiling project."

Luke's face brightened. "Well, alright! You like construction? I'll be happy to find out for you."

"You will?" Copper couldn't hide his hope.

"Sure."

"Can you also find out about Joel Goodson Tyler's human fulfillment business for me? I think it could help my mom."

Luke's feet came to a sudden stop. His hand flew to his cheek. "Hold on. Tyler's name is just Tyler."

"That's weird. He called himself Joel when we first spoke."

Luke kicked a twig over the edge of the sidewalk. "That's called delayed echolalia. When Tyler's stressed, borrowing language from movies is easier than forming his own sentences." He ground an acorn into the cement. His hair flew back as he looked up. "He was all about Tom Cruise movies this morning. And I think, maybe, human fulfillment might not be a good thing to suggest to your mother."

"She works a lot. A better job could—"

"Dude, trust me. I don't know a lot about women, but I'm certain this topic is not going to make her happy."

The last thing Copper needed to do was add to his problems with Pearl. "But—"

Luke tugged at his collar. "You'd have to see that movie to understand. And, from what I've seen, women don't like being told what kind of job they should take." He blinked one eye, turned, and resumed their walk.

"Ok. I still need to know about the sheetrock."

"Absolutely. Right now, I gotta keep up with my assistant tour guide. Come on." He jogged around the side of the building.

Copper noticed a reduction in the weight of the world. He no longer dragged an invisible boulder; the shackles had been sliced off. Luke was exactly the kind of person he had claimed to be—a helper. The other guys would probably enjoy their time here. But Copper would get his information, make a plan, and go home. He might have to stay through lunch, possibly the entire weekend, but then he would return to his home and make things right.

Around the corner, Keegan's grand gestures dominated the scene. "Some cottages have two people inside and others have four. My dad said that if we run out of room, we might add an apartment building in a few years." His cheeks were already changing color in the midday sun.

Tyler picked a tropical flower. Spinning the yellow bloom between his fingers, he slowly approached Copper. His eyes seemed so familiar. In the sunlight, they almost matched Sterling's eye color. His brother had inherited the icy blue gaze from Steele's side of the family. Pearl always said the Campbell eyes could melt your heart or pierce your soul, depending on whether they squinted or flashed. That was all he'd heard from her on the topic of Steele Campbell, but he knew Sterling hated that he'd inherited his father's eyes and last name.

Looking at Tyler, he thought of the good times he'd shared with his big brother. Sometimes Sterling had picked him up early from his day program. They'd hop in his little car, the Cozy Cocoon, and grab a quick meal at the diner before they had to eat whatever awful thing Pearl had prepared. They always ordered breakfast food because Sterling understood it was wrong to eat two dinners. Sterling called these delicious indulgences pre-gaming. Copper had always meant to ask what that meant. Now he'd never know.

He tasted the tear that slid down his cheek. Once or twice a year, Copper had let Sterling hug him. His brother was the only person whose touch didn't make his skin crawl. If he walked up right now, Copper would throw his arms around him. That would shock everyone...for multiple reasons.

He wiped his face with the back of his hand. Tyler was holding the flower out to him. There was no way Copper would turn down those eyes. The young man placed the flower in his palm and turned away. Tyler reached down and rubbed a huge knot on the back of his leg and whispered, "There's no place like home."[1]

Chapter Nine

KEEGAN

Sharing a meal offers a social opportunity.

- Friendship Knocks

"...and the inside says, 'Even if you ate something yucky.'" Keegan closed the card and looked at the families scattered across the dining hall. Each group formed their own little cluster at individual tables.

His mom's arm squeezed his waist. "Thanks, Keegan. That was lovely. Everyone, we hope you enjoy lunch today. We have two different restaurants on the property. Our residents have menus electronically delivered to the devices in their rooms. They can choose when and where they'd like to eat at no additional charge. Those with food allergies may prefer the cafeteria on the ground floor of the Terrace. That kitchen supplies meals to our medically fragile clients." Andrea pointed over her shoulder. "The Terrace is the four-story building located just beyond our extended stay facility, the Courtyard." She gestured in the opposite direction. "When you're finished eating, feel free to go to the Inn and explore the rooms before you say your goodbyes. We'd like the guys to have some downtime before we continue their orientation activities."

Keegan and his mother pulled out the green plastic chairs and sat at a small table for two. His plate was covered in clear plastic film. "I had your gluten-free cheeseburger brought over today." Andrea sipped her iced tea and picked at her food. Keegan shoved as much burger as he could into his mouth. Despite the low hum of conversation in the room, she still heard and corrected Keegan's smacking sounds. "Chew with lips closed, remember?" She rested her chin in her hand. "Are you extra hungry? I'd better text them to bring over the gluten-free chocolate chip cookies. Do you want grapes too?"

He nodded. "And milk."

"We'd better hold off on that, ok? When you drink a lot of milk, you get silly."

Keegan sat angled away from the table. "Fine. No milk party." He stuffed six french fries into his mouth. "The fries are good today."

"How's it going with the guys? Is Luke alright?"

A mound of smashed burger and fries rounded Keegan's cheeks to maximum capacity. "Good. Everyone will love it here. Luke seemed a little nervous, but I helped him out."

"I bet you did." She took a bite of her salad and looked at the next table.

Keegan glanced to the side and noticed Tyler's family. The boy was trying to pick something off the shoulder of the lady sitting next to him. Her head was facing the older gentleman on her opposite side. As though she were on auto-pilot, she gently set Tyler's hand aside and continued her conversation without a pause.

Keegan's mother asked, "Did you like Tyler?"

"Yes." Keegan swiveled in his seat to get a better look at his new buddy. "I gave him my hat, but he's not wearing it now."

"That was nice. I see you let your hair dry in it this morning. Turn back around, son."

Keegan angled back to face her.

"Did you notice the people with Tyler?"

Keegan, feeling a spark of energy, leaned forward. "That man has a huge stim stick. I wanted to talk to you about it!"

"Ok. We can chat about that later. That's Tyler's grandfather, Clement Edward Ramsey. He's very strict. Maybe wearing a hat at the table is against his rules."

"Oh." Keegan put his pencils on the table. "The lady in yellow has a beautiful smile. I saw it this morning."

"She sure does. That's Olivia, Tyler's governess."

"She works for the government? Wow."

"Not exactly. More like a nanny. She's kind and has a lovely accent. Once you're finished eating, I'll introduce you."

"Luke's here now," Keegan mumbled.

"How do you—"

"I smell his cologne."

Luke put a container of grapes and two large chocolate chip cookies on the table. "Somebody asked for reinforcements?" He raised an eyebrow and smirked at Keegan. His mouth broke into a wider grin as he looked at Andrea.

She stretched her hand out to him and he took it. "Thank you for doing an excellent job this morning. It had to be unnerving, jumping in there on your own. Nicola will be here soon."

"We managed. Hope she's alright."

"She'll be fine—"

"Luke, can you get an old cane pole out of storage for me?" Keegan interrupted. "I want to turn it into a giant stim stick."

Luke bobbed his head. "Will do, buddy. Look, Jay is sitting by himself. No one is here representing the Simmons family?"

His mother's hand covered her heart. "Oh! We should have invited him to our table."

"I got it." Luke grabbed a handful of Keegan's grapes and sauntered over to Jay's table.

Andrea watched him leave. "We got so lucky with him. He's such a good guy. Both of you are turning into wonderful young men, Keegan."

"Jay seems super-serious." Keegan thought about serious people as he bit into a cookie. "Maybe he's a genius!"

His mom picked up her fork again. "He has a cool job, but I'll let him tell you all about it. Now, what did you think of Copper?"

Determined to keep spirits high, Keegan chose a positive answer. "He really likes ceilings. He's going to be a builder."

Andrea rubbed the side of her neck. When they spoke to each other, she often held her head to the side. The Harris Head-tilt may have been her creation. Keegan liked to draw her in that pose. It was one way he instantly recognized his mother. He had many tricks to help him with facial blindness.

Staring at his last cookie, he considered how he might work those tips into a greeting card. "Andrea?"

"Yes, son?"

"My social skills book says sharing is friendly. Let's see if Tyler wants to eat this cookie."

"Good plan."

Tyler's group had finished their meal and stood near the door. His grandfather scowled. Olivia held Tyler at arm's length and touched him lightly on the cheek. "Yu fayva yuh madda. Dis gud luck."

The young man flashed his million-dollar smile and said, "Mi luv yuh." They both walked backward away from each other and turned around three times.

Keegan stood, held the cookie straight in the air, and spun. "Mom! He's a dancer."

Andrea touched Keegan's chest. "Careful." She looked at the other diners.

Keegan leaned in close. "Don't worry; I'll teach him English."

His mother tapped him lightly on the tip of his nose. "I'm going to check on Jay. Coming here alone had to be hard."

Keegan moved closer to Tyler. As his long arm floated down to shoulder height, he dipped his head in supplication and presented the chocolate chip cookie to Tyler. It slid from between his fingers. His offering had been accepted.

Luke took him by the elbow and led him a few steps away from the others. "We haven't had much time to talk. Is everything good so far?"

"It's not how I imagined it. I can't tell if they're happy. Nicola helps me figure these things out. Where is she?"

"She's tied up at the courthouse."

"Are you serious?"

"Yeah. I'm doing the best I can, but it's a little trickier than I thought it would be."

"Luke, this isn't about you. Off topic! Who's going to untie her? Is it a big knot? Can we use scissors? We need to rescue her!"

"Whoa. Sit down. She isn't actually tied with rope." Luke shook his head. "Figurative language, sorry. I mean she's busy with some legal issues. She'll be here as soon as she can."

"What time is that?"

Luke nudged him. "Careful. You sound like Jay..." The edge of his mouth curled.

"No jokes! We have team-building activities coming up. She needs to be here. Who's going to help me with all these emotions?"

"Hey...you and me, we got this! You know everything we're supposed to do today. Keegan, you helped make the schedule. What could go wrong?"

Keegan whipped his pencils out.

"Keeg, sit down for a minute."

Relieved his brother had chosen not to straddle the chair, Keegan resumed his seat.

"Do you really feel like you need those right now?"

Keegan's volume increased, his words laced with anxiety. "My pencils?"

"Yeah. I know you carry them around with you like a security blanket." Luke ran his hand through his hair and rested his forehead in his palm. "Are you super stressed out?"

Keegan rolled the pencils between his hands. "I have these pencils and you have your key collection."

"You see them as the same thing?"

"You jingle them when you fidget. They give you power. You carry them everywhere."

"Buddy, these keys are part of my job. I'm required to have them. I don't choose to…"

Keegan nodded. "Ah. That's true. I'm self-employed. Being my own boss gives me a lot of choices. Are you upset, Luke? Do you want to start a greeting card company?"

Luke's eyebrows tried to form one hairy line across his face. Perhaps in frustration that they would never reach that goal, they fell back apart. "Whatever." His dimples resurfaced with his smile. "It's fine. You do you, bro. I just want you to be ok."

Keegan patted his brother's hand. "That's nice, Luke. I know you don't have autistic abilities. It's not your fault you can't see my power." He rolled his wrist so his palm faced the ceiling like a waiter holding a tray. "If you would like some pencils, I can give you a pair. I have extra, but right now, I need to use this pair to build a team."

Chapter Ten

COPPER

A penny in a light socket

Copper sat across from his mother. While her chin wagged, her hands bent and swayed just like the chefs on the Entrée Network. She tossed, whipped, and folded invisible ingredients while spewing words like an overzealous meat slicer.

Over her shoulder, a stainless steel countertop caught his eye. *That must be the kitchen. Do they use All-Clad cookware? The ones with the copper core are the best.* He shook himself. *Focus.*

Pearl's voice rose, grating against his ears. He tried to listen, but his thoughts bounced from ads for kitchen appliances to the damaged ceiling back home. His memory cycled through the events of that awful day when the attic's insulation and sheetrock had offered little resistance to his full body weight. His foot had plunged through to the other side. He'd missed the electric current flowing into the light fixture by inches. While he'd imagined what it might feel like to fall from such a height, the glowing bulb warmed his leg. Fourteen steps. He'd counted them several times. Just thinking about the experience made his leg throb. Weeks had passed, but he could still hear himself screaming over the sound of people shouting, squawking radio voices, and strange smells. "Don't touch my box! It's for Sterling. He needs it!" There had been a big needle and then darkness. He'd woken to Pearl's tear-streaked face looking down at him. It was the worst day of his life.

Her cheeks were dry today. Orientation made her act nervous, but not sad. *I ruined her ceiling. I wasted it. We might not ever get a new one. I broke the rule and went into the attic. I deserve to be punished!* Copper considered how he might earn the money for ceiling repairs. He had no skills. The sum total of his activities in the adult day program at Pleasant Grove consisted of forty hours a week of video games and television. *Was there any money in watching the Entrée Network or playing* Passage?

His mother's intensified pace jolted him to the present. "So I was thinking, we could sign on for six months here." Pearl paused.

Copper stared at her.

She lowered her voice as the words continued to pour from her mouth. "...as part of a compromise...but only if you like it. It seems like a good place."

How had this experiment turned from two nights into six months? Her words skewered his heart. Sterling had always insisted an apology helped with damage control, so Copper said, "Mom, I messed up. I'm sorry." He forced his eyes to look deep into hers. They were the same shade of dark blue as his own—not like the sparkles in Sterling's light blue eyes, which had greatly increased their effectiveness. "I really am sorry." *Were there any other words a person should use in an apology?* Out of all the recommended therapies, he'd never had any instruction on relationship repair.

His mother bit her lip.

He couldn't maintain the eye contact any longer. "I broke the rules and I ruined the ceiling." He threw his hands halfway up in the air. He'd seen that gesture on some commercial. "But

I'm learning what to do to fix it. I'll find a way to get the money and put it back together, ok? Please let me come back home."

"Babe…"

It was his turn to talk faster. "The people here are nice, but weird. Some of them may be crazy."

"We're not here because of the ceiling." She propped her forehead against her hand. "I didn't know you were even thinking about that! Copy, you're here to see if this is a good option for your life. You're here because of Sterling." She pulled her head up and waved her hands around. "I thought you understood. The lawyers have these papers—"

The contents of his stomach whipped into a frothy, acidic foam. He pushed his chair back from the table. The familiar hazy rings started closing off his view of Keegan across the room. Blood roared in his ears. *This is worse than I'd imagined. Lawyers are talking about me and what happened to Sterling.* His back slid down the wall. He brought his knees up close to his body and used them as a place to rest his head.

Flashbacks of the ceiling, sirens, strangers, police, and his mother's sobbing all haunted him. It had been weeks, but he could still hear his mother saying, *"Sterling is dead, baby. He didn't make it."*

Someone from Ainsley Avenue whispered his name and rubbed his back. He shuddered at the touch and wanted to vomit. Then, much to his relief, he recognized the tinkling jingle from a set of keys. "Luke, is there someplace I can lie down? I need…"

"Yep. Can you walk, Copper, dude? Here, lean on me. We're right by the Inn. Let's go check out your room." Amid the sounds of whispering, chairs scraping the floor, and radio static, Luke's voice sounded mellow, almost lazy as he said, "We'd like a nurse to visit room 504. Thanks."

Chapter Eleven

KEEGAN

Competently directing an activity inspires trust.

- Lead the Way to Friendship

After all the excitement with Copper at the end of lunch, he'd been asked to take paperwork to his mom's office. Keegan needed to be even more responsible during Nicola's absence. These changes fell into the unexpected category, but he refused to let fear or random events derail his plans. He tossed the packet onto his mother's desk and tiptoed back to the art room.

The floor was lined with paper that crinkled as he dodged white canvases. Jay and Tyler stood near the door in awkward silence. Desperate for an ice-breaker, Keegan reached for the card he'd folded and stuffed into his pocket. "If you want to be friends, answer one important question," Keegan read, then opened the card. "Do you like to chase squirrels?"

The clock ticked loudly. There was no applause. His curls bounced when he shook his head. These guys didn't understand his art. Keegan hoped they enjoyed making things because he'd included painting in the team-building exercises.

The breakfast movie showed that engaging in creative pursuits was the best way to bond. He took a deep breath, gathered his courage, and moved to the next activity on the schedule.

A tall cylinder of dry spaghetti, a package of marshmallows, and some tape sat on a table in the center of the room. Keegan stuffed a large marshmallow into his mouth as he took a seat.

Jay stood by the door, gawking at the room. He pinched the bridge of his nose and reviewed his printed schedule for the millionth time. "This document neglects to mention any activity that involves squirrels. Do I not possess an updated version? Have alterations occurred due to Copper's health crisis? I require a current, clean copy." He patrolled the room, snapping photos with his phone. "It says team-building exercises." He peered under the table and searched the floor. "I do not work with squirrels."

Tyler sat with Keegan. He pulled the beanie out of his pocket and placed it back on his head. Keegan tossed him a marshmallow. His handsome face changed into a silly expression. With cheeks bloated by marshmallows, he garbled a word that sounded like "squirrel."

Keegan wanted to look relaxed and in charge so he leaned back in his chair. Just as his mother had always warned, he lost his balance. It was a close call, but he recovered the wobbling cylinder of pasta and gripped the edge of the table. "You guys don't understand how this works." He reached into his pocket and slapped his pencils onto the flat surface. "Step 1. I read a card. Step 2. You tell me it's wonderful and applause me."

Jay tapped his watch. "Applaud. The proper term is applaud."

One could not argue with a genius. Keegan gave a grateful nod and tried to produce his most cheerful smile. Luke was right. Leadership and hosting were tricky, indeed. He threw his hands up in the air. "I'll have to take over." He tried out his best teacher's voice. "We're going to make a tower using this tape and dried spaghetti. Then we'll place a marshmallow on top." He rubbed his chin. The *Gesture Dictionary* said that meant a person might be thoughtful or plotting. He hoped the others knew their gestures and could translate the move as thoughtful. "There's just one problem: it's supposed to be a timed race with teams and we don't have all of our people." He managed to keep the disappointment and frustration out of his voice. His speech therapist would have been proud. He'd spent hours talking to himself for practice.

Jay blurted, "The schedule can't accommodate additional delays. I'll be the timekeeper. I've got a stopwatch."

Keegan realized that this particular genius hadn't fully developed his social skills. *Politely Perfect* taught that it's rude to point out another person's flaws at your first meeting. Choosing to address it later, Keegan spoke with joy in his heart. "OK." He took some spaghetti and passed the jar to Tyler. "After this, we're supposed to paint those sketches on the floor. They're going to become pieces in a mural. Today's experience will become part of the property. Years from now, we'll be able to remember the weekend we became best friends."

Chapter Twelve

COPPER

Cut off without a penny

Luke handed Copper a key card. "After you, sir."

Copper swiped until the light turned green. The door opened to a kitchen that looked nothing like home or what he'd seen in cooking magazines. Equipped with only a tiny sink, mini fridge, and a microwave—he dismissed the toy kitchen. He passed over a small dining area to examine the living room. A sofa, chair, and coffee table filled the space. For a glorified prison, at least it was clean. "Are all the rooms at The Inn like this one?"

"Pretty much, but you haven't seen everything. Next to the TV, there's an entrance to the bedroom and a private bathroom."

Copper admired the built-in bookcase and shelves near the desk area. Without any enthusiasm, he noted the bathroom with a brief nod.

The hinges on the main door squeaked open. Apparently he didn't have the only key—so Ainsley Avenue's idea of privacy was an illusion. But at home, his door didn't even have a lock. He refused to care either way. *What difference did anything make now?*

Pearl walked in with a woman wearing a lab coat. Copper ignored them and switched on the second TV by the bed. At least they got the Entrée Network. The muted screen displayed a close-up of a manicured hand using a soft cloth to wipe an already clean pan. A red price flashed in the upper corner. Colorful vegetables poured out of another pan onto a stylish place setting. He considered his options and re-phrased the question. "Are all the Inn's *kitchens* like this one?"

"Yes, Baby. It's called a kitchenette." If artificial sweetener could make a sound, it would use the same tone as his mother's voice. "Will you let the nurse take your temperature?"

Copper flopped onto the bed and stared at the TV. The nurse touched his forehead and listened to his heart. She checked his blood pressure, gave him a quick smile, and whispered to Pearl that his vital signs were within the normal range. Then she left the room.

Pearl bumped his arm with a brochure. "Copy, this room looks just like the one in the picture. Do you want to go around and match everything up with me?" She spoke to Luke. "That always used to help him adjust to new places." His mother acted as though he needed an interpreter, as if she was an ambassador to the eccentricities of Copper Munro.

Luke nodded. "I'm familiar with the technique."

Copper exhaled. "Did you know Chef Pascal Chevalier only uses All-Clad cookware on his show? He's had 186 episodes and three specials." The commercial faded, and the program continued. "Oh, this is the one where he makes—"

"Copy Pie, do you want me to go?"

Leave it to his mother to ignore everything he found interesting. Chef Chevalier or cookware could have been conversation starters. She didn't understand him at all. He'd lost his brother, and his future, and now she expected him to play "Match the Picture" like he was five years old. Sanity had died with Sterling. Neither apologies nor polite conversation worked. There'd been death and destruction of property. He'd gained the attention and scrutiny of professionals who dealt in matters of law. *Maybe Pearl needed to make a clean getaway.*

His eyes never left the television. "You're leaving. I'm staying. This is my place now."

"Yes, for two nights. Copper, I promise, I will come back and—"

"Six months? Two years? You don't know the future. Nobody does. Stop pretending." His words were as sharp as the knives he'd seen advertised in *Bon Appétit* magazine. He flattened his face and his voice. "Go." He moved his hand the same way his fifth-grade teacher had when she sent students to the principal's office. "Leave."

"I…"

He refused to make eye contact. The blanket shifted under his leg as she smoothed the bedding. "He's never been much of a people person. Well now, you be a good boy and I'll see you soon. You can call me if you need…" She rushed toward the bedroom door, and thick, gooey sadness coated her vocal cords. "I'll come right away if you need me." Her voice sounded exactly like it had the day he'd fallen through the ceiling. "I'll miss you."

Luke called Pearl's name, but the front door slammed shut.

"Copper dude, we should talk, my man."

Copper turned up the volume just in time to hear Chef Chevalier's French accent say, "There's nothing worse than limp herbs." Copper put his hands over his nose and mouth. He tried to keep his lunch and his grief inside, but some bitterness escaped in a huff. *Really, chef? Nothing?*

Luke popped in with a second remote and lowered the volume. "I want to make sure you're healthy."

"I'm fine."

"But you almost collapsed in the restaurant."

"Life can be too much for me sometimes." He twitched his shoulders into the smallest shrug. "It's one of my problems."

Luke's fingers slid over his phone, texting like a freak of nature. His neck jerked sideways so his hair hung at an angle. Within a short time, it always fell back into his face. Eventually, he hid the longest strands behind his ear. "I need to check on the others. You want to come with me or rest in here for a little while?"

Copper refused to answer. He didn't want anything. Desire belonged to real people, and someone had pushed him around his entire life. Saddled with incompetence and irrelevant opinions, keeping up the pretense of being a real person required too much energy.

Luke fidgeted with his keys. "Oh! I found out about the ceiling project. It depends on the size of the room, but you're looking at—"

"Pearl torched that idea. Burned it to a crisp." Copper flicked his wrist like he was dusting crumbs off a table. "But thanks."

Luke muttered something about a nickel and cleared his throat. "I'm gonna come back and check on you in a little while, alright? If you need me before then, push this button." He handed Copper a tablet with several large icons on it. "This has maps, rules, schedules, and email. You can instant message most people who live and work here. There's a charging station by your dining room and one at your desk." He waved. "Be back soon."

Once the door closed, Copper grabbed his overnight bag. He dumped its contents all over the bed searching for his *Passage* T-shirt. As he focused on the clutter, he realized this probably looked like a mini-meltdown. He wasn't sure if he was looking for something or just making a mess because he finally could. His bag was stuffed with random items the same way his body held emotions without names.

Copper grew still and listened. He heard the pipes in the wall, the lawn care machines, the hum of the air conditioner, a few seagulls, and his own heartbeat. He choked back a sob. For the second time in his life, he was alone.

Chapter Thirteen

Include new people. Nobody likes feeling left out.

- Socially Satisfied

Keegan inspected the newest panels for the mural. Jay had selected subdued colors that matched his personality and painted with precision. Tyler's daring use of color contrasted with Jay's canvas. Keegan added several swirls and smiley faces to his own design. "Swirls are important. The swirlism is what makes Van Gogh's Starry Night so good."

He imagined all the paintings hung together. "It's not right. We're missing Copper's piece. Let's ask if he's feeling better."

504's door seemed thicker than the others. Cold against his fist, the door seemed stubborn and unfriendly, just like its occupant. All of the other doors opened with ease. As Keegan pounded, he wondered if Copper had replaced it while he wasn't looking.

On the opposite side of the narrow hallway, Tyler trained his eyes on the floor while Jay continued to be fascinated by his watch. Keegan's face and neck tightened. *Friendship Knocks* advised knocking three to five times and slowly counting to ten before knocking again. He waved his pencils and counted the blurs.

Over 1800 days. For five solid years, Keegan had been thinking about this Inn and the people who would live in it. Ever since he'd seen that crazy, frustrating movie, he could think of little else. The plan was to assemble a group and they would become real friends who counted on each other. Friends who shared secrets and jokes. The kind of close friends who grew old together. Five years of dreaming what it might be like to know other people and be known by them. He'd wondered how it would feel to be understood. He'd spent a lifetime of studying people and reading social skills books, trying to figure out how to be a friend.

And the day had finally arrived. New people were going to be fused with his heart, but Copper Munro was not cooperating. *How could he not want to be here?* The Inn was perfect. His family had thoughtfully considered each decision and every detail. The lights were covered. The building didn't stink. No weird smells were allowed. Keegan had made sure of that! There were no dogs. No need to be concerned about wild, licking monsters attacking, causing injury and an itchy death. Residents enjoyed a peaceful location, except for a few birds and the occasional hammer or saw. Schedules offered daily opportunities to learn something new, explore health and fitness, and be creative. Thanks to Terrance, residents had access to safe, convenient, and reliable transportation. The Inn provided freedom, fun, and security. As housing for people with special needs, the Retreat on Ainsley Avenue had no competition.

Was it him? Keegan reviewed his social skills tips. Charming, engaging, and cheerful, he'd been a fabulous host. *Why can't you make someone have fun at your party?* He wondered if scolding would work. "*You be fun or else!*" But he didn't need a book to know that threatening would be inappropriate. Friendship goals aside, he had to consider his family's situation. If he failed, they might need to divide the property. Worse still, they might have their hearts broken by disappointment. His chance for a good life would be over. He couldn't risk completely alienating the guy.

Keegan drummed a rhythm on the door with his pencils. His face fell. The muscles refused to hold his eyes open in a wide, alert, friendly fashion. His cheeks became inflexible, no longer willing to serve big smiles. He bent forward and leaned his head on the door.

The door swung open, and he fell inside. His body collided with Copper's shoulder. "Ow. Get off me!" Copper snapped.

Copper had obviously never listened to the bestselling audiobook, *Tone Tutor*. Rejection swept through Keegan's body. His chest filled with angry bees or butterflies. He touched his heart four times to match its rapid rhythm, then thrust the unsharpened pencils toward Copper. "You haven't been participating. You missed our team-building exercises. We have a blank spot in the mural because you haven't done your part."

One of Copper's hands held his belly while the other rubbed his shoulder. Keegan took a step back. He covered his nose and mouth with his arm. "Are you sick or something?" A stomach ache would make sense. This revelation brought Keegan some emotional relief, but there was no need to get all germed up.

He squinted and looked from the corner of his eye. Every chapter in *Social Eyes* stressed the importance of eye contact. In order to search for clues, he looked at the middle of Copper's face instead of the shape of his hair and head. A few orange spots lingered around his nose. *Copper might have chicken pox.* The books taught not to ask about bumps on a person's face. Keegan resolved to research the splotches on the Internet later.

Copper rubbed his hand over his eye and down his jaw.

Then he rested his chin in his hand. *Was there such a thing as heavy chin disease?* He looked past Keegan into the hallway. Jay and Tyler moved in closer to hear the exchange. Finally, the mysterious redhead spoke peacefully. "Keegan, I don't know what I'm going to do."

Jay smiled. "The itinerary states that in five minutes, Luke will take us on a pilgrimage to the waterfront."

A tear rolled down Copper's face. Tears were not part of the plan. The Inn was no place for tears. Keegan realized his tone must have been harsh. *Tone Tutor* warned that the sound of voices could hurt people. Maybe a compliment would fix things. "Yes!" Keegan clapped his hands. "You changed clothes. I like your robot shirt. Let's walk. Fresh air might help and we'll get back on task! You've got to see our super-awesome cool neighborhood."

Copper looked tired. "I'm really more of an inside person."

Keegan laughed. "That's funny. Except for treasure hunting, I'm happy to stay inside. Besides autism, that may be the first thing we have in common. C'mon!"

Chapter Fourteen

COPPER

Penny loafer

Copper looked down at his shirt. The letters were facing the wrong way, but he knew the *Passage* logo from any angle. The familiar brand rested above the drone's antenna. Short lines fanned out in every direction away from the antenna. He'd always seen rain drawn with lines, but Sterling swore these marks meant the drone's laser was armed and ready to face any intruder.

Tyler said "Activated" in an exact imitation of the game.

"You play *Passage?*"

The kid's smile was as white as sheetrock ceiling powder. And as if on cue, Copper's mind detoured onto the path of persistent memories. The last time he'd worn this shirt, he'd been strapped to a stretcher...

Lying on his back, the hole in the ceiling stared at him.

Strangers touched his leg. "I'm so stupid!" He scratched his face.

The neighbor named Ms. Peterson cried out, "His mother is on her way. Don't shout. He has autism. You're freaking him out."

He remembered Pearl looming over his face. Her words were muffled. She raised her voice. "Fill in the blank. I went in the attic to…"

"Get *Passage* stuff for Sterling so he can be well again."

She sobbed. The ceiling was a disaster. The hole wasn't a smooth oval-shaped portal like you made in *Passage*. It was jagged and ugly. If a person went through it, they'd crash straight down to the bottom of the stairs.

Some guy hugged his mother. Disappointment crushed her shoulders so hard they fell down and hung low. In between sobs, she moaned, "Look at the empty Toaster Treat boxes all over the kitchen. He can't even feed himself properly! I was gone too long. I didn't know Sterling's treatment would…Oh God. How can I tell him?"

Copper shouted, "I'm sorry! I can clean it. I just wanted—"

Pearl's face twisted. She ran back to him, her cheeks stained with tears. She threw herself against his chest. "The medicine didn't work. He got so sick. Sterling's dead, baby." She howled. "He's not going to get better. He's never coming home."

Copper's leg hurt. He heard the blood going through his veins, but couldn't move his body. "I can help him. He can use my *Passage* collection. He can keep it!" He screamed it over and over. Nobody listened.

His mother returned to the kitchen, broken. The straps around his body squeezed him tighter. A police officer with a holstered gun and handcuffs hanging from his belt spoke to Pearl.

"Don't take her to jail. I'll clean the kitchen! I'll fix everything."

The sound of the Inn's overhead lighting brought him back to Ainsley Avenue. The third bulb in the hallway would burn out within the next two days.

Tyler had disappeared. Copper had missed the boy's answer to his question about the video game. He crinkled his nose when he noticed the microwave tucked into the baby kitchen. The kitchenette. Whatever. The smell and texture of Toaster Treats tugged at the back of his mind. He pictured their crispy golden edges holding hot, sweet jelly in the center.

Copper stepped into the hallway and shut the door. "Keegan, does this place come with a toaster?"

Chapter Fifteen

KEEGAN

Include sensory breaks between activities.

- Busy Body

The breeze rubbed against Keegan's face like the caress of an old family friend. He loved the wind and everything about this day. Copper would cheer up—all they needed to do was buy him a toaster. Orientation was back on track. The Inn would be a success. His plan was working. He'd worried for nothing.

His senses sharpened as they moved away from his own little world to the wild space outside the gate. He made sure they crossed the street carefully, as a group. Soon they would be near Crescent Drive. The corner house on Crescent had a special iron fence that stretched over its driveway. Sometimes two mighty dachshunds played out there. All dogs were life-threatening, with their urge to lick, jump, and scratch him. They had strong jaws and made terrifying sounds. This would be a very dangerous walk, but in the movies, danger brought people together. Only a few iron rods kept those dogs from getting loose and running toward them. If the dogs had lost weight, they could easily slip through the bars and attack him. If they licked his skin, their germs would cause swelling. He was almost certain that meant he'd be minutes away from a gruesome death.

He strained his ears, trying to detect any hazardous activity well in advance. There wasn't any sound of their awful claws tapping on the pavement. No sound of metal tags bouncing against collars or fence gates. No barking. No dog sounds at all.

He skipped ahead of the group. As he neared the corner, he tried to sneak a peek at the house. The worst surprise was when dogs ran out snarling and growling. Those sudden changes were the most terrible, unexpected events of his life.

As luck would have it, the dogs were not outside. "No dogs, today!" He announced in his brightest, most encouraging voice.

Luke's voice held a hint of warning. "Wait for us, Keeg."

Attention RSVP trained readers to keep their bodies and brains present while in a group. Keegan waited patiently, but refused to take his eyes off the wrought-iron fence for one single second.

Luke skidded to a stop and touched Keegan on his elbow. "Someone's waving at you."

"Oh! Heeeeeey Mrs. Bray. It has been a long time since we last met." Keegan wagged his arm and rolled his wrist. The first thing people commented on when they saw him was how much he'd grown. None of his books mentioned this custom, but based on his experience, it seemed like a standard greeting. "Can you see how tall I'm getting?"

With a quick smile and a short sideways flick of her wrist, Mrs. Bray continued sweeping the sidewalk near her home.

"She may not hear very well," Luke explained, his voice low and quiet. He pulled out an A-shaped sticker from his back pocket.

Keegan grabbed the sticker and held it close to his heart. "Ooooh! Guys, look at this!"

Luke spoke to the group while walking backward. "You may notice some homes in the area have these decals in the windows. If you ever get lost or have an emergency, these mark houses as safe places for you to get help. Each resident with this sticker has donated to the Ainsley property. You can think of them as friendly, safer strangers. I have one I'd like to deliver, if y'all don't mind a quick stop."

Chapter Sixteen

COPPER

Feeling like a penny waiting for change.

Copper strolled down the sidewalk. They crossed a lane bordered by a series of beautiful lawns. Some had the same windswept oak trees as the Retreat, while others favored palm trees and tropical plants. Picture perfect mailboxes dotted the pavement. Not one house had an ambulance in the driveway. They probably didn't have holes in their ceilings. None of these homes bore the searing brand of death and loss.

He considered his companions. Like an overgrown preschooler, Keegan skipped down the lane. Professor Jay snapped photos with his phone, his lips in perpetual motion, whispering numbers. Tyler's steps mirrored Luke's as he led their small parade up to an old Victorian home. These people lived in a care-free world. They'd never destroyed homes or sifted through the wreckage after a tragedy. There was no way they'd ruined lives the way he had.

Copper looked at the sky. Pearl had told him about prayer but it seemed weird. *If you think words in your head and someone invisible hears them, why wouldn't everyone else be able to hear those thoughts?*

Many therapists had lectured him about something called the Theory of Mind. They insisted other people didn't always know the same things he knew. They always maintained that people couldn't "read his mind." It took a long time to realize they didn't mean that words were printed across the folds of brain tissue. For communication experts, they had a very strange way of saying people couldn't hear his thoughts.

The speech therapists had told him he must "use his words" more. They were paid for that sort of thing. If they convinced him he needed words, his mother would pay for more sessions. Sterling had told him about marketing, so Copper had decided long ago that speech therapy was probably a total scam. Either the therapists were mistaken or the whole concept of prayer was wrong. At least prayer didn't come with a bill so high that his mom would have to take a fourth job.

Sterling—if you can hear me, I'm sorry I didn't come see you at the hospital. I should have shared the Passage *stuff with you sooner. If I'd have sat by your side, you'd have recovered. It worked when we were kids and you had the flu. I was going to come, I swear. Please don't let the lawyers send me to jail.* From the movies he'd seen, prison seemed like a horrible place. It was dark and dirty. People hung from chains. Once someone got locked away with dangerous criminals, they were hidden forever. Lost. Nobody ever saw them again. Just like his father. Steele Campbell had probably gone to jail.

The door to the Victorian home opened, disrupting his thoughts about the kinds of torture that might happen in prison. Assaulted by the stench of baby powder and overly ripe roses, Copper looked down at a tiny woman with gray hair. Her strange face studied Luke.

"Hello, Miss Emily, ma'am," Luke said.

Keegan shouted, "It's Keegan!" He acted like the world was just waiting for an opportunity to give him a standing ovation. Copper mentally appended most of Keegan's sentences with the sound of "Ta-da."

The old woman winced and took a step back. Luke gave Keegan's shoulder a quick pat. "We're here to say thank you for your kind donation to the Retreat on Ainsley Avenue. We'd like to give you this to put in one of your front windows. It lets our residents know you're a safe house." He held the sticker out for her.

Her wrinkled claw snatched it from his hand. Her beady eyes and hawk-like nose bore into each of their faces. The silence extended for a few heartbeats. Jay stared at his phone. Keegan indulged his pencil addiction. Tyler's huge smile faded. He touched his shirt in search of lint or a stray string. Finding none, he shoved his hands into his pockets. When it was Copper's turn, he tried to hear her thoughts, but there was nothing.

Finally, her bony finger invaded Luke's personal space. She poked him in the chest. "I still hear a lot of beatin' and bangin' going on over there."

"Yes. We're finishing up our sensory spa in just a few weeks."

She looked at the sticker and licked her cracked lips. "Did y'all ever get those other shacks up to code?"

An expert at social hand ballet, Luke covered her hand with both of his and removed it from his body. In a fluid motion, he'd transitioned their physical contact into something resembling a warm greeting. "Oh, yes ma'am. You should come by for a tour."

She scrunched up her face and jerked her claw back. "Well, I might." She looked at each man one more time. "Is this your new bunch, then?"

Copper squinted back at her and hoped she could see his contempt.

Luke smiled with only one half of his mouth. "These are some new potential residents."

"They look like they might be able to garden or something. If one of them needs work, you can send him around."

"That's wonderful; I'll tell—"

The door slammed shut.

"C'mon guys. Let's go." His ring full of keys serenaded their return to the sidewalk.

Keegan slipped his pencils into his pocket. "Do you think I should send her a copy of *What's the Manner*? Or is she too old to read?"

Copper tuned out the chatter as he trudged along. This town was just like everywhere else: full of confusing, hostile people who didn't really see him. They barely listened and treated him like he was stupid. People everywhere recoiled and called some of his classmates "Those poor, sad, disabled people" when they thought he wasn't listening. *She didn't try to speak to any of us directly.*

This was the world. It was as if most people were born holding a ticket into society and a few, like him, had to earn their way in by being something…extra. Maybe the other guys hadn't lived as easily as he'd assumed. People without autism were ridiculous, but they held all the power. They got the free pass to whatever their mysterious club had to offer. Their secret society was The Culture, or at least, the only culture that mattered. Beyond the fantasyland walls of the Retreat, the world was a tough place. He looked at Luke's keys dangling from his pocket, each one a symbol of trust and responsibility. But that lady hadn't been nice to him. In this world, even Luke wasn't respected or admired.

Everyone had respected Sterling. People had called him Sir. Sterling wore suits to work. He had keys *and* money. He was everything: smart, athletic, good looking, generous, and kind. Girls loved him. Guys wanted to be like him. Most importantly, he was the only one who had completely loved and tried to understand Copper.

And Copper had let him down. Hot, stinging sand scoured his face as the weight of that reality forced him to his knees.

Chapter Seventeen

KEEGAN

Not every silence needs to be filled.

- A Primer on Conversation

Keegan lengthened his strides to catch up to Copper. For an indoor person who'd been sick an hour ago, he hiked with determination. The promise of a toaster seemed to have enhanced his energy level.

When they arrived at the beach park, Keegan stopped on the boardwalk and sat on a bench. Getting too close to the sand would spoil his starry sneakers. He used the edge of his Charlie Brown T-shirt to dry the sweat trickling from his hairline. On an August afternoon, his light springy hair was as hot as a fur coat.

Sloshing through the sand, Luke pursued Copper. "You walk like a man on a mission." He was breathing hard. "You must really love the beach. Are you feeling ok? Were you able to pay attention to the path we took to get here?"

Jay presented his phone screen. "I've charted our course."

Tyler started digging a trench with a seashell.

"Keeg, it looks like the guys want to build a sandcastle. Want to join in?"

As he sat on the hard bench, Keegan's pencils pressed into his back. He removed them from his pocket. "Nope. Too gritty and scratchy. I'm not even wearing my swimsuit!"

He took a well-deserved break, admiring the scene before him. The calm expanse of the sea mirrored his sense of peace. The guys were enjoying the coast together. Somehow his plan was working. The walk hadn't offered a sense of danger and drama like the one in the breakfast movie. Maybe it was enough that the guys had seen the safe neighborhood and friendly neighbors. Or maybe this walk had turned out to be like the film's soda mission. Either way, they were probably best friends now. His future was secure. Life was limitless like the horizon of the ocean.

Jay held his phone straight out in front of him, looking at the water. Maybe the ocean looked better through a screen. It looked awesome through his pencils. Since his mom was back at the Retreat, Keegan wiggled them so close to his eyes, their breeze kissed his eyelashes.

The rhythmic waves washed the shoreline. The blurring pencils animated the movement along the water's edge. A stunt kite appeared. It dove, looped, and swirled hypnotically across the light pink sky. Keegan's entire body turned soft like jelly. With great effort, he shifted his gaze toward the pier. The lonely wooden posts waited for the seagulls and pelicans to arrive. Families carried fishing poles, nets, and coolers. Midway between his bench and the pier, a young girl piloted the stunt kite. As his eyes zeroed in on her, he noticed his worst nightmare charging in his direction.

"DOG!" Keegan Harris ran for his life.

Chapter Eighteen

COPPER

Mean enough to steal pennies off a dead man's eyes.

Disappointment and loss roiled in Copper's belly. His face grew warm from the inside out. Copper rubbed it with his sleeve. Luke's boots accidentally flicked sand on him when he chased after Keegan, and he was desperate to feel clean again.

The platinum-colored water called to him. He stood, dusted the grit from his knees, and walked away from the group. All this time he'd been so angry with his brother. It wasn't Sterling's fault for dying—it was Copper's. If only he hadn't waited so long to visit him in the hospital. He'd been a selfish coward who was terrified of seeing his hero brought low. Sterling had been sick and frail, but Copper was weak in every other way. He'd been afraid of the weird sounds and smells, but he still should have gone. He hadn't even said goodbye. Not only had he failed to help Sterling recover, he'd probably broken his brother's heart. Copper had played enough video games to know once your heart cracks, that's it: Game Over. He belonged in jail, but there was no way he could live there. The noise alone would kill him.

Now his future would end before it even began. A lifetime of expensive therapies. What a waste. He remembered forcing his therapist's hands to make the sign language move for "all done." Pearl had introduced him to picture exchange cards instead. Later he'd traded those cards for a device. Eventually he had learned to use his voice to speak. "Use your words!" they'd demand, but be sure not to say the word "No." A snort escaped his nose.

He thought of the sensory lessons. *"Touch shaving cream, Copper. Get sticky, Copper." Ignore the tag in the back of the shirt that feels like bee stings and itchy ant bites, Copper. Only feel what we want you to feel, Copper.*

He looked at the endless horizon. The miles of waves were made of memories. Teachers had worked his hands for him, showing him how to use them in unison. But the moment he chose how to use them, they'd scold, "Quiet hands! Quiet body!" So what hung from his arms didn't belong to him. They were not his to command, direct, or control. He was only allowed the use of his hands for teacher-approved "normal" activities.

He'd been forced to study and recognize the feelings of other people using emotion flashcards. In order to earn rewards and praise, he'd suppressed his sadness and agitation. He had done whatever it took to please them. His life had been dedicated to mastering what other people knew almost instinctively. They promised this would make him fit into this crappy world. They were wrong. He didn't fit.

The high school counselor's words haunted his mind. He shook his head in an attempt to stop the endless loop. Of course, he was "developmentally delayed" and "behind his peers." This was his time to finally catch up and be set free. His time to become a real man.

He should be able to pass for non-autistic. That was the ultimate goal, right? To blend in? To be like everyone else? To improve. And by improve, they meant act less like his own nature. Be fake. Conform to be worthy…to matter…to belong. To take part in this waste of a world where people, like his Dad, leave. Where good people like his brother get cancer and die.

Acidic outrage burned his throat. Without Sterling to coach him, the best he could hope for was to continue as this version of himself—the one people either assumed was a fool or overlooked entirely. For all his time and effort, his grand reward boiled down to a life of being ignored or pitied, in a world where he had no place, and no opportunity to become anything or anyone.

He swallowed the taste of bile and shouted at the sea. "I'm not having it, Sterling!" A second later, his face crumbled. *I'm sorry, brother. I can't live in jail and I can't wait around for lawyers to make my choices for me.*

Copper mentally scrolled through his impressions of Ainsley Avenue: the gates that buzzed, the baby kitchen, the therapies, the rules and the kooky people who would live around him. That was no life for a real man, but jail would surely be worse. He considered returning home and remembered the hole in the ceiling. Every room held memories of better days. He imagined his mother's perpetually disappointed face, and sitting at Pleasant Grove for countless hours. Even then, he'd still be surrounded by strange people. He'd spend the rest of his life trying to avoid them while watching Chef Chevalier re-runs and playing *Passage* until his eyes fell out of his head. The noise and smell of that place made him gag. Nothing to look forward to but years of grief and wasted time.

He looked over his left shoulder. Luke was nowhere to be seen. This was his chance. He needed to get away. Killer or not, he refused to calmly wait for a ride to prison.

The scent of salt in the air grew stronger. The sand became

firmer under his feet. He could stomp right into the water and keep walking. If he stayed parallel to the shore, he might wade to another town. Maybe he'd be able to start over. He might try some more free prayer and see what happened.

The wild urge to seize this moment was too strong to reject. His feet seemed to propel him forward without any instruction from his brain. They accelerated. One foot in front of the other, straight toward the lazy waves. He looked at the horizon. The water would be dark soon.

As his shoes splashed, his right arm began to hurt. He took one more step and a sharp pain suggested he shouldn't continue. Caught in a strange grip, his wrist bent in a way that would break his bones if he tried to resist.

Jay stood next to him, half naked. He looked like one of those GI Joe dolls someone had given Copper for his eighth birthday. Shirtless, the man had a small frame but his skin stretched around lean, well-defined muscles. While maintaining a firm hold on his arm and wrist, the Muscular Professor guided him back toward the beach.

Copper opened his mouth to speak, but Jay bent over to pick his clothing off the ground. He shook the sand off his shirt and said, "Swimming is an unscheduled and therefore unapproved activity."

Chapter Nineteen

Hold up your index finger. People will pay attention.

- Gesturing: I'll Show You

Adrenaline coursed through Keegan's body. A long tongue flopped sideways through sharp fangs. Jowls seeped with drool. Car horns and screeching brakes confirmed his primal fear. Alarm bells should be ringing. *This is a level three event for sure.* All beasts who ran amuck focused on a single goal—kill Keegan Harris. His long, lean legs charged in one direction: away.

A man shouted after him, "Incoming! Frisbee."

Keegan raced forward, dodging the missile while sifting through his information about canines. *Cats could climb trees. What about dogs? Hillsides, sure, but not trees....* He needed a high place to hide. He searched for anything like a tree. He heard small children in a nearby playground. If he reached the jungle gym and balanced at the top, the dog might not eat him.

He threw himself onto the metal structure and scrambled up as high as he could go. Children shrieked. He wanted to shout, "Yes, a dog is coming. Take cover!" Instead, another sound crowded his mouth and the words refused to come out. Keegan wailed, and tears poured down his face. Children scattered.

From the top of the jungle gym, he searched the area for the wild animal. It was wrestling the man with the Frisbee. *Good. Let that guy get eaten first. The dog will be too full to want me.*

Tears and sweat mixed in his eyes. His chest hurt, and his breath wheezed in and out. *Level two, asthma! If the dogs don't get me, the lack of air will do me in.* His hands tapped against his chest like butterfly wings. They kept time with his racing heart. He chastised himself for mentally cursing.

Luke was running up, covering one eye with his hand. Keegan was saved! People surrounded the playground. Parents were clutching their children close, staring at him, all speaking at the same time. He didn't understand any of their words. They gawked in his direction, away from the mongrel. *Was there something scary behind him?* He glanced over his shoulder and saw nothing unusual. His burning throat loosened and his breathing improved.

"Luke," he wheezed, but his brother wasn't looking at him. Based on his social skills books, ignoring a person in an emergency was inappropriate. Luke was chatting with the parents. Keegan broke the rule about eavesdropping and strained to hear.

"...harmless. He's got a huge phobia about dogs..."

Keegan tuned out the words that followed "special needs" and looked at their faces. His body burned with the heat of confusion. *Was he in trouble? They thought he was scary while wild, snarling monsters were roaming the earth?*

He checked to see if the children were crying. They looked ok. One of them took the father's hand and pulled him to see the "cute, little puppy." That child was either deluded, brave, or insane. There was no time to process the information.

"Can you climb down, Keeg? These people should meet you."

"Am I in big trouble?"

"I don't think so, buddy. But you gave folks a scare. We're worried about you."

Keegan took no chances. "Is someone holding the dog? Is it on a string yet?"

"A leash?" Luke looked backward. "The dog situation is under control."

Keegan dropped to the ground. "Thank God."

His brother hugged him. "I hear your asthma. You alright?" He whispered, "Listen, you need to turn on the charm, ok? These people don't know you. That's Ms. Hadley over there. She writes for *The Tribune*. We don't want her publishing bad things about the family and the Retreat."

Over time, Keegan learned that "turn on the charm" meant "be awesome." Kelly-Jean Hadley was the third generation who wrote "Hadley's Helpful Hints." The whole town read the column. His family had worked too hard and sacrificed too much to make Ainsley Avenue a reality. If Keegan was going to have a place in this world, he had to protect the Inn's reputation.

Focus. He tried to find the energy for Keegan Harris' official Party-of-One personality to shine through. While he wiped away his tears, he imagined his brain boxes. Time to shut the fear box and open up the awesome box.

"Ladies and Gentlemen, Boys and Girls," he gave a grand wave and offered his best smile. "I'm Keegan Harris." He nodded at each of them, in case they'd already met. His fame usually preceded him. Sometimes folks became excited and said things like "You're so tall. I've been following you on your dad's social media account." Today, the faces didn't shine at the sound of his name. *Tourists.* He stretched his arms out and brought them into his chest. "I'm autistic." He wore his serious face and used the gestures he'd seen during political debates. "Dogs can be dangerous." For his big finish, he thought a small finger point would sell the last bit. He didn't know how pointing worked, but he folded all his fingers back except for his index and gave it his best try. "Stray dogs can be the most dangerous." He strained to make eye contact. Some very round eyes didn't blink. A few jaws unhinged and hung open.

One father put his tattooed hand over his child's mouth to shush it while he spoke to Ms. Hadley. Keegan remembered those days of childhood, when covering his mouth had filled him with fury. Such a rude way to treat a young person.

The people matched the drawing for shock in his social skills book, *Busy Body*. He would reference it later. Shock seemed reasonable, since they'd all just experienced a close brush with death. Unsure what to say or do next, he looked to his brother.

"We hope the children are ok—" Luke began.

Keegan jumped in. "Yes that was a close call with the dog." He awarded himself some extra social points for remembering the bizarre "close call" phrase.

"Keegan, buddy, when you come to the playground, please be careful not to bump into the small children."

Had he hurt someone? Another tear ran down Keegan's face. He always tried to be so careful, especially with little children.

Luke gave him a squeeze and wiped at his tear. One father stepped in and said "It's ok, son. Everyone is fine. You just surprised us."

This was not the best time to tell him that he wasn't this man's son. His last name was Harris. The words itched at the back of his throat. Then, Luke pressed the pencils back into his hand. Keegan didn't remember leaving them when he fled. His mouth formed a smile. "My pencils!"

Luke led him back to the beach, muttering about striking a deal with the local media. Some reporters would cover the

Retreat's community playgroup tomorrow. Keegan's pencils made beautiful silver streaks on their walk back. "Luke, you ran with your eye covered. Is it ok?"

Luke exhaled louder than usual. "Yep. My eye is still here, but Nicola will have my ass for running after you and leaving the others unattended."

He swallowed the urge to correct his brother's use of a level two word.

His brother tapped his scrunched forehead with crossed fingers. "Let's hope everyone else is safe. If anything's happened to them, we'll be sued out of existence."

Chapter Twenty

COPPER

Doesn't have two pennies to rub together.

Sitting on the curb outside the men's room, Copper rubbed his sore wrist. He was within arm's reach of the disheveled professor. There was zero chance he'd win a wrestling match against Jay. Avoiding eye contact, he picked seaweed out of his shoelaces. He weighed his words carefully. "Tyler's been in there for a long time."

Professor GI Joe checked his watch. "Precisely six minutes and thirty-seven seconds."

The Resident Trainer dragged his younger brother over by the hand. They darted across the street to regroup at the beach park facilities. Captain Crazy Curls set himself slightly apart from them. He slid down the brick wall and sat on the concrete. Vertical streaks of dirt lined his face.

The familiar jingle jangle of Luke's keys stopped. "Where's Tyler?"

Jay announced that Tyler had been in the men's room for seven minutes and forty-five seconds. Luke's eyes narrowed when he saw Jay's shirt. The buttons weren't lined up the same way as before.

Concern for his own appearance cramped the muscles deep inside Copper's stomach. The last thing he needed was to get into trouble with the Ainsley people. He relaxed a little when Luke focused on the bathroom door.

As soon as Luke reached for the handle, a man glided out. The lively stranger wore colorful clothing that didn't fully cover his grey chest hair or tan belly. Old or not, his reflexes were still quick, and he adjusted the trajectory of his roller skates, narrowly avoiding a head-on collision with Luke. Neon Grandpa appeared to be the sort of bold person Keegan would enjoy. Copper wondered which of them would draw the most attention, but the Master of Ceremonies' wild curls drooped. The back of his Charlie Brown T-shirt bunched against the brick wall. His legs stretched out across the sidewalk as he slumped in the heat.

Luke's boots ground against the gritty sidewalk. His laid-back appearance morphed into a more alert posture. "Have you seen—"

"There's an adorable fella in there. He stood close to me at the urinal and said, 'There's an awful lot you can tell about a person by their shoes.'"[1]

Professor Busybody inserted, "That's from *Forrest Gump*."

Luke squared his shoulders and coiled his hands into fists.

The restroom door swung open, and Mr. Teentastic strut toward the group, patting his hair into place. "There's a lot more to life than being really, really, ridiculously good looking."[2]

The vibrant gentleman beamed. "That's darling. Isn't he sweet?" He noted Luke's tense manner. "Oh honey, he's too young for me. Pretty, though."

"Thanks for looking out for him."

The man rolled away, and Tyler called after him, "On Wednesdays we wear pink!"[3]

Luke instructed everyone to sit on the curb. "Sorry I had to take off so fast. Here's a life tip: It's not the best idea to make friends in any restroom. Ever."

Jay interjected, "I regularly escorted my mother to the women's restroom. The social protocol is to issue a compliment such as 'nice top' or 'love that fragrance.'"

Keegan's voice boomed, "Jay's right. That's being *FRIENDLY*, Luke!"

Luke raked his hand through his hair. "The men's restroom has different rules."

Keegan continued ranting. "I ran from the dog. That's impulsive. But my social skills book says unexpected behaviors appear odd and potentially dangerous, so I've ruined everything! See? Tyler took off his beanie. We're doomed."

The Professor consulted his watch. "It's only ruined if we mismanage the schedule. Also, I'll require additional information that pertains to the pink Wednesdays Tyler referenced. I lack that documentation."

Luke pulled out his phone and stepped apart from the group. "Nicola, I need you. It's like herding drunk cats." He listened. "A restraining order against who?" He drifted farther away. "Not for anyone here, right? Ok. Get back fast."

Copper stood. Jay nodded at his wet shoes, grimaced, and shook his head. Glaring back at him, Copper's temper boiled over. "You hurt my wrist, you know!"

"I apologize. Perhaps I can make reparations. You require alternative footwear. Shall I requisition an additional pair of shoes on your behalf?"

For Copper, out of every sensation possible, exhaustion was the centerpiece. "I may not understand your words, but I know your shirt's buttoned incorrectly."

Luke returned, and declared they'd ride the trolley back to Ainsley Avenue.

Jay crossed his arms. "This is an unanticipated modification to the schedule. We must reverse our course to calculate the exact number of steps required for this excursion."

Copper's high-tops squished as he walked to the trolley stop. "Is that what you're counting? Multiply your number by two, Professor."

When the transportation arrived, Keegan gave a half-hearted wave to Terrance. Tyler shook the sand from his hat and stuck it back on his head. Jay hesitated. "This activity is irregular and therefore questionable. Human beings loathe uncertainty by nature. Definitive strategic coordination is key to our longevity."

Luke touched the trolley door. "Learning to be flexible will help you survive in the wild, Jay. Hop on, dude."

"I'm nothing if not compliant, but unexpected alterations bewilder, disorient, and confound."

As the trolley pulled away, Copper realized he'd missed his opportunity for escape, and all traces of hope evaporated. He tried to find comfort in the hard, plastic seat. It was the only source of stability in his life.

Chapter Twenty-One

KEEGAN

Listen twice as much as you speak.

- Listen With Both Ears

A musk of sweat and sunscreen filled the trolley. Enduring the odors served as part of Keegan's penance. He pinched his nose and stepped inside. Terrance's lined face broke into a grin. "Did you have a big time at the beach?"

"I'm an idiot. Everyone thinks I'm a scary fool."

"Best not to go with whatever most people think. You're smart enough to ride on my trolley. C'mon, climb aboard."

Keegan chose a seat near the middle of the bus. He hung his head out the window. When encountering foul odors, fresh air eased his tendency to dry heave. Jay sat in the first seat, closest to the door, and started hammering Terrance with a series of rapid-fire questions. On a bench near the front of the tram, Copper's lifeless pose provided a stark contrast to Tyler's carefree presence. The youngest in the group dusted sand from his shoes and leaned back in his seat. At least the guy had returned the beanie to its proper place. Luke relaxed across the aisle from the pair. His choice placed him next to Kelly-Jean Hadley. She looked like Easter every day with her pastel colors and floral prints.

An elderly woman floated down the aisle on a cloud of baby powder. She perched next to Keegan. *The circle of life must be made with baby powder. It was the most common fragrance for old people and brand new babies.* He wished he could switch places with Luke and sit beside Kelly-Jean. He imagined that she smelled like lemon cake. Plus, he had enough suggestions to fill a month's worth of "Hadley's Helpful Hints."

As the trolley's speed increased, Keegan moved his head back into the vehicle. Sticking his head out like a dog would be inappropriate. His new seat partner had twinkly eyes tucked inside wrinkled skin. Keegan wondered if she'd been part of the playground crowd earlier, so he offered an explanation. "These beach towns attract a lot of canines. We probably picked the wrong place to build the Retreat, but I couldn't find a dog-free state." The book *Make It Right* recommended a demonstration of dedication, so he hastily added, "I searched the Internet for hours. Fifty states and several territories. Not one single dog-free region."

Her shriveled hand covered the top of his wrist. She pressed her thin lips together into an even thinner line. Her head inclined at the same angle as her mouth curved. She had the official Harris Head-tilt down. *Maybe she's a relative.* They reached the stop for Go Fresh, his uncle's grocery store. The baby powder cloud lifted as she ambled to the front of the small bus.

A man carrying two bags almost knocked her over, shoving his way onto the car. He grabbed the spot in front of Keegan. A little girl planted herself beside his bags. She instantly wilted. "But Dad, I want to go to the playgroup tomorrow. Cecil, a boy from my class, will be there. He's in a wheelchair and—"

"Darla, I don't care if the Queen of England will be there.

You're not going near that place. I don't want their diseases rubbing off on you. Leave it to the handicapped. They'll just drool on you anyway."

The man's tattooed forearm reached backward to massage his thick neck. The vivid drawings ran together into a giant mass of scribbles, but one mark stood out from the rest. A strange symbol inside a circle occupied most of the prime real estate on his arm. The drawing looked like a capital letter "A" with one line angled back up to cross the two slanted lines. Keegan thought it was the beginning of a good star shape, but the line jutted out with an arrow on the end. The mark didn't match the Avengers, Star Trek, or the fountain at the Retreat.

The man's arm moved across the back of the girl's seat. "It's bad enough they put those mutants into the classroom with normal kids. They make it harder for regular students to get what they need."

Keegan stared at the man's artwork through his pencils. He'd met a few people who had tattoos, but they didn't have such ugly voices. *More than five tattoos puts too much ink in a body. Excessive ink upsets the blood and makes a person surly. Kelly-Jean Hadley should add that to her list of Helpful Hints.*

The little girl looked smaller. She shrank her shoulders into herself like a hermit crab going back into its shell. Darla's sadness spilled onto Keegan. *Tone Tutor* was right: raised voices hurt hearts. Her father's hatred for royalty and people named Cecil created a cloud Keegan couldn't smell, but it threatened to choke him just the same. He pushed his face against the window and the glass pressed against his cheek. He squeezed his pencils for reassurance as the trolley whizzed by the tidy lawns.

"Can I go sit with Aunt KJ?" Darla asked.

"You leave Kelly-Jean alone. She's workin.'" Her dad pulled her chin. "Listen. I don't want you mixing with their kind. I'll whup ya if you do. Your cousins will keep an eye out at school and tell me if you disobey. I'd rather die than have one of my own on that property. Shoot, after all those snobs have done to this town? After how they've treated your family? I ought to spank you for asking." Clenching the girl's wrist, he stood and dragged her down the aisle.

As they exited the trolley, Terrance told them to have a good day, but neither of them replied. *Everyone needs at least one book about social skills. Maybe the drivers could hand them out as people climbed into the vehicle.* Keegan resolved to ask his mom about donating them to the townspeople. He even wondered if he could get a job driving the streetcar. But unless he could enforce a "no dogs allowed" policy, he would have to keep making greeting cards.

Waving the pencils to a special rhythm, he recounted every big mistake he'd ever made. Today's dog incident made 475, but he'd only been counting since he was eight years old.

At the next stop, he slipped through the back exit and waited for his friends. He hoped he hadn't let everyone down too much. Terrance followed Copper off the car and dropped a penny into his hand. For such a sourpuss, that guy sure was a money magnet. The amount of change jingling in his pocket increased with every passing hour. Hopefully he'd see Ainsley Avenue as a lucky place and want to stay.

Chapter Twenty-Two

COPPER

A penny for your thoughts.

Copper could only think of two words to describe Keegan's living room: "visual festival." Room 502's decor, much like its occupant, was quirky and larger than life. A neon "No Dogs Allowed" sign hummed on the wall behind the couch, casting the room with a warm, red glow. Three feet from the ceiling, a shelf with a collection of desk toys lined the perimeter of the room. The sculptures rocked in a peculiar harmony. The windowsill held an assortment of hourglasses and colorful liquid timers. Copper remembered seeing those in a gift shop on his one and only family vacation.

The mass of movement hung around the room like a spastic halo. Like the host, the bits and baubles were hard to ignore. Exhaling through his first symptom of motion sickness, Copper focused on the others in the room.

From his seat at the kitchen table, Jay stared at his tablet. Tyler spun a tower rack full of greeting cards in the corner of the living room. Keegan lay on his couch, clutching a maroon beanie with one hand, his other arm bent across his face, covering his eyes.

Copper needed to relax and figure out his next move. He looked back at the window. "Keegan, can I flip one of those timers over? I want to watch the wheels spin while the drops fall to the bottom."

Keegan flung his arm out. Copper took that as a sign of permission and turned over a blue one. When no one was watching, he flipped a second timer. As the goo seeped down the side of a cylinder, he snuck a quick look at sleepy Stretchtastic Harris. *Could he turn all the timers over? Or just one more?* He tried to engage his host. "How do you keep so many kinetic objects moving?"

Slim grumbled about 9-volt batteries.

His irritated response sounded an alarm for the Professor. He actually peeled his eyes off his screen. "Keegan, I'm perplexed by your demeanor. Without your endorsement, you're under no obligation to display your dwelling. As much as it pains me to make yet another alteration to the schedule, I will omit this event out of respect for your privacy."

Tyler pulled some of the greeting cards out of the kiosk. "Do you understand the words that are coming out of my mouth?"[1]

Keegan's cap sailed across the room. "I hate being afraid. Dogs always make me act like a damned fool."

The card rack stopped squeaking. Tyler spoke as softly as if he had a soufflé in the oven. "Cursing?"

Keegan stormed to his kitchenette. "Yes. Cursing." At the sink, he shoved a bar of soap into his mouth. A few awkward seconds passed. He ejected the soap, rinsed his mouth, and dried his face.

Copper had never seen another person punish himself. The day had been so confusing and emotional, that he needed some time alone. The last thing he wanted was more drama. But if he had to share this space, he needed to bring back the cheerful Keegan. Through blurred vision, he whispered, "It's ok," and returned his gaze to the drops landing on the plastic wheel. They rode the wheel down and pooled at the bottom. His cheeks blazed.

He remembered Pearl driving all night. Sterling had helped with the map. They'd parked near the gates of the magic kingdom at dawn. By the end of the day, Copper had begged for a souvenir. He wanted to carry a piece of Florida home with him, but they couldn't afford trinkets. In the middle of the store, in front of all the other shoppers, he'd cried.

A man had barked, "Get a hold of yourself, kid. You're too big to act that way."

Sterling had placed the liquid timer shaped like Mickey Mouse back on the gift shop's clearance table and vowed, "It's ok, Cop. One day, I'll make lots of money and I'll buy you the best things."

It's ok. Those words always rang true when Sterling had said them. Copper's arm shook.

Keegan snatched the timer out of his hand and slammed it onto the window ledge. He inverted each timer and placed them in a neat row. "It's *NOT* ok. I've been trying to make today happen for years, and everything's going wrong. I have a plan, but Nicola's not here, and you people…and the dogs… and…" With glassy eyes, he flopped back down on the couch, swishing his pencils in front of his face. "It started with that stupid movie. I wasn't even supposed to be watching it. I thought it was about breakfast food, I swear. But the teens were doing crazy stuff while cursing and I couldn't take my eyes off it." He leaned forward, placing his elbows on his legs. His face rested in his hands, muffling his voice. "By the end, I realized I wanted what those characters had." His head shot back up. Wild hair swiveled from side to side. "But not the cursing part!" One hand palmed his face. "I put the movie on tomorrow's schedule. When you see it, you'll understand."

Jay swiped his finger across the glowing screen. "A film has been confirmed for tomorrow's agenda."

Tyler joined Keegan on the couch and pulled off the borrowed black beanie. He picked at a loose piece of fuzz and offered it back to Keegan.

Blond curls bounced as Keegan shook his head. He nudged Tyler's hand. "It's yours. You keep it." Keegan looked down at his shoes. "I've been imagining this weekend for more hours than even Jay can count. My parents have worked so hard to make this a safe place." He looked up at each of them, his eyes full of tears. "We really need to fill part of the Inn and we need the town on our side. But I freaked out today and scared people, and now some of them think I'm dangerous." Keegan pulled his feet under himself and rocked. "I'm stupid. But my family always says, 'It's ok.' But sometimes it's not ok at all. I have tons of social skills books." He flung his hand toward a bookcase, where bizarre titles filled all six shelves. "I try and try, but I still haven't learned how to fix it."

The sound of those words stirred Copper's memories of Sterling trying to reassure him. A tear rolled down his cheek.

Keegan glared at him. "And just how are you so sure it's ok, Copper? You haven't even tried to participate. Sometimes you don't even use our *actual* names. I bet your notes about us are blank. Are you aware Jay works as an inspector at the polymer plant? No! Because you don't even care." He stood, and his long bony finger shook when he thrust it into the air. "You're not part of the mural." He swept up the wine-colored beanie and smashed it down over his ears. "You don't know anything about anyone. You don't even want to *BE* here!"

Chapter Twenty-Three

KEEGAN

Good posture projects confidence.

- Social Security: Building Confidence for Social Encounters

Rage and disappointment spread throughout Keegan's body. He tried to remember the coping skills he'd learned. His most recent purchase, *How to Contain Your Crazy*, had a checklist, but it was too late to reference it now. He got upset the same way he got happy—all the way. He'd gone too far, and Copper's wet face proved he'd really messed things up again.

Caring Is Comforting mentioned a gift might reduce sorrow. He searched for his weighted blanket in the closet. He wasn't sure who needed it more at this moment, but the book stressed sharing to promote peace.

He tried to deliver the blanket, but Copper pushed it aside and exploded, "You're right! Maybe it won't be ok. I don't know anything." His arms flailed around. "I have no choices. I don't want to be here, but I may not even get to stay." Copper put his back to the group. Facing the window, he mumbled, "I'm probably a murderer and going to jail."

The quiet words fell like bombs. Everything in the room was the same. His toy collection moved in a perfect frenzy, but on the inside, Keegan's world had stopped. A bad guy visiting the Inn was the most unexpected event possible. Copper didn't look like an evil man, but Keegan had never seen one in real life. From the back, Copper looked like a normal person, except for his hair. *Were all red-haired men bad guys?* He cursed occasionally. Using the language of criminals might be a sign. Mentally sifting through all the books, none coached on conversing with murderers. *Confusion Requires Clarification* lay next to the lamp on his end table. He tried to keep his voice calm. "What do you mean, exactly?"

Swaddled in the rejected blanket, Tyler rocked on the couch and shouted, "You can't handle the truth!"[1]

Jay poked at his electronic device. His monotone voice sounded far away, and without looking up, he muttered, "A Few Good Men."

Copper paced like a madman. "It's a long story. Pearl said there are papers in your mom's office. Papers from lawyers about me and my dead brother. I need to see them."

Keegan took a ragged breath. "Alright. Tell me one thing. Did you use a weapon?"

Copper turned around, his eyes bulging. "Hell no! What kind of question is that?!"

Keegan held up his hands. "Do you have a weapon with you right now?" He tried to imitate Luke's hair trick, but his springy curls didn't swing or flop. "Be cool, man."

Copper wrapped his arms around his stomach. "I didn't shoot or stab my brother. Gah." With his back hunched, his shoulders drooped toward the floor. "Can a person die from a broken heart?"

Keegan's curls bobbed with affirmation. "Yes. Absolutely. Mom says Ainsley's mother died that way. It can totally happen. I've seen it in person. It's one of my top concerns."

The speed of Copper's hunchback pacing increased, and his voice made an animalistic groan. "I can't stand it. I need to read what those papers say. I have to know the truth."

Keegan knew it would be best not to hear any more growls and howls from a potential murderer. The important thing was to think fast and stay calm. So he hedged. "I can get us into my mom's office. We can find those papers, but we'll have to work together."

Everyone looked toward Jay. He thumped his screen.

"Hey Professor," Copper snapped. "What are you doing over there?"

The light from the device cast a green shadow over Jay's face. "I've discovered invigorating entertainment called Whack-a-mole."

With such a limited number of staff available, Keegan was responsible for the safety of the entire Retreat, so he took control of the situation with his best boss voice. "Inspector number 9! We need you to help break into my mother's office."

Jay's head shot up. He spoke through his hand covering his mouth. "That's a violation of several rules and definitely not on the list of scheduled activities."

Keegan strode to the dining area, pulled out a chair, and sat across the table. The wavy lines rippling across Jay's forehead made him look like a businessman, and Bill Harris negotiated with wrinkled business professionals. So Keegan thought of every tip in *Social Eyes* as he peered at his new companion, and gave his best impression of his father. "Copper might be a murderer. We need to determine if he killed his brother. Your job at the plant, Inspector 9, is quality control. It's time to control the quality right here on Ainsley Avenue."

Jay pulled at the buttons near his collar. "Keegan, I use a spectrometer to examine polymers for—"

"This is no time for your fancy talk, Jay. I need you to

focus." To his own ears, his "boss talk" made him sound important, like a school principal. He squared his shoulders and straightened the top of his body so he looked powerful. "Stay on topic. Keep your body and brain in the group. Will you help us or not?"

The Whack-a-mole screen flashed "Game Over," and Jay flung his hands. "Look at the schedule. Right now, we should be traveling to our evening meal. There's no time for illegal capers."

Visualizing leadership scenes from several movies, Keegan stood and announced, "I've got a plan. We'll break into the office after dinner." His mind raced. He'd just told his new best friends a lie. *This is what happens when you hang out with criminals.* He touched his pocket. It was flat. *Empty.*

Bile rose in Keegan's throat. He rushed to the desk and found two new unsharpened pencils, and he shook them with reckless fury. "Copper, I need you to promise me that you won't murder anyone here. That would be disrespectful to the Retreat, to my family, and to all the good people who work here."

Copper's body pitched forward. He grabbed his stomach and leaned against the wall. His voice passed through clenched teeth. "I promise."

Through his pencils, Keegan thought of the last few weeks of preparation. How many times had he stood in this very spot, imagining this visit? He'd made schematics of the shelf, carefully measuring so each of his favorite things would fit. Nicola had taken him to get all new 9-volt batteries so each kinetic toy would be at its best. Today hadn't matched his vision at all. Even with his new pencils, he felt like shrinking into himself, just like little Darla from the trolley. His body lost its energy. It burned when he swallowed. The hint of vomit was the flavor of his entire life breaking. "I don't know what we're going to do if the papers say you're a killer. It doesn't make sen—"

"Don't worry about it." Like a crack of lightning striking a tree, Copper's words spiked against Keegan's skin, making the hair on his arms stand up. The redhead's eyes shot daggers that punched holes into his chest. "Send Jay with me…" Copper paused. His face twisted. "…to make sure I don't go on a killing spree."

Pressure and responsibility threatened to crush Keegan, but that didn't happen in the movies. He looked through his pencils and animated the scene. He controlled how fast life moved. The Harrises needed to fill half the hall, but protecting the Retreat and the people in it was the most important thing. His family took bold action and got things done. Keegan Harris would protect their property, their dreams, and the people on Ainsley Avenue. He might only have two new friends today, but that was two more than yesterday. As written in *Socially Satisfied*, he would be happy with what he had. And hopefully, Nicola would help him with the townspeople. He could only handle so much.

Keegan watched the pencil's silver sparks streak in front of his eyes. "Fine. Working in teams is a good idea. Let's go to dinner." As Jay and Tyler approached the door, he added, "And act normal!"

Copper's sneakers squished and spattered across the floor. His face softened when he looked back at Keegan. "We were both wrong earlier. I know three things." He held up a finger. "Tyler likes that hat." He held up a second finger. "Jay is incredibly strong. He has huge muscles under that baggy shirt." His third finger popped up, joining the other two.

Keegan paid special attention to the hand gesture. If Copper gave him The Finger, he was certainly a murderer, and they needed to call the police.

Copper's face crumbled. "You're some kind of clown priest

who has agreed to help me break the rules." He sniffed. "And if I'm supposed to go to jail, I'll run away. I won't ruin your Inn." With that, he left the room.

Keegan tried to process the two statements at the same time. He called out, "But I'm not even Catholic!" He turned to make sure his door was locked, wondering if a clown priest would make a good greeting card. Whatever happened with Copper, he had his word that the Inn would be safe and full of good people. He exhaled and relaxed his shoulders. He hadn't realized he'd been holding his breath.

Relief curled Keegan's mouth. Clown, priest, or ringleader, getting orientation back on track required a solid plan, a little bravery, and a lot of luck.

Chapter Twenty-Four

COPPER

In for a penny, in for a pound.

Copper sped past the others, stopping short of the lobby. *Act normal. What did that mean in this place?* Thrust here unprepared and ignorant, they were all half-baked. He stepped to the side of the hall and waited for the band of misfits. *Would they keep his secret through dinner?*

Jay hurried past, checking his watch. Within a few strides, Keegan joined the Resident Trainer on the far side of the lobby. Luke twisted his mouth into half a smile. "Dinner for only three?"

Tyler casually dragged his hand on the surface of each door along the corridor. He crossed the hall with soft, slow steps. Despite the day's events, the kid looked as fresh as he did this morning. Even after screaming and huddling under a heavy blanket a few minutes ago, the back of his shirt was perfectly pressed.

"Tyler, are you coming with us?"

Tyler spoke with a confidence that didn't match his timid

footsteps. "I've come here to chew bubblegum and kick ass. I'm all out of—"[1]

"Cursing!"

Luke's hand shot out sideways and pressed against Keegan's chest. "Hold on, bro. I think he means he's coming with us." The other corner of Luke's mouth formed a full smile. "Tyler man, we need to talk about the movies you've been watching."

Copper's belly squeezed toward his spine when Luke aimed his smile at him next. He'd shared his worst fear with the others. Maybe he should wait in his room—nobody wants to dine with a delinquent, or worse, a murderer. Luke had been kind to him all day, even when he'd been a jerk calling him Rockstar Cowboy, and now, Copper had asked the group to betray his trust. Guilt was heavier than any weighted blanket.

"Copper, you gotta eat. There's no way you can survive on microwave popcorn. C'mon, what do ya say?"

Jay adjusted the straps on his backpack. "The human body will not function properly, solely on the nutritional content of corn."

Copper watched Keegan's foot tapping. He needed to make sure they kept his secret for as long as possible. If he could find out what kind of trouble he was in, he could figure out his next step. He was through letting life just happen to him. He needed to take action. *Act normal.* Today's version of normal meant maintaining an edge to his voice. He decided to be *super* normal. He emphasized the last word one syllable at a time. "Sure. I'll par-ti-ci-pate."

They approached the restaurant in silence. The evening air cooled Copper's burning cheeks. A few feet from the door, Keegan stopped and beat a rapid rhythm on his chest. Everyone except Luke froze in place. The minute Luke's boots stopped shuffling, the quiet reached a new depth. "What's goin' on, Keeg?"

Personal space be damned. Copper lunged ahead and stood close to Keegan. He peered into the blond bobblehead's face. "Are you ok? Do you need me to hold those *pencils* for you?"

Keegan's eyes squeezed shut. "The restaurant might smell. My heart is nervous." He grabbed Luke's shoulder. "There could be...gluten!"

Keegan pronounced the word *gluten* like it was the worst curse word of all, and Luke chuckled. Copper's shoulders released a small amount of tension—maybe in Bizzaro World, this *was* acting normal.

Luke swung his hair away from his eyes. "Alright. Here's how we'll do it. Stick your head in the door and take a big whiff. See if you can take it. If there's not a gluten-free menu, we'll have your food sent over from the Terraces."

Copper kept the conversation rolling. He would talk about anything, as long as it wasn't their after-dinner plans. "Oh yeah! You said the hospital—I mean, the Terraces—has another kitchen, right?"

Keegan stretched his neck to hold his head up high. His arms made a grand gesture toward the other building. He looked like one of those models Copper and Sterling had once seen at a car show. "They have a whole gluten-free area in their kitchen. No cross contamination." He tilted his head, pointed his chin down, and offered a melodramatic nod.

Jay tugged at the zipper on his backpack. "In addition to your erratic heartbeat, is there a complication with your neck? We can research your symptoms online."

Keegan threw his arms in the air. "I'm trying to do Luke's cool guy nod."

"Keeg, I don't—"

The ringleader opened the door to the restaurant and stuck his face inside, twisting his head right and left. Without warning, his wispy body slipped through the door and skittered across the floor. He chose a table as far from the kitchen as possible.

Luke ushered the rest of the group inside. "Did you just try to sneak in here?"

"Yeah! I saw that on a cartoon." Keegan plopped into a seat. "This place is so cool. It doesn't stink tonight!"

As the group settled into their places, Jay opened his backpack. Luke touched the table in front of Jay. "Whoa, Jay man. Let's leave the electronics off for now."

Jay's eyes darted to the side. "I'm acting normal." He slid the laptop back into its sleeve.

Copper seized control of the conversation. "Is there someone here to take your order or do we walk up to a counter?"

"For breakfast and lunch, it's a buffet. Afternoon snacks are ordered at the counter. At night, it's a full-service restaurant with a waitstaff and everything. It gives y'all a chance to practice different dining styles."

Keegan drummed on the table with his pencils. "It's preparing us for the real world. That's what my mom says."

Copper brushed his fingers along a cold penny in his pocket. "Then what world is this?"

Keegan pulled his phone out of his back pocket. "I can see today's menu on this app."

Jay fidgeted with his watch. "Should we inquire about the waitstaff? The restaurant appears to be vacant."

Luke pushed his chair back. "Copper, you like kitchens and cooking, right? Why don't you come with me? The rest of y'all can hang out while we see what's goin' on."

Copper stood up. Separating Luke from the others seemed like a great idea. A tour of the kitchen supplied the perfect distraction. Jay added the resident-issued tablet to his collection of gadgets on the table. Keegan and Tyler huddled around the glowing screens as Jay searched his bag. Knees in his seat, Keegan's elbows propped the rest of his body over the table. "You have more devices than anyone I know."

Through the kitchen's swinging door, Copper hoped he was the only one who could hear Keegan's forced enthusiasm.

Chapter Twenty-Five

KEEGAN

Ask simple, direct questions.

- Confusion Requires Clarification

Keegan's thoughts rippled like the screensaver on Jay's iPad. Being a liar was exhausting. Outwardly, he tried to be an entertaining and attentive host, while his mind scrambled to plan the heist. He hadn't outlined his course of action if the Retreat was truly at risk. After dinner, the guys were supposed to take a break from being social. A few precious minutes of solitude had been reserved so that the day would be less overwhelming. After a quick recharge, they were to enjoy some time by the fire pit. Now, he had to spoil the flow of the evening with additional clandestine activities. His guests needed to experience some big bonding moments in the firelight exactly as he'd planned. Without some rest, that would be next to impossible. Keegan pulled his legs out from under him and sat up in his seat. Serious situations called for serious thinking. He reached for his pencils.

In the movie that had inspired his original schedule, there

was a covert mission to get something from the rebellious guy's locker. Keegan had expected the students to score some waffles. During that first viewing, he'd kept waiting for breakfast to finally enter the story, but it never did. That was a disappointing plot hole. Even more shocking was learning the prize for their efforts wasn't a dried salad, but some kind of illegal drug. That revelation led to washing his eyes and his mouth with soap more than once.

Tomorrow's scavenger hunt would not include anything illegal. Nicola had explained orientation shouldn't be too exciting because it might make people more nervous. So he'd studied each encounter that encouraged the film's characters to connect, and he'd revised those activities to be safe and fun for this weekend. Nicola and Luke suggested that he use the word "appropriate" as a guideline.

His mother's perfume interrupted his stream of consciousness. Red-faced, he shoved the pencils back into his pocket as she approached the table. He hadn't seen her for hours, and so much had happened. Part of him wanted to cry and tell her everything, but he couldn't sob in front of his new friends. *Lead the Way to Friendship* said confidence and exhibiting a winning personality were like magnets that drew people into your life.

Andrea's arm reached out to her side. "Keegan, can we sit together for a few minutes?"

He pursed his lips. The Harris family got what they wanted. They created opportunities. They made things happen and they protected their own. Like it or not, he complied.

She gestured for him to move to a chair a few tables away from his friends. "I'm sorry I haven't been able to be with you much today. Nicola's extended absence has rearranged our schedules."

"Where is she? She's a huge part of our orientation plans."

His mother shifted in her seat and smoothed her hair. "Two

of our guests have complicated family situations, so she's been working hard behind the scenes. Boring stuff like finances—nothing for you to worry about. She's making sure everything is in place if they choose to live here."

Keegan's breath caught. "I thought this had all been arranged. You researched each of the guests months ago, right?"

She bent her elbow and let her chin rest in her palm. Her other hand rubbed one eye, before stifling a yawn. "Keegan, everything is fine. The Retreat has a lot of moving pieces, and every time we add something, we learn something new. We're doing our best to take care of people, like we always do." She folded her hands. "I came by to check on you, son. Luke mentioned the park situation. Are you ok?"

His hand clenched his pencils so hard his fingernails dug back into his palm. Luke had referred to the pencils as a security blanket. Keegan imagined a small child sucking its thumb. His teeth ground together and his jaw twitched as he made a special effort to keep the stim sticks still. "The dog didn't touch me. See? I don't need any medicine."

"I know, sweetheart. You look fine. But, I'm trying to see if you're upset or if you're happy. I can't tell." She pulled a crumpled napkin from her purse and squeezed it into a ball. Then she unwound the napkin and tore a piece off. "I know this weekend is important to you. It means a lot to all of us. Luke felt so bad. He thought he mismanaged the outing, and he's been concerned that the parents might be furious. They're trusting us, you know."

She exhaled. Some hair above her eye moved with the new wind. She swept the pile of paper fragments into her hand. "With your dad out of town, and Nicola's change of schedule, I'm relying on you and Luke to be responsible young men. Thank you for helping your new friends feel welcome today."

Then she stood and pushed her chair back. "I've got to

supervise the rec center events tonight. I'll come by later and you can tell me all about your day." She placed a light kiss on his forehead and left.

A piece of shredded napkin floated to the floor. Keegan loped to the garbage can and dropped it in. Chest lifted and head held high, he returned to his group with a plan. He would be the responsible young man his mother needed.

Chapter Twenty-Six

COPPER

A pretty penny

Copper loved the way the light played off the hanging pots and pans. It seemed as though tiny stars were embedded in the cookware, just waiting to turn a few ingredients into something magical.

Luke's voice startled him. "Have you been in a lot of commercial kitchens?"

Copper's gaze scoured the shiny metal countertops. "No. It looks like a set from the Entrée Network. I wonder if you have an immersion circulator here."

"An immer…What?!"

"They use it on Fastest Chef. It's for sous vide cooking." He glanced over his shoulder at Luke's blank face. "Never mind. They also have their own ice cream machines."

Luke's eyebrows bounced up and down. "Alright. I know a little something about ice cream." He pointed behind Copper.

"You have a machine here?"

"Well, it's probably not as fancy as Fastest Chef, but ice cream is available any time the doors are open. You can look at it, but don't touch, ok? Bart's in charge of the kitchen, and you do *not* want to get on his bad side. Wait here. I'm gonna run back to his office real quick."

As the rattle of the keys faded, Copper touched the cold countertop. He couldn't resist the temptation to make sure this kitchen was a real place. It looked like stainless steel heaven. With all these polished surfaces and equipment, he could live out every fantasy he'd ever had about being a chef. He walked closer to the giant sink and peeked in a few drawers. One was full of cutting boards. The next held knives. But these weren't like the knives at home. These were serious knives for real cooks. *Pointy and sharp.* They called to him. *So shiny.*

He noticed the drawers in this kitchen didn't have child-proof locks. No Pearl hovering around nearby to say, *Copy Pie, you really need to let me do that for you. You don't want to get hurt.* His mind flipped through mental snapshots. *Autism. His adult care center. Autism. Dead brother. Autism. Dead future. Autism. Knives. Weapons. Murder. Keegan's questions. Office papers and plots.*

But he would not be staying here. There would be no cooking fantasies—if he ran away, he'd be lucky to touch the garbage from a restaurant. He stood at the giant sink and let the warm water wash over his hands.

"I see you've found the sink. That's where the real magic happens."

Copper shut off the water and turned to find the source of the deep voice. A burly man in a bright, white apron walked in with Luke. He looked like he should be chopping wood or loading a cargo ship. "Magic? What do you mean?"

Apron Man rumbled. "Think about it. We can't do anything with dirty dishes!" He roared with laughter.

Copper's mouth twitched into a weak smile. "True."

Luke nudged The Apron. "That's the first real smile I've seen on his face. Thanks."

He edged closer to Copper. "Is your hand ok? Do you need a towel? Everything's cool, right?"

Copper wiped his hands on his pants. "I'm fine."

"Cool. Bart, this is Copper. He's checkin' out the Inn. Copper, this is Bart. He runs the kitchen."

Bart offered an easy smile. "Nice to meet you."

Copper gave Bart a quick appraisal and then looked away. "Do you also work on a ship?"

"Ha! I was in the Navy a long time ago. Worked in the galley. That's a great guess."

Copper shrugged. "I've seen one of those tattoos before."

Luke clapped his hands together. "Hey. I've got a small crew out there that may be bouncin' off the walls or gnawin' the furniture. Are you between shifts? I can grab the drinks."

Bart smiled. "There's one server tonight and she's got someone shadowing her. They're just getting started. I'll send them right over."

"Great. We gotta get back. I'm runnin' my tail off today. C'mon Copper."

Bart called after them. "Hey, is this your penny?"

Nice try, Sterling. Stop sending me pennies.

Bart bellowed, "If you like kitchens, you come back and visit me. But, if we're busy, I'll make you help."

Copper slipped through the swinging doors without touching them. He imagined Sterling's last moments and his own future opportunities being like those kitchen doors, slowly fluttering to a permanent stop.

Chapter Twenty-Seven

KEEGAN

Fast talking and interrupting others creates anxiety.

- Tone and Tension

Keegan reached across the table and covered Jay's screen. "Quick. We don't have much time. Is Copper really dangerous?"

Jay stared at the top of Keegan's hands. His eyebrows pulled a few more wrinkles into his forehead. "I'm not qualified to—"

"Ok. Great. I don't think he is either." Keegan strolled to the end of the table, and bent over to make eye contact with the quality control expert. "He trusts you. He said you could keep him from killing again. Can you?"

"I possess the skills of—"

"Perfect." Keegan stood, and paced the length of their table. "I know how to get into my mom's office. This really nice lady, Nicola, was supposed to be here. I don't know what's going on, but it's disrupted my mom's schedule today. She'll be in the rec center tonight, but that building is right beside her office." Keegan stopped and slammed his hands on the table in front of Jay. "Your job is to be the lookout and keep things running on time." He nudged the phone sitting on top of a mountain of other glowing rectangles. "Check your messages. I'm sending you the alarm codes. There won't be much time from the second he steps in until the alarm sounds."

Jay's arm wrapped around his stash of gadgets protectively. "This seems—"

"There's no time to argue." Keegan punched his phone screen. "This is an unscheduled activity, remember? You need the instructions before Luke and Copper return."

He moved to the opposite end of the table and flopped into his chair. "Tyler, we'll distract Luke while they go into my mom's office. Ok?"

"I'm looking for a dare-to-be-great situation."[1]

"I don't know what that means. Stick with me and be yourself, I guess. We'll visit Luke's room after dinner and I'll—"

Jay cleared his throat. "Keegan."

Keegan leaned forward to see past Tyler. "Level three, Jay! Interrupting people is terrible manners. I've got a book—"

Jay's jaw became soft. His voice sounded like Luke's when he talked in his sleep. "You never told me there'd be beautiful women here."

"Huh? We won't open the women's side of the Inn for…" Keegan stopped and turned around.

Two young women were advancing on their table.

Chapter Twenty-Eight

COPPER

Watching every penny.

Copper rounded the corner and stopped short. The scene held some strange quiet tension, like fruit suspended inside a jiggling gelatin mold. The laptop provided a pale blue filter for Jay's face. Keegan stared through his pencils at…nothing. Irritation replaced Tyler's smile. Two girls were near the table. The threat of exposure launched Copper into his seat.

A tall brunette with "Anne" on her name tag stood beside a cute blonde in a wheelchair. They both stared at Tyler. Anne's mouth hung open and her eyes looked glassy.

Tyler shouted, "I'll have what she's having!"[1]

Luke jogged to the table. "Whoa; easy, Tyler." He flipped his hair and slid smoothly into his seat. The slow, lazy Texas drawl poured over the crowd. "I'm sorry, Anne. He may be quoting *When Harry Met Sally*." He served his best "aw shucks, ma'am" smile. "Have you seen it?"

Anne shook her head. Her posture improved. She stood tall, pen poised over a tiny pad of paper. Copper studied her face. Her smile never quite touched her eyes. "I'm so glad you're here, Mr. Luke. Let's start over." She looked down toward the girl in the wheelchair and said in a low voice, "Sometimes, with these guys, you have to be good at puzzles."

The blonde looked at her with large, round eyes.

Anne sucked a deep breath through her nose. Her words spilled out as she exhaled. "Hi! I'm Anne. This is Ruby. She's shadowing me today. What would y'all like to drink?"

Jay kept his eyes glued to his laptop. "Milk."

"Did you want white milk or chocolate?"

This question earned Jay's full attention. He closed the lid on his computer. "Anne with an E, milk is, by its nature, white. Thus you have no need for the modifier. If I had wanted chocolate milk, I would have said so." He opened the laptop and resumed typing.

Anne looked at her pad. She closed her eyes, gave her head a quick shake, and angled herself toward Keegan. "And for you?"

Keegan turned around in his seat and faced away from the group. He studied the window, wiggling the ever-present pencils.

Luke nudged him. "Your turn, Keeg. Tell her what you'll drink."

"Just water."

Anne's gaze fell on Copper.

"Could I have lemonade?" Copper preferred to look at the blonde named Ruby. She wore a dark blue dress with white polka dots and white tights. A blue flower pinned her hair up on one side. She had soft, light pink cheeks. Ruby looked like a living doll. His throat went dry. "It's what the character drinks in *Passage*. I'm great at that game."

Anne stretched the word out as she scribbled on the pad. "Le...mon...ade." She leaned over to show Ruby her notes.

Tyler looked at Luke and pointed to a picture on a menu.

Luke nodded. "You tell her, man. You gotta practice."

Tyler displayed his set of giant white teeth. "I drink your milkshake."[2]

Anne smiled. She raised her voice and added space between each word. "That. Was. Good. Good Job! You. Did. It."

Ruby gave Anne the side-eye.

Then, Anne looked at Luke, who muttered something about being tired and requested a cup of coffee.

As the waitress turned to walk away, Ruby asked, "Did you want decaf or regular?"

Anne spun on her heel. "Ruby, you are the shadow. Just watch!"

Luke rubbed the back of his neck. "Thanks, Ruby; regular's perfect."

She smiled and rolled away.

Luke leaned forward. "Well guys, that was interesting. Keegan, what did you notice about those ladies?"

"One of them had shiny wheels."

"True. Buddy, it'd be great if you could face us when we sit together. Copper, did you get any impressions?"

"No. Why is one called a shadow? She looks real and fully formed to me."

"She stays as close to our server as a shadow while learning how to do the job. Grab a menu, guys. They'll be back any minute. The sooner we order, the sooner we can eat." He handed the last menu to Jay. "Your laptop could get wet when the drinks get here. You should stash it."

Keegan added, "Don't want it to get electrocuted."

Jay sucked the air out of the room, explaining how electricity worked while rummaging through his backpack. He snapped a few photos of the restaurant before storing his last gadget.

Copper listened for his name or the word "murder" to

come up in the conversation. He was too weary to care about anything else.

When the women came back, the ordering procedure went well until Anne got to Tyler. She spoke slowly, like a cavewoman sucking on helium rolled in confectioner's sugar. "What you eat?" Each word sounded like it had been dredged through thick, invisible syrup. Ruby frowned.

Tyler focused on his fingernails. He rubbed at the cuticle on one finger. Then he started scraping the underside of each his nails. The movement made a popping sound, similar to someone cracking their knuckles. Copper smashed his teeth together. His jaw hung loose when Tyler responded, "Why don't you go outside and jerk yourself a soda?"[3]

Anne's bright red face turned to Luke. "Did he call me a jerk?"

The blonde angel looked up at Anne. "That was from *Bugsy*. Released in 1991. Earlier, he quoted *There Will Be Blood* from 2007." Ruby adjusted the flower in her hair. "But he could have called you a jerk because you're talking to him like a toddler."

Copper checked over the group: Luke sipped his coffee, Tyler beamed, Keegan stimmed, and Jay played with the edge of his menu. At last, he'd encountered someone at The Retreat who seemed to understand what was going on and could speak plainly.

A tiny notebook fell into Ruby's lap. Anne stormed off.

Luke snickered. "You really know your movies, Ruby."

Tyler turned his menu toward her and touched a picture of a cheeseburger. "They call it a Royale with Cheese."[4]

She scribbled. "Yep. *Pulp Fiction*. You want everything on it?"

Tyler scrunched up his face. "There's something wrong with this yogurt. That's not yogurt, it's mayonnaise."[5]

Luke studied Tyler. "No mayo?"

Tyler's nostrils flared. His tongue made the universal sign for disgust.

The polka dot cherub was all business. "Ok, that's *Pulp Fiction,* hold the *Notting Hill.* How about you, Mr. Luke?"

He pointed at Tyler. "I'll have what *he's* having."[6]

Ruby rolled away from the table, and Copper wished he could go with her. "How can she do this job? She can't walk and carry things?"

Ruby's chair creaked as she spun around. "I'm sitting down, not deaf. And I won't stay in this chair forever. I'm getting better, Ginger Root." She whirled out of the room.

Luke blew into his coffee mug. "I'm no expert on women, but that one has some fire in her. Y'all better be careful."

"Yeah." Keegan's curls shook. "She's fast on those wheels."

Chapter Twenty-Nine

When asking for favors, a quiet, soft tone is best.

- Make It Right

Luke's room didn't have enough toys in it. Guitars lurked in each corner. He'd covered the walls with concert posters, vintage ads for musical instruments, and a few album covers. A birthday gift from Keegan provided the only bright, whimsical spot in the room. Using primary colors, he'd painted a group of broken instruments and included a custom card. They took center stage on his bookcase. Luke had stained the custom card with tears, but he'd framed it anyway. He'd strategically placed it so that the words shone under hot lights, proudly proclaiming to all who looked, "Just because something's broken, doesn't mean it's trash."

Tyler stuck his finger out. "Guitar?"

Luke clapped. "We've got a pointer!" He picked up the guitar and offered it to Keegan's co-conspirator.

After brightening the room with a huge smile, Tyler took

the guitar to Luke's dining room. He placed it flat on the table and lightly plucked each string.

Luke sat across from Keegan. "So brother, what's up?"

Keegan pulled the greeting cards out of his folder. "I thought we might go over some of my new designs. I didn't get any quality Luke Time today." His brother's eyes drifted toward Tyler. Aside from the confusing pointer comment, he could usually understand Luke's mind. "Tyler wanted to hang out and talk"—Keegan shot a quick glance at Tyler and added —"since he kind of speaks English now."

Tyler touched his own chest with one finger. "Point. Speak English. Hang out. Talk." His focus returned to the guitar strings.

Luke nudged a chair with his boot. "Sit. We'll talk, but just for a bit. It's been a long day especially since Nic—"

"Yeah. She's missed the whole day. I'm very disappointed."

"She'll get in late tonight or early tomorrow. Don't worry; she'll meet all of our new friends."

They'd better all be friends, but far too much was riding on the papers in his mom's office.

"Show me your cards."

"Oh." Lies warmed Luke's room. Keegan fanned his face with the small stack of prototypes. "Since Kiara is probably getting married this year, I thought I'd try some wedding cards."

"Gonna show off your romantic side, huh, Keeg?"

He wanted to correct Luke, but noticed his brother's smirk. It was another one of those odd jokes. His family tried to be funny. Keegan didn't have the heart to tell them that their sense of humor was weird. He swept the first card out with a gesture suitable for a royal audience. "I'll add flowers underneath the words 'On Your Wedding Day.' Inside, it says, 'I hope it works out for you.'"

"That's pure poetry, buddy."

Keegan beamed. He'd thought he'd nailed it with that card.

Luke's grin widened. "You sure have a gift."

Keegan's smile vanished. His hand shot forward. "I'm only selling cards, not gifts."

Chapter Thirty

COPPER

Penny wise, pound foolish

Jay's voice crackled through the radio speaker. "Schematics weren't furnished."

Copper hoped Jay hadn't decided to abandon his lookout post. "Forget it, Professor. I'll use the light from my phone screen." He held the screen side out in front of him. He didn't have time to find the flashlight app. His other hand stretched forward so he wouldn't accidentally smash his face into a chair or something. "There's five minutes from the time I use the key code before the alarm sounds. Set your timer for four minutes."

The silence brought no comfort. Copper's fears and uncertainties curdled into a nauseating mass in his belly. *If he found his paperwork, what would it say? What if his brother hated him? What if Pearl did?* He pictured jail cells as he stumbled in the darkness. He remembered how loud prisons sounded in the movies.

His foot landed on something slippery. Both hands flailed wildly in a desperate effort to catch himself as he fell. His phone clacked against the tile, and his hands slid through sticky goo.

In the distance, Jay's voice rang out, "Pandemonium? Should I initiate evasive measures to avoid capture?"

Copper raised his voice as he crawled toward the phone. "No. I slipped. What's all over the floor?" His hands felt like they were covered in blood.

The light from his phone revealed several wet canvases scattered across the floor. Vivid colors coated his shoes, and the knees of his pants were wet. "I fell. It looks like Walt Disney threw up in here."

"You've discovered our mural."

"Yes," Copper hissed. "Are there any more surprises waiting for me on the floor?"

"Unlikely. Prudence suggests we terminate this mission to avoid disciplinary action."

"Focus. Watch the clock and the door. That's it. Tell me if anyone's coming."

"Three minutes and...no, two minutes and fifty-nine sec... fifty-eight seconds remain. You've yet to arrive at your initial destination."

Copper tried to ignore the weight of his shoes as he hurled himself toward the far end of the room. Relief flooded over him as he opened the door to Mrs. Harris' office. This room made sense. The light switch hung in the proper place on the wall, just inside the door.

He tossed the phone next to a stack of folders on the desk. Keegan said his mom would probably still have the paperwork sitting there. He thumbed through the labels, then shouted at the phone. "How much time is left?"

"Two minutes and five seconds."

Copper's fingers flew through files. He read the top: the Tower, the Terrace, the Courtyard, the Inn, the Cottages. *Why did they make a new name for every damned building?* He flipped back to the one labeled "the Inn."

"Copper, I appear peculiar, loitering. This enterprise is unsuitable."

"Count and take pictures, Prof. That's your thing, isn't it?" Copper licked his fingers. The taste of paint and bile fought for dominance in his mouth. He separated the pages. *Tyler Ramsey, Tyler Ramsey, Tyler Ramsey…Come on! Jay Simmons…Jay…*

Jay scoffed. "Photographs? With this device, under the cloak of darkness? That's farcical."

Campbell. That was his brother's last name. Sterling Campbell. He'd never changed it to Munro. Copper pulled every page he could find with the words Campbell or Munro on them.

He looked up at the clock. "To Hell with it!" He snatched the entire folder, slammed the light switch, and ran for the front door.

Chapter Thirty-One

KEEGAN

Changing vocal tones adds interest to your words.

- Tone Tutor

Keegan continued reading. "'Your wedding is a special day.' On the inside, it says, 'You should have gone to Vegas!'" He gave his best version of a triumphant smile.

Luke's phone made the sound of a Howler monkey. His smirk folded in on itself, lips tucked tightly into his mouth. His eyes narrowed and creased as he looked at the screen.

Tyler covered his ears, and Keegan's guts twisted. He grabbed his stomach. "Oh, Luke, I may have gotten The Gluten."

His brother looked up, his jaw dangling. Keegan's mind raced. Music kept Luke busy. Playing the guitar might have been Luke's version of stimming. Keegan touched the pencils in his pocket. Bolstered by their presence he added, "Play me the song that always makes me feel better." He reached for the guitar to pass it from Tyler to Luke.

Tyler handed Keegan the guitar and paced. "Side effects

may include: stomach pain, nausea, vomiting, loss of appetite, vision problems, dizziness, mild headache, sweating, and mild skin rash."

The monkey screech filled the room, and Luke leapt to his feet.

Keegan produced a few dry heaves as Tyler wore a track in the floor.

"Sorry, Keeg. That's mom's office alarm. I gotta go."

Chapter Thirty-Two

COPPER

Penny pinched

Copper tore through the art room in a blind rush. The next few minutes would change his life. He had to get out, hide, and read the contents of the folder. He shot past the opposite side of the craft table, just missing the slick, sticky paintings. But his heavy, wet shoes were already ruined. He'd need to find some new ones while on the run. *Did prisoners get shoes to go with their uniforms?*

He planned to slam the door shut, but his foot caught on the threshold. As he stumbled outside, he noticed painted marshmallows covering his shoe. Before his mind could form a coherent thought about his feet, the rest of his body crashed into Jay's concrete arms. The force of the collision launched the folder out of his hands. It landed on top of Luke's boot.

Luke, Keegan, Tyler, and Andrea Harris stood a few feet outside the door on the sidewalk. The Resident Trainer retrieved the folder from the ground.

Copper's mouth, full of blazing heat, snarled, "I need to see it!"

Ms. Harris' eyes darted toward Luke. "Find his papers in the folder. I'll reset the alarm."

Keegan gawked at Copper's feet. His mouth hung wide open. He blinked twice, then lost all trace of charm. He ran after his mother shouting, "I'm sorry!"

Luke motioned toward some park benches. His face looked too serious when he suggested the guys sit down. Jay and Tyler shared a bench.

Copper sat alone. He tried to massage his shoulder. Crashing into Jay during his poor attempt at an escape reminded him of his earlier bump with Keegan's hard melon head this afternoon. Sore or not, the shoulder would have to wait. When he tried to rub it, he winced and grabbed his wrist. His arm may have been banged up during his fall in the art room or when the Professor pulled him out of the sea earlier. His time on Ainsley Avenue had been tough on his body, brain, and spirit.

Tears ran down his cheeks. His plans were over. Every time he thought he could save himself, things got worse. He listened for police sirens.

Tyler broke the silence. "You fake a stomach cramp, and when you're bent over, moaning and wailing, you lick your palms. It's a little childish and stupid, but then, so is high school."[1]

Copper heard steps in the gravel.

Keegan approached, taking long, deliberate strides toward the park benches. "Shut up, Tyler!" Keegan pulled his hat firmly over his ears. "I'm sorry. Every social skills book says that's rude."

Luke intercepted his mother. He handed her the folder covered in fingerprint-shaped smudges. "It's all here. I pulled the other sheets out."

Keegan's arms could have directed a plane down the tarmac if he'd had orange batons. "You wrecked our mural!

You destroyed our art room. There's paint all over my mom's light switch." He released a dramatic huff as he squat down to get a better view of Copper's shoes. His ear slid toward his shoulder, duplicating the angle of his mother's tilted head. "That is so disrespectful!" His tone became indignant. "Did you try to steal our marshmallows?"

"Keegan, that's enough!" His mother exhaled, adjusted her tone, and said, "Luke, could you take the guys back inside to drop off the pages and tidy up the mural? It's looking a little abstract in its current state."

With a nod and a mumbled "C'mon guys," they hung their heads and shuffled into the building.

Like an approaching thunderstorm, Copper rumbled, "I don't know why they're all upset. I'm the one who's going to jail!"

Ms. Harris sat next to Copper. She handed him some damp wipes for his hands. "Honey, I'm not going to press charges. I've already told the police the alarm was a mistake."

"But, what about my brother's murder?"

Ms. Harris shivered. "What murder?"

"That folder has papers about my brother's death...from attorneys." He clarified in case she didn't read her paperwork.

Andrea thumbed through the folder. She stopped and looked at him, wearing the expression of a dead fish. "Your mother didn't tell you?"

Copper looked down. He wiped his hands and shielded his stomach with his arms.

"I don't know about any murder, but your brother did have attorneys. These papers are about you. You're welcome to read them. I wish you'd have just asked." She flicked two pages, pinched three, and held them out. "These are some legal documents that we have for you."

Copper grabbed the pages. He walked over to the nearby

streetlight and scanned the lines. *Cancer. Will. Trust. His name.*
"Grantor intends this trust to provide Beneficiary…"

He looked back at Ms. Harris. In the half-light, she looked
tired, and a little older than he realized. He returned to the
bench and sat next to her. She handed him the folder. "Take a
look. You're old enough to be completely involved in this
process."

"I don't understand. Some of these papers are dated
several years ago." He handed the papers back to her.

"Yes, your brother was very smart. He took out a life
insurance policy as soon as he finished college. He put some
things in place for you, just in case…" She touched the outer
edge of her eye. "I can tell that he loved you very much." Her
hands rested on top of her lap. She crossed her legs at the
ankles and leaned back. "It looks like you loved him too."

"He was my whole world. He was also my future."
Copper's voice broke. He sounded like a child again. "And he's
gone. Just…gone." His body shook with tears.

Ms. Harris' arm wrapped around his shoulders. "Copper,
your brother died from cancer. I may not know a lot of things,
but I can promise you this: you didn't give him cancer. You
couldn't have cured his cancer. You did not kill your brother."
Her hand touched her forehead. "I really thought you and
your mom would have talked about this!" She took out her
phone.

Copper sniffed and swallowed. "Are you calling Pearl?"

Andrea's eyes wrinkled at the edges. "No, not tonight. I'm
going to call someone who will probably be a very good friend
for you. Her name is Nicola. She's been working with the
people listed on the legal documents." She touched a list of
names at the bottom of the page. "There's a board who will be
checking up on Ainsley Avenue to see if we're good enough for
you. Your brother had some very strong ideas about where you
might live."

Copper looked around. "But the Inn is great."

"Well, we kind of blew it on security today, didn't we?" She rubbed her lips together and raised her eyebrows.

"I'm really sorry." He covered his belly and bent forward.

"No, I'm the sorry one. It sounds like you've been having a difficult time." She put her hand on his back. "Is something wrong with your stomach, Copper?"

"I have a lot of big feelings. They go into my stomach."

She sat forward on the bench. "Have you had these belly pains for a long time or are they new?"

"I started having them more often when Sterling got sick."

"Your physical and emotional health are linked together. As you get older, it's important to learn how to take care of yourself and ask for help. Stress and grief can be very damaging. We might have some people to help you with it." She pushed some hair behind one ear. "But only if you want help. Our goal is to support you while you become the man you want to be."

Copper gave her a weak smile. Tears pooled in his eyes. "I don't know who that is."

"Oh, honey"—her eyes creased with a grin—"that's exactly how most people your age feel right now. This is a time of exploration. Your whole life is new from this moment forward. You can have a fresh start here." She scrolled through photos of her workshop on her phone. "See?"

Copper stared at a grayish brown lump sitting on a table. As she swiped her finger, the lump transformed. She stopped at a photo that looked like a crude figure. She advanced one more. A ballerina stood next to a tall man holding a golf club. She sniffed. "Whoops. Let's go back."

The muddy figure returned to the screen. "Days are like lumps of clay. We can mold them into a full life. But like every great work of art, it will take time and patience." She returned to the picture of the ballerina. Her finger hovered over the image. "Sometimes a lot of time and patience."

Copper sat up straighter and stretched his spine. "Are those lawyers going to let me stay here? I mean, if I want to...?"

"They're talking about money. There are conditions attached to the trust fund. I'm not so concerned with money. I should be, believe me, but the Inn is ready for residents. You have a room if you want it." She straightened up and smoothed her clothes. "Keegan likes you a lot. I can't put a price on how much his happiness means to me."

"I haven't been very nice to him—or anyone at all, really."

"Darling, he lied for you. He's never lied about anything. Ever." She bit her lip and swung her legs back and forth like a kid on a swing.

He wasn't sure why she was eating her smile or why lying was a good thing. Her son was odd, so that saying about the apple falling close to the tree was finally making sense.

Her shoes dragged across some coarse gravel. "Can I have my file back? I can give you copies tomorrow if you'd like."

Copper automatically handed her the file. He wasn't used to being asked and he sure wasn't going to argue with the woman who had single-handedly kept him out of handcuffs tonight.

She hopped off the bench. "Please excuse me; I've got to make a phone call."

The sound of keys announced Luke's presence, even at this distance. With her cell phone balanced between chin and shoulder, Ms. Harris formed a small huddle with the guys exiting the building.

In the distant foggy light, Keegan and Luke's mother danced as a slim figure joined them on the shadowed walkway. Ms. Harris sang out "Milestone!" and went inside.

The rest of the silhouettes grew larger as they drew near. Luke's keys competed with his voice. "...hug you but I'm dirty." Tyler and Jay were carrying large garbage bags. With them, a woman balancing on impossibly tall, pointy shoes replaced the spot usually occupied by Keegan's unique profile. She wore a tight skirt that ended right at her knees and carried a collection of shopping bags in each hand. She looked like the scales of justice figure he'd seen on one of Sterling's antique coins. They stopped at Copper's bench. She was pretty, her brown hair swept back into a neat ponytail. *Sterling would have loved her.*

"Copper, this is Nicola. She's been going over the terms of your paperwork all day." Nicola struggled, trying to shift the handles of her shopping bags all into one hand.

Jay pushed his garbage bag into Tyler's chest and reached for her bags. "Allow me."

"Thank you." Relieved of her burden, she extended her hand toward Copper. He'd made such a mess of things today. He resolved to get at least one thing right and engaged in the annoying social custom. His hand closed around hers.

"It's nice to meet you, Copper."

Her strong grip surprised him as they rocked their palms up and down a few times. Still grasping hands, she swung her almond-shaped eyes toward Luke.

Luke nodded. "Today has been full of surprises."

Copper wondered if she could read minds as she removed her hand from his grasp.

Luke disrupted his thoughts. "Copper man, you and I need to hang out for a little bit."

Nicola cleared her throat. "I've got some things for the sensory lab in those bags. I need to store them in the Inn. Tyler and Jay, would you help me with my bags?"

Tyler squeezed the trash bags closer to his chest. "Of all the gin joints in all the towns in all the world, she walks into mine."[2]

Jay offered his free arm. "Most exquisite lady, I will

accompany you to the ends of the earth enduring all hardships, such is my ardor."

Nicola didn't accept Jay's arm. She adjusted the purse on her shoulder. "Lucky for us, we're only walking across the property."

Chapter Thirty-Three

KEEGAN

Arms crossed with each hand holding the opposite elbow: feeling cold, or angry. See also: defensiveness, annoyance

- Gesture Dictionary

Keegan preferred the womb chair in the Inn's lobby to the uncomfortable seat in his mother's office. He missed his father. Bill Harris always knew the right thing to do. After reviewing the events of the day, he realized he'd missed Nicola too. She should have been here. She was the safeguard, the extra voice of reason slightly removed from the Harris family history.

He'd become flustered and made a series of poor choices. Things were a mess. Luke was angry with him. His mom was probably furious. They might be so upset that they close the whole Retreat down. If the other guys were in trouble, they'd never want to be his friends. They'd choose to live somewhere else. He'd go back to his old life, sitting alone, shut off from everyone. There'd be no school, no friends, and nothing to do but to sit and rot.

That's what he deserved. He hoped it wouldn't be too late for everyone to go back to their old lives and return to the dreams they'd left behind. Luke could go to college somewhere. He'd probably go far away, like their sister. His dad could focus on business. He wouldn't have to divide his time with permits, inspections, and fundraisers. Mom could be the artist she always should have been. She'd travel and show her work in galleries all over the world. As long as their hearts weren't broken by the failure, Keegan could sit and wait until everyone got old. Then he'd pick up where Ainsley left off, surviving years of loneliness, only to finish life in a place of abuse and neglect.

He shook. *Could his life really come to that? Had he made too many mistakes?* If his family died from broken hearts, he'd go straight to an institution. With his family, he had support. He had their love, companionship, and even a little power. With them, he was still a person. But without them…

The floor creaked. He straightened as his mom entered. She cracked open the door and glanced toward her desk. Keegan threw his arms around her. "I'm the worst. I'm so sorry."

His mother dropped the files on her desk. She hugged him hard, then held him away from her chest to study his face. "Oh, honey. You've had quite a day."

"Is Copper a murderer? Are we all gonna die?"

Her breath caught. "Son, what kind of director would I be if I didn't research those kinds of details? I do my best to make sure only good people come to the Retreat. I thought you knew that?!"

"I got confused." His pulse raced. He touched his pockets and scanned the room. "My plans. Our Retreat…" Keegan reached for his pencils.

His mother sat behind her desk. She waited. Once he

started adding sound effects to his stimming, she interrupted. "I remember your first ride on a school bus."

Keegan stood still and watched her through the blurry pencils. His mother's face and body looked calm, but sometimes people could be angry without yelling. She spoke the same way she did when she watched old home movies.

"It was a small bus designed for students with wheelchairs and things. You were three years old, and I worried you'd be confused and afraid. Up until that time, we were always together. You didn't go off in cars with other people, and we didn't have babysitters. It was a totally new experience for you. Days before you began school, I followed that bus and took pictures of the route. I counted the stops and took pictures at each one. I put them into a book that explained what was happening and where you were going. I made sure to tell you that you'd come back home. I asked the attendant to go through the book with you, pointing and reading along as you traveled. I did everything I could to be your guide, even when I wasn't able to be by your side. On your first day, I called the school and they assured me that you had arrived feeling happy."

She picked up the folder and shoved it into the drawer. "Back then, I thought I predicted your thoughts and feelings fairly well. I'd had years of practice, trying to understand and meet your needs while you learned to speak." She rubbed her tired face. "One afternoon, you came home upset. I thought you weren't sure they'd bring you home, or that you'd had a terrible time at school. But a boy named Ben was troubling you. Do you remember him?"

Keegan climbed back into the hard chair and sat on his feet. "With the legs?"

"Yes. He had mechanical legs. You screamed that a scary robot boy was on the bus. That was a sad day for both of you. You didn't mean to hurt his feelings. I explained that something had happened to Ben's legs, and the doctors gave him new ones. You wanted to fix his legs. Once I told you scientists had designed the special legs, you wanted to be a scientist."

"And they got to use science words for things we didn't say, so I thought they got to cuss. For a long time, I thought curse words were science words."

Andrea pulled lip balm from her desk drawer. "I didn't know that. Maybe part of you just really wants to cuss."

As she rubbed the tube against her lips, Keegan interjected. "Are you trying to tell me Copper has special legs?"

The tube fell into the drawer with a thunk. His mother crossed the room. "Son, you have a huge heart. Sometimes you connect to others like superglue, and you forget you're separate people. Copper is hurting. He's sad that his brother died. I love that you care about him and want us to fix his heart, but try not to wear his pain like it's your own, ok?"

"I thought friends shared feelings?"

"That probably means they talk about emotions. Don't worry. Most guys don't do that very often." She blinked her owl-like eyes. Her lip twitched.

"I do that with Nicola."

"Yes. She's here. I ran into her outside. Your friends are meeting her right now."

"Good." Maybe she could save the weekend. He thought of the last conversation he'd had with Nicola. "What does 'play the cards you're dealt' mean?"

His mother gathered him into a soft hug and held him close. She spoke into his hair. "It's more figurative language. If life was a card game, we have some helpful cards and some that present challenges. We need to make the best of our situation and use all the cards we've been given." She pulled away and looked at him. "We're doing that, aren't we?"

Keegan tightened his grip on the pencils and opened the

door. "It's not a good game. We need new cards. I'm going to my room for a while." Streaks of paint still spoiled the wall. They'd rushed the cleaning. It wasn't perfect. And neither was orientation. Not one part had gone according to plan.

His mother's voice followed him as he left the building. "Sometimes the challenging cards force us to do great things. We'll play a card game later. I'll show—"

He closed the door. Walking away while someone was talking broke the rule in *Listening With Both Ears*, but he needed to leave. If he had any hope of salvaging these friendships and his future, he had to start a fire.

Chapter Thirty-Four

COPPER

The penny dropped.

Luke dropped an olive green messenger bag on Copper's couch. Perched on the arm of an overstuffed chair, Copper asked, "Is everyone in big trouble?"

The Rockstar Cowboy wadded his plaid shirt into a ball. "I dunno. You guys sure know how to make me sweat." He shoved his laundry inside the bag.

Relieved the Resident Trainer still wore a white sleeveless undershirt, Copper tried to concentrate on the conversation. People were always doing things that had nothing to do with the topic.

"I didn't mean to stress everyone out. I was trying to figure my way out of a jam. Everything I do seems to cause trouble."

Luke sighed and ran his hand through his hair. "Well Trouble, you'll probably fit right in around here."

Copper tipped his head to the side.

A grin crept across Luke's mouth. "Man, now you're lookin' like family. Don't worry about the file. Sure, I wish you'd just asked me, but I can see why you were freaked out.

That's heavy stuff, dude. But, I'm on your side. I'd have fixed it all for you first thing this morning, if you'd trusted me."

"I didn't know you this morning."

"True." Luke detached the huge keyring from his belt. He spun the keyring around his finger once and set the keys on the table. "Keeping up with those and all that they stand for can be heavy too."

"Hey, you have a tattoo!"

"This?!" Luke touched his arm. "Got it when I turned 21. It's a phoenix."

"My brother had a tattoo. His wouldn't wash off either. You like birds?"

"I like this bird. There are legends that say the phoenix dies and comes back to life. This tattoo reminds me that my problems may feel like the end of everything, but I can keep going. Bad experiences can make me stronger."

Copper sat still. The quiet stretched on for a full minute. "Sterling died." His voice cracked. "He's not coming back stronger."

Luke ran his hand over his mouth and scratched his jaw. "Aw man, I'm sorry." He rubbed his neck, breathed the words "Level three, nickels," and leaned back in his seat. "What did Sterling's tattoo look like?"

Copper rolled off the edge of the chair and fell into his seat sideways. His head hung off the back of one of the chair arms and he draped his legs over the other. He thought back to the first time he'd seen Sterling's ink. "When it was new, it was slathered with a clear, greasy lotion and covered with cling wrap."

Luke nodded. "Mine was too."

"Sterling liked pennies. His tattoo was a 1980 Lincoln Memorial penny. He showed me that it had special letters on it and extra shading in places. My brother noticed things like that about money. Once he told me a penny might be worth more than one cent." Copper rubbed his forehead. "It's confusing. Anyway, he said the mark on his skin reminded him of me because it had more copper in it." He shifted his body into the proper seated position and leaned forward. His facial muscles shifted with revelation. "Sterling might have been mistaken. They might not have put copper into the ink." His hands tightened their grip on the chair. "I wish I could ask him."

Luke stood and stretched, then went to the window. "He might have meant the coin represented by the drawing had more copper in it." He shrugged. "I can see why you'd miss him." When he faced the window, his voice seemed far away. "Moving here might help you get stronger."

"Really?" Copper crossed the room to see what was so fascinating in the window. All he saw was an empty sidewalk lined with street lamps. "I really need to learn all the man stuff Sterling was going to teach me."

Luke turned. With his usual smirk etched into his face, he raised one eyebrow. "Well Copper man, you're in luck. I've been working on some of that man stuff lately. I'm gettin' pretty good at it. Maybe I can help." He shoved his hands into his pockets.

Copper looked him over. Ripped jeans, tank top, floppy hair, and motorcycle boots. Aside from the tattoo, Luke and Sterling were nothing alike. Then Copper winced. That wasn't true. Both had shown him patience and kindness. He re-examined the Resident Trainer. "We're almost the same height."

"Yeah, it looks like you'll outgrow me. Keegan did a long time ago. I don't come from large stock." He went to the coffee table and retrieved his keys. He regarded the heavy mass of metal in one hand. "This is as big as I'll ever be." His phone made a guitar sound. "Speaking of Keegan, that guy is gonna be miserable if I don't do this outdoor fire thing."

"Not as upset as Jay. That guy may self-destruct if we change the schedule."

Luke laughed. "You make an excellent point." He scooped up his bag. When he got to the front door, he turned back. "You comin'?"

Copper wriggled his toes in the disgusting sneakers. "These shoes are toast. I may have had enough new experiences for one day."

"It won't be the same without you, but I can respect your choice. I need to make a quick call if you're staying behind."

One more activity. After all he'd put the others through, he probably should face them, even if it was just to apologize. "No. Keegan would never forgive me if I missed another item on his list. Let's go." He'd lost track of how many apologies he'd given today. Hopefully, this one would go better than the others.

Chapter Thirty-Five

KEEGAN

Expect compromise to require multiple attempts.

- Changing Minds and Behaviors

A ring of garden chairs filled the extra space on the restaurant patio. In the center, Keegan removed the cover from a fire pit.

Tyler traced an invisible circuit around the outdoor space. He hit himself on the head as his speed increased. "Fire is a living thing, Keegan. It breathes, it eats, and it hates."[1]

Luke trudged to the restaurant's back door and flipped a switch. A twinkling canopy of white lights formed overhead. "Let's use these instead." Despite the festive atmosphere, none of the young men felt like celebrating. Luke straddled a chair. "Guys, it's been a crazy day. I don't even know what to do right now."

Jay glanced at his wrist. "We're late, but according to the schedule, we're supposed to be concluding a social skills activity by the fire."

Luke massaged the outer edges of his eyebrows. "Tyler doesn't like fire and I don't have the nerve to add an open flame to this mix of highly combustible personalities. Hopefully, the party lights will do."

"A fireless fire activity." Jay tapped on his electronic tablet.

Luke jerked his head to swing the hair from his eyes. When he leaned toward the group, his hair fell back to its original position. "I'm not going to give y'all a lecture, but please know that I'm here to help you. You could have told me that Copper was upset and wanted to see his files."

Jay rolled his head and cracked his neck. "Under the circumstances, we experienced difficulty determining the best course of action. Angering a violent criminal didn't seem wise."

Luke stared at the ground near Jay's feet. "Let me see if I can say this in a way that will mean something to you." He glanced up and gave Jay's face his full attention. "For future reference, if you think lives may be at risk, please divulge secrets at the earliest opportunity."

Jay's shoulders slumped in defeat. As ringleader, Keegan decided to defend his punctual friend. He stood on his chair. "I don't know what my brother just said, but I forced Jay to participate in our unscheduled activity. It's my fault." He bowed and returned to the ground level. His eyes shifted to Luke. "Your honor, please call your next witness."

The Resident Trainer offered a short prayer. He closed his eyes and breathed out, "Oh. My. God."

Keegan solemnly added, "Amen."

Copper angled his chair in a way that faced the other guests. "I should apologize. I've been agitated and confused. I'm sorry." His face dropped into his hands.

Luke got up and stood behind Copper's chair. "Just so we're clear, Copper did not kill his brother."

Keegan's eyebrows fell into sharp angles. "Who did he kill?"

"There's been no killing, ok?" Luke rubbed his forehead

and tucked the longest pieces of hair behind one ear. He dragged the messenger bag back to his seat.

Like two hyperactive spiders, Jay's fingers crawled all over his screen. "But his brother is deceased. Fatality or casualty, Copper is in a state of bereavement. We can concur that this is factual."

Tyler pulled the beanie over his face and hid his eyes from the group. "On a long enough timeline, the survival rate for everyone drops to zero."[2]

A pair of revolting shoes and socks flew across the patio. "My brother's body didn't react well to cancer treatment. Sterling died in a hospital. If I had visited him, he might have improved." Copper's face morphed into a series of expressions that were too fast for Keegan to decipher. The animated ginger-haired man clenched his fists. "I've helped him get well before. I didn't have a chance to say goodbye." His head fell back and he watched the sky. "I didn't go, and he died. He's dead, and so is my future. It's all gone."

"There's lawyer stuff. Are you a villain or not?" Keegan shook his pencils with fury. "Evil can't live here. I will break these pencils!" He held them out horizontally and set his jaw.

Luke touched Keegan's forearm. "The lawyers are sorting out some money matters between Copper and his brother. There's been no crime, I promise."

Jay yawned and checked his watch. "The current condition of his footwear should be illegal." He snapped a photo of the shoes.

"Great. That settles it." Keegan bounced on his toes and pointed his pencils to the sky. "Copper isn't a bad guy. He just has no future, for some weird reason." With a tilted chin, he swung his pencils like a conductor. "Let's do the social skills."

Jay's eyebrows lifted. "At last! We're adhering to the schedule."

Luke yawned. He looked around the group and his head shook. "I may be losing my mind."

Keegan's pencils touched his temple. "Check your bag."

Luke dragged the word "oh…" out for a few seconds and punctuated it with a terse "…kay." He pulled the pages from his satchel. "I'm using the notes you guys wrote about each other. I'll read a description and y'all guess who it's about. This one says, 'He likes ceilings.'"

Four of the five men smiled. Copper looked at their faces. "No! I fell through my mom's ceiling and made a hole in it."

"So he *hates* ceilings." Remembering his audiobook *Tone and Tension*, Keegan added enough emphasis on the word "hate" to make the statement an accusation.

"No. I don't care about ceilings." Copper stamped his foot and threw his arms up in the air. "Well, I care about *that* one." He crossed his restless arms and held them against his chest. "I only wanted to fix my mistake."

Keegan spilled out of his seat and allowed his legs to glide smoothly into the splits. "New rule at the Inn: No destroying the ceilings!"

Luke smirked. "Keegan, stop showing off." He looked away. "What *do* you like, Copper?"

Copper's scowl faded to a grimace. "Food." His shoulders twitched. "I watch Chef Pascal Chevalier on the Entrée Network. And I like the video game *Passage*."

"Cool." Luke flipped through some sheets of paper. "Let's try another. This one is too easy. 'Hates cursing.'"

Tyler pointed to Keegan while the others called out his name.

"Keeg, can we talk about your issues with foul language?"

"Sure." Keegan waited for the next question.

Copper broke the silence. "Do certain words hurt your ears? I hate the words 'moist flesh.' I also cringe when loud motorcycles or trucks go by. They make my body feel tight all over. There's a burning sensation in my spine all the way to a sore spot on my tailbone."

Keegan raised his hand as they'd taught him at school. That was the proper way to interrupt an info-dumper. "When I was young, I learned curse words from videos on the Internet. I knew they were powerful words." Luke's wrist flicked like he was trying to lift the air, so Keegan lowered his arm, released his gymnast pose, and continued with his story. "When I tried public school, we read a story about a mouse and a rabbit. One character called the other 'stupid and dumb.' I thought that meant we were allowed to use curse words at school. I couldn't call anyone stupid or dumb at home. I thought maybe there were home words and school words."

He put his hands on his knees and leaned forward. "My teacher sent my mom a note. She didn't like when I described an activity as effing stupid...only I used the real F-word."

Copper laughed the loudest. Luke's grin spread so wide his dimples appeared. "Tell them what mom did!"

Keegan sat back and wriggled his eyebrows up and down. "She taught me every curse word that night."

Copper's hand fell on his head. "She did?"

"Yep. We talked in the hot tub"—his hand waved at the patio lights—"while looking at the stars."

Jay gripped the edge of his seat with both hands. "Impossible!"

"Yes. I wouldn't lie to you. We sorted the words into groups. Some are ok to say in certain places, if I *want* to use them. We made a system of levels to help guide my choice, based on what might be appropriate. Eventually, I just started saying the level number. Everyone who knew the code understood, and I didn't have to curse at all."

Copper slapped his leg, winced, and then rubbed his wrist. "So have you been cursing this whole time? That's amazing."

Jay tapped his screen. "The purpose of verbal

communication, as I understand it, is to articulate thoughts, feelings, dislikes, and desires in a way that's understood by others."

Keegan swept one hand, palm up, out to the side of his body in an elegant arc. "Your English has improved, Jay. I understood most of what you said." He leaned back in his chair. "I have many speech books that say the same thing. But, if I say the level number, I can express myself without thinking about who hears me. They don't know the code so they don't get offended. If I say the wrong level, no harm is done." He touched his finger to his lips. "Figuring out what someone else thinks is appropriate has never been easy for me. And, with the code, I get to say exactly what I want, when I want."

"Ingenious and an elegant way to elevate the conversation. Society has become so crass. Please provide us with a cipher," Jay replied.

Keegan looked to Luke. "What?"

"He wants to know the code. If we search through the social skills books, I'm sure there's something about friends and inside jokes. It's a good idea to share this information, Keeg."

Keegan smiled. Perhaps the orientation was getting back on track. "It's easy!" Using his stim sticks, he imitated every maestro he could remember. "Level one words are ugly words that wouldn't shock grandparents, or people in school or church buildings. 'Stupid' and 'Dumb' are examples. Children's books contain these words"—he paused—"but I still think it's unkind for rabbits to call mice stupid."

He squeezed both pencils with the same hand and held up two fingers. "Level two words might be considered strong language or in poor taste by grandparents. 'Crap' is a good example. Also, certain words for butt fall into level two territory." He poked the sky with one finger for emphasis. "But they might also mean donkey."

After so much time standing, Keegan rocked from foot to

foot. He had their full attention. Finally, they were really listening. "Level three is an even stronger curse word. You might say it, but only if you're very upset. It's a four letter word that starts with the letter 's' and means poop."

Copper and Tyler chuckled. Jay typed with fervor. Keegan sliced the air with his hand like a lecturing ninja. "Shall I continue?" He paced. "Some people refer to other human beings as female dogs. So nasty. It's horrible to call someone any kind of dog. They're mongrels!" He recoiled. "Some words question the identity of your father or suggest you might be the son of a female dog. These are all on the third level." His hands made the umpire sign for "safe."

Copper moved to the edge of his seat. "Now we're getting somewhere! Are there words higher than level three?"

"Yes. Level four is the F-bomb. Also, any words used to describe body parts are level four curse words." He turned back to Luke. "I don't know why people call each other body parts. You un-autistic people are so strange."

Copper brought his chair closer inside the circle. "So that's it? Four levels?"

Keegan kneeled on the ground in the middle of the circle, and reduced his volume. "There's one final level. I don't know why anyone would ever need level four, really, but sometimes on the Internet people say level five. It's usually on those gamers' live streams. Can you believe some people add the word 'mother' before a level four? It's unbelievable! Since they bring mothers into it, it needs its own category." He stood and used his full voice. "Highly inappropriate."

Jay hopped out of his seat. "I agree wholeheartedly. Women are to be cherished."

Nicola's voice rang out from the covered porch. "Would it be ok if I joined you? I've wanted to spend time with you guys all day."

Jay called back. "Please do. Take my chair." He turned to the others and spoke in a soft voice. "That one is enchanting."

With a shake of her head, Nicola reached for the nearest chair and pulled it across the patio. She carefully stepped over Copper's shoes. "Oh what a great idea!" She shrank four inches when she peeled off her heels. "That's better."

Keegan raced to her side. "Nicola! I'm so glad you're here." He gave her a good squeeze, wrapped his arms around her, and told her ponytail, "I've been worried about you. My perfect plan has been a disaster. But now that you're here, we're saved." She was a social genius and could fix any mistake Keegan had made. He hoisted her chair above his head and marched toward the circle.

The patter of her bare feet accompanied her trek across the pavers. "Um…wow. I'll do my best, Keegan."

Chair aloft, Keegan put an extra bounce in his step. "I know you will. Also, you smell beautiful…like candy corn and marshmallows."

Luke met them half-way, and Keegan passed him the chair. His brother placed her seat next to his own. "We're getting to know each other. Did you know Copper loves cooking shows?"

Her shoulders rose to the same height as her chin. "As you can guess, my notes weren't very thorough."

Luke patted her shoulder and it fell down. "No problem. Keegan just explained all the cursing levels."

She put her hand on her heart. "Level two; I hate that I missed it."

Keegan offered her a quick bow, then he turned to Luke. "Let's do another one."

Luke shook a paper at the group. "Who do you think this is about? It says 'can imitate lots of movie stars.'"

Every head turned toward Tyler. Luke's smile crinkled his eyes. "You're up, T."

Tyler sat up straight. "You talking to me?"[3] His smile disappeared.

Luke's brow creased. "I'm sorry, Tyler man. I won't call you T."

The young man launched from his spot. "What we've got here is a failure to communicate."[4] He leapt over the low retaining wall and stumbled into the brushy garden. Two seconds later, he reappeared holding a large stick.

Luke grabbed his phone. "Nic this is new. I—"

Jay rolled his long sleeves up to his elbows. Tyler climbed back to the patio. "Houston, we have a problem."[5] He pointed the stick to the ground like a crude version of a cane, then his face crumpled. "I am your *grand*father."[6] He sliced the night with his stick.

Luke used his arm to shield Nicola. Tyler swung his makeshift cane at no one in particular, and in an instant, Jay appeared at his side, catching the stick in mid-air. Tyler slowly slid the prop out of Jay's grasp. He turned his back to the group and placed the stick in his chair. He lifted up his shorts. The backs of his legs were covered in bruises. With his head hung low, he grumbled, "I'll be back."[7]

Nicola and Luke jumped out of their chairs and ushered the boy away from the group. Whispered words trailed behind the trio as they hurried toward the porch. Soon, the area was filled with a bright new light, and Luke and Nicola bent to get a better look at Tyler's legs.

Jay picked up the stick. "That's unacceptable." He snapped it in half and threw the pieces on the patio.

Copper's head poked out from between his knees. "Sterling had some scars from things like that…from our father. That happened when I was little. Steele left, but it marked Sterling's heart forever."

Keegan perched in his chair. He lifted his chin up a fraction of an inch. "We will protect him!" He saluted.

Nicola and Tyler returned to the group. She thumped her phone's screen. "I'm on it." Tyler picked up the two halves of the broken stick. He tore some loose bark off the stick and watched them flutter to the ground. Without a backward glance, he tossed the sticks into the garden. The disturbance extinguished the cricket's nightly performance.

The new silence made the zipper on Luke's messenger bag seem loud by comparison. He stuffed the papers into his satchel. "Everyone seems tired. We should finish this tomorrow."

Jay wrung his hands. "Tomorrow's schedule has been finalized. We must complete today's agenda."

Luke let out a long, slow breath. "Alright. I'll read one more. He skimmed the last page as he filed it with the rest. "Who is a photographer?"

Copper and Keegan shouted at the same time. "Jay!"

Jay frowned at his phone. His voice broke. "Photography documents reality."

Luke put his elbows on his knees, leaned forward, and held his face up with his hands. "Jay, can you look up at us? We can't hear you."

Jay rubbed his nose with his sleeve and looked up. His eyes filled with tears. When he looked toward Nicola, horror washed across his face. He tugged at his dirty sleeve. "Dear lady, I apologize for my barbaric hygiene." He sniffed and wiped his eyes with the back of his hand.

It was Copper's turn to get up and pace. "Tell him what I wrote. It's an emergency!"

Luke reached back into the bag and shuffled the papers. "Remind me to clarify which events can be classified as emergencies." Nicola's head bobbed. The Resident Trainer's eyebrows fell down and he chewed his lip. "Uh…Copper says you are smart and strong." His mouth closed into a flat line, and his eyes darted from side to side. "That's nice, but I don't get it." His shoulders rose toward his ears and fell back into place.

Copper nodded. "Keep reading!"

Keegan scampered up beside the scrappy red one. "I like your marching style."

Luke resumed reading the note. "…and his favorite things are numbers, big clothes, and buttons."

Copper rushed to Jay's side. "See? Your favorite things! You should feel better now." He returned to his seat.

Keegan sat on the ground between them hugging his knees to his chest. He whimpered, "The Inn is supposed to be a happy place."

Chapter Thirty-Six

COPPER

Giving two cents.

Copper smacked his forehead in realization. "I've heard Luke talk about nickels all day. I thought he was obsessed with coins like my brother, but he meant Nicola."

Jay glanced at his watch—quite the technological marvel. "If our activity has concluded, I'll say goodnight."

Luke tapped his old-fashioned watch. "We have time for you to tell us about your pictures."

Jay set his timer. "I synthesize and arrange information into lists. Photos enhance the quality of the records. Quality is important." He sniffed and regarded his forearm. "There. Still on schedule."

Keegan sang out, "Quality! He's a controller of quality." He peeked up at Jay with a small grin. But then his spirit sagged and he adjusted his tune. "Oh no. He has a sad job. Quality makes people sad."

Hearing this, if the Professor's shirt had been fully fastened, the vein in his neck would have popped a button loose. "No!"

Luke scrambled to his feet and put a hand on the man's shoulder. "But it's not time to go."

Keegan rocked. "Quality makes people mad."

Jay's wrinkles deepened as his volume increased. "My job is important. Quality control ensures peak performance." He waved his arms up and down. "Lists keep you organized. Without quality lists and schedules, life is complete chaos!" He slammed his arms to his sides.

With the excitement of the day, Copper had forgotten how crazy they all were, even the mild-mannered Professor. He knew better than to stay within arm's reach of Jay when he got upset. He dragged his chair to a safer spot near Nicola. As the chair scraped across the patio, he noticed a penny was stuck underneath one chair leg, but chose to ignore it. Tyler followed his lead and slipped into Luke's chair.

The Rockstar Cowboy crouched down next to Jay. His words sounded like a low, sleepy hum. "It's ok. We're not having any chaos right now, are we?" Jay fiddled with the buttons on his long sleeves.

Copper gently rubbed his own forearm. The Professor was a secret ninja. He wondered if there would be a bruise tomorrow. *That guy should come with a warning.* "If you ever want to play guitar again, don't let him touch your wrist!"

Jay brushed Luke's hand away. "I require the use of my backpack." He rose and strode over to the patio tables.

The Resident Trainer's magical bird tattoo hadn't kept him from visibly aging. His face had found an extra ten years since this morning. "Alright." He backed up to his chair and bent his legs to sit down.

Tyler mimicked the high-pitched voice of a small child. "They're here!"[1]

Luke turned. "Sorry, Tyler. I didn't see you." He chose to relocate to Tyler's previous position.

Jay stormed back to the group, carrying a thick spiral

notebook. "See?" Like a preschool teacher, he opened the book wide and panned the pages around the group so everyone could get a good look. There were columns of pictures with check marks decorating each one. "My mom assembled visual schedules for me before I could read. These lists prepared me for the day." With each page, his face grew more relaxed. "They're comforting. Look! Here's one from junior high. The pictures were no longer necessary." He exhibited the text-based list for the group. "Here's when we'd expanded the grooming schedule." His finger touched the scribbled-in edits near 'wash hair' and 'brush teeth.' "That's when we added deodorant, shaving, and washing my face with special soap for acne."

Keegan's eyes widened. "Did you keep every list and paste them into this notebook?"

"No. Only when we made important alterations to the routine." Jay's hands sped through the notes. "Here's when we established more of my Man-of-the-House responsibilities." He leafed through a few more worn pages. "And here's when I got my QC job at the plant."

The Stimmer looked at the book through his pencils. "How come the pictures are back? Did you decide it was easier than reading?"

"My mom forgot her nouns so I resumed our old visual practice." Jay's voice sounded softer, and the words came slower. "Sometimes she got lost. I tabulated the number of steps to the locations featured in our routine. I expanded her lists to include directions, along with maps and—"

Copper wondered if they were up past his bedtime. "Can I see your book?"

With great care, Jay allowed Copper to take the book. He held it gently. One of the more recent entries had a folded corner. Underneath 'Krav Maga lesson,' 'Buy clothes' was crossed out. 'Look through Dad's clothes' had been scrawled over it. Copper regarded the loose clothing and the old man shoes.

"…One day when I came home from work, mom screamed when I entered the house. I retreated to the front lawn, and she phoned the police. The neighbors verified my identity, but my mother no longer remembered my face." He snatched the book out of Copper's hands. "She kept telling the officer that I was not her little boy. I'd neglected to record my own image. I didn't realize she would forget me too." He wiped his face again. "So, you see? Quality lists with accurate details are essential."

He turned his tablet toward the group. Photos of their time together appeared on the screen. He'd recorded snapshots of architectural details on the Ainsley buildings, as well as flowers, light fixtures, and the trolley stop. There were close-ups of signs and sidewalks. The next set included the beach, the public restroom door, and the power lines along the route they walked that morning. The final group contained candid portraits of the sun bouncing off Copper's red waves, Keegan stimming on a park bench, and Tyler holding a hibiscus to his nose.

"After I integrate the map data, I'll incorporate this into an app, so we can access it at any time. This tool increases your protection and provides a shield against mental frailty. I won't let you forget or lose your way."

Luke slowly pulled his chin back up to the rest of his mouth. He swallowed hard. "Thank you, Jay. That's very helpful." Nicola released her ponytail and raked through her hair, fixing her gaze on her lap. The lucky lady had long hair to hide her face. Shame and embarrassment heated Copper's face. He'd been wrong earlier. Crazy or not, their lives hadn't been care-free after all.

Keegan stood and clapped. "Yes! That is super-useful. It's good to have someone smart making the lists. With Jay here, I might not need to set so many timers." He spun in a few circles. When he stopped, his stim sticks were aimed at the Professor. "You can help me plan the parties!" He crammed his pencils back into his pocket.

With his beanie held near his heart, Tyler knelt at Jay's feet and lay his other hand on top of the book. His sad face contrasted with Keegan's grin. Part croak and part wheeze, the words "My precious"[2] fell from his mouth.

Keegan loped toward Jay and stood behind him. "We need a group picture. Everyone, gather around." Tyler remained kneeling on the ground. As usual, Keegan towered above everyone else. Copper meandered toward them, uncertain if he was really a part of this group.

Luke held his phone sideways. Then he turned it vertically, muttering, "It's so dark. I'm gonna use the flash, Keeg. Copper, you stand next to Keegan or sit beside Jay."

Nicola touched the Resident Trainer's arm. "Get over there. This one should be of all the guys." She stepped back and looked through the screen.

Luke scooted into the picture, and Keegan stretched his arms out as wide as possible. "Everyone say 'Teeeeeth.'"

As flashes lit up the patio, Jay turned back to Keegan. "The tradition is to say 'Cheese.'"

Keegan rested his hand on his shoulder. "Don't worry; I used to hear words incorrectly too. We show our teeth for a photo. That's why we say 'teeth.'"

Tyler's signature smile outshone everyone else's. "This is the beginning of a beautiful friendship."[3]

"Teeeeeeeeeeth."

Chapter Thirty-Seven

KEEGAN

Celebrate small victories.

- Caring Is Comforting

Keegan switched on the neon signs in his bedroom. They made their own special, satisfying buzz, eliminating his need to fill the space with humming. He jumped on his bed. Just a few times—he didn't want Luke to come in and complain. Then he flopped into his sleeping position and stared at the ceiling fan. The blades sliced a slow, soothing pattern through the air.

What a day. These people had been strangers this morning. Now they were becoming a family. He could feel it. Even though every event had spun wildly out of control, his fireside activity had saved orientation. He had been a little disappointed that Tyler didn't like fire, but then he remembered the circle scene in the film hadn't involved flames either. The firelight would have been his way of adding a little flair to the occasion, as the best plans always insured success, but he didn't need to complicate things. His new motto would be "Stick with the plan and push forward."

Tomorrow's program would be perfect. The guys were pretty much best friends now. They'd shared secrets. He'd taught them his cursing code. He looked at the empty frame leaning against his wall. Maybe he could make some prints out of Jay's snapshots. Nicola was back so Luke would have more time. Now both Resident Trainers could still organize the neighborhood inclusion playgroup and conduct the media tour, while his new crew went on their adventure. They'd learn their way around on the geocaching quest. A treasure hunt would help them bond, just like it did in the movie. Later they'd see the show that had inspired it all. Maybe they could help him understand parts of it.

And by the end of the second day, it would feel like they'd known each other forever. Everyone would hug and smile. The breakfast movie would become their favorite film of all time. They would grow old together on Ainsley Avenue, and his parent's mission would be a success. There was zero chance that giving up their lives to create this community would result in broken hearts. They wouldn't die the same way Ainsley's mom had.

Keegan had done everything he could to make sure it was an awesome plan. He couldn't fail. Afterward, with his family and his future secure, he could concentrate on changing the world. For the second night in a row, he was too excited to sleep. Everything was falling into place.

Chapter Thirty-Eight

COPPER

Penny press

Room 504's miniature kitchen presented a welcome respite from the day. *What a difference a few hours made.* Copper set his filthy shoes in the small sink. Warm water rinsed away some of the grime, but they were still sticky. Normally, Pearl would handle this sort of thing. Imagining her reaction to the ruined shoes inspired him to grab a bottle of bright green liquid from the counter. He squeezed it on a washcloth and scrubbed the sticky marshmallow residue. As the bubbles disappeared down the drain, he realized this might be considered an adult moment. *He was cleaning his shoes. All. By. Himself.* The warmth of pride spread across his chest. He was sorting out his own problems.

He'd been carrying a heaviness for such a long time, he'd come to think of it as normal. But right now, he felt lighter. The shoes looked much better. If only he had a stove, he might have been able to stir fry them dry. He gave them a quick shake. A penny plinked into the stainless steel basin. He picked it up and the cold, wet penny stung his hand. *Dated 1943.* He would need to ask Sterling about that year…then the sneakers fell on the floor.

Copper hit an invisible wall and his face hurt. His body shook and crumpled in on itself as the wall toppled over and buried him with its weight. *He couldn't ask Sterling anything ever again.* He reached out, and his hand moved along a very real, solid wall that led him from the kitchen to the bedroom.

Soft, cold sheets covered his bed. He turned the penny over in his hand while waiting for his body to create a warmth that was both comforting and familiar. He thought of his last-minute promise to join Keegan for a gluten-free breakfast. After all the drama he'd caused today, he owed the kid that much. Plus he might get to peek into another commercial kitchen. He rubbed his stomach. *How bad could gluten-free taste?* Keegan thought his stomach issues might be about his diet. That guy had an answer for everything. If confidence was a superpower, maybe he could change the world.

Pennies warmed faster than sheets. Copper's thumb ran over president Lincoln's profile. Images of pancakes made his stomach growl, but the bright red numbers on the digital clock proclaimed he had a long wait until breakfast. At least he hadn't fainted today. He flipped onto his side and covered his face with the pillow. As always, memories accompanied the darkness…

Tonight's feature was Sterling on another surprise visit from college. Amanda, the case manager at his day program, hadn't appreciated those unscheduled visits. But Copper never cared what she appreciated. She'd hardly ever had anything to do with him. But whenever his mom or Sterling signed in, she made sure to put in an appearance within five to ten minutes.

In this memory, his brother's strawberry blond hair had been cut to showcase his fine facial features and chiseled jawline. He turned every head. When he walked in wearing his pale blue long-sleeved shirt, even Mike the orderly stared. Sterling never seemed to notice the amount of attention he received.

"Hey Cop. Whatcha doin'?"

"Playing *Passage*."

"You still play that game?"

"Well this is *Passage 3*. I play it when I'm not watching the Entrée Network."

"Seriously? Mom spends a crazy amount of money on this place and all they do is give you TV and video games?"

"I like Entrée TV and you know this is one of the best video games ever created."

A new puzzle loaded on the screen. Copper shot a couple of teleportation paths in the wall. Then, he threw a robot with a laser inside one hole and it attacked several others waiting to ambush his character. He completed the level in less than sixty seconds.

"Whoa. How many times have you played that level?"

Copper studied the screen. "This is a new game. Got it yesterday. First time for this level. You smell different."

"Uh. Yeah, I've been somewhere different. But seriously, how did you just do that? You're so fast. That looked hard."

"I know where to put the teleportation shortcuts. It's easy for me." Copper looked at his brother. His shirt was untucked, there were wet circles under his arms, and he was breathing through his mouth. "Are you sick or something? Pearl says you'll eat flies if you keep your mouth open."

Sterling slapped Copper's shoulder. "Grab your stuff. I'm signing you out. Let's go."

Copper said "Surprise," like he'd heard on TV. He hoped he'd finally used the correct tone for sarcasm.

Sterling wiped beads of sweat from his forehead. "Sorry. Do you need a few minutes to mentally change activities?"

"Five minutes. Let me save my place and log out."

His babysitter's perfume filled the air. Copper looked at the kid sitting at the closest table. "Don't let him touch my game, Amanda. He drools and will short out the entire system."

Amanda's fragrance intensified as she rushed over to wipe the guy's chin. The soaked neckline of his shirt showed how little attention he was receiving. Copper loaded his backpack.

Amanda's whiny voice made him bristle. "Copper, what did I tell you about the computer?"

"That it belongs to everyone."

Amanda spoke like a child pretending to be a mother. "That's right. You have to share it."

"But he slobbers all over the place. Liquids and electronics don't mix."

"What he does is—"

"—not my business. I remember. I'm not stupid." He threw the backpack over his shoulder and stormed out.

At their favorite diner, Copper and Sterling snuck in an extra meal before dinner. As Copper poured syrup on his pancakes, he said, "You don't smell like college."

"I'm not sure what college smells like, but I don't spend much time there. I'm usually at the firm working on my internship." Sterling tapped a spoon on his coffee cup. "They say I'll get paid a lot more once I graduate."

"Then I can move to your place?"

"That's the plan, Copper." Sterling shoved a half-eaten bagel off to the side and began rolling up his sleeve. "Look what I got today!" Beneath a layer of cling film, Sterling revealed an area of red, irritated skin. An inflamed drawing of a penny and a few words decorated his arm.

Copper's fork hung in mid-air. Syrup cascaded toward his plate. "Is that going to wash off?"

"Nope. It's a tattoo. What do you think?"

"It covers your scar."

Sterling's bright blue eyes flashed as his mouth broke into a wide grin. "Yes. I got a 1980 Lincoln Memorial penny to cover it. Only one more step, and I'll be rid of every last thing that bastard ever gave me. I have to file the paperwork to get my surname changed to Mom's. Then I can be a Munro, like you."

Copper pushed the scrambled eggs around on his plate. "Pearl said that's why I didn't get Dad's last name. She wanted us to match. It would be good if our names matched too."

"I can't wait to be completely free from Steele Campbell." Sterling picked up the bagel and waved it. "Such a jerk." He scoffed and took a bite.

Copper wiggled the slice of bacon to see if it was floppy. Sometimes the diner got the bacon wrong. "Steele had a tattoo on his arm."

The noise from Sterling's fork hitting the table made Copper's shoulders shoot up toward his ears. "He did." Sterling rushed to grab the fork from hell. "I didn't think you remembered him."

Copper mumbled through the mass of pancakes crowding his mouth. "Some of our family pictures have an arm with a tattoo on it. The rest of that person, Steele, has been cut out."

"Pearl never was good at arts and crafts, huh?" Sterling threw the bread back onto his plate. "He probably got it in the military."

A tiny glob of butter sat at the corner of Sterling's mouth. Copper tried not to stare at it, and he looked at his brother's eyes again. "Are you going to wear colored contacts? Or an eyepatch or something?"

"Why?" Sterling rubbed a napkin over the lower half of his face.

"Pearl says you have his eyes, too."

At that moment, Sterling's eyes changed. What was normally white became red and glossy. "I swear Copper, I'm not going to be anything like that guy."

The Inn's air conditioner switched on. It whistled when it passed through the filter, breaking his concentration. Copper ripped the pillow from his face. It made a soft thump as it hit the bedroom door. "You sure didn't become like him, Sterling. You never had the chance."

The air conditioner's high-pitched noise persisted. He wondered if he could reach the vent by climbing on a chair, but with his history, he probably shouldn't touch the ceiling. It had been a long day. Tomorrow, he'd be on his best behavior. He could manage one more day. Trying to think beyond that was impossible.

His body heat overcooked the covers. He kicked them off. With a groan, he threw his head where his feet used to be and stared back at the headboard against the wall. He started to hum along with the whistle. He made a tune out of the building's sounds. Noisy or not, he was grateful the Inn had air conditioning. August nights were brutally hot in Texas.

During the summer, Sterling wore shirts, even in the pool, just to cover that scar. This year, since he'd been tattooed to cover it, he could have gone sleeveless like Luke. Copper decided the Resident Rockstar was ok. He'd stepped up every time he was needed. Like tonight with Tyler's legs. Those bruises haunted Copper's thoughts until sleep finally took him.

Day 2: Fitting Inn

Chapter Thirty-Nine

KEEGAN

Leaders encourage Positive Mental Attitudes.

- Lead The Way To Friendship

Keegan got fancy for day two. He wore his T-shirt with the tuxedo print and a pinstripe fedora. Equipped with ambient lighting and tablecloths, the Terrace's dining hall offered a more elegant atmosphere than the restaurant closest to the Inn. Since Copper's first day hadn't gone very well, he thought taking the opposite approach might yield a better result. An increase in the formality might help ensure a proper introduction.

When Copper arrived, Keegan cast his arms out, showcasing the dining room. This morning's task was to finish presenting the property to the newcomers, while building a sense of familiarity. To convince them to sign leases, they needed some time to experience the facilities as though they lived here.

But first, food. Breakfast, the most important meal of the day, was not to be missed...especially on the most magical day of the month: Pancake Day. "They have crepes, waffles, and pancakes. Since it's Pancake Day, there's every kind of flapjack you can imagine. Want to check it out?"

"Sure. Can I see the kitchen?"

"They have a whole, separate gluten-free kitchen here. It's amazing. C'mon!"

Copper seemed to be a different person. Dressed in an aqua polo shirt and light grey slacks, he looked like he was visiting a resort. A smile lit up his face. Formality and dining halls made Copper happy.

Keegan's eyes drifted toward his friend's feet. "Those shoes are much better." He nodded his head in approval. "No laces! I like the checkerboard pattern."

"Thanks. Someone left them on the doormat in my room. The other ones are still soaking wet."

"Those look just like a pair Luke used to wear." Keegan opened the kitchen doors. "My family isn't in charge of this part of the building, so we can only take a quick peek."

Copper stuck his hand out to catch the swinging door. "I'm really sorry about yesterday."

Keegan tipped his hat. "It's a different day and that's ok." Normally, he used that phrase to describe days that differed from his routine, as in a different *kind* of day, but the words seemed to put his guest at ease. *Don't correct him. Just go with it.*

Half an hour later, they set their trays on the table. Keegan admired Copper's selection of gluten-free pancakes, but his stack of bacon looked too small. He considered creating a life tip card. *If people ate as much bacon as he did, they'd be taller.* Keegan shoved four pieces of bacon into his mouth.

"Oh no."

He held his fifth slice of bacon in the air. "What is it?"

"I think this is a level two situation, right?"

Keegan nodded. "If it's bad, but not extra-bad." He stuffed

the bacon in his mouth and reached for his fork. "Is your food yucky?"

"It's good so far." Copper put the syrup down. "The thing is, I can't always tell if I've met a person before. My facial blindness is especially challenging with women. They change their hair too much."

"Facial blindness. That is so me." Keegan smiled. He and Copper had one more thing in common. "One time, in Vegas…Whoops. Info dump."

"No problem. It's why I use nicknames so much. So, do you have a lot of pretty blondes in wheelchairs here?"

Half a pancake balanced on Keegan's fork. "I don't think so."

Copper wiped his mouth with the napkin until it became red. "If that's Ruby, she should sit with us."

Mid-bite, partially chewed food proudly on display, Keegan asked, "Where?"

"She has wheels. You can't miss her. Look over by that person wearing the orange shirt. Do you see?"

Keegan watched a woman remove a glob of scrambled eggs from her orange shirt while a man with a tattoo on his hand dumped syrup on her plate. "I don't see any wheels, but that guy is floating her breakfast in a sea of maple syrup." As the dining hall attendant carried the syrup to another table, the wheels came into view. Keegan relaxed. "Ohhhh. I know *those* wheels. They're super sparkly. Ruby's a glittery girl."

Copper sat up straighter and dropped his napkin into his lap. "Invite her to sit with us."

Keegan got up and placed his pencils beside his plate. He counted his steps so he could tell Jay later. In four large strides, he was standing in front of Ruby. He bent his hand into a puppet, and his fingers—the puppet's mouth—moved. "Join us."

"Thanks, Keegan."

She followed him as he strutted back to the table and extended his long, languid arm toward his newest buddy. "Copper Munro." He shifted his hand toward the girl. "Ruby Cook."

Keegan sat down and resumed eating. "Copper will be a chef someday." His head popped up from his plate. "Hey...a Cook! And we were just talking about kitchens." He searched his plate for more bacon.

Copper took a bite and mumbled, "Do you like to cook, Ruby?"

"I guess. If I could work here, I'd want to make the pancakes." An assistant brought her tray over to her new spot. Her nose wrinkled when she poked the scrambled eggs with her fork. "I wouldn't want to cook the eggs. That shift would be so long. But the pancake makers stay busy with different flavors and shapes. I like variety. What kind did you get?"

Keegan looked at his empty plate. "Gluten-free for me. They were going to put some Nutella on the side so I could try a new food. Too late! I need more pancakes." He picked up his pencils.

"You eat like a machine." Copper poked at his plate. "I ordered white chocolate chip with raspberries. They taste best with whipped cream. The one I tried with maple syrup was a mistake." He lifted his head and looked toward Ruby. "If I worked here, I'd want to make the hash browns."

Ruby gasped. "That's worse than eggs! Hash browns aren't as disgusting, but you'd spend the hours doing the same thing over and over."

"Yeah, but the hash brown maker gets to stand next to the pancake maker." He smiled at her. "And she's pretty." He stared at his plate and swept up the last bits of food. "So if that's the price I'd have to pay, it'd be worth it."

Through his pencils, Keegan watched Ruby's face break

into a grin. The animation was lovely. Her cheeks grew pink. "Are y'all taking flirting lessons over there?"

Keegan concentrated on the blurring pencils. "I don't think we offer those, but after orientation, we're starting a new social skills group. I'll ask Nicola if you can come."

Copper looked at his phone. "Nicola! I promised to meet her after breakfast."

Ruby's pancakes were as pink as her dress. Keegan looked at the tuxedo image printed on his black T-shirt. He removed today's charcoal grey fedora. Hopefully, he hadn't broken any social rules by not matching his food to his clothes. A quick inspection of the room revealed the woman in orange hadn't matched her food either.

Ruby pushed her plate away. "I gotta roll. I've got PT on the patio."

Copper frowned. "PT?"

Keegan framed Copper's face with his pencils. "Physical therapy. You didn't get PT with ST and OT while you were young?" He invoked the Harris Head-tilt. "Maybe you don't have ASD at all."

Copper pushed his chair back. "Trust me, I did my time in plenty of therapies." He turned to Ruby. "Can I come with you? I'm supposed to meet Nicola over there."

Keegan's stomach made a sound. In ten more blurs, the server would reach him with a plate full of pancakes, banana slices, and Nutella. "Don't forget, you're a participant now. You'll be late to our geocaching scavenger hunt. Text me and I'll tell you where to meet us." Keegan thought he heard Copper's response, but the beautiful pile of whipped cream placed before him took center stage.

Chapter Forty

COPPER

A lucky penny

Copper watched Ruby navigate the crowded dining hall. He held the door open for her as they entered the lobby. "Would you like for me to push you?"

"Boy, if we raced, I'd beat you. I'm not some weak, helpless thing." She laughed and rolled in front of him.

"This place reminds me of a hospital. Is it really part of the Retreat?"

"They rent sections of it to medical people. My aunt cleans this building."

"For fun?"

Ruby paused. The pink ribbon in her hair tipped backward. "For her job, you goose. Nobody cleans for fun." She rolled forward.

"These are not my shoes," Copper groaned and rubbed his face. "Sorry. I'm terrible at small talk. I wasn't prepared to be here. This whole trip has been full of surprises."

She set her wheelchair at an angle. "This place takes some getting used to." Her cheeks rounded when she smiled.

Copper wanted to say more things to make her face look that way. But his phone made a noise. "That's the reminder to meet Nicola. She's waiting for me."

"C'mon, I know a shortcut. See if you can keep up." Ruby didn't just roll on those wheels; she flew.

They arrived on the patio much too soon. Even though idiotic words kept falling from his mouth, being with Ruby helped him relax. "Are you going to work in the restaurant later?"

"No. But I'll be around." She scanned the tables. "I wish I could sit and chat with Nicola this morning."

Copper's eyes widened with the rush of an idea. "You could probably join us." Instantly, he wondered if he'd said the wrong thing.

"Nope. I've got a goal. See ya!" She darted off toward a man wearing scrubs.

Close to the mess Ainsley Avenue called a garden, Nicola waited behind her laptop. Her coffee cup rested near a half-eaten danish. Copper dragged his feet like they each weighed 1000 pounds. He turned to take one last look at Ruby. He was shocked to discover she was staring back. For the first time in his life, he was grateful for his sensitive ears. The fair-haired angel called out, "Come find me later." Those were the best four words he'd heard in a long time. The next thing he knew, he'd arrived at Nicola's table. As he sat, he couldn't remember if he'd walked there or floated.

Nicola sipped her coffee. "Good morning. I hope you had a good breakfast." She bobbed her head toward Ruby. "You're making friends."

His cheeks burned. "Gluten-free pancakes were ok, and Ruby's not too bad." He chewed his lower lip.

Nicola looked younger in the daylight. Her long brown hair was tied up in a ponytail like the night before, but now she wore jeans and a V-neck blouse. Her kind, almond-shaped eyes were hazel green, not dark brown as he'd originally thought. She pulled a manila envelope from underneath her computer and handed it to him. "I made you a copy of the papers you wanted last night."

He clutched the folder to his chest. "Thank you."

"There's more." She dragged a white envelope out of her purse. "When I was with the attorneys yesterday, they found this." She flipped the envelope around. His name had been typed across the front. "It's from Sterling."

Chapter Forty-One

KEEGAN

Morning exercise can increase focus.

- Busy Body

Keegan held his nose. For once, it wasn't the restaurant that overpowered his senses. His brand-new buddy, Jay, swam through a sea of cologne this morning. It was way too much. Following his checklist for being a good host, Keegan held the door open for his friends.

On the far side of the patio, Copper and Nicola were engaged in an important conference. His fiery eyebrows were knit together while he studied a stack of paperwork. Lawyers and death meant serious business. Nicola noticed the group and gave a cheerful nod.

Jay adjusted the top button on his plaid shirt. "It's the pheromones. Women can't help but feel amorous when I apply this tincture."

Keegan lunged to the leadership position. He walked backward. "Is there something wrong with your eye, Jay? It keeps closing, and the way you walk has changed. That amount of cologne might cause blindness or seizures."

Jay's face went red. He moved his hand back and forth across his throat and coughed while widening both eyes.

Keegan's neck was growing sore from his inordinate use of the Harris Head-tilt. He swung his chin in the opposite direction to adjust the angle. "Fair-oh-moans seem to cause redness and a sore throat too. Is your shirt too tight at the neck? Are you having shortness of breath?"

The morning sun competed with the cloud of cologne, and Tyler shielded his eyes. "He was so deadly, in fact, that his enemies would go blind from overexposure to pure awesomeness!"[1]

Nicola's voice crossed the patio. "Hey guys! I didn't expect to see you here. What's up?"

Jay replied immediately. "Without your guidance, we are falling further behind schedule. Keegan has requested that I alter my selection of garments before we continue the geocaching activity."

Keegan whirled around just in time to catch Nicola crinkling her nose. This confirmed his suspicion; they were all going to choke to death. She hid her face with a napkin. "Excellent. Jay, we'll meet later to complete your housing decision."

Jay's eye twitched again. "Now that I know you're at the helm, I'm ready to sign a lease."

Keegan increased his pace. "C'mon guys. We'd better hurry. The toxic fumes are blinding him. The Inn may not be a proper living arrangement for those with impaired vision."

Tyler looked up from pulling the pilled fabric from his green sweater. "Love is blind, Wade."[2]

Keegan grabbed both his friends' arms and pulled. "Level two, the scent is so strong it's made Tyler forget my name. Hurry!"

Chapter Forty-Two

COPPER

Pennyweight

Copper held his brother's words with shaking hands. He rubbed the letter between his fingers. At one time, Sterling had touched this piece of paper. The thought pressed his body lower into his seat.

Copper,
Remember when we were kids, and I got the flu? It was the first time you played *Passage*. What am I saying? Your memory is amazing. You remember. That day, you built this gigantic Rube Goldberg machine all over the living room while I slept on the couch.

If you're reading this, we've experienced a terrible series of events. The dominoes have fallen in the wrong direction in the giant chain reaction of life. It's the worst Rube Goldberg machine ever. My body has failed me. And I have done the one thing I never wanted to do. I've failed you.

Life is so unfair. I'm sad this cancer came into my body. I want to fight it and win for you. I'm doing everything that I can. Many pieces of my insides are broken now. Some of my parts may have turned into garbage. Maybe the doctors can't fix them.

If I can't be here in person to keep my promise, then my life didn't go the way either of us wanted. I'm sorry I've let you down. I'm putting some plans in place, trying hard to make it right.

You can become a real man even if I'm not with you. As long as I've been on my own, I still haven't mastered manhood. Without some good examples, it's hard to figure out what it means to be a man. Our dad isn't one worth imitating. Becoming a man might be a long process. Be patient and keep trying.

I want you to live in a good place with great people who can teach you everything you need to chase after your dreams. Hopefully they will know more than I do. I'm going to be picky about what kind of place. You'll get the very best I can afford.

This situation is kind of like a *Passage* puzzle. The path you thought you would take has been blocked off. Place your new portals carefully. You can move around or through this obstacle and still make it to the other side.

As long as you're alive, you can grow and change. Live,

Copper. Learn. Become a man, but not just any man.
Be a good man.

I will miss you so much. I hope I can watch you succeed
from wherever I'm going next. I'm leaving you some
pennies. I love you.

Sterling

P.S. When you're ready, ask the lawyers or Mom for the
copies from my journal. I left you some pages. They're
memories from our time together.

A coin was taped to the bottom of the letter. It looked just
like Sterling's tattoo, with the words "Know Your Value"
scrawled beneath it. Except this was a 1989 D penny. Copper
would need to weigh it to be sure, but this one might be
enough to pay for most of culinary school.

He rubbed his face with the bottom of his shirt. "Can I
take this back to the room, now?"

"Sure. May I walk with you?"

Copper gave her a slight nod, and his mouth curved up on
one side. His brother had left him something priceless and a
little bit overwhelming. Copper Munro had inherited the
power to make choices.

Chapter Forty-Three

KEEGAN

Every social encounter is an opportunity to gain a friend.

- Friendship Knocks

Jay gasped as the elevators opened onto the third floor of The Terrace. "What an astounding use of symmetry. I approve of this decorative theme." He pressed his tablet's camera button so hard, it triggered the sound effect for a burst shot.

Keegan held the elevator doors. "Right this way, friends. We'll wait in the meeting room." He bowed before a large pane of glass. "Be careful. The first time I came here, I almost ran right into this wall. It's way too clean."

The room was full of young people sitting at desks, each paired with an adult. Some pairs were exchanging picture cards. One woman was steadying a guy's elbow while he pushed on a device. In the center of the room, Keegan's two new friends sat stiffly on the couch, their geocaching activity temporarily paused. Keegan looked at his phone and patrolled the area. Waiting for Copper was an exercise in patience, but in a way, it was good they'd split up. Copper had to use the Inn's official tablet so he could access the geocaching app. This would make an excellent tutorial for him. He would arrive trained and ready to go.

Tyler was picking at his sweater and tucking small bits of material into his pocket. Jay's tablet was zoomed in on the elevator. "Designating the wheelchair-accessible restrooms for humans, as opposed to men and women, was ingenious. Much more accurate." He took another photo.

Charming Chatter claimed it was the host's responsibility to keep small talk flowing. Keegan had no idea what small talk meant. Chatter was chatter. It advised to ask if they are enjoying and then insert the name of the activity when unsure of what to say at a social function. Unless you are attending a funeral—Keegan had learned that lesson the hard way. "Are you enjoying the treasure hunt?"

"I'm perplexed. You claimed this is a global enterprise. Are you suggesting people conspire to bestow covert rewards and tokens all over the world for fortuitous discovery?"

"If that means what I think it does, the answer is yes. It's fun! We set this hunt up just for today. It's a little different than true geocaching but it seemed like a good way for you to learn your way around."

Copper exited the elevator and found his way around the glass wall. "Hey guys!" Then he stopped short and his face hardened. "What are those people doing?"

"Glad you found us." Keegan tipped his fedora. "Which people?"

Copper rested his hands on his hips. "Why is that woman pushing his elbow?"

With his best game show announcer impression, Keegan replied, "They're typing."

Copper's eyebrow shot up. "She's *forcing* him to type?"

Keegan held his curved palm up to his mouth and spoke in

a stage whisper. "That's a facilitator. She's supporting his wiggly arm so he can choose his words carefully. He can't speak. Typing gives him a way to communicate." In one smooth motion, Keegan grabbed his fedora and swept it toward the desks. "Those people are like us. They're on the spectrum too." He bowed, flipped his hat, and placed it back on his head.

Jay gave a side-eyed glance. "Doubtful. That one's fingers are contorted. The fellow next to her oscillates and grouses so profusely, I can barely concentrate." He closed his eyes. "They're not like me."

Keegan bobbed his head. "That's true. Scott, that guy who's typing, is probably a little smarter than you."

Jay stood and his voice soured. "Preposterous. My typing skills are superior and I would only moan if I were in distress."

"Now that he types, we've learned his native language is physics. He's great. We play chess together sometimes, but he always wins."

Copper took Jay's seat on the couch next to Tyler, and steepled his fingers. "Are they all geniuses?"

"They might be. Or they could just be regular people. Claire has a lot of thoughts about animals. Sometimes she types about dogs and it makes me nervous because I'm allergic to them. If I have any questions about animals, she's the best person to ask."

Jay stomped his foot and earned a new fold in his forehead. "You converse with these people?"

"Why wouldn't I? They're amazing. I wish Ainsley could have been in this program, but we didn't know about some of these techniques back then." Keegan fidgeted. Jay made him lose focus so easily. "The point is, there are many people on the spectrum who may not seem like us, but they are us. They are everyone. Just as we are everyone. Same and different."

"I shall endeavor to unravel your riddle."

"They want friends too. There's really no reason not to socialize." Keegan tapped Jay's watch. "Except for our schedule, right? Let's go!"

With a cheerful grin, Copper helped Tyler up. "This is my first time searching for treasure. What does it look like?"

Keegan linked his arm through Copper's. For once, Copper didn't jerk his arm away. "C'mon. You'll see."

They crept down the hall passing modified hospital rooms. "What are these for?" Copper asked.

The redhead had a lot of questions, but Keegan welcomed the opportunity to take the lead. "For people who need more medical supervision." A flash of pink through one of the open doors caught his eye. "Hi, Ruby! We're on a treasure hunt. Have you seen any treasure around here?"

She was fiddling with some strange looking weeds on her window ledge. Two dried-up green things rested in her lap. "I haven't seen any treasure. I'm packing. I get to move to a room in the Courtyard today."

"That means you're getting better, right?"

"Yeah my breathing has improved a lot, but I'm not going home. My mom's out of town and they say someone needs to continue to look after me." She wrinkled her nose and crossed her arms in front of her chest. "I think I'm doing just fine."

In the doorway, Copper squeezed in beside Keegan. "Wow. You have a lot of plants. What the heck? They don't have any pots. Where's the dirt?"

"They're air plants. They don't need dirt. They were the easiest to bring with me from home, Ginger Root."

Copper leaned in as far as he could without crossing the threshold. "Can I see one?"

Ruby shrugged. "Sure. Come in."

Everyone except Jay squeezed into the small room. Keegan remembered his brother saying something about leaving no man behind. "You coming, Jay?"

"I prefer to remain focused on the objective. I'll peruse the hallway for treasure."

Copper held one of the rubbery plants from Ruby's window. "What if this whole time I've been like an air plant? Maybe I can do all sorts of things and people have underestimated me, like those kids in the meeting room back there. What if I don't need anyone or anything?"

"These plants would die if I didn't mist them once a week. Everybody needs something or someone, Copper."

Tyler poked a prickly plant with his finger. A tiny white flower had grown out of the center. He looked underneath it. There were no roots. His eyes bulged as he dropped the plant. "There's a great future in plastics. Think about it."[1]

Jay announced from the doorway, "Lady and gentlemen, I requisitioned this key from one of the potted plants at the far end of the hall. Since it was located at the exact coordinates given on the app, I've deduced this key is part of the treasure."

Keegan spoke into his pencils as an imaginary microphone. "Great job, Jay! I knew you were a genius. Did you pick up the capsule next to it?"

"No." Jay scratched his arms. "The container was embedded into an inordinate amount of Spanish moss. My epidermis—"

Keegan held up his hand. "Stop. English, please."

"You may continue the excavation."

"Almost English. Close enough. Let's go." Keegan ran down the hall and dug through the pot. The others followed him. Once he found the capsule, he unrolled the paper inside.

"What do we do now?" The redhead inquisitor's attitude and level of participation had greatly improved on day two.

Keegan held his tablet up high. "We enter coordinates. The app will guide us to the next spot."

Before they left, Copper stopped at Ruby's door. "Sure you don't want to come with us?"

"Not today. I'm breaking out of here."

The GPS sent them on a quest through the grand lawn. They'd just read a clue hidden under a stone, when they found the woman in the orange shirt slumped sideways on a park bench. All four men came to a full stop. Tyler turned to go back the way he came. "I see dead people."[2]

Copper stuck his arm out to stop the boy from leaving the group. "Should we call 911?"

Keegan browsed the lawn. They were the only people in the area. He remembered Luke's appointment with Kelly-Jean Hadley and other members of the local media. "Wait! You can't call 911 for just anything. Believe me, I *know*. We'll get in trouble with the police if it's not an emergency." He looked toward the sky. He needed to keep everyone calm. He couldn't risk the second day falling apart. Not after such a great morning. So he dialed up the charm. "Besides, we'll disturb the squirrels."

Copper tried out the Harris Head-tilt. "Don't tell me you're afraid of squirrels."

"The squirrels and I have an understanding. It's dogs who always want to lick me to death. That is *not* Ok."

Jay stared at his watch and counted in a whisper. "Quiet. She might be practicing the dragonfly technique."

Copper and Keegan spoke in unison. "What?"

"Some female dragonflies fake their own deaths when there's a large population of males nearby. It's a way to avoid mating with several aggressive males. When they are laying their eggs alone, they're vulnerable. This strategy allows them to live longer." Jay tipped his chin and squinted. "I'm not certain...women are mysterious...However, she's clearly more evolved than a dragonfly."

Keegan clasped his hands together and held them to his chest. "I like dragonflies. Can I use that for a card?" He took a step backward. "Let's back up and watch. Maybe she'll tire of the game and run off." The group took a few steps back. Keegan pulled a tiny notepad from his back pocket and scribbled.

In the excitement, Tyler had slipped away from the group. He stood about 20 feet behind them, trying to socialize with someone on another park bench. Copper's voice rang out. "Who's Tyler speaking to?"

"With whom is Tyler speaking?" Jay corrected.

"Sorry, Professor Brainy Buttons." Copper almost nudged Jay in the side, but he pulled away before he made contact.

Keegan peered over, giving half a salute to shade his eyes from the sun. "He's talking to…"

They watched as Tyler hopped and flailed his arms. The man on the bench jumped up, waved his tattooed hand, and ran away.

"…a Trekkie or Avengers fan," Keegan finished.

"What in the level two was that?"

Copper's adoption of the cursing code warmed Keegan's heart. "I've seen those people this weekend. They have these triangle tattoos that look pointy like a Star Trek communicator badge or the Avengers' A. They're not very friendly."

"Tyler's theatrical gestures are quite animated. Perhaps he has an aversion to women." Jay glanced at his watch and returned his gaze to the lady on the park bench.

"I hope he likes dragonflies. They're way better than dogs."

With his phone pressed against his face, Tyler rushed past them and touched the woman's neck.

Jay's eyebrows knit together. "It is unlawful to touch her. He must obtain her consent. My place of employment has a strict policy. I've signed affidavits to prove I understand this concept, in order to avoid litigation."

The quiet lawn became alive with sudden activity. They stood and watched as, like a choreographed stage production, people entered from every angle. A medical team dodged the fountain, two rolled a gurney, and the others ran over with radios and first aid kits. The people wearing blue scrubs fussed over the woman. Luke and Nicola swooped in from opposite sides of the property. Luke went straight toward the action while Nicola folded Tyler into her arms.

Jay crushed some acorns under his shoe. "She's incredible." He pulled out his phone and took two steps away from the group. "This is Jay Simmons. Please load up storage unit #950 and deliver my items to the Inn on Ainsley Avenue. It's a 20-minute drive. I'll text you the address. Tomorrow morning? I'll put it on the schedule. Thank you."

Luke tied his hair back as he walked to the group. The hairstyle revealed his large, round eyes and the freshly shaved sides of his head. "Thank God, Tyler used the speech to text function on his phone. His wording was a bit unusual but it did the job. Thanks to him, we were able to get her some help. Are you guys alright?"

"We were finishing up our treasure hunt when we found this woman resting." Keegan sucked air through his teeth and concentrated on the scene through his pencils' blurry frames. "Are the reporters here yet?"

"The reporters. Shh." Luke glanced at Keegan. "Level three, they're probably arriving now. Just my luck."

The medics moved the sleepy woman to the stretcher. One said, "Diabetic" as they rolled her toward the building. A woman that looked a lot like Kelly-Jean Hadley stood next to a cameraman at the fountain. He was snapping photos of the beautiful garden path.

Luke called over his shoulder. "Nic, we've got media attention."

Nicola walked Tyler back to the group. "You were very smart. Thank you. Guys, Luke and I need to do a little damage control, so can you move on to the next activity now?" She rubbed Keegan's shoulder. "You know what to do, right?"

He nodded. "Come on. I know what we're supposed to do with the key." He strode off toward the Recreation Center, and the others followed close behind.

Jay shuffled his feet in time with Tyler's steps. "What did you do to be rewarded with such an embrace?"

Tyler passed his phone to the eldest member of their party. Jay read aloud, "We all end up dead. It's just a question of how and why.[3] I have always depended on the kindness of strangers."[4] Then he tossed the phone back. "That's outrageous. I can only imagine the disconcertion you caused the man who brandished his middle finger."

Copper spoke into Keegan's right shoulder. "You knew what we would do with the key this whole time?"

Keegan's feet kicked up a small cloud of dust when they came to an abrupt stop. "We'll grab a bunch of my childhood toys from storage and set them up for the inclusion playgroup." He wiped sweat from his eyes. "Then, at long last, we'll watch that movie."

Once they reached a patch of grass, Copper had his first outburst of the day. "But why put us through geocaching?"

The redhead's fire was contagious, and heat rushed to Keegan's face. "We needed an adventure today." He bent at the waist and covered his face. "But it's all gone wrong. Again." He pushed the fedora back and checked to see if anyone had a camera trained on them. Unfamiliar people strolled through the park. "Level three. My mother should have named me Spectacle. C'mon." He groaned and strode across the street.

Tyler tapped his arm with the black beanie, and Keegan gave him a quick nod. "Thanks for calling for help. It was an emergency, after all." He walked backward. "I got all distracted with Jay's fancy dragonfly talk." He shook his head and spun around, almost tripping over the curb.

Tyler rushed ahead and opened the door to the rec center.

A blast of cold air shot out to greet them. "Would you like an adventure now or should we have our tea first?"[5]

Jay's face creased with worry over an unscheduled tea. Copper scowled.

As far as Keegan was concerned, orientation and his future at the Inn were doomed. He'd made the wrong judgment call again and someone could have died because of it. The media might pick up the story and ruin everything. Even if they didn't, he wasn't going to make the goal for the hall. Copper didn't like their programs.

Orientation may have been a bust, but Keegan would go through the motions and try to keep them out of trouble. He would do his best to preserve the rest of the Retreat. After all the mistakes he'd made, his family deserved that much.

Chapter Forty-Four

COPPER

One single penny

Copper and Keegan unloaded several boxes of toys and placed them on four long tables on the side of the basketball court. Tyler and Jay unpacked each box. Luke hustled in, looking every bit like Sokka from Avatar with half his hair shaved underneath. Copper huffed. He hadn't agreed to hard labor this weekend. "Hey, Last Airbender, where should we put this stuff?"

"Y'all set it up however you think is best. The kids will love it." Luke gave a thumbs-up sign.

Sometimes, his easy-going charm got on Copper's last nerve. Nobody was really that nice and that relaxed all the time. Despite starting the day with a fresh attitude, Copper's emotional experience was tangled up like a bunch of wet spaghetti. He needed someone he could trust, preferably someone who understood things, to help him process the recent events. He thought of the woman in the orange shirt leaving the park on a stretcher. There was something familiar about her.

"Copper, I can't bend air. Would you mind helping me with this big trunk?"

They each lifted one side from the bottom. "Sorry about the nicknames. Sometimes I use them to help me remember people. Then it becomes a habit."

"It's cool. We need to take this to the other side of the gym."

"What's in here, bricks?"

"Close. These are a few of Keegan's old musical instruments. They weren't supposed to be brought in this time. Trust me, you do not want a bunch of young kids playing with these in the gym." They set the box down. "Level two, that was a pain. Keeg has lost his mind. At least he didn't start bringing the drum kits out."

Copper tried to keep his voice casual. "Do you think we should contact Ruby about the woman on the park bench?"

"Why?" Luke asked as he lifted the lid off another large box. "Oh come on!" The container was full of noise makers typically used at a New Years Eve party. "My brother." Luke shook his head. "Sorry. What about Ruby?"

Copper stood with his hands in his pockets. "Her aunt works here. Except for the hair color, that lady looked a lot like her. That might be her relative. If you don't know her number, I could find her at the Terraces…"

The Resident Trainer placed three medium boxes on a nearby table. "Oh, Ruby has Down syndrome. So does the woman you saw in the park. I've met Ruby's aunt, and that wasn't her. Everything's alright."

Copper tested the weight of a large box, nudging it with his foot. He bit his lower lip. "I really thought my face blindness was improving." He closed his fist around the penny in his pocket. "What's Down syndrome?"

Luke dug inside a box and pulled out some Tinker toys. "She has an extra chromosome in her DNA."

Copper didn't move. "Is that ok?"

Keegan breezed by and tossed his fedora on a table, swapping it for a burgundy beanie. "Didn't you hear him? He said Ruby is extra. That's better than ok; it's fantastic. Follow me, please."

Jay lined the cars up while Tyler stuck colorful plastic tubes together for a marble run. Parts of the gym now looked like a toy store. Copper would have loved to have so many toys when he was younger. He could make some incredible Rube Goldberg machines with a fraction of what they had set up for the children. Keegan had a charmed life. "You had all of this growing up?"

Keegan reached into a closet and threw bean bags onto the floor. "This is a small part of my collection. Mom says I can't bring it all out because it's overwhelming. The toys are on a rotational schedule. Train Day is the best."

The blond dynamo had lost a bit of his razzle-dazzle. The corners of his mouth bent down. Copper couldn't figure him out. Maybe he wasn't happy to be sharing his toys or that his treasure hunt ended early. Keegan mumbled something about the lounge and left the room, carrying a load of bean bag chairs.

Copper threw his hands up, just like he'd seen his mother do a thousand times. "I guess we're supposed to help. Grab some bean bags, guys."

A few steps and a short ramp led to a sunken living room. The seating area was furnished with a couch and four white chairs shaped like globes. In the center of the floor, Keegan had built a mountain out of the cushions. He ran, launched himself, and landed face down on the pile.

The rest of the group stood, arms awkwardly loaded with shapeshifting sacks. Waiting for Keegan to perform his customary grand gestures and direct the activity grew tedious. Copper evaluated the situation. The bright blond hair and relative size seemed like Keegan, but he wasn't acting like the guy who'd been strutting around all weekend. "Keegan, do you feel bad?"

The lanky giant stood. Waving his pencils with erratic enthusiasm, his voice boomed, "I'm evil!"

The energy in the room changed. Tyler threw his bean bags toward the pile. He crawled inside the hollow ball that had been converted into a chair and slapped his hands over his ears. Jay set his bean bags down. With quiet confidence, he stood with his arms crossed, like a bouncer or a bodyguard. Copper wondered if the room had shrunk. The thick, stagnant air was hard to breathe. The black circles blocked his peripheral vision. Without a wall for support, his knees found the floor cushions. The cold, hard floor kissed his hot cheek. His world became submerged under a sea of cotton.

In the distance, just beyond a heap of fluff, Jay said, "Keegan, you're interfering with the quality of this activity. Are you feeling unhealthy?"

Keegan whimpered and rolled onto his back. "I'm worried about the Retreat. We need the local papers to love us, especially after my time at the park yesterday. And today's scene on the lawn wasn't good, either. The playgroup has to be perfect." He twisted a coil of his hair around his finger. "And I'm worried about you guys. It's time for the movie, and I really thought you'd like it, but I've been wrong about a lot this weekend. There's cursing. When I watched it, I ruined my childhood." He stared at the ceiling with his arm draped across his head. "And now Copper is taking a nap."

With Jay's help, Copper rolled to his knees grateful his peripheral vision had been restored. The human time-keeper wasn't finished with him yet. He nudged him in the ribs, urging him forward, "Come on. The schedule makes no allowances for naps." The Professor guided him to the couch and sat beside him. Jay addressed their host, "Keegan, how old are you?"

"Twenty."

"Then you're no longer a child. There's no childhood left to ruin. That part of life is finished. I would surmise everyone here is old enough to have heard profanity." He dusted off his hands and rubbed them on the knees of his pants. "You planned this activity, so let's return to the schedule. Resume your position of leadership. It will improve your disposition."

Keegan used his teacher voice. "Guys, I watched this entire movie, and I'm giving you a fair warning. It's confusing because it was made in the 1900s. There are lots of curse words and inappropriate conversations. It might even be rated R."

Copper spoke from between his knees. "Was it interesting?"

"Very! A group of kids did something wrong and had to spend the whole day at school being punished."

Jay bounced his legs. "Their disobedience is the cause of your anxiety?"

"No, Luke helped me with that part."

Copper rubbed his temples with circular motions. "So what's the deal? Why are you freaked out?" He lifted his head and peeked at the host. Blond ringlets bounced a million miles an hour. *The boy was back.*

Keegan stood tall on his bean bag mountain. "They dress weird." His arms moved like a baseball referee did when calling a runner safe. "And the title was about breakfast, but they don't eat breakfast one time in the whole movie!"

Copper wiggled his toes in the checkerboard shoes. "Level two. Spoiler alert, gah!"

Keegan continued. "The troublemakers are strangers at first, and they do a lot of bad things together. Later they defeat the harsh teacher man and become friends. I like that they were strangers at the beginning and left as friends at the end."

Copper shook his head, thankful that the guy had finally stopped talking. All of this active listening made his head spin.

Tyler broke the silence. "Eat...My...Shorts."[1]

Jay jerked back as though he'd been punched in the face. "Tyler! That's uncouth. You, of all people, should feel great enthusiasm for this adventure."

Keegan's hands pressed into his cheeks. "You've seen it, Ty?"

Copper looked at the Professor. "We should have seen that coming."

Jay stood. "Are we witnessing this cinematic masterpiece here or in the media room?"

The blond giant looked bashful. "We have to go to the media room so the kids in the gym can't hear it. The last thing we need is for the inclusion playgroup to become a tutorial for foul language and inappropriate topics of conversation."

Jay fumbled with his long sleeves. "We're overdue. Proceed." He moved toward the door. "As our unobtrusive advisor says, 'Walk and talk, people.'"

Tyler smiled. "Shut up, level three woman! Go fix me a turkey pot pie."[2] He followed Jay out the door.

Keegan groaned. "At least he used the code this time, but he can't keep quoting this movie!" Despite his protest, his mouth twitched into a grin. He galloped across the room to catch up.

Desperate for a break from the insanity, Copper wandered back to the gym. So many of the toys moved, danced, and twinkled. That was how Keegan behaved most of the time. No matter if he straddled the line between madness and genius, Keegan Harris was a force that couldn't be ignored. He was a random event generator, like a firework made flesh.

Suddenly, a wave of children poured through the gym door. Copper stood and watched them scatter across the tables full of toys. Some carried picture boards for communication. A few held hands. One boy added a vehicle to Jay's line of metal cars. In the corner, the tiniest girl he'd ever seen rolled a ball to a boy. The boy set his picture board to the side and rolled the ball back.

Over his shoulder, he heard the Professor. "Extraordinary."

Copper hadn't expected anyone to notice his absence. Since he'd missed a lot of yesterday's activities and had arrived late today, he suspected he was the odd man out. He was spectating on the perimeter of the group, still trying to understand things. He wasn't uncomfortable. That feeling of isolation accompanied him most of the time when he was with other people. He studied the children searching for signs of division or alienation within the crowd. "Did you ever have this as a kid, Jay?"

"No. Playtime was a solitary experience for me."

"Me too." He looked around the edges of the gym. There were a lot of adults nearby. "Looks like they still have helpers, but they're all supervising from a distance, not controlling things. That's so weird."

"Look in the northwest corner. The child in the wheelchair is receiving adult assistance with the modeling clay."

"Ah. That looks more familiar. See how the other kids——"

As Copper spoke, several children approached the boy in the chair. They invited him to join them. He followed them to an area where someone blew bubbles. "Never mind. I guess I was wrong." Copper watched for a few more minutes.

Jay cleared his throat. "We should attend the movie. Remember?"

As Copper ambled toward the next official activity, he wondered what it would have been like to belong in a group of peers. He tried to imagine being included, not pitied or cast aside. He lived life as an alien observer: close enough to see, but not to experience the world as others did.

Sometimes, Sterling invited his friends over. They'd play

Passage. Most of the time, Copper sat in the living room listening to the others play, while flipping through *Food* magazine. Once, they handed him the controller and admired how quickly he cleared the levels. Some of them wanted him to be on their team. He had fast reflexes and instinctively understood how buildings were arranged. It wasn't that much of a maze, really. He wasn't sure why the others found it challenging. That was the only time he'd fit in. He had to be amazing and special at something in order to be accepted. Something must have gone wrong because the friends no longer wanted to play *Passage* when they visited again.

Sterling tried to hang out with him when there was time, but the more his brother advanced in school, the less time there seemed to be. After college, they ran out of time permanently.

Copper stood outside the door to the media room. He could smell popcorn. He tried to settle his nerves and take a deep breath before re-entry into chaos. The plan had been for Sterling to show him everything necessary to become a real man. A real man had friends. Copper Munro needed to know the secret of how to make that happen. If he could learn it by watching a movie about breakfast companions, so be it. *The sooner, the better.*

Chapter Forty-Five

KEEGAN

Love yourself before you expect it from anyone else.

- Social Security: Building Confidence for Social Encounters

Relieved at Copper's return, Keegan set about resolving the next obstacle. Without direction, seat selection had become a complicated process. Freedom of choice disoriented his friends. Jay gave a lecture on sound waves and acoustics. He announced his strategy to locate the seat that provided the optimal view. He sat on the center seat in the middle row. Once he'd chosen, the other two sat as close to him as possible. Keegan took a position two rows lower. With so many seats, there was no need to sit in each other's laps.

They sat in silence, looking at a blank screen. Another roadblock. They should have bought the DVD. Keegan should have summoned the courage to ask his mother to buy a copy of the film. The best plans leave nothing to chance. But now everything hinged on Luke fixing the Internet issue so they could stream the movie.

Jay raised his voice. "While we squander inestimable

minutes, can we exchange views about the elephant in the room?"

Tyler set his head at an angle. "He has those ears that only a mother could love?"[1] He raised one eyebrow and folded his hands in his lap.

"Nice Harris Head-tilt, Tyler. Y'all talk about whatever you want. I'll check the sound. Back in a flash." Luke took the stairs two at a time.

Jay unbuttoned the top of his shirt. "Let's discuss autism."

"Great idea!" Keegan hopped over one row of chairs to close the gap and address them properly. He clapped his hands together. "I'll start. I love it. I'm incredible. People say that all the time!"

"Your attempts at levity never fail to mystify. Which brings me to my point: I find it dubious as well as unsettling that we allegedly share the same diagnostic label. Our expressions are varied. In terms of quality control, this assortment of characteristics isn't homogenous." He stood, tucked in his shirt, and moved to the outside of the row. "The clock is inaccurate. Flickering on twelve indicates a defective product."

With his fist clasping two pencils, Keegan twirled his wrist and lassoed the air. "They say my brain works differently." He bulged his eye and leaned toward Jay. "Different, but not in a bad way. I struggle with things, but everyone has challenges. So I can't see how that makes me very different at all. What other way is there to be? I can't be someone else. I'm Keegan and I'm happy." He bounced his shoulders and slipped the pencils back into his pocket.

Chapter Forty-Six

COPPER

Turn up like a bad penny.

Copper's midsection burned. "Have you ever read what they say on the Internet about us? We are every parent's worst nightmare. We are a gross disappointment, like"—he considered his present location for inspiration—"like burned popcorn! There are countless messages from upset parents who say we should be cured." His vision blurred and his voice broke. "But you can't fix popcorn. Once it's burned, it just stinks." He wiped his face. "I don't even understand what's wrong with us. If we were burned toast, we could scratch off the damaged parts. But we can't scrape away the autism. I've tried." Copper held his arms in front of his chest. "Keegan may be happy with it, but I don't enjoy being a mistake, or a disease, or a pitiful thing."

Keegan's mouth made a retching sound but nothing came up. "Let's not talk about burned smells." He grabbed his mouth and leaned back against the row of seats behind him. "My parents told me different isn't the same thing as wrong. Once I had a teacher who told me my autism was bad that day.

She didn't like my pencils. But Mom said autism can't be bad because that's like saying the color of someone's eyes or hair is bad and wrong, and that doesn't make any sense. My behavior can be annoying, but I've been annoyed by a lot of people who aren't on our spectrum."

The Professor stood next to the digital clock that flashed 12:00. "At the lab, if a sample varies from the standardized criteria, we shut down the equipment. We search for the anomaly and correct it to resolve the issue. Our product must be consistent. Perhaps that is the rationale with human populations...although we need a variety of DNA combinations to avoid defects." His busy hands stopped. "Copper states that others consider us to be substandard." His face fell. "My current emotional state might be classified as humiliation." He began pacing. "I *cannot* be substandard. My IQ and vocabulary are above average. I've been tested." His hands rested on his hips. "Clearly these people have drawn erroneous conclusions from unreliable data."

Keegan removed his burgundy beanie and waved it at the back of the room. "If we're talking about people, then *same* is boring. The world is so exciting and beautiful. So many of these *same* types can't even see it." He shook his cap and danced to a song that only he could hear. He practically sang the words, "I'm not a list of symptoms. Some of that stuff says I can't understand abstract language..." He put his hands on his waist and leaned forward. His eyes twinkled. "Hello? I made up my own cursing code!" He dusted off his cap, placed it back over his curls, and crossed his arms in front of his chest. With bobbing eyebrows he added, "People on the Internet don't know me. Some of them might have seen me in videos, but that's not the same as *really* knowing me."

Jay staggered across the row, avoiding toes and knees, to resume his center seat. "If *really* knowing you entails in-depth understanding and appreciation of your tendency toward the theatrical, I can see how that would be difficult to ascertain."

Luke stood at the back of the room near the projector, holding a tray loaded with striped bags of popcorn. "I don't have an autism diagnosis, but I interact with people every day who do. Would you like to hear the way it was explained to me?"

"As long as you pass out that popcorn, I don't care what you say."

Luke laughed. "Hungry, Keeg?" He instructed Tyler to grab a bag and pass it down. "I was told that your brains process data in a different way. This leads you to draw conclusions and connections that many of us wouldn't tie together. This can result in shortcuts that give you some genius abilities or you may miss some links we make with ease."

Once the other three had popcorn, Luke took the remaining bag to Keegan. "Your experience, using all five senses, can cause distress. Some people on the spectrum feel extremely uncomfortable in this world. There are physical illnesses that seem to be more common amongst people on the autism spectrum. That all complicates how people define the label."

Copper looked into his sack of popped corn. Perfectly prepared, it smelled delicious. "Ok, Luke. I can accept that my mind works differently. I still don't know how to change it. Just tell me one thing: why do parents and strangers all over the world hate us?" He scooped up some irresistible kernels and shoved them into his mouth.

Luke propped his foot up on the arm of a seat and rested his chin into his palm. "Parents want their kids to have a happy life. Some see their children struggling and feel powerless to help them, so they get tired and imagine a terrible future. I don't believe most of the people posting that stuff actually hate you. Fatigue, sadness, and fear are bad editors. Those conditions make all of us communicate without thinking about how our messages will be received by different audiences."

A piece of popcorn scratched the back of Copper's throat, and his mouth dried like he'd been eating crackers and sand. He coughed and his raspy voice grated against his own ears. "My diagnosis is Pervasive Developmental Disorder, Not Otherwise Specified. Pervasive. That means it's mixed throughout the core of my entire self. When someone says they hate something that is such a big part of who I am, and I can't separate myself from it, it seems like they hate all of me." He cleared his throat. "That hurts so much."

Tyler lifted his bag of popcorn into the air and proposed a toast. "Life is pain, Highness. Anyone who says differently is selling something."[1]

Jay shoved his popcorn into Copper's hand while he bent forward. After double-checking that his electronics were still tucked safely under his seat, he snatched his popcorn back. Balancing the snack precariously on his lap, he stared the picture paused on the movie screen. The word "Universal" loomed in front of a globe used to represent Earth. He wrinkled his forehead. "In order to have an accurate assessment of the sentiments of a large population, we'd need improved surveying methods and data collection. My sample size is small, but I've encountered some positive online messages. Not everyone hates us. And nature provides chemical reactions that assist in positive emotions toward progeny and romantic partners." He popped some popcorn into his overactive pie hole. "Never underestimate the power of chemistry."

Luke left the room and reappeared with bottled water. Keegan volunteered to distribute it so the Resident Trainer could start the movie. Then, the blond beanpole jumped back over the seats and announced, "Show time!"

Chapter Forty-Seven

KEEGAN

Casually tell someone that you enjoy their company.

- Charming Chatter

Keegan wondered which nuances divided a smile from a sneer. He smashed his teeth together and pulled his lips apart. Without a mirror, he struggled to duplicate facial expressions. His unsteady legs wobbled as he completed his bow. "Wasn't that the best movie ever?"

The quiet atmosphere forced him to add, "Except for the negative parts?" He wished Luke hadn't left. Their mother should have handled today's media tour, but his brother put people at ease, and that skill was in high demand this weekend.

Copper stretched. "I haven't seen a lot of movies, but that was really weird."

Keegan picked at his cuticles. "I know. Not even a mention of pancakes or anything breakfast-related. Do you think they accidentally used the wrong title?"

"Chef Chevalier has some wonderful breakfast episodes. You told us there wouldn't be breakfast, but I was all set for some French toast, omelettes, or quiche…something delicious. Brunch was an acceptable choice."

"That's a valid observation about the nonsensical identification. Since lunch is the only meal consumed, The Lunch Club is a superior option. Regardless, this motion picture presents several puzzles. I sympathize with your fascination." Jay retrieved his tablet from under his seat. "Perhaps there's a sequel."

Copper collected the trash. "It was a little heavy on the dialogue."

Keegan stamped his foot. "Ok, but…" He waved his hand at the frozen, overdressed figure posing with his fist in the air for eternity. "I watched this show and thought, 'I want that.' Do you understand?"

"You yearn to acquire favorable attention from fair-skinned females and to develop a passion for cannabis?"

"Level three, Jay!" Keegan shook his curls. "Cannabis! I don't break laws. We can't do that on Ainsley Avenue." He slapped his forehead. "Actually, we can't do that anywhere. No dogs and no criminals allowed. I'm very firm on these two points." He took a deep breath and exhaled slowly. "I liked the idea of a few random people coming together and becoming close friends. Not one of my social skills books fully explains the process." Keegan clambered to the ground level. He touched the screen. "I've studied this movie. Parts of orientation were designed to mirror it."

The group stopped. All eyes fell on Keegan. The garbage slipped from Copper's hands. "You did?"

Jay scanned his tablet. "At precisely what time were we under the influence of marijuana?"

Keegan ripped the beanie from his head, and crushed and twisted the soft hat. "Will you stop saying drug words? It's like you're obsessed."

Copper raised his hand. "I haven't had a chance to crawl

around in the ceiling, but I promise I'll be careful this time."
He bent to collect the trash again.

Jay's mouth twitched, but his face maintained its etched
expression. "Please abstain from all activities involving attics
and ceilings."

Keegan grabbed the wrappers away from Copper and took
them to a nearby bin. "Level two! You guys don't see? They
went on an adventure. I just substituted their illegal quest with
a perfectly safe and legal geocaching activity."

"Well, that turned into something memorable." Copper
rubbed his chin. "I'd already had experience with medical staff
and gurneys, but the reporters added some novelty."

Jay sat on the front row. "Who was the antagonist? Was it
the vice principal, John Bender, or both?" He sat upright in his
chair. "Keegan, did you embed an antagonistic force into our
orientation experience?"

"No. As usual, you're making things too complicated."

"Personally, I'm relieved. But you failed to act in
accordance with traditional story tropes. An antagonist may
have been a key component in obtaining your objective."

Keegan looked at the floor. "In our case, I thought life was
hard enough."

Copper tapped Keegan's shoulder. "So who were you
supposed to be? Not the jock...the brain? No." He paced the
length of the screen. "Basketcase?" Then his face lit up. "You
were the janitor." His feet planted themselves on the dark
carpet, and one hand landed flat on his chest. "Wait. Who am
I supposed to be? I'm not John, am I?"

Keegan pursed his lips. "I don't know. Let's go to the
lounge. They've delivered lunch by now."

Copper shook his head and held the door open. "There are
no ladies at the Inn. But the movie had girls. Are some of us
supposed to be female?"

As they filed into the hallway, Jay sighed. "If I were a

goddess, I wouldn't require these accommodations. Unfortunately, I lack the proper amount of femininity."

The other men stopped in the narrow corridor.

Copper was the first to say, "What?"

Jay's words were slow and deliberate. "Women provide our logistical framework. They restrain us from our barbaric, undisciplined ways and hold us accountable. Without their structure, it's bedlam. The organization and stability I expect from the Ainsley Avenue lifestyle wouldn't be necessary had I been born with two X chromosomes."

Keegan released a long breath as he lumbered to the head of the pack. "We need food."

Stacks of boxes and a small ice chest waited on the coffee table. Keegan hopped into the sunken space and offered a package to Tyler. "The restaurant sent over boxed lunches— probably sandwiches. I've got an extra gluten-free box if anyone wants one." He offered the special box to Copper.

Copper rejected that package and chose one without a gluten-free label. "It still doesn't quite work. There were five friends in the show, and we only have four."

Jay took charge of the ice chest, trading Keegan a cold drink for a box of food, and settled himself on the sofa.

Keegan took his lunch to the steps that led down into the conversation pit. "No. You're forgetting my brother, Luke. He counts!" Perched on the highest step, his feet almost reached the bottom of the stairs. "Maybe this is a big joke to you, but I've been dreaming about this weekend for years. This movie changed my life. It changed what I wanted for my future." He opened a bag of crispy snacks and tipped the edge of the bag into his mouth. His cheeks stretched to maximum capacity. If anyone had replied, Keegan couldn't hear it over the loud crunching from his overloaded mouth. As he swallowed the delicious glob of nacho cheese-flavored goodness, he realized all the other young men were equally interested in the contents of their lunchboxes.

Keegan scraped the bottom of the chip bag. He licked the savory orange powder from his fingertips. "I love this movie, even though it has profanity." He shaved the icing off a chocolate cupcake with his teeth. "I don't understand half of what they talk about. But something happens within that group. I'm not sure what it is." He threw the rest of the cupcake back into the box and dug around, avoiding the sandwich that rested on his lap.

Copper leaned out of the globe chair. He held a half-eaten apple in his hand. "They connected, Keegan." He turned the apple over, looking at it from every angle. "It's like my Rube Goldberg machines. Each piece is its own thing. I position them close together, so when I add a little push, there's a chain reaction. That's what they kept doing in that movie. Sometimes it resulted in bad things and I guess, other times, it turned out ok."

Keegan crumpled his empty plastic water bottle, then gathered the lunch debris. "I hope they're still friends on Monday. My plans were flawless. If you guys had gone along with them, we would be best friends." He chunked the garbage into the can. "But it's not working." He walked to the wheelchair access ramp and lay on the slope.

"Keegan, films are inaccurate depictions of reality."

"Pssht." Keegan stared at the ceiling. "Jay, it could have worked, but things kept going wrong."

Copper bumped his head on the roof of the iconic seat. "Ow. Damn chair." He rubbed his head. "How are we messing things up? By being ourselves?"

Keegan hopped to his feet. "Copper, your cursing is awful! If that chair wasn't a replica, Eero Aarnio would be offended." Sucking air through his teeth, he pulled out his pencils and released the breath in a huff. "I probably committed a crime for you. Breaking into my mother's office…What were we thinking?" He waved his pencils while gazing at his shoes. "And the craziest part of that is, it was all for nothing."

Copper approached the ramp. "Sorry. I screwed up everyone's day. But Keegan, I have real problems and you've lived a charmed life. Maybe you don't have much experience in the real world. Like Jay tried to say, life doesn't always go according to a script."

Tyler peeked his head out from under his round pod. "I know who I am. I'm the dude playin' the dude, disguised as another dude!"[1]

Copper stuck a hand out toward Tyler's chair. "There, listen to Tyler. He probably works from more scripts than all of us combined." He lowered his voice. "And look where that got him."

Keegan stopped waving his pencils. "You don't want to be here, Copper? Fine. I give up." He walked toward some storage cabinets and rummaged through them. "We may not have the right number of people to make my plan work, so we'll have another empty room at the Inn. Not even gonna fill one side of that hall."

Copper's hands rested on his hips. "I may not have things figured out, but I'm tired of being told who to be, how to act, or what to feel all the time! I'm not a puppet."

Keegan slammed some drawers shut. "Look, I don't know what you were doing before you came here. Your brother died. That's sad and I'm sorry." He returned to the conversation pit with one hand behind his back, then pressed a cold, lumpy baggie into Copper's hand and curled his fingers around it. "Whatever you want to do with your life is totally up to you. Just don't dump all over Ainsley Avenue. There are many people who would love to live here."

Copper opened his fist. He held a clear sandwich bag with several coins in it. "What's this?"

"Sometimes we find loose change. I put it in this sack."
Keegan's shoulders bounced. "You stim by playing with a coin,
so I thought you might like these." Keegan climbed on top of
the coffee table and addressed the group as he had during their
first meeting. "Gentlemen, your attention please. I apologize,
but I do not have a greeting card for this occasion." He swept
his arms up, each hand holding an unsharpened yellow pencil.
"I wanted a group of true friends." He angled his head toward
Jay. "I hear other people have them. In. Real. Life." He put his
hands together like he was going to pray, holding his pencils
vertically between his palms. "I have to change the world.
That's a big project. I thought it would be better if I had
friends by my side." He turned the pencils sideways, his fists
positioned on opposite ends. "I have failed." Keegan Harris
bent his wrists, snapping the pencils in half.

Jay rushed to help him down from the coffee table. "Now
you've done it. You've wasted valuable resources. Look at
Tyler! He's retreated into his sweater like a terror-stricken
turtle. I'm not an expert on affinity, but I assume a profuse
amount of time must be invested to cultivate trust. At least,
that's the consensus from most of the women I've met.
Actually, they suggest my intense devotion is unsettling." His
scruffy cheeks flushed and he rubbed his brow. "Perhaps your
accelerated timetable is overzealous."

"You don't understand. It's like we're speaking two
different languages. For years, I've known that I'd like you
guys." Keegan stuffed the four pencil fragments into his pocket.
"It's a little weird that Copper is the only other person besides
me who speaks English, but——"

Jay removed his hand from Keegan's shoulder. "Slander!
People often compliment my ability to convey information in a
clear, concise manner. Occasionally, I'm ridiculed because my
brevity confounds——"

Keegan placed his fingertips lightly on Jay's forearm. "It's ok. Some of the best people I've known can't utter a word in any language." He grinned. "If I may continue…Out of a group of applicants, you were selected as the perfect person to live here. I knew you would be Quality." Keegan left Jay and moved closer to Copper.

Copper recoiled. "Ugh. Personal space."

Keegan put his hands behind his back. "Even though your application came in late and you were the last to be added on our list, you were chosen. I had complete faith in the process. I liked you years before I actually met you."

He rushed over to Tyler, who was still hiding, although part of the black beanie was still sticking out of the top of his sweater. Keegan tapped him on the top of his head. "You are meant to be here. You are part of my life and I'm glad."

Tyler peeked out of the sweater. "How come you're being so nice to me?"[2]

Keegan laughed and adjusted the hat on the young man's head. "I'll play along. The next line is 'Because you're letting me,'[3] and that's totally true, by the way." Keegan put his hand out like a stop sign. "But I'm not going to put lipstick on while wearing a bra like the girl in the movie, so don't get too excited."

Tyler nodded. He hugged his feet to his chest and slid deeper inside the orb.

Keegan used the Harris Head-tilt. "Don't worry; we'll work on your English later."

A voice like Yoda came from the chair. "Do, or do not. There is no try."[4]

Chapter Forty-Eight

COPPER

Penny savers

Deep in contemplation, Copper squeezed the bag of coins. While he was relieved that he had choices, he was still confused about what he wanted to do with his life. If he returned home and kept attending the program at Pleasant Grove, he'd have no educational opportunities. The adult daycare offered zero chance of having a real man's life. Their resources maxed out at video games and TV. He'd sit there day after day…year by year…just existing. Had Sterling survived, he would have been Copper's whole world. That might not have been ideal, but they'd never discussed an alternate plan. He rubbed his eyes. He didn't want anyone to see him crying. Real men probably didn't cry.

He stole a quick glance around the room. Jay had his face buried in electronics. Tyler had dissolved into the furniture. Keegan was sitting in the pile of bean bags with his head hung low. Keegan sighed. "I'm so disappointed. I thought we could be a group. I even had a name picked out: The Innsiders. I can't believe it's not going to happen."

Jay looked at the orientation mastermind. "I'm sufficiently perplexed. Please explain this moniker."

Keegan threw his head back into the cushions and sighed. "Because we're inside people. We love the great indoors. And we may not know much about the rest of the world, but we understand autism in a way that other people can't." He yawned and folded his arms behind his neck. "And we live at the Inn, so I-N-N-siders." He rolled over to his side. "I thought it was very cool."

Jay resumed his scrolling and swiping. "Preposterous. Spelling isn't arbitrary. Ancillary characters can't be added to common words. You'll make a mockery of the entire Middle English *and* English Reformation eras."

Keegan's head crashed back down into the bean bags. "Don't worry; it's not happening. Besides, nobody would write it on paper and I haven't ordered embroidered jackets. I'm not an idiot. Besides, I didn't know which sizes to get. "

Copper shook his head. He needed some physical distance in order to process the insanity. He walked to the window and considered the group. Tyler's sleeve fell out of the ball chair and flopped loosely, well past his hand. His knees were tucked underneath the sweater, stretching it completely out of shape. Keegan crouched at the edge of the boy's chair, tying his shoelaces for him like he was a toddler. The Professor was squinting so hard at his phone a new vertical line had formed between his eyebrows. He seemed to be arguing with no one in particular.

Some group. They were absurd. If those raising a fuss online were right and their DNA had been arranged incorrectly, maybe this cluster could be weird and wrong together. Maybe they each had just enough of the right qualities that all combined, they could form a socially acceptable man. And somehow, they might stumble their way to friendship. That wouldn't be so bad. Copper squeezed the bag of coins, his mind turning over the possibilities. One thing was certain: they couldn't follow that crazy movie.

He looked out the window. The construction crew had gone on a lunch break. A corner of his mouth rose. The sensory spa sounded luxurious. His gaze rested on an elderly man and middle-aged woman poking around the slab. Copper searched through his memories as they marched away toward the far side of the new building. He vaguely remembered seeing a similar man sit with Tyler.

The distinguished-looking gentleman poured liquid from a glass bottle, and it splashed on the ground. His companion passed him a plastic bag that was dripping. Copper scrunched up his eyes in suspicion, when the man removed a dead chicken from the sack. They weren't anywhere near a kitchen, and a person didn't need to watch the Entrée Network to recognize the threat salmonella presented. It was poison. Food poison.

The old man shoved the chicken back at his companion, while taking a few swallows from the bottle. She stuffed it into the sack with a frown and marched back toward the window, her hand stained with blood. The word sailed out of his mouth before he had a moment to think. "Blood!" At that, the others charged toward the window. "Tyler's people have alcohol and a bag of raw, bloody chicken."

Keegan's hand flew to his mouth. "That's completely unexpected. I'm filing this into the scary category." Copper, Jay, and Keegan considered Tyler. The young man had crossed his legs and was standing the way children did when they tried not to wet themselves.

Keegan pulled his burgundy beanie down tight around his ears. "His legs! We've got to get Tyler out of here." He threw his head backward and covered his face with his hands. "Level three, I wonder if the photographers are still on the property."

Copper glanced at the other buildings and the lawn. He

would not allow Tyler to be beaten or poisoned. Not today. Not on his watch. "I can get Tyler back to the Inn without being seen."

"Are you sure?"

"Yes, I have a talent for finding shortcuts and alternate routes. I've got video game badges to prove it. I'll get him to safety." Copper held his hand out to the young man.

"If you notify Nicola, she'll subjugate this gruesome debacle."

"I have an idea, Professor: I'll take him to Nicola. If we can't find her, I'll help him hide."

"You're reiterating, essentially, what I—"

Copper licked his dry lips. "Keegan, you need to stall them. Jay, you can either physically restrain them or talk them to death."

Tyler peeked out the window. "The greatest trick the devil ever pulled was convincing the world he didn't exist."[1] He squeezed Copper's hand hard. They ran.

Chapter Forty-Nine

KEEGAN

If you want a loyal friend, be a loyal friend.

- Make It Right

For the guy who only strolled around on low-stress treasure hunts, running with Jay proved to be challenging. Keegan's lungs burned as they crossed the lawn. Creating greeting cards and geocaching weren't cardiovascular activities. He was definitely more of an "inside person."

But alcohol, a dangerous drug, had come to Ainsley Avenue, and drug use guaranteed unexpected events. Many of his social skills books stressed the importance of appearing calm during a crisis, so Keegan slowed his breathing. He hunted for fallen acorns to hide his face and catch his breath.

Jay hadn't broken a sweat. His slow, even breathing proved he was an athletic champion. "Acorns are inadequate defensive weapons."

On the eastern wall of the Inn, a cane pole caught Keegan's eye. "Luke is making a huge stim stick for me. Grab it, Jay. You may need it to control the quality."

Jay retrieved it and returned, tapping the giant staff on the sidewalk. "What's our targets' position?"

For once, Keegan needed to be taller. He backed up to a tall tree. "I'll climb this and be the lookout. Don't worry; I do it all the time." He scaled the windswept oak and checked out the property. A squirrel chittered on the branch above him, but Keegan wasn't bothered by that particular creature—his treaty with the squirrels remained firmly in place. The sea breeze knocked a couple of acorns to the ground. The sound of an owl and rustling leaves startled him—there were no peace agreements with owls. He craned his neck and rolled his head searching for the bird.

A whinny distracted him. His father claimed that hippotherapy would be beneficial for the residents, but Keegan opposed the use of livestock on the premises. He'd shown his father a machine that simulated the motion of riding a horse as a suitable alternative. Surely everyone knew it was a superior option to feeding and cleaning up after such a large animal?

A disturbance in the shrubbery below drew his attention. Copper's head rose out of the hedge, and if the situation hadn't been so tense, Keegan would have laughed at the peek-a-boo gesture. Relieved, he called down, "You made it! Where's Nicola?"

Copper cupped his hands around his mouth. "We couldn't find her." Like a lost prairie dog, Tyler's head popped out of the leaves.

Keegan continued to look for a large bird with sharp claws and a dangerous beak. "There's an owl but I can't find it anywhere."

Copper duplicated the owl sound. Tyler gave a realistic imitation of a horse.

"It was you!" Keegan frowned. "Take your sound effect show and go find Nicola."

Jay strode toward them, holding the stick horizontally in

front of his chest. "Superior coverage options can be located within the building."

Hide-and-seek paired with bloody animals and alcohol made Keegan nervous. The first pocket he explored contained useless, broken pencils. He shifted his weight and reached for his phone in the other pocket. He'd learned a lot this weekend. The safety of the Retreat was at risk, and one of his new friends was truly in danger. This time he would ask for help. He sent a quick group text message.

The branch made a low, creaking sound. Jay stood beneath the tree and said, "Have you verified whether that branch can withstand your body weight?"

"I'm watching for Mr. Ramsey. How do you like that stick?"

Jay twirled it with one hand. Straight out of a kung fu movie, he made some practice strikes through the air. "The balance is adequate, but it's hollow. That significantly reduces its efficacy for bludgeoning purposes."

Keegan spotted movement on the lawn. "I see them." The woman was sitting on a park bench. Red splatters had ruined her pale blue dress. Shadows shifted. He announced, "The mean grandpa is coming!"

Mr. Ramsey wiped his neck with a handkerchief as he trudged toward them. He wrapped the top of his cane with the cloth. The bottle of booze swung from his other hand.

Jay hissed into the shrubbery. "You have exceeded the allotted time for subterfuge. Your deception would have been far more effective if you'd selected a more obscure location."

"Can I get that in English, Professor?"

"Get down and stay hidden." Jay carried the pole as an impromptu walking stick and strolled to the trolley stop.

Crouching in the bushes, Tyler tugged Copper's hair. "You can be my wingman any time."[1] He disappeared into the leaves.

A squirrel scampered across the old man's path. He skipped a step. "Wh'appen?" Keegan sprinkled acorns onto the ground. Tyler's grandfather covered his head. "Gweh duppy!"

Keegan asked, "Do you love to hate squirrels?"

Mr. Ramsey shook his bottle up at Keegan. "Ease up nuh, man." Jay cut across the grass to stand in front of Mr. Ramsey on the sidewalk.

Luke flung the Inn's doors open and stepped outside, holding the security radio in his hand. Keegan could always count on his brother to take bold, decisive action. He thanked his lucky stars for group texting technology. Adopted or not, Luke executed the perfect Harris Head-tilt. "Jay?" He tucked his hair behind his ear. "Mr. Ramsey, you're a day early."

"My grandson, Tyler. Please."

"Sir, we're not fond of rum being consumed on the property." Luke sauntered toward him. "Why don't we go to the local bar and talk for a while?" He reached for the gentleman's elbow. "Excuse us, Jay. We're gonna take a little walk."

Clement Ramsey pulled his arm away. "No. I speak to my boy. Now."

"Mr. Ramsey, I think we all know Tyler isn't much for conversation. He's having a good time. Let's let him be."

The scent of rum wafted up into the oak tree. "That mother of his, she cut his hair before he said his first words. Everyone knows that creates problems." Mr. Ramsey shook his head and took another sip.

Luke touched the bottle. "May I?" Mr. Ramsey passed it to Luke, who took it and held it behind his back. A wide grin fell across his face. "Tyler is a great guy. He's been a pleasure to have around. The language—"

The grandpa's face twisted into a pout. "I don't like to speak about the dead, but his parents—"

Ainsley Avenue's finest Resident Trainer offered his hand to the man. "Maybe we can sit down somewhere and talk—"

The sound of crinkling leaves and tiny twigs snapping interrupted Luke's offer. Tyler crawled out of the bushes, tears lining his cheeks. "Screws fall out all of the time, the world is an imperfect place!"[2]

Mr. Ramsey jabbed a finger toward Tyler. "See? What's that mean? The boy's mother failed him. Sat him in front of the TV while she always going to that law school." He swiped the bottle from Luke's hand. "Look at him! Wearing that heavy thing during a Texas summer. He's almost destroyed it too. Boy don't have any sense. Come here! Take off that rag!"

Like a soldier, Jay stood guard between Mr. Ramsey and Tyler.

Clement Ramsey raised his cane a foot off the ground. "They say, 'Ben di tree while it young, cause when it old, it a go bruk.'"

Jay spun his makeshift staff like a warrior. He sliced it through the air in a series of arcs and slashes. The rod circled around his back and over his head. It crashed straight down like a hammer right in front of him. Had anyone been standing there, they would have been hurt. If the pole had been solid wood, they'd have been unconscious.

Luke's smile disappeared. He stuck his hand out in front of the elderly man. "Easy, Jay. Mr. Ramsey, we've seen bruises on the boy. Looks like you've bent him enough."

Andrea Harris' voice permeated the tense air. "Hello Clement." Arms waving wildly, she crossed the street as fast as her feet would carry her. Tyler's governess and Nicola were following close behind. Ms. Kelly-Jean Hadley, from the local paper, trailed a distant third place.

Keegan heard someone mutter, "Level four." His eyes darted to the bushes. Copper stood and tried to remove the leaves from his hair. *This crew was terrible at following instructions.*

Keegan's mom engaged everyone's full attention. "Luke…

Tyler's lovely governess, Olivia, was just describing a charming Jamaican custom involving chickens and"—she gnawed her lower lip and raised an eyebrow—"blood, and all sorts of things. It's a ceremony to bring safety and good luck when breaking ground on a new building. And Ms. Hadley suggested that she write an article about it. Isn't that marvelous?" She stared at Luke with eyes as wide as dinner plates.

Jay gave a hint of a bow to Nicola and the governess as they joined the group at Andrea's side. Even though Nicola's ponytail looked like it had been through a windstorm, her voice was calm. "Let's all go back to the Welcome Center. We have so much to discuss."

As Ms. Hadley started to cross the street, the trolley's brakes squeaked. It came to a full stop in front of the Inn, blocking her view. A man stood in the open door of the trolley with a leash wrapped around his tattooed hand. A furry monster appeared at his side. Its tongue flopped between sharp teeth. At the precise moment the man let go of the leash, Tyler shouted, "When you grow up, your heart dies!"[3]

The sidewalk crowd was so invested in the boy's words that they didn't notice the mongrel coming to destroy them all. The beast was lunging toward Tyler, and Keegan didn't have time to think about consequences. Tyler was the one sure thing of the entire weekend. He may not have been able to save Ainsley, but he would not fail his new friend Tyler. Keegan could not let the Retreat down. All he wanted was for his family and friends to be safe and happy. "I'm going off script!" he yelled, and plummeted from the tree into the path of the hound from Hell.

The wind escaped Keegan's lungs. Fur covered his face and fell into his mouth. The dog's paws danced all over his body as he collided with the ground. A warm, slimy, wet thing slathered across his arm. Everything happened all at once. His senses were overloaded. An odor of musk and mildew. Pain. Shrieking.

Andrea Harris ditched professional decorum and screamed, "Oh my God!"

Luke rolled on top of Keegan. He pushed and wrestled the heavy creature, shouting, "Call it off!"

The man shouted, "Bella, heel!"

Somehow, there was an absence of fur, and time slowed down again. A small voice in the distance said, "Sorry." The trolley's tires crunched acorns as it rolled away.

Nicola murmured something he couldn't quite make out. Keegan thought his eyes were open, but he couldn't see. His mother screeched something about stretchers and new pencils. He moaned, "Broken pencils. No wonder time feels so..."

Copper's voice sounded close. "Holy craaaa—uh...level two. Your face. I've never seen anything like it."

A warm hand brushed across his cheek. "We set out to save the Shire, Sam. It has been saved."[4]

Keegan's swollen lips made his words sound strange to his own ears. "I can't see. I may not be breathing. Am I dead?"

"No way. Level four, Keeg. I can't believe you did that, buddy."

"Me either." He tried to move, but his whole body hurt. He was beginning to feel the unbearable prickles of the intense itch. "Sometimes life is the level threes and the level fours." He groaned, wishing his skin suit came with a zipper or an escape hatch. "Are all the guys still here? Don't let them take Tyler!"

"Present and accounted for, Keegan. Your current countenance is alarming."

"Great. Jay is here. Keep controlling the quality, please." Someone slid his body onto a firm board. "Wait..."

"Sure, buddy. Go ahead."

Keegan hoped the odor of Luke's hair products mixed with wet dog wouldn't be the last smell he experienced. "Since I'm dying of dog germs, I've got one last wish. Can you guys please be the Innsiders now?"

Chapter Fifty

COPPER

A penny saved is a penny earned.

Bland and minimally furnished, the clinic was cold and sterile. In the waiting alcove just outside Keegan's room, the hard plastic chairs provided little comfort. Without even a poster on the wall for distraction, Copper winced and steeled himself to engage in conversation with the others. As always, Jay's attention was buried in electronic screens. Tyler was working at removing each pilled pebble from his sweater. When Copper cleared his throat, the boy's blue eyes pierced his heart. Tyler placed a finger over his lips, shook his head, and stared at the ceiling. Luke stalked past them and went to look in on his brother. He left the door open. Copper crossed his arms in front of his chest and rubbed his elbows for warmth while he listened to the events unfolding in the next room.

"...going to put him on the nebulizer to help with his asthma. The facial swelling should resolve soon. I've got some ointment for the rash. Since he landed on the sidewalk, we want to get x-rays. Ok?"

A member of the light blue scrub brigade wheeled

Keegan's gurney down the hall. Ms. Harris' voice rang like bells. "He's so upset, Nicola. I don't know if the hives are from the dog or stress."

Noisy shoes scraping the floor interfered with Copper's ability to hear some of Nicola's response. "...sweet that he tried to save his friend from danger. We'll sort it out."

"Thanks, hun. For everything. I don't know how you got rid of Clement Ramsey, but I'm glad you did."

"Things should be ok. We gave Kelly-Jean a feel-good story with the inclusion playgroup. That's a better fit for her column."

"Let's hope so. Is Tyler allowed to stay?"

"Mr. Ramsey plans to return in about six weeks. I've got a lot to research: different culture, different norms, and a whole new set of laws." Nicola snickered. "Looks like I get to spend a lot more time with lawyers."

Andrea Harris groaned. "Keegan's going to be so loopy from the medication. If he has to miss out on the rest of the orientation…"

"Let's wait and see."

Keegan returned to the hall in a wheelchair. Copper assumed he had been through the x-ray process and had been cleared to sit upright. Somewhere along the way, he'd accessorized his hospital gown with two new pencils. Behind a few wild curls that had escaped his beanie, Keegan's facial features looked more familiar. As the doctor rolled him back into the examination room, he gave a half-hearted wave.

Copper thought the guy looked ready to go. But, he heard the physician's report through the open door. "Good news: no broken bones. He'll have some nasty bruises, but that's not so bad. The injection will make him drowsy. Let's set him up with a breathing treatment and then he can rest."

Keegan wheezed. With ragged breath and a reedy tone, he

refused. "No rest. It's orientation weekend. Give me the good stuff."

His mother cautioned, "That prescription makes your head tingle."

"Don't worry," Keegan urged. "I'll stay awake."

Andrea Harris sounded just like Sterling after he'd stayed up all night studying. "Fine, but we're going to have a talk about jumping out of trees later."

"I was brave, right, Nicola?"

"I need to check on your friends. I'll be back."

Nicola appeared in the doorway. Behind her, a machine hummed. She smoothed the stray hairs sticking up around her face. "Hey, guys. Keegan will be ok."

As if by magic, her words allowed Jay to surgically remove his eyes from the glowing screen. "Marvelous," he breathed.

Nicola crouched down, resting her hands on her knees. "You guys still have one evening left. I'm sorry, but we'll need to adjust the schedule, Jay."

"It would be indecorous to object. Allowances must be made for emergencies and accidents."

She nodded. "Thanks. You guys have been through a lot. Would you like to relax in your rooms for a little bit? I'll walk you over."

Tyler and Jay prepared to leave, but Copper looked toward Keegan's room. "Could I stay here?"

Nicola smiled. "Sure, if that's what you want." She looked into his eyes. "Thanks for trying to help Tyler today." She gave his hand a quick squeeze and left.

Copper removed Keegan's gift from his pocket. He drew one coin from the small plastic bag. As he turned the nickel in his hand, the mechanical humming stopped. Clunky shoes clopped along the tile floor. An unfamiliar voice said, "There. That should feel a lot better." A woman wearing the light blue uniform breezed out of the examination room pushing a cart loaded with medical equipment.

Keegan's voice was clearer but had lost its usual confidence. "I'm sorry, Mom. After all the family has done for me, I messed things up."

"Honey, honey...No. What are you talking about? We're ok."

"No, I've ruined everything. Orientation has been a disaster."

Copper rubbed the coin with the hem of his shirt, and admired its mirror-like finish. Keegan's next outburst startled him. "When we get shut down, I'll have to go to that horrible place where Ainsley died!" A disturbing melody of weeping and retching drifted across the threshold and into the waiting area. Copper selected another coin for examination.

"Sit down, young man. You've been through a lot and you're too upset."

Copper, already sitting, looked around. The Harris family drama continued to provide the soundtrack for his time in the waiting area. He poured all the coins onto Jay's empty chair.

"Darling, I'll never—"

"I remember everything. We were standing at the front desk with his mother. She got called away, and we turned to look for her. The attendant screamed, 'Stop him!' Then Ainsley's legs passed through the sliding glass doors. His shoelaces flew behind him like streamers." Keegan's voice sounded like a wounded animal. After a small coughing fit, he continued. "I always helped him with his shoelaces. Ainsley hated them. At the bus stop, kids tied his shoes together. Once, they used them to strap his feet to his desk..."

Andrea Harris murmured something Copper thought might be a level six.

Keegan's voice sounded thick and cracked. "I can still hear the horn and the brakes screeching, and that terrible thump.

He rolled over the hood of the SUV. I ran to him, but his body was twisted into strange angles. His shoes weren't tied. Maybe he tripped. I should have—"

"You can't blame yourself for what happened. Ainsley is the one who ran outside."

"He was miserable there. He'd stopped making his music— his humming wasn't the same." Keegan's words mixed with tears. "Nobody ever really listened to Ainsley. He did everything he could to communicate, but they thought it was noise. They didn't even *try* to know him."

Copper turned a coin over in his hand and cringed when he heard someone blow their nose. He looked at the coins he'd sorted on the chair. He'd taken all of the pennies out, so he threw the rest back into the sack.

A chair grated against the floor. "Son, you are my heart floating outside of my body. We'll always do everything to keep you safe. We'll provide whatever we can to give you the best chance for happiness, and that includes teaching you how to do things for yourself. I promise."

Luke reappeared, walking through the waiting area holding a second black T-shirt. "Hey, Copper. What's up?"

"Just waiting in the room designed for it."

"Alright. There's probably a TV in the next room over. They might have the Entrée Network. Want me to check for you?"

"Nah. I'll just sit here and simmer on low."

"Cool." He took his swagger into the examination room. "Keeg, dude. I brought you a fresh, fur-free tuxedo T-shirt. This one has the bow tie untied and the collar open. It's good to be casual after a long day. There. You look like a champ. I told ya; nobody ever dies from a little dog spit."

Keegan's tongue was thick with chemical sleep. "Level three?"

"Spit. S-P-I-T." Luke laughed.

Copper laughed too. Then he slapped his hand over his mouth and hoped they hadn't noticed him.

"Do you think the townspeople will try to shut us down, Luke?"

"What?! No way. And if they do, we'll take them all on. Right, Ma?"

"Yes. That's why we're here. To help people like Ainsley, as well as the Tylers and Keegans of the world. We will fight until our very last breath for people to be valued, included, and safe."

"But you've changed your lives to make this place for me and people like me. If anything happens, your hearts will break, and I can't let that happen."

"Sweet boy, you can't keep our hearts safe from everything."

"But I have to! You can't die."

"What?"

"From broken hearts, like Ainsley's mom…"

Luke's voice cracked. "Whoa. Dude. Keeg, I—"

"Son, you've already broken my heart, but in a very good way. Having you in my life has made my heart bigger. Since you came into my life, I can love people with much more strength. The things that happen here…well, you're not going to kill us, son. Cheryl Mitchell's broken heart was complicated. She had no help taking care of Ainsley. Remember, when we'd go over to their house? We'd keep him company so she could go grocery shopping. Honey, that woman never got any rest. She'd been sick for a long time."

Copper put the last coin away. None of the dates matched the valuable ones Sterling had taught him, but it didn't matter. These were still special. He'd keep them forever. He got up and stuck his head inside his friend's room. "Are you ready to go home, Keegan? I'll walk with you."

Keegan stood, wiped his face, and started down the

hallway. The medicine he was huffing through that machine must have lit a fire under his feet, and Copper had to hurry to grab his bag of coins from the alcove. As he rounded the corner, he heard Andrea Harris crying with Luke. "I don't know if I can ever explain Cheryl's suicide, but…"

At his regular pace, Copper had to take two steps to match one of the blond giant's strides. If he was going to walk with Keegan, he'd have to jog.

Chapter Fifty-One

KEEGAN

Sometimes it's best to just breathe.

- How To Contain Your Crazy

The group sat in the lobby where they first met. Each guy took the same seat as before. Keegan decided he would ask his mother to buy a second womb chair—Tyler probably needed one as much as he did. Next to the mailboxes, Nicola and Luke traded whispers. Keegan's skull buzzed and his heart jittered. His insides moved at a different speed than the rest of him. He was sloshing around inside his skin, and his brain was too busy to report if his body held pain. Some part he couldn't name was relieved that his people would not die from broken hearts. If folks simply said what they meant, life would be a lot less confusing.

He waved his fresh new pencils and tried to make sense of this crazy, upside-down weekend. Images of Copper's shoes covered in marshmallows, Tyler's head emerging from the shrubbery like some kind of jack-in-the-box toy, and Jay swirling that stick around like a superhero flooded his mind. "Jay, how'd you learn to work a stick like that?"

Copper perked up. "Yeah, Professor. Was that from your fancy Krav Maga classes?"

"No. I obtained proficiency through the scrutinization of Internet videos and practice."

"Professor, all I heard was blah, blah, blah...Internet videos."

Keegan held two fingers up. "And practice! Isn't it funny how some words in other languages sound so much like English?"

Nicola scurried into the room. She sat on the coffee table in the middle of the group. "Guys, you've got one more night together. What's something"—she swiveled her head to look at each one of them—"*calm* we could do as a group?"

Keegan's neck was made out of jelly. He pulled the beanie over his ears. "Let someone else decide. Everything I plan is doomed."

Copper rubbed the top of his checkerboard foot. "What do real men do?"

"You look pretty real to me." Nicola laughed. She was the only one who was amused. "Um...Some guys play cards. Do y'all know how to play poker?"

She looked briefly at Luke. He shook his head and mouthed the word "No." Keegan had seen that gesture a thousand times.

Nicola tried again. "I don't think anyone wants to learn a new game tonight. But I have an idea. Follow me." She walked across the lounge to the other hallway. "This may eventually be the ladies' side of the Inn. My room is the first one on this hall."

"Noted." Jay punched the screen on his tablet and snapped a photo of the door.

"On the floor plan, this room was reserved as a multi-use room. But, I"—she slipped a key card into the door—"took the liberty of creating a game room."

They shuffled into the new room. Floor to ceiling cabinets lined one wall. Air hockey and foosball games occupied the opposite wall. A few tables of various sizes were scattered throughout the space. One round table had been divided into four workspaces, each equipped with a computer and headset. "That's for multiplayer video gaming." She paused. "I suppose it could also be used for studying."

On cue, Keegan groaned. "Not homeschool again. What's the shelf above it for? There are holes in it."

Nicola walked to the wall of cabinet doors. The first one she opened revealed several boxes of new gaming systems. "Those are for the ugly cords. I don't know much about video games, but these should be fun." She waved her hand at the unopened packages. "I'm hoping Luke, or some other genius, will help me set up these XStationBoxes."

Keegan held his hands up to his cheeks. "Wonderful, but you really are clueless about games."

"I know poker." She stuck her tongue out and nudged him with her elbow.

"Ow."

"Oh! I forgot about the bruises. Did I get you?"

"Nope. My body is flowing with powerful medicine. I got you."

"Pretty good joke, Keegan Harris." She stood on a chair and touched the top of his head. "You almost gave me a heart attack."

"Did I really? Mom just said I wasn't going to…Level two! Please say what you mean."

"Sorry. It's a bad habit." After giving him a quick hug, she hopped down, and opened another cabinet. "These cabinets are full of tabletop games, building sets, and other group projects you might want to try. Can we hang out in here tonight?" Then she turned and waved at a chair. "Luke go test out the recliner. You're exhausted, my friend."

Luke stretched out on the recliner with a satisfied sigh. The guys milled about, looking at the items in the cabinets. Copper spotted an unopened *Passage* game disc. "Wow! It's just like I remember."

"It was probably on sale." Nicola removed her hair tie and shook out her ponytail. "It's a weird time of day. I think we're going to need to stock up on snacks. Since I didn't get to spend much time with you yesterday, how about we take a trip to the grocery store? You feel like going, Keegan? I'm sure your uncle would love a quick visit."

Luke pulled the bar on the side of the recliner. His feet went to the floor and his back was straight. "Are you sure, Nic? Yesterday was—"

"Stay here. You need a break. I got it. I need to get to know our crew and I owe you after yesterday."

Luke raised one eyebrow.

"Look how they worked together today. I feel good about this, plus they need to be able to get around town if we're going to roll some semi-independence into this program."

Jay frowned. "While I'm amenable to accompanying you anywhere, this unanticipated event may clash with our dining program. I wonder if a journey of this magnitude could be conducted at an acceptable pace?"

Nicola straightened the collar on Jay's shirt. "I think we can make time."

His cheeks bloomed red. "Technologically impossible. Highly erroneous lang—"

"I promise we'll get enough food so that if you miss dinner, you'll be ok." As Nicola turned to grab her purse, her hair fanned out and landed beautifully on her shoulders. The motion made blurs similar to Keegan's wiggling pencils. She applied some lip balm, and asked, "Jay, would you sit by me on the trolley?"

Jay rubbed his mouth with his index finger. "Absolutely!"

Chapter Fifty-Two

COPPER

Opinions are ten a penny.

Terrance's squeaky brakes stopped in front of the Inn. "Y'all hop on. There's a few spots left. It gets busier on Saturday evening."

Jay tapped his watch. "Good afternoon, Terrance."

"Same to ya, Jay!"

Copper followed the Professor and Nicola down the aisle. They chose the last available bench seat. An elderly woman slid over one space, opening the aisle seat next to her. She spoke as Copper sat, but the whistle from her false teeth stole his ability to concentrate on her words.

Tyler sat close to the driver, while their still-drugged master of ceremonies chose to stand. Keegan faced the remaining passengers, squeezing the hand strap with one hand. Had the top of the trolley not been curved, his head might have touched the ceiling.

Terrance called back. "You better hang on, Keegan. Don't want you to fall down and add another scrape to your leg."

Nicola answered. "Only one stop, Terrance. Just a quick trip to Go Fresh."

As the car rolled forward, Keegan hugged his body against the nearest pole. He wrapped one leg around its base, leaving his long, floppy arms free to display points of interest with his customary flair.

A voice from behind competed with the sounds of crushed acorns and seagulls. "Such a fine woman. You're already fresh enough." The man's laugh sounded wrong, like when kids used to tease him at school. That sound slowed everything down and made the hairs on the back of his neck grow longer. Copper turned to see who made the comment. A man wearing a black T-shirt corrected his greasy seat partner. "Shhh. Didn't you see where she got on? Maybe she's simple."

Nicola's face pinched with irritation. Jay tensed. His rigid body didn't touch the back of his seat.

Everything about the man behind them was oily. His hair, his skin, even the buttons on his shirt were smudged with grease. He put his tattooed hand on the seat in front of him and leaned forward. "Hey, darlin'? You ain't simple, are you?" He turned to his buddy. "Simple might be nice and easy." His eyes crinkled as he stuck his tongue between his dirty teeth and wiggled the slimy pink and yellow mouth tentacle around. His laughter transformed into a coughing fit.

Nicola's eyes rolled to the side. Jay's eyebrows fell into a hard line. His jaw tightened and his chest heaved. After that, only his Adam's apple moved.

The loud pair continued their conversation. Mr. Black T-shirt crossed his arms in front of his chest, tucking his hands into his armpits. "I don't know why we're stopping over here now. Another change just for them that's going to throw everyone else off. Damn family bought up half the town, and now property taxes are going through the roof. No consideration for those of us who belong here."

The greasy tattooed cougher let go of the seat in front of him and flopped back into his chair. "Hey, I like the new grocery store!"

"Starting the store was one thing. It created some jobs, but then they bought all these houses"—Mr. Black T-shirt's hand waved around in the air—"and brought in all these freaks and weirdos." He shook his head and pursed his lips. "They're changin' the whole neighborhood."

Copper's belly coiled in on itself. He tried to focus on something peaceful. When he turned to face forward, he saw Keegan swaying like his muscles were made from melted butter. The medication had finally taken full control of their tour guide, and his pencils conducted a symphony that only he could hear.

The human grease factory grunted to Terrance. "Is that boy on drugs? Stop the car, I don't want to be in a vehicle with this garbage."

Jay called out from his seat. "Terrance, permit me to provide assistance? I shall expedite the departure with efficiency."

Terrance hit the brakes and steered the trolley to the side of the road. "Mighty fine, sir."

The men stood and filed into the aisle. Black T-shirt led the way while Greasy followed close behind. They walked toward Keegan, and as the first man passed, Copper noticed Mr. T-shirt and his slick buddy had similar tattoos. T-shirt Guy turned red with anger. "Ain't gonna be living in a town full of dumb whores and freaks." He spat on the floor.

Jay stepped into the aisle and stood between the two men. Copper froze, and the familiar sensation of warm cotton filled his ears. His heartbeat grew louder. Time slowed. Moments stretched like taffy.

Jay's back was turned away from the first man. He leaned

forward and grabbed Greasy's outside shoulder-blade near his neck.

One word fell from Greasy's lips. "Eli?"

The world became blurry as four men moved simultaneously. Keegan lunged closer to the driver as the spitting man named Eli, turned back to see the commotion. Greasy's tattooed hand became a swinging fist aimed right at the Professor. Jay blocked the blow and caught his opponent by the arm. In one fluid motion, Jay pushed the guy's head down, drove his other elbow forward, and lay his forearm against the man's throat. With a quick combination of pushing and pulling, he pivoted and swung the creep around, so that Jay was no longer in between the two jerks. Using Greasy's locked-up body as a battering ram, the Professor pushed the grease monster into his friend.

As he steered the two men forward, Jay turned to Copper. "This is Krav Maga. It's called stacking." He shoved them out the front door and leaned forward. "Gentlemen, you were delaying our progress." They stumbled to the gravel on the side of the road, and Terrance closed the door. He tipped his head toward Jay.

Nicola rushed to the front of the vehicle. "Jay! Terrance, I...Please!"

The kind driver touched her shoulder. "I won't say anything, if you won't. But you need to research those tattoos, ma'am."

Tyler stuck his face out of the window. "You mess with the bull, you get the horns."[1]

Still in his fog, Keegan wobbled toward the recently vacated bench. Frustration, fear, and confusion brewed in Copper's belly. Adding adrenaline to his emotional mix churned uncomfortably in his stomach, but it had cleared his vision. He looked at his seat partner, the old woman, patiently staring out the window. There was an open notebook on her lap. The word "loyalty" was scratched across the top page. He studied Nicola and Jay. Her face looked tired, and Jay stared straight ahead with his hands folded in his lap. There wasn't an electronic device anywhere in sight. Keegan teetered as he sat down. For someone larger than life, in that moment, he looked small.

Copper's face was blazing, and his hands curled into fists. He stood and faced the few other people sitting on the trolley behind him. Hot, angry tears filled his eyes. He squeezed them shut, preventing them from falling down his cheeks, and swallowed hard. His voice began with a quiver but grew stronger and more determined with each word. "I have autism. I'm autistic. Whatever." He waved his hand. "However I choose to describe myself, I'm not garbage. If anyone else has a problem with me or my buddies, this is your stop."

The trolley was silent. A moment passed and someone coughed. He opened his eyes and found nothing unusual in the faces of bored passengers.

Copper sat next to Keegan. "Are you ok? That was crazy. Jay just…"

The skinny giant smiled. "Controlled the quality."

The shuttle rolled back to the paved road. Keegan's pencils fell as he leaned out the window, "We're not just going to change the neighborhood. We're going to change the entire world!"

Copper grabbed the pencils before they rolled away. He cleaned the stim sticks with his shirt, and offered them back to his friend. "You're damn right we will. We're the Innsiders."

Keegan tilted his head and waved the pencils in front of his nose. As his eyebrows reached new heights, his thin lips bent up at the corners. His eyes slid sideways in Copper's direction. "Cursing. Level two."

Chapter Fifty-Three

COPPER

Worth every penny.

The next morning, Copper followed Ruby across the patio. A low, stone wall failed to hold back the disorganized green mess. He dropped into a chair and fidgeted with the penny in his pocket. "They call this a garden? It's chaos. There's a bush with tiny roses getting buried by grassy mounds of lilies. The tangled ground cover spilling over the wall is fit for the trash."

Ruby rolled her chair toward the garden. "Two different kinds of ivy are growing here. I doubt they planned for the lilies to do so well when they stuck them near the miniature rose bush, but the sun makes this a perfect spot for bulbs."

"You know a lot about plants, even though they're boring." Immediately after saying it, Copper wanted to slap his own face. *How do men show interest if they're ignorant about the topic?* He tapped his fingers on the table. "I mean, you could talk about anything and I'd want to listen. What's the pointy one next to that pathetic bush on the other side?"

Ruby rolled closer to the plants. "The pointy thing is aloe

vera. Good for scratches and sunburns. But this"—she touched the limp thing—"you should see this up close."

Copper jumped at the chance to get closer to her.

She held the plant. "Touch it, but be careful—there are thorns. Can you tell what it's doing?"

Copper's stomach swam toward his throat. His ignorance wouldn't impress her. Men knew things; they were confident and made judgments. Manly men on TV gave orders and got respect. His mouth felt unusually dry. "They should weed it out. It's practically dead. None of these plants look right piled together like this." He hoped he sounded powerful.

Ruby let go of the plant and crossed her arms. "These are gifts people send to the hospital rooms. Sometimes patients don't take them home, so rather than waste them, the Harris' stick them in the dirt out here." She turned to face him, and her angled, angry eyebrows made listening difficult. Even though her face moved too much, she was still so pretty. "And this *Thing* you want weeded out…"

The last "t" in "out" sounded sharp to his ears.

"…is a Meyer lemon tree. It's been through a lot but it's growing new branches anyway." Her hands moved all over the place, her words increasing in speed and volume. "All you can see are the problems, but I know that one day, it's going to make a lemon. What can you do, Copper? You'd be lucky to be half as good as this lemon tree."

He sat down on the stone wall, his back to the prickly weeds. Ruby's face was red. *What had he done wrong?* His version of acting like a man was a disaster. She was so smart, and she'd already figured out his secret: he had no skills. "You're right. I can't do anything. I don't want to be left on Ainsley Avenue and forgotten like one of these plants."

Ruby's soft, warm hand lightly covered his own, and her face relaxed. "These plants are in a good place. They've been saved from the garbage, and they're not being forgotten.

They're growing. People sit and trade air with them while they add color to a dreary day. They all have something to give, even if they don't look perfect." Catching sight of something, her eyes moved to the side. She jerked her hand away from his. "See a penny, pick it up…"

"…All day long, you'll have good luck," Copper finished. "My brother used to say that."

"I can't bend over, so that one's for you."

Copper reached down to get the penny.

Her voice came from a distance. "My PT is here. I gotta go. See ya later, Ginger Root."

He'd planned to give the coin to her, but she'd already rolled away. Those wheels made her way too fast. He flipped the penny in his hand. It wasn't worth a lot of money. He could almost hear Sterling say, "Good looking out, Copper. Know your value." He slid it into his pocket. This penny was another keeper.

"I hope you'll remember to empty those pockets later, son." He recognized Pearl's voice anywhere, and he turned just in time to be engulfed by her arms.

He told the mass of perfumed red hair, "Hi, Mom."

"Baby, I missed you." She gave him a huge hug. "Let's go grab your stuff." They had only taken three steps before she asked, "Who was that girl?"

Copper's face grew warm. "Her name is Ruby." He looked at his mother out of the corner of his eye and wiggled his eyebrows.

Soon, his mother was cooing about how clean Copper's room still looked. He handed her the special penny from Sterling's note and told her to put it some place safe. She left to chat with Ms. Harris while Copper stuffed his laundry into the duffel bag. When he was finished, he found an envelope resting on his desk and opened it. Inside, the front of the card said,

Hi! My name's Keegan. Your name is Copper.

Copper unfolded it to read the interior.

You're not a killer. Everything checks out. Let's be
friends.

A grin stretched across his face as he tossed the card into
his bag. He shuffled through his kitchenette and cracked open
the door. Luke's unmistakable drawl lazily wafted down the
hall. "Yep, that matches the tattoo. Keegan's been drawin' it."

Nicola's words spewed out at a hundred miles an hour.
"Luke, this is a Nazi symbol for the brownshirts. I can't say it
right, but it's called Sturmabteilung."

Copper wanted to hear more, but his mom would return
soon, looking for her Copy Pie, so he had no time to try and
unravel the word puzzles that people without autism always
used. Instead, he slid into the room next door. Keegan's
computer screen had his undivided attention, so Copper
tiptoed to get a closer look. Half the screen had unfamiliar
software running, while the other half rested on a website:
chuandchother.com. "I should have knocked."

Keegan jumped out of his chair. "Level three!" His hand
tapped the famous painter's face on his T-shirt. He ran his
other hand over the slogan: 'There are no mistakes, only happy
accidents.' "You got me good."

"I came to say thanks for the card. Are you working on
some more?"

"Yep."

"Is that your greeting card shop? Chu and Chother?"

"Yeah. I'm thinking about getting into T-shirts." Keegan
tapped the desk with his pencils.

"I don't understand the name."

"Songwriters are in love with Chu. There are so many

songs written to or about Chu. They can't live without Chu, so Chu must be an amazing muse. Other tunes talk about hugging E. Chother, and how we need E. Chother to get through life. I've never met those people but I thought their names might help my business, so…ChuAndChother."

"Sounds whimsical and interesting, just like you, Ringlet Leader." Copper pushed the back of Keegan's chair. "You gotta look outside: the Inn is bubbling with activity."

Keegan clapped his hands. "Yes! I knew it would be a popular destination. I'll catch up with you in two minutes."

Chapter Fifty-Four

KEEGAN

Friendship is an investment that increases in value over time.

After Copper left, Keegan jammed another card into an envelope. Rushing toward the door, he almost ran over Luke and Nicola.

"Whoa. You in a hurry, Keeg?"

"Kinda."

"Alright. I wanted to show Nic that A-shaped thing you were workin' on earlier."

Keegan stretched his arm out to his side. "Ta-da?" His eyebrows raised up, hoping this was an acceptable time to show off.

Nicola touched the paper. "This is a wonderful drawing. I can tell you worked hard on it." Then her lips pressed together as she crossed her arms in front of her chest. "But I wouldn't try to use it for work."

Keegan's hands flopped to his sides. "Why?"

She tightened her ponytail as she joined Luke in the hall. "I've seen it before."

"Yes! It's all over town. I saw it on the trolley, in the park, and the dining hall."

Her breath caught and a flood of words flowed out. "That's the thing. It might be protected by copyright." She flipped her hands over and showed her palms. This matched the *Gesture Dictionary* sign for "I don't know."

Keegan offered half a bow as he slid past them and out the door. "No problem. Lots of ideas." He touched the pencil erasers to his head. A few long strides carried him down the hall, and he considered how often his plans failed. He opened the Inn's double doors and squinted against the sunlight.

Tyler, Jay, and Copper were unloading boxes from the back of a yellow moving truck. Two floor lamps waited in the grass near the shrubs. "And sometimes things work out anyway," he mumbled. He hoped Ainsley could see the scene from his bed made of clouds.

The front doors would need to stay open for the movers. After Keegan fixed the latches, he jogged down to his friends. Copper didn't pull away or even flinch when he touched his shoulder. "Are you going to live here?"

"Pearl said I could try it for a few months." Copper passed a box to Jay. "But this stuff belongs to the Professor. I gotta go home and get mine."

Keegan's smile faded. He rubbed his All Star shoe in the dirt. "Ok."

"Hey Curly, it's a different day, but that's ok, remember?" Copper blew some dust off a fake plant and set it on the ground.

Keegan tugged on his beanie. "What if life is one really long different kind of day?"

"That's impossible! A day consists of twenty-four hours. For it to be anything else would completely throw off our entire calendar."

Keegan's hand flew over his mouth. "Jay, you spoke English!"

Copper joined in. "Even I understood that, Professor."

"Last night, Nicola told me I could use common terminology and people would still recognize my intelligence."

Keegan put his pencils in his front pocket. "Well, that was a good try, and I'm sure you'll improve. You just need more practice." He extended the greeting card toward Jay. "I've got a card for you. It's so romantic, it will get you married. Wait and see!"

Jay set down his box, rolled up his sleeves, and opened the envelope. "That's a lovely rendition of a dragonfly."

Copper tapped his foot. "Read it, Professor. Let's hear the magic."

Jay cleared his throat. "It says, 'You are beautiful and clearly more evolved than a dragonfly.' And the inside reads, 'If you're not too busy faking your own death, maybe we could have coffee together.'"

Tyler poked his face through the leaves of an artificial tree. "We're all pretty bizarre. Some of us are just better at hiding it, that's all."[1]

Pearl called over, and Copper waved at his mother. He turned to Keegan and imitated the jock's stupid dance from the movie. "Write me, Ringleader."

"I'll send you a card." Both guys struck their fists in the air. Their pose from the movie was so synchronized, it looked like they'd planned it. Keegan laughed. "You know, if this was a movie, we'd stop here and be frozen like this."

Jay shook his card at Keegan. "We've agreed that life isn't a movie."

Keegan wrapped his long arms around his new crew and brought them together into a tight circle. "You're right. Sometimes it's better."

Epilogue

Keegan threw open the French doors. Voices bounced off the tile floor. He crept to the art studio entrance and peeked inside. His mother and Nicola were admiring a huge canvas.

"Nic, I can't file a police report. We don't know if anyone tried to hurt the diabetic woman on purpose. Dining halls get busy. Maybe the attendant made a mistake with the syrup. Besides, I didn't see the tattoo. Lots of people are marked up these days. Maybe it's not what you think."

"But even Terrance said—"

"There's no way we've selected the most hateful town in America to build this community." She touched Nicola's arm. "But I will keep an eye out. Now, tell me about Copper's case."

"The board will check on his living conditions and progress. The real issue will be his father, Steele Campbell."

"Didn't he leave the family years ago?"

"He did, but he's hellbent on getting that money. Pearl's attorneys tried to put some restraining order in place. She wants to make Copper's living arrangements a secret to protect his privacy."

When Keegan shifted his weight, his pencils slipped from his hand and rolled into the studio.

"Son? Come in here. I want to show you something."

Nicola lightly brushed his arm on her way to the door. "Looks like I need to add eavesdropping to our social skills curriculum. See ya later, Keegan."

His mother put her arm around his waist. "What do you think?" She waved at her painting. Four figures studied the seascape.

"I see you chose my burgundy beanie."

"Adds more color."

"And I'm wearing jeans."

"Darling, I'll never capture the pale majesty of your legs. I'm good, but not that good."

Keegan bowed. "Fair enough. Why not show our faces?"

His mother put her finger to her lips. "Privacy."

"It's missing something." He tipped his wrist in an exaggerated pose. "May I?"

She passed him a paintbrush. "I suppose this could be a collaboration." He dipped it into white paint and scrawled the words "The Insiders Club" over their heads. His mother paired her smile with the Harris Head-tilt. "That looks good, but I thought you were the Innsiders? With the extra *n*?"

Keegan gave her the brush. "On that point, we could not agree. It's a good thing I canceled the order for the jackets." He exhaled and relaxed into a smile. "But I'm not worried. The most important thing is we're friends."

Thank you so much for attending orientation on Ainsley Avenue. I hope you enjoyed *The Insiders Club*. Leaving a quick 2 line review helps others discover this story and would be greatly appreciated. To get an exclusive look at Keegan's first greeting card, join me in the Echo Chamber. Subscribers will receive bonus content in addition to updates about the *Life on the Innside* series, please visit this special link www.echomillerbooks.com/echo.

Acknowledgments

To say writing fiction has been a challenge diminishes the meaning of the word "challenge." This book could have been called Orientation for the characters, the reader's journey, and for me as a storyteller. I live in my own bubble, but nothing happens in a vacuum. I could not have begun, continued, or completed this story without the help of many people.

Special Thanks To....

Mariah S,
The beautiful cover you created inspired me to weave it into the epilogue. Thank you for taking a bunch of random information and turning it into a wonderful work of art.

James M,
Everyone needs an editor and I certainly needed you. You went above and beyond the call of duty. Thank you. (*If you're a reader and you find a big mistake, don't blame James. I probably missed a piece of his advice or stubbornly chose to leave it technically incorrect.*)

Liz S,

Thank you for "it's a different day and that's ok." That phrase got us through some tough times. I'm happy to have it in this book.

Amy T,

The first non-family member to read the book: Your enthusiasm and excitement gave me the courage to keep going. The book might not have ever been released "into the wild' without you.

The SPP/Story Studio podcasters: Johnny, Sean, and David.

Through your efforts, I connected with my tribe of fellow creative weirdos. Those gatherings were perfect examples of how grace and inclusion can be life changing. Dave, I'm not sure how the president of our Eeyore club became an excellent encourager, but you did. They say friendships aren't always 50-50 in terms of effort. Thanks for doing the heavy lifting on several occasions.

To my author friends on fitbit:

Without our workweek hustles, I'd be rusted to my laptop and weigh 500 lbs. You fit folks are hard to beat, but easy to love.

Danny C,

Thanks for embracing my family. You set a great example of how people should treat each other. You help me remember my value.

Lamar,

You had to tell us that we could be a force for positive change multiple times, but it finally sank in. Thanks!

Carol,
My friend since the 1900s and my expert on all things swirlism: You were the second person outside our home to read this story. And you finished it! "They" say your friends and family won't read your book. Thanks for proving "them" wrong. Your encouragement and friendship has been priceless.

Other Megan,
How can someone who is my ally in over-analyzing everything also make me giddy with laughter? That must be some of your Snow Queen magic. You live in a chilly place, but you have one of the warmest hearts I've ever encountered. Thanks for letting me hang out in there. So cozy.

Jami and Sara,
My locally-sourced, fellow TexMex enthusiasts: You've been so much more than "writer friends." There's no way to list all the ways you've helped me. Thanks for taking my life from approximately 5.5 to a 9. My world is much better with you in it.

To my family of origin,
Thanks for all of my quirky DNA and telling me I'm capable of doing anything. That's not true, (*mixing numbers & letters together and calling it math- pssht*) but it's an inspiring fib.

Family-in-law/love,
Thanks for making me feel like I'm one of your own and always being so supportive. The way you embrace people… well, now I know how your kids grew up to be so confident.

Megan Cupcake,
My fellow word nerd: You are a breath of fresh air when I'm a little too confined. Thank you for expressing interest in the

story. Knowing that a young person might want to read it, helped push me forward on the days I didn't feel like writing. No pressure but you give me hope for the future of humanity. *(just by being yourself and doing your thing)* ha!

Son,
Sharing this trip through the world with your unique spirit has been a whimsical journey. I'm tired but I'm happy. Never forget: You are exactly the way I'd ever wish for you to be. Without you, this book would have never been written. Thanks for the joy, laughter, and tears. I dedicate my laugh lines and the trench between my eyebrows to you, sir.

To my partner in all things,
Thank you for being my biggest fan and my best cheerleader. You valued my voice and convinced me that I had something to say. It might be a whisper or a scream, but I made a sound thanks to your unwavering support. Thanks for loving me more than I can understand.

To fellow parents of kids with diagnostic labels,
I know I didn't describe your child. I didn't paint an accurate picture of your reality. But I thank you for your grace, patience, and support. The spectrum is vast and wide. There will be more stories to come.

To the people living all along the spectrum:
Thank you for teaching me about life. You opened a window and let me see a different way to experience every single thing. I'd be honored to hold the door for you as we step into a more compassionate world.

Endnotes

Chapter 6

1. Brickman, Paul. *Risky Business*. Film. Directed by Paul Brickman. USA: Warner Bros., 1983.
2. Gould, Heywood. *Cocktail*. Film. Directed by Roger Donaldson. USA: Buena Vista, 1988.
3. Cameron Crowe. *Jerry Maguire*. Film. Directed by Cameron Crowe. USA: Sony, 1996.
4. Schulman, Tom. *Dead Poets Society*. Film. Directed by Peter Weir. USA: Buena Vista, 1989.
5. Schulman, Tom. *Dead Poets Society*. Film. Directed by Peter Weir. USA: Buena Vista, 1989.
6. Stone, Oliver. *Scarface*. Film. Directed by Brian De Palma. USA: Universal, 1983.
7. Siefert, Lynn and Michael Ritchie, Tommy Swerdlow, and Michael Goldberg. *Cool Runnings*. Film. Directed by Jon Turtletaub. USA: Buena Vista, 1993.
8. Bergstein, Eleanor. *Dirty Dancing*. Film. Directed by Emile Ardolino. USA: Vestron, 1987.

Chapter 7

1. Carol, Lewis (books) and Carol Woolverton (screenplay). *Alice In Wonderland*. Film. Directed by Tim Burton USA: Buena Vista, 2010.
2. Carol, Lewis (books) and Carol Woolverton (screenplay). *Alice In Wonderland*. Film. Directed by Tim Burton USA: Buena Vista, 2010.

Chapter 8

1. Baum, Frank L. (book), Noel Langley, Florence Ryerson, and Edgar Allen Woolf (screenplay). *The Wizard of Oz*. Film. Directed by Victor Fleming. USA: MGM, 1939.

Chapter 20

1. Groom, Winston (novel) and Eric Roth (screenplay). *Forrest Gump*. Film. Directed by Robert Zemeckis. USA: Paramount, 1994.
2. Sather, Drake, Ben Stiller, and Jon Hamburg. *Zoolander*. Film. Directed by Ben Stiller. USA: Paramount, 2001.
3. Fey, Tina. *Mean Girls*. Film. Directed by Mark Waters. USA: Paramount, 2004.

Chapter 22

1. LaManna, Ross and Jim Kouf. *Rush Hour*. Film. Directed by Brett Rattner. USA: New Line, 1998.

Chapter 23

1. Sorkin, Aaron. *A Few Good Men*. Film. Directed by Rob Reiner. USA: Columbia, 1992.

Chapter 24

1. Carpenter, John. *They Live*. Film. Directed by John Carpenter. USA:Universal, 1988.

Chapter 27

1. Crowe, Cameron. *Say Anything...* Film. Directed by Cameron Crowe. USA: 20th Century Fox, 1989.

Chapter 28

1. Ephron, Nora. *When Harry Met Sally...* Film. Directed by Rob Reiner. USA: Columbia, 1989.
2. Sinclair, Upton (novel) and Paul Thomas Anderson. *There Will Be Blood*. Film. Directed by Paul Thomas Anderson. USA: Paramount Vantage, 2007.
3. Toback, James. *Bugsy*. Film. Directed by Barry Levinson. USA: TriStar, 1991.
4. Avary, Roger and Quentin Tarantino. *Pulp Fiction*. Film. Directed by Quentin Tarantino. USA: Miramax, 1994.

5. Curtis, Richard. *Notting Hill*. Film. Directed by Roger Michell. USA: Universal, 1999.
6. Ephron, Nora. *When Harry Met Sally...* Film. Directed by Rob Reiner. USA: Columbia, 1989.

Chapter 32

1. Hughes, John. *Ferris Bueller's Day Off*. Film. Directed by John Hughes. USA: Paramount, 1986.
2. Epstein, Julius J., Philip G. Epstein, and Howard Koch. *Casablanca*. Film. Directed by Michael Curtiz. USA: Warner Bros., 1942.

Chapter 35

1. Widen, Gregory. *Backdraft*. Film. Directed by Ron Howard. USA: Universal, 1991.
2. Palahniuk, Chuck (novel) and Jim Uhls (screenplay). *Fight Club*. Film. Directed by David Fincher. USA: Fox, 1999.
3. Shrader, Paul. *Taxi Driver*. Film. Directed by Martin Scorsese. USA:Columbia, 1976.
4. Pearce, Donn and Frank Pierson. *Cool Hand Luke*. Film. Directed by Stuart Rosenberg. USA: Warner Bros., 1967.
5. Kluger, Jeffrey and Jim Novell (novel: Lost Moon) and William Broyles Jr. and Al Reiner (screenplay) *Apollo 13*. Film. Directed by Ron Howard. USA: Universal, 1995.
6. Lucas, George (story) and Leah Brackett and Lawrence Kasdan (screenplay) *Star Wars: Empire Strikes Back*. Film. Directed by Irvin Kershner. USA: Fox, 1980.
7. Cameron, James. *The Terminator*. Film. Directed by James Cameron. USA: Orion, 1984.

Chapter 36

1. Spielberg, Steven, Michael Grais and Mark Victor (screenplay) *Poltergeist*. Film. Directed by Tone Hooper. USA: MGM, 1982.
2. Tolkien, J. R.R. (novel), Fran Walsh, Philippa Boyens, Peter Jackson, and Guillermo del Toro (screenplay) *The Hobbit: An Unexpected Journey*. Film. Directed by Peter Jackson. NZ and USA: Warner Bros,. (New Line), 2012.
3. Epstein, Julius J., Philip G. Epstein, and Howard Koch. *Casablanca*. Film. Directed by Michael Curtiz. USA: Warner Bros., 1942.

Chapter 41

1. Aibel, Jonathan and Glenn Berger. *Kung Fu Panda*. Film. Directed by Mark Osborne and John Stevenson. USA: Paramount (Dreamworks), 2008.
2. Nicieaza, Fabian and Rob Liefeld (story) Rhett Reese, Paul Wernick (screenplay) *Deadpool*. Film. Directed by Tim Miller. USA: Fox, 2016.

Chapter 43

1. Webb, Charles (novel) Buck Henry and Calder Willingham (screenplay) *The Graduate*. Film. Directed by Mike Nichols. USA: AVCO Embassy (United Artists), 1967.
2. Shyamalan, M. Knight *The Sixth Sense*. Film. Directed by M. Knight Shyamalan. USA: Buena Vista, 1999.
3. Wallace, Randall Braveheart. Film. Directed by Mel Gibson. USA: Paramount (Fox international), 1995.
4. Williams, Tennessee (play and screenplay) *A Streetcar Named Desire*. Film. Directed by Elia Kazan. USA: Warner Bros., 1951.
5. J.M. Barre, *Peter and Wendy* (novel) UK: Hodder & Stoughton, 1911

Chapter 44

1. Hughes, John. *The Breakfast Club*. Film. Directed by John Hughes. USA: Universal, 1985.
2. Hughes, John. *The Breakfast Club*. Film. Directed by John Hughes. USA: Universal, 1985.

Chapter 45

1. Aberson, Helen and Harold Pearl (novel) Otto Englander, Joe Grant, and Dick Huemer (screenplay) *Dumbo*. Film. Directed by USA: RKO, 1941.

Chapter 46

1. Goldman, William (novel and screenplay) *The Princess Bride*. Film. Directed by Rob Reiner. USA: Fox (Vestron International), 1987.

Chapter 47

1. Theroux, Justin with Ben Stiller and Eric McLeod. *Tropic Thunder*. Film. Directed by Ben Stiller. USA: Paramount (DreamWorks), 2008.
2. Hughes, John. *The Breakfast Club*. Film. Directed by John Hughes. USA: Universal, 1985.
3. Hughes, John. *The Breakfast Club*. Film. Directed by John Hughes. USA: Universal, 1985.
4. Lucas, George. *Star Wars*. Film. Directed by George Lucas. USA: Fox, 1977.

Chapter 48

1. McQuarrie, Christopher. *The Usual Suspects*. Film. Directed by Bryan Singer. USA: Gramercy, 1995.

Chapter 49

1. Cash, Jim and Jack Epps, Jr. *Top Gun*. Film. Directed by Tony Scott USA: Paramount, 1986.
2. Hughes, John. *The Breakfast Club*. Film. Directed by John Hughes. USA: Universal, 1985.
3. Hughes, John. *The Breakfast Club*. Film. Directed by John Hughes. USA: Universal, 1985.
4. Tolkien, J. R.R. (novel, The Return of the King), Fran Walsh, Philippa Boyens, Peter Jackson (screenplay) *The Lord of the Rings: The Return of the King*. Film. Directed by Peter Jackson. NZ and USA: New Line, 2003.

Chapter 52

1. Hughes, John. *The Breakfast Club*. Film. Directed by John Hughes. USA: Universal, 1985.

Chapter 54

1. Hughes, John. *The Breakfast Club*. Film. Directed by John Hughes. USA: Universal, 1985

About the Author

Echo Miller writes fiction featuring unconventional personalities who explore societal norms, pursue self-acceptance, and discover the value of inclusion. Through character-driven stories, Echo broadcasts the universal truth that everyone wants to belong. Self-described as quirky and contrarian, Echo enjoys inventing imaginary people, creating new traditions, and adding whimsy to ordinary experiences.

www.echomillerbooks.com

Printed in Great Britain
by Amazon

46005669R00175